BEST PRACTICES
IN LITERACY INSTRUCTION

Best Practices in Literacy Instruction

FOURTH EDITION

Edited by

Lesley Mandel Morrow
Linda B. Gambrell

Foreword by Nell K. Duke

THE GUILFORD PRESS
New York London

A Division of Guilford Publications, Inc.
72 Spring Street, New York, NY 10012
www.guilford.com

Printed in the United States of America

This book is printed on acid-free paper.

Last digit is print number: 9 8 7 6 5 4 3 2 1

Library of Congress Cataloging-in-Publication Data

Best practices in literacy instruction / [edited by] Lesley Mandel Morrow, Linda B. Gambrell ; foreword by Nell K. Duke. — 4th ed.
p. cm.
Includes bibliographical references and index.
ISBN 978-1-60918-178-9 (pbk.) — ISBN 978-1-60918-179-6 (hardcover)
1. Language arts—United States. 2. Reading comprehension—United States. 3. Literacy—United States. I. Morrow, Lesley Mandel. II. Gambrell, Linda B.
LB1576.B486 2011
372.6—dc22

2011000859

About the Editors

Lesley Mandel Morrow, PhD, is Professor and Chair of the Department of Learning and Teaching in the Graduate School of Education at Rutgers, The State University of New Jersey. Her research, which she conducts with children and families from diverse backgrounds, deals with early literacy development and the organization and management of language arts programs. Dr. Morrow has published more than 300 journal articles, chapters, and books. Her work has been recognized with awards including the Outstanding Teacher Educator in Reading Award and the William S. Gray Citation of Merit from the International Reading Association (IRA), and Oscar S. Causey Award from the Literacy Research Association. Dr. Morrow is past president of the IRA and is a member of the Reading Hall of Fame.

Linda B. Gambrell, PhD, is Distinguished Professor in the Eugene T. Moore School of Education at Clemson University. Her major research interests are in the areas of reading comprehension strategy instruction, literacy motivation, and the role of discussion in teaching and learning. Dr. Gambrell has published numerous books and articles on reading instruction. She is a recipient of the Outstanding Teacher Educator in Reading Award from the IRA, the Albert J. Kingston Award from the National Reading Conference, and the Laureate Award from the College Reading Association. She is past president of the IRA and is a member of the Reading Hall of Fame.

Contributors

Peter Afflerbach is Professor of Reading in the Department of Curriculum and Instruction at the University of Maryland. He began his teaching career as a Chapter 1 teacher in grades K–6 and then taught remedial reading and writing in junior high school and high school English. Dr. Afflerbach's research interests focus on reading assessment and reading comprehension strategies. He has published in numerous research and practitioner journals, including *The Reading Teacher, Journal of Reading, Journal of Adolescent and Adult Literacy, Elementary School Journal, Journal of Literacy Research, Reading Research Quarterly,* and *Cognition and Instruction.* He is an associate editor of the journal *Metacognition and Learning* and an editor of the *Handbook of Reading Research.* He has served as chair of the Reading Assessment Committee of the International Reading Association (IRA) and on the Reading Committee of the National Assessment of Educational Progress. His most recent books include *Understanding and Using Reading Assessment, K–12* and *Essential Readings on Assessment.* He was elected to the IRA Reading Hall of Fame in 2009.

Richard L. Allington is Professor of Education at the University of Tennessee. He is a past president of the International Reading Association (IRA), the National Reading Conference, and the Reading Hall of Fame, and a recipient of the President's Award for Excellence in Research from the University of Albany; the Outstanding Dissertation Award, the Albert J. Harris Award, and the William S. Gray Citation of Merit from the IRA; the A. B. Herr Award from the College Reading Association; and the Outstanding Reading Educator Award from the New York State Reading Association. Dr. Allington serves on the editorial boards of *Reading Research Quarterly, Remedial and Special Education, Language Arts, Journal of Literacy Research, Journal of Disability Policy Studies,* and *Elementary School Journal.* He has been principal investigator on a number of research projects funded by the U.S. Office of Educational Research and Improvement, the Office of Special Education and Rehabilitation, and the National Institutes of Health. He is the author/coauthor of over 100 research articles and a number of books, including *Classrooms That Work, Schools That Work, No Quick Fix, Learning to Read, Reading to Learn, Big Brother and the National Reading Curriculum, What Really Matters for Struggling Readers, What Really Matters for Fluency, What Really Matters for Response to Intervention,* and *Handbook of Reading Disability Research.*

Janice F. Almasi is the Carol Lee Robertson Endowed Professor of Literacy Education at the University of Kentucky. She received the International Reading Association's Outstanding Dissertation of the Year Award in 1994 and the National Reading Conference's Outstanding Student Research Award in 1993. She is currently a co-principal investigator on the evaluation of Kentucky's Striving Readers project. She has published several books, and her research has been published in journals such as *Reading Research Quarterly, Journal of Educational Psychology, Journal of Literacy Research, Elementary School Journal,* and *Educational Psychologist.* She is currently serving on the Board of Directors of both the International Reading Association and the Literacy Research Association.

Jessica Baxter is a graduate of the University of Georgia's doctoral program in the Department of Language and Literacy Education. With 3 years invested in working with elementary literacy learners as a classroom teacher, she has developed a passion for providing effective instruction for striving learners and English language learners. Dr. Baxter has also served as a teaching assistant for the University of Georgia, as an instructor of courses preparing preservice teachers to teach literacy and use assessment as a means to guide instruction for elementary learners. Her current research focuses on exploring how technology influences the teaching of classroom teachers and the nature of learning experiences for striving students. In addition, she serves as an instructional technology specialist for the Clarke County School District in Athens, Georgia.

Rita M. Bean is Professor Emerita, University of Pittsburgh. Prior to joining the university, she taught at the elementary level and also served as a K–12 reading specialist. She served as a member of the board of the International Reading Association and was president of the College Reading Association. Her newest book, the second edition of *The Reading Specialist: Leadership for the Classroom, School, and Community*, focuses on the role of the reading specialist. Dr. Bean has written chapters on literacy coaching and on the importance of professional development for teachers. Her current research focuses on the development and evaluation of early literacy reading programs, instruction for struggling readers, and the role of reading specialists/literacy coaches as change agents and in improving student learning. Dr. Bean received the Distinguished Teacher Award and the Distinguished Service Award from the University of Pittsburgh.

Alain Bengochea is a PhD candidate in the Language and Literacy Learning in Multilingual Settings program at the University of Miami, where his interests include bilingual first-language acquisition, cross-linguistic transfer, and vocabulary development through children's television. He earned a bachelor's degree from the University of Florida, where he majored in French and political science. He later joined the New York City Teaching Fellows and taught fourth- and fifth-grade students in the Bronx while obtaining his master's degree in bilingual education at Fordham University.

Camille L. Z. Blachowicz is Professor of Education at National-Louis University, where she also directs the reading program and the reading center. She is the author of several books and numerous chapters, monographs, and articles on vocabulary and comprehension instruction and on working with at-risk readers. Dr. Blachowicz was a Fulbright Fellow to Italy and is active in professional organizations and staff development nationally and internationally. She is co-director of the Literacy Partners: Advanced Reading Development Demonstration Project (ARDDP), a project on coaching and school literacy improvement in the Chicago Public Schools. In 2003, she was named to the roster of Outstanding Teacher Educators in Reading by the International Reading Association.

Karen Bromley is a SUNY Distinguished Teaching Professor in the School of Education at Binghamton University. Currently, she is a member of the board of the International Reading Association. Previously she was a third-grade teacher and K–12 reading specialist in Maryland and New York. Her research interests are comprehension and vocabulary development, literacy instruction and assessment, and writing. Her most recent books are *Writing for Educators: Personal Essays and Practical Advice; Stretching Students' Vocabulary;* and *50 Graphic Organizers for Reading, Writing, and More.*

María S. Carlo studies bilingualism in children and adults. Her research focuses on the cognitive processes that underlie reading in a second language and on understanding the differences in the reading processes of bilinguals and monolinguals. Dr. Carlo obtained a doctorate in psychology from the University of Massachusetts at Amherst. She is currently Associate Professor of teaching and learning in the School of Education at the University of Miami in Coral Gables, Florida.

Byeong-Young Cho is a former high school teacher in Korea and currently a doctoral student in the Reading Center at the University of Maryland, College Park. He is interested in literacy assessment and adolescents' Internet literacy practices.

Kristin Conradi is Assistant Professor in the Department of Curriculum, Instruction, and Counselor Education at North Carolina State University. She has taught literacy at several grade levels in inner-city schools and has worked as a K–3 reading specialist and a K–2 mentor and coach. Ms. Conradi is the coeditor of two recent books: *Issues and Trends in Literacy Education* and *Promoting Early Literacy.*

Maria Elliker Crassas is a former elementary classroom teacher, former elementary music teacher, and a certified reading specialist. She is currently a doctoral student and graduate assistant in the Reading Center at the University of Maryland, College Park. Her research interests include new literacies and multicultural education.

Patricia M. Cunningham is Professor of Education at Wake Forest University. Dr. Cunningham's passion has always been finding alternative ways to teach struggling readers. In 1991, she wrote *Phonics They Use: Words for Reading and Writing,* which is currently available in its fifth edition. She is coauthor, with Richard L. Allington, of *Classrooms That Work* and *Schools That Work.*

Jennifer Renner Del Nero is a doctoral student in the Language and Literacy program at Rutgers University and an instructor of college courses in general education and English education. She was previously a sixth- and seventh-grade language arts literacy instructor for inclusion, regular, and advanced classes at Green Brook Middle School in Green Brook, New Jersey. Ms. Del Nero's research interests surround adolescent literacy motivation.

Nell K. Duke is Professor of Teacher Education and Educational Psychology, and Co-director of the Literacy Achievement Research Center, at Michigan State University, East Lansing. Her research focuses on early literacy development, particularly among children living in poverty. Her specific areas of expertise include development of informational literacies in young children, comprehension development and instruction in early schooling, and issues of equity in literacy education. Dr. Duke has a strong interest in the preparation of educational researchers and has published and presented on this topic.

Patricia A. Edwards is Distinguished Professor of Language and Literacy in the Department of Teacher Education and Senior University Outreach Fellow at Michigan State University. She served as a member of the board of the International Reading Association (IRA) from 1998 to 2001 and as the first African American President of the National Reading Conference, the world's premier reading research organization, for the 2006–2007 term. Currently, she serves as the 2010–2011 President of the IRA. Her publications are rich with evidence and insights into issues of culture, identity, equity, and power that affect families and schools. She is the author of two nationally acclaimed family literacy programs—*Parents as Partners in Reading* and *Talking Your Way to Literacy*—and of *Tapping the Potential of Parents* and the forthcoming *It's Time for Straight Talk*; coauthor of *A Path to Follow, Change Is Gonna Come,* and the forthcoming *Reaching Nontraditional School Families in Nontraditional Ways*; and coeditor of *Best Practices in ELL Instruction.*

Douglas Fisher is Professor of Language and Literacy Education in the College of Education at San Diego State University and a classroom teacher at Health Sciences High and Middle College in San Diego. He is a recipient of the Celebrate Literacy Award from the International Reading Association, the Paul and Kate Farmer *English Journal* Writing Award from the National Council of Teachers of English, and a Christa McAuliffe Excellence in Teacher Education Award from the American Association of State Colleges and Universities. Dr. Fisher has published numerous articles on reading and literacy, differentiated instruction, and curriculum design, as well as many books.

Peter J. Fisher is Professor of Education in the National College of Education. Dr. Fisher's research interests include vocabulary development and instruction, and teaching students storytelling. He is coauthor of *Teaching Vocabulary in All Classrooms* and the author of numerous chapters and articles. He was coeditor of the *Illinois Reading Council Journal* from 1992 to 1996. In 1997, Dr. Fisher was inducted into the Illinois Reading Council Hall of Fame. As a staff developer, he has been involved in many long-term projects in schools in Chicago, Evanston, Skokie, and other school districts in the Chicago area. He has been a featured speaker at state and local conferences.

Nancy Frey is Professor of Literacy in the School of Teacher Education at San Diego State University (SDSU). She received the 2008 Early Career Achievement Award from the National Reading Conference, as well as the Christa McAuliffe Excellence in Teacher Education Award from the American Association of State Colleges and Universities. In addition to publishing with her colleague Douglas Fisher, she teaches a variety of courses in SDSU's teacher credentialing and reading specialist programs on elementary and secondary reading instruction, literacy in content areas, and supporting students with diverse learning needs. Dr. Frey is a credentialed special educator and reading specialist in California. She is privileged to learn with and from students and teachers at Health Sciences High and Middle College every day.

Linda B. Gambrell (*see* About the Editors).

Vicki Benson Griffo is a doctoral candidate at University of California, Berkeley. Her research interests are in reading development and disabilities, refining instructional methods, and developing teacher education. These interests first took root while she served as a first/second-grade teacher working with bilingual students in a rural, high-poverty district in central California. In 2002, Ms. Griffo earned her MA as a reading specialist at the University of California, Berkeley. In the course of 10 years, Ms. Griffo has conducted educational research on a variety of topics such as improving reading comprehension and reading assessment and remediation of at-risk students.

John T. Guthrie is the Jean Mullan Professor Emeritus in the Department of Human Development at the University of Maryland. He is a member of the International Reading Association's Reading Hall of Fame and received the Oscar S. Causey Award from the National Reading Conference. Dr. Guthrie is a Fellow of the American Educational Research Association and the American Psychological Association and principal investigator of a 5-year National Institute of Child Health and Human Development-funded grant targeting adolescent reading engagement of information text, focusing on all grade 7 students in a district from 2007 to 2012. Coauthored with former students, *Engaging Adolescents in Reading* is his latest book.

Susan J. Hart is a full-time doctoral student at the University of Kentucky, where she also received a master's degree in elementary education with a reading and writing endorsement for kindergarten through 12th-grade students. She is a former elementary school teacher who taught in the District of Columbia public school system. As a research assistant for Dr. Janice F. Almasi, she has assisted with various research endeavors, including collecting and analyzing data related to the Kentucky Reading Project and implementation of response to intervention across the state of Kentucky. Ms. Hart's dissertation research examines an online interactive community of practice that seeks to better support teachers, specifically as it relates to literacy and strategy instruction.

Jong-Yun Kim was a former high school language teacher in South Korea. He is a doctoral student at the University of Maryland, College Park, and works for a reading center in the university. His research interests are reading assessment, adolescents' comprehension of multiple texts, and their metacognitive strategy use.

Melanie R. Kuhn is Associate Professor in Literacy and Language at Boston University. She has authored two books on fluency instruction, as well as numerous articles and chapters. Her research interests also include literacy instruction for struggling readers, comprehension development, and vocabulary instruction. She currently teaches courses on reading methods and content-area literacy instruction.

Linda D. Labbo is Professor Emerita in the Department of Language and Literacy Education at the University of Georgia, Athens, and continues to teach graduate courses on media in literacy education, new literacies, theoretical models of the reading process, and early childhood literacy education. She has received several grants and awards, including an American Library Association Award for an Outstanding Academic Book of the Year, the Edward Fry Book Award from the National Reading Conference, the Phi Delta Kappa Faculty Research Award, the Ira Aaron Award for Teaching Excellence and Collegiality, and a National Science Foundation grant. She received the Computers in Reading Research Award from the Technology in Literacy Education Special Interest Group of the International Reading Association for demonstrating a dedication to promoting literacy and technology through instruction, research, and collaboration. Her consulting work currently focuses on the semiotic interactivities of children's e-books, online games, and transmedia involved in televised educational series and related social networking sites.

Laura Lang is a high school literacy coach in Madison, Wisconsin, and a doctoral student in the Department of Curriculum and Instruction at the University of Wisconsin–Madison. Previously, she worked as an English teacher and reading specialist/literacy coach in the Chicago Public Schools and at New Trier High School in suburban Chicago. Ms. Lang spearheaded the development of interdisciplinary literacy teams at both New Trier High School and Madison West High School, where she continues to work. Her current research interests include the professional identity development of secondary literacy coaches and literacy coaches as critical change agents.

Diane Lapp is Distinguished Professor of Education in the Department of Teacher Education at San Diego State University (SDSU). Her major areas of research and instruction regard issues related to struggling readers and writers who live in economically deprived settings, their families, and their teachers. Dr. Lapp directs and teaches field-based preservice and graduate programs and courses. She was the coeditor of *The California Reader* from 1999 to 2007 and is currently a coeditor of *Voices from the Middle,* published by the National Council of Teachers of English. She has also authored, coauthored, and edited many articles, columns, texts, handbooks, and children's materials on reading and language arts issues and has also chaired and co-chaired several International Reading Association (IRA) and National Reading Conference committees. Her many educational awards include being named as the Outstanding Teacher Educator and Faculty Member in the Department of Teacher Education at SDSU, the Distinguished Research Lecturer from SDSU's Graduate Division of Research, and IRA's 1996 Outstanding Teacher Educator of the Year. Dr. Lapp is also a member of both the California and the IRA Reading Halls of Fame.

Christina L. Madda is Assistant Professor in the Department of Reading at Northeastern Illinois University. She began her career teaching English as a second language. Her research interests include writing instruction in bilingual classrooms, teachers' instructional responses to policy, and university–community partnerships that strengthen teacher preparation.

Jacquelynn A. Malloy is Assistant Professor in the Graduate School of Education at George Mason University in Fairfax, Virginia. She is affiliated with the elementary education and literacy program areas and teaches literacy methods courses as well as differentiation and assessment and research methods. Dr. Malloy is also a university facilitator at two elementary schools in Prince William County, Virginia, where she supervises interns and collaborates with teachers and school administrators as part of a professional development school partnership. She recently coedited (with Barbara Marinak and Linda Gambrell) a volume on motivation for the International Reading Association's *Essential Reading* series. Her research interests include instructional methods for improving comprehension and engagement and supporting students' online reading comprehension skills and strategies.

Susan Anders Mazzoni is an independent literacy consultant who works with administrators and teachers to improve literacy practices in elementary school classrooms. For the past 10 years, she has worked with teachers on implementing guided reading practices for the purpose of building reading fluency, miscue analysis and prompting, and comprehension instruction. She has taught reading courses and served as a research assistant for the National Reading Research Center. Her work has been published in *The Reading Teacher, Reading Psychology*, and the *International Journal of Learning.*

Michael C. McKenna is the Thomas G. Jewell Professor of Reading at the University of Virginia. His research interests include comprehension in content settings, reading attitudes, technology applications, and beginning reading. Dr. McKenna has published 16 books and more than 100 articles, chapters, and technical reports. He was appointed by the U.S. Department of Education to the Expert Review Panel of Reading First and has worked closely with reform initiatives in seven states.

Aimee L. Morewood is Assistant Professor in the Department of Curriculum and Instruction, Literacy Studies, at West Virginia University. She teaches online graduate courses in children's literature and motivation, interest, and engagement, as well as undergraduate courses in primary reading instruction. Dr. Morewood works in a professional development school, where she collaborates with primary grade teachers. Her early career, working as a learning support teacher in an urban elementary school, guided her toward her current position and research agenda in literacy education with a focus on exemplary literacy teaching practices, and professional development of both inservice and preservice teachers.

Lesley Mandel Morrow (*see* About the Editors).

Donna Ogle is Professor of Reading and Language at National-Louis University (NLU) in Chicago, Illinois, and is active in research and professional development projects. She is currently senior consultant to the Chicago Striving Readers Project; co-director of the Reading Leadership Institute; and co-director of the Literacy Partners Project, a collaboration among the Chicago Public Schools, NLU, and the Chicago Community Trust. Dr. Ogle also serves as a literacy consultant internationally, including with Critical Thinking International and Grupo SM in Latin America. She is on the editorial review boards of *Lectura y Vida, The Reading Teacher,* and the *Journal of Adolescent and Adult Literacy.* She is past president of the International Reading Association and an elected member of the Reading Hall of Fame. She also conducts research on visual literacy and content comprehension, having developed both the K–W–L and PRC2 (Partner Reading and Content, Too) frameworks.

Jeanne R. Paratore is Professor and Program Coordinator of the Reading Education and Literacy Education programs at Boston University. She has been a classroom teacher, a reading specialist, and a Title I director. In 1989, she founded and now serves as advisor to the Intergenerational Literacy Program, a family literacy program that serves immigrant parents and their children. Dr. Paratore has conducted research and written widely on issues related to family literacy, classroom grouping practices, and interventions for struggling readers. She is currently principal investigator on a funded study of the effects of a family literacy intervention on the literacy and language performance of children in prekindergarten to second grade. Dr. Paratore is a frequent speaker on literacy instruction and has presented at local, national, and international conferences as well as in school districts throughout the United States.

P. David Pearson is a professor in the Language, Literacy, and Culture Program in the Graduate School of Education at the University of California, Berkeley, where he served as Dean from 2001 to 2010. He has written scores of articles and chapters and written or edited several books about research and practice, most notably the *Handbook of Reading Research,* now in its fourth volume. He has received numerous honors, including the William S. Gray Citation of Merit and the Albert Harris Award from the International Reading Association, the Oscar S. Causey Award from the National Reading Conference, the Alan Purves Award from the National Council of Teachers of English, and the Distinguished Contributions to Research in Education Award from the American Educational Research Association.

Taffy E. Raphael is on the Literacy, Language and Culture faculty at the University of Illinois at Chicago and President of SchoolRise LLC, supporting whole-school literacy improvement through professional development. Dr. Raphael's research has focused on strategy instruction in comprehension and writing, frameworks for literacy curriculum and instruction (e.g., Book Club *Plus*), and whole-school reform in literacy. Dr. Raphael has published several books and more than 100 articles and chapters. Her work has been recognized through the International Reading Association's (IRA) Outstanding Teacher Educator in Reading Award, the University of Illinois at Urbana–Champaign Distinguished Alumni Award, and the National Reading Conference Oscars S. Causey Award for Lifetime Contributions to Literacy Research. She is a Fellow of the National Council of Research in Language and Literacy and a member of the IRA Reading Hall of Fame. She has served on the board of the IRA.

Timothy Rasinski is Professor of Literacy Education at Kent State University. He has written more than 200 articles and has authored, coauthored, or edited over 50 books or curriculum programs on reading education. He is author of the best-selling book *The Fluent Reader,* now in its second edition. His scholarly interests include reading fluency and word study, reading in the elementary and middle grades, and readers who struggle. Dr. Rasinski's research on reading has been cited by the National Reading Panel and has been published in journals such as *Reading Research Quarterly, The Reading Teacher, Reading Psychology,* and the *Journal of Educational Research.* He recently served a 3-year term on the board of the International Reading Association (IRA) and is past president of the College Reading Association. From 1992 to 1999, he was coeditor of *The Reading Teacher* and also served as coeditor of the *Journal of Literacy Research.* He won the A. B. Herr and Laureate Awards from the College Reading Association for his scholarly contributions to literacy education and was elected to the IRA Reading Hall of Fame in 2010.

D. Ray Reutzel is the Emma Eccles Jones Distinguished Professor and Endowed Chair of Early Childhood Literacy at Utah State University. Dr. Reutzel is the author of more than 190 refereed research reports, articles, books, book chapters, and monographs. He has received more than $7.9 million in research and professional development funding from private, state, and federal funding agencies and more than $25 million in private foundation gifts and donations. He was the coeditor of *The Reading Teacher* from 2002 to 2007. Dr. Reutzel received the A. B. Herr Award from the College Reading Association in 1999 and the John C. Manning Public School Service Award from the International Reading Association (IRA) in 2007. He served as President of the College Reading Association from 2007 to 2008 and also served as a member of the board of the IRA from 2007 to 2010. He was elected to the IRA Reading Hall of Fame in 2011.

Jennifer Rowsell is a Canada Research Chair in Multiliteracies at Brock University in St. Catherines, Ontario. The author/coauthor of several books in the areas of new literacy studies, multimodality, and multiliteracies, she has also published many journal articles and attends national and international conferences. Her current research is an Elva Knight-funded research project that examines how adolescents adopt a design-based approach to learning literacy and language arts. She has two new books, *Design Literacies* (with Mary P. Sheridan) and *Artifactual Literacies* (with Kate Pahl).

Diane H. Tracey is Associate Professor of Education at Kean University, where she specializes in theories and models of literacy education. Coauthor of *Lenses on Reading: An Introduction to Theories and Models,* she has written widely on topics related to literacy achievement and is an active presenter at national conferences. Dr. Tracey currently serves as Secretary of the Literacy Research Association (formerly the National Reading Conference) and is coeditor of the *Journal of School Connections.* In addition to university teaching, Dr. Tracey is a literacy consultant for school districts and educational software companies. Prior to her work at the university level, she was an early childhood educator and a research assistant on a large, federally funded grant studying children's reading disabilities.

Foreword

The term *best practices* has been used in a wide variety of domains—for everything from growing tomatoes to managing file servers. Simply stated, a best practice is "the best, most effective way to do something."[1] The *Business Dictionary* defines best practice as "methods and techniques that have consistently shown results superior [to] those achieved with other means, and which are used as benchmarks to strive for."[2] This book is about the best and most effective ways to develop literacy.

To say that something is *the* or *a* "best" practice is a weighty claim in any domain, but certainly in a domain such as literacy instruction, in which such a wide variety of practices are available and in which so much research and professional experience have been accumulated. The editors of this volume chose authors who are widely admired in their respective areas to identify best practices in that area. I urge you to take the time to read the contributor bios, and prepare to be impressed. And I urge you to take full advantage of these contributors' perspectives and expertise by reading what they have written, of course, but also by reading the research and research reviews they invoke in their chapters. Much as we are inclined to read the works a novelist recommends, we should, as much as possible, read the research these scholars value.

Best practices have never been more important. We now have the highest expectations for literacy that we have ever had for students in the history of the United States. Yet time available to meet these expectations is not substantially different than it was decades ago. In many schools across the country we still have only about 6 hours a day with students for only about 180 days of the year. And there is pressure on this time from a host of domains other than literacy. Given the constraints on time to focus on literacy during the school day, we simply cannot afford, if we ever could, *not* to use best practices.

---

[1] *www.macmillandictionary.com/dictionary/british/best-practice.*

[2] *www.businessdictionary.com/definition/best-practice.html#ixzz13Kje8BSw.*

The circumstances that make best practices so important also make them difficult to implement. We are so pressed for time that it can be overwhelming to think about yet more content to add to your curriculum or yet more strategies to add to your instruction. For this reason, I encourage you to read the chapters in this book not only for what *to* do, but for what *not* to do. In some cases, contributors are quite explicit about ineffective practices. For example, in Chapter 14, Douglas Fisher and Nancy Frey identify as ineffective a practice in which students complete a graphic organizer by simply copying one the teacher has placed on an overhead projector, rather than doing the analysis or thinking themselves. If you, or a teacher you know, has provided students with already completed graphic organizers (and indeed, a number of commercially available programs include them), you can eliminate this practice and devote that time to the more effective practices described in the book. In other cases, it is a matter of reading between the lines of a chapter—reading for what is not there as well as what is there. For example, the word *worksheets* never once appears in Patricia M. Cunningham's chapter (Chapter 8) on best practices in teaching phonological awareness and phonics, despite the ubiquity of worksheets in teaching these topics. And nowhere in Camille L. Z. Blachowicz and Peter J. Fisher's chapter (Chapter 9) on best practices in vocabulary instruction do the authors recommend having students look up a list of words in the dictionary and write sentences for each, though this is arguably the most common vocabulary practice used in U.S. schools today.[3] The absence of these practices implies that they can be either eliminated or at least reduced. Scrutinizing our practice for these less-than-best practices may allow you to make room for the best practices that should be our highest teaching priority.

Finally, it is important to note that what we view as a "best practice" can, in fact should, change over time as additional research is conducted and experience gleaned. We must be ready to supplant practices we once held dear in favor of those that have proven to be more effective. For this reason, it is wise that the editors have regularly updated this text, now in its fourth edition with the first edition published only 12 years ago. I end by thanking them, and all of the contributors to this important text, for their ongoing efforts to give students what they deserve—*the best.*

NELL K. DUKE, EdD
Michigan State University

[3]Blachowicz and Fisher do note that instruction that *combines* definitional information with "active processing, such as adding contextual information, writing contextual discovery, or rich manipulation of words" (p. 236) is effective.

Contents

Part III. Evidence-Based Strategies for Literacy Learning and Teaching

Part IV. Perspectives on Special Issues

Introduction

Jennifer Renner Del Nero
Lesley Mandel Morrow
Linda B. Gambrell

> If I have seen further than others, it is by standing upon the shoulders of giants.
>
> —ISAAC NEWTON

Today's literacy teachers face more challenges than ever before. They must negotiate state and national pressure for students to meet stringent standards of college and career readiness, increased classroom diversity, and an ever-growing concern for the overall well-being and success of every student. All of these challenges must be met amid rapid transitions from print to digital-based media that have dramatic implications for how teachers instruct and students learn. The fourth edition of *Best Practices in Literacy Instruction* serves as a powerful guide that teachers can use to navigate the complex and dynamic components surrounding contemporary reading and writing instruction. It contains the latest insights and research from literacy leaders in their respective fields with direct implications for classroom instruction. This is a resource for literacy practitioners; like the past editions, it contains innovative knowledge and advice to help educators improve their pedagogy and practice. These authors are fully cognizant of the unique pressures and demands of today's literacy classrooms; they tailor their writing to help teachers succeed amid these challenges.

The third edition of this book encouraged preservice and practicing teachers alike to develop a *vision*, defining what they hope to achieve regarding the literacy development of their students under the advantages and constraints of their respective school districts. The fourth edition calls on teachers to *expand* that vision in order to embrace the complex notion of what it means to be a successful literacy instructor amid current challenges and evolutions. Today's literacy teachers have to see further into every aspect of their instruction for the future success and well-being of their students. They have to nurture global, dynamic, and creative thinkers who will live and work in future industries and endeavors, some of which do not yet exist in our world today. Although this book is designed for practicing teachers, the authors hope it will also be utilized with teacher educators and professional development, for graduate students and reading specialists, as well as by administrators who seek schoolwide literacy success.

Literacy researchers approach their projects from a multivariate perspective. They consider overarching perspectives on literacy, specific populations of students with unique needs, classroom contexts, pedagogy, motivation, and various social interactions and relationships. The contributors to this volume remain in contact with classroom teachers and students through classroom-based research initiatives and literacy program innovations. They believe literacy teaching is at its best when educators are informed about research-based literature that they can apply to their specific classroom circumstances and student populations. Each author was asked to write about current research, theory, and practices in their area. Specifically, they were asked to include recent research and findings pertaining to response to intervention (RTI), motivation, English language learners (ELLs), content-area reading, technology, new literacies, policy issues that affect classroom practice, and the new common core standards, where applicable.

This book is organized into four parts: Perspectives on Best Practices, Best Practices for All Students, Evidence-Based Strategies for Literacy Learning and Teaching, and Perspectives on Special Issues. In Part I, the authors explore fundamental beliefs and ideals surrounding the teaching of literacy for all grade levels; in particular, the authors focus on comprehensive literacy instruction that touches upon all facets affecting reading and writing development. It introduces and previews more specific topics that arise in later sections. Part II adopts a more precise lens in regard to particular student populations and their unique literacy needs, specifically early childhood students, struggling readers, ELLs, and adolescent learners. Part III presents the latest evidence-based research and strategies for the following components of literacy instruction: motivation, phonological awareness, vocabulary instruction, comprehension, fluency, writing, and assessment. Part IV introduces new perspectives on specific issues surrounding effective literacy practices: content-area literacy, technology usage, new literacies integration, instruction organization, the family's role and influence on literacy development, and professional development.

PART I. PERSPECTIVES ON BEST PRACTICES

In Chapter 1, Linda B. Gambrell, Jacquelynn A. Malloy, and Susan Anders Mazzoni discuss 10 evidence-based best practices for literacy instruction. The authors maintain that narrow views of literacy do not serve students well in their development as readers and writers. These practices are grounded in a comprehensive literacy framework that looks at the development of the whole child. At the heart of all 10 practices lies the need for effective teachers. The authors also maintain that in order for any program to be effective, teachers must be allowed the vision, latitude, and agency to alter programs in order to best meet the needs of their students.

Christina L. Madda, Vicki Benson Griffo, P. David Pearson, and Taffy E. Raphael begin Chapter 2 with a discussion on what it means to have a balanced literacy program, with the understanding that the notion of "balance" constantly evolves. The authors look at past perspectives of what defined a balanced approach to reading and writing, as well as how external forces continuously reshape and redefine this idea. The historical analysis serves as a springboard for the authors to discuss what entails today's balanced approach to literacy instruction. The authors insist that in order to achieve balance, flexibility and creativity are paramount.

PART II. BEST PRACTICES FOR ALL STUDENTS

In Chapter 3, Lesley Mandel Morrow, Diane H. Tracey, and Jennifer Renner Del Nero provide an overview of what "best practices" means for early childhood education. The authors present a brief research and theoretical overview of past literacy initiatives in early childhood education. This section is followed by practical activity suggestions and instructional strategies that nurture all the various components related to early reading and writing development. The chapter concludes with a specific case study that illustrates how these ideals can be effectively integrated into the classroom environment. Overall, there is attention directed at ELLs, technology, the new common core standards, RTI, and reading content materials.

Within the framework of supporting struggling readers, Richard L. Allington, in Chapter 4, discusses how the number of struggling readers correlates to the number of effective literacy teachers. The chapter details the experiences of two highly effective teachers to serve as models for other educators in terms of their ability to promote high-quality reading instruction and effective intervention for students with reading difficulties. Essentially, Dr. Allington argues that innovative and effective reading lessons must be made available to all students in order to truly conquer this problem.

The understanding that ELLs need an integrated and comprehensive approach to language acquisition is discussed by María S. Carlo and Alain Bengochea in Chapter 5. They begin by considering the theory and research that guides the teaching of ELLs, with a particular focus on their oral language proficiency in terms of overall literacy achievement. The authors reiterate the unique challenge of trying to read in an unfamiliar language and how a focus on oral language can help students overcome this obstacle. This section is followed by a review of recent literature focusing on early reading instruction that builds on learners' strengths and oral language needs. The chapter closes with a look at recent initiatives that focus more on vocabulary development and less on general language proficiency.

In Chapter 6, Donna Ogle and Laura Lang take into account the unique needs of adolescent literacy learners. They begin by looking at current research-supported components of adolescent reading and writing instruction with a specific emphasis on the need for schoolwide support and consistency in literacy practices across content domains. The authors acknowledge the unique challenges of adolescent literacy instruction and offer two examples of interdisciplinary teams that overcame these obstacles. They offer practical tips for addressing the needs of adolescents and provide an additional list of references that readers can refer to for more information on effective adolescent literacy instruction.

PART III. EVIDENCE-BASED STRATEGIES FOR LITERACY LEARNING AND TEACHING

John T. Guthrie, in Chapter 7, discusses literacy motivation and its direct relation to students' interest, confidence, and dedication to reading and writing tasks. Guthrie outlines research on evidence-based classroom approaches that include autonomy support and teacher support through care and commitment. Finally, classroom practices that are built on relevance, choice, success, collaboration, cross-curricular connections, and social justice principles are provided as exemplars of practices that cultivate literacy motivation.

In Chapter 8, Patricia M. Cunningham considers the role phonemic awareness plays in learning to read. She explores the recent research on topics surrounding the teaching of phonics, including multisyllabic word decoding, in the classroom context. Aligning pedagogies and practices are outlined, and Cunningham ends the chapter with practical examples and tips for fostering phonological awareness.

Camille L. Z. Blachowicz and Peter J. Fisher explore best practices surrounding vocabulary instruction in Chapter 9. The authors present research-based guidelines for effective vocabulary instruction. Each guideline is supported by the research that defined it, and practical suggestions for enacting each guideline follow. The authors describe, in rich detail, a classroom that exemplifies these principles. The chapter culminates with additional resources for learning about and successfully implementing vocabulary instruction in the classroom.

In Chapter 10, Janice F. Almasi and Susan J. Hart urge readers to shift their teaching focus from specific reading comprehension strategies to an approach that teaches readers how to become independently strategic readers. In order to foster an environment where strategic reading habits are learned, Almasi and Hart insist that the following classroom conditions must be in place: students must feel free to take risks, metacognition must be encouraged, explicit instruction must be provided, and new information must be scaffolded for students. These ingredients allow readers to feel supported, while also allowing teachers to be change agents in improving their comprehensive ability to train strategic readers.

In Chapter 11, Melanie R. Kuhn and Timothy Rasinski expand the traditional concept of fluency, or one that strictly focuses on rapid word recognition. Instead, they delve into the nuances of fluent reading and critical corresponding elements such as intonation. The chapter also explores more creative fluency practices than traditional repeated reading exercises. The authors also offer assessment measurements for teachers to use alongside this expanded view of fluency.

Karen Bromley focuses on effective writing instruction in Chapter 12. She briefly reviews the research and theory surrounding the teaching of writing as it pertains to kindergarten through grade 8 students. Bromley discusses topics such as grammar, spelling, conventions, and specific student populations within this framework. The majority of the chapter details evidence-based best practices for writing instruction that include developing a context for writing, successful integration of technologies, ideas for explicit instruction, and assessment measures. Bromley concludes by looking toward the future of writing instruction and its implications.

Peter Afflerbach, Jong-Yun Kim, Maria Elliker Crassas, and Byeong-Young Cho take up the discussion of literacy assessment in Chapter 13. The authors begin by providing an overview on how classroom-based reading assessment tools are developed. They explain that these assessments are the result of a fusion between curriculum and instruction, teachers and students, and tradition and policies. This results in the privileging of certain assessments, which can potentially lead to assessment imbalance. Afflerbach et al. pinpoint the areas of imbalance and discuss potential strategies to remedy the problem. The chapter concludes with a discussion of the "best practices" components surrounding classroom-based assessments.

PART IV. PERSPECTIVES ON SPECIAL ISSUES

In Chapter 14, Douglas Fisher and Nancy Frey delve into best practices surrounding content-area literacy. The chapter opens with the realization that, although reading for information is vital in secondary classrooms, many "good" readers struggle with content-area text comprehension. The authors discuss probable causes for this phenomenon, such as utilizing reading techniques better suited for narrative texts. This section is followed by a discussion of the recent research and practice surrounding effective reading of content-specific texts for true reader understanding.

Michael C. McKenna, Linda D. Labbo, Kristin Conradi, and Jessica Baxter discuss the effective use of technology in literacy instruction in Chapter 15. They first offer an overview of how technology has been utilized in the classroom and then examine the importance of appropriately situating technology in social contexts within the classroom milieu. Evidence-based approaches for younger children are imparted, as well as techniques that are effective with more skilled readers. Finally, the authors detail how technology can enhance and support the literacy experience of special student populations, such as ELLs.

In Chapter 16, Jennifer Rowsell and Diane Lapp explore new literacies and corresponding implications for literacy instruction. The authors trace the history of this topic from the seminal research of authors of past decades to a present view of what new literacy studies entails for wide-ranging issues, such as linguistic diversity and alternative communicative modes. The theory presented in the first half of the chapter is made tangible by the practical suggestions given in the latter portion. The case studies of this chapter exemplify the complexity surrounding literacy practices. Rowsell and Lapp argue that literacy is a social and cultural practice that can successfully be developed through an array of modes. Finally, the authors consider what it means to teach literacy in a global and digital context; they call for dramatic changes to teacher pedagogy, student practices, achievement standards, and professional development opportunities that will help teachers meet these new literacy demands.

In Chapter 17, D. Ray Reutzel expounds on the topic of differentiated instruction through a review of related theoretical and research perspectives, including response to intervention (RTI). Components from evidence-based research instruction that align with differentiation and RTI are presented, as well as related use of literacy assessments as they support these domains. An array of research-supported instructional practice, such as concept-oriented reading instruction (CORI), is described for readers to utilize in their classrooms. The chapter wraps up with a look at scheduling considerations to effectively support differentiation and RTI.

Jeanne R. Paratore and Patricia A. Edwards reflect on the complex dynamic of the family and its effect on literacy development in Chapter 18. The goal of this chapter is to provide ideas for the classroom teacher to foster positive and meaningful home–school partnerships. The authors provide a pithy synopsis of the research detailing parental involvement and student achievement, with a focus on the teacher's role in fostering such involvement. They also discuss particular initiatives and ultimately provide teachers with advice that will help them develop meaningful relationships with students' families.

Best Practices in Literacy Instruction concludes with a look at professional development. Rita M. Bean and Aimee L. Morewood begin Chapter 19 with a summary of the recent research on best practices surrounding professional development, followed by an analysis of the research findings. Bean and Morewood assert that meaningful professional development is embedded in the work of teachers, has content emphasis, and allows teachers to practice, apply, and receive feedback and further support on the new knowledge presented in professional development sessions. This section is followed by a glimpse into several promising professional development endeavors, such as literacy coaching and professional learning communities.

Education is at its best when ideas are shared. The collaborative energies of these literacy experts and teachers directly affecting students paves the way for educative success. *Best Practices in Literacy Instruction* is a vehicle for that fusion. It allows practitioners to "stand on the shoulders" of the "giants" in their respective literacy fields, renowned by their peers for their exceptional research and classroom expertise, and learn from that knowledge. Literacy teachers can then take the wealth of wisdom that lies between the pages of this resource and create a new and unique version of "best practices" as it relates to their own students, with an expanded vision of what it means to successfully teach literacy today.

PART I

Perspectives on Best Practices

CHAPTER 1

Evidence-Based Best Practices in Comprehensive Literacy Instruction

Linda B. Gambrell
Jacquelynn A. Malloy
Susan Anders Mazzoni

> There is hard work ahead as we strive to improve reading education and provide comprehensive literacy instruction for all our students.
>
> —PRESSLEY (2007, p. 404)

This chapter will:

- Present and discuss features of evidence-based best practices for comprehensive literacy instruction.
- Discuss the importance of determining and differentiating best practices to provide *all* students with opportunities for literacy learning.
- Discuss the important role of teachers as visionary decision makers.
- Present 10 evidence-based best practices for comprehensive literacy instruction.
- Propose a mindset for thoughtful incorporation of best practices for comprehensive literacy instruction.

Students must be literate in order to succeed in school and in the workplaces of tomorrow. However, evidence across the past four decades indicates that the achievement has not been equal for all children in American schools

(Morrow, Rueda, & Lapp, 2009; National Assessment of Educational Progress, 2007). There is considerable evidence of a growing gap in reading achievement among (1) minority and nonminority students, (2) students from poorer and richer families, (3) students who are native English speakers and those who are English language learners (ELLs), and (4) students identified for special education services and those in regular education (Morrow et al., 2009). Consider the following statistics that further substantiate the achievement gap:

- By age 2, children who are read to regularly by an adult have greater language comprehension, larger vocabularies, and higher cognitive skills than children read to less often (Raikes et al., 2006).
- In middle-income neighborhoods the ratio of books per child is 13 to 1, while in low-income neighborhoods the ratio is 1 age-appropriate book for every 300 children (Dickinson & Neuman, 2006).
- In the United States, approximately 13 million children live in poverty. Poverty places children at higher risk for a number of problems, including those associated with brain development and social and emotional development (Every Child Matters, 2008, *www.everychildmatters.org/homelandinsecutity/geomatters.pdf*).
- Each school day, seven thousand students become dropouts. That adds up to 1.2 million students who will not graduate high school each year (Alliance for Excellent Education, 2007).
- Approximately 78% of juvenile crime is committed by high school dropouts (*www.edubook.com/causes-and-prevention-of-high-school-dropouts/10917/*, retrieved August 7, 2010; *www.readingfoundation.org/Economics_of_Early_Childhood_Literacy.jsp*, retrieved August 7, 2010).
- The average annual income for a high school dropout in 2004 was $16,485, compared with $26,156 for a high school graduate, a difference of $9,671 (*factfinder.census.gov/jsp/saff/SAFFInfo.jsp?_pageId=sp2_economic&_submenuId*, retrieved August 7, 2010).
- The Progress in International Reading Literacy Study (Programme for International Student Assessment; PISA) concluded that finding ways to engage students in reading may be one of the most effective ways to leverage social change. According to the PISA report, being an enthusiastic and frequent reader was more of an advantage than having well-educated parents in good jobs (Programme for International Student Assessment; PISA, 2006; *nces.ed.gov/surveys/pirls/pirls2006.asp, retrieved August 7, 2010*).

These statistics reflect the many challenges teachers face in classrooms, as well as the importance of providing effective literacy instruction for all students. Gordon (2009) contends that "every child must be visible if we are to succeed as a world-class nation" (p. ix). According to Gordon:

> It is a source of shame that our society has moved slowly to achieve the necessary accommodations and differentiations in educational treatments, and has essentially avoided serious effort at providing improved circumstances of life for our most seriously socially disadvantaged children. . . . It is the society's good fortune that some of us have taken seriously the need for accommodation and differentiation in the teaching and learning transactions made available to diverse populations of students. (2009, p. x)

The authors of the chapters in this volume are among the educators who take seriously the need for accommodation and differentiation to enhance literacy development for all students, many of whom struggle because of life circumstances. Any serious effort to close the reading achievement gap will require attention to all aspects of literacy teaching and learning. This challenge can only be met with instruction and assessments that are grounded in evidence-based best practices and the continued search for principles of learning that work for all our students (Garcia & Wiese, 2009).

We must acknowledge that some students are at risk of academic failure because of their life conditions. Furthermore, we need to acknowledge that school cultures require specialized academic abilities. Life conditions and experiences that do not support and encourage the development of those specialized academic abilities "tend to produce children who are deficient in the ability to handle academic work" (Gordon, 2009, p. ix). We think Gordon has it right when he states, "We know in the 21st century that the absence of a certain developed ability because of the absence of opportunity to learn should not be interpreted as absence of ability to learn, and the recognition of the fact of diverse human characteristics demands accommodation and differentiation in pedagogical treatment" (p. x).

During the past decade (2000–2010) literacy instruction has continued to be a hot topic in education, in the media, and with politicians at every level of government. Federal programs and national reports from the previous decade, such as No Child Left Behind (NCLB, 2002) and the National Reading Panel (NRP) report (NICHHD, 2000), continue to influence both assessment and instruction in our schools. As we move into the next decade it is clear that the following initiatives will influence literacy research, policy, and practice: response to intervention (NASDSE, 2010), Race to the Top (U.S. Department of Education, 2010), and Common Core State Standards for English Language Arts (Common Core State Standards Initiative, 2010).

RESPONSE TO INTERVENTION

Response to Intervention (RTI) is a federally funded program designed to integrate assessment and intervention within a multilevel prevention system to maximize student achievement. As an early intervention framework, RTI provides a system for identifying students who require intervention and the subsequent supports to meet their needs, as well as a process by which students may be identified to receive special services. The major feature of RTI is a leveled intervention system that often includes: the core reading program for all students; supplementary instruction for students with early reading difficulties; and intensive intervention for students who still struggle. RTI involves educators in identifying students at risk for poor learning outcomes, monitoring student progress, providing evidence-based interventions, adjusting the intensity and nature of those interventions depending on student responsiveness, and identifying students with learning or other disabilities. An increasing number of states have developed RTI models to address students at risk of school failure that may involve new assessment techniques, data management tools, and instructional methodologies for teaching and monitoring students showing the least progress.

RACE TO THE TOP

Race to the Top (R2T) is a federally funded initiative that provides competitive grants to encourage and reward States that develop educational plans that emphasize the following: creating the conditions for innovation and reform; achieving significant improvement in student outcomes; making substantial gains in student achievement; closing achievement gaps; improving high school graduation rates; and ensuring student preparation for success in college and careers. The state proposals must include specific educational plans in four core areas:

- Initiating standards and assessments that prepare students to succeed in college and the workplace and to compete in the global economy.
- Developing data systems that measure student achievement and inform teachers and principals about how they can improve instruction.
- Recruiting, developing, rewarding, and retaining effective teachers and principals, especially where they are needed most.
- Turning around our lowest-achieving schools (U.S. Department of Education, 2010).

COMMON CORE STATE STANDARDS FOR ENGLISH LANGUAGE ARTS

In the spring of 2010 the Common Core State Standards for English Language Arts (CCSSELA) were released. This effort to develop common core state standards for the United States was guided by the National Governors Association (NGA) Center for Best Practices and the Council of Chief State School Officers (CCSSO) in collaboration with content experts, states, teachers, school administrators, and parents. The standards articulate a vision of what it means to be "a literate person in the twenty-first century" (CCSSI, 2010). According to the CCSSI mission statement the standards

> provide a consistent, clear understanding of what students are expected to learn, so teachers and parents know what they need to do to help them. The standards are designed to be robust and relevant to the real world, reflecting the knowledge and skills that our young people need for success in college and careers. With American students fully prepared for the future, our communities will be best positioned to compete successfully in the global economy. (CCSSI, 2010)

Most educators agree that the federally funded programs, RTI and R2T, as well as the CCSSELA will have a dramatic impact on literacy instruction and assessment in American classrooms in the coming decade.

THE CONTINUING INFLUENCE OF THE NRP

The report of the National Reading Panel (NICHHD, 2000) led us to focus on five factors of instruction—phonemic awareness, phonics, fluency, vocabulary, and comprehension—perhaps to the exclusion of others. Although these areas of skill development are essential to reading instruction from the viewpoint of basic reading processes, they are by no means a magic bullet that will lead to successful literacy achievement by all students, and they do not address areas of reading and writing that are seen by many states, districts, schools, and teachers as being equally important. We must be cautious about viewing the act of reading as a sum total of discrete processes, whereby instruction in one weak area will magically improve students' "reading achievement." Instead, we argue for consideration of evidence-based best practices within a comprehensive literacy framework. Such a framework includes attention to motivation; opportunities to read and write; differentiated assessment and instruction; and reading, writing, listening, and speaking for wide, authentic, and varied purposes.

MOVING FORWARD

There is universal agreement in our field that the foundation for all instructional practice, regardless of one's theoretical or pragmatic orientation to reading, is the goal of improving reading achievement for all students. Indeed, there are many points of agreement in the reading profession, even among individuals with diverse philosophies (Braunger & Lewis, 2006; Flippo, in press; Rasinski, 2001). In a study designed to explore the contexts and practices on which literacy experts could agree, Flippo (1998, 2001, in press) conducted a survey of literacy experts representing a wide spectrum of beliefs and philosophies. She found that these literacy experts agreed about the contexts and practices that both facilitate learning to read and make learning to read difficult. According to Rasinski (2001), the major finding of Flippo's study of literacy experts is that "the perceived gulf that exists between orientations to research and practice in literacy education by literacy researchers and scholars is not as large as it may seem" (p. 159).

Although we have learned a great deal about literacy and instruction over the past few decades, there remains significant controversy over what constitutes "best practices" in literacy instruction. Interestingly, our developing understanding of the literacy process appears to contribute to the ongoing debate. While we agree that there is no *single* best practice, we do suggest that teachers remain abreast of the current research so that they can judiciously select from evidence-based instructional practices to meet the diverse needs of their students.

We have become increasingly aware of the complexity of reading development and instruction; consequently, many researchers have adopted broader perspectives regarding the nature of literacy and how literacy learning occurs (Braunger & Lewis, 2006). For example, since the 1970s, researchers have moved from performing laboratory-controlled experiments, in which one aspect of learning was studied independently of the learning context, to conducting research in naturalistic classroom settings where contextual variables such as affective environment, authenticity of tasks, social interaction, parental involvement, or types of materials can be considered and evaluated. Research has shown that, indeed, many contextual variables affect literacy learning.

Formative and design experiments (Reinking & Bradley, 2008) are emerging as a means of investigating promising instructional methods and classroom practices while taking into account the myriad variables that affect teaching and learning in classrooms. These research studies seek to *design* or *form* the practice, method, or intervention in a classroom—or several classrooms—over a period when factors that *enhance* progress toward a pedagogical goal can be noted in each classroom context. Similarly, factors that *inhibit* progress toward the pedagogical goal can be addressed by the teacher/researcher team, who can then develop modifications based on theory and professional knowledge or judgment.

Furthermore, as workplace demands have evolved due to changes in industry and technology, so has our definition of what it means to be literate. Simply being able to decode and answer low-level literal questions about a piece of text is no longer sufficient. Becoming fully literate in the 21st century has come to mean, among many things, using strategies independently to construct meaning from traditional as well as electronic texts, using text information to build conceptual understanding, effectively communicating ideas orally and in writing, and developing the intrinsic desire to read and write (Biancarosa & Snow, 2004; Braunger & Lewis, 2006). To compete effectively in a global economy, students must acquire expertise in moving across multiple platforms for reading and communicating. Explicit and supported instruction in the use of the Internet and other information and communication technologies is essential to preparing future generations for the constantly changing technological landscape of their future professions (*www.21stcenturyskills.org*).

EVIDENCE-BASED BEST PRACTICES

Although no single instructional program, approach, or method has been found to be effective in teaching all students to read, *evidence-based best practices* that promote high rates of achievement have been documented. An evidence-based best practice refers to an instructional practice with a record of success that is both trustworthy and valid. There is evidence that when this practice is used with a particular group of children, the children can be expected to make gains in reading achievement (International Reading Association, 2002a, 2002b). Providing comprehensive literacy instruction in today's increasingly diverse classrooms requires teachers to differentiate student needs and assess skillfully in order to design appropriate instruction to meet the individual needs of all students. In addition, the classroom teacher must be adept at identifying student needs through ongoing formative assessments and providing appropriate whole-group, small-group, and individual instruction.

What counts as evidence of reliable and trustworthy practice? A position paper published by the International Reading Association (2002b) asserts that such evidence provides:

- *Objective* data that any evaluator would identify and interpret similarly.
- *Valid* data that adequately represent the tasks children need to accomplish to be successful readers.
- *Reliable* data that will remain essentially unchanged if collected on a different day or by a different person.
- *Systematic* data that were collected according to a rigorous design of either experimentation or observation.
- *Refereed* data that have been approved for publication by a panel of independent reviewers.

Allington (2005) asked "What counts as evidence in evidence-based education?" In our view, evidence-based instruction involves teachers making decisions using "professional wisdom integrated with the best available empirical evidence" (Allington, 2005, p. 16). This definition of evidence-based instruction honors the wisdom and evidence derived from professional experience and recognizes the important role of empirical research (Allington, 2005; Pressley, 2007).

Furthermore, no single investigation or research study ever establishes a practice as effective. When evaluating claims of evidence for best practices, we must determine whether the research was data based, rigorous, and systematic (Bogdan & Biklen, 1992; International Reading Association, 2002b). It is important to note that the *convergence of evidence* from an array of research studies, using a variety of research designs and methodologies, allows us to determine best practices.

In order to provide instruction using best practices as well as make appropriate instructional and assessment decisions, teachers need a strong knowledge of good evidence, drawn from both professional wisdom and the research. One of the most important questions a teacher can ask is "What evidence is available that suggests that using this practice in my classroom will support comprehensive literacy instruction and increase reading achievement for my students?"

COMPREHENSIVE LITERACY INSTRUCTION

The goal of comprehensive literacy instruction is to ensure that all students achieve their full literacy potential. This instruction should prepare our students to enter adulthood with the skills they will need to participate fully in a democratic society that is part of a global economy. Students need to be able to read and write with purpose, competence, ease, and joy. Comprehensive literacy instruction emphasizes the personal, intellectual, and social nature of literacy learning and supports the notion that students learn new meanings in response to new experiences rather than simply learning what others have created. Thus comprehensive literacy instruction is in keeping with constructivist learning theory and social learning perspectives that emphasize the development of students' cognitive abilities, such as critical thinking and decision making. Our students need and deserve comprehensive literacy instruction that is well informed and based on a broad model of the reading process.

Comprehensive literacy instruction:

- Is a balanced approach that involves appropriate emphasis on meaning making and skill instruction.
- Incorporates evidence-based best practices to suit the needs of all students in whole-group, small-group, and individualized instruction.
- Builds on the knowledge that students bring to school.
- Acknowledges reciprocity among reading processes (e.g., decoding, vocabulary, comprehension, motivation) and between reading and writing.
- Recognizes that comprehension is the ultimate goal of literacy instruction.

- Emphasizes meaning construction through open and collaborative literacy tasks and activities that require critical thinking.
- Offers opportunities for students to apply literacy strategies in the context of meaningful tasks for real-world purposes.
- Provides for differentiated assessment and instruction in accordance with the diverse strengths and needs of students (i.e., struggling readers, ELLs).

Teachers who provide comprehensive literacy instruction have a broad vision of literacy that is continually informed by evidence-based best practices. They understand literacy learning well enough to adapt the learning environment, materials, and methods to particular situations and students. Packaged program approaches typically lack such adaptability. Thus, in the final analysis, comprehensive literacy instruction rests on the shoulders of teachers who make informed decisions about the instructional and assessment approaches and practices that are most appropriate for each student.

TEACHERS AS VISIONARY DECISION MAKERS

Researchers who have entered classrooms in the past few years to observe and record the types of instruction that are occurring in high-achieving learning environments found that, beyond a carefully orchestrated integration of skills and strategies, content, and literature, successful classrooms are led by teachers who motivate and support individual students in ways that cannot be prescribed by any one program, method, or practice (Pressley, 2007; Pressley, Allington, Wharton-McDonald, Block, & Morrow, 2001; Wharton-McDonald, Pressley, & Hampston, 1998). What has become increasingly clear through research that probes more deeply into the inner workings of effective classrooms is that the teacher is the crucial factor in the classroom. In fact, study after study points to teacher expertise as the critical variable in effective reading instruction. The teacher who is knowledgeable and adept at combining and adjusting various methods, practices, and strategies to meet the needs of a particular set of students with a differentiated set of needs is most likely to lead students to higher levels of literacy achievement and engagement. Effective teachers are able to differentiate and contextualize their instruction and to support the practices they choose through evidence provided by research and through discussions and collaborations with colleagues in their schools and districts. In particular, research on effective teachers reveals the following common themes:

- Effective teachers are supported within a context of strong school and faculty commitment to improving student achievement. Teachers work within and across grades to coordinate the curriculum in ways that will enhance student growth and development. Ongoing professional development is provided so that teachers can become apprised of research-based practices and share evidence from their classrooms (Frey, Fisher, & Allen, 2009; Taylor, Pearson, Peterson, & Rodriguez, 2003).

- Effective teachers are much like coaches. Instead of telling students what they must do to become better readers and writers, they use discussion and inquiry to guide students in constructing meaning from text (Allington & Johnston, 2002; Malloy & Gambrell, 2010; Taylor, Pearson, Clark, & Walpole, 2000).

- Effective teachers incorporate higher-level responses to text, both oral and written, and emphasize cognitive engagement during literacy activities. They are explicit in tying strategy instruction to authentic literacy activities that are meaning centered while teaching skills as needed to whole groups, small groups, and individual students (Purcell-Gates, Duke, & Martineau, 2007; Taylor et al., 2003).

- Effective teachers provide access to a variety of books and time to engage with print in authentic ways, in an effort to encourage students to be lifelong learners (Baumann & Duffy, 1997; Cunningham, Cunningham, & Allington, 2002; Gambrell, 1996, 2009; Hiebert & Martin, 2009; Neuman & Celano, 2001; Reutzel & Smith, 2004; Routman, 2003).

Students who are taught in these classrooms are engaged, strategic, and see a clear path between instruction and real-life literacy tasks. The instruction provided for students in these classrooms is both differentiated and contextualized to address all aspects of literacy required of students as they progress through the grades. Teachers are ultimately the instructional designers who implement best practices in relevant, meaningful ways for their particular community of learners. In other words, best practices can be *described*—but not *prescribed*.

BEST PRACTICES IN ACTION

Literacy researchers have converged on a word to describe the driving force that guides teachers in coordinating and integrating practices effectively—*vision*. Although this is not a word you might expect to see in a discussion of evidence-based practices, the teacher's vision of literacy achievement has long been heralded as the crucial factor in ensuring that the goal of improving literacy instruction for all students is met. According to Calfee (2005), ensuring that "children have the opportunity to acquire the level of literacy that allows them full participation in our democratic society depends on a corps of teachers who possess extraordinary minds and hearts" (p. 67).

Calfee asserts that teachers not only must possess a domain of skills and knowledge to lead students to acquire this level of literacy success but also must acquire a sensitivity to student needs and be passionate in their willingness to make their vision work. Duffy (2003, 2005) describes the teachers' ultimate goal as that of *inspiring students to be readers and writers*—to engage students in "genuinely literate activities" where they are doing something important with literacy. This engagement should reflect the teachers' instructional vision—the reason they are passionate about teaching reading and writing.

Teachers who are visionary decision makers are empowered to identify and select evidence-based literacy practices to create an integrated instructional approach that adapts to students' differentiated needs. A teacher's vision should clearly be knowledge based and should encompass what he or she wishes to achieve for each student. How detailed one's vision becomes is certainly an individual matter and subject to personal experiences and situations, but without a vision the teacher is left to sway and sputter as a candle facing the winds of curricular change and federal, district, and school-level impositions. The teacher with vision is able to stand firm in the belief that, with knowledge and heart, evidence-based best practices can be selected and adapted to meet the needs of each student every day.

TEN EVIDENCE-BASED BEST PRACTICES FOR COMPREHENSIVE LITERACY INSTRUCTION

In keeping with the characterization of teachers as visionary decision makers, we present 10 evidence-based best practices for comprehensive literacy instruction that are generally accepted by experts in the field (Table 1.1). These practices are based on a broad view of the reading and writing processes, one that incorporates the full range of experiences that students need in order to reach their literacy potential. We believe that best practices are characterized

TABLE 1.1. Ten Evidence-Based Best Practices for Comprehensive Literacy Instruction

1. Create a classroom culture that fosters literacy motivation.
2. Teach reading for authentic meaning-making purposes: for pleasure, to be informed, and to perform a task.
3. Provide students with scaffolded instruction in phonemic awareness, phonics, vocabulary, fluency, and comprehension to promote independent reading.
4. Give students time for self-selected independent reading.
5. Provide students with high-quality literature across a wide range of genres.
6. Use multiple texts that build on prior knowledge, link concepts, and expand vocabulary.
7. Build a whole-class context that emphasizes community and collaboration.
8. Balance teacher- and student-led discussions of texts.
9. Integrate technologies that link and expand concepts.
10. Differentiate instruction using a variety of instructionally relevant assessments.

by meaningful literacy activities that provide students with both the *skill* and the *will* they need to become motivated and proficient literacy learners.

The chapter authors throughout this book address and expand on the broad research consensus that supports the following 10 evidence-based best practices.

1. Create a classroom culture that fosters literacy motivation. Motivation often makes the difference between superficial and shallow learning and learning that is deep and internalized (Gambrell, 1996). Clearly, students need both the *skill* and the *will* to become competent and motivated readers (Guthrie, McRae, & Klauda, 2007; Guthrie & Wigfield, 2000; Paris, Lipson, & Wixson, 1983). Best practices include ways that teachers support students in their reading development by creating classroom cultures that foster reading motivation, such as providing a print-rich classroom environment, opportunities for choice, and opportunities to interact socially with others. The most basic goal of any literacy program should be the development of readers who *can read* and who *choose to read.* Teachers can provide instruction in the most essential literacy skills, but if our students are not intrinsically motivated to read, they will never reach their full literacy potential (Gambrell, 2009).

2. Teach reading for authentic meaning-making purposes: for pleasure, to be informed, and to perform a task. Authentic literacy activities are reading and writing events like those that occur in people's lives, as opposed to reading and writing solely to learn (Purcell-Gates, 2002, 2005; Purcell-Gates et al., 2007). We know that as young children learn and use their developing oral language, they do so for real reasons and purposes (Halliday, 1975). Therefore, in order for literacy learning to be meaningful to students, teachers must be mindful of the reasons and purposes they establish for reading and writing tasks.

Authentic literacy activities are often designed to focus on communicating ideas for shared understanding rather than simply to complete assignments or answer teacher-posed questions. Authentic literacy events include activities such as authoring or recommending books, reading to discover how to do or make something, and collaborating on a report of group findings. Students are more likely to transfer their classroom literacy learning to real life and future applications when they engage in authentic literacy learning in the classroom (Gambrell, Hughes, Calvert, Malloy, & Igo, in press; Teale & Gambrell, 2007; Teale & Sulzby, 1986; Teale, Zolt, Yokota, Glasswell, & Gambrell, 2007).

Teachers can raise the value of literacy learning by making reading, writing, speaking, and listening authentic tools for learning in their classroom. Students who see literacy as a means to understanding their world and gaining both knowledge and pleasure will be more engaged in the types of collaborative, meaning-making, and problem-solving activities that mirror those of their future workplaces.

3. Provide students with scaffolded instruction in phonemic awareness, phonics, vocabulary, fluency, and comprehension to promote independent reading. The report of the National Reading Panel (NICHHD, 2000) identified phonemic awareness, phonics, vocabulary, fluency, and comprehension as critical to the development of the reading process and provided research support for instruction in these areas. Students often need concentrated instructional support in these areas in order to learn important skills and strategies that they might have difficulty discovering on their own. The gradual-release-of-responsibility model provides such scaffolded instruction.

In general, the gradual-release model describes a process in which students gradually assume a greater degree of responsibility and independence for a targeted learning outcome. During the first stage, the teacher assumes most of the responsibility by modeling and describing a particular skill or strategy. In the second stage, the teacher and students assume joint responsibility; students practice applying a particular skill or strategy, and the teacher offers assistance and feedback as needed. As students are ready, instruction moves into the third stage, in which students assume all, or almost all, of the responsibility by working in situations where they independently apply newly learned skills and strategies. This gradual withdrawal of instructional support is also known as scaffolded instruction, because "supports" or "scaffolds" are gradually removed as students demonstrate greater degrees of proficiency.

We view the gradual-release model as consistent with the notion of explicit instruction. During each phase of the gradual-release model, teachers can—and should—be explicit in their instruction and feedback. For example, during the first phase, teachers should provide clear explanations and modeling for a specific skill or strategy. As responsibility is gradually released, feedback to students should be specific and understandable. Small-group and one-on-one configurations can be particularly effective in differentiating the scaffolding of strategies for students with similar learning needs. The gradual-release model and scaffolded instruction are in keeping with constructivist principles when they are used within meaningful, authentic contexts (Graham & Harris, 1996; Harris & Graham, 1994). Indeed, many authors in this book provide examples of how to integrate these models within meaningful reading and writing programs that include use of literature, technology, authentic writing experiences, choice, and collaborative learning.

4. Give students time for self-selected independent reading. "Practice makes perfect" is an old adage that rings true. Practice may not make you a perfect reader, but the consensus among reading researchers is that practice will make you a better reader (Allington, 2009; Gambrell, 2009; Hiebert, 2009). Hiebert and Martin (2009) contend that opportunity to read is a critical component of the reading curriculum. The effectiveness of these opportunities to read is influenced by a number of variables including time, text difficulty, text genre, and dimensions of the task as well as the readers' engagement and reading proficiency (Hiebert & Martin, 2009). We know it takes much more than just providing students with time to read. The role of the teacher is critical in motivating students to read for their own reasons by assuring an appropriate student–book match so that time spent reading is both profitable and enjoyable for the reader.

There is clear evidence from reading research that the amount of time spent reading (reading volume) is a major contributor to increased vocabulary and comprehension (Allington, 2009; Hayes & Ahrens, 1988; Nagy & Anderson, 1984; Stanovich, 1986). In a classic study, Anderson, Wilson, and Fielding (1988) found a significant relationship between the amount of reading schoolchildren do and their reading achievement. In this study of 155 fifth graders, the amount of book reading that students reported was the best predictor of performance on several measures of reading achievement. In addition, other studies have supported the inclusion of time to read during the school day (Linehart, Zigmond, & Cooley, 1981; Reutzel & Hollingsworth, 1991; Reutzel, Jones, Fawson, & Smith, 2008).

According to Cunningham and Stanovich (1998), lack of reading practice delays the development of fluency and word recognition skills. Thus struggling readers may be hindered in comprehending, frustrated in the reading experience, and avoid further practice. Time for reading is important for all readers, but it is especially important for struggling readers. Good readers tend to have more practice in reading, and consequently they become more and more proficient, while poor readers spend less time reading and have fewer experiences with appropriately leveled reading materials (Allington, 2009).

During independent reading, students practice and consolidate the skills and strategies they have been taught, and thereby come to "own" them. According to Allington (2009), such practice provides students with the opportunity to develop the autonomous, automatic, and appropriate application of reading skills and strategies *while actually reading*. Adequate time for reading is essential so that students have the experience that is needed to increase reading proficiency.

5. Provide students with high-quality literature across a wide range of genres. Although early readers benefit from the decodable support of leveled texts (Clay, 1993; Fountas & Pinnell, 1996), the effective teacher makes use of high-quality literature during teacher read-alouds, during teacher-guided instruction, and for independent reading. Pressley and his colleagues (2001; Pressley, Mohan, Raphael, & Fingeret, 2007) reviewed research on exemplary first-grade classrooms and found that direct teaching, when supported by immersion in high-quality literature, promotes reading engagement and growth. Duke (2000) reported on the scarcity of information texts in first-grade classrooms, raising concern about the lack of experience young children have with respect to informational text. As content-heavy expository texts become more prevalent in the later elementary years, we are remiss if we do not provide exposure to and explicit instruction in comprehending the full range of genres our students are expected to read. According to Cervetti, Jaynes, and Hiebert (2009), "evidence is mounting that experiences with nonfiction texts can be most powerful when they are related to and situated within content area instruction that has the potential to build students' skills with, and extend their conceptual understandings of, several different genres of text" (pp. 92–93).

6. Use multiple texts that build on prior knowledge, link concepts, and expand vocabulary. The best predictor of what students will learn is what they already know (Dochy, Segers, & Buehl, 1999; Hailikari, Nevgi, & Komulainen, 2008). Prior knowledge is the foundation upon which new meaning (or learning) is built. Effective teachers assess students' conceptual understanding, beliefs, and values and link new ideas, skills, and competencies to prior understandings. They also provide experiences that equip each child with sufficient background knowledge to succeed with literacy tasks. Such practices are also consistent with Vygotsky's (1978) notion of the "zone of proximal development," which suggests that optimal learning occurs when teachers determine students' current level of understanding and teach new ideas, skills, and strategies that are at an appropriate level of challenge.

Using a variety of texts on common topics promotes concept and vocabulary development as well as critical thinking. Hartman (1995) found that good readers are able to construct meanings from text that connect with those derived from other texts, as well as from their cultural and social–experiential knowledge. These meanings are initially imprecise in nature but change and adapt as new meanings are acquired and concepts are continually shaped and solidified. Presenting new information through a variety of related texts offers multiple opportunities for students to attach new knowledge to their existing and developing schemas on a topic. Lenski (2001) extends this work to include intertextual connections that are enhanced by teacher questioning and student discussion. Furthermore, students who have authentic purposes for reading and a variety of quality literature, both narrative and expository, are able to construct meanings and develop concepts through reading multiple texts for real-world purposes (Moje & Sutherland, 2003; Soalt, 2005).

Thematic and integrated units can also help learners build conceptual knowledge across content areas to deepen a developing knowledge base in one or more domains. By integrating literacy instruction across content areas, students can read fiction and nonfiction texts and write for real-world purposes in the pursuit of a targeted learning outcome. For example, sixth-grade students can explore the topic of plate tectonics by reading geology and geography trade books and texts. But when asked to work in groups to predict where the continents will be situated in 100,000,000 years, students will need instruction and practice in mathematical simulation and distance/time calculations. They may also need to read newspaper and online accounts of earthquakes and volcanoes to understand the effect of these geological activities on plate movements and integrate them into their calculations and predications. At the end of the unit, the groups can present their findings in a "geological summit" or "news briefing" by writing a report and creating a model, which serves as an assessable culminating product for the unit. Through this instruction, students combine and integrate knowledge in ways that present multiple opportunities to build and demonstrate a knowledge base, link concepts across domains, and use new vocabulary in meaningful ways.

7. Build a whole-class context that emphasizes community and collaboration. Research reports and commentaries of literacy instruction make increasing reference to the power of teachers and students learning together in a community (Pressley, 2007). Brown and her colleagues (Brown, 1992; Brown et al., 1993; Brown & Campione, 1994; Campione, Shapiro, & Brown, 1995) introduced this idea of a "community of learners" through their research in classrooms where teachers facilitated learning through collaborative and student-centered lines of inquiry. Similar contexts, such as those described in the research on concept-oriented reading instruction (Guthrie et al., 1996), were associated with increased levels of conceptual learning and literacy engagement.

Students need assistance in developing the interpersonal skills required for effective collaborative learning. They also need a degree of teacher assistance and influence in order to stimulate new learning within the community. However, research has shown that the rewards are great. Collaborative learning contexts have been found to result in greater student achievement and more positive social, motivational, and attitudinal outcomes for all ages, genders, ethnicities, and social classes than individualized or competitive learning structures (Johnson & Johnson, 1983; Johnson, Johnson, & Maruyama, 1983; Johnson, Maruyama, Johnson, Nelson, & Skon, 1981; Sharan, 1980; Slavin, 1983, 1990).

The development of a "community of literate souls" (Malloy, Marinak, & Gambrell, 2010) is the product of a teacher's vision and dedication to the shared learning and the collaborative construction of meaning that has been associated with increased learning and engagement (Pressley, El-Dinary, Marks, Brown, & Stein, 1992; Pressley & Woloshyn, 1995). An effective learning community can be developed even in the increasing diversity that we find in our classrooms today. In her ongoing research into the literacy practices and values that are situated in learning communities and cultures, Purcell-Gates (2005) suggests that educators should become aware of the differences between the types of texts and purposes for literacy that are found in students' home environments and those presented at school. By incorporating culturally meaningful teaching methods in literacy instruction, teachers can build classroom communities that view literacy as a valuable means of getting information and pleasure from reading text and for communicating students' knowledge through writing.

8. Balance teacher- and student-led discussions of texts. The term *collaborative learning* is also used to refer to the exchange of ideas that results in co-constructed understanding. From a social-constructivist perspective, literacy is a social act. Readers and writers develop meanings as a result of co-constructed understandings within particular sociocultural contexts. This means, among many things, that text interpretation and level of participation are influenced by the size and social makeup of a group, the cultural conventions of literacy (e.g., What are reading and writing for? What are the literacy goals of the community?), as well as the different perspectives others convey about text.

Collaborative learning and the social perspective have brought to the fore the importance of peer talk. Interest in the positive benefits of the role of discussion in learning has resulted in new classroom participation structures, such as book discussion groups, literacy clubs, and small-group investigations of specific topics related to a content area and communication of findings to others.

Several studies provide evidence that discussions of text promote reading comprehension, motivation to read, and higher-order thinking skills (Almasi, McKeown, & Beck, 1996; Almasi, O'Flahavan, & Arya, 2001; see the review of research by Gambrell, 1996). We know, however, that discussions do not just "happen"—they occur because teachers plan for them and explicitly teach the skills required. When students are provided with the skills and opportunities to think and talk about shared texts, they bring their personal interpretations into a *shared workspace* (Malloy & Gambrell, 2010). In the shared workspace of a peer-led discussion, students gain from the insights and interpretations of their peers, allowing students to share their background knowledge and initial interpretations. Similarly, the shared workspace allows students to see how others have thought through the text, thus allowing for the modeling and appropriation of interpretive tools for comprehending. Following a well-run peer-led discussion, students leave with new understandings and well as new *tools* for understanding. Discussions that are teacher led and student led are enhanced when students can share ideas and build upon their prior knowledge (Gambrell, 2004; Kucan & Beck, 2003), question the author or challenge the text (Almasi, 1995), and read books that are engaging and that promote discussion (Evans, 2002).

9. Integrate technologies that link and expand concepts. Increasingly, teachers are using technologically enhanced instruction. Interactive and projected display boards are becoming more commonplace in the classroom. Technology that provides varied displays of knowledge, ways to manipulate knowledge for encoding, or opportunities to locate and communicate knowledge may provide exciting new avenues for teaching and learning. Aside from the possible instructional benefits, students must learn to be proficient in working with and learning from these technology resources, while also becoming adept and competent with conventional print documents (Pressley, 2007).

Although the integration of Internet use and other computer-mediated instruction in the K–12 classroom is increasing, the empirical evidence to support instructional strategies for using these technologies is just beginning to emerge (Azevedo & Cromley, 2004; Coiro & Dobler, 2007; Malloy, Castek & Leu, 2010). Recommendations from teachers and researchers who focus on these "new literacies" are available for teachers to adapt to their classrooms (Eagleton & Dobler, 2007; Karchmer, Mallette, Kara-Soteriou, & Leu, 2005; Leu, Castek, Henry, Coiro, & McMullan, 2004). What we are coming to understand is that reading on the Internet requires different skills than reading traditional text and that it is important we understand these differences in order to provide appropriate instruction for our students (Coiro, 2003; Malloy, Castek & Leu, 2010). It is incumbent on teachers, therefore, to acquaint themselves with new research as it emerges and to incorporate this new knowledge into their classrooms as suits their particular instructional needs. Our students are entering an age when knowledge of technology is a necessity and not a luxury. As educators, we are obligated to prepare them for that reality.

10. Differentiate instruction using a variety of instructionally relevant assessments. One of the core issues driving today's concerns about reading instruction is the pressure for students to perform well on state and national assessments. The stakes are high, and the penalties for inadequate performance on these tests are great. Schools are directed to show adequate yearly progress (AYP) on state assessments or face sanctions such as school takeover by the state or allowing parents to choose other schools, perhaps in other districts, for their children to attend. In each school, principals are called upon to meet federal, state, and district-level requirements while providing for teachers and students with varying needs and abilities. And in every classroom, it is the teacher who struggles to meet the challenge of providing appropriate literacy instruction for his or her students.

Johnston and Costello (2005) situate their discussion of literacy assessment within current understandings of literacy as a complex construct and the need to view assessment as a social practice. Whether assessments are formal or informal, summative or formative, they influence the amount and type of support provided the teacher in tailoring instruction to specific students, whole classrooms, and district-level needs (Harlen & Crick, 2003; McDonald & Boud, 2003; Tomlinson & McTighe, 2006). Thus we caution against the use of a single, narrow assessment to drive instruction, as doing so loses sight of the reciprocity that we know exists among reading processes. We must ensure that the assessments we use reflect an authentic, comprehensive literacy framework, or the instruction we provide will fall woefully short for the demands that will be placed on our students in adulthood.

Differentiated instruction involves assessing and addressing differences among students (Tomlinson, 2003). It runs counter to the notion of *one-size-*

fits-all, teach-to-the-middle instruction, which can result in some students not being challenged while others fall behind. Differentiated instruction is central to the RTI concept. Educators are being called upon to intervene early by assessing students and differentiating instruction to provide the level of service each student requires. There is strong evidence to suggest that struggling readers need the instructional intensity of excellent, differentiated classroom instruction *and* intervention instruction (Foorman & Torgesen, 2001; Gersten & Domino, 2001; Leslie & Allen, 1999; McGill-Franzen, 2005; Stahl, Heubach, & Holcomb, 2005; Wasik & Slavin, 1993).

SUMMARY

Once teachers are empowered by their vision and have at their disposal a plethora of practices and instructional methods from which to choose, they are free to orchestrate an integration of evidence-based practices to provide comprehensive literacy instruction. No matter how well a particular practice is shown to be effective by research, *optimal literacy teaching and learning can only be achieved when skillful, knowledgeable, and dedicated teachers are given the freedom and latitude to use their professional judgment to make instructional decisions that enable students to achieve their full literacy potential.*

As we increase our understanding of effective literacy instruction, our conceptions of best practices will continue to broaden and deepen. Our students need and deserve instruction that embraces the richness and complexity of the reading process as well as instruction that is both evidence based and comprehensive. This is no easy task. It requires commitment, time, and knowledge. It begins with a teacher who is a visionary decision maker, one who can identify the strengths and needs of each individual child and plan instruction accordingly. It begins with a commitment to provide comprehensive, differentiated literacy assessment and instruction for all our students. While the challenge is daunting, the rewards are great as we nurture and support students in becoming engaged lifelong readers and writers.

ENGAGEMENT ACTIVITIES

1. Articulate your vision for literacy teaching and learning. Commit to writing what you wish to accomplish as a literacy teacher as well as what you wish for each of your students to achieve. Refer to this vision statement often as you teach or as you learn more about teaching. Be certain to adjust and enhance your vision statement as new knowledge and expertise dictate.
2. Reflect on your vision statement for literacy teaching and learning. Does your classroom environment, instructional

practice, and classroom management support your vision statement?

3. Richard Allington defines evidence-based instruction as "professional wisdom integrated with the best available empirical evidence" (2005, p. 16). Identify a literacy instruction method or practice that you have observed or used in the classroom and discuss how it meets Allington's definition of an evidence-based practice.
4. In this chapter, we list 10 evidence-based best practices for comprehensive literacy instruction (pp. 21–29); however, this list is not meant to be exclusive or exhaustive. Consider the literacy instructional practices that you think should be added to this list and give reasons why you, as a literacy professional, think they should be included. Provide evidence to support your decision.

REFERENCES

Alliance for Excellent Education. (2007, January). *The high cost of high school dropouts: What the nation pays for inadequate high schools* (Issue brief). Washington, DC: Author.

Allington, R. L. (2005). What counts as evidence in evidence-based education? *Reading Today, 23*(3), 16.

Allington, R. L. (2009). If they don't read much . . . 30 years later. In E. H. Hiebert (Ed.), *Reading more, reading better* (pp. 30–54). New York: Guilford Press.

Allington, R. L., & Johnston, P. H. (2002). *Reading to learn: Lessons from exemplary fourth-grade classrooms.* New York: Guilford Press.

Almasi, J. (1995). The nature of fourth graders' sociocognitive conflicts in peer-led and teacher-led discussions of literature. *Reading Research Quarterly, 30,* 314–351.

Almasi, J. F., McKeown, M. G., & Beck, I. L. (1996). The nature of engaged reading in classroom discussions of literature. *Journal of Literacy Research, 28*(1), 107–146.

Almasi, J. F., O'Flahavan, J. F., & Arya, P. (2001). A comparative analysis of student and teacher development in more proficient and less proficient peer discussions of literature. *Reading Research Quarterly, 36*(2), 96–120.

Anderson, R. C., Wilson, P. T., & Fielding, L. G. (1988). Growth in reading and how children spend their time outside of school. *Reading Research Quarterly, 23*(3), 285–303.

Azevedo, R., & Cromley, J. G. (2004). Does training on self-regulated learning facilitate students' learning with hypermedia? *Journal of Educational Psychology, 96*(3), 523–535.

Baumann, J. F., & Duffy, A. M. (1997). *Engaged reading for pleasure and learning: A report from the National Reading Research Center.* Athens, GA: National Reading Research Center.

Biancarosa, G., & Snow, C. E. (2004). *Reading Next—a vision for action and research in middle and high school literacy: A report to Carnegie Corporation of New York.* Washington, DC: Alliance for Excellent Education.

Bogdan, R. C., & Biklen, S. K. (1992). *Qualitative research for education: An introduction to theory and methods* (2nd ed.). Boston: Allyn & Bacon.

Braunger, J., & Lewis, J. P. (2006). *Building a knowledge base in reading* (2nd ed.). Newark, DE: International Reading Association.

Brown, A. L. (1992). Design experiments: Theoretical and methodological challenges in creating complex interventions in classroom settings. *Journal of the Learning Sciences, 2,* 141–178.

Brown, A. L., Ash, D., Rutherford, M., Nakagawa, K., Gordon, A., & Campione, J. C. (1993). Distributed expertise in the classroom. In G. Salomon (Ed.), *Distributed cognitions: Psychological and educational considerations* (pp. 188–228). New York: Cambridge University Press.

Brown, A. L., & Campione, J. C. (1994). Guided discovery in a community of learners. In K. McGilly (Ed.), classroom lessons: Integrating cognitive theory and classroom practice (pp. 229–270). Cambridge, MA: MIT Press/Bradford Books.

Calfee, R. (2005). The mind (and heart) of the reading teacher. In B. Maloch, J. V. Hoffman, D. L. Schallert, C. M. Fairbanks, & J. Worthy (Eds.), *54th yearbook of the National Reading Conference* (pp. 63–79). Oak Creek, WI: National Reading Conference.

Campione, J. C., Shapiro, A. M., & Brown, A. L. (1995). Forms of transfer in a community of learners: Flexible learning and understanding. In A. McKeough, J. Lupart, & A. Marini (Eds.), *Teaching for transfer: Fostering generalization in learning* (pp. 35–68). Hillsdale, NJ: Erlbaum.

Cervetti, G. M., Jaynes, C. A., & Hiebert, E. H. (2009). Increasing opportunities to acquire knowledge through reading. In E. H. Hiebert (Ed.), *Reading more, reading better* (pp. 79–100). New York: Guilford Press.

Clay, M. M. (1993). *An observation survey of early literacy achievement.* Portsmouth, NH: Heinemann.

Coiro, J. (2003). Exploring literacy on the Internet. *The Reading Teacher, 56,* 458–464.

Coiro, J., & Dobler, E. (2007). Exploring the online comprehension strategies used by sixth-grade skilled readers to search for and locate information on the Internet. *Reading Research Quarterly, 42,* 214–257.

Common Core State Standards Initiative. (2010). *Common Core State Standards Initiative: Preparing America's students for college and career.* Retrieved July 31, 2010, from *corestandards.org/.*

Cunningham, A. E., & Stanovich, K. E. (1998). What reading does for the mind. *American Educator, 22*(1), 8–15.

Cunningham, P. M., Cunningham, J. W., & Allington, R. L. (2002). *Research on the components of a comprehensive reading and writing instructional program.* Clemmons, NC: Four Blocks Literacy Model.

Dickinson, D. K., & Neuman, S. B. (2006). Introduction. In D. K. Dickinson & S. B. Neuman (Eds.), *Handbook of early literacy research* (Vol. 2, pp. 1–10). New York: Guilford Press.

Dochy, F., Segers, M., & Buehl, M. M. (1999). The relation between assessment practices and outcomes of studies: The case of research on prior knowledge. *Review of Educational Research, 69*(2), 145–186.

Duffy, G. G. (2003). *Explaining reading: A resource for teaching concepts, skills, and strategies.* New York: Guilford Press.

Duffy, G. G. (2005). Developing metacognitive teachers: Visioning and the expert's changing role in teacher education and professional development. In S. E. Isreal, C. C. Block, K. L. Bauserman, & K. Kinnucan-Welsch (Eds.), *Meta-cognition in literacy learning: Theory, assessment, instruction and professional development* (pp. 299–314). Mahwah, NJ: Erlbaum.

Duke, N. K. (2000). 3.6 minutes a day: The scarcity of informational texts in first grade. *Reading Research Quarterly, 35*(2), 202–224.

Eagleton, M. B., & Dobler, E. (2007). *Reading the Web: Strategies for Internet inquiry.* New York: Guilford Press.

Evans, K. S. (2002). Fifth-grade student's perceptions of how they experience literature discussion groups. *Reading Research Quarterly, 37*(1), 46–68.

Flippo, R. F. (1998). Points of agreement: A display of professional unity in our field. *The Reading Teacher, 52*, 30–40.

Flippo, R. F. (Ed.). (2001). *Reading researchers in search of common ground.* Newark, DE: International Reading Association.

Flippo, R. F. (Ed.). (in press). *Reading researchers in search of common ground* (2nd ed.). Newark, DE: International Reading Association.

Foorman, B. R., & Torgesen, J. (2001). Critical elements of classroom and small-group instruction promote reading success in all children. *Learning Disabilities Research and Practice, 16*(4), 203–212.

Fountas, I. C., & Pinnell, G. S. (1996). *Guided reading: Good first teaching for all children.* Portsmouth, NH: Heinemann.

Frey, N., Fisher, D., & Allen, A. (2009). Productive group work in middle and high school classrooms. In S. R. Parris, D. Fisher, & K. Headley (Eds.), *Adolescent literacy, field-tested: Effective solutions for every classroom* (pp. 70–81). Newark, DE: International Reading Association.

Gambrell, L. B. (1996). Motivating contexts for literacy learning. In L. Baker, P. Afflerbach, & D. Reinking (Eds.), *Developing engaged readers in school and home communities* (pp. 115–136). Mahwah, NJ: Erlbaum.

Gambrell, L. B. (2004). Exploring the connection between oral language and early reading. *The Reading Teacher, 57*(5), 490–492.

Gambrell, L. B. (2009). Creating opportunities to read more so that students read better. In E. H. Hiebert (Ed.), *Reading more, reading better* (pp. 251–266). New York: Guilford Press.

Gambrell, L. B., Hughes, E., Calvert, W. L., Malloy, J. A., and Igo, B. (in press). Authentic reading, writing, and discussion: An exploratory study of a pen pal project. *Elementary School Journal.*

Garcia, E. E., & Wiese, A. (2009). *Policy related to issues of diversity and literacy: Implications for English learners.* In L. M. Morrow, R. Rueda, & D. Lapp (Eds.) *Handbook of research on literacy and diversity* (pp. 32–54). New York: Guilford Press.

Gersten, R., & Domino, J. (2001). The realities of translating research into classroom practice. *Learning Disabilities Research and Practice, 16*(2), 120–130.

Gordon, E. W. (2009). Foreword. In L. M. Morrow, R. Rueda, & D. Lapp (Eds.), *Handbook of research on literacy and diversity* (pp. ix–xi). New York: Guilford Press.

Graham, S., & Harris, K. R. (1996). *Making the writing process work: Strategies for composition and self-regulation.* Cambridge, MA: Brookline Books.

Guthrie, J. T., McRae, A., & Klauda, S. L. (2007). Contributions of concept-oriented reading instruction to knowledge about interventions for motivations in reading. *Educational Psychologist, 42*(4), 237–250.

Guthrie, J. T., Van Meter, P., McCann, A. D., Wigfield, A., Bender, L., Poundstone, C. C., et al. (1996). Growth of literacy engagement: Changes in motivations and strategies during concept-oriented reading instruction. *Reading Research Quarterly, 3l*, 306–325.

Guthrie, J. T., & Wigfield, A. (2000). Engagement and motivation in reading. In M. L. Kamil, P. B. Mosenthal, P. D. Pearson, & R. Barr (Eds.), *Handbook of reading research* (Vol. 3, pp. 403–422). Mahwah, NJ: Erlbaum.

Hailikari, T., Nevgi, A., & Komulainen, E. (2008). Academic self-beliefs and prior knowledge as predictors of student achievement in mathematics: A structural model. *Educational Psychology, 28*(1), 59–71.

Halliday, M. A. K. (1975). *Learning how to mean.* London: Arnold.

Harlen, W., & Crick, R. D. (2003). Testing and motivation for learning. *Assessment in Education: Principles, Policy and Practice, 10*(2), 169–207.

Harris, K. R., & Graham, S. (1994). Constructivism: Principles, paradigms, and integration. *Journal of Special Education, 28*(3), 233–247.

Hartman, D. K. (1995). Eight readers reading: The intertextual links of proficient readers reading multiple passages. *Reading Research Quarterly, 30*(3), 520–561.

Hayes, D. P., & Ahrens, M. (1988). Vocabulary simplification for children: A special case of "Motherese"? *Journal of Child Language, 15*, 395–410.

Hiebert, E. H. (2009). *Reading more, reading better.* New York: Guilford Press.

Hiebert, E. H., & Martin, L. A. (2009). Opportunity to read: A critical but neglected construct in reading instruction. In E. H. Hiebert (Ed.), *Reading more, reading better* (pp. 3–29). New York: Guilford Press.

International Reading Association. (2002a). *Evidence-based reading instruction: Putting the National Reading Panel report into practice.* Newark, DE: Author.

International Reading Association. (2002b). *What is evidence-based reading instruction?* (Position Statement). Newark, DE: Author.

Johnson, D. W., & Johnson, R. T. (1983). The socialization and achievement crisis: Are cooperative learning experiences the solution? In L. Bickman (Ed.), *Applied social psychology* (Annual 4). Beverly Hills, CA: Sage.

Johnson, D., Johnson, R., & Maruyama, G. (1983). Interdependence and interpersonal attraction among heterogeneous and homogeneous individuals: A theoretical formulation and a meta-analysis of the research. *Review of Educational Research, 533*, 5–54.

Johnson, D., Maruyama, G., Johnson, R., Nelson, D., & Skon, L. (1981). Effects of cooperative, competitive, and individualistic goal structures on achievement: A meta-analysis. *Psychological Bulletin, 89*, 47–62.

Johnston, P., & Costello, P. (2005). Theory and research into practice: Principles for literacy assessment. *Reading Research Quarterly, 40*(2), 256–267.

Karchmer, R. A., Mallette, M. H., Kara-Soteriou, J., & Leu, D. (Eds.). (2005). *Innovative approaches to literacy education: Using the Internet to support new literacies.* Newark, DE: International Reading Association.

Kucan, L., & Beck, I. L. (2003). Inviting students to talk about expository texts: A comparison of two discourse environments and their effects on comprehension. *Reading Research and Instruction, 42*, 1–29.

Lenski, S. D. (2001). Intertextual connections during discussions about literature. *Reading Psychology, 22*, 313–335.

Leslie, L., & Allen, L. (1999). Factors that predict success in an early literacy intervention project. *Reading Research Quarterly, 34*(4), 404–424.

Leu, D. J., Jr., Castek, J., Henry, L. A., Coiro, J., & McMullan, M. (2004). The lessons that children teach us: Integrating children's literature and the new literacies of the Internet. *The Reading Teacher, 57,* 486–503.

Linehart, G., Zigmond, N., & Cooley, W. (1981). Reading instruction and its effects. *American Educational Research Journal, 18,* 343–361.

Malloy, J. A., Castek, J. M., & Leu, D. J. (2010). Silent reading and online reading comprehension. In E. H. Hiebert & D. R. Reutzel (Eds.), *Revisiting silent reading: New directions for teachers and researchers* (pp. 221–240). Newark, DE: International Reading Association.

Malloy, J. A., & Gambrell, L. B. (2010). The contribution of discussion to reading comprehension and critical thinking. In A. McGill-Franzen & R. Allington (Eds.), *Handbook of reading disabilities research* (pp. 253–262). Mahwah, NJ: Erlbaum.

Malloy, J. A., Marinak, B. A., & Gambrell, L. B. (2010). We hope you dance: Creating a community of literate souls. In J. A. Malloy, B. A. Marinak, & L. B. Gambrell (Eds.), *Essential readings in motivation* (pp. 1–9). Newark, DE: International Reading Association.

McDonald, B., & Boud, D. (2003). The impact of self-assessment on achievement: The effects of self-assessment training on performance in external examinations. *Assessment in Education: Principles, Policy and Practice, 10*(2), 209–220.

McGill-Franzen, A. (2005). In the press to scale up, what is at risk? *Reading Research Quarterly, 40*(3), 366–370.

Moje, E. B., & Sutherland, L. M. (2003). The future of middle school literacy education. *English Education, 43,* 149–164.

Morrow, L. M., Rueda, R., & Lapp, D. (Eds.). (2009). *Handbook of research on literacy and diversity.* New York: Guilford Press.

Nagy, W., & Anderson, R. C. (1984). How many words are there in printed school English? *Reading Research Quarterly, 19,* 304–330.

National Assessment of Educational Progress. (2007). Retrieved July 19, 2010, from *nces.ed.gov/nationsreportcard/.*

National Association of State Directors of Special Education. (2010, August 6). *Response to Intervention (RTI) project.* Retrieved August 19, 2010, from *www.nasdse.org/Projects/ResponsetoInterventionRtIProject/tabid/411/Default.aspx.*

National Institute of Child Health and Human Development (NICHHD). (2000). *Report of the National Reading Panel. Teaching children to read: An evidence-based assessment of the scientific research literature on reading and its implications for reading instruction* (NIH Publication No. 00-4769). Washington, DC: U.S. Government Printing Office.

Neuman, S. B., & Celano, D. (2001). Access to print in low-income and middle-income communities: An ecological study of four neighborhoods. *Reading Research Quarterly, 36*(10), 8–26.

No Child Left Behind Act of 2001. (2002). Pub. L. No. 107-110, 115 Stat. 1425. Retrieved July 15, 2010, from *www.ed.gov/policy/elsec/leg/esea02/index.html.*

Paris, S., Lipson, M., & Wixson, K. (1983). Becoming a strategic reader. *Contemporary Educational Psychology, 8,* 293–316.

Pressley, M. (2007). Achieving best practices. In L. B. Gambrell, L. M. Morrow, & M. Pressley (Eds.), *Best practices in literacy instruction* (pp. 397–404). New York: Guilford Press.

Pressley, M., Allington, R. L., Wharton-McDonald, R., Block, C. C., & Morrow, L. M. (2001). *Learning to read: Lessons from exemplary first-grade classrooms.* New York: Guilford Press.

Pressley, M., El-Dinary, P. B., Marks, M. B., Brown, R., & Stein, S. (1992). Good strategy instruction is motivating and interesting. In K. A. Renninger, S. Hidi, & A. Krapp (Eds.), *The role of interest in learning and development.* Hillsdale, NJ: Erlbaum.

Pressley, M., Mohan, L., Raphael, L. M., & Fingeret, L. (2007). How does Bennett Woods Elementary School produce such high reading and writing achievement? *Journal of Educational Psychology, 99*(2), 221–240.

Pressley, M., & Woloshyn, V. (Eds.). (1995). *Cognitive strategy instruction that really improves children's academic performance* (2nd ed.). Cambridge, MA: Brookline.

Programme for International Student Assessment (PISA). (2006). PISA technical report. Retrieved October 29, 2010, from *nces.ed.gov/surveys/pisa/.*

Purcell-Gates, V. (2002). Authentic literacy in class yields increase in literacy practices. *Literacy Update, 11*(1), 9.

Purcell-Gates, V. (2005, December). *What does culture have to do with it?* Oscar S. Causey Research Award address, National Reading Conference, Miami Beach.

Purcell-Gates, V., Duke, N., & Martineau, J. (2007). Learning to read and write genre-specific text: Roles of authentic experience and explicit teaching. *Reading Research Quarterly, 42*, 8–46.

Raikes, H., Luze, G., Brooks-Gunn, J., Raikes, H. A., Pan, B. A., & Tamis-LeMonda, C. S. (2006). Mother–child bookreading in low-income families. Correlates and outcomes during the first three years of life. *Child Development, 77*, 924–953.

Rasinski, T. V. (2001). A focus on communication with parents and families. In R. F. Flippo (Ed.), *Reading researchers in search of common ground* (pp. 159–166). Newark, DE: International Reading Association.

Reinking, D., & Bradley, B. A. (2008). *On formative and design experiments: An approach to language and literacy research* (A NCRELL Volume). New York: Teachers College Press.

Reutzel, D. R., & Hollingsworth, P. M. (1991). Investigating topic-related attitude: Effect on reading and remembering text. *Journal of Educational Research, 84*(6), 334–344.

Reutzel, D. R., Jones, C. D., Fawson, P. C., & Smith, J. A. (2008). Scaffolded silent reading: A complement to guided repeated oral reading that works! *Reading Teacher, 62*(3), 194–207.

Reutzel, D. R., & Smith, J. A. (2004). Accelerating struggling readers' progress: A comparative analysis of expert opinion and current research recommendations. *Reading and Writing Quarterly, 20*, 63–89.

Routman, R. (2003). *Reading essentials: The specifics you need to teach reading well.* Portsmouth, NH: Heinemann.

Sharan, S. (1980). Cooperative learning in small groups: Recent methods and effects on achievement, attitudes, and ethnic relations. *Review of Educational Research, 50*, 241–271.

Slavin, R. E. (1983). *Cooperative learning.* New York: Longman.

Slavin, R. E. (1990). *Cooperative learning: Theory, research, and practice.* Englewood Cliffs, NJ: Prentice Hall.

Soalt, J. (2005, April). Bringing together fictional and informational texts to improve comprehension. *The Reading Teacher, 58*(7), 680–683.

Stahl, S., Heubach, K., & Holcomb, A. (2005). Fluency-oriented reading instruction. *Journal of Literacy Research, 37*(1), 25–60.

Stanovich, K. E. (1986). Matthew effects in reading: Some consequences of individual differences in the acquisition of literacy. *Reading Research Quarterly, 21*(4), 360–406.

Taylor, B. M., Pearson, P. D., Clark, K., & Walpole, S. (2000). Effective schools and accomplished teachers: Lessons about primary-grade reading instruction in low-income schools. *Elementary School Journal, 101*, 121–166.

Taylor, B. M., Pearson, P. D., Peterson, D. S., & Rodriguez, M. C. (2003). Reading growth in high-poverty classrooms: The influence of teacher practices that encourage cognitive engagement in literacy learning. *Elementary School Journal, 104*, 3–28.

Teale, W. H., & Gambrell, L. B. (2007). Raising urban students' literacy achievement by engaging in authentic, challenging work. *The Reading Teacher, 60*, 728–739.

Teale, W. H., & Sulzby, E. (1986). *Emergent literacy: Writing and reading.* Norwood, NJ: Ablex.

Teale, W. H., Zolt, N., Yokota, J., Glasswell, K., & Gambrell, L. B. (2007). Getting children In2Books: Engagement in authentic reading, writing, and thinking. *Phi Delta Kappan, 88*, 498–502.

Tomlinson, C. (2003). Fulfilling the promise of the differentiated classroom: Strategies and tools for responsive teaching. Alexandria, VA: Association for Supervision and Curriculum Development.

Tomlinson, C. A., & McTighe, J. (2006). *Integrating differentiated instruction and understanding by design.* Alexandria, VA: ASCD.

U.S. Department of Education. (2010). *Race to the Top Fund.* Retrieved July 31, 2010, from *www2.ed.gov/programs/racetothetop/index.html.*

Vygotsky, L. S. (1978). *Mind in society.* Cambridge, MA: Harvard University Press.

Wasik, B. A., & Slavin, R. E. (1993). Preventing early reading failure with one-to-one tutoring: A review of five programs. Reading Research Quarterly, 28, 179–200.

Wharton-McDonald, R., Pressley, M., & Hampston, J. M. (1998). Literacy instruction in nine first-grade classrooms: Teacher characteristics and student achievement. *Elementary School Journal, 99*, 101–128.

CHAPTER 2

Balance in Comprehensive Literacy Instruction

Evolving Conceptions

Christina L. Madda
Vicki Benson Griffo
P. David Pearson
Taffy E. Raphael

This chapter will:

- Consider how conceptions of balance have changed over time.
- Revisit the research base that supports the importance of balance in the literacy curriculum.
- Offer our reconceptualization of balance in light of current research, insights, and contexts.
- Consider the implications of external forces and the challenges they present to ensuring balance in comprehensive literacy instruction.

EVIDENCE BASED BEST PRACTICES: DEFINING BALANCE IN THE LITERACY CURRICULUM

The concept of balance in the literacy curriculum has continued to gain currency over the past decade. Balance, a key term of the late 1990s, was born out of what the popular press (e.g., Lemann, 1997; Levine, 1994) and the research community (e.g., Pearson, 2004) termed the "Reading Wars." In the past, the idea of balance has drawn advocates from two distinct camps—one advocating for a whole language perspective as "ground" from which we could achieve a balanced approach (e.g., McIntyre & Pressley, 1996; Pressley, 2006) and another viewing an early code emphasis as the cornerstone of a balanced framework (e.g., Lyon, 1997). Each side claimed to be the balanced party in this debate, thus proliferating confusion and contributing to an obscured vision of balance in comprehensive literacy instruction. Moreover, as we have argued in previous editions of this volume, the unidimensional views of balance that often emerged from these debates never captured its true complexity. The political context of the debate has privileged some curricular decisions, such as how much or how little phonics to include over others, thus watering down the notion of balance by minimizing the importance of many other facets of literacy teaching and learning.

Recently, a force promoting a new vision of balance has emerged in the United States in the form of the Common Core Standards (2010). These voluntary standards, sponsored and promoted by the Council of Chief State School Officers (CCSSO) and the National Governors Association (NGA) (2010), offer a vision of balance for the English language arts that reflects much of the research conducted in the last decade. Comprehension and composition play a central role in these standards, with strong supporting roles played by word-level processes, vocabulary, oral discourse, and the conventions of written language. Another "balanced" feature of these new standards is disciplinary balance, for the standards illustrate in vivid ways how different standards for comprehension and composition get realized in literature, science, and social studies, thus demonstrating both commonalities and differences across disciplines. We find these new standards to be consistent with our view of balance across the language arts and urge readers to use them as a benchmark against which to test the applicability of the conceptualization we offer in this chapter.

Looking back at the first edition of this volume, we can assert that what was at stake then, and what continues to be at stake as we aim to reconceptualize and enact balance in light of current research and insights, is the schooling experience of students as they engage processes of learning to read, write, and talk about a variety of texts across disciplines, genres, and learning contexts.

As we reflect on balance more than a decade after our first entry into this space, not only is it important to remind ourselves of where we've been, but also to consider what is unique about where we currently stand. The presence of new and changing literacy demands of the 21st century (Bruce, 2003), as well as today's "back-to-basics" and high-stakes accountability climate, holds implications for what it means to achieve balance in literacy instruction. The contributors to this volume want the literacy experience to be what research suggests, and we believe to be "fully" balanced: to focus on a range of texts, to build strategies for working with today's texts and other media, and to prepare students to manage the vast sources of information they encounter across settings and for different purposes. We begin this chapter by revisiting past conceptions of balance and the forces that have shaped them. We also consider what we've learned from research about the core elements that constitute a balanced literacy program and why they are crucial. We then extend the discussion as we consider today's educational and political context and the ways in which it calls for a more progressive and reconceptualized notion of balance.

Evolving Conceptions of Balance

Determining the range of best practices for a balanced literacy curriculum requires the fundamental step of defining the construct—balance—and the components to which the research base applies. Two questions frame this section:

1. How have conceptions of balance evolved over time?
2. What research base supports the need for balance in the literacy curriculum?

Our initial conceptions of balance—as described in earlier editions of this book (Pearson & Raphael, 1999, 2003; Pearson, Raphael, Benson, & Madda, 2007) grew out of the antagonistic "Reading Wars" debate (Pearson, 2004). In these renditions, the debate positioned skills (i.e., phonics) against holistic (i.e., whole language) approaches to teaching reading, or—in its more current framing—literacy as a set of cognitive skills (Snow, Burns, & Griffin, 1998) versus a set of cultural practices that, in turn, shape and influence cognition and identities (Gee, 2000, 2002). The content of the debate has played out in issues involving curricular content, the nature of texts, teacher preparation and professional development, and, particularly, who controls decisions within these areas.

These debates are not new or unique. A century ago, the reading debates pitted ABCs (synthetic phonics) against analytic phonics (words first, then the letters) (Mathews, 1966). Right after World War II, the debate focused on look–say (exemplified by the classic Dick and Jane readers) versus phonics (see Chall, 1967; Mathews, 1966). In one form or another, the debate has always been about the *emphasis* during earliest stages of formal reading instruction—whether to focus on *breaking the code* (i.e., code-emphasis) or *understanding what we read* (i.e., meaning-emphasis) (see Chall, 1967, 1997, for a historical treatment of the debate).

The code-emphasis side takes a "simple view of reading" (Gough & Tunmer, 1986; Hoffman, 2009; Tumner & Nicholson, 2011): reading comprehension = decoding × listening comprehension. Those who advocate the simple view argue that because the code (the cipher that maps letters onto sounds) is what students do not know, the sooner they learn it, the better they will be able to read. That is, get phonics and decoding out of the way early so that students can begin to engage in regular reading by translating letters into the sounds of oral language and then using the same cognitive processes that facilitate listening comprehension to understand what they read (Cain, 2010).

The meaning-emphasis side argues that because making meaning is the ultimate goal of reading, it is best to start students off with that very expectation. If teachers provide relevant "scaffolding" to help students determine textual meaning(s), learners will, as a natural by-product, acquire the cipher for mapping sounds onto letters. Moreover, in their emphasis on meaning, advocates argue for beginning simultaneously on many fronts such as the following three: oral reading activities; shared reading (where teachers and students together read and study a book); and writing through pictures and temporary spellings. Ultimately, the code-emphasis side argues that we should teach students what they do not directly know, while the meaning-emphasis side argues that we should bootstrap what they do not know by relying on what they do know (see Harrison, 2010; Hoffman, 2009; Pearson, 1976; Tumner & Nicholson, 2011, for more extensive discussions of these issues).

In addition to the early debates about emphasis, literacy educators debated about the *instructional focus.* The concern was whether the growth of each individual *child* or the sanctity of the *curriculum* should dominate the teachers' decision-making processes. One camp wanted to make sure that each child experienced the optimal curriculum for his or her development. For example, Harste, Woodward, and Burke (1984) wrote about approaches that made the child the primary curriculum informant. The individual-child camp argued that there are many paths to reading acquisition; while the curricular-sanctity camp argued that there are many variations in the way the single path is traversed. The question was how to balance curricular-driven instructional decisions (i.e., all my students must learn *X*) with child-driven instructional decisions (i.e., Jason will learn *X* when he is ready).

Over the past decade, the context for debates about balance has broadened. As painful and enduring as the Reading Wars have been, they did help educators and researchers see the problems of a single-dimension, dichotomous, either–or approach (Pearson, 2004). We currently argue in favor of a conception of balance that responds to the complex and challenging settings that characterize today's literacy teaching and learning. While we have become more sophisticated as a field about what and how we teach, we continue to struggle to ensure that all students are able to participate in a full range of meaningful literacy practices. Today, we must recognize that balance is not an external construct achieved by coordinating phonics and whole language components. Rather, achieving balance is a complex process that requires flexibility and artful orchestration of literacy's various contextual and conceptual aspects. Reconceptualizing balance requires attention to the wide array of components at work, to their interconnectedness, and to the contextual elements that influence how balance manifests itself in today's classrooms.

Balance Today

Three sources of evidence point to the importance of a balanced literacy curriculum today. First, a look at U.S. students' achievement levels, as reflected in standardized norm-referenced tests (e.g., the National Assessment of Educational Progress [NAEP]), indicates that there is still work to be done to ensure that all students are achieving the highest levels of literacy. Second, research syntheses, as well as large-scale studies of effective literacy instruction, suggest that there is a broad range of skills, strategies, genres, and contexts that must be considered in a complete literacy curriculum—and a finite amount of time in which teachers have to teach it. Third, a critical analysis of "balanced literacy" as a historical construct worthy of our attention divulges some limitations of long-standing models and the need to reconsider the construct.

Current State of Achievement

Results from large-scale assessments of students' literacy achievement in U.S. schools are cause for concern about current practices. As the U.S. student population grows more diverse, disparities in performance levels on national assessments persist between students of diverse backgrounds (i.e., from ethnic and racial minority groups, speaking a first language other than English, living in poverty) and their "mainstream" peers (i.e., white, middle class, native English speaking). According to the NAEP 2009 Executive Report in Reading, there have been no significant changes in reducing the racial/ethnic gaps, gender gaps, or social class gaps at either grade 4 or 8 compared with 2007. Compared with 1992, only the white–black gap at grade 4 and female–male gaps at grade 8 have narrowed slightly (National Center of Educational Statistics, 2010).

For example, the achievement data in Figure 2.1 reflect students' performance levels on the 2002 NAEP (Grigg, Daane, Jin, & Campbell, 2003). Using Figure 2.1, compare the scores of black and Hispanic students in 12th grade to those of white and Asian–Pacific Islander students in grade 8. You'll notice that by 12th grade, as a group, students from diverse backgrounds have fallen 4 years behind their mainstream peers. The average 12th-grade black

Ethnicity	Grade 4	Grade 8	Grade 12
White	229	272	292
Black	199	245	267
Hispanic	201	247	273
Asian–Pacific Islander	224	267	286

FIGURE 2.1. Achievement gap.

student's gain score (267) is at the same level as the average eighth-grade Asian–Pacific Islander student (267), and slightly below that of the average eighth-grade white student (272). An average 12th-grade Hispanic student's gain score (273) is only 1 point above that of an average eighth-grade white student. Such a large disparity in average scores suggests that a variety of instructional support will be required to meet students' needs.

Effective Literacy Instruction

There are many ways to explain the achievement gap reflected in tests such as the NAEP. These explanations include such factors as economic disparities and related differences in experiential background before entering school, high mobility rates, and so forth—factors that are well beyond the control of a classroom teacher or school staff. Yet we know from research that there are important factors that we can control within schools and classrooms that influence student achievement levels—those of curriculum that frame instruction (i.e., *what* to teach) and the quality of teaching in implementing the curriculum (i.e., *how* it is taught). For example, a review of research that led to the National Reading Panel Report (National Reading Panel, 2000) suggests that a complete reading program must include instruction in comprehension and fluency as well as basic understanding of the symbol system at the word level (i.e., phonics and phonemic awareness); the full report suggests that as important as phonics instruction is, it must always be set within a broader pedagogical context in which it is surrounded by meaning-making activities. These more cautionary themes are also reflected in several of the chapters in the most current (i.e., Volume IV) *Handbook of Reading Research.*[1]

Others have demonstrated the centrality of concept knowledge or vocabulary learning in general, particularly for students who do not speak English as their native language (Carlo et al., 2004). Taylor, Pearson, Peterson, and Rodriguez (2003, 2005) identified a set of classroom practices, dubbed "teaching for cognitive engagement," that support higher levels of achievement; the set includes teacher coaching rather than telling, high levels of questioning, students' active participation in activities that require high levels of thinking (e.g., book club discussions, inquiry groups), and time for students' sustained engagement in reading and writing.

How do these findings connect with the achievement gap? Research has documented that students from diverse backgrounds often have limited

---

[1]The full citation of the currently in press *Handbook* is M. L. Kamil, P. D. Pearson, E. Moje, & P. Afflerbach (2010). *Handbook of reading research, Vol. IV.* London: Routledge. In particular, the chapters by Tumner and Nicholson on word identification instruction, by Duke and Carlisle on comprehension development, by Foorman and Connor on primary-grade reading, and by Paratore, Cassano, and Schickendanz on early literacy development reflect this more balanced perspective.

exposure to high-quality instruction, even within what teachers believe to be a balanced curriculum. Researchers have documented that, when compared with "mainstream" peers, low-income or minority students tend to receive a great deal of instruction in lower-level skills and little instruction in reading comprehension and higher-level thinking about text (see Amendum & Fitzgerald, 2010; Amendum et al., 2009; Darling-Hammond, 1995, 2004; Kong & Fitch, 2002). It may be a conspiracy of good intentions—one that might be labeled "first things first," where the logic is something like "Let's get the words right and the facts straight before we get to the 'what ifs' and 'I wonders' of classroom instruction." And, of course, the conspiracy is that many lower-performing students spend their entire school careers getting the words right and the facts straight, never reaching that higher-level thinking. One reason for this disparity and conspiracy—lowered expectations for the achievement of students from historically marginalized communities and limited instructional focus areas—is something we can and should change.

Unpacking the Components of Balanced Literacy

Thus historically different proponents have excluded or privileged certain literacy components (e.g., pitting instruction in basic skills *against* use of authentic, meaningful literature and literacy experiences). For many years the term *balance*, as appropriated by either side in the Reading Wars debate, led to an oversimplified notion—one that applies only to balance within literacy instructional elements. In the remainder of this chapter, we unpack the construct of balance with an eye toward what it might become. In doing so, we argue for the need for a comprehensive literacy curriculum that gets at all components of literacy (Au & Raphael, 1998; Pearson & Raphael, 1999; Pressley, 2006) while avoiding the potential problem of literacy becoming the curricular bully, driving out and overshadowing other important school subjects.

BEST PRACTICES IN ACTION

By deconstructing and then reassembling the phenomenon known as balance, we believe we can build a case for the rich knowledge bases teachers need to implement comprehensive literacy instruction that is truly balanced. In so doing, we "complexify" balance by moving beyond the code versus meaning debate (i.e., balance in the past) to argue that there are many independent elements of literacy that must be simultaneously balanced (i.e., balance today). As a beginning, we find it useful to consider a series of continua that reflect multiple dimensions of literacy instruction. These include (1) contextual continua and (2) content continua.

Contextual Continua

While there are many contextual aspects that literacy educators attempt to balance in their daily teaching activities, we have chosen to focus here on four: authenticity, classroom discourse, teachers' roles, and curricular control (see Figure 2.2). Illustrations of these four concepts exemplify why a mere meeting in the middle between code- and meaning-emphasized instruction is not enough to achieve that balance we seek in literacy instruction.

First, the notion of *authenticity* has been identified as important to students' literacy learning (Florio-Ruane & Raphael, 2004; Purcell-Gates, Duke, & Martineau, 2007). The argument underlying the promotion of authenticity is that too many school tasks are inauthentic, unrealistic, and, by implication, not useful for engaging in real-world literacy activities; that is, instead of teaching kids how to "do school," we should be teaching them how to "do life." The content students read, write, and talk about and the activity settings in which

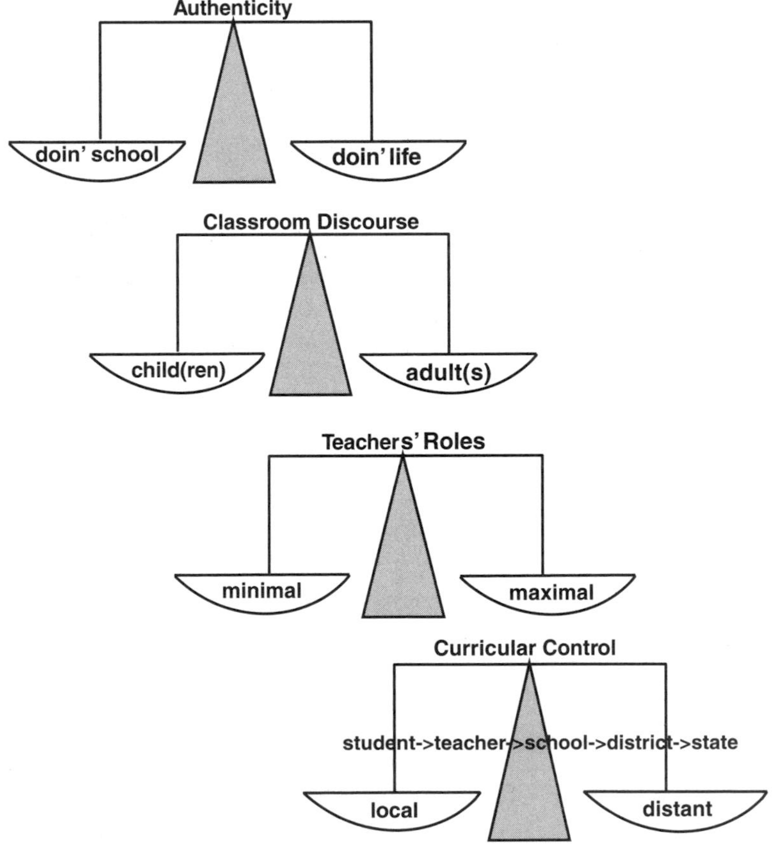

FIGURE 2.2. Balancing contextual factors.

students work should be grounded in authentic tasks and goals. These include writing for real audiences and purposes (e.g., Cappello, 2006), writing to make sense of their lives (Dyson, 2003; Genishi & Dyson, 2009; Schultz, 2006, 2009), and reading to engage in book club or other discussions with teachers and peers (e.g., Raphael, Florio-Ruane, George, Hasty, & Highfield, 2004). To be downplayed are activities such as writing solely to demonstrate knowledge of conventions or reading to successfully answer a set of comprehension questions. On the face of it, it might seem hard to disagree with an emphasis on authenticity. However, if authenticity were pursued too single-mindedly, some useful skills might never be acquired. If all instruction were held to the authenticity criterion, there might be no occasion for treating formal features of language (e.g., its structure, sound–symbol system, punctuation) as objects of study. For example, children arguably need to understand the "code"—how sounds are captured in written language, conventions for conveying stress and intonation—in order to engage in lifelong literacy; yet the hazard is that the practice activities associated with becoming fluent in such areas may be limited to school practice tasks or reading practice readers. One way of labeling what might be lost under a regime of hyperauthenticity is knowledge *about* language and how it works in different contexts. Clearly, balance is important across the continuum bounded by "doing school" and "doing life."

A second contextual aspect is the type of *classroom discourse* that students experience. Sociolinguists such as Cazden (2001) and Philips (1972) note the importance of control, specifically over topics and turn taking. Teachers may control topics and turns, topics but not turns, turns but not topics, or neither topic nor turn. Students can exert similar control. Depending on the goal of the literacy event, activity, or lesson, different patterns of classroom talk are appropriate. Moreover, many scholars today underscore the variations in children's experiences with the discourse of the classroom or school setting more generally. Gee (2002, 2007) and others point out how inextricably linked literacy development is to oral language and its use. Thus the discourse patterns and related identities students bring to school may align differentially with how language is used in schools. Students' primary language practices directly influence the degree to which they can participate in the literacy practices of schooling. Balance, then, must take into account not only who is controlling the topics and turns under discussion, but also which language(s) and discourses are practiced in the context of schooling.

The *teachers' roles* within a classroom are closely related to types of classroom discourse. Au and Raphael (1998) characterize variations in teachers' roles in terms of the amount of teacher control and student activity. They define five teacher roles: (1) explicit instructing, (2) modeling, (3) scaffolding, (4) facilitating, and (5) participating. These reflect decreasing control by the teacher and increased activity on the part of the student (see Figure 2.3). Thus students are most passive when teachers are engaged in direct instruction and most active when they assume more conversational control. Au and Raphael's description implies that it is just as mistaken to assume that

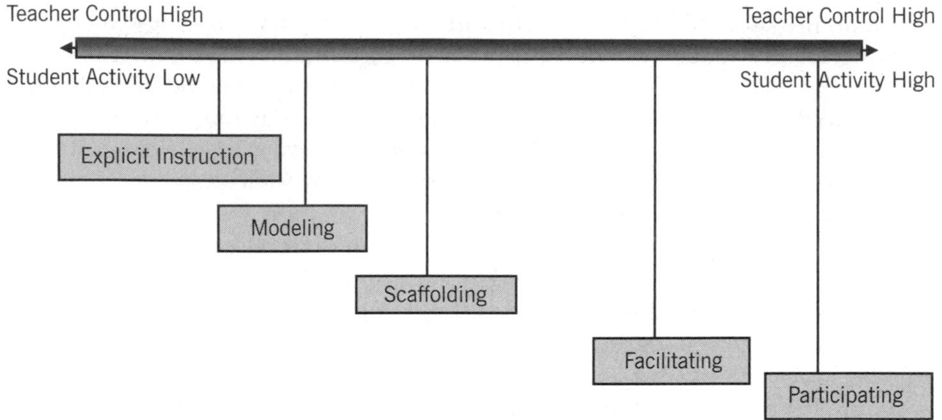

FIGURE 2.3. Teachers' roles.

literacy learning is limited to situations in which the teacher is engaged in explicit instruction as it is to assume that learning is meaningful only when the teacher is out of the picture. Maloch (2002) found that just because the teacher shares her thinking does not mean that students are taking on the language they are hearing for their own uses and purposes. It is important to have variability in support levels if students are to take up learning. Furthermore, researchers such as Rodgers (2004) have demonstrated how teachers' roles vary even within these different discourse settings. Rodgers's observations of teaching and learning over time illustrated the lack of an apparent scope or sequence to the teaching contexts and related teacher and student roles. That is, teachers did not start out with greater control and move steadily to lesser. Rather, teachers varied the amount of support they provided and the related degree of teacher control and student activity levels according to their perceptions of what students needed, thus demonstrating that the delicate element of balance is one partially crafted by the teacher.

A fourth aspect is *curricular control*—who, or what, "calls the shots" in terms of how teachers and students spend their time in classrooms. At one extreme, control is most distant from the classroom (e.g., at the national or state levels) where curriculum is controlled by those least familiar with the specific students who study the curriculum. Such control may be exerted through mandating the textbooks to be used, specifying standards or benchmarks of performance, or (as appears to be increasingly dominant) the tests that students, teachers, and schools are held accountable to. At the other extreme, control is in the hands of those most intimately involved with the students, specifically classroom teachers or grade-level teams. And in some classrooms, teachers cede curricular control to their students in terms of the books they read, the pieces they write, and the artifacts they choose to bring forward to represent their learning.

Balancing across these two extremes is crucial. On the one hand, all educators must make clear those standards to which they would hold students accountable as these students move through the curriculum. Fourth-grade teachers have the right to assume that certain curriculum content was covered and mastered prior to the students' entering grade 4. Similarly, the fourth-grade teacher has a right to know what information these students will be held accountable for when they matriculate to their next grade level. However, perhaps only the parents of these fourth graders know them better than their classroom teachers. Thus to dictate specific instructional methods and even specific curriculum materials for reaching benchmarks and standards is to deny students the right to have those decisions made by the individuals who know them best—their teachers. In short, when curricular control is too distant from the classroom, it is difficult for schools and teachers to adhere to their basic professional responsibility to adapt to individual differences.

Content Continua

Balancing the contextual aspects of literacy instruction sets the stage for balance within the content of what is taught. We highlight several aspects of the curricular content, some of which have been central to debates about literacy instruction and some of which have been implicit or understated in the debates. All, we think, are essential to a complete view of balance. They are (1) skill contextualization, (2) text genres, (3) text difficulty, (4) response to literature, (5) subject-matter emphasis, (6) balance within the language arts, and (7) balance within reading instruction (see Figure 2.4).

Skill contextualization (Pearson & Raphael, 1990) refers to the primary "context" from which the instruction of a particular skill or strategy arises. At the one extreme, teachers may rely on a predetermined curriculum of skill instruction, often tied to a curricular scope and sequence that operates within and across grade levels. At the other extreme, the texts and the tasks that arise in the course of instruction, or, even more common, the needs that a given student or set of students demonstrate, are the determining force behind what is taught. In the latter view, the curriculum is unveiled as teachable moments occur, with the text, the tasks, and the students functioning as springboards to skill or strategy instruction.

We suggest the need for teachers to operate flexibly between these two extremes. It makes a great deal of sense, for example, to teach about point of view as students read historical fiction related to the American Civil War, even if point of view happens to be scheduled at some other point in the academic year's guide to curriculum. Conversely, it makes little sense, in the context of reading Bunting and Diaz's (1994) *Smoky Night* to a group of second graders, to highlight the /fl/ blend in *flames*, simply because it appeared in the text at the same time that the /fl/ blend popped up in an instructional scope and sequence plan. However, strict reliance on emerging questions, issues, or

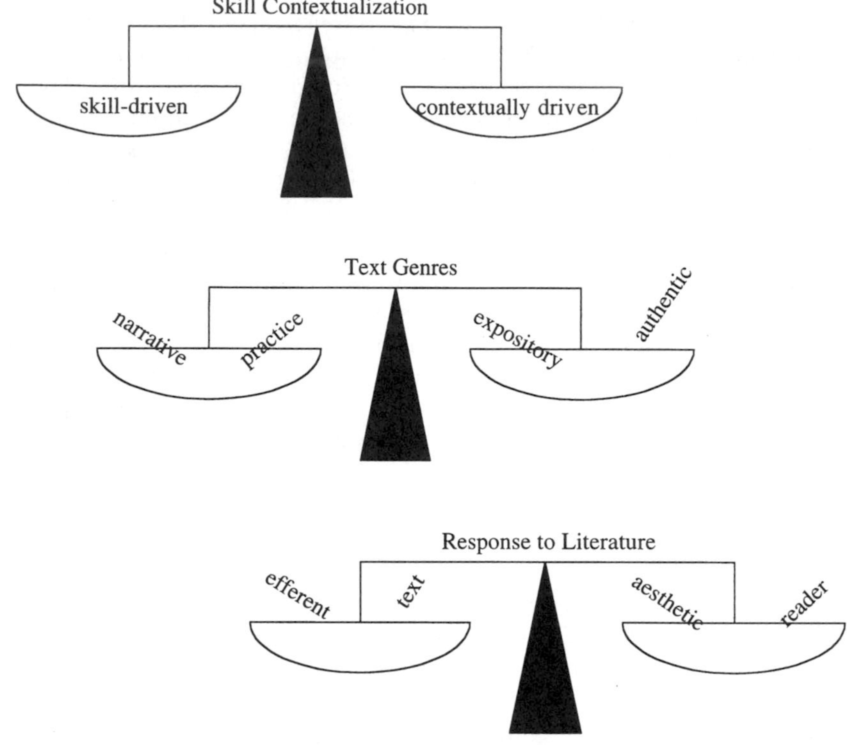

FIGURE 2.4. Balancing curricular content.

teachable moments as the standard by which teachers determine the content of the literacy curriculum creates problems or uncertainties because, at some point, aspects of the literacy curriculum really do have to be covered.

A second area of content balance is *genre* (e.g., Duke & Purcell-Gates, 2003; Hicks, 1998; Nodelman, 1992; Pappas & Pettegrew, 1998). Genre refers to the types of texts that form the basis of the literacy curriculum—stories, personal narratives, poems, essays, descriptions, and a range of specific expository structures. However, literacy can no longer be defined simply as the reading and writing of printed text. Instead, we need to consider the multiple and overlapping forms of literacy, including digital, visual, spoken, and printed forms, that require the reader to critically analyze, deconstruct, and reconstruct meaning across a variety of texts for various purposes (Anstey, 2002; Anstey & Bull, 2006; New London Group, 2000). For example, Web-based multimedia formats combine text, sound, color, images, and layout to convey meaning. It is critical that we help students develop literate competencies within such forms of "new literacies" (see Gee, 2007; Kist, 2005, 2010; Kress, 2001, 2003; Lankshear & Knobel, 2003). Furthermore, new literacies include blogging, Tweeting, console games, instant messaging, looking up "cheats" on the Internet for game playing, and social networking sites (Pahl & Rowsell, 2005). Thus students today engage in multiple genres that transcend traditional notions contrasting informational with narrative texts. Related literate actions are complex, varied, sophisticated, and extend beyond school-based literate activities (Moje, 2008). These new technologies raise questions about what it means to balance teaching across genres and what new genres students need to learn to control to achieve different purposes (Cervetti, Damico, & Pearson, 2006). They also raise questions of how new genres can support students' learning within more traditional genres.

The debate about genre isn't limited to defining text forms. It also involves questions of balancing authentic and instructional texts. Some literacy educators argue that young readers learn best when reading and responding to authentic literature, which reflects purposeful use of language, complex natural language, and compelling story lines (e.g., Dyson, 2003). Others have argued that such literary criteria make little sense in selecting books that young readers need to become fluent readers (e.g., Hiebert, 1998). Teachers need the flexibility to travel the full range of positions on this axis as well. Even our youngest students must be able to handle, read (even if it's "pretend-read"), and respond to high-quality literary texts—texts written by authors to inform, persuade, entertain, and inspire. However, when it comes to acquiring the skills that enable authentic reading, relying on traditional literature to promote skill development may serve neither the literature nor the skills well. Factors ranging from word placement on a page to relationships between words and pictures may actually make wonderful literary texts though poor materials for practicing and fine-tuning skills. Also, the sheer amount of practice reading that early readers need to engage in calls for a host of easy-to-read books students can read at their independent level. As engaging as these books may be to young and enthusiastic readers, many, and perhaps most, may never qualify as quality literature. Neither high-quality trade books nor practice books can serve as the sole diet of books for young readers to become proficient in literacy activities.

The third dimension of content balance relates to *text difficulty*, regardless of genre. For students to gain the literacy skills and strategies they need, teachers today have two responsibilities (see Raphael et al., 2004). First, they must ensure that excellent diagnostic decisions are made about where to place students instructionally—to make sure that students are taught what they need using texts written for their instructional reading level. But today, that means realistically that many students will be taught to read using texts that are below or far below what is appropriate for their age level. So the second responsibility teachers have is one of access. They must ensure that all students are given access to age-appropriate texts and held accountable for writing in response to the text and talking about issues with their peers and the teacher—in settings such as "Book Club" (Raphael, Pardo, & Highfield, 2002). Thus teachers must balance students' exposure to texts of high quality that requires engagement in high levels of reading, writing, and talk with students' opportunity to improve their independent reading abilities through focused teaching using texts written at their instructional level.

The newly released Common Core Standards (2010) have upped the ante for text difficulty, for they have suggested that, at every grade level, students need to be exposed to and supported in reading a higher proportion of more challenging text. The rationale for this approach is based on the sobering observation that, when students finish secondary school (in grade 12 in the United States), the average level of challenge of the texts they are reading is about a whole grade level below what they will be expected to read as freshmen in college. The authors of the standards point to, and we think rightly so, the tremendous amount of resources devoted to remedial education in the first year of college—not only in community colleges (where one might expect less well-prepared students to comprise a significant proportion of the population) but also in regional and even research-intensive universities. Their solution to closing this text complexity/text challenging gap is to gradually increase the expectations (and instructional support) at every grade level from the primary years onward so that by 12th grade, it stands a chance of being closed altogether. Our view is that we have only begun to understand how we might possibly meet this challenge; we'll know a lot more if and when we write the sequel to this chapter.

The fourth dimension of content balance is *response to literature* (Sipe, 2008). The debate here stems from complex issues related to readers' individual interpretations of text and the tensions concerning social and cultural values that almost inevitably arise in literature discussions (Galda & Beach, 2001). This debate has been traveled along two axes—reader-driven versus text-driven understandings, and conventional (i.e., culturally sanctioned) versus personal interpretations. As our field has moved toward authentic literature as the basis for our reading programs, teachers find themselves face to face with students' response to the content of literature: the enduring themes of the human experience (love, hate, prejudice, friendship, religious values, human rights, etc.). Fourth and fifth graders reading Taylor's (1990) *Mississippi Bridge* will undoubtedly initiate conversations about how African Americans were treated by southern whites in the 1930s, which can lead to conversations about race relations today. Third graders reading and responding to McLerran's book (1991) *Roxaboxen* unpack their own family stories and memories and consider the relationships they have with family members across generations.

Debates about response are deeply rooted in beliefs about the functions of schooling, the separation of church and state, and the roles of parents and teachers. Furthermore, they are rooted in beliefs about the development of students' interpretive dispositions—whether we privilege each reader's interpretation of the story's meaning or author's message, or whether there is a "correct" (official or conventional) meaning that teachers are obligated to help students learn for later demonstration that they have acquired that conventional meaning. Balancing response to literature actually involves balancing the tension between the two goals of schooling—connecting to the past and preparing to meet an uncertain future. On the one hand, schools are obligated to teach students about dominant societal perceptions of cultural lore, history, cultural and linguistic tools, norms for interaction, and so forth. On the other hand, schools must build our future citizenry, helping students become adults who can live in a world that will undoubtedly differ significantly from the world we live in today. This tension between convention and invention must be addressed through a curriculum that balances the individual with the culture.

A fifth dimension of content balance turns on the relationship between literacy and other *subject-matter domains*, such as mathematics, science, social studies, art, music, and the like. The point here is simple but important: as much as we might like to see literacy assume a central role in the school curriculum, we are keenly aware of the dangers we will face if the elementary or secondary curriculum becomes too literacy-centric. There are at least three reasons for all literacy educators to press for greater balance across subject-matter areas: (1) to assure a steady source of knowledge to fuel the comprehension and composition processes; (2) to find contexts in which students can authentically apply their literacy strategies; and (3) to ensure the integrity of disciplinary knowledge as a goal in its own right.

It is foolhardy for those who care about reading and writing acquisition to press for its emphasis at the cost of disciplinary knowledge. Reading and writing are not abstract processes. When we read, when we write, we read and write about something in particular—a text lies in front of us in reading or just behind the mind's eye in writing. We create or understand texts that are grounded in knowledge and experience. If we deny access to the knowledge that comes from rich curricular experiences in the disciplines, we ultimately deny progress to students' reading and writing accomplishments. Indeed, the most recent iteration of a set of national English language arts standards represents a current attempt to bring balance to the curriculum by integrating the language arts with other subject areas as a means to helping students "acquire a wide range of ever more sophisticated knowledge and skills" (CCSSO & NGA, 2010, p. 1).

The second reason is, in a sense, the logical complement of the first. Earlier, in discussing the contextual continuum of authenticity, we made an implicit argument for applying reading and writing skills and strategies to contexts in which reading and writing were put to service in "real" reading and writing tasks. Nowhere in the school curriculum is this authenticity better portrayed than in the acquisition of disciplinary knowledge and processes.

The benefits of reading and writing are rendered transparent when they are viewed as tools for the acquisition of knowledge and insight typically found in subject-matter learning. Indeed, much has been written (e.g., Cervetti, Pearson, Bravo, & Barber, 2006; Magnusson & Palincsar, 2005; Palincsar & Magnusson, 2001) about the efficacy of reading and writing as tools to support inquiry-based science learning. In fact, we believe that if one regards literature (with its inherent emphasis on the stuff of human experience—love and hate, friendship and betrayal, humankind and nature) as a discipline—on par with science and social studies and mathematics, for example—then we can view reading and writing (and we would add oral language) as tools for learning across all of these domains. The third reason is moral in nature: students need a fair shot at all of these subject matters because each area is a critical part of the human experience. To deny their place in the curriculum or to delay their curricular emphasis until after the basics of reading, writing, and language are acquired is to harm both their integrity and the efficacy of good literacy instruction. The literacy curriculum is the better for strong and complementary disciplinary emphases. As Cervetti et al. (2006) put it, reading needs to be transformed from being a curricular "bully" (which it pretty much is in the wake of the No Child Left Behind Act of 2001 and the Reading First Act of 2002) into serving as a curricular "buddy" to enhance both the learning of disciplinary knowledge and its own application in that learning.

In considering the sixth content aspect, *balance within the language arts*, one of the great virtues of the language arts (traditionally thought of as reading, writing, listening, and speaking) is that, while they are surely distinct in function, they are mutually synergistic. What we learn in and through oral language can be put to work in reading and writing, and vice versa. For example, we learn new vocabulary through oral language that allows us to call up the meaning of a specific word when we encounter it in print and later use it in an essay. Conversely, a word we first encounter in a story or an article, such as *glorious* or *misanthrope*, might well make it into our oral language and later our writing. And the new knowledge that we acquire when we listen to a teacher read a book or a story that is beyond our reading level can become the prior knowledge we will use to understand a new text on our own tomorrow. The point? Just because you as a teacher love reading and view it as the nucleus of early schooling does not mean that you will want to privilege it over the other language arts for the very reason that reading is enhanced by progress in listening, speaking, and writing. Hence the need for balance within the language arts becomes apparent.

Finally, in considering *balance within reading instruction*, we earlier touched on this most salient issue in the debate by emphasizing the distinction of code versus meaning. But we are now armed with strong evidence to ensure this sort of balance, for we know—by virtue of the work of the National Reading Panel (2000) and a long tradition of research curriculum and pedagogy stemming back into the 1980s (e.g., Anderson, Hiebert, Scott, & Wilkinson, 1984), the 1960s (e.g., Chall, 1967), and even earlier (e.g., Gray, 1948)—that the research confirms the importance of mastering lower-level processes such as phonics and phonemic awareness, as well as thoroughgoing instruction in comprehension and vocabulary. We would add, to go one level deeper into curriculum, that the research also supports balance within each of these important areas of reading and writing instruction—phonemic awareness, phonics, comprehension, and vocabulary (we combine these last two in our discussion as a pair of meaning-emphasis approaches).

Phonemic Awareness

Here the research (National Reading Panel, 2000) suggests that explicit instruction in various elements of phonological awareness, such as rhyming, phonemic segmentation (breaking a word into its phonemic units—*bat* → /buh/aa/tuh/), and phonemic blending (putting the parts together—/buh/ /aa/ /tuh/ → *bat*) pays dividends in the long run in terms of its transference to beginning-reading achievement. But we also know that the instruction can include many engaging oral language games (see Snow et al., 1998) and even invented spelling (see Adams, 1990; Clarke, 1988). There is no need to privilege dense skill-oriented programs over engaging language activities.

Phonics

If we recast phonics as word-reading strategies (Ehri, Nunes, Stahl, & Willows, 2001), we find the need for balance here too. We know that the National Reading Panel report, its narrow sample of subject populations notwithstanding, concluded that what mattered was early emphasis on the code, not an emphasis on any particular approach to phonics. We know from other work (e.g., Ehri et al., 2001; Gaskins, Ehri, Cress, O'Hara, & Donnelly, 1996/1997) that approaches to word reading are complementary and that students need a full repertoire of tools to do justice to the challenge of pronouncing unknown words encountered in text.

Ehri (1995) talks about four strategies that we find particularly useful as ways of conceptualizing the curricular goals of teachers and the learning needs of students. Ehri suggests that students need to learn to read words using four approaches: sequential decoding, analogy, contextual analysis, and sight-word recognition. Sequential decoding, or letter-by-letter decoding, is the stuff of which the time-honored ABC approach is made, and students can indeed sound out words in this way. Analogy should be focused on word families or phonograms—words that are spelled and pronounced similarly, such as *cat, fat, sat, bat,* and the like. Gaskins (2005) found, in building the Benchmark School curriculum, that analogy instruction is much more effective after sequential decoding has been established among readers. Contextual analysis is an ad hoc form of problem solving—what you do when you come to a word you cannot pronounce, and it involves both intraword (morphological analysis) and extraword (the surrounding context) analysis in order to work. Finally, there is immediate sight-word recognition, and it plays two roles in word reading. First, some words, such as *give, have, the,* and *get,* must be learned as sight words because they violate the principles one learns from instruction in sequential decoding and analogy. Second—and this is the really important face of sight-word reading—the goal of the other three approaches is to move words from students' repertoire of "arduously analyzable" (I can figure these out if I work at it) to "immediately recognizable" (I know that word; it's *irrefutable*). In short, the goal of phonics and context instruction is to get to the point where readers need them only minimally, freeing up their thinking skills for higher-level processes. Balanced phonics instruction—or, more accurately, balanced word-reading instruction—is essential to skilled reading.

Balanced Comprehension Instruction

We know from the National Reading Panel that comprehension can be improved by explicit strategy instruction and by a variety of approaches to vocabulary instruction. We also know from previous work (see Murphy & Wilkinson, 2005; Pearson & Fielding, 1991) that rich conversations about text can improve comprehension of both the texts within which the instruction is embedded and new texts that students subsequently read on their own. Hence we are prepared to conclude that all three of these approaches—strategy instruction, rich talk about text (of the sort described in the earlier section on students' responses to literature), and semantically rich conversations about word meanings (see Beck, McKeown, & Kucan, 2002; Blachowicz & Fisher, 2009) should all be a part of a balanced curriculum. At this point in our research history, there seems to be no basis for privileging any one of the three over the other two, and they do seem to relate well to one another as a complementary set.

REFLECTIONS AND NEW DIRECTIONS: RETHINKING BALANCE

In thinking about balance then and now, it has become clear that we need to avoid overemphasizing any one particular dimension of literacy instruction. Instead, balance today requires attention toward multiple dimensions that fall along the context and content continua. We borrow from environmental science the concept of "ecological balance," which suggests a system that works to support each individual component—a comprehensive literacy curriculum that doesn't pit one aspect against another. In doing so, we hope to suggest that we must shift the debates about balance *away* from single-dimension discussions of what to teach and what not to teach, and *toward* the notion that achieving a balanced literacy curriculum is a logical goal of all literacy educators. The ecologically balanced curriculum that follows is based on research focused on a literature-based program, Book Club and Book Club *Plus* (Raphael et al., 2002, Raphael, Kehus, & Damphousse, 2001; Raphael et al., 2004), and a K–5 literacy curriculum designed for the Kamehameha Early Education Program (Au & Carroll, 1997). Both programs are grounded in the belief that ownership of literacy is central to students' lifelong success (see Au & Raphael, 1998). The literacy instructional content that forms the ecological system consists of four areas: (1) comprehension, (2) composition, (3) literary aspects, and (4) language conventions (see Figure 2.5).

Comprehension	Composition	Literary Aspects	Language Conventions
Background Knowledge: prediction Text Processing: summarizing sequencing identifying importance Monitoring: clarifying planning	Process planning drafting revising Writing as a Tool Writing from Sources On-Demand Writing	Literary Elements: theme plot character setting Response to Literature: personal creative critical	Sound/Symbol Grammar Syntax Interaction

FIGURE 2.5. An ecologically balanced curriculum.

Each of these four areas is supported by extensive bodies of research using a range of rigorous research methods (see Raphael & Brock, 1997). We must be conscious not to weigh in too heavily against any particular curriculum aspect, such as downplaying the role of phonics, as depicted in Figure 2.6. Nor should we be overly optimistic about teaching only a small part of the curriculum and hoping the rest will follow, as depicted in Figure 2.7. And, if we take seriously the idea that instruction must be balanced within the language arts and between the language arts and other subject areas, then we need an even more complex picture, as in Figure 2.8.

Comprehension	Composition	Literary Aspects	Language Conventions
Background Knowledge: prediction Text Processing: summarizing sequencing identifying importance Monitoring: clarifying planning	Process: planning drafting revising Writing as a Tool Writing from Sources On-Demand Writing	Literary Elements: theme plot character setting Response to Literature: personal creative critical	Sound/Symbol Grammar Syntax Interaction

FIGURE 2.6. Balance askew when curriculum is ignored.

Comprehension	Composition	Literary Aspects	Language Conventions
Background Knowledge: prediction Text Processing summarizing sequencing identifying importance Monitoring: clarifying planning	Process: planning drafting revising Writing as a Tool Writing from Sources On-Demand Writing	Literary Elements: theme plot character setting Response to Literature: personal creative critical	Sound/Symbol Grammar Syntax Interaction

FIGURE 2.7. Balance askew when curriculum is overemphasized.

So, now we want to wed these two driving metaphors of ecological balance and orchestrating balance on multiple balance beams simultaneously to create a truly complex but, we think, apt model of good teaching. Unpacking the cluster of dimensions in our balance beam metaphor, focusing on the specifics of content and contextual facets that constitute reading instruction demonstrates some of the complexities in that debate. If we allow teachers the prerogative, for particular situations and students, of positioning themselves on each of these scales independently of the others, then we avoid the

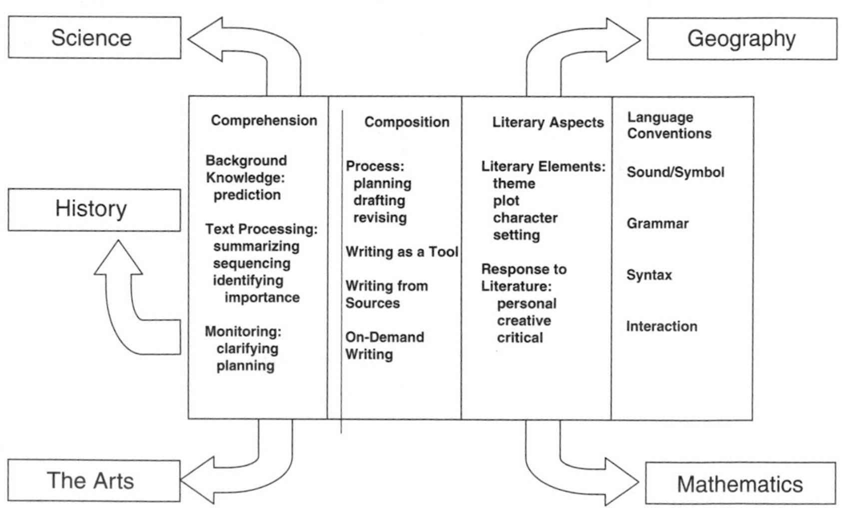

FIGURE 2.8. Balancing within the language arts and between the language arts and other subjects.

overemphasis of any single dimension and move toward the balance we need to achieve today.

Effective teachers cannot easily be pigeonholed into curricular boxes. If they are good at what they do—orchestrating a complex curriculum in the face of an enormous range of individual differences among students—then they learn to slide along each of these dozen or so contextual and content continua we have identified. At any given moment, they might be at different points along each of the continua, and then, with the slightest change in the instructional ecology of the classroom, change their position on half of them, knowing that in the very next minute they might make another four or five minor shifts in emphasis. Call it orchestration, call it a curricular dance (more like a ballet), call it responsive teaching—no matter what label we use, it is the essence of professional practice. We believe there is merit in the metaphor of multiple balance beams, each with at least one and sometimes two axes that must be traversed thoughtfully and independently. It makes balance a more elusive construct, but also a more powerful one—one that we hope we can all strive to achieve in our teaching.

ENGAGEMENT ACTIVITIES

1. Obtain your school, district, or state's standards and/or curriculum related to literacy. Given the ecologically balanced system proposed here, discuss the degree to which these materials reflect or obscure balance within and across contextual factors (i.e., authenticity, classroom discourse, teachers' roles, and curricular control) and curricular content (i.e., skills contextualization, genre, text difficulty, response to literature, subject-matter emphasis, balance within language arts, and balance across reading instruction). Consider the question "What can I do?" based on your findings.
2. The argument for balance in this chapter places much of the responsibility in the hands of the classroom teacher. This teacher must make professional decisions about how to teach particular students with specific needs, use a specific curriculum to achieve particular goals, and so forth. How can the profession best support those teachers who lack the professional experiences that may be important to making wise decisions and creating balance?
3. Given your professional experiences, where do you think the challenges to providing or creating a balanced curriculum emerge? What can you do, as an individual as well as a member

of a particular professional community, to infuse balance throughout the literacy curriculum and general classrooms for which you share responsibilities?

RESOURCES FOR FURTHER LEARNING

Connelly, F. M., He, M. F., & Phillion, J. (Eds.). (2008). *The Sage handbook of curriculum and instruction.* Thousand Oaks, CA: Sage.

Hoffman, J. V., & Goodman, Y. M. (2009). *Changing literacies for changing times: A historical perspective on the future of reading research, public policy, and classroom practices.* New York: Routledge.

Li, G., & Edwards, P. A. (Eds.). (2010). *Best practices in ELL instruction.* New York: Guilford Press.

Morrow, L., Rueda, R., & Lapp, D. (Eds.). (2009). *Handbook of research on literacy and diversity.* New York: Guilford Press.

www.ciera.org—Center for the Improvement of Early Reading Achievement

www.corestandards.org—Common Core State Standards Initiative

www.SchoolRiseUSA.com—School Rise: Enlightened Teaching

REFERENCES

Adams, M. J. (1990). *Beginning to read: Thinking and learning about print.* Cambridge, MA: MIT Press.

Amendum, S., & Fitzgerald, J. (2010). Reading instruction research for English-language learners in kindergarten through sixth grade: The last 15 years. In R. Allington & A. McGill-Franzen (Eds.), *Handbook of reading disability research.* New York: Routledge.

Amendum, S., Li, Y., Hall, L., Fitzgerald, J., Creamer, K., Head-Reeves, D. M., et al. (2009). Which reading lesson instruction characteristics matter for early reading achievement? *Reading Psychology, 30*(2), 119–147.

Anderson, R. C., Hiebert, E. H., Scott, J. A., & Wilkinson, I. A. G. (1984). *Becoming a nation of readers: The report of the commission on reading.* Washington, DC: U.S. Department of Education.

Anstey, M. (2002). "It's not all black and white": Postmodern picture books and new literacies. *Journal of Adolescent and Adult Literacy, 45,* 444–457.

Anstey, M., & Bull, G. (2006). *Teaching and learning multiliteracies: Changing times, changing literacies.* Newark, DE: International Reading Association.

Au, K. H., & Carroll, J. H. (1997). Improving literacy achievement through a constructivist approach: A KEEP demonstration classroom project. *Elementary School Journal, 97,* 203–221.

Au, K. H., & Raphael, T. E. (1998). Curriculum and teaching in literature-based programs. In T. E. Raphael & K. H. Au (Eds.), *Literature-based instruction: Reshaping the curriculum* (pp. 123–148). Norwood, MA: Christopher-Gordon.

Beck, I. L., McKeown, M. G., & Kucan, L. (2002). *Bringing words to life: Robust vocabulary instruction.* New York: Guilford Press.

Blachowicz, C., & Fisher, P. (2009). *Teaching vocabulary in all classrooms* (4th ed.). Columbus, OH: Prentice Hall.

Bruce, B. C. (2003). *Literacy in the information age: Inquiries into meaning making with new technologies.* Newark, DE: International Reading Association.

Bunting, E., & Diaz, D. (1994). *Smoky night.* San Diego: Harcourt.

Cain, K. (2010). Reading for meaning: The skills that support reading comprehension and its development. In K. Hall, U. Goswami, C. Harrison, S. Ellis, & J. Soler (Eds.), *Interdisciplinary perspectives on learning to read: Culture, cognition, and pedagogy* (pp. 74–86). New York: Routledge.

Cappello, M. (2006). Under construction: Voice and identity development in writing workshop. *Language Arts, 83*(6), 482–491.

Carlo, M. S., August, D., McLaughlin, B., Snow, C. E., Dressler, C., Lippman, D. N., et al. (2004). Closing the gap: Addressing the vocabulary needs of English-language learners in bilingual and mainstream classrooms. *Reading Research Quarterly, 39*(2), 188–215.

Cazden, C. B. (2001). *Classroom discourse: The language of teaching and learning.* Portsmouth, NH: Heinemann.

Cervetti, G. N., Damico, J. S., & Pearson, P. D. (2006). Multiple literacies, new literacies, and teacher education. *Theory into Practice, 45*(4), 378–386.

Cervetti, G., Pearson, P. D., Bravo, M. A., & Barber, J. (2006). Reading and writing in the service of inquiry-based science. In R. Douglas, M. Klentschy, & K. Worth (Eds.), *Linking science and literacy in the K–8 classroom* (pp. 221–244). Arlington, VA: National Science Teachers Association Press.

Chall, J. S. (1967). *Learning to read: The great debate.* New York: McGraw-Hill.

Chall, J. S. (1997). *Learning to read: The great debate* (3rd ed.). New York: McGraw-Hill.

Clarke, L. K. (1988). Invented versus traditional spelling in first graders' writings: Effects on learning to spell and read. *Research in the Teaching of English, 22*(3), 281–309.

Council of Chief State School Officers & the National Governor's Association. (2010). *Common Core State Standards Initiative.* Retrieved July 22, 2010, from *www.corestandards.org/about-the-standards/key-points-in-english-language-arts.*

Darling-Hammond, L. (1995). Inequality and access to knowledge. In J. A. Banks & C. A. M. Banks (Eds.), *Handbook for research on multicultural education* (pp. 465–483). New York: Macmillan.

Darling-Hammond, L. (2004). What happens to a dream deferred? The continuing quest for equal educational opportunity. In J. A. Banks & C. A. M. Banks (Eds.), *Handbook of research on multicultural education* (pp. 607–630). San Francisco: Jossey-Bass.

Duke, N. K., & Carlisle, J. (2010). The development of comprehension. In M. L. Kamil, P. D. Pearson, E. B. Moje, & P. Afflerbach (Eds.). *Handbook of reading research, Vol. IV* (pp. 199–228). London: Routledge.

Duke, N., & Purcell-Gates, V. (2003). Genres at home and at school: Bridging the known to the new. *The Reading Teacher, 57*(1), 30–37.

Dyson, A. H. (2003). *The brothers and sisters learn to write: Popular literacies in childhood and school culture.* New York: Teachers College Press.

Ehri, L. C. (1995). Phases of development in reading words. *Journal of Research in Reading, 18,* 116–125.

Ehri, L. C., Nunes, S., Stahl, S., & Willows, D. (2001). Systematic phonics instruction helps students learn to read: Evidence from the National Reading Panel's meta-analysis. *Review of Educational Research, 71*(3), 393–447.

Florio-Ruane, S., & Raphael, T. E. (2004). Reconsidering our research: Collaboration, complexity, design, and the problem of "scaling up what works." *National Reading Conference Yearbook, 54*, 170–188.

Foorman, B. R., & Connor, C. M. (2010). Primary grade reading. In M. L. Kamil, P. D. Pearson, E. B. Moje, & P. Afflerbach (Eds.), *Handbook of reading research, Vol. IV* (pp. 136–156). London: Routledge.

Galda, L., & Beach, R. (2001). Response to literature as a cultural activity. *Reading Research Quarterly, 36*(1), pp.64–73.

Gaskins, I. W. (2005). *Success with struggling readers: The Benchmark School approach.* New York: Guilford Press.

Gaskins, I. W., Ehri, L. C., & Cress, C., O'Hara, C., & Donnelly, K. (1996/1997). Procedures for word learning: Making discoveries about words. *The Reading Teacher, 50*(4), 312–327.

Gee, J. P. (2000). The limits of reframing: A response to Professor Snow. *Journal of Literacy Research, 31*, 355–374.

Gee, J. P. (2002). A sociocultural perspective on early literacy development. In S. Neuman & D. Dickinson (Eds.), *Handbook of Early Literacy Research* (pp. 30–42). New York: Guilford Press.

Gee, J. P. (2007). *Social linguistics and literacies: Ideology in discourses* (3rd ed.). London: Routledge.

Genishi, C., & Dyson, A. (2009). *Children, language, and literacy: Diverse learners in diverse times.* New York: Teachers College Press.

Gough, P., & Tunmer, W. (1986). Decoding, reading, and reading disability. *Remedial and Special Education, 7*, 6–10.

Gray, W. (1948). *On their own in reading: How to give children independence in attacking new words.* Chicago: Foresman.

Grigg, W. S., Daane, M., Jin, Y., & Campbell, J. R. (2003). *The nation's report card: Reading 2002* (No. NCES 2003-521). Washington, DC: U.S. Department of Education, Institute of Education Sciences.

Harrison, C. (2010). Why do policy-makers find the "simple view of reading" so attractive, and why do I find it so morally repugnant? In K. Hall, U. Goswami, C. Harrison, S. Ellis, & J. Soler (Eds.), *Interdisciplinary perspectives on learning to read: Culture, cognition, and pedagogy* (pp. 207–218). New York: Routledge.

Harste, J. C., Woodward, V. A., & Burke, C. L. (1984). *Language stories and literacy lessons.* Portsmouth, NH: Heinemann.

Hicks, D. (1998). Narrative discourses as inner and outer word. *Language Arts, 75*(1), 28–34.

Hiebert, E. H. (1998). Selecting texts for beginning reading instruction. In T. E. Raphael & K. H. Au (Eds.), *Literature-based instruction: Reshaping the curriculum* (pp. 195–218). Norwood, MA: Christopher-Gordon.

Hoffman, J. V. (2009). In search of the "simple view" of reading comprehension. In S. E. Israel & G. G. Duffy (Eds.), *Handbook of research on reading comprehension* (pp. 54–66). New York: Routledge.

Kamil, M. L., Pearson, P. D., Moje, E. B., & Afflerbach, P. (Eds.). (2011). *Handbook of reading research, Vol. IV.* London: Routledge.

Kist, W. R. (2005). *New literacies in action: Teaching and learning in multiple media.* New York: Teachers College Press.

Kist, W. R. (2010). *The socially networked classroom: Teaching in the new media age.* Thousand Oaks, CA: Corwin.

Kong, A., & Fitch, E. (2002). Using Book Club to engage culturally and linguistically diverse learners in reading, writing, and talking about books. *The Reading Teacher, 56*(4), 352–362.

Kress, G. (2001). *The modes and media of contemporary communication.* New York: Oxford University Press.

Kress, G. (2003). *Literacy in the new media age (literacies).* New York: Routledge.

Lankshear, C., & Knobel, M. (2003). *New literacies and changing knowledge in the classroom.* Buckingham, UK: Open University Press.

Lemann, N. (1997, November). The reading wars. *The Atlantic Monthly, 280,* 128–134.

Levine, A. (1994, December). The great debate revisited. *The Atlantic Monthly.* Retrieved June 16, 2005, from *www.theatlantic.com/politics/educatio/levine.html.*

Lyon, G. R. (1997). *Report on learning disabilities research.* (Adapted from testimony by Dr. Reid Lyon before the Committee on Education and the Workforce in the U.S. House of Representatives on July 10, 1997.) Retrieved January 2, 2002, from *www.ldonline.org/ld_indepth/reading/nih_report.html.*

Magnusson, S. J., & Palincsar, A. S. (2005). Teaching and learning inquiry-based science in the elementary school. In J. Bransford & S. Donovan (Eds.), *Visions of teaching subject matter guided by the principles of how people learn.* Washington, DC: National Academy Press.

Maloch, B. (2002). Scaffolding student talk: One teacher's role in literature discussion groups. *Reading Research Quarterly, 37,* 94–112.

Mathews, M. M. (1966). *Teaching to read: Historically considered.* Chicago: University of Chicago Press.

McIntyre, E., & Pressley, M. (1996). *Balanced instruction: Strategies and skills in whole language.* Boston: Christopher-Gordon.

McLerran, A. (1991). *Roxaboxen.* New York: HarperTrophy.

Moje, E. B. (2008, Spring). The complex world of adolescent literacy: Myths, motivations, and mysteries. *Harvard Educational Review,* 107–154.

Murphy, P. K., & Wilkinson, I. (2005, April). *Making sense of group discussions: What the studies tell us: A meta-analysis.* Paper presented at the annual conference of the American Educational Research Association, Montreal.

National Center of Educational Statistics. (2010, March). The Nation's Report Card: Reading 2009 (Publication No. NCES 2010458). Retrieved March 19, 2010, from *nces.ed.gov/pubsearch/pubsinfo.asp?pubid=2010458.*

National Reading Panel. (2000). *Teaching children to read: An evidence-based assessment of the scientific research literature on reading and its implications for reading instruction* (National Institute of Health Pub. No. 00-4769). Washington, DC: National Institute of Child Health and Human Development.

New London Group, The. (2000). A pedagogy of multiliteracies: Designing social futures. In B. Cope & M. Kalantzis (Eds.), *Multiliteracies: Literacy learning and the design of social futures* (pp. 9–38). London: Routledge.

No Child Left Behind Act of 2001, Public Law No. 107-110 (2002). Retrieved September 22, 2006, from *www.ed.gov/policy/elsec/leg/esea02/index.html.*

Nodelman, P. (1992). *The pleasures of children's literature.* New York: Longman.

Pahl, K., & Rowsell, J. (2005). *Literacy and education: Understanding the new literacy studies in the classroom.* London: Chapman.

Palincsar, A. S., & Magnusson, S. J. (2001). The interplay of firsthand and text-based investigations to model and support the development of scientific knowledge and reasoning. In S. Carver & D. Klahr (Eds.), *Cognition and instruction: Twenty-five years of progress* (pp. 151–194). Mahwah, NJ: Erlbaum.

Pappas, C., & Pettegrew, B. S. (1998). The role of genre in the psycholinguistic guessing game of reading. *Language Arts, 75*(1), 36–44.

Paratore, J., Cassano, C., & Schickendanz, J. A. (2010). Supporting early (and later) literacy development at home and at school: The long view. In M. L. Kamil, P. D. Pearson, E. B. Moje, & P. Afflerbach, *Handbook of reading research, Vol. IV* (pp. 107–135). London: Routledge.

Pearson, P. D. (1976). A psycholinguistic model of reading. *Language Arts, 53*(3), 309–314.

Pearson, P. D. (2004). The reading wars: The politics of reading research and policy—1988 through 2003. *Educational Policy, 18*(1), 216–252.

Pearson, P. D., & Fielding, L. (1991). Comprehension instruction. In R. Barr, M. L. Kamil, P. Mosenthal, & P. D. Pearson (Eds.), *Handbook of reading research, Vol. 2* (pp. 819–860). New York: Longman.

Pearson, P. D., & Raphael, T. (1990). Reading comprehension as a dimension of thinking. In B. F. Jones & L. I. Idol (Eds.), *Dimensions of thinking and cognitive instruction: Implications for reform, Vol. 1* (pp. 209–240). Hillsdale, NJ: Erlbaum.

Pearson, P. D., & Raphael, T. E. (1999). Toward an ecologically balanced literacy curriculum. In L. B. Gambrell, L. M. Morrow, S. B. Newman, & M. Pressley (Eds.), *Best practices in literacy instruction* (pp. 22–33). New York: Guilford Press.

Pearson, P. D., & Raphael, T. E. (2003). Toward a more complex view of balance in the literacy curriculum. In L. M. Morrow, L. B. Gambrell, & M. Pressley (Eds.), *Best practices in literacy instruction* (2nd ed., pp. 23–39). New York: Guilford Press.

Pearson, P. D., Raphael, T. E., Benson, V. L., & Madda, C. L. (2007). Balance in comprehensive literacy instruction: Then and now. In L. M. Morrow, L. B. Gambrell, & M. Pressley (Eds.), *Best practices in literacy instruction* (3rd ed., pp. 30–54). New York: Guilford Press.

Philips, S. U. (1972). Participant structures and communicative competence: Warm Springs children in community and classroom. In C. Cazden, V. P. John, & D. Hymes (Eds.), *Functions of language in the classroom* (pp. 370–394). New York: Teachers College Press.

Pressley, M. (2006). *Reading instruction that works: The case for balanced teaching* (3rd ed.). New York: Guilford Press.

Purcell-Gates, V., Duke, N., & Martineau, J. (2007). Learning to read and write genre-specific text: Roles of authentic experience and explicit teaching. *Reading Research Quarterly, 42*(1), 8–45.

Raphael, T. E., & Brock, C. H. (1997). Instructional research in literacy: Changing paradigms. In C. Kinzer, D. Leu, & K. Hinchman (Eds.), *Inquiries in literacy theory and practice* (pp. 13–36). Chicago: National Reading Conference.

Raphael, T. E., Florio-Ruane, S., George, M., Hasty, N. L., & Highfield, K. (2004). *Book Club Plus: A literacy framework for primary grades.* Littleton, MA: Small Planet Communications.

Raphael, T. E., Kehus, M., & Damphousse, K. (2001). *Book Club for middle school.* Lawrence, MA: Small Planet Communications.

Raphael, T. E., Pardo, L. S., & Highfield, K. (2002). *Book Club: A literature-based curriculum* (2nd ed.). Lawrence, MA: Small Planet Communications.

Rodgers, E. (2004). Interactions that scaffold reading performance. *Journal of Literacy Research, 36*, 501–532.

Schultz, K. (2006). Qualitative research on writing. In C. A. MacArthur, S. Graham, & J. Fitzgerald (Eds.), *Handbook of writing research* (pp. 357–373). New York: Guilford Press.

Schultz, K. (2009). *Rethinking participation: Listening to silent voices*. New York: Teachers College Press.

Sipe, L. R. (2008). *Storytime: Young children's literary understanding in the classroom*. New York: Teachers College Press.

Snow, C. E., Burns, M. S., & Griffin, P. (Eds.). (1998). *Preventing reading difficulties in young children*. Washington, DC: National Academy Press.

Taylor, B. M., Pearson, P. D., Peterson, D. P., & Rodriguez, M. C. (2003). Reading growth in high-poverty classrooms: The influence of teacher practices that encourage cognitive engagement in literacy learning. *The Elementary School Journal, 104*(2), 3–28.

Taylor, B. M., Pearson, P. D., Peterson, D. P., & Rodriguez, M. C. (2005). The CIERA School Change Framework: An evidenced-based approach to professional development and school reading improvement. *Reading Research Quarterly, 40*(1), 40–69.

Taylor, M. (1990). *Mississippi bridge*. New York: Skylark.

Tumner, W. E., & Nicholson, T. (2010). The development and teaching of word recognition skill. In M. L. Kamil, P. D. Pearson, E. B. Moje, & P. Afflerbach (Eds.), *Handbook of reading research, Vol. IV* (pp. 405–432). London: Routledge.

PART II

Best Practices for All Students

CHAPTER 3

Best Practices in Early Literacy

Preschool, Kindergarten, and First Grade

Lesley Mandel Morrow
Diane H. Tracey
Jennifer Renner Del Nero

This chapter will:

- Present several theoretical perspectives that frame early literacy learning.
- Offer instructional strategies that facilitate early literacy growth.
- Discuss technology, English language learners, response to intervention, and the K–12 Common Core State Standards.
- Illustrate best practices in early literacy through the presentation of a case study.

There has been controversy about the importance of intentional explicit instruction and informal spontaneous early literacy instruction for preschool and kindergarten children. The controversy has to do with two questions: (1) When should we begin literacy instruction? and (2) What is the appropriate nature of the instruction? Research demonstrates that children who attend quality preschool that includes language and literacy instruction are likely to be more successful in literacy development than children who do not; this holds true in all types of communities. Those who benefit the most are children from disadvantaged backgrounds (Barnett, 1998). We know that literacy instruction must take place with young children, but we still agonize about the methods that should be used. Should we have a systematic skills-based curriculum or should the curriculum be child centered, where learning is spontaneous and allows for teachable moments? To answer these questions, we will look at historical views, theory, research, policy, and practice to see whether these varied perspectives share any common ground.

EVIDENCED-BASED BEST PRACTICES: A RESEARCH SYNTHESIS

Child-Centered Theories

Historical Influences

The child-centered approach in early childhood literacy education has been widely accepted. From this perspective, early literacy classrooms are places for natural social, emotional, physical, and intellectual development. The child-centered approach suggests that learning is best facilitated by providing children with motivating opportunities to explore and experiment in playful environments. Historically, many philosophers, theorists, psychologists, and educators addressed early childhood learning from a child-centered theoretical perspective that has implications for early literacy instruction. Rousseau (1712–1778) believed that children's learning evolved naturally as a result of their innate curiosity. He advocated that educators follow children's leads regarding what and when they wanted to learn. Pestalozzi (1746–1827) also believed in natural learning, but felt that children needed informal instruction and adult facilitation to enhance development. He was also a strong proponent of nurturing warm and caring classroom climates to optimize learning. Froebel (1782–1852) emphasized the importance of play as a vehicle for learning and coined the term kindergarten, which literally means "children's garden." Piaget believed that a child acquires knowledge by interacting with objects and experiences and subsequently changes and reorganizes his or her own knowledge in response to those objects and experiences (Piaget & Inhelder, 1969). Piaget's theory of cognitive development suggests that children's thinking evolves and becomes more sophisticated over time.

John Dewey's (1916) philosophy of early childhood education led to the concept of the child-centered curriculum built around the interests of children. He believed that students learn best through play and in real-life settings. He maintained that social interactions encourage learning and emphasized a problem-based learning approach. Dewey rejected the idea of teaching skills as ends unto themselves. He believed that learning is maximized through integrating content areas. Today Dewey is well known for his learning centers and thematic instruction.

Social Constructivist Influences

The theory of social constructivism was put forth by Lev Vygotsky (1896–1934). Vygotsky's work became widely read in the early 1970s; he has become one of the world's most influential theorists regarding how children learn. Vygotsky is prominent for recognizing that children learn as a result of social interactions with others. He argued that children's learning is most affected by their mastery of language and that children naturally acquire language from their informal interactions with the people around them. He believed that new tasks and information needed to be modeled for children. To enhance children's learning, the teacher models and provides scaffolding and guidance. When the child no longer needs guidance the teacher allows the child to practice the skill independently. This moment is referred to as the child's *zone of proximal development.*

Emergent Literacy Theory

The term *emergent literacy* refers to a period in a child's life between birth and when the child can read and write conventionally. Marie Clay (1966) coined the term *emergent literacy*. This theory is based on the belief that children's development in the areas of listening, speaking, reading, and writing are all interrelated. Literacy development begins at birth and grows in the contexts of home, school, and community through authentic experiences. Emergent literacy recognizes the crucial role of the child's family and home environment in literacy development and that a child's scribble on a page and pretend reading of a book are real literacy behaviors although they are not conventional. These behaviors are important for all children to experience.

Skills-Based Theoretical Influence

Skills-Based Instruction

Skills-based instructional models involve systematic explicit teaching of literacy. This approach views early childhood as a time when children are ready to learn early reading and writing skills that will improve literacy achievement in the future (Barnett, 1998; Hart & Risley, 1999). Skills-based instruction has its roots in *behaviorism* that suggests complex cognitive activities, such as reading and writing, can be broken down into their composite skills that are taught one at a time and mastered (Tracey & Morrow, 2006b).

Direct Instruction

Direct reading instruction is clearly linked to a skills-based approach. In direct instruction, teachers explicitly focus students' attention on specific, isolated reading skills and provide information to students about those topics (Kame'enui, Simmons, Chard, & Dickson, 1997; Shaywitz, 2004; Slavin, 1997). According to Carnine, Silbert, Kame'enui, and Tarver (2004), direct instruction is the most effective and efficient approach to reading instruction. It is based on the teaching of six steps: (1) specifying objectives, (2) devising instructional strategies, (3) developing teaching procedures, (4) selecting examples, (5) sequencing skills, and (6) providing practice and review. This is the means by which most skills-based instruction is delivered. These steps are often scripted for the teacher.

Reading Readiness

Reading readiness is also a form of reading instruction that is closely associated with skills-based instruction. In the reading readiness approach, educators focus on facilitating reading development through direct instruction of skills identified as prerequisites for reading. A skill associated with reading readiness is auditory discrimination, which includes identification of like and different sounds and eventually letter sounds. Visual discrimination is also a reading readiness skill and includes identification of colors, shapes, and letters, as well as left-to-right progression, visual–motor skills (cutting on a line), and large-motor abilities (skipping and hopping). Worksheets were used often in reading readiness instruction.

FEDERAL POLICIES AFFECTING EARLY LITERACY INSTRUCTION

In 1965 President Lyndon Johnson authorized the first federal policy directed at preschool education by creating the Head Start program. The goal of the initiative was to prepare low-income children for kindergarten. Federal Head Start grants are made directly to public and private nonprofit organizations. Consistent with a child-centered model of early literacy education, the services address children's cognitive, physical, emotional, and social needs. All families receiving services must be below federal guidelines for poverty, and parental involvement is critical. The National Association for the Education of Young Children (NAEYC), the primary accrediting agency for independent preschools in the United States, follows a child-centered model for learning as well.

In 1997 Congress requested that the National Institute of Child Health and Human Development (NICHHD) establish the National Reading Panel to determine the most effective practices for teaching reading. Made up of a group of distinguished scholars, the panel reviewed scientifically based reading research and then published *The National Reading Panel Report: Teaching Children to Read* (NICHHD, 2000). From the research, five key areas were identified for effective reading instruction: (1) phonemic awareness, (2) phonics, (3) vocabulary, (4) comprehension, and (5) fluency. It is mandatory for early childhood teachers to teach these skills at a level appropriate for their children.

Another group was formed and charged with creating and overseeing the National Early Literacy Panel (NELP). The NELP was charged with conducting a synthesis of the scientific research related to early literacy development from birth through kindergarten. The variables the panel identified as essential to early literacy success include (1) expressive and receptive oral language development; (2) knowledge of the alphabetic code (alphabet knowledge, phonological and phonemic awareness); (3) use of invented spelling; (4) print knowledge (can read some environmental print, knows concepts about print, writing one's name); and (5) other skills including rapid naming of letters and numbers, visual memory, and visual perceptual abilities (Shanahan & Lonigan, 2010). This information affects educational policy, curriculum development, and professional development decisions. Preschool and kindergarten teachers are responsible for teaching their students these particular skills.

In 2010 the National Governors Association Center for Best Practice (NGA Center) and the Council for Chief State School Officers (CCSSO) released the K–12 Common Core State Standards. The complete document is available at *www.corestandards.org/articles/8-nationa-governors-association-and-state-education-chiefs*. Most likely, these national standards will eventually replace state standards. Proponents hope that a unified set of national literacy standards will merge instruction in the United States, resulting in increased student achievement both nationally and internationally. The overall goals for the CCSSO are to define general cross-disciplinary literacy expectations that must be met for students to be prepared to enter college and workforce training programs ready to succeed. There are grade-specific standards that define end-of-year expectations and a cumulative progression. The standards must leave room for states to determine how goals should be reached and additional topics that might need to be addressed. The standards are divided into reading, writing, speaking, listening, and language strands for clarity; however, these processes are connected and taught concurrently. Teaching the English language arts (ELA) must be a shared responsibility with the entire school. All subjects (such as science and social studies) must have a place for developing ELA skills in their content areas. There are five major categories in the K–12 Common Core State Standards:

1. Reading Literature
2. Reading Informational Text K–3
    - Key Ideas/Details (recognizing important text components, concepts, and ability to retell part or all of a story)
    - Craft and Structure (recognizing and differentiating among text types, people who create a text, word study, text form, and point of view)
    - Integration of Knowledge and Ideas (impact of illustrations on texts, identifying theme, mood, text comparisons, and author comparisons)
    - Range of Reading and Text Complexity (engage in oral reading, collaborative, and independent reading of a variety of texts)

3. Foundational Skills
    - Print Concepts (word study, language development, and decoding)
    - Phonological Awareness (phonemes, syllables, and rhyming patterns)
    - Phonics/Word Recognition (high-frequency words and long/short vowels)
    - Fluency (reading with purpose and understanding)
4. Writing
    - Text Types/Purposes (drawing, dictating, writing, and identifying/producing different text types)
    - Production/Distribution of Writing (shared writing, respond to adult/peer feedback, respond to questions)
    - Research to Build/Present Knowledge (where to find information and collaborative writing experiences)
    - Range of Writing (write for extended/short times, remain task oriented, and demonstrate ability to stay focused in different settings)
5. Speaking and Listening
    - Comprehension/Collaboration (engage in successful conversations, answer/ask questions, and express thoughts)
    - Conventions of Standard English (identify parts of speech, upper/lower case letters, etc.)
    - Knowledge of Language
    - Vocabulary Acquisition/Use

A BALANCED AND COMPREHENSIVE LITERACY INSTRUCTION MODEL

The following documents showcase approaches to early literacy education that integrate child centered and skill-based instruction: *Learning to Read and Write: Developmentally Appropriate Practices* (IRA & NAEYC, 1998), *Using Multiple Methods of Beginning Reading Instruction* (IRA, 1999), and *Literacy Development in the Early Years* (Morrow, 2007). These publications suggest that there is no single method or combination of methods that successfully teach all children to read. Teachers need to know and utilize a variety of strategies when teaching literacy that involve spending time learning about individual student needs. A comprehensive balanced perspective in reading instruction means the careful selection of the best theories and the use of instructional strategies to match the learning styles of individual children. This might mean using more skill-based explicit instruction for some children and more child-centered, problem-solving strategies for others. According to Pressley (2007), teaching explicit skills is a good start for constructivist problem-solving activities, which allows for consolidation and elaboration of those skills. One method does not preclude or exclude the other. A balanced perspective is not simply a combination of random strategies. A teacher may select strategies from different learning theories to provide balance. One child, for example, may be a visual learner and benefit from sight-word instruction. Another child may be an auditory learner and will learn best from phonics. The balanced approach focuses more on what is important for each child than on the latest fad in literacy instruction. Balanced instruction acknowledges the importance of both form (phonics mechanics, etc.) and function (comprehension, purpose, and meaning) of the literacy process.

States, professional organizations, and the federal government have proposed standards for children to achieve at each grade. The following section is a general outline created by blending standards observed from different groups for preschool and kindergarten children. In order to fully describe best practices coinciding with the large number of early literacy standards, we would need to write a separate chapter for each major area. Instead, we present some important standards categories and describe a few exemplary strategies based on research and practice.

GENERAL READING STANDARDS FOR EARLY LITERACY

Emergent Reading Behaviors: Concepts about Books and Print

- Knows that letters make words and words are separated by spaces.
- Recognizes that words have meaning.
- Realizes that a book has a title, author, and illustrator.
- Understands the difference between print and pictures in a book.
  - Pictures have meaning.
  - Print is read.
- Demonstrates an interest in books and reading.
- Enjoys listening to and discussing books.
- Requests being read to and retells the same story by looking at the pictures.
- Understands that print is read from left to right and top to bottom.
- Attempts to read and write.
- Understands that reading is a way to obtain information.

It is important to recognize that emergent reading behaviors need to be taught because children do not possess these skills naturally. Teachers must help students develop a love for several favorite story books. This will happen when they hear the same text repeatedly. Select a text that the child knows quite well and ask him or her to retell the story looking at the pictures. Then, ask students to retell the story by looking at the pictures and pointing from left to right as they pretend read. Eventually, children will begin to point out some words they learn from repeating the book so often and notice that letters in their names are in some of the words in the book. Pretend reading demonstrates comprehension. In addition, with repeated readings, questions and discussions become more sophisticated (McGee & Morrow, 2005).

Letter Knowledge and Early Word Recognition

Phonemic awareness is the ability to:

- Hear the different sounds in words.
- Segment sounds in words.
- Blend the sounds back together.
- Substitute new sounds at the beginning of a word to create a new word with the same ending (e.g., *fat, cat, rat, bat, mat*).
- Identify the parts or syllables of words.
- Recognize rhyming words and think of a word that rhymes with another.
- Develop a large sight vocabulary of meaningful words.
- Identify all upper- and lower-case letters.
- Notice beginning letters in familiar words.
- Start to make some letter–sound matches.
- Learn initial and ending consonant sounds.
- Gain knowledge about short and long vowels.
- Learn some irregular consonant and vowel chunks (e.g., digraphs and blends).
- Identify some high-frequency words.

Although there are other methods, learning the letter of the week in consecutive order is one of the most popular ways to learn the alphabet. The first letters a child should learn are those in his or her name. These should be followed by letters such as *S, P, T,* and *B* because of their frequent occurrence in words and because you can hear their name in the letter. Teach the letters seen on signs in the child's environment, such as *M* for McDonald's or, *D* for Dunkin' Donuts. Learning the letters in their friend's names will also have meaning for children. Letter learning can also be incorporated into class themes. For example, when teaching a unit on the fall season, emphasize letters that are used in words in the theme such as *F* for *fall, L* for *leaves,* and *T* for *trees.* Expose children to the same letters often. Learning one letter a week only focuses on that letter once in the year. It is recommended that you focus on more than one letter a week, so that when you reach the end of the alphabet, you can start from the beginning again allowing for multiple reviews (Reutzel, 2010). Many activities exist for learning the names of letters. Children also enjoy learning about letters tangibly and kinesthetically through the use of magnetic letters, wooden letters, and those made of sandpaper. Teachers have children shape their bodies into letters, make letters in sand, and with Play-Doh. Digital technologies intrigue young children; many websites and software packages reinforce the learning of letter names.

The term "phonemic awareness" became well known after the release of the National Reading Panel report (NICHHD, 2000). The report found that phonemic awareness is a precursor to learning phonics, and it is important for children to engage in activities that promote that skill (Castiglioni-Spalten & Ehri, 2003). Phonemic awareness involves the ability to know that words are made up of different sounds. Children need to identify sounds in words, segment parts of words, blend words together, substitute new initial sounds with a word ending to make new words, and clap out parts of words or syllables. Chanting a poem that rhymes helps develop phonemic awareness, as does clapping the parts of words while singing a song. Ask children to take apart or segment the word *cat* and altogether as a class say /k/ /a/ (short *a* sound) /t/. Then the teacher can ask the students to blend that word back together, and everyone says "CAT." The teacher models substitution using the *-at* word ending. The teacher says "CAT" and then says, "If I make the sound 'sssss' and put it in front of *-at*, what would the word be?" The group replies, "SAT." The teacher then says, "Now if we put a 'buh' in front of *-at*, what word do we make?" The children reply, "BAT." Sound and symbol relationship does not come into play here. These are auditory activities without naming letters or looking at the letter symbols.

Research illustrates that mastering phonics skills has a positive correlation with reading success in early childhood (Allington & Baker, 2007; Cunningham, 2007; NICHHD, 2000). There are many skills and strategies to choose from. Select the most important skills, such as initial and ending consonant with regular and irregular sounds, short and long vowels, and a few rules such as "When two vowels go walking, the first one does the talking." When adding an *E* at the end of a consonant–vowel–consonant (CVC) word such as *mat*, you make a new word, *mate*. The first vowel becomes long and the *E* is silent. Finally, with CVC words such as *sat*, the vowel is usually short. Most other rules do not transfer to many words and therefore are not worth learning. One effective strategy is blending and segmenting onsets, the initial consonant in the word, and the rime or the ending of the word. This is similar to what was discussed in phonemic awareness, but instead letters are written down and children must make the sound–symbol relationship. Work with ending rimes such as *-at*, *-in*, *-an*, *-ack*, *-op*. Rimes are also called phonograms and word families. The student segments the initial consonant from the word ending and then substitutes a new consonant at the beginning. The consonant and rime are blended together to make a new word (Adams, 1990). Activities based on word families include matching, classifying, sorts, puzzles, arranging magnetic letters on white boards, and making words with oak tag letters in a pocket chart. Students can create small physical or digital books containing words and pictures for word families. This type of instruction strengthens knowledge of the way our language works (Adams, 1990). Fluent readers learn high-frequency words such as *the*, *and*, and *but*. These words have little meaning, but they are important. The best way to learn them is memorization. Words that are a part of thematic instruction are a source of interesting "Very Own Sight Words" (Tracey & Morrow, 2009). According to

Pressley, Allington, Wharton-McDonald, Block, and Morrow (2001), the ultimate goal of reading instruction is for a child to understand or comprehend what he or she reads. Phonics helps students to become fluent independent readers.

Language Development

- Demonstrates an increase in listening and speaking vocabulary.
- Uses language for a variety of purposes.
- Uses sentences of increasing length and syntactic complexity.
- Tells a simple personal narrative.
- Asks questions.
- Begins to retell stories in sequence.
- Uses new vocabulary in daily communication.
- Refines understanding of words.
- Increases listening vocabulary.
- Pronounces words with increased ease and accuracy.
- Experiments with language.
- Incorporates digital literacies into reading and writing activities.

The beginning of reading occurs when a child learns some decoding skills and acquires a large sight-word vocabulary. Many young readers can decode, but they must be able to attach meanings to the words that they identify in order to comprehend the text. Children come to school with wide variations in vocabulary knowledge. Hart and Risley (1995, 1999) found that within a year, children from professional homes are exposed to 11.2 million words, children from working-class homes are exposed to 6.5 million words, and children in homes on public assistance are exposed to 3.2 million words. Based on these figures, children from professional homes enter kindergarten with exposure to approximately 30 million more words than do children from economically disadvantaged homes. From the time they are 2, children need to acquire about 10 new words a day. This will only happen if they hear 10 new words each day and if the words are repeated (Rupley & Nichols, 2005). An inadequate vocabulary for a 3-year-old can plague a child throughout her entire school career. Vocabulary is a significant factor to literacy success, particularly for English language learners (ELLs). Research provides many reliable strategies for building children's vocabulary. Reading aloud is the most popular approach. There is a positive correlation between how often children listen to read-alouds and the size of their vocabulary. This depends on the interaction between those involved in the story reading (Walsh & Blewitt, 2006). There are reading styles associated with increasing vocabulary such as repeated readings and discussion of new vocabulary in the book prior to reading (Penno, Wilkinson, & Moore, 2002). When teachers read with expression, ask open-ended questions, and model language expansion, vocabulary will improve. When teachers ask children to chant rhymes in the story and repeat phrases in the book, vocabulary will improve (Beck & McKeown, 2001; Brabham & Lynch-Brown, 2002; Justice, Meier, & Walpole, 2005). For ELLs, these strategies represent nonthreatening and motivating means to acquire additional vocabulary in an unfamiliar language. Surround children with interesting objects and talk about them in relation to the five senses. Experiences in thematic instruction using science, social studies, art, music, dramatic play, technology, math, blocks, and outdoor play are sources for vocabulary development. Thematic instruction around topics of interest will cause children to naturally converse. For example, for a plant unit, add to your science center items such as a terrarium, green and flowering plants, magnifying glass, microscope, seeds, soil, and materials for children to plant themselves. In addition, have paper, pencils, and books to read and write about plants. Allow children to use the computer to look up information on plants using the Internet.

If you are teaching about another country, such as Spain, put maps in the social studies center to find where the country is. In addition, have native costumes and songs in the language of the country, food from the country, pictures, DVDs, and of course include paper, pencils, and books. If the technology is available, use an electronic white board or projector to showcase visuals of the country, as well as audiovisual clips from venues such as Teachertube (*www.teachertube.com*). Consider creating a unit around the countries of your ELL students. This will make them feel that their culture is valued in the classroom and fellow students will better understand the customs unique to those students. Art will create discussion with paint, markers, crayons, scissors, pipe cleaners, pieces of fabric, and wool. For a winter theme, have blue and black construction paper, white cotton balls, white lace doilies, silver foil, and white wool to create a winter collage or picture. These visual activities also stress the notion of multimodality, or communicating through various modes, and not just the written word. Such multimodal activities are particularly useful for students acquiring a new language. Wasik and Bond (2001) found that the use of tangible objects to portray target words increased at-risk preschoolers' vocabulary (Fisher & Blachowicz, 2005).

In music with a theme about Spain have Spanish music on CDs, musical instruments from Spain, DVD performances from Spain, and clips from the Internet about Spain. Continue the theme in dramatic play with Spanish costumes and figures for bullfights. When engaging in these motivating activities, take advantage and expand upon the language they can produce. Visuals will stimulate talk. Within the *context method* of vocabulary development, children learn how to independently figure out word meanings from informational cues in the text.

Listening Comprehension and Reading Comprehension

- Responds to literal questions about text.
- Responds to inferential questions about text.

- Predicts outcomes.
- Can retell a text.
- Has a sense of story structure for narrative text:
  - Setting, Theme, Episodes, and Resolution.
- Has a sense of structure for informational text:
  - Description, Sequence, Cause and Effect, Problem/Solution
- Engages in discussions about books.
- Asks questions about the information or events in a book.
- Connects information and events in books to real life.
- Uses technology to find out information.
- Has ability to use and comprehend digital literacies such as audio books, computer programs, websites, digital stories, and so on.
- Reads fluently with automaticity at an appropriate speed. Decodes accurately with expression, indicating comprehension of the text.

Comprehension is the ultimate goal of reading experiences. Strategy instruction in comprehension is important from the time children enter preschool. When reading or listening to a story, we teach children to be involved in prereading activities to prepare for text comprehension. This is accomplished when we familiarize the learner with the content and vocabulary of the selection. A "picture walk" is such an activity. The children and teacher look and talk about every picture in the book and discuss what the story might be about. Prereading activities build background knowledge, which helps with vocabulary during reading. When you come to a crucial moment while reading aloud, ask the children to predict what they think will happen next. Then continue reading and discuss whether their predictions were correct (Brown, 2008). Students can generate questions regarding texts, and then asked to read (or listen) to find the answers (Brown, 2008). A graphic organizer, whether digital or paper based, helps students organize the material they read. When reading a story, a graphic organizer aids students in listing details, character names, story sequence, themes, episodes, and resolution. Graphic organizers for informational text will engage students in sequencing details, describing concepts, determining cause and effect, and problem solution (Morrow, 2007).

During reading, visualizing can assist with comprehension. Students close their eyes and think about the sounds, smells, and tastes in the story, the clothing worn by the characters, and the setting (Dougherty-Stahl, 2004). Beginning readers can be taught to use Post-it notes to record questions and thoughts during reading. These responses can be organized into many groupings such as (1) connections between the text and the student's own life and (2) connections between the text and other books the student has read.

After reading, students benefit from experiences that help them to better understand the story. In addition, concepts are clarified. Story retelling is an important skill for young children to develop (Morrow, 2007). Similarly, summarizing helps students learn to identify the most important information

(Harvey & Goudvis, 2007). Responding to texts is useful. In early childhood, the responses are often a piece of artwork. Young children's responses are often naturally multimodal, artistic, and creative.

In our quest for skill development, we often forget about *motivating children to want to read.* We must provide children with choices of books to read, challenges that fit into children's "zones of proximal development," social interaction when reading, authentic and meaningful reading experiences, and success. Guthrie (2004) has spent a great deal of his professional life researching how to engage children in voluntary reading. He called his program concept-oriented reading instruction (CORI). This program recognizes that you must engage children in order for them to want to read. CORI has five parts: (1) thematic-based instruction, (2) an emphasis on student choice for both what students read and how they respond, (3) the use of hands-on activities for responding to readings, (4) the availability of a wide variety of text genres at different reading levels chosen to interest students, and (5) the integration of social collaboration into reading response activities. The foundational component of CORI thematic instruction can be based on literary genres, an author study, and social studies and science themes. Research on the effects of CORI indicates that students involved in this program demonstrate increased motivation for reading, increased use of metacognitive skills, and increased gains in conceptual knowledge (Tracey & Morrow, 2006b). This approach is particularly useful for ELL students as they move from reading sight words to longer texts. It is important to integrate the basic concept of CORI into reading instruction for creating excitement, engagement, and lifelong readers. In addition, technology is changing the face of reading and writing instruction. These developments have major implications for how teachers instruct and students learn. New literacies such as digital books, websites, and blogs are also motivating activities for children as they naturally engage in these literacy practices outside of school (Sheridan-Rabideau & Rowsell, 2010). Teachers must meaningfully integrate new literacies into their literacy instruction if they wish for reading experiences to be relevant and authentic to contemporary students. In addition, the new national standards are calling for students to be global and dynamic thinkers who will be ready for new academic and professional ventures.

Writing

- Can dictate ideas to an adult who records them on paper.
- Attempts to write themselves.
- Uses letters to represent written language.
- Attempts to connect the sounds in a word with their letter forms.
- Imitates special language in a book.
- Participates in narrative writing.
- Engages in informational writing.
- Takes part in functional writing tasks, such as making lists.

- Uses proper writing mechanics: spelling, punctuation, and so on.
- Expresses self in multiple modes (e.g., through visuals, artifacts, discussion, written).
- Successfully utilizes technology and new literacies in communicative practices.

Since the 1970s, educators have included writing as an integral part of best practices in early literacy (Morrow, 2007). Because of emergent literacy theory, writing is seen as integrated with the other language arts: listening, speaking, and reading. Improvement in one of these domains tends to be associated with improvement in the others. Similarly, writing ability begins in a child's first year of life and is further facilitated through authentic learning activities. Young children begin writing when they make their first scribble on a page. Scribbles become controlled, and the child can tell you what he or she has written. Later, scribbles become random letters, and children engage in invented spelling that is writing without concern for correct spelling or punctuation. Communicating through drawing is particularly useful for ELLs, as pictures are universal in terms of meaning and can act as a bridge to communication in writing. As with reading, writing must have an authentic purpose and be relevant in a child's life. Examples of authentic activities include writing notes and letters that are actually mailed (electronically or through the postal service), writing recipes that will be shared, writing in online or physical journals that will be read and responded to, and writing stories and poetry that will be listened to by others. Writing in the classroom includes the use of a writing center and minilessons in which teachers explicitly teach skills and mechanics. Children should share what they have written to receive formative and constructive feedback to improve their writing. They should also have the opportunity to read finished products to the class. Young children are motivated by topics that are familiar and that stem from literature read aloud in the classroom. There is a strong connection between learning to read and write. When reading and writing are learned concurrently they help the development of both skills.

NEW LITERACIES IN THE EARLY CHILDHOOD CLASSROOM

Regardless of their background, children come to preschool and kindergarten having some experiences with technology. Their families probably have cell phones, an iPhone, or a computer. They could have Wii games or some type of small electronic Game Boy. Children know how to click on these devices and how to search for games they want to play. They understand how to tap screens to get to a particular space, drag screens, push numbers and letters, and so on. Some know more than others and have more access to technology than others. As we continue to use more digital and global texts, it is critical that we introduce and incorporate them in the early childhood literacy classroom. Chapters in this volume are dedicated to technology and new literacies, but it is important to recognize the importance of technology as it pertains specifically to early literacy and some available practices.

When schools have Internet access, they can use e-mail, create class websites, blogs, and utilize electronic books, to name just a few of the numerous possibilities. Flip cameras can easily tape children playing, conversing, writing, and reading. They are equipped with USB ports, so the video can be immediately transferred to the computer. You can use this tool for assessment, for children to watch themselves and learn to improve behaviors, and story retelling. Teachers can make class books that look like published materials with particular programs where photos can be manipulated on the computer into a book with print on the pages. The teacher can teach whole-class lessons using an electronic interactive white board. By moving letters and words on the screen children can use the white board to practice skills such as classifying and sorting colors, shapes, letters, and sound–symbol relationships.

Classroom websites are a space you create on your computer for your class to share their work by scanning it onto the website. The teacher or students can scan resources onto the website that will be useful for students and upload videos to watch. Students can have their own page on a class website to share information with others. A podcast is a digital media file containing audio and/or visual recordings that can be uploaded to a class website. For example, if a teacher created a class website, he or she could upload a podcast on the opening page. Students could then click on the podcast and hear and/or see their teacher talking to them. What a wonderful way to welcome students to a new and exciting year! A podcast can be viewed on any computer, so children and their families can click on the podcast at home and become immediately acquainted with the teacher before school starts. After seeing their teacher model a successful podcast, students can also (with teacher assistance) create podcasts for class projects and activities. A free program for audio podcasting that can be downloaded and used by educators is Audacity (*tinyurl.com/4gx3j*). For video postcasting, teachers can use external webcams (if the computer does not have one already built in). Corresponding computer programs, iMovie for Mac users or Windows Movie Maker for Windows users, assist in recording, editing, and saving videos. This is a snapshot of the digital possibilities in an early childhood classroom.

ELLs IN EARLY CHILDHOOD CLASSROOMS

In a discussion of early literacy, we cannot forget to address the demographics of the U.S. population, which are becoming more racially and ethnically diverse daily. It is projected that by 2030, 40% of the school-age population in U.S. schools will be ELLs. Over 400 different languages are spoken in the United States.

We need to welcome diversity in our schools; it adds a rich dimension to the classroom. Most important, every child has the right to be respected and to receive a quality education. By recognizing students' diverse backgrounds, we will enhance their self-image. Differences should be the norm, rather than the exception. It is, however, necessary for children who speak other languages to learn standard English while simultaneously maintaining their ethnic identity and native language. Teachers must have a vast understanding of cultural differences, such as divergent lifestyles and values, to better work with children from diverse backgrounds. Similarly, children need to learn to function successfully in the U.S. culture and to relate positively with individuals from varied backgrounds.

Shanahan, August, Gray, and McCardle (2010) participated on the National Language Panel. This group conducted a comprehensive review of research, supported by several federal agencies, on literacy development and reading instruction for language-minority children. Some important findings for teaching ELLs were:

- The most important knowledge to help ELLs is English vocabulary.
- Although ELLs do need to learn decoding skills and usually learn them easily, there is too much emphasis placed on teaching these skills.
- Decoding skills of ELLs can become equivalent to decoding skills of native English speakers with instruction over a short period of time.
- Learning English is related to reading comprehension ability in English.

Early childhood teachers are at an advantage over teachers who teach past the first grade in helping their ELL students with English. Children in preschool, kindergarten, and first grade still have a natural ability to learn language. If they are given an English speaking buddy and become immersed in the classroom, before long they will speak English. Those who come from a literate background and have parents who are literate in their primary language will learn English easily. Those students whose families are not literate in their own language will have more difficulty. Good teaching strategies are good for all children; however, there are activities that will encourage English learning more than others.

Some goals for teachers and children in our multicultural society to make them feel comfortable and help them learn English are:

- Include print in the classroom in children's first language, such as labels on objects.
- Suggest that ELL students write books in their first language and share it with others.
- Be sure ELLs have the opportunity to read and write with others who speak their language such as parents, aides, and other children in the school.

- Assign an English-speaking child as a buddy for the ELL to help with that child's oral language development, reading, and writing.
- Provide thematic instruction that elicits talk, reading, and writing.
- Write charts based on children's home life and experiences in school.
- Encourage children to copy experience charts; have them dictate their ideas for you to write and encourage them to write themselves.
- Have predictable routines so the ELLs will feel comfortable in their new environment.
- Give ELL students nonverbal class jobs such passing out folders or watering the plants at the beginning of the year so they can contribute immediately.
- Speak slowly and clearly. You do not have to speak loudly.
- The classroom library should contain a variety of texts in English and a variety of books in the primary languages of students.
- Provide daily, extensive, and explicit vocabulary instruction. Vocabulary development is the key to learning English and learning to read.
- Select school words, familiar words, and phrases to teach, such as playground, cafeteria, bathroom, gymnasium, centers, books, pens, and pencils.
- Play word games like Picture Puzzler and Action Jeopardy! (Carlo & Bengochea, Chapter 5, this volume).
- Children collect "very own word" (VOW) cards for new English vocabulary. They can request words for their VOWs on 5×8 index cards. On one side, write the word in English, and on the other in their native language. Use an accompanying picture for visual reinforcement.
- Use manipulative materials in the form of games, puppets, and visual figures.
- Provide a computer for additional support. Many digital programs and games are available to support ELLs. For example, Gmail (Google mail) has a "Google translator" device that can translate e-mails into many languages.
- Research Internet sites that can support ELL learning. Some examples are: *www.teachchildrenesl.com*, *www.eslkidstuff.com*, and *www.everythingesl.net*.
- Record simple stories on CDs and have ELLs follow the text as the story is read.
- Cut up short stories into sentences for children to sequence.
- Cut up sentences into words to be sequenced into the sentences.
- Involve parents by demonstrating strategies for them so they can help at home.
- Encourage parents and family members to come into the classroom to share their cultural experiences and customs through stories, songs, artifacts, and food.
- Empower the parents of ELL students by ensuring that they are informed about important school procedures, routines, and events.

AT-RISK EARLY CHILDHOOD STUDENTS AND RESPONSE TO INTERVENTION

Research illustrates that early intervention initiatives in reading decrease classification rates. The earlier the intervention begins, the more likely it is to work. In the past we did not include early intervention in preK or kindergarten. First grade was the place this would begin. Response to intervention (RTI) written into the Individuals with Disabilities Education Act (IDEA) must start as soon as we can reach children.

The RTI law allows 15% of IDEA funding to be used with nonclassified children. This means that a child who is struggling can receive intensive and targeted intervention to avoid classification. After receiving this more tailored and intense instruction, students who do not demonstrate adequate progress are then evaluated for possible classification. Many will improve because of the help received and not need to be classified as special education students. RTI is geared toward assisting unclassified children who experience difficulty with oral expression, listening comprehension, written expression, basic reading skills, fluency skills, and reading comprehension. This initiative helps some children get the assistance they need and avoid classification.

In a particular program in a public district in New Jersey, RTI evolved from an extension of their basic skills program. The district's RTI teachers are called intervention specialists. They are certified teachers and preferably hold a reading specialist certification. They select or hire the most qualified teachers to work with the most at-risk learners. The district decided not to use a specific program or curriculum since one size does not fit all. Children are evaluated, and then programs are designed to meet their needs. All children are eligible including PreK and kindergarteners. The school district has used multisensory reading techniques, teaching of essential strategies, Reading Recovery, and other programs. Lessons include preteaching of concepts, reteaching a lesson or concept, additional practice of a skill with an alternative method, and making sure that lessons are interesting and relevant. The district has monthly meetings with all those involved in RTI, such as reading specialists, coaches, interventionists, administrators, speech pathologists, ELL teachers, special education, and regular teachers.

When deciding to implement intervention programs, consider the children involved, the resources you have, and how best to use the talent within your school. Recognizing the need and then taking measures to help is the first step. RTI is a prevention approach based on best practices; it includes proactive and reactive features. Children who receive intervention also receive regular literacy instruction in their classrooms; therefore, it interfaces with typical classroom teaching and classification procedures. Early intervention in literacy decreases classification rates. The earlier the intervention begins, the more likely it is to succeed.

CREATING A LITERACY-RICH CLASSROOM ENVIRONMENT

A classroom's physical environment sets the foundation for literacy learning. The classroom should be inviting, with well-defined centers around the room. Ideally, displays on the walls reflect a theme being studied and demonstrate evidence of the children's growing literacy development. Nearly all of the displays should include charts with samples of children's writing and/or artwork. In the whole-group area (a large, carpeted space), there should be an easel with chart paper for the morning message, a calendar, a weather chart, a helper chart, a daily schedule, classroom rules, a hundreds chart to count the days in school, a pocket chart, and a Word Wall.

The literacy center should contain a rug for independent reading and multiple bookshelves for storing books. There should be baskets of books grouped by level of difficulty that coordinate with small-group reading instruction. Other shelves can hold baskets organized by topics and authors, such as dinosaurs, sports, and books by Dr. Seuss or Eric Carle. Books should be rotated monthly. Colored stickers on the books and baskets help students return them to the correct spot. Student-made books are displayed in another basket. Books about the current theme can be placed on a special open-face shelf. Ideally, the literacy center has a flannel board and flannel board characters, puppets, and props for storytelling. There is a rocking chair for the teacher and other adults to read to the class. The listening area in the center can have a CD player for listening to stories. There are manipulatives for learning about print. These include magnetic letters, puzzle rhyme cards, and letter chunks on small tiles for making words.

The writing center is an extension of the literacy center. There is a round table for small groups of children to meet with the teacher. If possible, at least one computer should be a part of the literacy center for typing, Internet searching, and other activities. There are shelves with many types of paper, a stapler, markers, crayons, colored pencils, dictionaries, alphabet stamps, and ink stamp pads. A Word Wall in the writing center has each of the letters of the alphabet taped on horizontally. When the children learn a new word, it is taped under the letter it begins with. Children use the words when they need help spelling or to practice reading. During instruction, children may be asked to think of words that begin with the same letter and sound as a word on the Word Wall or to think of words that rhyme with a Word Wall word. Other classroom centers include science, math, dramatic play, and art.

Classroom Management and Affective Climate

Having a motivating classroom environment in which children are on task and engaged begins with the teacher (Gambrell, Malloy, & Mazzoni, 2007).

Phelan and Schonour (2004) published *1-2-3 Magic for Teachers,* which offers a highly effective approach to classroom management. When consistently applied, their approach leads to smoothly run classrooms and, subsequently, positive affective classroom climates. The classroom management approach does not concentrate on behaviors that students need to cease. Instead, it focuses on behaviors that students need to use, referred to as *starting behaviors.* Examples of unacceptable behaviors are calling out, inattention, and off-task activities. Examples of starting behaviors are engaging in schoolwork, cooperating with others, and successfully transitioning between activities. *1-2-3 Magic for Teachers* helps educators learn the differences between these two types of student behaviors and apply appropriate strategies depending on whether teachers want to stop or start student behavior. Stopping unwanted student behavior is based on a technique called the *counting method.* Initiating desirable student behavior uses eight techniques: positive reinforcement, simple requests, the kitchen timer, the docking system, natural consequences, charting, counting for brief start behavior, and cross-dialogue. Best practices in literacy instruction takes place in classrooms that are well managed and have a sense of community. Teachers and parents are encouraged to read *1-2-3 Magic: Effective Discipline for Children 2-12.* We will share a case study of an exemplary teacher to illustrate how the factors described can be integrated in a real classroom.

It is May, and the children in Katie Nero's kindergarten room are familiar with the classroom routines. They have already acquired many skills that are expected in kindergarten. Katie Nero has been teaching kindergarten for the past 7 years. She recently completed a master's degree with a reading specialist certification. She teaches in a working-class community and has 22 students of diverse backgrounds in her all-day kindergarten.

Katie's philosophy of teaching includes integration of the curriculum so that students can build connections between content areas. She purposefully integrates her literacy skill development in reading, writing, listening, speaking, and viewing with her social studies and science themes as much as possible. Her small-group literacy instruction is explicit by emphasizing specific skill development. Her approach to teaching reading, in which she attends to individual differences, requires her to have a large collection of print, audio, and digital books that range in difficulty from a single word or two on each page to books with one or two sentences per page. The range of books paves the way for literacy success.

Ms. Nero has a special interest in using informational texts with her children. She recognizes that background knowledge and vocabulary are enhanced by using expository material and that students need to read informational text in a variety of forms such as reading how-to manuals, applications, instructions, and digital texts such as websites. She has also found that at-risk students and boys are particularly drawn to expository or informational text.

Center Management

Ms. Nero uses her centers daily; 5-year-olds learn best when they are manipulating materials such as those found in centers. To ensure that students visit two specific centers a day, Katie has designed a contract on which she indicates the centers where children are expected to work. The contract has the name of each center and an icon representing it. These same labels and icons are at the actual centers. When children complete work in a center, they check it off on their contracts. The completed work is placed in the basket labeled "Finished Work." At the end of each day, Katie discusses and reviews with the children completed work from the centers and assigns centers for the next day. Any incomplete work or work that indicates a child needs help with a concept is placed in the "Unfinished" folder. There is a time during the day for completing unfinished work. This system allows for differentiation among the students. When children complete their two assigned centers, they can work at any center they choose.

Assessing Students to Determine Instructional Needs

In order to provide instruction to meet the varied levels of reading and writing of her students, Ms. Nero spends considerable time assessing them with formal and informal measures. This is particularly critical for ELLs and at-risk students, so that potential problems are effectively dealt with in a timely manner. In September, January, March, and June, she assesses students' knowledge about print and book concepts, phonological and phonemic awareness, ability to recognize and write letters of the alphabet, knowledge of letter–sound relationships, ability to read sight words, vocabulary skills, listening comprehension, and writing ability. Katie plans instruction based on the needs she identifies. As children begin to read conventionally, she takes monthly running records for each child. This system of recording children's reading behavior assesses the types of errors or miscues that children make, the decoding strategies they use, and their progress. Ms. Nero also takes anecdotal notes about students' behaviors that indicate both progress and points of difficulty. She collects samples of children's writing four times a year, analyzes them, and places them in student portfolios. Ms. Nero also observes students' social, emotional, and physical development.

Small-Group Reading Instruction

Ms. Nero works with small groups of children for reading instruction. With the assessment information she collects, she places students with similar needs together. As she works with the children, she takes careful notes regarding progress in literacy and adjusts the members of her various groups as needed. While in small groups, Ms. Nero provides instruction in phonological awareness, letter identification, letter–sound relationships, knowledge about books and print concepts, vocabulary, listening comprehension, oral language, and writing. She presently has four small groups and meets with each group three times a week. On Fridays, she attends to any special needs that come up during the week.

A Typical Day in Katie Nero's Classroom

Children Arrive at School (8:45 A.M.)

It is a Monday morning, and chatter begins to fill the classroom as Ms. Nero's students arrive. Quiet music plays in the background as children complete their morning routines. Children move their name tags on the attendance board from the side labeled "Not Here" to "Here," and they place their name sticks into the "Buy Lunch" or "Milk" can. Some children cluster around the easel, where they work together to read the morning message and discuss the question of the day. Today's message says: "Good Morning. Today is Monday, May 16, 2011. We will have Art today. Do you like animals? *Yes No.*

Students know it is time for writing their weekend news in their journals. Ms. Nero circulates among the writers, gently reminding some children to use spaces between words, suggesting others use classroom tools such as the Word Wall to spell needed words. As she listens to completed entries, she has the opportunity to chat with the children about their weekend. When the 2-minute warning bell rings, several children are already in the meeting area on the rug in the literacy center, reading books alone or with a partner. Those still writing begin to put away their materials and place their unfinished work in the "Unfinished" basket. They will be able to complete their entries later during center time. Once a student shakes the tambourine announcing morning meeting, everyone gathers and forms a circle on the carpet.

The Morning Meeting (9:00 A.M.)

"Good morning, Emily," Ms. Nero begins as they shake hands around the circle. Because they are beginning a new month, May, they echo-read a poem called "May" from *Chicken Soup with Rice* (Sendak, 1962). Katie has written the poem on chart paper. At the end of the month, the children will illustrate personal copies of this poem that will be placed in their Poem Books, along with other poems used throughout the year. As the calendar person, weather reporter, and scheduler lead the class in these activities, Katie records the attendance and lunch count, which the messenger takes to the office.

Ms. Nero guides the class in discussing the results of the tally of the day's question, "Do you like animals?" She then asks what kind of animals they like and writes responses on the Morning Messages. Ms. Nero then discusses the punctuation marks at the end of each sentence in the Morning Message. She has a new animal story for the theme called *Animals Should Definitely Not Wear Clothing* (Barnett, 1988). Ms. Nero reads the humorous book to the class and tracks the print with a pointer. After the first reading, she has the children echo-read each page with her. She then uses her LCD and computer to show the students a collection of PowerPoint slides she has of jungle animals she downloaded from the Internet

Center Time (9:30–10:30 A.M.)

Ms. Nero spends a few minutes reviewing the center activities. Centers have materials that are in place over a period of time and are enriched with activities that reflect the current theme. A description of what has been added to each center relating to the dinosaur theme follows.

- *Writing Center*: There are books about farm, jungle, and forest animals. Animal stickers, an animal dictionary, and black books are available for students to make their own animal books.
- *Literacy Center*: There are fiction and nonfiction animal books, animal books with accompanying CDs, an animal puzzle with labels on the animals, an animal concentration memory game, and an animal lotto game. There is an electronic white board with projected farm, jungle, and forest animals. Children move the figures around and place them under the correct heading. The names of the animals are also on the board to be moved next to the appropriate animal.
- *Computer Center*: There is software to view a virtual reality multimedia program for printing animal stationery, postcards, and masks, and for visiting a virtual museum exhibit about farm, forest, and jungle animals.
- *Science*: There are pictures and small figures of farm, forest, and jungle animals to discuss the characteristics of these animals and why they live where they do, as well as animal cards to sort into farm, jungle, and forest. There are recording sheets for all activities.
- *Math*: There is a set of pictures Ms. Nero got off the computer of several jungle, farm, and forest animals to talk about their sizes, colors, shapes, and body coverings such as feathers and fur, little plastic animals in an estimation jar, a basket containing 50 little animals numbered from 1 to 50, the aim being to put the animals into sequential order.
- *Blocks*: There is an area called the farm, one called the jungle, and one called the forest. Each has been decorated with plastic foliage and other items to make them look like the location they are supposed to be. Toy animals of the appropriate type are placed in the farm, jungle, or forest.
- *Art Center*: Animal stencils and animal stamps are added to the art center. There are pictures of farm, forest, and jungle animals and Play-Doh for children to make models of an animal of their choice.
- *Dramatic Play*: The dramatic play area is transformed into a veterinarian's office. There is a phone for the nurse to take appointments, paper for

the doctor to write a report on problems animals are having, a stethoscope, and other items found in such an office.

After Katie reviews center activities, her students look at their contracts and proceed to their "have-to" activities. The activities that must be done are often skills in which the students need practice, such as matching pictures with letters to reinforce letter–sound knowledge. When they complete their required activities, children may select any center, such as blocks or dramatic play. Children check off the centers they have worked in on their contract.

Small-Group Reading Instruction (9:30–10:30 A.M.)

The first group that Ms. Nero sees is reviewing a book they have read before, *We Went to the Zoo* (Sloan & Sloan, 1995). It is a simple patterned text with repeated words and phrases with some slight variations in the pattern. Katie provides a guided introduction as children look through the book and stop to talk about each page. During the book introduction, the students are asked to find the words *saw* and *many,* since these words caused some difficulty during the first reading. They also discuss the names of the animals in the book. As the group reads, Katie notices that one student makes no errors in reading and finishes quickly. Ms. Nero makes a note to think about moving him to a more advanced guided-reading group. During guided reading, she was able to complete a running record on one child. She noted that this student reads *seals* instead of *otters* and said *pander bears* instead of *bears.* Ms. Nero decides that she will help this child to pay more attention to the print in the words as he reads. She calls two more small reading groups in the remaining time.

Snack and Play (10:30–10:45 A.M.)

By midmorning everyone needs a break. The snack is animal crackers and what Ms. Nero is calling "animal juice."

Writing Workshop (10:50–11:45 A.M.)

The children gather for writing in the whole-class meeting area. Ms. Nero introduces the writing activity for the week. The children will be writing informational texts about an animal of their choice. Students have the option of working with a partner, which is particularly beneficial for ELLs and at-risk learners. Ms. Nero has paired off some children. In particular, she paired Juan with Jose, since they both speak Spanish. Juan only speaks Spanish and Jose is fluent in Spanish and English. They are to select an animal they like and mention as many facts about that animal as they can from their discussions and books she has in the room. She says, "You can write what your animal looks like, what it eats, what products it gives us if it is a farm animal, and what it does." Next, the students brainstorm about their animals and discuss what they look like, what they eat, what products they give, and what they do. On Tuesday, they will begin to browse through books about their animal for information and start to write. Children will write facts and draw pictures. There are many levels of writing, such as picture for writing, scribble writing, letter strings, invented spelling, and conventional writing. At the end of the week, Ms. Nero takes everyone's writing and makes it into a class book.

Play, Lunch, and Rest (11:45 A.M.–1:00 P.M.)

Children play either outside or in the gym, depending on the weather. Lunch is in the cafeteria, and children have rest time on rugs after lunch. Ms. Nero plays a CD of the story *Barnyard Banter* (Fleming, 2010) during rest time.

Math (1:30–2:15 P.M.)

There is a specific math curriculum followed in Ms. Nero's kindergarten. We describe here only the theme-related literacy activities that she added. Today the class brainstorms a list of as many farm, forest, and jungle animals as they can. There are books about each type of animal and there are four computers in the classroom. Children take turns looking at the books related to their type of animal and on the Internet to copy down as many as they can. At the end of the activity they each share the kind and numbers of animals they found from the farm, jungle, and forest. The farm group has the most.

Art, Music, and Gym (12:15–2:45 P.M.)

The class goes to a special teacher for art, music, or gym. Ms. Nero has coordinated with these teachers about the theme being studied, so the art teacher is working on papier-mâché animal sculptures with the children, the music teacher has found some great animal songs, and the gym teacher has thought of some movements to help the students walk and run like chickens on the farm, monkeys in the jungle, and bears in the forest.

Closing Circle with Read-Aloud (2:50–3:00 P.M.)

At closing time, students clean up and gather in the meeting area for their closing circle and a read-aloud. Today Ms. Nero has chosen an informational book titled *Animal Babies* (Hamsa & Dunnington, 1985). After reading, she helps children list the characteristics of the baby animals, what they eat, what they do, and writes it on a chart. Finally, she and the children review the activities of the day and plan for tomorrow.

Family Involvement

Before the animal unit began Ms. Nero, as she did with all units throughout the year, sent home a short note about the activities that would be done in school, the skills being taught, and suggestions for activities for parents to do at home. During the unit she asked for volunteers to come and read animal books and she asked for artifacts about animals that parents might share with the class. Ms. Nero asked for parent volunteers during writing workshop to assist students with words they couldn't spell and asked for help during center time to assist children with activities while she worked with small groups of children. She offered multiple options and multiple time periods for participation. At the end of the unit, parents were invited to school to see all the work done about animals. She also put many of the projects on the class website. Ms. Nero found that parent participation helped her program run more efficiently and her students carried out their work with a higher level of achievement. Parents respected the work she was doing, and the more they helped, the more they wanted to. Parents who hadn't volunteered in the past asked about getting involved. All of the students in Ms. Nero's class are on their way to becoming lifelong motivated readers and writers. In addition, she is preparing these youngsters to successfully meet the demands of the new national standards and become dynamic, creative thinkers.

REFLECTIONS AND FUTURE DIRECTIONS

We know a lot about early literacy development. We must stop looking for the silver bullet and refine what we know. We need to master differentiated instruction to meet the needs of our diverse society. We need parent involvement to be required as children enter public preschools and kindergartens. We need effective ways to meaningfully integrate technology that will enhance instruction. The most crucial goals are to ensure universal preschool for 3- and 4-year-olds and all-day kindergarten for 5-year-olds. If children do not get a good start in school, it can have a negative influence on the rest of their education (Hart & Risley, 2003). Many problems we face in the elementary and high schools would be eliminated with excellent preschool and kindergarten programs for all. Every child deserves this opportunity.

ENGAGEMENT ACTIVITIES

1. After reading the case study in Ms Nero's room, compare it to your own early childhood room or one that you observe. Discuss the theory-, policy-, and research-based practices used.
2. Is there evidence of the use of specific standards in Ms. Nero's

room? If yes, mention them. If some appear to be missing, mention what else she needs to include.

3. Create a lesson plan that meaningfully integrates new literacies.
4. Prepare a second lesson plan that shows modifications for the ELLs.
5. Compare the management of your classroom or a teacher you know to Ms Nero's. How would you improve her organization and management and your own, or the teacher you observed?

REFERENCES

Professional Literature

Adams, M. J. (1990). *Beginning to read.* Cambridge, MA: MIT Press.

Allington, R. L., & Baker, K. (2007). Best practices for struggling readers. In L. B. Gambrell, L. M. Morrow, & M. Pressley (Eds.), *Best practices in literacy instruction* (3rd ed., pp. 83–103). New York: Guilford Press.

Barnett, W. S. (1998). Long-term effects on cognitive development and school success. In W. S. Barnett & S. S. Boocock (Eds.), *Early care and education for children in poverty: Promise, programs, and long-term results* (pp. 11–44). Albany: State University of New York Press.

Beck, I. L., & McKeown, M. G. (2001). Text talk: Capturing the benefits of read-aloud experiences for young children. *The Reading Teacher, 55,* 10–20.

Brabham, E., & Lynch-Brown, C. (2002). Effects of teachers' reading-aloud styles on vocabulary acquisition and comprehension of students in the early elementary grades. *Journal of Educational Psychology, 94*(3), 465–473.

Brown, R. (2008). The road not yet taken: A transactional strategies approach to comprehension instruction. *The Reading Teacher, 61*(7), 538–547.

Carnine, D. W., Silbert, J., Kame'enui, E. J., & Tarver, S. G. (2004). *Direct reading instruction.* Upper Saddle River, NJ: Pearson.

Castiglioni-Spalten, M. L., & Ehri, L. C. (2003). Phonemic awareness instruction: Contribution of articulatory segmentation to novice beginners' reading and spelling. *Scientific Studies of Reading, 7*(1), 25–52.

Clay, M. M. (1966). *Emergent reading behavior.* Doctoral dissertation, University of Auckland, New Zealand.

Cunningham, P. M. (2007). Best practices in teaching phonological awareness and phonics. In L. B. Gambrell, L. M. Morrow, & M. Pressley (Eds.), *Best practices in literacy instruction* (3rd ed., pp. 159–177). New York: Guilford Press.

Dewey, J. (1916). *Democracy and education.* New York: Macmillan.

Dougherty-Stahl, K. A. (2004). Proof, practice, and promise: Comprehension strategy instruction in the primary grades. *The Reading Teacher, 57*(7), 598–609.

Fisher, P., & Blachowicz, C. (2005). Vocabulary instruction in a remedial setting. *Reading and Writing Quarterly, 21,* 281–300.

Gambrell, L. B., Malloy, J. A., & Mazzoni, S. A. (2007). Evidence-based best practices for comprehensive literacy instruction. In L. B. Gambrell, L. M. Morrow, & M. Pressley (Eds.), *Best practices in literacy instruction* (3rd ed., pp. 11–29). New York: Guilford Press.

Guthrie, J. (2004). Teaching for literacy engagement. *Journal of Literacy Research, 36*(1), 1–29.

Hart, B., & Risley, T. R. (1995). *Meaningful differences in the everyday experience of young American children.* Baltimore: Brookes.

Hart, B., & Risley, T. R. (1999). *The social world of children: Learning to talk.* Baltimore: Brookes.

Hart, B., & Risley, T. R. (2003). The early catastrophe: The 30 million word gap. *American Educator, 27*(1), 4–9.

Harvey, S., & Goudvis, A. (2007). *Strategies that work.* Portland, ME: Stenhouse.

International Reading Association. (1999). *Position statement: Using multiple methods of beginning reading instruction.* Newark, DE: Author.

International Reading Association and the National Association for the Education of Young Children. (1998). *Learning to read and write: Developmentally appropriate practices.* Newark, DE: International Reading Association.

Justice L., Meier, J., & Walpole, S. (2005). Learning new words from storybooks: An efficacy study with at-risk kindergarteners. *Language, Speech, and Hearing Services in Schools, 36,* 17–32.

Kame'enui, E. J., Simmons, D. C., Chard, D., & Dickson, S. (1997). Direct reading instruction. In S. A. Stahl & D. A. Hayes (Eds.), *Instructional models in reading* (pp. 59–84). Mahwah, NJ: Erlbaum.

McGee, L. M., & Morrow, L. M. (2005). *Teaching literacy in kindergarten.* New York: Guilford Press.

Morrow, L. M. (2007). *Literacy development in the early years: Helping children read and write* (7th ed.). Needham Heights, MA: Allyn & Bacon/Pearson.

National Institute of Child Health and Human Development. (2000). *Teaching children to read: An evidence-based assessment of the scientific research literature on reading and its implications for reading instruction* (NIH Publication No. 00-4769). Washington, DC: U.S. Government Printing Office.

Penno, J., Wilkinson, I., & Moore, D. (2002). Vocabulary acquisition from teacher explanation and repeated listening to stories: Do they overcome the Matthew effect? *Journal of Educational Psychology, 94*(1), 23–33.

Phelan, T. W., & Schonour, S. J. (2004). *1-2-3 magic for teachers: Effective classroom discipline pre–K through grade 8.* Glen Ellyn, Illinois: Parent Magic.

Piaget, J., & Inhelder, B. (1969). *The psychology of the child* (H. Weaver, Trans.). New York: Basic Books.

Pressley, M. (2007). Achieving best practices. In L. B. Gambrell, L. M. Morrow, & M. Pressley (Eds.), *Best practices in literacy instruction* (3rd ed., pp. 397–404). New York: Guilford Press.

Pressley, M., Allington, R. L., Wharton-McDonald, R., Block, C. C., & Morrow, L. M. (2001). *Learning to read: Lessons from exemplary first-grade classrooms.* New York: Guilford Press.

Reutzel, R. (2010, May). *Something old is new again: Teaching alphabet letter names and sounds to develop young students' reading and writing.* Paper presented at the conference of the International Reading Association, Chicago.

Rupley, W., & Nichols, W. (2005). Vocabulary instruction for the struggling reader. *Reading and Writing Quarterly, 21,* 239–260.

Shanahan, T., August, D., Gray, J., & McCardle, P. (2010, May). *A meta-analysis of studies of reading instruction for English Language Learners.* Presentation at the conference of the International Reading Association, Chicago.

Shanahan, T., & Lonigan, C. J. (2010). The National Early Literacy Panel: A summary of the process and the report. *Educational Researcher, 39*(4), 279–285. *doi10.3102/0013189X10369172*

Shaywitz, S. (2004). *Overcoming dyslexia: A new and complete science-based program for reading problems at any level.* New York: Knopf.

Sheridan-Rabideau, M. P., & Rowsell, J. (2010). *Design literacies: Learning in digital environments.* London: Routledge.

Slavin, R. E. (1997). *Educational psychology: Theory and practice* (5th ed.). Needham Heights, MA: Allyn & Bacon.

Tracey, D. H., & Morrow, L. M. (2006a). *Best practices for phonics instruction in today's classroom. Professional Development Series, Volume 13.* New York: Sadlier.

Tracey, D. H., & Morrow, L. M. (2006b). *Lenses on reading: An introduction to theories and models.* New York: Guilford Press.

Tracey, D. H., & Morrow, L. M. (2009). *Best practices for phonics instruction in today's classroom.* New York: Sadlier.

Walsh, B., & Blewitt, P. (2006). The effect of questioning style during storybook reading on novel vocabulary acquisition of preschoolers. *Early Childhood Education Journal, 33*(4), 273–278.

Wasik, B., & Bond, M. (2001). Beyond the pages of a book: Interactive book reading and language development in preschool classrooms. *Journal of Educational Psychology, 93*(2), 243–250.

Children's Literature

Barrett, J. (1988). *Animals should definitely not wear clothing.* New York: Simon & Schuster.

Fleming, D. (2010). *Barnyard banter.* New York: Holt.

Hamsa, B., & Dunnington, T. (1985). *Animal babies.* New York: Scholastic.

Sendak, M. (1962). *Chicken soup with rice.* New York: Harper & Row.

Sloan, P., & Sloan, S. (1995). *We went to the zoo.* Boston: Sundance.

CHAPTER 4

Best Practices with Struggling Readers

Richard L. Allington

This chapter will:

- Discuss how most children experiencing reading difficulties can have their literacy development accelerated when they have access to sufficient appropriate instruction.
- Discuss how teachers who provide personalized interactive lessons, skills instruction within context, and substantial reading and writing opportunities are most effective.
- Discuss how a comprehensive system with three components—prevention, acceleration, and long-term support—is needed in schools to meet the needs of students experiencing literacy difficulties.

EVIDENCE-BASED BEST PRACTICES

Not all children, unfortunately, acquire literacy easily. Although there has always been much debate as to just why some children struggle to become readers and writers, in this chapter we focus on how exemplary instructional support might be provided to such children and leave the issue of the etiology of learning difficulties for others to consider. In my view, children who find learning to read and write more difficult are best served not by identifying some label for them, but by designing and delivering sufficient and appropriate instruction and substantial opportunities to actually engage in high-success reading and writing activities. Thus I draw on our experiences in two long-term school-based research projects to offer detailed descriptions of interventions that we consider exemplary in nature and outcomes.

The Critical Role of Classroom Reading Lessons

Providing all children with exemplary classroom literacy instruction is an essential first step in addressing the needs of children who find learning to read and write more difficult. In our studies of exemplary first-grade teachers (Pressley, Allington, Wharton-McDonald, Block, & Morrow, 2001), for instance, we found that the greatest impact of the exemplary teachers we studied was on the development of reading and writing proficiency in the lowest-achieving children. In other words, in the classrooms of the exemplary first-grade teachers, there were far fewer children who ended first grade still struggling with reading and writing. Likewise, Mendro, Jordan, and Bembry (1998) studied the effects of three consecutive years of high-quality teaching on student reading development. They compared the achievement of children placed in high-quality classrooms with that of students who were unfortunate enough to have attended lower-quality classrooms over the same period. Although the children's average standing on national norms rose consistently year after year in the high-quality classrooms, the standing of children in the lower-quality classrooms dropped each year. After 3 years, the achievement of children who had similar initial achievement now differed by almost 40 percentile ranks! The results of this large-scale study have been replicated with respect to the impact of quality classroom instruction on reading development (Allington & Johnston, 2002; Pressley et al., 2001; Snow, Barnes, Chandler, Goodman, & Hemphill, 1991; Taylor, Pearson, Peterson, & Rodriguez, 2003), especially the reading development of struggling readers.

Now, it would not have seemed necessary, in some senses, actually to conduct studies showing that access to high-quality teaching is important—essential, in fact. Who would argue against providing high-quality classroom instruction? But then, who argues for it? How often are resources allocated to improving classroom instruction from funding provided by the Title 1 program of the No Child Left Behind Act (NCLB) or special education under the Individuals with Disabilities Education Act (IDEA)? How often are such funds allocated for the purchase of needed classroom instructional materials, for instance, to purchase a classroom supply of texts of an appropriate level of complexity for use by students with reading difficulties? Or how often are funds allocated to provide professional development opportunities for classroom teachers to learn how better to document the development of children who are struggling with literacy learning?

Instead, these programs more often fund additional personnel, including specialist support teachers (reading teachers, learning disabilities teachers, speech and language teachers), school psychologists, social workers, or paraprofessional personnel. There may be a role for any and all of these extra personnel, but in our view a necessary first step is ensuring that children have access to high-quality classroom instruction regardless of their label or participation in a special program.

One question that I now routinely pose is whether there is evidence that specialized personnel enhance the quality of classroom instruction. In other words, what evidence is available that points to the ways that the school psychologist has improved classroom teaching? The same question might be asked about the roles of the social worker, the learning disability specialist, the reading teacher, or the paraprofessional. If the presence of specialized personnel is not improving classroom instruction, at the very least we should reconsider the role demands for such positions so that improving the quality of classroom teaching becomes a central attribute of each specialist's role (Walmsley & Allington, 2007).

One unintended effect of federal education programs targeted at improving the education of struggling learners may be a reduced professional responsibility that many general education teachers have for the reading instruction and outcomes of struggling readers served by specialized teachers in special programs. A recent study (Scharlach, 2008) found that two-thirds of new teachers report having no responsibility for teaching reading to students with disabilities. In other words, teaching struggling readers to read is seen as primarily the responsibility of the special education teachers. But struggling readers spend perhaps 15–20% of their school day in special programs. The rest of the day they sit in the general education classroom. In order to adequately address the problems faced by struggling readers, we must also be concerned with the quality of instruction encountered in the other 80–85% of the day—the time spent in the general education classroom. We like to think of this as a plan that extends the notion of intervention as necessary all day long.

Intervention all day long means, simply, that struggling readers have books they can read in their hands all day long and lessons that address their learning needs all day long. This would mean not only reorganizing classroom reading instruction so that it matched struggling readers' needs but also assuring that science and social studies lessons would require texts that struggling readers could read accurately, fluently, and with understanding and that address the requisite content. Such is rarely the case now, but the use of such multilevel curriculum materials was one feature of the exemplary fourth-grade classrooms we studied (Allington & Johnston, 2002).

Supplemental Support for Struggling Readers

However, even exemplary classroom teachers cannot do it all. Although such teachers dramatically reduce the incidence of reading difficulties, a few children typically continue to struggle even in these exemplary classrooms. Some children have enormous instructional needs that simply cannot be met in the day-to-day bustle of the classroom. Their needs for close and personalized teaching simply exceed the capacity of even exemplary teachers. It seems to be both a quantity and quality problem.

Most of these children simply need closer and more explicit teaching than can be accomplished by a teacher with the responsibility for a classroom filled with 25 children. These children need, for instance, more guided reading opportunities and more high-success independent reading. As Guthrie (2004) notes, because good readers typically spend 500% more time reading than struggling readers, "Educators should attempt to increase engaged reading time [for struggling readers] by 200%–500%. This may require substantial reconfigurations of curriculum" (p. 1).

Most classrooms will need a substantially expanded supply of books and textbooks at appropriate levels of difficulty for those struggling readers—typically, levels different from those used in the daily classroom lessons and activities. Some struggling readers will need particularized instruction—an emphasis on hearing sounds in words, for instance—that may require not only more time to provide than the classroom teacher has available but also a particular instructional expertise that classroom teachers do not routinely acquire, even exemplary classroom teachers (Allington, 2006). Thus another feature of exemplary intervention efforts is the useful and targeted deployment of special support teachers and personnel who provide the intensive and personalized instruction that those few children need in order to thrive in school.

Unfortunately, it is common today also to find that a school employs a large number of paraprofessionals in attempting to meet the instructional needs of children who find learning to read difficult, usually funding such personnel with disbursements allocated by Title 1 or IDEA. In other words, huge numbers of paraprofessionals are employed in remedial and special education programs (Howes, 2003; International Reading Association, 1994). However, there is substantial evidence that students gain little academic benefit when paraprofessionals deliver intervention instruction (Achilles, 1999; Anderson & Pellicier, 1990; Croninger & Valli, 2009; International Reading Association, 1994). In fact, the use of paraprofessionals in classrooms of any kind has been shown to have no positive effect on student achievement (Boyd-Zaharias & Pate-Bain, 1998; Gerber, Finn, Achilles, & Boyd-Zaharias, 2001). The key to understanding these findings is located in the need children have for access to expert instruction. Too often, it seems, school programs are designed such that children who find learning to read difficult are paired with inexpert paraprofessional staff for instruction and practice.

Paraprofessionals might provide supportive practice opportunities, but such activities seem more successful when the lessons are planned and the materials selected by the teacher or reading teacher. Paraprofessionals can be provided with professional development that allows them to successfully use one or more lesson routines (Allington & Cunningham, 2007), but unfortunately many paraprofessionals receive little, if any, such professional development.

So what might an exemplary program for addressing the needs of struggling readers look like? It would, of course, begin with exemplary classroom teaching. Support for exemplary classroom teachers would be available in the form of expert specialists, who provide appropriate and intensive services for children in need of such added attention. This support might be offered during the school day, after school, or during the summer. It might be offered in the classroom or in another location. There might be paraprofessional support for either the classroom teacher or the specialist teacher, or for both. But the efforts of the paraprofessional would be to focus on providing supportive reading and writing practice, organized and closely monitored by the classroom or reading teacher.

A grand scheme, you say, but what exactly would it look like? In the following sections, you will meet (1) an exemplary first-grade teacher and spend

RESPONSE TO INTERVENTION

Since we observed these teachers, another federal initiative for struggling readers has been written into law. Passed in 2004 as part of the reauthorization of IDEA, response to intervention (RTI) is a general education initiative focused on reducing the number of children identified as being learning disabled (LD). Since approximately 80% of pupils with disabilities have reading difficulties (and for many that is their disability), RTI requires schools identify pupils with learning disabilities differently.

Once RTI is in place in a school, at that point the older "discrepancy" formula for identifying children with LD can no longer be used. In its place is the requirement that the school provide expert, intensive reading instruction of increasing tiered intensity. Tier 1, classroom reading instruction, may be the most important tier, since the research indicates that almost all children with LD can learn to read but that they need daily high-quality reading lessons. Tier 2 is expert additional reading lessons provided to the child in a small-group format. Because RTI is a general education initiative, using certified reading specialists in Tier 2 seems the most appropriate option. Tier 3 is daily expert one-to-one tutoring. If after providing one or more years of daily Tier 1, 2, and 3 additional reading lessons, no acceleration of reading progress is noted, then the child can be identified as LD.

Congress wrote this act such that RTI initiatives are general education responses to reading difficulties. But school districts are allowed to remove 15% of their total special education budget from special education and use those funds to fund RTI initiatives.

If you would like to read more about RTI see the books below:

Allington, R. L. (2009). *What really matters in response to intervention: Research-based designs*. Boston: Allyn & Bacon.

Howard, M. (2009). *RTI from all sides: What every teacher needs to know.* Portsmouth, NH: Heinemann.

Johnston, P. H. (Ed.). (2010). *RTI in literacy: Responsive and comprehensive.* Newark, DE: International Reading Association.

a day in her classroom, and (2) an exemplary support teacher—certified and experienced in both reading and special education—and spend a day with her as she goes about supporting teachers and children as they learn to read and write.

BEST PRACTICES IN ACTION

Exemplary Classroom Instruction for Children Who Find Learning to Read and Write Difficult

Georgia teaches in a small rural district in northern California. Nearly two-thirds of the children come from low-income families, and one-sixth of them are members of ethnic minority groups. Seasonal employment in agriculture supports a mobile low-wage workforce in this community. Because of the transient nature of agricultural work, Georgia's class membership had a 50% changeover during the latest school year.

However, when you walk into Georgia's first-grade classroom, the mood is one of a community that is actively engaged and interested in what it is doing. Students are working in groups and alone, reading and writing, sharing and exchanging ideas and information. Georgia integrates reading and writing throughout the day and across subjects. Print surrounds the students on all four walls, including students' stories, students' artwork with labels, charts of songs and poems, and a pocket board for sentences about the basal story from guided reading.

Georgia's language arts program involves a weekly schedule of varied reading and writing activities, not the more common daily schedule. At least three times a week, the students have independent reading time while Georgia holds individual reading conferences. A literature-based core reading program is used twice weekly for guided reading, supplemented with appropriately leveled little books for additional guided reading lessons. The class is divided by reading ability into four groups for the twice-weekly guided reading sessions, but it is heterogeneously grouped for daily independent reading time and often for the small-group guided reading lessons drawn from a large supply of leveled books. While Georgia meets with guided reading groups, the other students have center activities. Friday is an independent reading day for all groups. Each day after lunch, the students have independent reading time.

Georgia also reads aloud daily, offering a chance for predictions, sharing of personal knowledge and experiences, and vocabulary building. Often, she chooses books that enhance a math, science, or social studies concept on which the class is working.

Writers' Workshop is a vital component in the planned weekly literacy program. Twice a week, students are composing for at least 45 minutes and engaged in small-group and individual writing lessons. Other writing assignments, responses to their reading, personal journals, and whole-class generated big books offer diverse writing opportunities. The students have cubbies and are encouraged to write notes to one another.

A Day in First Grade

Students enter school at 8:20 A.M., quickly hang up their jackets, put away lunches, and group on the rug. On Mondays, there is oral sharing time, when students have the opportunity to participate in telling an experience. Georgia quickly takes lunch count, attendance, and has two student helpers who write the day of the week and the date. (At the beginning of the school year, she modeled this and, by January, handed it over to students to do on their own.) While this is going on she engages the rest of the class in "reading the room"—reading words from the Word Wall and from the poems and songs around the room. When the students finish their calendar information, the class reads it silently and then in unison. Then the Pledge is said and a patriotic song is sung, with a student pointing to the large printed words on a chart. Again, an activity that Georgia did at first has been taken over by the students. This usually takes 10 to 15 minutes, and by 8:35 A.M. the class is engaged in guided reading and centers, independent reading, or Writers Workshop. Georgia has organized a time block of 90 minutes for literacy activities. Over two-thirds of this period involves students daily in individual reading and writing. Writers Workshop, guided reading and centers, independent reading, and conferences are included throughout the week.

Guided reading revolves around both a basal selection and books drawn from Georgia's large collection of leveled little books. Georgia has all the students gather on the rug as she performs a prereading activity. With this week's basal story, *Over in the Meadow* (Keats, 1993), she has the children close their eyes and think about animals and plants in a meadow. She tells them, "There is a creek, not as big as our local creek, and a tree trunk nearby, with ants crawling on it. Up in the blue sky are clouds. If you were sitting back in this meadow, you would be smelling things, seeing things, and hearing things."

Georgia then directs the students to the story, illustrated by Ezra Jack Keats. A discussion ensues about the fact that this is an old story—Keats did not write it—and how they have read other retold stories. Georgia reads it aloud from a big book edition, and the students comment that it is a counting book, a rhyming book, and a repeating book. *Muskrat, snug,* and *chirp* are discussed as vocabulary as she reads, because they are hard words to determine from the pictures. Georgia asks questions about the muskrat; she has just elaborated on *snug* by saying "I like snug. It reminds me of being warm and comfortable." She demonstrates *chirping* when asked "What is *chirp*?" by a student.

Georgia had the written numbers *one* through *ten* on cards and arranged them, using a pocket board, in a column and placed blank cards across from them in another column. As the students worked on remembering which animal matched which number in *Over in the Meadow,* they flipped the cards to reveal the correct names. Georgia also used this exercise to stress sounds and words. She used the word numbers *one* and *eight* to talk about how *one* starts with the /w/ sound, not /o/, and how *e* and *i* says /ay/ in *eight.* As students matched the animals to the number from the story, they silently—in their heads—read. Then in unison they read the story again, with all the students appearing to be able to read. At their seats, using the table of contents, they all found the story in individual books and read chorally.

Then Georgia directed her students to write in their journals about their favorite baby animal and why it was their favorite. During this time, Georgia and her aide circulated, helping students sound out words. With *cheetah,* Georgia directed a student to look at her mouth as she said the word, stretching it out. The student said, and then wrote *ch—ee—ta.* This sound stretching was a common feature in the classroom during writing. Georgia linked the students' sound spelling to developing phonemic segmentation by modeling word stretching and encouraging the students to do this on their own. This, in and of itself, has been shown to be a powerful activity for fostering growth in phonemic awareness (McGill-Franzen, 2006).

The next day, in the students' smaller guided reading groups, Georgia worked with the pocket board, using sentences from the story but leaving blank the animals and their activities. The students filled in these missing words by reading the sentence in their heads, talking with one another, and deciding what should fit. Afterward, they read it silently or whisper-read, then read aloud together. Finally, Georgia directed the students to read from individual books, loud enough for her to hear when she moved around but not loud enough to disturb their neighbors.

The reading specialist, who provides instruction to five students in a pull-out program, now arrives and takes those students to her room for an added small-group lesson. The reading specialist coordinates what she is working on with Georgia. Later, she pulls one student for a lesson geared toward the specific phonological difficulties that child is having. She has trained Georgia's aide and supervises the aide's work with another student. In this case the aide implements the pause–prompt–praise strategy for fostering fluency and growth of self-regulation while reading (Allington, 2006), having the child read and reread books selected by the reading teacher as appropriate.

The aide is in the classroom all morning and spends most of her time working in a similar manner, providing extended high-success reading practice with a focus on self-monitoring, with other students while Georgia oversees her interactions and offers bits of advice about each student. Next, the students who have been with the reading teacher move up to work with Georgia. She shares pages from several books about bees. Then she introduces the Storybox book *The Bee,* by Joy Cowley (1990), preparing the students by activating their background information about bees, previewing the cover and the following pages, and setting the readers up to whisper-read successfully on the first try. She then has them reread it two times, stressing that the sentences make sense. Next, she does a minilesson on the double *ee* sound, starting with *bee* and making a list with *see, meet, beet, cheetah,* and *bees,* all words from this story and a recently read book. The students think of sentences about what bees can do: *Bees can sting. Bees can collect nectar. Bees can drink.* Although they know only the beginning letter of *collect,* the students spell everything else as Georgia writes. As Georgia writes *collect,* she models stretching out the sounds of the word to better be able to hear and spell them. Students whisper-read the chart, read all the sentences together, and then each student picks a sentence to read alone. This high-success minilesson lasts about 20 minutes, and then these children return to their seats to engage in independent reading.

Guided reading is alternated with independent reading of books chosen from the baskets. The baskets are filled with teacher-selected books that the students have encountered during previous lessons. This is a quiet reading time, but students share with one another or sometimes read with partners, taking turns. With the groups heterogeneously mixed and a variety of leveled books available, students model good reading strategies and fluency for one another.

During this time, Georgia has individual reading conferences, takes running records, jots down notes, and offers personal instruction in reading strategies to encourage self-monitoring, multiple strategy use, and independence. In one reading conference with a struggling emergent reader, Georgia encourages his use of multiple strategies: self-monitoring, decoding, and—most important—meaning making. *Apples and Pumpkins* by Anne Rockwell (1994) is a new book for this reader, so Georgia encourages talking about it a little bit, looking at the title and discussing the opening illustration and what he thinks is going on. When the student reads "country farm" instead of "Comstock Farm," Georgia praises the attempt, saying it was a really good word that made sense. She then claps out the syllables in *Comstock,* directing the student to look closely at the letters, and he is able to sound it out by syllables. Early in the story the student reads "greens and chickens" for "geese and chickens." Georgia draws attention to the mistake, asking, "Does that make sense?" The student quickly rereads the phrase correctly. She then encourages the use of multiple strategies, using picture cues, making sense, use of letter–sound relationships, and reading on to find out what happens.

The student slowly but successfully reads "The geese and chickens and a big fat turkey walked with us on our way to the . . . where the apples grow." The word skipped is *orchard.* Georgia builds upon the student's knowledge, asking, "Where do apples grow? What do we call a lot of trees? What parts of the word look familiar?" until the student uses existing prior knowledge and the word part *or-* to correctly pronounce *orchard.*

As the student reads on, he becomes more fluent. Another mistake, "for me vine"/ "for the vine"/ "from the vine" is a quick succession of readings. The student is self-correcting as Georgia asks, "Does that make sense?" Another self-correction leads Georgia to ask, "How did you figure out that it was 'carry'?" The student does not know how to verbalize what strategies he used, so Georgia suggests some: "Did you look at all the letters? Did you look at the pictures? Did you go on?" For a final miscue, *fake* for *face*, Georgia again stresses making sense: "Read it again and see if that makes more sense to you, from the beginning." Thus she encourages another strategy, rereading along with meaning making, in cross-checking. The student successfully reads "At home we carve a jack-o-lantern face on our big orange pumpkin." Georgia praises him for his use of multiple strategies and for sticking to the reading even though the book has many hard words.

The days that students have reading from the literature baskets are also Writers Workshop days. The teacher and the aide give individual attention and encouragement to the writers. Checklist cards for editing encourage correct final punctuation, capitals, and spelling. Most of the students spell phonemically, sounding out words and stretching the sounds. Back in January, Georgia created a priority word list of 25 nonphonemic and high-frequency words. The students have a list of them on their tables and are expected to refer to it whenever they need to use these words in writing. After 3 months, students were spelling them correctly without looking at the lists. Today, there is much use of the Word Wall (Cunningham & Allington, 2007) for spelling other words.

A typical example is a boy adding to a story on giant sea turtles. He is reading from a book about sea turtles to gather new information. He has already written two drafts that have been revised and edited. As he writes, he uses the Word Wall and the information and spelling from the book he is using as a resource. Another student is working on a chapter book about animals, because she has decided to combine two works in progress, one on horses and one on dogs.

After recess, Georgia has a math lesson on telling time on the hour and on the half-hour. It begins as a whole-class discussion on the rug as Georgia models the time for reading, for recess, and for leisure reading, using a large yellow clock with movable hands. Again literacy is stressed. To tie in with this unit on telling time, she reads aloud *The Bear Child's Book of Hours* by Anne Rockwell (1987). Students then proceed to more individualized work back at the tables, each writing his or her own *My Book of Hours and Half-Hours.* Each student fills in clocks and composes sentences that match personal experiences, with Georgia assisting with scaffolding when necessary. Lunchtime and another recess end this busy morning.

When students return from lunch, they settle down for independent leisure reading time. Crates of books of different reading levels are available, including many easy ones, as well as magazines and student-published books. Students share responses with one another, partner-read, or read segments to one another from the books they have chosen. There is a very low hum to this reading time. Twenty-five minutes later, students go to the gym. When Georgia picks them up from the gym, she comes prepared with clipboards, paper, and pencils. They discuss the various sights and smells they envisioned earlier on the rug, before reading *Over in the Meadow* (Keats, 1993). Then Georgia directs them to write down anything they observe as they go on their 10-minute playground/meadow walk. Students are busy talking, smelling, looking, and sharing ideas as they gather data and write their own observations.

This day, the students have written in response journals, in their individual "book of hours," and now on clipboards about their trip to the meadow, writing in their own words everything they have seen, smelled, or heard. Georgia teaches both reading and writing skills explicitly, typically in the context of a reading or writing activity. She is opportunistic, selecting multiple occasions daily to provide explicit skills information during whole-group, small-group, and individual meetings. But Georgia is also systematic, incorporating much of her strategy and skills instruction into her guided reading lessons, Writers Workshop conferences, and reading conferences. All of these activities offer students instruction on a personalized basis.

Before the children leave for the day, Georgia makes sure each student has selected a well-practiced little book to take home to read that night to his or her parents.

Exemplary Instructional Support for Children Who Find Learning to Read and Write Difficult

Joyce is a reading specialist in an old mill town on a river in the Northeast. The school serves a significant number of at-risk students, with 40% of the children eligible for free or reduced-price lunch. Joyce starts her day at 8:00 A.M., snatching small conferences with the various teachers whose rooms she pushes into, getting plastic baskets ready with books for the various first-grade rooms she enters, and setting up her small, cozy room for the two pullout sessions she does each day. At 9:00, she enters the first of five first-grade classrooms she visits on a daily basis.

The "warm-up" involves 10 students who come over immediately as Joyce spreads out multiple copies of eight little books. These are all rereads in which students quickly engage, with comments such as "I can read this one" (e.g., *The Ghost*; Cowley, 1990) or "Let's read this one together" (e.g., *In a Dark, Dark Wood*; Ross, 1990). Joyce works with and listens to each student read in a whisper, their version of silent reading. As they finish one book, students take or trade for another. After 10 minutes, Joyce collects those texts and gives each child a copy of *Where's the Halloween Treat?* (Ziefert, 1985), first introduced the preceding day.

Joyce starts the guided reading with "Where are your eyes going to be?" The students chime in: "On the words." Working on the title, one student knows the word *the*, another, *Halloween*; still another guesses *trick*. Noting that *trick* makes sense, Joyce asks, "Is that *trick* or *treat*?" The student answers, "*Treat* because of the *t* at the end." Students read the text together, misreading *us* for *me*. When asked, "Is that *us*?" they reread, saying that the word starts with an *m*, and self-correcting to *me*. Joyce points out, "I hear a rhyme. Listen for two words," and rereads the pages. Students quickly suggest *eat/treat*. "Detective ears" are used to find more rhyming words as the story progresses. Joyce picks up the pace; so does the group, self-correcting individually as they go along. When they finish the story, Joyce has them turn back to page 6, finding the words *good, eat,* and *six*. She cues each word with "What's it going to start with?" This reread with a minilesson on rhymes takes about 10 minutes.

For the final 10 minutes, Joyce introduces a new book, *Going Up?: The Elevator Counting Book* (Cummins, 1995). Finger-pointing to the first word, she asks, "What does it say?" As she covers the *-ing,* students quickly chant "go"; then they chant "going" as she uncovers the whole word. From the title, students predict where the character is—in an elevator. Joyce asks the students, "Why is this a good name for a book about an elevator, and how does it know when to stop?" Students have various responses, which are all accepted positively. Then they begin to read as Joyce finger-points to each word. The elevator stops at floor number 5. She then asks them to predict what will happen next: the numbers go down as the elevator goes down. Then they all read the rest of the text together. Before leaving, Joyce tells the students that they will work on writing books tomorrow.

Joyce quickly goes back to her small room, where she picks up the next basket of books and hurries on to her second first-grade class. In this class, students start their warm-up with *Jack-o'-Lantern* (Frost, 1990). Each student has his or her own copy. Joyce has extra copies for those children who took the book home and forgot to bring it back. Joyce spreads out other books for warm-up, with the instruction, "Everyone find one page to read to me. When I have heard you read your page, take a different book." Joyce encourages rereading, thinking of a word that makes sense, and starts with the beginning sound and voice–print match. One student, who picked the first page of *Scarecrow* (Bacon, 1993), reads. Joyce asks him how the book ends, which he does not know. She tells him to find the end of the book, and together they read the last pages, working on self-correcting and understanding. After the 10-minute warm-up, the students are directed to put the books in the middle and are told they can keep *Jack-o'-Lantern* and take it home again.

In this group, she introduces *Where's the Halloween Treat?* (Ziefert, 1985). Looking at the title, students are directed to the *H* and asked "What sound does it make?" Students all say /h/ and start thinking of a word that makes sense with the cover picture. They offer *haunt, house, Halloween*. Another student reads "Where's the," and everyone choruses "Halloween." Joyce begins the book, finger-pointing to the words as she goes along. By the second page, students are chiming in and predicting a good thing to eat behind the door. *Sandwich* and *apple* are accepted; the word *skeleton* prompts "Is that something good to eat?" By the third page, the students are using the repetition and their knowledge of numbers to read with no assistance. When asked how they know it is *seven,* students say it starts with an *s,* and another adds that it ends with *n*. Near the end of the book, Joyce asks the students to predict: "What do you think they did when the ghost said 'Boo'?" Answers vary from "They stayed," to "They ran," to "They were afraid." The children finish the story to see what would happen and revise their predictions as needed.

With 5 minutes left, Joyce has the students begin writing their own book, modeled after the book they just read. The classroom teacher allows them to continue writing as Joyce leaves.

Joyce's third first-grade class does a warm-up reading time for 10 minutes. Then *Where's the Halloween Treat?* is read chorally, a reread for three students and new to two others. With this group, Joyce takes from her basket of *My Journal* books, with each child's name at the bottom of the cover. In the book, they are working on patterns and words they can make from them to use in writing. The students are directed to make a box, then a *u* in the box, then a vertical line, and then an *s*. Joyce asks, "What's that word?" Students respond, "Us." After writing it under the box, Joyce asks, "What would rhyme with *us*?" Students think of *bus*. Joyce models on a pad, writing *us* and putting a *b* in front of it, while she thinks aloud, "If we can write *us*, we can write *bus*. We need to put the *b* first, then *us*." Students are now directed to write *Give* on the bottom of their page; the students and Joyce spell it. Next they are asked to write *us* from above, read the two words, and add a number: *Give us 7*. Then together they spell *good things to eat*, with the students spelling the beginning and ending sounds and the *-ing*. Joyce ends her half-hour by telling the students, "When I come back tomorrow, we will cut up these sentences and do a new book."

It is now 10:30 A.M. and time for Joyce's fourth first-grade class. Six students in this classroom quickly dive into the warm-up books Joyce brought in a plastic basket. As she comments positively to one student, "I like the way you are finger-pointing," other students start finger-pointing. Joyce works individually with each student. Then, a new book for this group is introduced, *Jack-o'-Lantern* (Frost, 1990). The end of the lesson revolves around the word *made*. "We are going to write the word *made*. Think about it. How big a box?" Joyce asks. She uses a small easel blackboard to model a box with three spaces, the last divided with a dotted line. The students fill in *m, a, d*, as Joyce ends by saying, "There is a letter we don't hear at the end." Students predict *n* or *t*, and Joyce tells them *e*. They add the *e*, commenting that there are three sounds but four letters. Students now write in their journals about the kind of face they would make on a pumpkin. Joyce has each student say the sentence he or she wants to write, concentrating on adjectives. Students quickly write "I made a," and then Joyce helps them stretch the words *vampire, scary, wolf, happy*, or *mad*. She then directs them to the word *face* in their book. On a blank piece of paper, she writes each sentence, cuts it up, and puts it and a copy of *Jack-o'-Lantern* in a Ziploc bag for each student to take home.

Joyce is a little behind schedule, arriving in the fifth classroom at 11:10. The children do warm-up reading and then Joyce holds up the new book, *Jack-o'-Lantern*, saying, "Look at the cover. What do you see?" The students say, "Pumpkin." Joyce responds, "Do you think that word says *pumpkin*?" The students reply, "No." Her "Why?" is answered with "Because it starts with a *j*." Joyce prompts them: "What is another name that starts with *j*?" They answer "jack-o'-lantern." Different students take turns finger-pointing and reading with Joyce. Then the students read in pairs from their own copies of the book. Joyce then has each student pick one page to read out loud to her after first practicing it in pairs.

Joyce now has a prep time and lunch, which she spends preparing the different baskets for the five first-grade lessons tomorrow. Over lunch, she talks with the fourth-grade teacher in whose room she will work for an hour.

Joyce is giving daily intensive tutoring to the two first graders who are struggling most with reading. As several studies have shown, individual tutoring provides the best chance for the lowest readers to accelerate reading development and get caught up with their peers before the end of first grade (Mathes et al., 2005; Phillips & Smith, 2010; Scanlon, Vellutino, Small, Fanuele, & Sweeney, 2005). At 12:30 she provides a one-on-one pullout session with one of the first graders. She picks up the student, quickly walking with her to her small tutoring room. Out of a packet kept in the reading room, the student picks a copy of *The Monster's Party* (Cowley, 1990) with her name on it. She reads it, finger-pointing as Joyce listens. Then Joyce picks *Sing a Song* (Melser, 1990) out of her packet. As the student reads it, she takes a running record. When she gets stuck on the word *about*, Joyce prompts, "What can you do if you don't know it?" The student says, "Read on," and she does. Although she does not self-correct here, she does so later on when reading *together* for *bed* and *tuck* for *us*. In both cases, she appears to use both letters and meaning to help self-correct. As the student completes the book, Joyce asks, "Can you tell me one thing in this story you liked?" The girl likes the splashing. Joyce continues, "What else happened in the story?" The student replies, "They got out." Joyce asks, "How did they get out?" The student answers, "Jump." She is asked to find the word and does.

The next book they read is *Hairy Bear* (Cowley, 1990). They discuss that *we* and *together* mean more than one tiger. Up on the blackboard Joyce and the student work on the word *out*, making a box with one wall and one segment divided with a dotted line. The student fills in the *t*, Joyce the *o* and *u*. They then work on a box for *about*, the word the student missed in her reread for the running record. The student hears and writes each sound, then practices writing *about*. Then, she writes *out* and *about* on 3″ × 5″ cards that will be added to her word box, a recipe box. For 2 minutes, they practice words from the box. Then, while the student picks another story to read, Joyce writes a sentence on jumping from *Sing a Song* (Melser, 1990): "Out, Out, Out we jump." The student reads the sentence. Joyce cuts it up, has her assemble it, and read again. Into a bag go the cut-up sentence, the book, and the 3″ × 5″ cards *out* and *about* to go home for practice.

In the last 3 minutes, they discuss real and make-believe as a new book, *Dan the Flying Man* (Cowley, 1990), is introduced. Joyce begins reading, with the book in front of the student, and has the student finger-point to the words.

Joyce leaves blanks at the end of the sentence, and the student correctly supplies *trees* and *train*. Halfway through, the student takes over. Joyce joins in again at the ending, which has a change of wording.

Note how Joyce has the students in her groups reading or rereading for most of the intervention periods. This is similar to the design of effective interventions that researchers have used. If we want struggling readers to become proficient readers, we must ensure they read successfully and read more every day than normally developing readers.

Joyce now goes to the fourth-grade classroom. The fourth-grade teacher has requested that Joyce work with her to enhance her writing instruction. In September, Joyce had modeled the writing process, brainstorming, rough drafts, revising, conferencing, editing, and publishing. She and the teacher worked on modeling peer conferences that sensitively gave feedback, constructive criticism, and specific ideas to the writer. With the writing process smoothly working in late October, Joyce continued to help with writing conferences but also was available for reading conferences and small heterogeneously grouped work. Language arts time was structured so that Joyce provided assistance for students with special needs who were working on reading and writing material at their independent and instructional levels. More frequent conferences in reading and writing were provided for them.

Joyce enters the room as the teacher is reading the beginning of *The Eerie Canal* (Reber, 1991). The introduction to the book had taken place earlier. Joyce points out at the end of the chapter, "I met a lot of characters. They keep mentioning Tom. I think he will be important." A student adds that another character, Sandy, is being described in detail and must be important too. As the teacher reads, Joyce and the children discuss the opening chapters, and inferences and predictions flow. Questions such as "Is anybody else getting a funny feeling?", "What do you think right now?", "What do you feel?", "Can you picture that?", and "What made you think it?" all encourage responses, the sharing of ideas, and predictions.

Both teachers then lead the discussion to important characters and significant events that happen to them. In groups of two or three, they discuss, share ideas, and write about the two main characters and important events they experienced in the opening chapters. Joyce and the teacher circulate among the students, listening, prompting, and asking questions to expand ideas and encourage examples. In the return to whole-class discussion and a composite list of events, the conversation also includes the author's style and how he pulled the reader right into the story. They contrast it to Cynthia DeFelice's style in *The Light on Hogback Hill* (1992), the current read-aloud, which has a much slower beginning and draws the reader in slowly. As this discussion continues, Joyce leaves.

It is now 2:00 P.M. and time to pick up the other first grader for intensive one-on-one tutoring. After this, Joyce visits a third-grade classroom. This third-grade teacher worked with Joyce for several weeks earlier this year, and now Joyce stops in to observe and then discuss her observations with the teacher about once a month. This is an extension of the coaching role that provides teachers with long-term support and professional conversation about the successes and concerns they are experiencing. After this debriefing session it is time for Joyce to be ready to respond to any number of queries or requests from teachers in her school. Sometimes the requests are easy, sometimes not, but supporting classroom teachers in their attempts to offer higher-quality reading instruction is central to Joyce's vision of her role.

How Joyce Developed Her Role

Joyce and her school have participated in a variety of studies with a nearby university for 10 years. Organizational support from a former administration allowed and even encouraged change involving teachers and their ideas. Earlier, some 12 years ago, when Joyce was a special education teacher, she started pushing into the classrooms. She started with one teacher:

> "It was contagious. People were upset I couldn't come into their room. Part of it was that they were getting something back. They were learning how to teach with literature, and they really wanted to have their special education kids with them more of the time. We were learning together how best to do this."

When she earned her reading specialist credential and shifted from special education to reading teacher several years ago, both the remedial reading and special education programs were completely pullout. At that time, an administrator wanted to start a brand-new kindergarten and first-grade reading program that incorporated a push-in model for supplemental instructional support.

> "The K–1 teachers never had exposure to working with someone in their rooms before. They might not have invited me in, but I just couldn't feasibly do a pullout in K–1. Plus it was really successful with the way my special ed program was operating. . . . I don't think people like to see you come in with a halo of authority. I would always say we should sit and talk. First, we had discussion time. I would say to them, 'I need to know what I'm doing, when I'm in the room, so let's decide what your goals are and what you want to accomplish, and I'll talk about some of my goals and what I want to accomplish. Then let's figure out how we can do this together in the room at the same time.' Every person was different."

One teacher and Joyce worked on flexible grouping, with students rolling in and out between them. For another teacher, she modeled read-alouds and having the children respond to stories: "I had to give her something concrete, something predictable, something she could do every day by herself."

In subsequent years Joyce's role changed:

> "The teachers have gotten comfortable with providing reading instruction from leveled book collections. I don't have to spend much time giving whole-class lessons. I'm spending more time with students, individualizing more. I try to do a lot more things quickly—quicker than I used to. I make sure they read lots of books when I'm with them. I'm seeing the kids more often. The real secret has to be that the classroom teachers really know how to do instruction, and that we figure out a plan, where some days I'm integrated in everything and other days maybe I'm not integrated. I'm working with my kids, but also I'm pulling out other kids who have that same problem."

Joyce and the teachers she works with feel "that we are both responsible for all of the kids in that room," yet she works primarily with the kids who really need the additional instruction.

The remedial program has become very collaborative. Several days throughout the year, substitutes come in, rotate, and relieve the classroom teachers so that they can attend roughly hour-long conferences with Joyce. Planning focuses on the very specific needs of certain children and how those needs will be addressed. Joyce has changed from a complete push-in model to primarily a push-in model, with two periods a day in which she pulls out students for one-on-one tutoring. One positive outcome of all these changes has been a large reduction in the number of children being labeled and placed in special education because of continuing reading difficulties.

REFLECTIONS AND FUTURE DIRECTIONS

Certainly more studies that continue the research into exemplary classroom and reading teachers and their instructional practices are needed.

Another area in which there has been little or no research involves looking at comprehensive intervention programs that include long-term support. This crucial component needs to be better understood so that schools can offer professional development, create budgets, and coordinate instructional support that will provide exemplary support programs for children throughout their schooling.

Exemplary early literacy interventions begin with an emphasis on ensuring that all children have access to high-quality classroom instruction. But classroom teaching is complex, and classroom teachers will likely never to be able to meet the substantial demands on time and expertise that a few children pose. This suggests, then, two roles for special program personnel. The first involves working with classroom teachers to enhance the quality of literacy instruction offered as part of the general education experience (often labeled coaching). This might occur in any number of ways, but in the cases that we observed the specialists offered training, advice, information, and appropriate materials to classroom teachers in order to enhance classroom instruction. The second role is to provide direct instruction to children who find learning to read difficult—but instruction that extends classroom lessons and is offered in a more intensive and personalized manner. Delivering such instruction requires working with classroom teachers over a period of time, but the benefits suggest that the effort pays substantial dividends.

CONCLUDING COMMENTS

What have we learned about addressing the needs of struggling readers? First, high-quality classroom reading instruction is absolutely essential. Struggling readers need high-quality instruction all day long. That means texts they can read not just in reading/language arts lessons but in science and social studies as well. One reason struggling readers read so much less than better readers is that they are, too often, sitting all day in classrooms where there are few books they can read accurately, fluently, and with understanding. Second, struggling readers need a steady supply of essential strategy lessons accompanied by extensive opportunities to independently practice and apply those strategies in high-success reading materials (Allington, 2009; Swanson & Hoskyn, 1998). Finally, even when high-quality classroom reading instruction is available, some struggling readers will need more expert and more intensive reading instruction than classroom teachers will be able to provide—thus the critical role of reading specialists. In the most effective supplemental support programs, care is taken to link the supplementary lessons to classroom instruction while still attending to the specific needs of individual students. In other words, struggling readers do not need a more fragmented reading curriculum than better readers. What they need is more expert, more intensive, and simply more reading lessons than we typically provide children. Once we figure out how to deliver what struggling readers need we will eliminate struggling readers from our schools.

ENGAGEMENT ACTIVITIES

1. Track the volume of reading that struggling readers in your classroom (or school) do over a 1-week period. Compare this to the volume of reading better readers do. Are struggling readers doing at least as much reading as better readers? If not, what can be done to expand the reading volume of struggling readers?
2. Examine the texts you find in any struggling reader's desk. How many of the texts can that child read accurately, fluently, and

with comprehension? Is the desk filled with books that are too difficult?

3. Interview an elementary school principal and ask about the school's literacy program. How does it meet the needs of all students? What components are in place for preventing reading and writing difficulties? What support is there for intervening and accelerating the progress of students who struggle with reading and writing?
4. Research how many fourth-grade students in your district will need additional support in middle school.
5. Find out about preventive, accelerated, and longer-term support plans in place in your school district. Are there clear links between preschool and elementary school programs, and elementary and middle school programs?

ACKNOWLEDGMENTS

The development of the case studies reported in this chapter was supported in part under the Educational Research and Development Program (Grant Nos. Rll7GIOO15 and R305A60005) and the National Research Center on English Learning and Achievement, as administered by the Office of Educational Research and Improvement, U.S. Department of Education. However, the contents of this chapter do not necessarily represent the positions or policies of the sponsoring agencies. Dr. Kim Baker of Russell Sage College provided research assistance and editorial support for this project. Georgia and Joyce continue as exemplary teachers benefiting the struggling readers in their schools.

REFERENCES

Professional Literature

Achilles, C. M. (1999). *Let's put kids first, finally: Getting class size right.* Thousand Oaks, CA: Corwin Press.

Allington, R. L. (2006). *What really matters for struggling readers* (2nd ed.). Boston: Allyn & Bacon.

Allington, R. L. (2009). *What really matters in response to intervention: Research-based designs.* Boston: Allyn & Bacon.

Allington, R. L., & Cunningham, P. M. (2007). *Schools that work* (3rd ed.). New York: Longman.

Allington, R. L., & Johnston, P. H. (2002). *Reading to learn: Lessons from exemplary fourth-grade classrooms.* New York: Guilford Press.

Anderson, L. W., & Pellicier, L. O. (1990). Synthesis of research on compensatory and remedial education. *Educational Leadership, 48*(1), 10–16.

Boyd-Zaharias, J., & Pate-Bain, H. (1998). *Teacher aides and student learning: Lessons from Project STAR.* Arlington, VA: Educational Research Service.

Croninger, R. G., & Valli, L. (2009). "Where is the action?": Challenges to studying the teaching of reading in elementary classrooms. *Educational Researcher, 38*(2), 100–108.

Cunningham, P. M., & Allington, R. L. (2011). *Classrooms that work: They can all read and write* (5th ed.). Boston: Allyn & Bacon.

Gerber, S. B., Finn, J. D., Achilles, C. M., & Boyd-Zaharias, J. (2001). Teacher aides and students' academic achievement. *Educational Evaluation and Policy Analysis, 23*(2), 123–143.

Guthrie, J. T. (2004). Teaching for literacy engagement. *Journal of Literary Research, 36*(1), 1–28.

Howes, A. (2003). Teaching reforms and the impact of paid adult support on participation and learning in mainstream schools. *Support for Learning, 18*(4), 147–153.

International Reading Association. (1994). Who is teaching our children? Implications of the use of aides in Chapter 1. *ERS Spectrum, 12*, 28–34.

Mathes, P. G., Denton, C. A., Fletcher, J. M., Anthony, J. L., Francis, D. J., & Schatschneider, C. (2005). The effects of theoretically different instruction and student characteristics on the skills of struggling readers. *Reading Research Quarterly, 40*(2), 148–182.

McGill-Franzen, A. (2006). *Kindergarten literacy.* New York: Scholastic.

Mendro, R. L., Jordan, H., & Bembry, K. L. (1998, April). *Longitudinal teacher effects on student achievement and their relation to school and project evaluation.* Paper presented at the annual meeting of the American Educational Research Association, San Diego, CA.

Phillips, G., & Smith, P. (2010). Closing the gaps: Literacy for the hardest to teach. In P. Johnston (Ed.), *RTI in literacy: Responsive and comprehensive* (pp. 219–246). Newark, DE: International Reading Association.

Pressley, M., Allington, R. L., Wharton-McDonald, R., Block, C. C., & Morrow, L. (2001). *Learning to read: Lessons from exemplary first-grade classrooms.* New York: Guilford Press.

Scanlon, D. M., Vellutino, F. R., Small, S. G., Fanuele, D. P., & Sweeney, J. M. (2005). Severe reading difficulties—can they be prevented? A comparison of prevention and intervention approaches. *Exceptionality, 13*(4), 209–227.

Scharlach, T. D. (2008). These kids just aren't motivated to read: The influence of preservice teachers' beliefs on their expectations, instruction, and evaluation of struggling readers. *Literacy Research and Instruction, 47*(3), 158–173.

Snow, C., Barnes, W., Chandler, J., Goodman, I. F., & Hemphill, L. (1991). *Unfulfilled expectations: Home and school influences on literacy.* Cambridge, MA: Harvard University Press.

Swanson, H. L., & Hoskyn, M. (1998). Experimental intervention research on students with learning disabilities: A meta-analysis of treatment outcomes. *Review of Educational Research, 68*(3), 277–321.

Taylor, B. M., Pearson, P. D., Peterson, D. S., & Rodriguez, M. C. (2003). Reading growth in high-poverty classrooms: The influences of teacher practices that encourage cognitive engagement in literacy learning. *Elementary School Journal, 104*(1), 4–28.

Walmsley, S. A., & Allington, R. L. (2007). Redefining and reforming instructional support programs for at-risk students. In R. L. Allington & S. A. Walmsley (Eds.),

No quick fix: Rethinking literacy programs in America's elementary schools: The RTI edition (pp. 19–41). New York: Teachers College Press.

Children's Literature

Bacon, R. (1993). *Scarecrow.* Crystal Lake, IL: Rigby.
Cowley, J. (1990). *The bee.* Bothell, WA: Wright Group.
Cowley, J. (1990). *Dan the flying man.* Bothell, WA: Wright Group.
Cowley, J. (1990). *The ghost.* Bothell, WA: Wright Group.
Cowley, J. (1990). *Hairy bear.* Bothell, WA: Wright Group.
Cowley, J. (1990). *The monster's party.* Bothell, WA: Wright Group.
Cummins, P. (1995). *Going up?: The elevator counting book.* Glenview, IL: Celebrations Press.
DeFelice, C. (1992). *The light on Hogback Hill.* New York: Scribner's.
Frost, M. (1990). *Jack-o'-lantern.* Bothell, WA: Wright Group.
Keats, E. J. (1993). *Over in the meadow.* New York: Scholastic.
Melser, J. (1990). *Sing a song.* Bothell, WA: Wright Group.
Reber, J. (1991). *The eerie canal.* Unionville, NY: Trillium Press.
Rockwell, A. (1994). *Apples and pumpkins.* New York: Aladdin Paperbacks.
Rockwell, A. (1987). *The bear child's book of hours.* New York: Crowell.
Ross, C. (1990). *In a dark, dark wood.* Bothell, WA: Wright Group.
Ziefert, H. (1985). *Where's the Halloween treat?* New York: Viking Press.

CHAPTER 5

Best Practices in Literacy Instruction for English Language Learners

María S. Carlo
Alain Bengochea

This chapter will:

- Provide background information relevant to understanding the demographic and policy context surrounding instruction for English language learners (ELLs).
- Highlight differences in learning to read a first versus a second language.
- Highlight the role of oral language proficiency in the development of ELLs' knowledge about English alphabetics and reading comprehension.

In this chapter we consider research and theory that can guide the design and delivery of English literacy instruction for English language learners (ELLs) and highlight the role of oral English proficiency in ELLs' literacy achievement. In writing a review piece of this sort, one risks portraying ELLs as a homogeneous group of learners who stand to benefit uniformly from the instructional practices one happens to review. Such a portrayal of ELLs would be, of course, incorrect. The ELL designation applies to youngsters who vary by age, country of origin, mother tongue, socioeconomic status, degree of access and exposure to formal schooling, and so on. Variations along these factors influence the extent to which instructional practices can favorably influence learning to read in a second language. Indeed, strategies that may prove effective with 10-year-old English learners who have already learned to read in their first language may have little applicability for teaching 15-year-old English learners who have been denied access to formal schooling prior to entering the United States. Hence, a first step in a principled approach to ELL reading instruction involves identifying the various ways in which ELLs differ from one another and from native English speakers. It should also indicate the need to examine the role that these differences may play in determining the success of an instructional intervention. Thus a goal throughout this chapter will be to bring attention to sources of differences in ELL language and literacy development that may dictate the need to adapt instruction in English literacy to achieve better alignment with students' needs (Harper & de Jong, 2004).

The influence of the report of the National Reading Panel (NRP, 2000) on the delivery of reading instruction to schoolchildren in the United States has prompted questions about the extent to which the findings of the NRP apply to children who are learning to read in a language that they do not speak natively. The 2006 publication of August and Shanahan's *Report of the National Literacy Panel on Language Minority Children and Youth* has addressed many of these questions. An important finding gained from this report was that the literacy achievement difficulties of ELLs appear to be more related to problems in the acquisition of English vocabulary, English proficiency, and other higher-level text processing skills than to the acquisition of lower-level skills in English alphabetics. The report suggests that ELLs achieve parity with English-only peers on low-level skills but fail to catch up to their peers on text-level skills. Recent findings by Nakamoto, Lindsey, and Manis (2007) further suggest that English learners who achieve parity with English monolinguals on English reading comprehension in the early grades may fall behind as the language demands of text increase. Moreover, ELL students who began first grade with lower oral proficiency in English experienced more "rapid deceleration of growth" (Nakamoto et al., 2007, p. 713) in reading comprehension when they reached the upper elementary and middle school grades. For these reasons, this chapter highlights the interplay between oral language development in English and the development of skills that underlie reading achievement.

This discussion on best practices for ELLs begins with a description of the demographic shifts in the U.S. school population and a brief discussion of the policy context surrounding ELL instruction in the United States. The focus on demographic and policy changes serves to highlight the fact that both are creating increasing demands for expertise in ELL reading instruction from all literacy practitioners.

THE DEMOGRAPHIC AND EDUCATIONAL POLICY CONTEXT

The most recent estimates available from the National Clearinghouse for English Language Acquisition (NCELA), recorded during the 2005–2006 school year, indicate that there are approximately 5.1 million students designated as ELLs in the United States school system. Although there was a slight increase of 3.7% in overall growth of the school-age population, there was a markedly larger increase in the number of ELLs enrolled in schools throughout the United States, with 57.2% growth. Misconceptions about this population remain, such as ELLs' length of residence within the United States. Most ELLs in elementary and secondary grades are, in fact, native born and are larger in number than those who are foreign born. Foreign-born ELLs, or first-generation Americans, only comprise 24% of all ELLs in the elementary grades, while also representing 44% of all ELLs in secondary schools (Capps et al., 2005).

Although there has been an increase in the number of immigrant families moving to parts of Middle America, there are but a few states where a majority of ELLs reside. Five states—California, Texas, New York, Florida, and Illinois—provide instruction to 68% of all elementary-age ELLs in the United States (Capps et al., 2005). ELLs tend to vary in language of choice at home. Approximately 10.9 million, or 21%, of children ages 5 to 17 speak a language other than English at home, and 5%, or 2.7 million students, speak English with difficulty (Aud et al., 2010). With an ever-increasing ELL population, it is projected that this group will comprise more than 40% of elementary and secondary students by 2030 (Thomas & Collier, 2002). Concerns about ELL student performance should therefore be well heeded. While 76% of English-proficient students achieved at or above basic reading level scores, about 30% of ELLs achieved these levels in reading achievement (NCES, 2007).

At the same time that the number of ELLs is increasing, the availability of varied pedagogical models for serving this population is decreasing, despite the fact that every study that has compared English-only and bilingual models has failed to find evidence suggesting that bilingual programs are detrimental to ELL academic learning (August & Shanahan, 2006). The passage of ballot initiatives in California, Arizona, and Massachusetts has resulted in the elimination or limited the availability of instructional models that are based on bilingual instruction. In some cases, this has also limited the availability of English as a second language (ESL) instruction for ELLs. In California for example, Proposition 227 prescribes that "children who are English learners shall be educated through sheltered English immersion during a temporary transition period not normally intended to exceed one year" (Unz & Tuchman, 1998).

The demographic trends, coupled with reports of a disappointing level of success toward closing the educational achievement gap for ELLs (August & Shanahan, 2006), accentuate the urgent need for instructional approaches that attend to the linguistic needs of ELLs. The causes of the educational achievement gap are complex, and the solutions surely do not reside exclusively in the realm of literacy education. But increasing the effectiveness of our efforts in literacy development for ELLs is an important part of the solution.

LEARNING TO READ IN A SECOND LANGUAGE

One way to gain appreciation of the challenges children encounter when learning to read a language they does not fully command is to reassess what a native English-speaking child knows about the English language when he or she begins formal instruction in reading and after at least 5 years of sustained exposure to the language. During this time, a child has acquired the ability to perceive (although not necessarily to isolate and manipulate) pretty much all the sounds of her language (Menn & Stoel-Gammon, 2000). He or she is able to recognize changes in the meanings of words in relation to changes in sound. For example, recognizing that the addition of a single sound /s/ to *cat* significantly alters its meaning. Not only does he or she understand how the phoneme /s/ works in *cats*, but also implicitly knows its function as an inflectional morpheme that when added to other words signals "more than one" (Tager-Flusberg, 2000).

At the time a child begins formal reading instruction, his or her vocabulary will consist of several thousand words and will have command over most of the grammar of her language (Tager-Flusberg, 2000). In fact, in terms of the simplest grammatical forms, the child's usage will be comparable to that of adult native speakers (Tager-Flusberg, 2000). In addition, the child will have acquired some fairly sophisticated knowledge of language pragmatics. It will be possible to understand, for example, that if mom asks whether it is time to do homework, mom is not really asking for a clock check. The difference between intended meanings and stated meanings is in some cases already apparent (Bryant, 2000).

The books the native speakers will use to learn to read have been designed with their language abilities in mind. The words that appear in the books are words that they use orally, and that others in their linguistic community use on a daily basis. The children learn that print is talk written down, and fortunately the books contain examples of how others in their world talk.

In this light, the challenges associated with learning to read in a language one does not speak or understand become more obvious. Learning to read builds on a child's capacity to communicate orally. Learning to read in a language one does not command orally can present multiple challenges for a child. A very basic example of such challenges involves recognizing what constitutes a word in the new language, something we assume most native speakers have mastered in relation to oral language when they are ready to learn to read. Yet, at the very early stages of learning, second-language learners must confront the challenge of figuring out a reliable way of recognizing boundaries for words in the new language (Saffran, Senghas, & Trueswell, 2001). Natural speech is a continuous blend of words, so word boundaries are not clearly identifiable. The pauses one hears between words are not really present in the acoustic signal. In developing their first language, children are aided by multiple linguistic and social scaffolds that gradually build their skill to recognize the boundaries for words in speech.

The theoretical and empirical evidence signaling an important role for oral language proficiency in second-language literacy development (Gottardo, 2002; Lindsey, Manis, & Bailey, 2003; Proctor, Carlo, August, & Snow, 2005), coupled with pressures for accountability in student literacy outcomes, demands that we think creatively about ways of designing reading instruction that explicitly attends to weaknesses in oral proficiency so that ELLs can benefit from the reading instruction they will receive. Properly scaffolded reading instruction can become an additional source of language input, and well-chosen print materials can, by virtue of the modality, afford opportunities to revisit, reexamine, and contrast that input in a manner that is conducive to language learning.

INSTRUCTION IN ALPHABETICS

Like all children, ELLs will benefit from opportunities to learn in an environment that is affirming of their individual and social identity and from instruction that builds upon their strengths and recognizes their instructional needs. The following sections review literature that can help inform decisions about how to adapt early reading instruction so that it builds on learners' strengths and addresses their oral language needs in relation to the development of phonological awareness and phonics knowledge. As suggested by the National Reading Panel (2000) and the NRC (Snow, Burns, & Griffin, 1998), the two skills are foundational components for learning to read in English.

Phonological Awareness

Phonological awareness is often defined as awareness that words are made of smaller units of sound that can be manipulated and changed (Moats, 2000; Snow et al., 1998). This awareness is fundamental to learning to read in languages that employ an alphabetic writing system. The ability to isolate sounds and correlate them to the orthographic system is essential for grasping the alphabetic principle and is an essential step toward developing the ability to effortlessly retrieve the meaning of printed words from the oral lexicon.

In order to learn to read in English, ELLs, like native speakers, must develop phonological awareness (PA). The review by the National Literacy Panel (NLP) (August & Shanahan, 2006) on the development of reading readiness skills among ELLs concluded that there was a great deal of variation in the level of attainment of PA among ELLs and that this variation in levels of attainment was related to factors such as age, level of second-language proficiency, language and literacy experiences, as well as degree of mastery of each language relative to each other (Lesaux & Geva, 2006). However, as noted earlier, difficulties in PA are not placing ELLs at risk for reading difficulties at a higher rate than native speakers (Lesaux & Geva, 2006). The NLP also points out that achievement in PA does not appear to function in a purely language-specific manner. Rather, the evidence suggests that PA skills developed in the native language may be instrumental to the development of second-language PA as evidenced by the fact that assessments of PA in the first language predict reading outcomes in the second language (see Lesaux & Geva, 2006, for a review). Given the variation in PA attainment among ELLs, it is important to understand the possible sources of variation. In particular, it is worth considering how differences in oral language proficiency might affect the development of PA in a second language (Roberts, 2005).

Those who study the development of PA among native speakers often point to two properties of natural speech that make it difficult for children to grasp on their own the concept that words are made of smaller units of sound (Moats, 2000). In natural speech, phonemes are unsegmented and coarticulated (Moats, 2000). That is, words are not uttered one sound at a time; instead, sounds blend into one another. In addition, phonemes are influenced by the phonemes that precede and follow them. To develop PA, children need to be able to ignore what is most salient to them in a word, namely its meaning, and create discrete units out of a speech signal that is seamless (Moats, 2000). To complicate matters further, those discrete sounds that are extracted from speech are never identical to the sounds as they occur within a word. This is because, in making the sounds discrete, one strips them of the qualities they achieve when pronounced in a coarticulated manner in natural speech (Moats, 2000). Thus when one asks a child to decide whether the sound /p/ appears in the word *plant,* one is not exactly asking the child to compare two identical entities.

Now consider an additional characteristic of speech perception—the categorical perception of phonemes—that can differentially affect second-language speakers and native speakers (Bialystok & Hakuta, 1994). Even though phonemes are articulated as a continuous acoustic signal, the perception of phonemes is categorical. A classic illustration of this exists in the acoustic feature that allows one to contrast the phonemes /b/ and /p/; namely, voice–onset–timing (VOT). These two phonemes differ in the time lapsing between the output of air on the lips and the vibration of the vocal cords. Technically speaking, /b/ fades into /p/ as VOT increases, but perceptually and thus experientially, /b/ changes to /p/ at a particular time point in VOT (Bialystok & Hakuta, 1994; Moats, 2000). The point at which this change in perception occurs varies by language. Spanish speakers perceive the switch earlier than English speakers, for example (Bialystok & Hakuta, 1994). What is relevant to the present analysis is the fact that the boundaries for the perception of phonemes are set very early in development. Moreover, the boundaries that are set in one's first language are the same that one applies when processing phonemes in a second language, at least during the initial stages of second-language development (Bialystok & Hakuta, 1994). Over time, and with exposure to the second language, the boundaries shift closer to those applied by native speakers, but they never quite correspond exactly to the boundaries of native speakers (Bialystok & Hakuta, 1994).

When applied to the previously described task of deciding whether the sound /p/ appears in *plant,* the second-language speaker is confronted with the following challenge. Just like the native speaker, he/she must compare the discrete phoneme /p/ articulated by the examiner and compare it to the coarticulated /p/ in *plant.* Unlike the native speaker, the second-language speaker is affected by the phonemic categories set by his or her first language (Brown, 1998; Escudero & Boersma, 2004; Roberts, 2005).

ELLs are capable of mastering this seemingly complicated task. How they come to master it is not fully understood, nor are the reasons why they fail to master it. One might speculate that those who succeed are aided by the metalinguistic skills—including PA skills—they have developed in their first language, as evidence suggests that systematic exposure to more than one language can in fact enhance metalinguistic abilities in bilingual children (Bialystok, 1997). In addition, one would expect that systematic instruction in PA also aids the process. Nevertheless, it is important to understand the complexity of the process in order to make instructional decisions that address differences in the rate of attainment of this skill among ELLs.

While it may appear that giving ELL students practice with sound discrimination activities may be one fruitful way to encourage development of phonemic perception abilities, two arguments are offered against doing so or at least against doing so, at the expense of opportunities for exposure to meaningful communication. The report on Preventing Reading Difficulties in Young Children (Snow et al., 1998) reviews evidence that links phonological awareness development to language proficiency among native speakers of English (see also Goswami, 2000). The report states, for example, that

> performance on phonological awareness tasks by preschoolers was highly correlated with general language ability. Moreover, it was measures of semantic and syntactic skills, rather than speech discrimination and articulation, that predicted phonological awareness differences. Correlations between metalinguistic and more basic language abilities have similarly been reported by others (e.g., Bryant, 1974; Bryant et al., 1990; Smith & Tager-Flusberg, 1982). These findings indicate that the development of phonological awareness (and other metalinguistic skills) is closely intertwined with growth in basic language proficiency during the preschool years. (p. 53)

If language proficiency differences among native speakers can impact the development of PA, it stands to reason that any investments in developing the language proficiency of ELLs could also have an effect on their ability to discriminate phonemes in the second language and, further down the line when coupled with phonological awareness instruction, on their ability to reflect upon and manipulate phonemes in English (Rolla-San Francisco, Carlo, August, & Snow, 2006).

On theoretical grounds, it is also worth noting that while phonemes are not in and of themselves a unit of meaning, they are the smallest unit of sound *that makes a difference in meaning*. The differences in meaning that are signaled by phoneme changes may provide a stronger motivation to attend to the changes in sound than might be afforded by discrimination tasks in which semantic contrasts are irrelevant.

Word Identification

In order to read with comprehension ELLs, like native speakers, must be able to recognize printed words accurately and effortlessly (Birch, 2002; Perfetti, 1992). Research on the development of word recognition among young ELLs has generated some understanding about the degree of success they experience in achieving accurate identification of printed words. In the NLP report Lesaux and Geva (2006) concluded that, as a group, second-language learners do not differ from native speakers in their attainment of the ability to accurately decode and apply grapheme–phoneme correspondences to words in print and in their spelling. However, caution in interpreting this finding is recommended because, as Lesaux and Geva point out, the prevalence of differences in the efficiency of word identification skills has not been thoroughly studied in child populations. Research on adults suggests that differences in speed of word identification can be significant (Mägiste, 1979; Ransdell & Fischler, 1987).

ELLs, like their native-speaking peers, need to develop what Perfetti (1992) refers to as impenetrable word recognition processes. This means that identification of the word via phonological and orthographic information occurs quickly and that it does so with little demand for attention. It also means that the outcome of this process is activation of the word's *meaning* (not just pronunciation) without reliance on contextual or other higher-order information. If one aims to develop the autonomous word reading skills displayed by fluent monolingual readers among ELL readers, one must move beyond teaching practices that restrict performance to the achievement of accurate word pronunciation. Word identification instruction must be designed to enable students to pronounce the word *and* access its meaning or meanings. In a study of Spanish speaking ELLs, Proctor et al. (2005) reported evidence suggesting that, "given adequate [second-language] decoding ability, [second-language] vocabulary knowledge is crucial for improved English reading comprehension outcomes for Spanish-speaking ELLs" (p. 246). For students to be able to access the meaning of words once they have activated the appropriate phonological codes, they need to develop a deep and broad oral vocabulary.

INSTRUCTION IN VOCABULARY AND READING COMPREHENSION

The gap in English vocabulary knowledge between ELLs and their native-speaking counterparts is wide (August, Carlo, Dressler, & Snow, 2005; Nation, 2001). A number of recent studies have provided estimates of the vocabulary achievement of English learners documenting their percentile rank performance below the 50th percentile, with a large number of studies indicating percentile ranks below 16% (Cirino, Pollard-Durodola, Foorman, Carlson, & Francis, 2007; Lanfranchi & Swanson, 2005; Manis, Lindsey, & Bailey, 2004; Proctor et al., 2005; San Francisco, Mo, Carlo, August, & Snow, 2006; Vaughn et al., 2006). Low vocabulary achievement is believed to be a major factor in the low levels of literacy attainment observed for ELLs (August & Shanahan, 2006; NCES, 2007). In addition to differences in performance from native speakers, ELLs can be expected to vary from one another in both the breadth and quality of their vocabulary knowledge (Ordonez, Carlo, Snow, & McLaughlin, 2002), depending on the richness of the English and first-language input to which they are exposed.

There is a wealth of research and theory that informs vocabulary instruction for native speakers (Beck, McKeown, & Kucan, 2002; Graves, 2005; Hiebert, 2005; Stahl & Nagy, 2006). Over the past decade, there have been several efforts to study the effectiveness of vocabulary interventions using principles and strategies gleaned from the research literature on monolinguals (Biemiller & Boote, 2006; Carlo et al., 2004; Kieffer & Lesaux, 2007; Lesaux, Kieffer, Faller, & Kelley, 2010; Pollard-Durodola, Mathes, Cardenas-Hagan, Linan-Thompson, & Vaughn, 2006; Proctor, Uccelli, Dalton, & Snow, 2009; Silverman, 2007; Snow, Lawrence, & White, 2010; Spycher, 2009; Townsend, 2009; Ziplo, Coyne, & McCoach, 2010). The results suggest that direct and systematic vocabulary instruction for ELLs can follow the principles that guide best practices in vocabulary instruction for native speakers. These research efforts have also included modifications intended to better meet the needs of ELLs. Before we describe these interventions in more detail, we highlight features that are common to several of them.

Several of the vocabulary interventions for ELLs have relied on text-based strategies where vocabulary is presented in context using read-alouds or text selections that are organized as thematic units (Biemiller & Boote, 2006; Carlo et al., 2004; Kieffer & Lesaux, 2007; Lesaux et al., 2010; Pollard-Durodola et al., 2006; Proctor et al., 2009; Silverman, 2007; Snow et al., 2010; Spycher, 2009; Ziplo et al., 2010). Also common across studies is the choice of general-purpose academic words as the target for instruction. The approaches for identifying academic words vary, but all seem to converge on words that are frequent in academic texts and that span different subjects. Fewer studies focus on instruction of basic words of the kind Beck et al. (2002) term Tier I words. These are words needed by the most emergent ELLs who need to amass a large number of basic words that are part of the vocabulary of most

5-year-old native speakers (Tran, 2006). Early and systematic introduction of these basic words is important because they are used frequently in speech and in print, and instruction of more sophisticated words builds on these more basic concepts (Beck et al., 2002).

At least four of the interventions have incorporated explicit morphological instruction to teach ELLs about word structure in an attempt to increase their knowledge of English derivational morphology and as a strategy for inferring the meaning of unknown words through analysis of word parts (Carlo et al., 2004; Kieffer & Lesaux, 2007; Lesaux et al., 2010; Proctor et al., 2009; Snow et al., 2010). Recent research points to the importance of morphological awareness in literacy development (Carlisle, 2003; Kuo & Anderson, 2006). In addition, Goodwin (2010) found that English morphological awareness made a significant and meaningful contribution to passage comprehension and reading vocabulary among ELLs when controlling for phonological recoding skills in English.

Another common feature of vocabulary interventions for ELLs involves making them aware of the resources for vocabulary learning that they already have in their first language. In some cases, this involves use of bilingual dictionaries and glossaries (Carlo et al., 2004). In others, it involves exploiting cross-language morphological relationships such as those present in cognates (Carlo et al., 2004; Keiffer & Lesaux, 2007; Lesaux et al., 2010; Proctor et al., 2009).

Cognates are words from other languages that have common etymological roots with English and hence have similar spelling and meaning in two languages. Often, cognates can also have similar-sounding pronunciations. Cognates can contain orthographic patterns that make the relationship between the words in the two languages highly transparent, as is the case with the word *doctor–doctor* in Spanish and English. Sometimes the orthographic patterns make the relationship somewhat more opaque as in *jardín–garden* or *frenesí–frenzy*. Children who can recognize these similarities in spelling and meaning and combine them with context-checking strategies can use cognate recognition strategies as sources of information about unfamiliar words they encounter in text (Garcia & Nagy, 1993; Jimenez, Garcia, & Pearson, 1996; Nagy, Garcia, Durğunoglu, & Hancin-Bhatt, 1993).

Another common feature across these interventions involves the use of visuals and other extralinguistic strategies. While it may be sufficient for native speakers to work with linguistically contextualized explanations of word meanings, ELLs may require images and other extralinguistic sources of information (such as the use of total physical response) about words in order to fully grasp their meaning.

BEST PRACTICES IN ACTION

In this section, we describe recently developed classroom-based intervention programs aimed at improving ELLs' vocabulary and reading comprehension performance through instruction that targets vocabulary development specifically and language proficiency more generally. These interventions cover a wide range of ages and methods but share many of the features reviewed above.

Silverman (2007) carried out a kindergarten vocabulary intervention to test whether research-based practices implemented across classrooms containing ELLs and English-only learners had similar effects for both groups. Specifically, ELLs and native English speakers were assessed on whether vocabulary growth and knowledge of target words taught throughout the intervention increased at similar rates. The Multidimensional Vocabulary Program was carried out over the course of 14 weeks to three mainstream English classrooms, one structured immersion classroom, and a two-way Spanish–English bilingual classroom. In this vocabulary intervention, words were introduced through rich context of authentic children's literature; clear, child-friendly definitions and explanations were given of target words; questions and prompts were presented to help children think critically about the meaning of words; examples of how words are used in other contexts were shown; opportunities were given for children to act out the meaning of words; visual aids were displayed to illustrate meanings of words; children pronounced the target words; children were guided to notice the spelling of words; words were compared and contrasted; and words were repeated and reinforced. Five to 10 words varying in difficulty were selected from storybooks read in class each week. The two weeks following every storybook reading were designated for a review of the words. Silverman found that ELLs and native English speakers improved significantly in knowledge of target words after the intervention. Although ELLs differed significantly before the intervention, they seemed to catch up to their monolingual peers in knowledge of the target words. The findings showed that ELLs can learn words from instruction as fast or faster than English-only learners, at times achieving faster rates of growth in vocabulary.

Carlo et al. (2004) focused on instructing students on 10 to 12 general-purpose academic words that were likely encountered in texts from different content areas as well as instructing students on word-learning strategies. In this quasi-experimental study lasting 15 weeks, 254 bilingual and monolingual children from nine fifth-grade classrooms in four schools in California, Virginia, and Massachusetts were the locations serving differing working-class Latino communities. One hundred forty-two of the students in the study were ELLs, and 112 were English-only monolingual students. Ninety-four of the ELLs and 75 of the monolingual students were in the treatment condition while 48 ELLs and 37 monolingual students were in comparison classrooms. Instruction took place over 4 days each week for 30 to 45 minutes per day. As a means of promoting reading comprehension and retaining the students' attention, words were selected from texts that were of interest to the learners and grade-level appropriate. The texts were also available in Spanish to facilitate ELLs when reading the same text in English. Students were provided with multiple opportunities for exposures to target words in various contexts and tasks. The intervention aimed to instruct students on depth of meaning of words, polysemy, morphological structure, cross-language structure, spelling, and pronunciation. A variety of instructional strategies were employed to instruct students on the utility of context to infer word meaning, recognize the possibility of polysemy, use a bilingual glossary, notice similarities between cognates, as well as to build on depth of word meanings. The curriculum designed for this study, which focused on the aforementioned word-learning skills, improved performance for both ELL and monolingual fifth graders at equal levels. The participants learned explicitly taught words and gained the ability to learn new words independently through incidental learning. The intervention also indicated that improvement in vocabulary and word analysis skills was associated with improvement in reading comprehension, although the gains were less robust than those found in students' vocabulary knowledge.

Townsend (2009) investigated whether interventions that have been deemed effective for elementary students would serve similar purposes in augmenting general academic vocabulary for 52 middle school ELLs in southern California. The program, described as Language Workshop, was designed to teach 60 of the most common academic words found in Coxhead's (2000) Academic Word List (AWL) throughout engaging after-school activities. Two groups were tested in three phases. While one group participated in the treatment, the other group acted as its control group, allowing for between- and within-group testing. All the words were taught through direct instruction and discussions about them as they were encountered from informational texts found in discovery book series that contain diagrams and pictures. Following the discussion around the text, students would participate in interactive games. During the Picture Puzzler exercise, students discussed how a word's meaning might relate to the picture being displayed. For instance, the word *function* would first be defined as a verb and noun, and a picture of a sponge or computer would be shown. Students would describe the function of these items. Music Puzzler enabled the students to talk about the favorite songs using target words such as *interpret, specific,* and *similar.* During the Matching Game, a set of cards was created for every target word. A word, definition, or sentence would be displayed on the card. Students with the word card would search for those students who held the matching definition or sentence. The intervention provided different opportunities for students to process words in different contexts. Other activities that followed the discussion include Pictionades, Action Jeopardy! and the Dice Game. Throughout these activities, ELLs were encouraged to personalize the meanings of words through different activities. Visual supports were provided or generated by the students themselves. Participants in the after-school program showed more growth than in the controlled condition. The results also showed that the ELLs' general vocabulary knowledge was a significant predictor of their academic word knowledge. Language skills in English mediated the levels of words learned throughout the intervention. Consequently, students with higher levels of English proficiency learned academic words at a faster rate than those whose language proficiency did not meet a certain level of English proficiency.

Snow et al. (2010) investigated whether implementation of the Word Generation program (*wordgeneration.org*) would improve scores of language-minority and monolingual English students' on state-mandated standardized assessments. Five schools where Word Generation was implemented with 697 students were compared to three schools that did not receive the treatment. The treatment group was composed of three middle schools and two K–8 schools, totaling 697 students, which included only grades 6–8, all located in high-poverty areas in Boston. The comparison schools, from which 319 students participated, had higher standardized test scores and were somewhat less disadvantaged than those in the treatment group. All the schools in the study had a very high proportion of students coming from second-language homes. The Word Generation program had a duration of 24 weeks discussing grade-level text that presented five all-purpose academic words and activities relating to math, science, and social studies. Initially, teachers along with the students read a short text containing five target words. The text presented students with a controversial issue that would have them take a stance. Following the reading, guided questions were discussed in order to aid comprehension. The target words would be further elaborated by presenting student-friendly definitions. Throughout the week, additional activities took place in which the same academic words were once again encountered. Math teachers assigned no more than two problems surrounding the issue previously discussed. In the science lesson, students came across the same issue with a text. A debate was organized around the controversial issue during social studies. At the end of the school week, students wrote an essay arguing their stance about the issue. In the end, students participating in the Word Generation program learned more of the target words than those students in schools that had performed better at the outset. The language-minority students showed more improvement than monolingual English students on the curriculum-specific assessments, which have a predictive value on how they would fare on the statewide assessments.

Lesaux et al. (2010) examined the effects of a vocabulary intervention program developed for use in English instruction classrooms that enroll a high proportion of ELLs. In this quasi-experimental mixed-methods study, Lesaux et al. (2010) implemented an academic vocabulary program, entitled Academic Language Instruction for All Students (ALIAS), that strove to bolster vocabulary and reading comprehension skills amongst urban middle school students. The main focus of this study was to incrementally build up students' word knowledge based around authentic informational text that middle school students would encounter. The researchers also investigated the program's ease of implementation in order to assess teachers' perspectives on its usefulness and applicability in different mainstream classrooms. Carried out over 18 weeks in 21 classes of seven low-performing middle schools, the intervention consisted of eight 2-week units, an 8-day lesson cycle, and two 1-week review cycles. The daily lessons instructing 476 sixth-grade students (346 ELLs and 130 native English speakers) went on for 45 minutes, delivered over 4 days per week in the various mainstream classrooms, in which language-minority students were predominant. The lessons were based on informational text found in *Time for Kids* magazines, from which eight to nine high-utility academic words were selected. As a means of teaching academic words that are frequent yet difficult as a result of their abstract nature, words were selected based on their presence in the AWL. A total of 72 words were taught by the end of the program. Instructors took on a procedural approach that is different than the vocabulary instruction that traditionally took place in the participating classrooms. The eight control classrooms proceeded to teach words as they had previously done—introducing a list of words, requiring students to memorize definitions, and having them perform basic activities using the words. The ALIAS program in the 13 treatment classrooms provided lessons that would present students with grade-level informational text around topics that would keep the students engaged. Students did not encounter the entire group of target words in one day's lesson to ensure the instruction was meaningful and authentic. In each unit lasting 8 days, students engaged in whole-group, small-group, and independent activities, also presenting the students with opportunities to encounter and employ the words through listening, speaking, reading, and writing. Students began the unit by first being exposed to the word through text; then activating prior knowledge of the word; completing work related to the word's meaning in context; analyzing the morphology of different forms of the word; and finally using the word in their own writing. The 1-week review units took place in the first half and at the end of the program as a way to revisit vocabulary that remained unclear to the students in the units preceding the review sessions. At this time, instructors had opportunities to reteach target words, morphological skills, and provide them with a chance to engage in cooperative games focusing on the target vocabulary. In this study, significant program effects were found on researcher-developed vocabulary measures targeting knowledge of the words taught, knowledge of word meanings in context, and morphological skills. There were marginally significant effects on students' performance on standardized measures of word knowledge and reading comprehension. No effects were present on a measure of students' performance on vocabulary knowledge. The effects were similar for both language-minority students and their native-English peers. Due to the small differences across treatment and control classrooms and the positive program effects after the intervention, the present study seems to provide potential benefits to mainstream urban classrooms with large numbers in language-minority students and monolingual English speakers. Language-minority students achieved similar gains to their English-speaking peers; however, they remained at a disadvantage.

Additional research would help further understanding of how middle school language-minority students could attain equivalent levels of achievement already reached by native-English speakers through multifaceted vocabulary instruction.

SAMPLE ACTIVITIES

Below we describe two activities that illustrate the use of morphology and cognate awareness instruction used with ELLs.

Morphology

One of the recommendations of Kieffer and Lesaux (2007) is to teach derivational morphology explicitly and in context. One of their suggested activities involves teaching students about how words are transformed by the addition of affixes. Figure 5.1 is an example of a word chart created by Kieffer and Lesaux (2007). They recommend guiding students through the process of adding word forms and discussing meaning changes across word class. We would add that such charts can also be modified to attend to the language needs of less proficient ELLs who may need assistance in understanding inflections. The nouns and verbs on this chart can further be analyzed in relation to number and tense, respectively.

Cognate Awareness Instruction

The activity illustrated in Figure 5.2 is intended for ELLs who are readers and speakers of Spanish. It formed part of a curriculum developed to increase ELLs' awareness of cognates in Spanish and English. The effectiveness of this curriculum is being tested in a joint study by researchers at the Center for

Noun	Adjective	Verb	Adverb
economy	economical	economize	economically
analysis	analytic	analyze	analytically
subsidy	subsidiary	subsidize	subsidiarily
stimulus	poststimulus	stimulate	stimulatingly
recovery	recoverable	recover	irrecoverably
profitiability	profitable	profit	profitably

FIGURE 5.1. Sample completed word form chart. Based on Kieffer and Lesaux (2007).

Show students the following Likert Scale on the overhead. Explain that some of the cognates sound more alike than others. On the overhead projector, direct students to identify how alike or different the sets of cognates sound on a scale of 1 to 4. There are no right or wrong answers.

edifice/edificio

Sounds completely different	Sounds slightly different	Sounds similar	Sounds exactly alike
1	2	3	4

mass/masa

Sounds completely different	Sounds slightly different	Sounds similar	Sounds exactly alike
1	2	3	4

FIGURE 5.2. Identification of sound differences.

Applied Linguistics and the University of Miami.[1] This particular activity was designed to increase learners' awareness of the variation in degree of orthographic and phonological similarity in Spanish–English cognates. It aims to encourage learners to look deeply into an English word's orthography to find similarities to words they may know in Spanish.

REFLECTIONS AND FUTURE DIRECTIONS FOR COMPREHENSIVE LITERACY INSTRUCTION

In recent years, we have witnessed the enormous effort involved in trying to ensure that every primary-grade teacher develops the knowledge, skills, and dispositions that are required to provide excellent reading instruction to young children. For these efforts to benefit ELLs, they must include appropriate attention to the role of language in the development of reading.

Teaching ELLs to read in English also requires a commitment to teaching English. To the extent that efforts toward preparing reading teachers have ignored the teaching of language, they have failed to address one of the greatest challenges ELLs face in becoming highly skilled readers of English. The NLP review (Lesaux & Geva, 2006) suggests that ELLs catch up to their native speaking peers on low-level components of the reading process such as PA and accuracy of word reading. The NLP review also suggests that ELLs

[1]Transfer of Reading Skills in Bilingual Children. Research grant awarded by the National Institute of Child Health and Human Development and the Institute for Educational Sciences to Diane August, Principal Investigator, Center for Applied Linguistics, as part of the program project entitled Acquiring Literacy in English Cross-linguistic, Intralinguistic, and Developmental Factors.

don't catch up to their native speaking peers on aspects of text processing that make demands on syntactic and semantic language processes.

Closing the gap in reading comprehension of ELLs does not require abandoning the progress that has been achieved in improving the teaching of foundational reading skills to ELLs. Rather, it requires that the teaching of foundational skills like PA and word identification be linked to an equally comprehensive, explicit, and systematic model for teaching oral English to ELLs.

CONCLUDING COMMENTS

Throughout this chapter, research and theory on first-language reading development has been combined with research and theory on second-language learning to stress the importance of attending to the language–literacy link in designing reading instruction for ELLs. Research and theory speak directly to the involvement of oral language proficiency in the development of skills considered to be foundational to reading even among children who speak English natively. The language needs of ELLs cannot be comprehensively addressed through reading instruction alone. However, it is possible to capitalize on the many opportunities for language development that present themselves in the context of the reading lesson. The success of early reading instruction with native speakers of English depends in part on helping children establish a bridge between the orthography they need to learn and the language they already know. A step toward greater success in ELL reading instruction requires awareness of the fact that ELLs need to be supported as they build a bridge between the orthography they need to learn and a language they are still learning.

ENGAGEMENT ACTIVITIES

1. Find pictures depicting places or activities that one encounters routinely at home and places and activities one encounters routinely at school or in the greater community. Assess your ELL students by asking them to point to an object you name. Compare their identification of items (receptive vocabulary) to their production of the names of items you point to (productive vocabulary). Are there differences in their knowledge of English labels for the "at-home" words and the "out-of-home" words? If so, what might explain such differences?
2. Find a piece of expository text and a narrative text of roughly the same difficulty. Circle words that you believe would be most

challenging to Spanish-speaking ELLs. Look them up in a Spanish–English dictionary and note how many of the words in each text are cognates to Spanish. Are there differences in the prevalence of cognates across the two genres? If so, what might explain such differences?

RESOURCES FOR FURTHER LEARNING

wordgeneration.org—Strategic Education Research Partnership (SERP) website for word generation.

Nash, R. (1997). *NTC's dictionary of Spanish cognates thematically organized.* Chicago: NTC Publishing Group.—Spanish–English cognate dictionary.

REFERENCES

Aud, S., Hussar, W., Planty, M., Snyder, T., Blanco, K., Fox, M., et al. (2010). *The condition of education 2010* (NCES Publication No. 2010-028). Washington, DC: U.S. Department of Education.

August, S., Carlo, M., Dressler, C., & Snow, C. (2005). The critical role of vocabulary development for English language learners. *Learning Disabilities Research and Practice, 20*(1), 50–57.

August, D., & Shanahan, T. (2006). *Developing literacy in second-language learners: report of the National Literacy Panel on Language Minority Children and Youth.* Mahwah, NJ: Erlbaum.

Beck, I. L., McKeown, M. G., & Kucan, L. (2002). *Bringing words to life: Robust vocabulary instruction.* New York: Guilford Press.

Bialystok, E. (1997). Effects of bilingualism and biliteracy on children's emerging concepts of print. *Developmental Psychology, 33,* 429–440.

Bialystok, E., & Hakuta, K. (1994). *In other words: The science and psychology of second language acquisition.* New York: Basic Books.

Biemiller, A., & Boote, C. (2006). An effective method for building meaning vocabulary in primary grades. *Journal of Educational Psychology, 98*(1), 44–62.

Birch, B. (2002). *English L2 reading: Getting to the bottom.* Hillsdale, NJ: Erlbaum.

Brown, C. M. (1998). L2 reading: An update on relevant L1 research. *Foreign Language Annals, 31,* 191–202.

Bryant, J. B. (2000). Language in social contexts: Communicative competence in the preschool years. In J. B. Gleason (Ed.), *The development of language* (5th ed.). Needham Heights, MA: Allyn & Bacon.

Capps, R., Fix, M. E., Murray, J., Ost, J., Passel, J. S., & Herwantoro, S. (2005). *The new demography of America's schools: Immigration and the No Child Left Behind Act.* Retrieved May 1, 2006, from the National Clearinghouse for English Language Acquisition and Language Instruction Educational Programs, *www.ncela.gwu.edu/stats/2_nation.htm.*

Carlisle, J. F. (2003). Morphology matters in learning to read: A commentary. *Reading Psychology, 24,* 291–332.

Carlo, M., August, D., McLaughlin, B., Snow, C. E., Dressier, C., Lippman, D. N., et al. (2004). Closing the gap: Addressing the vocabulary needs of English-language learners in bilingual and mainstream classrooms. *Reading Research Quarterly, 39,* 188–215.

Cirino, P. T., Pollard-Durodola, S. D., Foorman, B., Carlson, C. D., & Francis, D. J. (2007). Teacher characteristics and language in bilingual kindergarteners and their relation to student outcomes. *Elementary School Journal, 107*(4), 341–364.

Coxhead, A. (2000). A new academic word list. *TESOL Quarterly, 34*(2), 213–238.

Escudero, P., & Boersma, P. (2004). Bridging the gap between L2 speech perception research and phonological theory. *Studies in Second Language Acquisition, 26,* 551–585.

Garcia, G. E., & Nagy, W. E. (1993). Latino students' concept of cognates. In D. J. Leu & C. K. Kinzer (Eds.), *Examining central issues in literacy research, theory, and practice.* Chicago: National Reading Conference.

Goodwin, A. (2010). *Does meaning matter for reading achievement? Untangling the role of phonological recoding and morphological awareness in predicting word decoding, reading vocabulary, and reading comprehension achievement for Spanish-speaking English language learners.* (Doctoral dissertation). Retrieved January 12, 2010, from *ProQuest* (3424784).

Goswami, U. (2000). Phonological and lexical processes. In M. Kamil, P. Mosenthal, P. D. Pearson, & R. Barr (Eds.), *Handbook of reading research, Vol. III* (pp. 251–267). Mahwah, NJ: Erlbaum.

Gottardo, A. (2002). The relationship between language and reading skills in bilingual Spanish–English speakers. *Topics in Language Disorders, 22*(5), 46–70.

Graves, M. F. (2005). The vocabulary book: Learning and instruction. New York: Teachers College Press.

Harper, C., & de Jong, E (2004). Misconceptions about teaching English-language learners. *Journal of Adolescent and Adult Literacy, 48*(2), 152–162.

Hiebert, E. (2005). In pursuit of an effective, efficient vocabulary curriculum for elementary students. In E. H. Hiebert & M. Kamil (Eds.), *Teaching and learning vocabulary: Bringing research to practice* (pp. 243–263). Mahwah, NJ: Erlbaum.

Jimenez, R., Garcia, G. E., & Pearson, P. D. (1996). The reading strategies of bilingual Latina/o students who are successful English readers: Opportunities and obstacles. *Reading Research Quarterly, 31,* 90–112.

Kieffer, M. J., & Lesaux, N. K. (2007). Breaking down words to build meaning: Morphology, vocabulary, and reading comprehension in the urban classroom. *The Reading Teacher, 61*(2), 134–144.

Kuo, L.-J., & Anderson, R. C. (2006). Morphological awareness and learning to read: A cross-language perspective. *Educational Psychologist, 41,* 161–180.

Lanfranchi, S., & Swanson, H. L. (2005). Short-term memory and working memory in children as a function of language-specific knowledge in English and Spanish. *Learning and Individual Differences, 15,* 299–319.

Lesaux, N., & Geva, E. (2006). Synthesis: Development of literacy in language-minority students. In D. August & T. Shanahan (Eds.), *Developing literacy in second-language learners: Report of the national literacy panel on language-minority children and youth.* Mahwah, NJ: Erlbaum.

Lesaux, N. K., Kieffer, M. J., Faller, S. E., & Kelley, J. G. (2010). The effectiveness and ease of implementation of an academic vocabulary intervention for linguistically diverse students in urban middle schools. *Reading Research Quarterly, 45*(2), 196–228.

Lindsey, K., Manis, F., & Bailey, C. (2003). Prediction of first-grade reading in Spanish-speaking English-language learners. *Journal of Educational Psychology, 95*(3), 482–94.

Mägiste, E. (1979). The competing language systems of the multilingual: A developmental study of decoding and encoding processes. *Journal of Verbal Learning and Verbal Behavior, 18,* 79–89.

Manis, F. R., Lindsey, K. A., & Bailey, C. E. (2004). Development of reading in grades K–2 in Spanish-speaking English-language learners. *Learning Disabilities Research and Practice, 19,* 214–224.

Menn, L., & Stoel-Gammon, C. (2000). Phonological development: Learning sounds and sound patterns. In J. B. Gleason (Ed.), *The development of language* (5th ed.). Needham Heights, MA: Allyn & Bacon.

Moats, L. C. (2000). *Speech to print: Language essentials for teachers,* Baltimore: Brookes.

Nagy, W. E., Garcia, G. E., Durğunoglu, A., & Hancin-Bhatt, B. (1993). Spanish–English bilingual students' use of cognates in English reading. *Journal of Reading Behavior, 25,* 241–259.

Nakamoto, J., Lindsey, K. A., & Manis, F. R. (2007). A longitudinal analysis of English language learners' word decoding and reading comprehension. *Reading and Writing, 20,* 691–719.

Nation, I. S. P. (2001). *Learning vocabulary in another language.* Cambridge, UK: Cambridge University Press.

National Center for Education Statistics. (2007). *National Assessment of Educational Progress (NAEP), 2007 reading assessment.* Washington, DC: Author. Retrieved July 18, 2010, from *nces.ed.gov/nationsreportcard/nde/.*

National Clearinghouse for English Language Acquisition and Language Instruction Educational Programs. (2005–2006). *National and regional numbers and statistics.* Retrieved May 1, 2006, from *www.ncela.gwu.edu/stats/2_nation.htm.*

National Reading Panel. (2000). *Teaching children to read: An evidence-based assessment of the scientific research literature on reading and its implications for reading instruction* [online]. Available at *www.nichd.nih.gov/publications/nrp/report.cfm.*

Ordonez, C. L., Carlo, M. S., Snow, C. E., & McLaughlin, B. (2002). Depth and breadth of vocabulary in two languages: Which vocabulary skills transfer? *Journal of Educational Psychology, 94*(4), 719–728.

Perfetti, C. (1992). The representation problem in reading acquisition. In P. Gough, L. Ehri, & R. Treiman (Eds.), *Reading acquisition* (pp. 145–174). Hillsdale, NJ: Erlbaum.

Pollard-Durodola, S. D., Mathes, P., Cardenas-Hagan, E., Linan-Thompson, S., & Vaughn, S. (2006). The role of oracy in developing comprehension in Spanish-speaking English language learners. *Topics in Learning Disorders, 26*(4), 362–381.

Proctor, C. P., Carlo, M. S., August, D., & Snow, C. E. (2005). Native Spanish-speaking children reading in English: Toward a model of comprehension. *Journal of Educational Psychology, 97,* 246–256.

Proctor, C. P., Uccelli, P., Dalton, B., & Snow, C. E. (2009). Understanding depth of vocabulary online with bilingual and monolingual children. *Reading and Writing Quarterly, 25*, 311–333.

Ransdell, S. E., & Fischler, I. (1987). Memory in a monolingual mode: When are bilinguals at a disadvantage? *Journal of Memory and Language, 26*, 392–405.

Roberts, T. A. (2005). Articulation accuracy and vocabulary size contributions to phonemic awareness and word reading in English language learners. *Journal of Educational Psychology, 97*(4), 601–616.

Rolla-San Francisco, A., Carlo, M., August, D., & Snow, C. (2006). The role of language of literacy instruction and vocabulary in the English phonological awareness of Spanish–English bilingual children. *Applied Psycholinguistics, 27*(2), 229–246.

Saffran, J. R., Senghas, A., & Trueswell, J. C. (2001). The acquisition of language by children. *Proceedings of the National Academy of Sciences, 98*(23), 12874–12875.

San Francisco, A. R., Mo, E., Carlo, M., August, D., & Snow, C. (2006). The influences of language of literacy instruction and vocabulary on the spelling of Spanish–English bilinguals. *Reading and Writing, 19*(6), 627–642.

Silverman, R. D. (2007). Vocabulary development of English-language and English-only learners in kindergarten. *The Elementary School Journal, 107*(4), 365–383.

Snow, C., Burns, S., & Griffin, P. (1998). *Preventing reading difficulties in young children.* Washington, DC: National Academy Press.

Snow, C. E., Lawrence, J. F., & White, C. (2010). *Generating knowledge of academic language among urban middle school students.* SREE Conference Abstract.

Spycher, P. (2009). Learning academic language through science in two linguistically diverse classes. *The Elementary School Journal, 109*(4), 359–379.

Stahl, S., & Nagy, W. E. (2006). *Teaching word meanings.* Mahwah, NJ: Erlbaum.

Tager-Flusberg, H. (2000). Putting words together: Morphology and syntax in the preschool years. In J. B. Gleason (Ed.), *The development of language* (5th ed.). Needham Heights, MA: Allyn & Bacon.

Thomas, W., & Collier, V. (2002). *A national study of school effectiveness for language minority students' long-term academic achievement.* Santa Cruz, CA, and Washington, DC: Center for Research on Education, Diversity, and Excellence.

Townsend, D. (2009). Building academic vocabulary in after-school settings: Games for growth with middle school English-language learners. *Journal of Adolescent and Adult Literacy, 53*(3), 242–251.

Tran, A. (2006). An approach to basic vocabulary development for English-language learners. *Reacting Improvement, 43*(3), 157–162.

Unz, R. K., & Tuchman, G. M. (1998). *Proposition 227: English language education for children in public schools.* Retrieved May 1, 2006, from James Crawford's Language Policy Web Site and Emporium, *www.humnet.ucla.edu/humnet/linguistics/people/grads/macswan/unztext*.htm.

Vaughn, S., Mathes, P., Linan-Thompson, S., Cirino, P., Carlson, C., Pollard-Durodola, S., et al. (2006). Effectiveness of an English intervention for first-grade English language learners at risk for reading problems. *The Elementary School Journal, 107*(2), 153–180.

Ziplo, R. P., Coyne, M. D., & McCoach, B. (2010). Enhancing vocabulary intervention for kindergarten students: Strategic integration of semantically related and embedded word review. *Remedial and Special Education, 20*(10), 1–13.

CHAPTER 6

Best Practices in Adolescent Literacy Instruction

Donna Ogle
Laura Lang

This chapter will:

- Describe the challenges of providing literacy instruction to adolescent readers in middle and high schools.
- Explain the importance of schoolwide approaches to reading development.
- Outline key components of reading instruction.
- Provide supporting research that informs the focus on these components.
- Share an example from a ninth-grade high school campus that has established a schoolwide literacy committee.
- Include resources for reading instruction.
- Suggest ways readers can apply some of these ideas in their own schools.

The challenges of helping middle and secondary students develop the reading and thinking skills and strategies they need are significant and multifaceted. Reading permeates the curriculum; however, content-focused teachers generally don't feel responsible for developing the sophisticated reading strategies that students need to be successful. At upper levels there is no common pattern for instruction in content literacy. Schools struggle to find engaging and effective methods to build students' competence with the different skills and strategies they need to make sense of texts in science, mathematics, social studies, practical arts, and literature (Moje, 2010; Snow, Griffin, & Burns, 2005).

Most of the texts students need to read are expository and not necessarily user-friendly or "considerate." These informational texts and reports can be organized in a variety of ways, and the content-specific vocabulary is critical to their meaning. In addition to its own discourse, each discipline also offers its own unique way of representing information to readers. As a result, students need to become flexible in developing strategies for engaging with varying text and content demands (Jetton & Alexander, 2004; Moje, 2007; Shanahan, 2009). They need to read primary-source documents, scientific reports, visual displays and charts, and mathematical representations. They also need to learn to analyze pieces of literature, evaluate the accuracy of information, determine authors' points of view, and use multiple sources in their inquiry and research.

Reading and learning from different types of texts is complicated by the fact that most students have not received much instruction in reading and learning with informational texts and textbooks in upper elementary school (Pressley, Wharton-McDonald, Hampson, & Echevarria, 1998). Therefore, content teachers with little experience in teaching reading must provide this instruction as they teach content. The reality is that content-area teachers have been reluctant to incorporate reading instruction into their teaching. Despite preservice preparation in literacy strategies, most studies have shown that young teachers do not maintain their attention to literacy teaching (Bean, 1997; Conley, 2005; Sturtevant, 1996). Therefore, both students and teachers often lack requisite confidence and commitment.

Complicating the situation is the increasingly wide range of student interests and competencies. Many are good readers; however, they may spend most of their time online pursuing particular interests. For teachers, even within one class the range of knowledge, interests, confidence, and abilities is often great. Middle and secondary teachers are also challenged by adolescents who often appear disinterested in the demands of the content-area curriculum. Issues of motivation and perseverance in learning are significant at the upper levels (Cooper, 2005; Guthrie, Alao, & Rinehart, 1997; Miller & Faircloth, 2009; Reed, Schallert, Beth, & Woodruff, 2004).

What can middle and high schools do? What approaches are being implemented successfully? This chapter takes the perspective that continued literacy development for adolescents requires the cooperative efforts of whole-school teams of teachers and administrators. Literacy instruction needs to occur across the school (Carnegie Council on Advancing Adolescent Literacy, 2010; Irvin, Meltzer, Mickler, Phillips, & Dean, 2009). Students requiring particular support should also have those opportunities provided in literacy labs or added reading courses. However, while these courses are an important component of a school-wide literacy program, they are not sufficient in and of themselves. In addition to basic literacy development, students also need to understand that each content area places its own literacy demands on readers and writers. Each content area has its own discourse and incorporates different types of texts and modes of writing (Fang & Schleppegrell, 2010).

These texts place unique demands on the reader. For example, in order to be successful in a laboratory science course students must be able to read and follow steps in a laboratory experiment, and they also must know the difference between writing detailed observation notes and conclusions/summary statements. In a social studies class, students must be able to read primary source documents with particular attention to the author's point of view and inherent biases. They also need to be able to craft analyses of issues that emerge within the course and argue their own point of view. Since each content area has its own types of texts and resource materials, students need and deserve guidance in knowing how to use them successfully. Therefore, coordinated efforts across school departments are needed to support students' literacy development (Carnegie Council on Advancing Adolescent Literacy, 2010; Santa, Havens, & Maycumber, 2005). One of the roles of the literacy coach is to identify common strategies and approaches that can be used by all content areas, but they also need to identify subject-specific strategies that can support a more sophisticated approach to reading and learning.

This chapter begins by describing key components of successful reading instruction in middle and secondary schools. The information is grounded in school-based projects, both our own and those described in the literature. This section is followed by examples from high schools and middle schools where teachers work together on campus literacy teams to enhance their effectiveness in promoting thoughtful literacy. The chapter concludes with a section describing a new energy that is emerging for adolescent literacy research.

For those readers who are reading teachers or coaches in middle and high schools, we hope this chapter provides support for your goals as part of a team in a school. We believe that reading teachers working alone are not likely to be highly effective. Literacy needs to be conceived of as a schoolwide commitment, and particular attention must be given to informational, multisource, and multimodal literacy development.

EVIDENCE-BASED BEST PRACTICES: HOW SCHOOLS ARE ABLE TO CREATE THIS SCHOOLWIDE MODEL OF LITERACY

This section describes five keys to successful adolescent literacy programs. The essential foundation is that teachers together build a knowledge base about the complex and varied strategies readers need to be successful with challenging texts, the kinds that teachers regularly assign but too seldom scaffold for students. From this common understanding, teachers can build frameworks that help them identify good teaching strategies or activities that lead to student independence in strategy use. A third key is involving students in understanding the active nature of reading and evaluating their own reading progress. This metacognitive control and monitoring is a hallmark of maturing readers. For students to succeed it is also important that they have texts available that are within their instructional range as readers. Providing a range of texts with varied text features is essential in helping students engage with content. Finally, utilizing the energy and motivation that come from students learning together, with and from their peers, is important.

Building Common Understanding of the Reading Process

Teachers need to know what good reading entails. This is the first step. Many middle and secondary teachers initially avoid thinking about reading, considering it a primary-level set of decoding tasks. In fact, the national focus on beginning reading has contributed to this misperception, as if once children master foundational reading skills, no more attention to literacy is required. To raise secondary-content teachers' awareness of the complexity of reading, secondary staff development efforts now often begin by involving teachers in reading difficult, unfamiliar expository texts. This lets them experience reading as their students do—as novices in content. By modeling and thinking aloud about their own reading processes during such experiences, teachers can better identify the supports needed to help their students develop thoughtful reading in difficult materials.

From these experiences, teachers can build a language to talk about the kinds of strategies and "moves" good readers utilize as they engage with informative and technical texts. When teachers reflect on what they do to make sense of the text (or when an activity is done with a text on an overhead and group thinking aloud), they generate a list of mental activities, such as predicting, inferring, questioning, visualizing, rereading and revising, problem solving, and summarizing. This can be a foundation for further discussion of what is involved in reading, and it enables teachers to model how their strategy use differs when they approach different types of texts, such as lab reports, field notes, websites, or primary-source documents. A great deal is known about the basic processes needed for readers to make sense of individual texts. Studies of mature readers engaged in thinking aloud while reading have been very helpful in identifying how readers actively construct meaning and monitor their engagement with texts before, during, and after reading. From their review of more than 40 studies involving readers thinking aloud, Pressley and Afflerbach (1995) concluded that mature readers use a variety of processes flexibly as they read, including being aware of their purpose, previewing the material, reading selectively, connecting ideas to their prior knowledge, revisiting and revising ideas, interpreting and evaluating the text, and thinking about how to apply ideas and information.

Comparing the types of reading needed for various content materials can help teachers build their understanding that the term *reading* is a broad one that encompasses many different kinds of engagement with texts. In some of our school-based projects (Ogle, Newman, & Spirou, 2005), these reflections have led teachers to focus on visual literacy and strategies to help students use their visual skills in learning. This is especially important, given the variety of types of both print and electronic texts that students are reading both in and out of school. Issues of reading multiple sources and thinking deeply about authors' perspectives and purposes are also the subject of much discussion.

Creating middle and high school teams of teachers who work together for literacy goals has been shown to be effective (Carnegie Council on Advancing Adolescent Literacy, 2010; Irvin, Meltzer, Dean, & Mickler, 2010).Our own work within schools in Chicago and Madison, Wisconsin, has involved interdisciplinary literacy teams focused on improving academic literacy and students' strategic development. Donna Ogle has worked with these teams in several capacities, beginning with a Goals 2000 Project (Ogle & Hunter, 2000), a Middle-Level Literacy Project, and most recently in the Chicago Striving Readers Research Grant and the Transitional Adolescent Literacy Project (TALL)(Kallemeyn, Schiazza, Ogle, McKnight, & Livingston, 2010). In addition, Laura Lang's facilitation of literacy teams in suburban Chicago and in Madison also confirms the importance of schoolwide reflective collaborations. In each of these collaborations, we have spent time addressing the variety of texts that students are expected to use.

Creating a Framework for Teaching and Student Strategy Control

Translating the information about reading into ways teachers can work together to provide instructional support for students and monitor their reading is important. Adolescent readers who move from teacher to teacher during the day must know how to successfully negotiate a variety of school literacy tasks. Too often, students do not internalize the strategies or routines teachers use, and they fail to maintain an active approach to learning across their content subjects. When teachers work together in establishing particular strategies and shared vocabulary for those strategies, more students develop the habits of strategic reading and learning (Ogle & Hunter, 2000; Sailors, 2009).

Using a framework that describes the reading process as occurring before, during, and after reading texts provides a clear way for teachers to think of their role in modeling and encouraging active reading. Students need to learn to approach texts actively, thinking about their purposes for reading, surveying the organization and presentation of content, and activating what they already know. Then, as they read, they monitor their comprehension, connect ideas, consider how the text is organized, and discern the author's point of view. After reading, it is important to consolidate and connect ideas and critically assess the author's argument and relation to other texts. Teachers need to provide and model instructional activities that build their students' active reading behaviors. Table 6.1 provides a framework through which teachers can think about the processes involved in reading, both from the perspective of how they can model important strategic behaviors and how they can help students transfer the modeled activity into independent reading and learning strategies.

TABLE 6.1. Reading and Learning Processes

Learning process	Teaching activities	Student applications
Anticipation		
Preview text	• Text preview guide; textbook feature analysis • Determine text frame • THIEVES preview • PLAN graphic	• Survey text • Identify external features and graphic displays • Identify internal organization • Create a PLAN outline
Activate knowledge	• Anticipation guide • Rate your knowledge • K-W-L+ • Concept sort	• Preview text questions • Reflect on information in graphics • Brainstorm ideas • Identify key terms and make a vocabulary list
Focus interest and set purpose	• Read a timely article or show a short video clip to help students connect to topic • Guide thinking with K-W-L+ • Create a group PLAN • Explanation of lesson goals and rubric for group evaluation; connect to standards	• Ask and think, "What's important to me in this lesson?" • Create a list of questions • Mark text sections by familiarity • Read an easier article or book to help connect to other experiences and readings
Building knowledge		
Construct meaning	• Model thinking along with a short introductory text piece • Create a group semantic map • Use a reading–thinking guide • Model INSERT or Cornell notemaking • Model paired reading and questioning • Demonstrate mind mapping	• Read with pencil in hand and make INSERT or Cornell notes • Visualize ideas; mind map • Add information to PLAN graphic organizer • Summarize sections with a partner
Clarify ideas	• Model INSERT notemaking • Model questioning the author • Lead group discussions around confusions and questions of students	• Make notes and connect ideas • Question the author • Reread text sections; graphic displays • Read additional sources • Monitor confusions with notes in text

(cont.)

TABLE 6.1. *(cont.)*

Learning process	Teaching activities	Student applications
Consolidate learning		
Construct meaning	• Model GRASP; create group summary of key ideas • Complete PLAN graphic • Use point of view guide to discuss text • Use Predicting/Reflecting ABCs Chart	• Use Cornell notes and write summary • Complete PLAN notations • Review mind map and extend
Consolidate ideas and make connections	• Use Discussion Web to guide reflections • Revisit K-W-L+ chart and create model synthesis of known and new information • Provide a guide for student writing using RAFT	• Use mnemonics for basic facts • Make notes on personal connections • Create synthesis of learning with KWL+ • Go online and extend ideas • Create a multimedia summary
Assess achievement of goals	• Revisit PLAN graphics and discuss any remaining questions and uncertainties • Return to standards or objectives for lesson and use rubric for group reflection	• Evaluate success in meeting personal and class goals • Compare entry knowledge to learning; clarify misconceptions • Use the class rubric to monitor own learning

Making this connection between teacher-led reading activities and students' appropriation of the important strategies when reading either on their own or in small groups is a critical link that often is overlooked. Conley (2009), in his recent review of comprehension in content areas criticizes both methods textbooks and research reviews for failing to make this connection. He laments that "The research reviews for content-area literacy and then adolescent literacy do not improve upon this picture [from methods textbooks], preferring to treat teaching activity and the development of comprehension strategies as distinct activities" (p. 536). We agree that the strategies recommended for teachers should serve as the model for students' reading and that the connections need to be made explicit to students.

It is important to think about the variety of instructional tools teachers can use to help students make sense of individual texts and about what teachers do to empower students to take control of their own reading. The focus needs to be on ways to turn control of reading over to students. Therefore, teaching activities and strategies are best considered in light of how they can further both students' understanding of active reading and their independent use of strategies.

Teachers may use a graphic organizer, for example, to help students understand the underlying structure of a difficult piece of text. The example in Figure 6.1 is a graphic organizer that was developed to help students make their way through James Madison's *The Federalist Papers, No. 10.* Students who use this will be better able to understand the argument Madison makes in this essay. These difficult readings can be found in every content area. In an elective English course called Introduction to Mass Media, a teacher in Madison, Wisconsin, wanted his students to critique an author's contention that our minds have been "polluted" by modern media. However, the text itself had been a challenge for many students in prior years. As we worked together to plan this lesson, we (L. L. and the teacher) realized that the difficulty stemmed partly from an extended analogy that the author drew between the pollution of the natural environment and the media's pollution of what he

TEXT ANALYSIS FRAME
The Federalist Papers, No. 10

Major argument:

The union needs to control the violence of faction . . .

First option:	Second option:
Remove the causes by	Control the effects by
1.	1.
results are . . .	
2.	2.
results are . . .	

Conclusion:

Advantage of a republic over a democracy and large over small republic because . . .

FIGURE 6.1. Text structure analysis of *The Federalist Papers, No. 10.*

termed the "mental environment." In collaboration, we developed a graphic organizer that would both build students' prior knowledge and introduce the conceptual analogy upon which the author's argument and organizational structure were built (see Figure 6.2). Used together with a knowledge rating activity and a think-aloud, the graphic helped students confidently enter this challenging text. Although the above examples depict the ways that graphic organizers were created by teachers to help students access challenging texts, we feel that it is also crucial to give students multiple opportunities to identify these structures on their own. This can be done most effectively after teachers have modeled the various types of text structures and discussed how each structure helps authors convey ideas about a particular topic.

A middle-level team at Cole Middle School in Rhode Island does just that. Students are introduced to the basic expository text structures early in the year, and they are given experiences identifying each. Then, as part of their social studies activities, this knowledge is applied each week as students are asked to locate and share one current-events story that is appropriate for their social studies classroom. The teachers give students a guide they can use in reading and summarizing their selections (see Figure 6.3). The evaluation is explicitly laid out for the students (Figure 6.4). In this way, students apply what they learn about text structure and content as they read and share current events articles. This ongoing experience using text structures to summarize and share what has been read exemplifies how teachers can help students learn to look independently for the underlying organization of ideas in texts and to use that knowledge to make sense of what they read. And when teachers across the content disciplines engage in using the same language as they help students identify and use text structures in their learning, students gain confidence in reading expository texts.

The research on developing learning strategies makes clear that students need extended opportunities to develop strategic approaches to their learning (Bransford, Brown, & Cocking, 1999). Simply introducing a strategy, like previewing and identifying highlighted vocabulary, is not enough (Deshler et al., 2001; Pearson & Gallagher, 1983). Teachers need to model the strategy several times with the course content they have assigned students to use. They need to ensure that students are able to preview actively and identify important terms. Students need opportunities to compare their efforts with those of other classmates. Then the same approach to previewing and focusing on vocabulary needs to be reinforced in other content courses. The science and social studies teachers need to model using the strategy, think through with students the issues that confront them as they try to implement the strategy, and provide diagnostic help and support. All the content areas need to hold students accountable for using the previewing approach, collect sample pages on which students indicate their thinking as they preview a text page and give feedback, create rubrics so students can see what is required of good previewing, and continue to use the system over time until students make notes in this

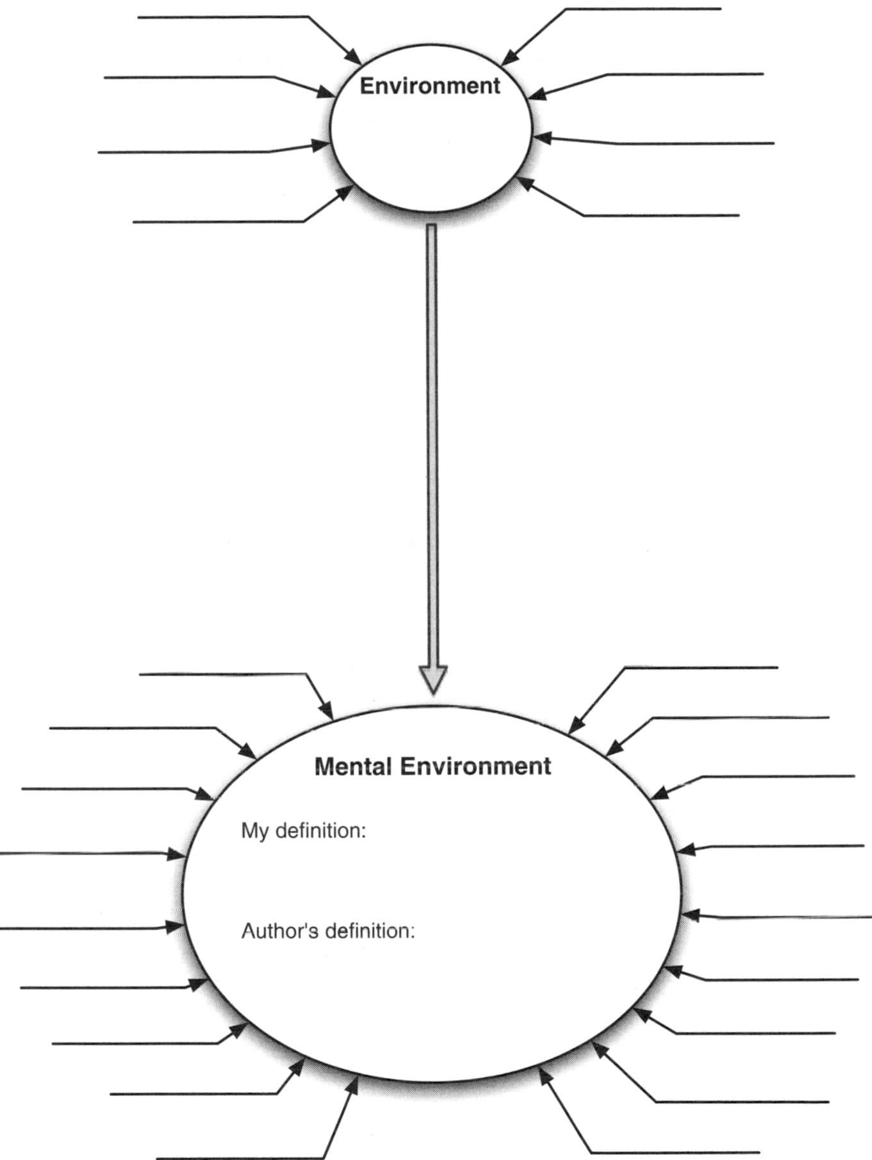

FIGURE 6.2. Volume organizer.

Name ______________________________

Steps When Reading a News Article

Title of article:

____

News source:

____

Date of publication:

____

What is your purpose for reading? What do you want to learn from this article? (Use the article's heading to form a question.)

As you read, think about the important facts. Record them below.

Think about the article you just read. What questions are you left with? Is there anything that you don't understand?

Think about the article you read. What happened? Record all effects below.

Why did it happen? Record all causes below.

FIGURE 6.3. Causes and effects in news articles.

Using at least one cause and effect signal word (list below), write the cause and effect sequence.

Signal words:

Cause	Effect
Because	As a result
The reason for	Outcome
On account of	Finally
Bring about	Consequently
Give rise to	Therefore
Created by	For this reason
Contributed by	Hence
Led to	Effect
Due to	Then
Since	So

FIGURE 6.3. (*continued*)

format automatically. Students learn and internalize a systematic approach to reading that can serve them well when strategies are taught carefully and students are monitored on their use of the same strategies across various content areas and different years in school (Pressley et al., 1994).

To help teachers consider how to prioritize their time most effectively, it is valuable to differentiate what teachers and students do during instruction. There are several useful teaching strategies or routines that model active engaged reading, such as conducting think-alouds (Bereiter & Bird, 1985), questioning the author (Beck, McKeown, Hamilton, & Kucan, 1997), and having students work in small groups, as in collaborative strategic reading (Kim et al., 2006) Partner Reading and Content, Too (Ogle, 2010), and Book Club (Raphael & McMahon, 1994). As teachers use these approaches for helping students learn, they also need to explain their purpose and value and show students how to translate them beyond the classroom into independent reading and study practices.

Current Events Assignment

Purple Team Social Studies

Cole M.S. East Greenwich, RI

Ms. Bethany Friel

THE ASSIGNMENT:

Social studies students are required to complete one current events assignment each week. Current events assignments are due in class each Monday.

- News articles must be current and come from credible nontabloid news sources (examples: *Providence Journal, New York Times*, *cnn.com*, etc.).
- Articles must be appropriate for the social studies classroom. Therefore, articles involving death, crime, and entertainment news will not receive full credit. (Articles about death resulting from war *are* permitted, as well as the death of major public figures such as a former U.S. President.)

CONTENT AND GRADING:

Each current events assignment can earn a maximum of 10 points. The criteria and grading policy for the current events assignments are listed below.

- *List three facts.* You are retelling the story with three facts, so it is important to choose three very important main ideas. To receive full credit, your facts must be written in your own words and in complete sentences.—*3 points*
- *List two questions* about the article. Questions may be a phrase you do not understand, a concept that you do not understand, something you still wonder about, etc.—*2 points*
- *Identify a major example of problem and solution* from your news story. In one paragraph, you must describe the problem from the story, the solution described in the article, AND explain your own idea(s) for solving the problem. If your article doesn't describe a solution that has taken place, you can only state the problem and offer your own solution.—*3 points*
- *Attach a map of the location* in which the story takes place (maps can be easily found on *mapquest.com*)—*2 points*

Additional Requirements:

All current events assignments should also include the following format requirements:

- Heading: Student's name at top, title of article, news source (*Providence Journal, cnn.com*) and article's date of publication.
- News article should be stapled to the *back* of your written work.

FIGURE 6.4. Current events assignment.

Learning to Read with a Critical Eye

With the increasing popularity of using online sources and with the incorporation of an increasingly biased mass media into curricula, it is critical that teachers orient students to looking for the perspective and bias embedded within texts. Students need to identify the authors of the texts they are using, and they need to be able to determine the credibility of these sources. In order to do so, they need to read multiple sources—not only online sources, but also those that have been edited for accuracy. One of the recommendations we make to teachers is that they give students an opportunity to see how multiple authors have represented the same content.

Teachers are approaching the challenge of authority and accuracy in online sources from the perspective of social networking tools, too. Students' portrayal of themselves online and their use of these tools (Facebook, MySpace, blogs, wikis, animations, YouTube, remixing, etc.) is an avenue for discussing the need for careful and critical reading of these texts. As Alvermann (2008) explained:

> In my opinion, the most striking insight to be gained from the research on adolescents' remixing of multimodal content to create new texts is this: Those who create online content recognize that authorship is neither a solitary nor completely original enterprise. . . . In fact, I propose that young people's engagement with these kinds of ideological messages and materials is central to their becoming the critical readers and writers we say we value. (p. 17)

Engaging Students Metacognitively

Students need to understand what it means to be strategic readers. The term *strategy* is widely used to refer to specific processes or strategies like prediction and visualizing. However, when engaged in reading, we generally use many different strategies, depending on the text and our purposes. The extensive strategy research that has been done includes studies both on individual strategies and on more extensive routines that involve more than one strategy. Pressley et al. (1994) and others have called this more fluid use of strategies "transactional strategies." Readers who possess a set of strategies or processes use them as needed to construct meaning when texts are challenging. Therefore, the goal of instruction needs to be that students know or internalize a variety of strategies they can use when they encounter challenging texts. This involves metacognitive control—knowing what the task involves, considering possible ways of approaching it, and then selecting and implementing an approach and monitoring its success. This knowledge about one's own strategy use constitutes what is called the reader's executive function, or metacognition.

The research on strategy instruction supports the value of students learning to make their own decisions about which strategies to implement. Studies (El-Dinary, 2002; Paris, Cross, & Lipson, 1984; Pressley et al., 1994) confirm that students, even in elementary grades, can learn to be in control in these ways. By the time students are in middle school and high school, assessing their knowledge and involving them in thinking about their own reading and learning are both important keys to improving literacy. Students who know what they can do to be successful in reading texts are much more likely to engage than are those without such understanding (Anderson & Roit, 1993). Therefore, giving students a language to talk about their reading and learning strategies and opportunities to monitor their own use of strategies is important.

One of the easiest ways we have found to begin this process is to teach students to read with a pencil in hand and make regular notations in the margins of the texts they are reading. The INSERT notemaking system developed by Vaughan and Estes (1986) works well and is especially effective with students who argue that annotating a text takes too much time and disrupts the flow of their reading. Students learn to use a common notation system (+ for important ideas; ? for items that are unclear; – for things the reader disagrees with; ! for surprising ideas). After reading a portion of a text or an article, students gather in small groups of three to four to discuss their annotations. The items for which they have questions are often the first to be discussed. It is often helpful for the group to have a sheet of paper with a matrix on which they can record their responses to the text reading. In this way there is a shared record of their thinking, and it can be saved for later assessment by both the teacher and students (see Figure 6.5).

In helping ninth graders become more self-reflective about how they annotate a fictional text, Laura created a rubric for students to use after they have completed an assigned reading. As a class, the freshmen had already discussed the goals of note taking, and Laura had modeled the process with a short passage. Each student then used the rubric to evaluate how successful he or she was in using this form of active reading independently (see Figure 6.6). Students were encouraged to use this form of notemaking in other content areas, too. A Spanish teacher included it on the guidelines for reading the selection "Pobre Ana"; the science teacher included it on directions for reading the chapter on the circulatory system. This process of teaching students to use active processing strategies as they read and then to turn the process over to them creates better readers. This is a real shared example of formative assessment; both the teacher and students participate in determining how well they are learning to use the targeted strategies. The more students take ownership of their reading and learning, the more likely they are to participate fully in school.

In a book on formative assessment Clarke (2005) summarizes the concept:

> Doing formative assessment is about changing the way in which a lesson is constructed and managed, the culture and ethos of the classroom and the quality of questioning and feedback. Most of all, it is about the involvement

Name ______________________________

Name ______________________________

Name ______________________________

?	−	!	+

FIGURE 6.5. Insert notes group chart.

of students in the learning process, beyond anything traditional teaching has previously allowed. The proven effect of teaching in this way is that students do better at tests than before, and become lifelong independent learners. (p. 3)

Students are often unaware of what is involved in learning successfully. Teachers can do a great deal to make explicit the components of reading and learning and engage students in their own self-monitoring and assessment. Having students work with others as partners at the same level or tutoring younger students also puts students in powerful roles. When students teach others, they often develop more understanding of the reading process and more confidence in their own abilities.

Annotation Rubric: How Did I Do?

Name ______________________________

Chapter Title/Number ________________

Pages Nos. __________________________

Directions: For each category below, place an *X* on the line above the word that best describes your annotations.

N.A. = This category was not applicable on these pages.

I circled the names of all new characters who were introduced.

____

Always Sometimes Never N.A.

I underlined any words or phrases that revealed the setting (time, place, weather, etc.).

____

Always Sometimes Never N.A.

I wrote a summary at the top of every page.

____

Always Sometimes Never N.A.

I put a question mark in the margin if there was something I didn't understand.

____

Always Sometimes Never N.A.

I wrote an exclamation point in the margin if something crazy or unexpected happened.

____

Always Sometimes Never N.A.

The grade I would give myself on my annotations: ________

Why?

FIGURE 6.6. Annotation rubric, Laura Lang.

M. Duderstead developed a program called Tall Friends in which struggling middle-grade readers tutored elementary students in basic reading strategies. Before each tutoring session, Duderstead provided instruction to the older students, reviewing skills they also needed. As these middle graders worked with younger students, they built their own understanding and gained confidence in themselves as readers.

Ensuring That Students Have Materials Available That They Can Read

Teachers are increasingly aware that many students in their classes lack some of the basic reading abilities needed for success with their texts. Finding appropriate materials that students can read is another key to their being willing and able to learn from text. Schools that have tried to circumvent having students read by developing totally hands-on science classes or providing all materials on audiotapes are shortchanging students. Instead, schools should use the full resources of the librarians and the reading teachers and specialists to create environments full of interesting and accessible materials. Such resources are generally available with some effort, especially now that so many materials are on databases and accessible through Internet-based services.

One of our current middle school projects in Chicago (Chicago Striving Readers, 2006–2011). revolves around developing content support materials for units in the science and social studies curricula (Ogle, 2010). This project responds to the reality that too many students are reading substantially below their grade placement and struggle with designated textbooks. Central to these units are sets of short topical books at varied reading levels—from second grade to appropriate grade level. Teachers receive one to three copies of each of the books in the set. They conduct 1-minute fluency assessments with the students to get a general idea of their reading levels. Based on this information, they partner students with someone reading at approximately the same level so that each pair of students can share a book and read together. Students learn to use the question–answer–relations framework (Raphael & Au, 2005) to write questions for each other on their first silent reading of each page of text. Teachers have developed different ways to help students monitor their reading; in some classrooms students write their questions on Post-it notes. In others, students work from a graphic organizer sheet to record their questions, answers, and pages read during each 20-minute session. Teachers involved in the project have reported that many students eagerly await their partner reading time and are asking to read these content books when they have choice times or when they can self-select activities.

Some of the power inherent in this project is that students are able to engage in learning about important curricular topics from materials that are not overly challenging. The new small texts are generally full of visual and graphic information and help all students, particularly the struggling readers and English-language learners, develop an understanding of content through pictures and diagrams. The size of the books also is inviting; most students feel they can read these skinny books!

As we follow the classrooms in this project we are also aware that students in urban schools often lack self-confidence as learners. The partner reading routine that puts them in the role of teacher for each other in materials in which they can succeed has increased many students' interest and engagement. Opportunities for increased self-control and successful collaboration can have a sustaining impact on students who struggle with content learning (Guthrie & Davis, 2003; Kim et al., 2006; Walczyk & Griffith-Ross, 2007).

Creating Contexts for Students to Learn Together

A final consideration is that students do well when they can learn together (Bransford et al., 1999). In both the example from Laura's lesson using a modified form of INSERT notemaking and in partner reading, students learn from each other. Teachers can create more engaged learning in classrooms by establishing settings in which students work together in partnerships and teams rather than isolated as individuals. Much of the current work with adolescents has affirmed the importance of situating instruction in the social and shared context of classrooms and school (Guthrie & Davis, 2003; Moje et al., 2004; Oldfather, 2002).

Students like to work together and learn from one another. In Laura's class, students became much more involved with the text as they listened to one another describe what they had marked in the text and why than if they had just been reading independently. They began to see new questions and ways to interpret what they had read. One student remarked, "I had no idea you could read that much into it!" Approaches that encourage shared exploration, study, and reflection by students deepen those students' interest and understanding. They help students understand the constructive nature of comprehension and how tenuous the connection between authors and readers can be. Perhaps most important, they give students opportunities to take on the roles of experts and teachers, fully participating in the learning possibilities created in stimulating classrooms.

Friends and significant others are powerful forces in motivating adolescents and in determining what and how they read. Many students become more deeply engaged when they have opportunities to engage socially in discussing reading material. As Schallert and Reed (1997) explain:

> Under ideal circumstances and for many students, talking with peers to negotiate an understanding of what was read is highly motivating. Not only are students likely to become involved in the active interaction often associated with peer-led discussion groups, they may be more interested in what they are reading as they anticipate what will happen when they meet in groups to discuss what they have read. (p. 81)

Student-to-student discussions are particularly helpful with English language learners. A growing and important area of research involves minority and English language learners in middle and high schools. These students face particular challenges, since they may have acquired conversational English but lack familiarity with the academic routines and norms of American schools. They often encounter challenges with academic content vocabulary and disciplinary structures needed for success.

With the increasing diversity of our population, learning about and being interested in students' lives is imperative. This includes being more conscious of the varied cultural and social values and experiences of students and learning about students' lives outside of school, in their families and communities. Some research has shown that when teachers intentionally connect students' culture to instruction students are more likely to engage and learn. Lee (2005), for example, has used signifying, a black cultural communication tool, as a cultural bridge to high school students' learning Shakespeare.

As more researchers examine the social contexts for learning and the sociocultural dimensions of literacy development in schools (Bean, 2000; Hinchman & Zalewski, 1996; Moje, 2010; Oldfather, 2002), several questions emerge. These relate to how well schools know and respond to adolescents' interests and sense of well-being (Moje, 2007; Oldfather & McLaughlin, 1993), foster students' own inquiry and engaged learning (Guthrie et al., 1997; Ivey, 2004), and accommodate the differences among adolescent students—in gender-related interests and needs (Allison, 2009; Brozo, 2000; Cole, 1997; Ivey, 2004; Smith & Wilhelm, 2004), learning abilities (Boudah, Deshler, Schumaker, Lenz, & Cook, 1997), and culture (Ball, 2005; Gutierrez, 2005)—in providing literacy instruction. Moje (2007) challenges teachers to work in the third space—the intersection of students' home cultural formats and values with school priorities. She proposes that teachers can involve students more actively by relating students' everyday knowledge to content-area learning. Several recent publications have explored ways teachers are moving into this "third space" (Benson, 2010; de la Piedria, 2010; Lynch, 2009).

BEST PRACTICES IN ACTION: HOW SCHOOLS CAN DEVELOP STRONG INSTRUCTIONAL PROGRAMS—TWO EXAMPLES

One of us (Laura Lang), a reading specialist at New Trier High School, in Chicago, from 1998 to 2006 and a current literacy coach at Madison West High School, has worked with the faculty and administration to develop a comprehensive program to support students' literacy learning needs. Although her role remains varied, one of the highlights of her job was the creation of and continued participation in interdisciplinary literacy teams at each school. These teams encourage all teachers to provide support to all students in meeting the varied reading demands. Laura explores the evolution of these teams in the following section.

Identify the Need

During the summer of 2004, department coordinators from New Trier High School's freshman campus joined forces to explore the role of literacy in content-area classes. Students were not reading as carefully or critically as they had in years past, and this was hindering their ability to learn the course content or, in some cases, even to follow simple written directions. Their teachers wanted to become more comfortable offering direct reading skills instruction to the students. Other teachers wanted to incorporate more literacy-rich experiences into their classrooms. Most significantly, we all recognized that the reinforcement and repetition of strategy use and instruction are essential to developing lifelong critical literacy skills, but at that point there was no uniform schoolwide approach to teaching those strategies.

With the support of our building principal and a stipend from our assistant superintendent for curriculum, a summer grant materialized.

Establish Team Goals and a Team Structure That Respects the School Culture

After some illuminating discussions about the role literacy plays in each of our disciplines, the summer grant collaborators proposed the creation of a Literacy Team on the freshman, or Northfield, campus. The team would have two primary goals.

1. Raise teachers' awareness of the components of successful literacy education by:
   - Establishing a schoolwide shared vocabulary for teachers to use in their classrooms and with one another.
   - Supporting and developing literacy staff development opportunities for teachers.
   - Examining current curriculum to identify existing connections to our literacy goals.
   - Helping teachers choose the most appropriate activities to achieve a specific instructional objective.
   - Disseminating research findings regarding best practices.
2. Identify a set of literacy skills that all freshmen students should use by the end of freshman year and develop assessments that determine whether the skills have been learned.

As one of the campus reading specialists, I would coordinate the team, and ideally we would recruit representatives from every department in the school. Because our school operates through a shared leadership model, we knew that in order to promote this program we would have to demonstrate its relevance to every discipline in the school and that every discipline would have to be involved in determining the direction that our literacy work would take. We would meet once monthly during the school day.

Get the Right People on Board

At this point, I would be remiss if I didn't explain why we felt confident proceeding with our proposal—how we knew that a Literacy Team was a viable approach at New Trier's freshman campus. First, our building principal was our most vocal advocate. She encouraged us to "dream big," and she was particularly savvy to the politics of bringing a new program to fruition. When we first presented the Literacy Team to the faculty, the principal wanted to explain publicly why she supported this initiative. She consistently attended the Literacy Team meetings once they got under way, and, most important, she gave us the gift of time. Administrative support and participation is essential for successful school-wide literacy reform (Carnegie Council on Advancing Adolescent Literacy, 2010) (Irvin et al., 2009). The second factor that was key to our success was the support of most of the department coordinators. They were excited about the future of the Literacy Team and agreed that it could address a genuine need in their individual departments. In addition, the coordinators were able to identify one or two teachers in their respective departments who they knew would be interested in pursuing this kind of work.

At the end of September, the summer grant team of department coordinators presented the idea of a Literacy Team to the freshman teachers at a Northfield campus staff meeting. As promised, the principal introduced our proposal and expressed her genuine support of our goals. After the meeting, interested teachers had an opportunity to sign up and be part of the inaugural Literacy Team.

By the time our inaugural meeting arrived in October, we had amassed a wonderful group of teachers, administrators, and department coordinators who spanned a wide range of content offerings: French, Spanish, practical arts, performance arts, English, social studies, science, special education, mathematics, and health.

My work with the Literacy Team at Madison West High School in the fall of 2008 began slightly differently. Volunteers had already been identified, and I was new to both the school and the district. Because I was not yet familiar with the specific instructional needs of students or teachers, I was truly dependent on the team members and the administrator to shape the direction of our work together. However, one reality shapes much of my work at West High School: I was hired under a federal grant that aims to reduce the existing achievement gap within the district. Although the goals of West's Literacy Team in many ways mirrored the goals that New Trier's team had established, they took on a different meaning, given the diverse student population and the daily challenges that our lower-income students of color, in particular, faced within the school building.

Give the Participants the Opportunity to Shape the Team's Work

Regardless of the school context in which they are operating, in order for literacy teams to be successful, participants must want to participate, and they must share a common passion: to help every student in the school become a more confident and competent reader of diverse texts. During their first year of existence at both New Trier High School and at Madison West High School, the Literacy Team members came together to identify teacher and student literacy needs, and we explored research about best-practice literacy instruction. Although we accomplished a lot, we were trying to cover a lot of ground. We wanted to address all facets of literacy instruction, but we realized that we needed to focus our efforts a bit more during the upcoming year. Both groups decided that reading would be our focus.

At this point, I realized that I needed to make some recommendations about how we could proceed. I reflected on the conversations that had already taken place, and it became clear that the participants valued most the opportunity to share—and ultimately tackle—the frustrations that emerged in their individual classrooms. They had shared an incredible amount during those first few meetings, including lessons that they and their colleagues were using to address their students' reading problems. They were interested in the reading research, but they were even more excited about learning from their colleagues' efforts. Those sharing and collaborative learning sessions drew the most positive reviews. The echoes of our conversations had lingered, one teacher from New Trier said, and had woven their way into her daily lesson planning.

Our challenge, then, was to share our discoveries with the rest of the school. Best-practice reading instruction was occurring in every discipline, but often teachers did not have the opportunity to see it firsthand. The literacy team members agreed that all teachers should be able to view the wonderful lessons that were occurring in classrooms throughout the school, but classroom observations were not an immediately practical alternative.

At New Trier, this conversation compelled us to create a reading strategy guide for our faculty. I knew that a number of districts had created such guides, and that spring I brought a few samples for the team to consider. When I brought the samples into our spring Literacy Team meetings, we agreed that we too would set out to create a guide of our own. Before long, we started discussing logistics. The literacy guide had to look professional, and it had to be personalized to our faculty's needs. We also agreed that, once created, these guides could not be imposed upon—or simply handed to—our faculty. Literacy Team participants reminisced about all of the instructional guides and packets that they had received over the years, many of which now sat untouched on their desks.

We also knew that we wanted to try to get the guide out in the fall. Every Literacy Team participant was to scour his or her department for best-practices lessons that could be included in the guide. A small group of teachers volunteered to continue the work during the summer. As expected, our work continued long into the fall.

Those many hours of collecting resources, writing, typing, editing, formatting, and checking the printer's proofs eventually resulted in the *Northfield Literacy Guide*, which offers not only basic reading research and strategies but also specific examples of the way that New Trier teachers use reading strategies in their own classrooms. The *Literacy Guide* was published on November

23, 2005, and it helped propel the work that we embarked upon during our second year together.

At West High School, the Literacy Team was afforded a formal opportunity to share its work with the entire high school staff. A little more than a year after we started working together, our administration asked us to prepare a 3-hour presentation during the January staff inservice. The Literacy Team members decided it was imperative that the "presentation" was content specific, teacher generated, and interactive. However, we also decided that it was important for the staff to share a basic common vocabulary around literacy strategies.

The team members were released from their teaching responsibilities for one full day so that we could plan the staff inservice. We spent our time looking at school data, identifying school- and subject-specific needs, and continuing our exploration of best-practice strategies. Because we had engaged in our own professional development during the prior months, we were able to get to work quickly. At the end of that day, we selected the three strategies that they thought were most applicable across content areas. Our strategy selection was also driven by the reality that the AVID (Advancement via Individual Determination) program had been rolled out at the school that year. Although only 30 freshmen students were enrolled in the program, the ultimate goal was to have all teachers using components of the program in their classes. Because of this, we knew that our strategies had to be consistent with the strategies proposed within the AVID curriculum. As a result, we realized that we could not engage in our work in isolation. We needed to consider how both our vision and our recommendations fit within the broader context of ongoing school reforms.

In January the Literacy Team members presented the Vocabulary Knowledge Rating, Think Aloud, and the INSERT text-marking strategies to their departments. They used content-specific materials to present these strategies, and they tailored their agendas to meet the needs of each department.

Offer Training in Reading Research and Strategies: Make It as Easy as Possible for Interested Teachers and Administrators to Be Involved

In both schools, literacy teams met, at a minimum, once per month during the lunch hour. In addition, both teams elected to pursue their own exploration of reading instruction during at least part of their meeting time. Subsequently, each Literacy Team member was given a copy of Cris Tovani's *Do I Really Have to Teach Reading?* (2004) and a tentative agenda for future meetings. The meeting topics ranged from choosing the most accessible texts for students to establishing a clear purpose for reading to making our content-specific comprehension strategies visible to students. At both schools, each meeting began with lunch and time for teachers to read a short section of Tovani's book and, at New Trier, the *Literacy Guide* pages that corresponded with that day's topic. Surprisingly, teachers told me that they relish being given time to actually sit and read during a meeting! The second half of the meetings run much like an informal book club meeting—participants are free to share their reactions to Tovani's ideas and are prompted to consider how to incorporate some of her ideas into their own classroom practice. We laugh, share frustrations, and question what we are currently doing in our classrooms. Finally, we share strategies for bringing the substance of these discussions back to each teacher's department. After exploring Tovani's work, the West High School Literacy Team continued their own staff development this year through a discussion of Alfred Tatum's *Teaching Reading to Black Adolescent Males* (2005). Our lower-income students of color continue to struggle within the district; therefore, we are especially interested in approaches that will help engage, support, and validate the experiences and funds of knowledge (Moll, Amanti, Neff, & Gonzales, 1992) that all of our students bring into our classrooms.

Because of my experiences with the literacy teams at both New Trier High School and Madison West High School, I am convinced that it is the relationship and collaboration among teachers of disparate disciplines that truly fuels their excitement and engagement in this important work. Every student benefits when teachers share a common language and a common passion for literacy instruction.

LESSONS LEARNED/OUR CONTINUED JOURNEY

Since the last edition of our chapter, both of us have continued to work in adolescent literacy in new settings. Laura is now a literacy coach at Madison West High School and a PhD student at the University of Wisconsin–Madison, and Donna is serving as senior consultant to the Chicago Striving Readers project. These contexts have helped us deepen our conversations and our reflections regarding the issues and possibilities that accompany implementing best practices in adolescent literacy. Laura's experience working across grade levels at an urban high school and Donna's current experience in 30 middle schools (grades 6–8) in Chicago provide new contexts for us to deepen our understanding.

We were surprised at how many common challenges we encountered, such as:

- The universal conflict between curricular breadth versus depth. Many teachers perceive the need to cover so much information that they don't feel there is much time available to incorporate alternative approaches, assessments, or texts.
- School structures and cultures that are not conducive to instructional change.
- The challenge of developing professional development opportunities

that take into account teachers' wide range of knowledge about what strategies work for students.
- The increase in teachers' workloads (more students per class) and more time spent on test preparation means less time available to devote to professional development.
- The challenges of sustaining effective learning communities.
- A dearth of existing assessment measures that truly inform instruction, as well as too few formative assessments being used.
- Inadequate textbooks that drive teachers to stop using them altogether.
- Financial obstacles to purchasing alternative texts that address multiple reading levels.
- Lack of support required to effectively meet all students' needs; teachers support the need for differentiation, but they don't always feel that they have possibilities to make it happen.

Our experiences have strengthened our belief that no one-size-fits-all program will be able to address the needs of all of our middle and high school students. We also know that any single stand-alone strategy will not bring about the kind of systemic instructional change that will truly make a difference for all of our students. Instead, we know that the success of adolescent literacy programs relies on teachers who have a deep understanding of both general and discipline-specific reading processes and who know that they must help their students internalize those understandings as well. Despite all of the challenges we listed above, we both work with exceptional teachers and administrators who are fully committed to addressing the needs of adolescent readers and writers. We understand that, as reading professionals, it is our responsibility to support these teachers and to value and celebrate their hard work.

REFLECTIONS AND FUTURE DIRECTIONS

Secondary students spend most of their school reading time engaged with content-area texts. The work done on establishing strategies readers can use to make sense of text has consistently shown that the use of thoughtful approaches to reading produces gains in comprehension.

Reading across Texts and Multimodal Reading

Most of these studies, however, have involved students reading single texts. There is little research on how students read and use multiple texts and sources. How do students make sense of primary-source documents in history? How do they compare different presentations of graphic data in science and mathematics? Are students able to read and think analytically and critically when they are engaged in more extensive research and when they use Internet sources for this research (Robnolt, Rhodes, & Richard 2005)? Reading across electronic sources, among the most frequent type of reading done by adolescents, has barely been studied (Coiro, Knobel, Lankshear, & Leu, 2008). However, Leu's team at the University of Connecticut has shown how different "online reading" can be from traditional text-based reading and that many students can be successful in one context and not the other. Research is needed to explore how teachers can help students use multiple texts and text types in their learning (Alvermann, 2008). The potential for much more self-guided learning using a variety of resources exists. Both pilot programs and research on these programs are needed; perhaps new relationships among learners (teachers, students, and the community) in the "third space" can evolve.

Part of the recent wave of interest in literacy has been inspired by the New London Group's call for critical literacy and their attention to out-of-school literacies and the uses of technology (Alvermann, 2004; Luke & Elkins, 2000). This research is important and provides a lens through which teachers and schools can assess their own approaches to literacy; it also challenges the rigid focus on achieving knowledge "standards" and "authorial" reading of texts. These researchers remind us of the ever-expanding nature of literacy; the immediacy with which students can be in contact with others and the need for a "critical stance" with regard to any position or theoretical orientation are important.

Attention to Academic Vocabulary

Another issue that is basic to adolescent literacy development is the development of students' vocabularies. A major component of reading in middle and high schools involves attending to academic and technical vocabulary. It is a central issue in comprehension for English language learners, but certainly transcends this population and affects all students in secondary schools. Vocabulary researchers differentiate general vocabulary from academic vocabulary specific to content areas (Blachowicz & Fisher, Chapter 9, this volume). Students continue to expand both types of vocabulary during the adolescent years. How to assist this growth is a major challenge. Secondary school content, in particular, consists largely of technical terms that are unfamiliar to students. How can students build their understanding of the enormous amount of content-specific terminology they are expected to learn across their subjects? The Vocabulary Knowledge Rating (Blachowicz, 1986) has proven particularly effective in introducing content-specific vocabulary that is central to a given topic or reading, and we have seen this applied successfully in all content areas (see Figure 6.7). Robert Marzano (2004) also offers a variety of instructional strategies designed to increase students' academic vocabulary.

Words/concepts/ allusions	Know it well	Have heard or seen it	No clue	Notes/definitions
Global warming				
Pacific turtles				
Delicacy				
Coastal development				
Hatchery				
Biologist				
Endangered				
Environmentalist				

FIGURE 6.7. Vocabulary Knowledge Rating. "Turtles Are Casualties of Warming in Costa Rica" sample used in literacy committee meeting.

Comprehension at the Center

Attention has been so focused on primary-level literacy that what instruction students should receive later and how to make it effective have received little research attention until very recently. In fact, when the U.S. government's Office of Educational Research and Improvement (OERI) funded a group of 14 researchers to develop a research agenda for the most pressing issues in literacy for the 21st century, it determined that reading comprehension was the most crucial. This study (Snow, 2002) was funded through the RAND Corporation and was directed by Catherine Snow of Harvard University. Part of the group's rationale for choosing to focus on comprehension was the recognition that, while society requires higher levels of literacy from high school graduates than in the past, students in the United States are not showing achievement growth comparable to the growth students are achieving in other countries. On the recent international comparison of 15-year-olds (Progress in Student Achievement, or PISA), U.S. students emerged in the middle of the rankings, about 16th—well below the top countries. As a result of the growing attention to adolescent literacy, the Institute for Educational Studies (IES) has funded several studies of programs and basic research. The results of these efforts can help inform the development of approaches to literacy for older readers.

Advocacy for Adolescent Literacy

The Carnegie Corporation, in conjunction with the Alliance for Excellent Education, a group formed with the explicit purpose of getting more resources and programs for adolescent literacy, has published a series of reports highlighting the needs and potential for adolescent literacy. Their first report, *Reading Next: A Vision for Action and Research in Middle and High School Literacy* (Alliance for Excellent Education, 2004), established 15 key elements of effective adolescent literacy programs—nine related to instruction and six to structural conditions necessary for the instructional recommendations to be well implemented. The Carnegie Corporation also convened its own Council on Advancing Adolescent Literacy and recently published its own report, *Time to Act: An Agenda for Advancing Adolescent Literacy for College and Career Success* (2010). That report challenges America to provide "all students with a high-quality and challenging educational experience aimed at developing intellectual skills, critical thinking, and effective communication" (p. viii). Carnegie has also supported the work of the National Literacy Center in producing two excellent guides for secondary schools (Irwin et al., 2010).

These calls for action in adolescent literacy build on the growing recognition of the need to extend reading instruction into secondary schooling. The International Reading Association's Commission on Adolescent Literacy in 2001 published the important Adolescent Literacy Position Statement, and later the National Reading Conference commissioned Donna Alvermann (2004) to write a position paper on adolescent literacy. Both of these papers identify the need for quality instruction at the secondary level and the importance of involving students actively and personally in their learning. Recently the role of the secondary literacy coach has also received attention as part of the interest and expansion of the practice of using literacy coaches.

Emergence of Middle/Secondary Literacy Coach Positions

Within just the last few years, many districts have developed literacy coaching positions within their secondary schools. Although the way these positions are defined and carried out vary (Blamey, Meyer, & Walpole, 2009–2010), literacy coaches have the potential to serve a crucial role in literacy reform efforts (Sturtevant, 2003). Nancy Shanklin (2006) identifies seven characteristics of effective literacy coaching: effective coaches collaborate with teachers of all disciplines and levels, help develop a vision of adolescent literacy, make data-driven decisions, increase teacher capacity, observe classroom instruction, and support rather than evaluate the teachers with whom they work. In 2006 the International Reading Association, in conjunction with the National Council of Teachers of English, National Council of Teachers of Mathematics, National Science Teachers Association, and the National Council for the Social Studies, published *Standards for Middle and High School Literacy Coaches* (IRA, 2006). This document situates the literacy coach as a potential agent of change within his or her school and district context, one who can affect instructional reform that will enable schools to better meet the needs of struggling adolescent readers.

Striving Readers Research and Implementation Grants

The Striving Readers Research Grant Program of the U.S. Department of Education (2006), which allocated up to $25 million for each of eight winning grants that were awarded to school districts and consortia of schools to implement research-based programs, is completing the 5 years of implementation in 2011. This large-scale effort focuses on three key elements: cross-school team efforts for literacy instruction, support for struggling readers (defined as 2 years or more below their grade level in reading), and ongoing assessment to guide instruction. Finally, the grants require extensive research on the designs and their implementation. Following the implementation of this research initiative, the department has also made many smaller awards to districts to implement promising practices in schools. Lessons are already being derived from these projects (Ayers & Miller, 2009).

More intervention programs for struggling secondary readers have been developed recently. Alvermann and Rush's (2004) review and the Deshler, Palincsar, Biancarosa, and Nair (2009) review of these programs indicates that we can expect more attention to and support for adolescent readers in the coming years. These reviews also underscore the complexity of changing secondary reading instruction. The introduction of the response to intervention (RTI) framework and mandates to districts to provide more diagnostic and "progress monitoring" of students needing more support in reading adds to the urgency of developing strong adolescent literacy programs. One of the variables that works in our favor is that, with the RTI initiative and an increased focus on inclusion, there will be more support for differentiation, therefore providing more support for students. The attention being given to RTI and special education inclusion are both realities that we can use to develop more appropriate instruction for kids.

CONCLUDING COMMENTS

With these new efforts and perspectives on literacy for the 21st century, we can certainly expect to know much more about adolescent literacy instruction and practices within the next several years. Our students clearly deserve this support. In a global community, we can all gain from understanding what it means to be literate in this digital age. We can learn to select texts that are most useful in meeting our needs from the wide variety that are available. We can help students think more deeply by challenging interpretations and engaging in real-time dialogues with learners and experts around the world. We need to support students as they develop the habits of checking the perspective and authority of texts read and consulting a variety of sources. Teachers and larger community groups must also advocate so that *all* students have access to this new digital environment, not just those in more affluent districts. The potential is great for a global learning community replete with motivated and engaged learners, but it won't happen automatically. Schoolwide shared commitments and articulated instructional practices are needed. It takes teachers and administrators with vision who are willing to develop knowledge and to experiment with more collaborative teaching as well as with an openness to including all students and the wider community in these efforts.

ENGAGEMENT ACTIVITIES

1. Reflect on the reading and learning processes in Table 6.1. Add to the middle column teaching activities you use to support students before, during, and after reading. If you find yourself short in one area, make a plan including more modeling. Then talk with your students about how they, too, can be more engaged with greater teacher support.
2. Review for students the various expository text structures widely used in English texts and create a graphic organizer for a text you will use with your students. The organizer included in Figure 6.1 can serve as a guide. After using it, discuss with your students how it did or didn't increase their attention to the author's main ideas and argument.
3. If you are not part of a team effort to help students apply active reading strategies across their school subjects, make a copy of

the section detailing the examples of the two literacy teams and find teachers with whom you can begin a dialogue about a more cooperative effort to improve students' reading.

RESOURCES FOR FURTHER LEARNING

Books for Reflection

Alliance for Excellent Education. (2004). *Reading next: A vision for action and research in middle and high school literacy: A report to the Carnegie Corporation of New York.* Washington, DC: Author.

Buehl, D. (2008). *Classroom strategies for interactive learning* (3rd ed.). Newark, DE: International Reading Association.

Carnegie Council on Advancing Adolescent Literacy. (2010). *Time to Act: An agenda for advancing adolescent literacy for college and career success.* New York: Carnegie Corporation.

Ganske, K., & Fisher, D. (Eds.). (2010). Comprehension across the curriculum: Perspectives and practices K–12. New York: Guilford Press.

International Reading Association. (2005). *Standards for middle and high school literacy coaches.* Newark, DE: Author.

Jetton, T. L., & Dole, J. A. (Eds.). (2004). *Adolescent literacy research and practice.* New York: Guilford Press.

Tovani, C. (2004). *Do I really have to teach reading?: Content comprehension, grades 6–12.* Portland, ME: Stenhouse.

Teaching Strategy Resources

Buehl, D. (2009). *Classroom strategies for interactive learning* (3rd ed.). Newark, DE: International Reading Association.

Burke, J. (2007). *Tools and texts for 50 essential lessons.* Portsmouth, NH: Heinemann.

Ogle, D. (2010). *Partnering for content literacy: PRC2 in Action.* Boston: Pearson.

Ogle, D., Klemp, R., & McBride, W. (2007). *Building literacy in social studies.* Alexandria, VA: Association for Supervision and Curriculum Development.

Zwiers, J. (2010). *Building reading comprehension habits in grades 6–12* (2nd ed.). Newark, DE: International Reading Association.

REFERENCES

Alliance for Excellent Education. (2004). *Reading next: A vision for action and research in middle and high school literacy: A report to the Carnegie Corporation of New York.* Washington, DC: Author.

Allison, N. (2009). *Middle school readers: Helping them read widely, read well.* Portsmouth, NH: Heinemann.

Alvermann, D. (2004). Effective literacy instruction for adolescents. *Journal of Literacy Research, 34,* 189–208.

Alvermann, D. (2008). Why bother theorizing adolescents' online literacies for classroom practice and research? *Journal of Adolescent and Adult Literacy, 52*(1), 8–19.

Alvermann, D. E., & Rush, L. S. (2004). Literacy intervention programs at the middle and high school levels. In T. L. Jetton & J. A. Dole (Eds.), *Adolescent literacy research and practice* (pp. 210–227). New York: Guilford Press.

Anderson, V., & Roit, M. (1993). Planning and implementing collaborative strategy instruction for delayed readers in grades 6–10. *Elementary School Journal, 94*(2), 121–137.

Ayers, J., & Miller, M. (2009). *Informing adolescent literacy policy and practice: Lessons learned from the striving readers program.* Washington, D.C. Alliance for Excellent Education.

Ball, A. F. (2005). Culture and language: Bidialectical issues in literacy: A response to Carol Lee. In J. Flood & P. L. Anders (Eds.), *Literacy development of students in urban schools: Research and policy* (pp. 275–287). Newark, DE: International Reading Association.

Bean, T. W. (1997). Preservice teachers' selection and use of content-area literacy strategies. *Journal of Educational Research, 90,* 154–163.

Bean, T. W. (2000). Reading in the content areas: Social constructivist dimensions. In M. Kamil, P. B. Mosenthal, P. D. Pearson, & R. Barr (Eds.), *Handbook of reading research* (Vol. 3, pp. 629–644). Mahwah, NJ: Erlbaum.

Beck, I. L., McKeown, M. G., Hamilton, R. L., & Kucan, L. (1997). *Questioning the author: An approach for enhancing student engagement with text.* Newark, DE: International Reading Association.

Benson, S. (2010). I don't know if that'd be English or not": Third space theory and literacy instruction. *Journal of Adolescent and Adult Literacy, 53*(7), 555–564.

Bereiter, C., & Bird, M. (1985). Use of thinking aloud in identification and teaching of reading comprehension strategies. *Cognition and Instruction, 2*(2), 131–156.

Blachowicz, C. (1986). Making connections: Alternatives to the vocabulary notebook. *Journal of Reading, 29,* 643–649.

Blamey, K., Meyer, C. K., & Walpole, S. (2009–2010). Middle and high school literacy coaches: A national survey. *Journal of Adolescent and Adult Literacy, 52*(4), 310–323.

Boudah, D. J., Deshler, D. D., Schumaker, J. B., Lenz, K., & Cook, B. (1997). Student-centered or content-centered?: A case study of a middle school teacher's lesson planning and instruction in inclusive classes. *Teacher Education and Special Education, 20*(3), 189–203.

Bransford, J. D., Brown, A. L., & Cocking, R. R. (1999). *How people learn: Brain, mind, experience, and school.* Washington, DC: National Research Council.

Brozo, W. (2000). *To be a boy, to be a reader: Engaging preteen boys in active literacy* (2nd ed.). Newark, DE: International Reading Association.

Carnegie Council on Advancing Adolescent Literacy. (2010). *Time to act: An agenda for advancing adolescent literacy for college and career success.* New York: Carnegie Corporation of New York.

Clarke, S. (2005). *Formative assessment in the secondary classroom.* London: Hodder Education.

Coiro, J., Knobel, M., Lankshear, C., & Leu, D. J. (2008). Central issues in new literacies and new literacies research In J. Coiro, M. Knobel, C. Lankshear, & D. Leu (Eds.), *Handbook of research on new literacies* (pp. 1–21). Mahwah, NJ: Erlbaum.

Cole, N. (1997). *The ETS gender study: How females and males perform in educational settings.* Princeton, NJ: Educational Testing Service.

Conley, M. W. (2005, October). *Reconsidering adolescent literacy: From competing agendas to shared commitment.* Paper presented at Michigan State Symposium on Literacy Achievement, East Lansing.

Conley, M. (2009). Improving adolescent comprehension: Developing comprehension strategies in the content areas. In S. Israel & J. Duffy (Eds.), *Handbook of research on reading comprehension* (pp. 531–550). New York: Routledge.

Cooper, E. (2005). It begins with belief: Social demographics is not destiny. *Voices from the Middle, 13,* 1.

de la Piedria, M. T. (2010). Adolescent worlds and literacy practices on the United States–Mexico border. *Journal of Adolescent and Adult Literacy, 53*(7), 575–586.

Deshler, D., Schumaker, B., Lenz, K., Bulgren, J., Hock, M., & Knight, J. (2001). Ensuring content-area learning by secondary students with learning disabilities. *Learning Disabilities Research and Practice, 16*(2), 96–108.

Deshler, D., Palincsar, A., Biancarosa, G., & Nair, M. (2009). *Informed choices for struggling adolescent readers.* Newark, DE: International Reading Association.

El-Dinary, P. B. (2002). Challenges of implementing transactional strategies instruction for reading comprehension. In C. C. Block & M. Pressley (Eds.), *Comprehension instruction: Research-based best practices* (pp. 201–215). New York: Guilford Press.

Fang, Z., & Schleppegrell, M. J. (2010). Disciplinary literacies across content areas: Supporting secondary readers through functional language analysis. *Journal of Adolescent and Adult Literacy, 53*(7) 587–597.

Guthrie, J. T., Alao, S., & Rinehart, J. M. (1997). Engagement in reading for young adolescents. *Journal of Adolescent and Adult Literacy, 40,* 438–446.

Guthrie, J. T., & Davis, M. H. (2003). Motivating struggling readers in middle school through an engagement model of classroom practice. *Reading and Writing Quarterly, 19,* 59–85.

Gutierrez, K. D. (2005). The persistence of inequality: English language learners and educational reform. In J. Flood & P. L. Anders (Eds.), *Literacy development of students in urban schools: Research and policy* (pp. 288–304). Newark, DE: International Reading Association.

Hinchman, K. A., & Zalewski, P. (1996). Reading for success in a tenth grade global-studies class: A qualitative study. *Journal of Literacy Research, 28,* 91–106.

International Reading Association (IRA). (2006). *Standards for middle and high school literacy coaches.* New York: Carnegie Corporation.

Irvin, J., Meltzer, J., Mickler, M. J., Phillips, M., & Dean, N. (2009). *Meeting the challenge of adolescent literacy.* Newark, DE: International Reading Association.

Irvin, J., Meltzer, J., Dean, N., & Mickler, M. J. (2010). *Taking the lead on adolescent literacy.* Newark, DE: International Reading Association.

Ivey, G. (2004). *Content counts with struggling urban readers.* In D. Lapp, C. C. Block, E. Cooper, J. Flood, N. Roser, & J. V. Tinajero (Eds.), *Teaching all the children: Strategies for developing literacy in an urban setting* (pp. 316–326). New York: Guilford Press.

Jetton, T. L., & Alexander, P. A. (2004). Domains, teaching and literacy. In T. L. Jetton & J. A. Dole (Eds.), *Adolescent literacy research and practice* (pp. 15–39). New York: Guilford Press.

Kallemeyn, L., Schiazza, D., Ogle, D., McKnight, K., & Livingston, C. (2010, May). *Student literacy learning and transition to high school assessments: Tools developed and lessons learned.* Paper presented at the American Educational Research Association conference, Denver, CO.

Kim, A., Vaughn, S., Klingner, J. K., Woodruff, A., Reutebuch, C., & Kouzekanani, K.

(2006). Improving reading comprehension of middle school students with disabilities through computer-assisted collaborative strategic reading. *Remedial and Special Education, 27,* 235–249.

Lee, C. D. (2005). Culture and language: Bidialectical issues in literacy. In J. Flood & P. L. Anders (Eds.), *Literacy development of students in urban schools: Research and policy* (pp. 241–274). Newark, DE: International Reading Association.

Luke, A., & Elkins, J. (2000). Re/mediating adolescent literacies. *Journal of Adolescent and Adult Literacy, 43,* 396–398.

Lynch, T. L. (2009). Rereadings and literacy: How students' second readings might open third spaces. *Journal of Adolescent and Adult Literacy,* 334–342.

Marzano, R. J. (2004). *Building background knowledge for academic achievement.* Alexandria, VA: Association for Supervision and Curriculum Development.

Miller, S., & Faircloth, B. (2009). Motivation and reading comprehension. In S. Israel & G. Duffy (Eds.), *Handbook of research on reading comprehension* (pp. 307–312). New York: Routledge.

Moje, E. (2007, April). *Social and cultural influences on adolescents' literacy development.* Paper presented at the AERA, Chicago.

Moje, E. (2010). Comprehending in the subject areas: The challenges of comprehension, grades 7–12, and what to do about them. In K. Ganske & D. Fisher (Eds.), *Comprehension across the curriculum* (pp. 46–75). New York: Guilford Press.

Moje, E., Ciechanowski, K. M., Kramer, K., Ellis, L., Carrillo, R., & Collazo, T. (2004). Working toward third space in content area literacy: An examination of everyday funds of knowledge and discourse. *Reading Research Quarterly, 39*(1), 38–70.

Moll, L., Amanti, C., Neff, D., & Gonzalez, W. (1992). Funds of knowledge for teaching: Using a qualitative approach to connect homes and classrooms. *Theory into Practice, 31*(1), 132–141.

Ogle, D. (2010). *Partnering for content literacy: PRC2 in action.* Boston: Pearson.

Ogle, D., & Hunter, K. (2000) Developing leadership at Amundsen High School: A case study of change. In M. Bizar & R. Barr (Eds.), *School leadership in times of urban reform* (pp. 179–194). Mahwah, NJ: Erlbaum.

Ogle, D., Newman, M., & Spirou, C. (2005, March). *Visual literacy (reading maps and photographs) in teaching history.* Presentation at the Association of Teacher Educators Conference, Chicago.

Oldfather, P. (2002). Students' experiences when not initially motivated for literacy learning. *Reading and Writing Quarterly, 18,* 231–256.

Oldfather, P., & McLaughlin, H. J. (1993). Gaining and losing voice: A longitudinal study of students' continuing impulse to learn across elementary and middle school contexts. *Research in Middle Level Education, 3,* 1–25.

Paris, S. G., Cross, D. R., & Lipson, M. Y. (1984). Informed strategies for learning: A program to improve children's reading awareness and comprehension. *Journal of Educational Research, 76,* 1239–1252.

Pearson, P. D., & Gallagher, M. (1983). The instruction of reading comprehension. *Contemporary Educational Psychology, 8,* 317–344.

Pressley, M., & Afflerbach, P. (1995). *Verbal protocol of reading: The nature of constructively responsive reading.* Mahwah, NJ: Erlbaum.

Pressley, M., Almasi, J., Schuder, T., Bergman, J., Hite, S., El-Dinary, P. B., et al. (1994). Transactional instruction of comprehension strategies: The Montgomery County, Maryland, SAIL program. *Reading and Writing Quarterly, 10,* 5–19.

Pressley, M., Wharton-McDonald, R., Hampson, J. M., & Echevarria, M. (1998). Strategies that improve children's memory and comprehension of text. *Elementary School Journal, 90,* 3–32.

Raphael, T. E., & Au, K. H. (2005). QAR: Enhancing comprehension and test-taking across grades and content areas. *The Reading Teacher, 59*(3), 206–221.

Raphael, T., & McMahon, S. (1994). Book club: An alternative framework for reading instruction. *The Reading Teacher, 48,* 102–116.

Reed, J. H., Schallert, D. L., Beth, A. D., & Woodruff, A. L. (2004). Motivated reader, engaged writer: The role of motivation in the literate acts of adolescents. In T. L. Jetton & J. A. Dole (Eds.), *Adolescent literacy research and practice* (pp. 251–282). New York: Guilford Press.

Robnolt, V. J., Rhodes, J. A., & Richardson, J. S. (2005, December). *Study skills for the twenty-first century "demographic group differences."* Paper presented at the National Reading Conference, Miami.

Sailors, M. (2009). Improving comprehension instruction through quality professional development. In S. Israel & J. Duffy (Eds.), *Handbook of research on reading comprehension* (pp. 645–657). New York: Routledge.

Santa, C., Havens, L., & Maycumber, E. (2005). *Creating independence through student-owned strategies.* Dubuque, IA: Kendall/Hunt.

Schallert, D. L., & Reed, J. H. (1997). The pull of the text and the process of involvement in reading. In J. T. Guthrie & A. Wigfield (Eds.), *Reading engagement: Motivating readers through integrated instruction* (pp. 68–85). Newark, DE: International Reading Association.

Shanahan, C. (2009). Disciplinary comprehension. In S. E. Israel & G. G. Duffy (Eds.), *Handbook of research on reading comprehension* (pp. 240–260). New York: Routledge.

Shanklin, N. (2006). *What are the characteristics of effective literacy coaching?* (Brief written for the Literacy Coach Clearinghouse). Retrieved July 1, 2010, from *www.literacycoachingonline.org/briefs/CharofLiteracyCoachingNLS09-27-07.pdf.*

Smith, M., & Wilhelm, J. D. (2004). "I just like being good at it": The importance of competence in the literate lives of young men. *Journal of Adolescent and Adult Literacy, 47*(6), 454–461.

Snow, C. E. (2002). *Reading for understanding: Toward an R & D program in reading comprehension.* Santa Monica, CA: RAND Corporation.

Snow, K., Griffin, P., & Burns, M. S. (2005). *Knowledge to support the teaching of reading.* San Francisco, CA: Jossey-Bass.

Sturtevant, E. G. (1996). Beyond the content literacy course: Influences on beginning mathematics teachers' uses of literacy in student teaching. In D. J. Leu, C. K. Kinzer, & K. A. Hinchman (Eds.), *Literacies for the 21st century: Research and practice: Forty-fifth yearbook of the National Reading Conference* (pp. 146–158). Chicago: National Reading Conference.

Sturtevant, E. (2003). *The literacy coach: A key to improving teaching and learning in secondary schools.* Washington, DC: Alliance for Excellent Education.

Tatum, A. (2005). *Teaching reading to black adolescent males.* Portland, ME: Stenhouse.

Tovani, C. (2004). *Do I really have to reach reading?: Content comprehension, grades 6–12.* Portland, ME: Stenhouse.

U.S. Department of Education. (2006). *Striving readers.* Retrieved January 25, 2006, from *www.ed/gov/programs/strivingreaders.*

Vaughn, J., & Estes, T. (1986). *Reading and reasoning beyond the primary grades.* Boston: Allyn & Bacon.

PART III

Evidence-Based Strategies for Literacy Learning and Teaching

CHAPTER 7

Best Practices in Motivating Students to Read

John T. Guthrie

This chapter will:

- Present the prevailing motivations that impact students' reading, including interest, confidence, and dedication.
- Describe a sample of research documenting these motivations and teaching practices that foster them.
- Portray classroom approaches consisting of autonomy support, teacher support through caring, and commitment.
- Present individual practices of assuring relevance, providing choices, generating success, arranging collaborations, setting up thematic units, and emphasizing importance to build valuing.

WHAT DO WE MEAN BY MOTIVATION?

Many teachers think of a motivated reader as a student who is having fun while reading. While this is often true, motivation is diverse. What we mean by motivation are the values, beliefs, and behaviors surrounding reading. Some productive values and beliefs may lead to excitement, yet other values may lead to determined hard work. We talk about three powerful motivations that drive students' reading. They operate in school and out of school, and they touch nearly every child. Some students may have all of these motivations and some may have only one. For some students, these motivations appear in the positive form driving students toward reading. Other motivations are negative and push students away from books. When we talk about reading motivations we refer to (1) interest, (2) dedication, and (3) confidence. An interested student reads because he enjoys it, a dedicated student reads because he believes it is important, and a confident student reads because he can do it.

KEY MOTIVATIONS TO READ: INTEREST, CONFIDENCE, DEDICATION

Interest

When we think of motivation our mind first turns to interest. Motivation is enjoying a book, being excited about an author, or being delighted by new information. Researchers refer to interest as intrinsic motivation, meaning something we do for its own sake. On a rainy day, we might rather read our favorite book than do anything else. We are not trying to get a reward when falling into a novel.

Motivation also brings to mind the reward for success. Who doesn't like to win a trinket for hitting the target with a dart at the state fair? Who doesn't want to earn serious money for working hard in a career? These are extrinsic rewards because someone gives them to us. We do not give them to ourselves, and these rewards do propel us to put out effort, focus energy, and get up in the morning. Yet extrinsic rewards do not motivate reading achievement in the long term. Students who read only for the reward of money, a grade, or a future job are not the best readers. The reason is that if you read for the reward of a good quiz score, what happens after the quiz is that you stop reading. If the test score is the only thing that matters, it is OK to take shortcuts, not really understand, or cheat. It encourages students to become more interested in the reward than the learning. None of these generate long-term achievement. Sometimes a reward, such as candy or early recess, will jump-start a group of students to read in this moment for this purpose. But if the motivation is not intrinsic, it will not increase achievement in the long term (Wigfield & Guthrie, 1997).

Confidence

Believing in oneself is more closely linked to achievement than any other motivation throughout school. The reason is that confidence, which is belief in your capacity, is tied intimately to success. This link occurs for simple daily reading tasks. A student who reads one page fluently thinks he can read the next page in the same book proficiently. The link is also forged for reading in general. A student who reads fluently and understands well is also sure of himself as a reader. In and out of school, people like the things they do well.

Conversely, students who struggle begin to doubt their abilities. They expect to do poorly in reading, writing, and talking about text. The real dilemma is that lower-achieving students often exaggerate their limitations. Believing they are worse than they really are, they stop trying altogether. Retreating from all text interactions, they reduce their own opportunity to do what they want to do more than anything—to be good readers. Their low confidence undermines them even further in a cycle of doubt and failure. By middle school, breaking this cycle is a formidable challenge for teachers.

Dedication

Although intrinsic motivation is desirable, this type of motivation is not always possible in school. There are assignments that are not desirable to a student, yet are part of the curriculum. There are books that do not appeal to some individuals, yet at a given moment in a given school, it is necessary to read them. What motivation enables students to read in this situation? The reason to read in this case is the students' belief that reading is important, and the students' persistence in reading, whatever the assignment. We call this dedication and researchers call it behavioral engagement (Skinner, Kindermann, & Furrer, 2009).

Every student has the potential to be dedicated. Skills are hard for some students to develop, but dedication is related to will. It is up to a student to decide whether to be dedicated. Students are either avoidant, dedicated, or somewhere in between the two. Students who value reading are dedicated in the sense that they devote effort, time, and persistence to their reading. These are the three key signs of dedication in students.

Persisting

One of the most important distinctions between dedicated and avoidant students is that avoidant students do not make the connection between their efforts and the outcomes. A fourth-grade teacher, Taysha Gateau-Barrera, told us that "dedicated students know that they don't improve by mistake. They make continued efforts to try hard and be well organized because they want to be successful in school." Avoidance is a particularly powerful sign because it stops all learning abruptly. If a student wants to read and tries to read well, she may learn. If another student refuses to interact with text, all hope for gaining skill, knowledge, or experience from text is dashed.

Valuing Knowledge from Reading

Dedicated students read to attain information that expands their knowledge of their perceived world. Reading is a vehicle to take them to the knowledge they want. Unlike the kids who are reading for practice, these students are reading to know. In our interview study (Guthrie, Klauda, & Morrison, in press), one middle school student said reading was important because "it informs us because we read about the Titanic, and it happened on April 12.

It's not boring, it's more like fun because they give you information and stuff about the past." Others remarked, "Reading actually teaches you things and makes you really think about life that's going on this Earth." Another said, "In science [we read about] this bacteria that I didn't know about and it's called hiking disease. When you're hiking and you get some water from the pond, and it's this little bug that if it hits you too long it can make you very sick."

Values for the Future

Dedicated middle school students think about their future. Here is one example: "Well, I guess if you are a good student and get a good education then you can go somewhere in life." Another said, "By being a good student you get in good colleges, and that's what I'm trying to do." One claimed, "Being a good reader will help you in the future because like if you got a job, you read a lot, like, even if you didn't like it. If you didn't read in school, you wouldn't know the meaning of it." A fourth said, "I sort of want to be a vet when I get older, so readings in science and learning about chemicals help me. Learning how to write things and all that stuff will help me later on." Belief in the importance of reading fuels dedication to wide and frequent reading (Guthrie et al., in press).

EVIDENCE-BASED PRACTICES IN CLASSROOM MOTIVATION

Autonomy Support

We turn next to the path from classroom practices to students' motivation. One of the most widely promoted and documented classroom practices that affects students' motivation is autonomy support (Reeve, Jang, Carrell, Jeon, & Barch, 2004; Zhou, Ma, & Deci, 2009). Based in self-determination theory (Ryan & Deci, 2000), this construct refers to taking the students' perspectives, acknowledging their feelings, and providing them with opportunities for self-direction. Teachers who support students in this way minimize the use of controlling pressures and demands. Across a range of subjects, including English, students who were afforded autonomy support by the teacher were more likely than other students to believe in the importance of reading. These students tend to identify with school and believe that schoolbooks are important and useful. Beyond valuing, autonomy support increases intrinsic motivation, which involves "doing an activity out of interest because it is rewarding in its own right" (Zhou et al., 2009, p. 493). Thus autonomy support fosters valuing and intrinsic motivation (Zhou et al., 2009). In elementary school, autonomy support may assume the form of providing challenging and interesting texts for reading (Miller & Meece, 1999).

Middle and high school students are motivated when teaching is relevant to their lives and useful for their goals. In these conditions, students showed higher volumes of reading activity (more reading engagement) than students who perceived the instruction as less relevant to them. The effect of relevance as a teaching practice was on behavioral engagement, as measured by amount of reading, and was fully mediated by intrinsic motivation and social motivation for younger secondary students. The effect of relevance of instruction was mediated for older secondary students by intrinsic motivation only. The dedication influenced by this instruction was educationally significant. Highly engaged students were reading eight times more than disengaged students on a scale that measured frequency, time spent, and breadth of materials (Lau, 2009).

Teacher Support

Vital to the classroom is the quality of teacher–student relationships. When teachers emphasize positive interpersonal relationships, student motivation increases. Believing that their teachers think they are important, students participate more socially in the classroom (Furrer & Skinner, 2003). According to both teachers and students, the quality of teacher–student relationships enhances engagement (Decker, Dona, & Christenson, 2007). For African American students in particular, collaborative learning environments enhance students' recall of stories and their desire to participate in similar activities in the future (Dill & Boykin, 2000). Across a range of contexts, explicit arrangements for student collaborations in reading and writing increased students' satisfaction of the social interactions in the classroom (Guthrie, Mason-Singh, & Coddington, in press).

In this line of research, teacher support represents student centeredness of instruction. It contrasts with a domineering or controlling approach by the teacher. Teacher support refers to students' perceptions of teacher involvement (warmth, knowledge, and dependability), and classroom structure (clarity of goals and expectations) (Skinner et al., 2009). Furrer and Skinner (2003) found that teacher support was associated with increases in students' engagement in classroom activities from fall to spring for students in grades 4 to 7. Students' engagement referred to their self-reported effort, attention, and persistence while participating in classroom learning activities. In contrast, students' behavioral disaffection decreased from fall to spring as a consequence of teacher support. This decrease consisted of a reduction in students' lack of effort or withdrawal from learning activities. Although teacher support is not a specific practice, but rather a broad attribute that may be associated with a number of specific practices such as assuring success, providing relevance, offering choices, arranging collaborations, and providing themes for learning, it was strongly associated with students' increases in behavioral engagement and decreases in behavioral disaffection.

Akin to these findings, Shih (2008) reported that Taiwanese eighth graders who reported autonomy support from their teachers were likely to show relatively high levels of behavioral engagement. They listened carefully in class, persisted with hard problems, and participated in class discussions. They did not ignore classroom activities or avoid challenges. In this case, perceived autonomy referred to the instructors' openness to students' interests.

A burgeoning literature shows that emotional support from teachers affects students' academic performance (Wentzel, 2009). In these studies, teacher support refers to students' perceptions that teachers enable them to perceive the goals of teaching clearly. Students believe that their teachers will help them attain the goals efficiently in a safe and trusting environment. The findings on the favorable effects of emotional support range from grade 1 (Hamre & Pianta, 2005; Perry, Donohue, & Weinstein, 2007) to college classrooms (Filaka & Sheldon, 2008). For example, teacher support was found to increase competence in reading words and passages in the middle of first grade, especially for at-risk students. In fact, the benefits of emotional support were stronger than the benefits of excellent pedagogy for cognitive learning in beginning reading (Hamre & Pianta, 2005).

Social relationships and teacher support in the classroom are pivotal in middle schools. In overviewing the literature on social motivation, Juvonen (2007) stated:

> Of school-based social relationships, teacher support is probably the most salient. When students feel supported and respected by their teachers they are presumed to comply with the expectations and norms set by instructors and engage in the behaviors endorsed by these authority figures. When students lack a bond or do not get along with a teacher, students are presumed to disengage themselves from school-related activities and the institution. (p. 200)

She continues, "Perceptions of positive teacher regard at seventh grade have been shown to predict improved academic competence, mental health, and higher academic values in eighth grade" (p. 200). Likewise, lack of sense of belonging in school frequently predicts adolescents' dropout rates (Finn & Rock, 1997). Based on her review, Juvonen proposes that educators should "capitalize on affiliative needs to engage students" (p. 203). Such a recommendation might include cooperative learning, peer collaboration, and building teacher–student relationships. A few studies have shown the positive effects of collaborative arrangements on motivation, especially for African American students (Guthrie, Rueda, Gambrell, & Morrison, 2009). Although social structures in classrooms have been evaluated rigorously from the perspective of their contribution to developing cognitive skills (Murphy, Wilkinson, Soter, Hennessey, & Alexander, 2009), they have rarely been investigated for their motivation benefits in literacy learning.

Teacher caring is central to teacher support (Wentzel, 2009). Students who say, "The teacher cares about me" are higher achievers than those who do not feel that the teacher cares. However, the specific ways in which teachers express caring for students has been little studied. It is unclear how teacher caring relates to some of the other practices discussed earlier, such as helping students to see the relevance of instruction and making meaningful choices during learning. Unfortunately, it is not easy to enable teachers to "care" through professional development or preservice education. However, teachers can learn the practices of caring about students. The practices will be presented in the next section.

Intervention Research in Reading Motivation

Although interventions are rare in motivation research, a few studies can be identified. Vansteenkiste, Lens, and Deci (2006) compared experimental groups who received either intrinsically motivating goals for reading or extrinsically motivating goals for reading the same text. In the intrinsic condition, students who were obese were asked to read a text on nutrition for their own purposes. In the extrinsic condition, similar students were asked to read the same text for the extrinsic goal of memorizing facts to score well on a test. The students with intrinsic goals recalled the text more fully and reported more involvement in the reading than students with the extrinsic goals (Vansteenkiste et al., 2006). Furthermore, when a brief computer-based instructional unit was embellished with personalized features and inconsequential choices, students showed more intrinsic motivation for the activity than if the program did not have the embellishments (Cordova & Lepper, 1996). Following a meta-analysis of motivation studies involving text interaction, Guthrie and Humenick (2004) concluded that a variety of positive motivations were increased by experimental conditions related to relevance, content goals, choices, and collaborations.

In summary, a variety of correlational, experimental, and qualitative research confirms the positive affects of motivational practices on students' interest, confidence, and dedication in reading. This body of research undergirds the broad approaches of autonomy support and teacher support. It also affirms the effectiveness of specific practices described next, including making reading relevant, affording choices, assuring success, arranging for collaborations, emphasizing the importance of reading, organizing thematic units, and integrating multiple motivation supports during instruction.

BEST PRACTICES IN ACTION

Relevance

Appealing to students' interest is a popular motivational approach. In a book-length treatment on building reading motivation for boys, Brozo (2002) found that boys respond when teachers become aware of their students' personal interests and needs. Some boys may want to read about heroes, adventurers, magicians, or tricksters. If their curiosities can be identified through interest inventories, they may become engrossed in a book or a topic and learn to find satisfaction through literacy. Although this suggestion is useful for book clubs or free reading activities, it is not easily used for instruction with information books and is not easy to relate to curriculum-connected academic accountabilities that are widespread in middle schools.

Real-World Materials

When it is possible to bring media based in the real world into classroom instruction, the text becomes relevant. For example, in a social studies class studying civil rights, the teacher found a poignant newspaper article. It described an elderly female protester who was on a picket line objecting to racist policies. Although she was a civil rights activist she behaved hypocritically by owning a segregated grocery store. The article captivated students' attention and through their critical analysis of the text and the historical situation, they developed keen insights about the economic and moral pressures surrounding racism (Johnson & Cowles, 2009).

Relevant texts are commonplace in vocational schools or courses. One vocational school's students worked in shops that were run like real job sites. Students were presented many opportunities to participate in work-related scenarios. As well as providing services to the community such as changing the oil or repairing people's car brakes, they read texts on auto mechanics, construction, electricity, plumbing, graphic design, and computer technology. The school did not have to stretch to provide students with authentic tasks or reading materials. Because of their relevance, the students valued these reading tasks. The vast majority of students dedicated themselves to mastering these texts despite their complexity (Darvin, 2006). Whether they are newspapers, job-related texts, or part of the popular culture, texts from the real world are relevant in themselves.

For elementary school students in urban settings, a team of teachers built relevance by forming linkages between students in the upper elementary grades and adult pen pals in local businesses, nonprofit organizations, and government agencies in the area. Adult pen pals read the same books as the students and wrote questions and commentaries guided by a website. Teachers selected grade-level books from five domains: fiction, social studies, biography, folk tales, and science. In a final look at the program, the author stated:

> A key to active student engagement was the series of literacy activities reflective of real-life experiences. Students interacted purposefully above all with their adult pen pals. They read to answer real questions, compose responses to their pen pals' questions, and to build conceptual knowledge. The pen pal context provided powerful motivation for students to read and write strategically and learn skills in order to make their letters as good as possible for the real person to whom they wrote. For many students the motivation extended beyond the particular book and the particular letter. They

were motivated enough to read many other books at their grade level on the same topic or the same genre. Kelley & Clausen-Grace, 2009, p. 736)

In this case, it was not the real-world materials, but the real-world members of their community and authentic questions that inspired reading dedication.

Poignant Topics

A powerful source of relevant texts for young adolescents is novels or biographies on the theme of freedom. As Bean and Harper (2006) showed, young adolescents are captivated by *The Breadwinner* (Ellis, 2001), a novel about Parvana, a 12-year-old girl living in Afghanistan under Taliban rule. In an act of survival, Parvana poses as a boy selling goods to earn money for her family. She achieves some freedom by making her femininity invisible, but she loses some of her ethnic identity. Reading this book, students became immersed in her losses of religious and gender identity as she gained economic freedoms. Many of them discovered they had paid a price for freedoms as well. Relevance of this text to their lives generated dedicated reading.

The quickest way to locate topics relevant to students' interests is to enable them to select a topic for project-based activities. In one example, students in an upper elementary school class selected topics on social justice, which was new to them. In the media center and on the Internet they found books and articles on injustices in housing, employment, and access to health care. Reading these multiple self-selected texts, students composed five-panel comic strips using computer software to explain their particular topic. They read deeply and wrote sharply to portray and explain the injustice they unearthed.

In a study at the elementary school level, students volunteered that their personal interests were the main factor that made them want to read a narrative text. In asking why they chose certain books students replied:

- "I like dolphins. I think they are cool because they live in the ocean and I like oceans."
- "It was important because I like different cultures."
- "Because it was about an Indian and I am interested in Indians."

Identifying students' topical interests through a conversation or a questionnaire can enable teachers to heighten the relevance of books and entice students into dedicated reading.

Teachers Create Relevance

It is often impossible to locate real-world materials. On many occasions, the teacher needs to create relevance by designing events that enable students to see connections of text to themselves. For example, a middle school class was reading *Night* by Elie Wiesel (1960), an account of the author's experiences during the Holocaust. Taking place on another continent in an earlier generation, students did not take much interest in the scene in which Jewish individuals were herded like cattle into a railroad car. To render the scene more personal, the teacher made a large rectangle of red tape on the classroom floor. He asked the class to crowd into this limited space. After students' giggling and complaining subsided, the teacher explained that this is how Jews stood for days at a time on a moving train. Following this weak simulation, students began to ask about the people and their circumstances, and their reading was reignited.

A teacher-guided event that generates relevance consists of enabling students to create their own questions about text. In one social studies class, students wrote their questions about the freedoms of religion, speech, assembly, petition, and the press. Students were expected to learn about the five basic freedoms embodied in the Constitution. They read for definitions, historical origins, and limits of all these freedoms and prepared a 6- to 8-minute oral report. Their report centered on a single person, event, battle, or place during the Civil War that was connected to one of these freedoms. By enabling students to be guided by their own questions, as well as the curriculum framework, students bring their knowledge, interests, and idiosyncrasies into their reading activities. As a consequence, their willingness to spend time and effort grows and their products display the benefits of dedicated reading.

For students at many ages, the teacher may set up situations involving a discrepant event, a reality that conflicts with what the students might expect to see. For example, as Duke, Purcell-Gates, Hall, and Tower (2006) reported in a study on light, one teacher set up a prism on the overhead projector while her class was out of the room. This caused rainbows to appear on the ceiling. When the students returned there were many oohs and aahs and a rush of questions about how the rainbow effects occurred. Teachers led students to find and read information text on light to help them answer their questions. Such discrepant events may be created for literature and fiction as well. If students are asked to predict the outcome of a chapter or what a character will do in a scene, the teacher can create a discrepancy between the students' expectations and the events in the book. Exploring and explaining the discrepancies between students' predictions and the actual events can lead to teachable moments that deepen students' comprehension and enhance their reading dedication.

Relationships of teachers and students in elementary school can often be built around finding the right books for students. If teachers use an interest inventory to determine topics that students enjoy, they can often find great books based on this information. Highlighting these books in book talks, book commercials, or other means helps build students' faith in teachers' ability to find relevant materials for them. In teacher–student conferences during independent reading, teachers can help students find and stick with a good book. As students gain trust in the teacher as an ally in finding and enjoying books, students' all-important reading time grows.

Relevance is an instructional practice central to Concept-Oriented Reading Instruction (CORI) activities (Guthrie, Mason-Singh, et al., in press). In this context, relevance refers to linking books and reading activities to the students' personal experiences. These connections to "me" as a person are especially poignant for adolescents who are centered on thinking about who they are. Such links to self can be tied to long-term history, such as students' cultural experiences in their ethnic group, to a personal interest such as skateboarding, or to a recent personal experience. In CORI for middle school students, we give context through videos related to the conceptual theme. For example, in Week 1, we present a video on predation in which a cheetah is capturing a gazelle on the Serengeti plain. After watching the 3-minute video, students make observations about it, draw inferences, and make connections between the events. The students then read a paragraph of text to learn more about predation in cheetahs and other animals. They draw inferences from the text and share their observations with peers.

In this 20-minute activity, reading information text is made relevant by connecting it to a vivid personal encounter with the phenomenon through video. Needless to say, the color, audio effects, and drama rivet the students' attention and arouse their interest. Asking students to perform the processes with the video that we later ask them to perform with the text brings a linkage not only in content but also in the process of learning across the media. Thus relevance is established through the immediacy of experience with video and text. It is relevance situated in a disciplinary domain and information texts on the subject matter. We believe that this level of relevance is effective as a starting point for learning the relevance of other texts on other topics in the future.

When students view a video on predation in the Serengeti the experience is effortless, eye opening, and interesting. It activates what they already know and arouses natural curiosities. Watching the video is intrinsically motivating, which means that students will do it for their own enjoyment. Students often ask to see the video many times. Linking a readable trade book to this interesting event projects the qualities of the video enjoyment into the text interaction. For this moment, in this situation, reading becomes interesting. Thus the students' interest in reading is scaffolded by creating situated interest in an extremely concrete situation. Then we extrapolate outward from it. Students are weaned from the relevance-generating event and learn to find interest in other texts and other topics.

Choices

The most widespread recommendation for motivation is providing choices. In the classroom, students are often thrilled to have a choice in their reading.

They rise to it with enthusiasm, at least temporarily. A theoretical framework for choice in the classroom is self-determination theory (Ryan & Deci, 2000), which argues that students' development of autonomy, or being in charge of their lives, is central to their academic achievement and emotional adjustment. After reviewing Self-Determination Theory, Reed, Schallert, Beth, and Woodruff (2004) stated, "When it comes to addressing specifically the motivational processes of adolescents in literacy-focused classrooms, the single most powerful suggestion we can make is to encourage teachers to develop learning environments that are autonomy supportive" (p. 274).

Autonomy support in this context refers to enabling students to become self-directing and self-controlling of their literacy and academic work. Reeve (1996) explained autonomy support in the classroom in a book-length treatment entitled *Motivating Others: Nurturing Inner Motivational Resources.* As Reeve said:

> Autonomy support refers to the amount of freedom a teacher gives a student so the student can connect his or her behavior to personal goals, interests, and values. The opposite of autonomy support is coercion or being controlled. Teacher autonomy support expresses itself when teachers allow students choices, respect their agendas, and provide learning activities that are relevant to personal goals and interests. (p. 206)

Among the proposals for instructional practices described in this section, autonomy support may enjoy the largest amount of empirical verification, which has been reviewed in Guthrie and Humenick (2004).

Providing choice is a motivational support system in CORI for middle school that enables students to develop self-direction in the classroom. Teachers provide the following kinds of choices within the 6-week CORI program: self-selection of books or sections of books, student input into topics or sequence of topics, student suggestions for strategy use for comprehension, options for demonstrating learning from text, and selecting partners for teams. As these examples show, we are not affording students open opportunity to take complete charge of everything they do for a week in Reading/Language Arts. These are mini-choices during literacy lessons. Yet as small as these choices may appear, they enable students to feel a stronger sense of investment and to commit larger amounts of effort to their reading work. We have given many examples of the roles and ranges of choices that are possible in middle school elsewhere (McRae & Guthrie, 2009).

On a daily basis effective teachers can give mini-choices. They empower students to increase their investment in learning. When appropriate, in every lesson have students do at least one of the following:

1. Select a story.
2. Select a page to read.
3. Select sentences to explain.

4. Identify a goal for the day.
5. Choose three of five questions to answer.
6. Write questions for a partner exchange.

Success

Support for students' self-efficacy in reading and other subjects is crucial. Without the belief in themselves, students in the upper elementary and middle school grades often retreat from books. As portrayed by Schunk and Zimmerman (2007), several explicit teaching practices increase students' self-efficacy. The self-efficacy-fostering framework consists of providing students' process goals. These are steps for performing reading tasks successfully. Teachers provide feedback for success in the process goals rather than feedback for the students' products or outcomes. That is, teachers give specific direction to students about the effectiveness of their strategy for performing work. They help students set realistic goals for reading. Also beneficial to students' self-efficacy is their perception of coherence in the texts and tasks of instruction. When students can identify the links across contents of reading and perceive themes in the substance of their reading materials, they gain a belief that they can succeed in reading and writing about text (Guthrie, Mason-Singh, et al., in press).

To afford your students practices that boost success, assure that at least one of the following is very prominent in every lesson:

1. Text matched to students' reading levels.
2. Frequent feedback for reading.
3. Authentic reading merged with skills.
4. Multiple opportunities for reading.
5. Sharing competency with peers.
6. Student goal setting.
7. Rewarding effort.

Collaboration

Collaboration is a central process in CORI. Teachers implementing collaboration are initiating the following activities: (1) reading in partners or small groups, (2) exchanging ideas and sharing expertise, (3) student-led discussion groups, (4) book talks, (5) team projects such as a poster-making activity, and (6) peer feedback. As with the other motivation supports, these activities are contextualized within the conceptual theme and books related to the theme. For example, partners may be given 5 minutes to discuss the inferences they generated from reading three pages of text on the conceptual question of the day. In each 90-minute lesson, teachers arrange for students to work in whole class, partnerships, small-team interactions, and individually. The structure for small-team interaction is collaborative reasoning, based on research from

Chinn, Anderson, and Waggoner (2001). In this interactive structure, students make claims about the text, add to each other's interpretations, raise clarifying questions, and attempt to synthesize their own brainstorming. Shown to affect higher-order thinking about text, collaborative reasoning is not merely a social break from learning or an open discussion, but a scaffolded process of cumulative contributions based on reading about a topic. The outcome is a collective understanding about text.

Collaboration can occur in every lesson. It may be a broad plan or a brief event. Each lesson can include one of the following:

1. Have partners read aloud together.
2. Partners exchange questions to answer over text.
3. Team summarizes a chapter.
4. Literature circles.
5. Collaborative reasoning.
6. Organize a jigsaw.
7. Set up peer editing about text.

Emphasizing Importance

Too many students avoid reading because they believe it is not important to them now or in the future. They do not value reading and do not think it will benefit them. To address this dilemma, we believe in providing students with a concrete experience rather than an abstract principle. Rather than attempting a global strategy of persuading students that reading will enable them to go to college or enter a career of their choice, we attempt to situate the benefit of literacy in a concrete situation. For example, have students view a video of plant–animal relationships. Then have them read a related text and share their new learning with a partner. After the lesson, ask, "What were your sources of new learning today?" Students will respond by saying, "the video" or "my partner" or "my writing." Soon they will discover that it was the text that enabled them to gain knowledge most effectively on this topic on this day. This recognition is an awareness of the value of reading. It often comes as a surprise to the students. The teacher may also ask how a choice made during the lesson benefitted them. Students' awareness of how well they enjoyed the choice, and how it helped them focus cognitively, raises their estimate of the value of reading.

Valuing literacy is the motivational process we attempt to facilitate with the practice of emphasizing importance. When the students begin to reflect on how the text helped them speak effectively with their team or write effectively, they begin to view the book reading process as beneficial in a new way. Obviously, a single event is limited to one topic in one day in one classroom. This cannot create a lifelong value. However, it is a starting point for the journey of finding literacy to be important. It is a first step in working hard because reading is valuable. If 5 minutes of concentrated effort paid off in today's activity, the ethic of hard work in reading activities can be acquired and applied to broader reaches of schooling.

For each lesson you can ask students to show the importance of reading. Have them:

1. Identify the portion of text they used to answer a question.
2. Point to a text that was most informative about a character in literature.
3. Identify a text that enabled them to explain a concept in information text.
4. Compare what they learned from a text versus what they learned from a video on the topic.
5. Contrast the content they learned from reading, writing, or discussing in a lesson.
6. Explain how the content of a text could help them in an out-of-school situation.

Thematic Unit

Thematic units can be taught on many topics. First you begin with a main theme or big idea. Next identify supporting concepts to explain the big idea. Then identify texts that contain the concepts. Texts should also afford you the opportunities to teach reading strategies, such as concept mapping. In one unit of CORI for grade 7, the theme is the Diversity of Plants and Animals in Community Interactions. The superordinate idea of the unit is *symbiosis*, including such forms as mutualism and parasitism. To accentuate the conceptual theme, teachers give students a big question for each week, as well as daily questions related to the week's big question. This does not preclude student questioning, but sets a frame for the topic. In Week 1, the following four questions were presented on the first 4 days of instruction:

1. "What are the characteristics of an ecosystem?"
2. "How does predation contribute to balance in an ecosystem?"
3. "How do different species of animals rely on their environment for feeding?"
4. "In what ways do animals adapt to their environment for survival?"

To provide resources for literacy in this theme all books are unified around it for the 6 weeks. Texts for whole-class instruction, individual guided reading, and individual books for group projects are selected to be relevant to the theme. Strategies that are taught for comprehension, including summarizing and concept mapping, are placed within the context of the conceptual theme. For example, student summaries represent their reading related to a particular question on a given day. Motivation supports, such as choice, are provided in the context of thematic learning. For example, the teacher may provide a choice for which chapter in a selected book to read on a given day. Students make their selections based on their view of what will enable them to learn about the question of the day and to discuss it effectively with a peer. Thus motivational support of choice is not global, but is framed by the content question of the day and undergirded by the content learning of yesterday.

Self-efficacy is the motivational process that is fostered by the thematic unit. The theme empowers students to answer questions, talk with peers, and write opinions confidently. The conceptual theme feeds students' sense of competence because it makes the learning from text more sensible; texts are linked to what they have recently learned in the classroom. Thus students' self-efficacy for reading derives more from their sense of competency with the content of the texts than their sense of being fluent or writing answers to questions. When the clarity of content is enhanced, the confidence in learning from text is extended.

Build in the following qualities to your thematic units:

1. Instructional units have conceptual complexity and duration.
2. Students learn big ideas of survival, war and peace, discovery, oppression.
3. Topics persist over days and weeks.
4. Students write concept maps of pages, chapters, books, and unit.
5. Connect diverse genre (stories, nonfiction, poems) to each other.
6. Have overarching guiding questions that link texts.

Integration of Motivational Practices

It is entirely possible to integrate multiple motivation practices into a coherent teaching unit. Following are two examples, one at the elementary level and one at the primary level.

We and our colleagues have examined how CORI influences third-, fourth-, fifth-, and seventh-grade students' reading comprehension and engagement in reading (Guthrie et al., 2004). CORI includes the classroom practices of providing relevance, choices, collaboration, leveled texts, and thematic units. This cluster of practices is designed to increase intrinsic motivation, self-efficacy, social motivation, and valuing for reading (Guthrie, Wigfield, & Perencevich, 2004). Guthrie, McRae, and Klauda (2007) performed a meta-analysis of CORI's effects across 11 experiments with 75 effect sizes. CORI was found to surpass comparison treatments in increasing students' competence according to standardized tests of reading comprehension, 2-day reading and writing tasks, passage comprehension, reading fluency, and word recognition. CORI also fostered students' reading motivation and engagement in reading. This confirms that an integrated cluster of motivational practices over extended time can increase students' performance on educationally significant measures of reading comprehension. The bulk of the evidence shows that CORI affected reading comprehension outcomes, although one study also showed that this instructional effect was mediated by behavioral engagement (Wigfield et al., 2008; see further discussion below). Furthermore, these effects were confirmed by investigators who showed that an intervention that added motivational supports to instruction in self-regulation increased students' self-regulated reading more effectively than instruction that did not include motivational practices (Souvignier & Mokhlesgerami, 2006).

Integration is also shown to be effective at the primary level. For example, in Hamre and Pianta's (2005) study of reading instruction in kindergarten, classroom quality was assessed in terms of teachers' provision of effective instruction while building warm, emotional connections with students, which included support for students' self-regulation, a balance of activities for children's diverse skill levels, and sensitivity to students' interests. Classrooms with high global quality induced high levels of student behavioral engagement, which consisted of attending to tasks, completing reading activities, following rules, persisting in the face of difficulty, and exercising control. Students with high behavioral engagement showed higher gains in reading competencies than students with lower behavioral engagement and lower global quality of instruction (Ponitz, Rimm-Kaufman, Grimm, & Curby, 2009). What motivating teachers were doing was being responsive to students' interests (reading a story the students preferred), providing abundant praise, giving students time to complete their work, showing their appreciation for individual students, and expressing confidence in students' ability to learn. At the same time, motivating teachers were not too teacher centered, authoritative, or controlling.

Double-Edged

Teachers' motivational practices are so powerful that they can have deleterious effects. Some teachers behave in ways that are devaluing for students. For example, negative feedback from teachers may be devaluing for students. When teachers consistently scold or make students feel badly for having the wrong answers, students respond by devaluing academic work, as indicated by their expressions that they do not care about learning or grades (Strambler & Weinstein, 2010). In addition, students who experience no choices or limited choices in reading in language arts or science classes, show losses of intrinsic motivation for reading. Likewise, when books are extremely difficult to read, students report declines in self-efficacy for reading. When books are irrelevant, as indicated by students' failure to connect the content to their prior knowledge or their life experiences, they report low levels of interest or dedication to reading (Guthrie, Klauda, et al., in press).

What this shows is that classroom practices are swords that cut in two directions. Affirming practices may foster motivational growth. But undermining practices, such as negative feedback, controlling instruction, and irrelevance may generate losses in motivation. These findings are consistent with the correlational findings reported by Assor, Kaplan, and Roth (2002) and reciprocal relationships between classroom instruction and student motivations found by Skinner and Belmont (1993).

CONCLUDING REFLECTIONS

In one regard, every teacher is a motivator. Teachers empower students to become active with print. Otherwise reading never happens. On the other side of the coin, motivating students to their fullest is rare. Teachers seldom put motivation first, but when they do, students become interested, confident and dedicated. And almost every teacher is rewarded by having motivated readers.

That is what makes motivation inevitable. We know what motivates students to read—interest, confidence and dedication. We know what teachers are doing that fuels these motivations. They are using the practices in this chapter. Tools for motivation are at hand, and teachers are discovering them daily. Because using these tools for motivation boosts achievement, many stakeholders benefit. Administrators shine when motivated students achieve. Parents swell with pride when their children succeed as readers. Because the repercussions of reading radiate from the motivated student to her surrounding village and back again to the learner, reading engagement is expanding.

ENGAGEMENT ACTIVITIES

1. *Reflection.* To grapple with the ideas in this chapter, first make an appraisal of where you are. Many teachers support motivation—some more than others. Where are you? For each motivational practice, such as providing relevance, ask the following questions. You might do it alone or in a grade-level school team. Take a few notes on each question and share your perceptions. Almost certainly you, especially along with your colleagues, can take steps forward.
   a. Do I do this practice already?
   b. How often do I do this?
   c. When do I do this?
   d. How well does it work?
   e. How can I do this more?
   f. How can I do this better?
   g. How can I connect this practice more deeply to my teaching?

2. *Appraisal.* To understand how your students experience your classroom, ask them. You can give a brief questionnaire with statements such as, "The teacher relates the reading to my interests." You may be surprised at what they say. Some questionnaires for students and teachers are available in the Appendix of *Engaging Adolescents in Reading* (Guthrie, 2008). They are easily used or adapted for students in grades 3–12.
3. *Application.* Select a lesson coming up in the next week. Ask yourself, "What choice am I going to give during the lesson?" Give that small choice. Then compare how the lesson went with a lesson where you did not give any choice. How did the students respond? Do this application for each motivational practice including relevance and so on. Then enrich your lessons by giving two motivation supports, say, choice and relevance, in the same lesson. How do your students respond, and how can you improve those supports? Your students will become a bit more dedicated to reading. Build momentum.

REFERENCES

Assor, A., Kaplan, H., & Roth, G. (2002). Choice is good, but relevance is excellent: Autonomy-enhancing and suppressing teacher behaviours predicting students' engagement in schoolwork. *British Journal of Educational Psychology, 72,* 261–278.

Bean, T. W., & Harper, H. J. (2006). Exploring notions of freedom in and through young adult literature. *Journal of Adolescent and Adult Literacy, 50,* 96–104.

Brozo, W. G. (2002). *To be a boy, to be a reader: Engaging teen and preteen boys in active literacy.* Newark, DE: International Reading Association.

Chinn, C. A., Anderson, R. C., & Waggoner, M. A. (2001). Patterns of discourse in two kinds of literature discussion. *Reading Research Quarterly, 36,* 378–411.

Cordova, D. I., & Lepper, M. R. (1996). Intrinsic motivation and the process of learning: Beneficial effects of contextualization, personalization, and choice. *Journal of Educational Psychology, 88,* 715–730.

Darvin, J. (2006). "Real-world cognition doesn't end when the bell rings": Literacy instruction derived from situated cognition research. *Journal of Adolescent and Adult Literacy, 49,* 10–18.

Decker, D. M., Dona, D. P., & Christenson, S. L. (2007). Behaviorally at-risk African American students: The importance of student–teacher relationships for student outcomes. *Journal of School Psychology, 45,* 83–109.

Dill, E. M., & Boykin, A. W. (2000). The comparative influence of individual, peer tutoring, and communal learning contexts on the text recall of African American children. *Journal of Black Psychology, Special issue: African American culture and identity: Research directions for the new millennium, 26,* 65–78.

Duke, N. K., Purcell-Gates, V., Hall, L. A., & Tower, C. (2006). Authentic literacy activities for developing comprehension and writing. *The Reading Teacher, 60,* 344–355.

Ellis, D. (2001). *The breadwinner.* Toronto: Groundwood Books.

Filaka, V. F., & Sheldon, K. M. (2008). Teacher support, student motivation, student need satisfaction, and college teacher course evaluations: Testing a sequential path model. *Educational Psychology, 28,* 711–724.

Finn, J. D., & Rock, D. A. (1997). Academic success among students at risk for school failure. *Journal of Applied Psychology, 82,* 221–234.

Furrer, C., & Skinner, E. (2003). Sense of relatedness as a factor in children's academic engagement and performance. *Journal of Educational Psychology, 95,* 148–162.

Guthrie, J. T. (Ed.). (2008). *Engaging adolescents in reading.* Thousand Oaks, CA: Corwin Press.

Guthrie, J. T. & Humenick, N. M. (2004). Motivating students to read: Evidence for classroom practices that increase reading motivation and achievement. In P. McCardle & V. Chhabra (Eds.), *The voice of evidence in reading research* (pp. 329–354). Baltimore: Brookes.

Guthrie, J. T., Klauda, S. L., & Morrison, D. A. (in press). Motivation, achievement, and classroom contexts for information book reading. In J. T. Guthrie, A. Wigfield, & S. L. Klauda (Eds.), *Adolescents' engagement in academic literacy.* Sharjah: UAE. Bentham Science Publishers.

Guthrie, J. T., Mason-Singh, A., & Coddington, C. S. (in press). Instructional effects of Concept-Oriented Reading Instruction on motivation for reading information text in middle school. In J. T. Guthrie, A. Wigfield, & S. L. Klauda (Eds.), *Adolescents' engagement in academic literacy.* Sharjah: UAE. Bentham Science Publishers.

Guthrie, J. T., McRae, A., & Klauda, S. L. (2007). Contributions of Concept-Oriented Reading Instruction to knowledge about interventions for motivations in reading. *Educational Psychologist, 42,* 237–250.

Guthrie, J. T., Rueda, R. S., Gambrell, L. B., & Morrison, D. A. (2009). Roles of engagement, valuing, and identification in reading development of students from diverse backgrounds. In L. M. Morrow & R. S. Rueda (Eds.), *Handbook of research on literacy and diversity* (pp. 195–216). New York: Guilford Press.

Guthrie, J. T., Wigfield, A., Barbosa, P., Perencevich, K. C., Taboada, A., Davis, M. H., et al. (2004). Increasing reading comprehension and engagement through Concept-Oriented Reading Instruction. *Journal of Educational Psychology, 96,* 403–423.

Guthrie, J. T., Wigfield, A., & Perencevich, K. C. (Eds.). (2004). *Motivating reading comprehension: Concept-Oriented Reading Instruction.* Mahwah, NJ: Erlbaum.

Hamre, B. K., & Pianta, R. C. (2005). Can instructional and emotional support in the first-grade classroom make a difference for children at risk of school failure? *Child Development, 76,* 949–967.

Johnson, A. S., & Cowles, L. (2009). Orlonia's "literacy-in-persons": Expanding notions of literacy through biography and history. *Journal of Adolescent and Adult Literacy, 52,* 410–420.

Juvonen, J. (2007). Reforming middle schools: Focus on continuity, social connectedness, and engagement. *Educational Psychologist, 42,* 197–208.

Kelley, M. J., & Clausen-Grace, N. (2009). Facilitating engagement by differentiating independent reading. *The Reading Teacher, 63,* 313–318.

Lau, K. (2009). Reading motivation, perceptions of reading instruction and reading amount: A comparison of junior and secondary students in Hong Kong. *Journal of Research in Reading, 32*, 366–382.

McRae, A., & Guthrie, J. T. (2009). Beyond opportunity: Promoting reasons for reading. In E. H. Hiebert (Ed.), *Reading more, reading better: Are American students reading enough of the right stuff?* (pp. 55–76). Newark, DE: International Reading Association.

Miller, S. D., & Meece, J. L. (1999). Third graders' motivational preferences for reading and writing tasks. *The Elementary School Journal, 100*, 19–35.

Murphy, K., Wilkinson, I., Soter, A., Hennessey, M., & Alexander, J. (2009). Examining the effects of discussion non students' comprehension of text: A meta-analysis. *Journal of Educational Psychology, 101*, 740–764.

Perry, K. E., Donohue, K. M., & Weinstein, R. S. (2007). Teaching practices and the promotion of achievement and adjustment in first grade. *Journal of School Psychology, 45*, 269–292.

Ponitz, C. C., Rimm-Kaufman, S. E., Grimm, K. J., & Curby, T. W. (2009). Kindergarten classroom quality, behavioral engagement, and reading achievement. *School Psychology Review, 38*, 102–120.

Reed, J. H., Schallert, D. L., Beth, A. D., & Woodruff, A. L. (2004). Motivated reader, engaged writer: The role of motivation in the literate acts of adolescents. In T. L. Jetton & J. A. Dole (Eds.), *Adolescent literacy research and practice* (pp. 251–282). New York: Guilford Press.

Reeve, J. (1996). *Motivating others: Nurturing inner motivational resources.* Boston: Allyn & Bacon.

Reeve, J., Jang, H., Carrell, D., Jeon, S., & Barch, J. (2004). Enhancing students' engagement by increasing teachers' autonomy support. *Motivation and Emotion, 28*, 147–169.

Ryan, R. M., & Deci, E. L. (2000). Self-determination theory and the facilitation of intrinsic motivation, social development, and well-being. *American Psychologist, 55*, 68–78.

Schunk, D. H., & Zimmerman, B. J. (2007). Influencing children's self efficacy and self-regulation of reading and writing through modeling. *Reading and Writing Quarterly: Overcoming Learning Difficulties, 23*, 7–25.

Shih, S. (2008). The relation of self-determination and achievement goals to Taiwanese eighth graders' behavioral and emotional engagement in schoolwork. *The Elementary School Journal, 108*, 313–334.

Skinner, E. A., & Belmont, M. J. (1993). Motivation in the classroom: Reciprocal effects of teacher behavior and student engagement across the school year. *Journal of Educational Psychology, 85*, 571–558.

Skinner, E. A., Kindermann, T. A., & Furrer, C. J. (2009). A motivational perspective on engagement and disaffection: Conceptualization and assessment of children's behavioral and emotional participation in academic activities in the classroom. *Educational and Psychological Measurement, 69*, 493–525.

Souvignier, E., & Mokhlesgerami, J. (2006). Using self-regulation as a framework for implementing strategy instruction to foster reading comprehension. *Learning and Instruction, 16*, 57–71.

Strambler, M. J., & Weinstein, R. S. (2010). Psychological disengagement in elementary school among ethnic minority students. *Journal of Applied Developmental Psychology, 31*, 155–165.

Vansteenkiste, M., Lens, W., & Deci, E. L. (2006). Intrinsic versus extrinsic goal contents in self-determination theory: Another look at the quality of academic motivation. *Educational Psychologist, 41,* 19–31.

Wentzel, K. R. (2009). Students' relationships with teachers as motivational contexts. In K. R. Wentzel & A. Wigfield (Eds.), *Handbook of motivation at school* (pp. 301–322). New York: Routledge/Taylor & Francis Group.

Wiesel, E. (1960). *Night.* New York: Bantam Books.

Wigfield, A., & Guthrie, J. T. (1997). Relations of children's motivation for reading to the amount and breadth or their reading. *Journal of Educational Psychology, 89,* 420–432.

Wigfield, A., Guthrie, J. T., Perencevich, K. C., Taboada, A., Klauda, S. L., McRae, A., et al. (2008). Role of reading engagement in mediating effects of reading comprehension. *Psychology in the Schools, 45,* 432–445

Zhou, M., Ma, W. J., & Deci, E. L. (2009). The importance of autonomy for rural Chinese children's motivation for learning. *Learning and Individual Differences, 19,* 492–498.

CHAPTER 8

Best Practices in Teaching Phonological Awareness and Phonics

Patricia M. Cunningham

This chapter will:

- Describe the role of phonemic awareness in learning to read.
- Explore what research says about the best way to teach phonics.
- Summarize what we know about multisyllabic word decoding.
- Describe classroom practices consistent with what we know about phonemic awareness, phonics, and multisyllabic word decoding.

Phonics is and has been the most controversial issue in reading. Since 1955, when Rudolph Flesch's book *Why Johnny Can't Read* became a national best-seller, educators and parents have debated the role of phonics in beginning-reading instruction. A variety of published phonics programs have been touted as the "cure-all" for everyone's reading problems. Enthusiasm for these programs has lasted just long enough for everyone to relearn that thoughtful reading requires much more than just the ability to quickly decode words. As the chapters of this book demonstrate, the most effective literacy frameworks include a variety of instruction and activities that provide children with a balanced literacy diet. This chapter focuses on phonemic awareness and phonics. When the knowledge from this chapter is combined with that from all the other chapters, good balanced research-based literacy instruction will result.

EVIDENCE-BASED BEST PRACTICES

To become good readers and writers, children must learn to decode words. In the beginning stages of learning to read, phonemic awareness is crucial to success. As children move through the primary grades, their phonics strategies must be developed. Successful reading in the intermediate grades requires children to have strategies for decoding multisyllabic words. There is research to guide us as we guide children through all stages of successful decoding.

Phonemic Awareness

One of the understandings that many children gain from early reading and writing encounters is the realization that spoken words are made up of sounds. These sounds (phonemes) are not separate and distinct. In fact, their existence is quite abstract. Phonemic awareness has many levels and includes the concept of rhyme and the ability to blend and segment words and to manipulate phonemes to form different words. Phonemic awareness develops gradually for many children through exposure to songs, nursery rhymes, and books with rhymes and alliteration that promote word play.

Phonemic awareness is one of the best predictors of success in learning to read (Ehri & Nunes, 2002; National Reading Panel, 2000). Upon learning that phonemic awareness is such an important concept, some people have concluded that phonemic awareness is all we need to worry about in preparing children to read. Phonemic awareness training programs have been developed and mandated for every child every day for 30–40 minutes. The classroom reality is that there are only so many minutes in a day, and if something gets 30–40 minutes, other important things get less time. In addition to phonemic awareness, children who are going to learn to read successfully must develop print tracking skills and begin to learn some letter names and sounds. They need to develop cognitive clarity about what reading and writing are for, which you can only learn when you spend some of your time each day in the presence of reading and writing.

Another problem with the overreaction to the phonemic awareness findings is that some children enter school with sufficient phonemic awareness to begin to learn to read and others will develop it solely from engaging in emergent literacy activities such as shared reading of books that play with sounds and writing with invented spelling. Yopp and Yopp (2000) argue for phonemic awareness instruction as only *one* part of a beginning literacy program:

> Our concern is that in some classrooms phonemic awareness instruction will replace other crucial areas of instruction. Phonemic awareness sup-

> ports reading development only if it is part of a broader program that includes—among other things—development of students' vocabulary, syntax, comprehension, strategic reading abilities, decoding strategies, and writing across all content areas. (p. 142)

Phonics

While there is general agreement on the need to develop children's decoding strategies, there is little agreement on which methods are most successful in doing this. Stahl, Duffy-Hester, and Stahl (1998) reviewed the research on phonics instruction and concluded that there are several types of good phonics instruction and that there is no research base to support the superiority of any one particular type. The National Reading Panel (NRP, 2000) reviewed the experimental research on teaching phonics and determined that explicit and systematic phonics is superior to nonsystematic or no phonics but that there is no significant difference in effectiveness among the kinds of systematic phonics instruction:

> In teaching phonics explicitly and systematically, several different instructional approaches have been used. These include synthetic phonics, analytic phonics, embedded phonics, analogy phonics, onset–rime phonics, and phonics through spelling. . . . Phonics-through-spelling programs teach children to transform sounds into letters to write words. Phonics in context approaches teach children to use sound–letter correspondences along with context clues to identify unfamiliar words they encounter in text. Analogy phonics programs teach children to use parts of written words they already know to identify new words. The distinctions between systematic phonics approaches are not absolute, however, and some phonics programs combine two or more of these types of instruction. (pp. 2–89)

Several studies published since the NRP report suggest that effective phonics instruction might include a variety of approaches. Davis (2000) found that spelling-based decoding instruction was as effective as reading-based decoding instruction for all her students but more effective for children with poor phonological awareness. Juel and Minden-Cupp (2000) noted that the most effective teachers they observed of children who entered first grade with few literacy skills combined systematic letter–sound instruction with onset–rime analogy instruction and taught these units for application in both reading and writing. McCandliss, Beck, Sandak, and Perfetti (2003) investigated the effectiveness of Isabel Beck's instructional strategy, word building, with students who had failed to benefit from traditional phonics instruction. They found that the children who received this word building instruction demonstrated significantly greater improvements on standardized measures of decoding, comprehension, and phonological awareness.

Multisyllabic Word Decoding

Little research has been conducted on multisyllabic word decoding, but what we do know leads us to believe that morphemes—prefixes, suffixes, and roots—are the building blocks of big words. In 1984 Nagy and Anderson published a landmark study in which they analyzed a sample of 7,260 words found in books commonly read in grades 3–9. They found that most of these words were polysyllabic words and that many of these big words were related semantically through their morphology. Some of these relationships are easily noticed. The words *hunter, redness, foglights,* and *stringy* are clearly related to the words *hunt, red, fog,* and *string.* Other more complex word relationships exist between such words as *planet/planetarium, vice/vicious,* and *apart/apartment.* Nagy and Anderson hypothesized that if children knew or learned how to interpret morphological relationships, they could comprehend six or seven words for every basic word known. McCutchen, Green, and Abbott (2008) examined the development of morphological knowledge among older elementary students and the relationship of their morphological knowledge to decoding. They found that morphological awareness continued to develop from fourth to sixth grade and that children's skill with morphology made a unique contribution to decoding ability. To move children along in their decoding and spelling abilities in upper grades, instruction needs to focus on morphemes—prefixes, suffixes, and roots—and how these morphemes help us decode, spell, and gain meaning for polysyllabic words.

BEST PRACTICES IN ACTION

While research does not tell us what kind of phonemic awareness and phonics instruction is most effective, we can use some research-based findings to evaluate classroom activities. Activities designed to develop phonemic awareness should be done in the context of reading and writing so that children develop the other concepts necessary for successful beginning reading. Because children vary in their level of phonemic awareness, phonics activities for young children should include opportunities to develop phonemic awareness. Because it is not clear how phonics is best taught (and because all children might not learn best with any single method), phonics instruction should include a variety of activities, including letter–sound, spelling, and analogy instruction. As children encounter more big words in their reading, they should learn to use morphemes to unlock the pronunciation, spelling, and meaning of polysyllabic words. The remainder of this section describes activities to teach phonemic awareness, phonics, and multisyllabic word decoding in ways that are consistent with research.

Focus on Rhymes to Develop Phonemic Awareness

Children who come to school with well-developed phonemic awareness abilities have usually come from homes in which rhyming chants, jingles, and songs were part of their daily experience. These same chants, jingles, and songs should be a part of every young child's day in the classroom.

There are so many wonderful rhyming books, but because of their potential to develop phonemic awareness, two deserve special mention. Along with other great rhyming books, Dr. Seuss wrote *There's a Wocket in My Pocket* (1974). In this book, all kinds of Seusssian creatures are found in various places. In addition to the wocket in the pocket, there is a vug under the rug, a nureau in the bureau, and a yottle in the bottle! After several readings, children delight in chiming in to provide the nonsensical word and scary creature which lurks in harmless-looking places. After reading the book a few times, it is fun to decide what creatures might be lurking in your classroom. Let children make up the creatures, and accept whatever they say as long as it rhymes with their object:

"There's a pock on our clock!"

"There's a zindow looking in our window!"

"There's a zencil on my pencil!"

Another wonderful rhyming book for phonemic awareness is *The Hungry Thing* by Jan Slepian and Ann Seidler (1967). In this book a large, friendly dinosaur-looking creature (you have to see him to love him!) comes to town, wearing a sign that says "Feed Me." When asked what he would like to eat, he responds, "Shmancakes." After much deliberation, a clever little boy offers him some pancakes. The Hungry Thing eats them all up and demands, "Tickles." Again, after much deliberation the boy figures out he wants pickles. As the story continues, it becomes obvious that The Hungry Thing wants specific foods and that he asks for them by making them rhyme with what he wants. He asks for *feetloaf* and gobbles down the meatloaf. For dessert, he wants *hookies* and *gollipops*!

The Hungry Thing is a delightful book, and in many classrooms teachers have made a poster-size Hungry Thing, complete with his sign that reads "Feed Me" on one side and "Thank You!" on the other. Armed with real foods or pictures of foods the children try to feed The Hungry Thing. Of course, he won't eat the food unless they make it rhyme. If they offer him spaghetti, they have to say "What some bagetti?" (or "zagetti," or "ragetti"—any silly word that rhymes with *spaghetti*!). To feed him Cheerios, they have to offer him "seerios," "theerios," or "leerios"!

Focus on Blending and Segmenting to Develop Phonemic Awareness

In addition to hearing and producing rhymes, the ability to put sounds together to make a word—blending—and the ability to separate out the sounds in a word—segmenting—are critical components of phonemic awareness. Blending and segmenting are not easy for many children. In general, it is easier for them to segment off the beginning letters—the onset—from the rest of the word—the rhyme—than it is to separate all the sounds. In other words, children can usually separate *bat* into /b/ and /at/ before they can produce the three sounds /b/, /a/, and /t/. The same is true for blending. Most children can blend /S/ and /am/ to produce the name *Sam* before they can blend /S/, /a/, and /m/. Most teachers begin by having children blend and segment the onset from the rime and then move to blending and segmenting individual letters.

There are lots of games children enjoy that can help them learn to blend and segment. The most versatile is a simple riddle-guessing game. The teacher begins the game by naming the category and giving the clue: "I'm thinking of an animal that lives in the water and is a /f/ /ish/ [or /f/ /i/ /sh/, depending on what level of blending you are working on]." The child who correctly guesses *fish* gives the next riddle: "I'm thinking of an animal that goes 'quack' and is a /d/ /uck/ [or /d/ /u/ /ck/]." This sounds simplistic, but children love it, and you can use different categories to go along with units you are studying.

A wonderful variation on this guessing game is to put objects in a bag and let children reach in the bag and stretch out the name of an object they choose and then call on someone to guess "What is it?" Choose small common objects you find in the room—a cap, a ball, chalk, a book—and let the children watch you load the bag and help you stretch out the words for practice as you put them in.

Children also like to talk like "ghosts." One child chooses an object in the room to say as a ghost would—stretching the word out very slowly—"dddoooorrr." The child who correctly guesses *door* gets to ghost-talk another object—"bbbooookkk." Both the ghost-talk game and the guessing game provide practice in both segmenting and blending as children segment words by stretching them out and other children blend the words together to guess them.

Encourage Writing with Invented Spelling

When young children write, they need to spell many words that they have not yet learned to spell. If teachers demonstrate how you can stretch out words and put down letters for the sounds you hear, young children will write a lot more than if they think they have to spell all the words correctly or wait for someone to spell the words for them. As they stretch out words, they are segmenting those words into their component sounds. Segmenting is an important—and difficult—phonemic awareness ability that will develop more quickly if children are encouraged to stretch out words while writing.

How Emphasizing Rhyme, Segmenting, and Blending Reflects What We Know

Rhyme awareness—the ability to make and recognize rhymes—is one of the earliest developed phonemic awareness abilities. Many children come to kindergarten with developed rhyme awareness. These children were not given any direct instruction in rhyme, but they were immersed in an environment of songs, jingles, and books in which rhyme played a large role. Including rhyming songs, jingles, and books as part of every early-childhood day allows all children to begin developing their phonemic awareness.

Segmenting and blending words are two of the more difficult phonemic awareness abilities. Children need lots of practice with oral activities in which they put sounds together to create words and pull words apart into their component sounds. When children are encouraged to stretch out words while writing, they get a lot of practice with segmenting. Writing also gives students a way to apply the letter–sound knowledge they are learning. Many children can read their own writing before they can read the same words in books.

Make Words to Include a Variety of Phonics Approaches

Making Words is a popular activity with both teachers and children. Children love manipulating letters to make words and figuring out the secret word that can be made with all the letters. While children are having fun making words, they are also learning important information about phonics and spelling. As children manipulate the letters to make the words, they learn how small changes, such as changing just one letter or moving the letters around, result in completely new words. Children develop phonemic awareness as they stretch out words and listen for the sounds they hear and the order of those sounds. Making Words lessons are an example of a type of instruction called Guided Discovery. In order to truly learn and retain strategies, children must discover them. But some children do not make discoveries about words on their own. In Making Words lessons, children are guided toward those discoveries. Every Making Words lesson has three parts. First, children manipulate the letters to make words. This part of the lesson uses a spelling approach to help children learn letter sounds and how to segment words and blend letters. In the second part of the lesson, children sort words according to rhyming patterns. We end each lesson by helping children transfer what they have learned to reading and spelling new words. Children learn how the rhyming words they sorted help them read and spell lots of other rhyming words.

Each Making Words lesson begins with short easy words and moves to longer, more complex words. The last word is always the secret word—one that can be made with all the letters. As children make the words, a child who has it made successfully goes to the pocket chart and makes the word with big letters. Children who don't have the word made correctly quickly fix their word to be ready for the next word. The small changes between most words encourages even those children who have not made a word perfectly to fix it because they soon realize that having the current word correctly spelled increases their chances of spelling the next word correctly.

In Step 2 of a Making Words lesson, children sort the words into patterns. Many children discover patterns just through making the words in the carefully sequenced order, but some children need more explicit guidance. This guidance happens when all the words have been made and teachers guide children to sort them into patterns. Children sort the words into rhyming words and notice that words that rhyme have the same spelling pattern.

Many children know letter sounds and patterns and do not apply these to decode an unknown word encountered during reading or spell a word they need while writing. This is the reason that every Making Words lesson ends with a transfer step. Once words are sorted according to beginning letters, children apply these beginning letter sounds to new words. Once words are sorted according to rhyme, children use these rhyming words to spell new words. Here is an example of how you might conduct a Making Words lesson and cue the children to the changes and words you want them to make.

Beginning the Lesson

The children all have the letters: *a e u c c k p s*. These same letters—big enough for all to see—are displayed in a pocket chart or on the active board. The vowels are in a different color and the letter cards have lowercase letters on one side and capital letters on the other side.

The words the children are going to make are written on index cards. These words will be placed in the pocket chart as the words are made and will be used for the Sort and Transfer steps of the lesson.

The teacher begins the lesson by having the children hold up and name each letter as the teacher holds up the big letters in the pocket chart.

> "Hold up and name each letter as I hold up the big letter. Let's start with your vowels. Show me your *a*, your *u*, and your *e*. Now show me your two *c*'s, *k, p*, and *s*. Today you have eight letters. In a few minutes, we will see if anyone can figure out the secret word that uses all eight letters."

Step 1: Making Words

"Use two letters to spell the word *up*. I got *up* at 6:30."

Find someone with *up* spelled correctly and send that child to spell *up* with the big letters.

"Change one letter to spell *us*. The fifth graders put on a play for *us*."
"Add a letter you don't hear to spell *use*. We *use* our letters to make words."
"Move the same letters to spell the name *Sue*. Do you know anyone named *Sue*?"

Find someone with *Sue* spelled with a capital *S* to spell *Sue* with the big letters.

"Change one letter to spell *cue*. When you are an actor, you listen for your *cue*."

Quickly send someone with the correct spelling to make the word with the big letters. Keep the pace brisk. Do not wait until everyone has *cue* spelled with their little letters. It is fine if some children are making *cue* as *cue* is being spelled with the big letters. Choose your struggling readers to go to the pocket chart when easy words are being spelled and your advanced readers when harder words are being made.

"Change one letter in *cue* to spell *cup*. The baby drinks from a sippy *cup*."
"Change the vowel to spell *cap*. Do you ever wear a *cap*?"
"Add a silent letter to change *cap* into *cape*. Batman wore a *cape*."
"Change one letter to spell *cake*. Do you like chocolate *cake*?"
"Change one letter to spell *sake*. I hope for your *sake* that it doesn't rain during the game."

> "Change the last two letters spell *sack*. A *sack* is another name for a bag."
> "Change one letter to spell *pack*. *Pack* your clothes for the sleepover."
> "Change the last letter to spell another four-letter word, *pace*. The racers ran at a very fast *pace*."
> "Add one letter to spell *space*. When we write, we leave a *space* between words."
> "I have just one word left. It is the secret word you can make with all your letters. See if you can figure it out."

Give the students 1 minute to figure out the secret word and then give clues if needed. Let someone who figures it out go to the big letters and spell the secret word—*cupcakes*.

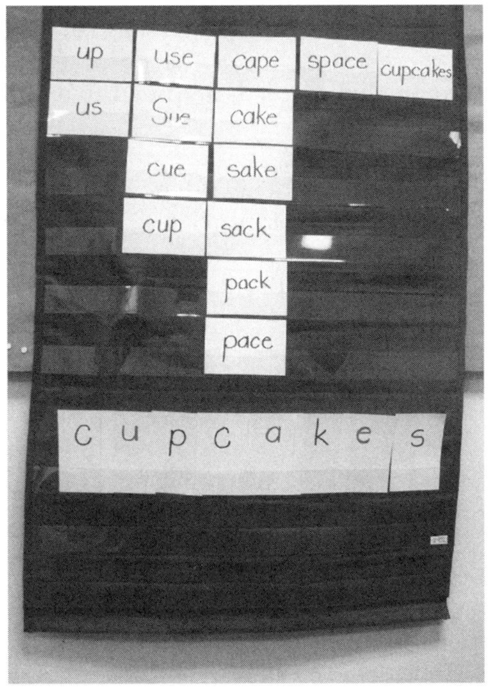

Step 2: Sorting the Words into Patterns

Put the index cards with words you made in the pocket chart having children pronounce and chorally spell each. Give them a quick reminder of how they made these words:

> "First we spelled a two-letter word, *up, u-p*.
> We changed the last letter to spell *us, u-s*.

We added the silent *e* to spell *use, u-s-e.*
We used the same letters with a capital *S* to spell *Sue, S-u-e.*
We changed the first letter to spell *cue, c-u-e.*
We changed the last letter to spell *cup, c-u-p.*
We changed the vowel to spell *cap, c-a-p.*
We added the silent *e* to spell *cape, c-a-p-e.*
We changed one letter to spell *cake, c-a-k-e.*
We changed one letter to spell *sake, s-a-k-e.*
We changed two letters to spell *sack, s-a-c-k.*
We changed one letter to spell *pack, p-a-c-k.*
We changed the last letter to spell *pace, p-a-c-e.*
We added a letter to spell *space, s-p-a-c-e.*
Finally, we spelled the secret word with all our letters,
cupcakes, c-u-p-c-a-k-e-s."

Next have the children sort the rhyming words. Take one of each set of rhyming words and place them in the pocket chart.

Sue *cake* *pace* *sack* *cup*

Have three children come and find the other words that rhyme and place them under the ones you pulled out.

Sue	*cake*	*pace*	*sack*	*cup*
cue	*sake*	*space*	*pack*	*up*

Have the children chorally pronounce the sets of rhyming words.

Step 3: Transfer

Tell the children to pretend it is writing time and they need to spell some words that rhyme with some of the words they made today. Have children use white boards or half-sheets of paper to write the words. Say sentences that children might want to write that include a rhyming word. Work together to decide which words the target word rhymes with and to decide how to spell it.

> "Boys and girls, let's pretend it is writing time. Terry is writing about what he likes to eat for a *snack*, and he is trying to spell the word *snack*. Let's all say *snack* and stretch out the beginning letters. What two letters do you hear at the beginning of *snack*?"

Have the children stretch out *snack* and listen for the beginning letters. When they tell you that *snack* begins with *sn*, write *sn* on an index card and have the children write *sn* on their papers or white boards.

Take the index card with *sn* on it to the pocket chart and hold it under each column of words as you lead the children to chorally pronounce the words and decide whether *snack* rhymes with them:

> "Sue, cue, snack": Children should show you "thumbs down."
> "Cake, sake, snack": Children should again show you "thumbs down."
> "Pace, space, snack": Children should again show you "thumbs down."
> "Sack, pack, snack": Children should show you "thumbs up."

Finish writing *snack* on your index card by adding *ack* to *sn* and place *snack* in the pocket chart under *sack* and *pack*. Have children write *snack*. Make up sentences and use the same procedure to demonstrate how you use *pace* and *space* to spell *brace, Sue* and *cue* to spell *blue, up* and *cup* to spell *pup*, and *sack* and *pack* to spell *track*.

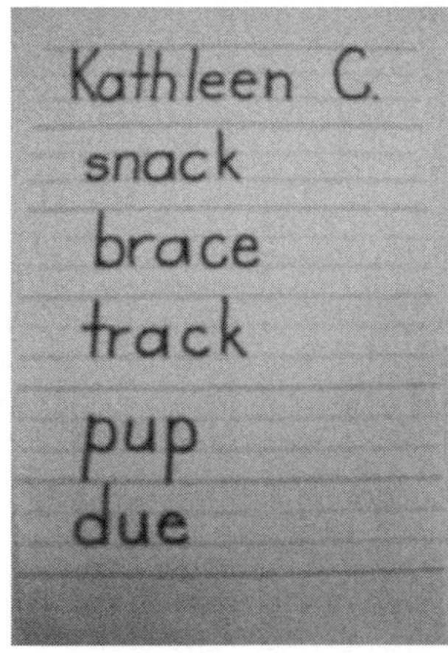

We hope this sample lesson has helped you to see how a Making Words lesson works and how Making Words lessons help children develop phonemic awareness, phonics, and spelling skills. Most important, we hope you see that in every lesson children will practice applying the patterns they are learning to reading and spelling new words.

Teach Children to Use the Words They Know to Decode and Spell Other Words

Another activity that includes a variety of approaches to phonics is called Using Words You Know. To plan a Using Words You Know lesson, pick three or four words that your children can read and spell and that have many rhyming words spelled the same way. You can use any words your students know that have lots of rhyming words. *Play,* for example, will help you decode and spell many other words, including *stray, spray, clay, delay,* and *betray. Rain* helps you decode and spell *brain, Spain, chain, sprain,* and *complain.* You can also use brand names that have lots of rhyming words. Bring in packages with the product names and then use those names as the known words. Children are highly motivated by these products and are fascinated to see how many other words these products can help them read and spell. Here is a sample lesson[1] using ice cream and Cool Whip.

Begin the lesson by displaying the products, then let the children talk a little about them. Draw the children's attention to the names and tell them that these names will help them spell and read a lot of other words. Using the board, chart, or overhead, make columns and head each with one of the key words, underlining the spelling pattern. Have your students do the same on a sheet of paper. At the beginning of the lesson, their papers look like this:

<u>ice</u> cr<u>eam</u> c<u>ool</u> wh<u>ip</u>

Show the students words that rhyme with *ice, cream, cool,* or *whip.* Do not say these words and do not allow them to say the words but rather have them write them in the column with the same spelling pattern. Send one child to write the word on the chart, board, or overhead. When everyone has the rhyming word written under the original word that will help them read it, have them say the known word and the rhyming word. Help them to verbalize the strategy they are using by saying something like "If *c-r-e-a-m* is *cream, d-r-e-a-m* must be *dream.*" "If *c-o-o-l* is *cool, d-r-o-o-l* is *drool.*" After showing them eight to ten words and having them use the known word to decode them, help them practice using known words to spell unknown words. To help them spell, don't show them a word. Instead say a word, such as *twice,* and have them say the word and write it under the word that it rhymes with. Again, help them verbalize their strategy by leading them to explain:

---

[1]Adapted from Cunningham (2009). Copyright 2009 by Patricia Cunningham. Adapted by permission.

"If *ice* is spelled *i-c-e, twice* is probably spelled *t-w-i-c-e*."
"If *whip* is spelled *w-h-i-p, strip* is probably spelled *s-t-r-i-p*."

To show children how they can decode and spell bigger words based on rhyming words, end the lesson by showing them a few longer words and having them write them under the rhymes and use the rhymes to decode them. Finally, say a few longer words, help them with the spelling of the first syllables and have them use the rhyme to spell the last syllable. Here is what their papers would look like with at the end of the lesson:

ice	cream	cool	whip
nice	dream	drool	tip
mice	stream	pool	skip
slice	scream	fool	trip
twice	gleam	spool	strip
dice	beam	stool	clip
sacrifice	mainstream	whirlpool	equip
device	downstream	preschool	spaceship

It is very important for Using Words You Know lessons that you choose the rhyming words for them to read and spell rather than ask them for rhyming words. In English, there are often two spelling patterns for the same rhyme. If you ask them what rhymes with *cream*, or *cool*, they may come up with words with the *e-e-m* pattern such as *seem* and words with the *u-l-e* pattern such as *rule*. The fact that there are two common patterns for many rhymes does not hinder us while reading. When we see the word *drool*, our brain thinks of other *o-o-l* words such as *cool* and *school*. We make this new word *drool* rhyme with *cool* and *school* and then check out this pronunciation with the meaning of whatever we are reading. If we were going to write the word *drool* for the first time, we wouldn't know for sure which spelling pattern to use, and we might think of the rhyming word *rule* and use that pattern. Spelling requires both a sense of word patterns and a visual checking sense. When you write a word and then think "That doesn't look right!" and then write it using a different pattern, you are demonstrating that you have developed a visual checking sense. Once children become good at spelling by pattern, you can help them develop their visual checking sense. During Using Words You Know lessons, we are trying to get them to spell based on pattern, and we "finesse" the problem of two patterns by choosing the words we present to them.

Using Words You Know lessons are easy to plan if you use a good rhyming dictionary, such as the *Scholastic Rhyming Dictionary* (Young, 1994). Children enjoy Using Words You Know, especially if the words you use are popular products such as *Coke, Crest,* and *Cat Chow.*

How Making Words and Using Words You Know Reflect What We Know

Making Words and Using Words You Know are examples of lesson formats that teach phonics in a variety of ways. When the children are making words with their letters, they are engaging in a spelling approach to phonics. They are told the word, and they must figure out which of their letters to use to spell it. This spelling approach is also used in Using Words You Know when the teacher says a word that rhymes with the key words and the children decide how to spell them based on their known rhyming words.

Both lesson formats also teach children to decode words based on pattern and analogy. In a Making Words lesson, there are always several sets of rhymes with the same spelling pattern. Children sort out these rhyming words and then use these words to decode two new words and spell two new words with the same pattern. Analogy and pattern instruction is also obvious in Using Words You Know lessons in which children use known words to decode and spell rhyming words with the same pattern.

While not the focus of the lesson, both Making Words and Using Words You Know provide opportunities for children to develop phonemic awareness and firm up their beginning-letter knowledge if they still need to do that. Teachers encourage the children to stretch out words as they are making them. In the transfer step, children blend the beginning letters with the rhyming patterns to spell or read the new words.

Sorting rhyming words is included in every Making Words lessons, but there are also opportunities to sort for beginning-letter patterns if children still need their attention focused on those. Whenever possible, we include words such as *cup* and *cupcakes*, which share the same base word. Although this is not the focus of instruction in primary grades, children do need to begin to notice the morphemic patterns that are the basis for the decoding and spelling of polysyllabic words. In Using Words You Know lessons, we always include some words with two or more syllables to help children extend their decoding strategies to longer words.

Making Big Words

You can use the making words lesson format to help your older students discover the morphemic patterns they can use to decode, spell and build meaning for big words. The Making Big Words lesson format has three steps. In the first step, the students make words. Rather than little letter cards, they are given a letter strip with the appropriate letters (in alphabetical order so as not to give away the secret word). Once they have made words, they sort the words according to morphemic patterns and then use these patterns to spell other words. Here is a sample Making Big Words lesson.[2]

[2]Adapted from Cunningham and Hall (2009b). Copyright 2009 by Patricia Cunningham. Adapted by permission.

The students all have a letter strip with these letters: *a a e i u l m n p r t*. One student is assigned the job of "letter manipulator" for today's lesson. As students make each word at their desks, the teacher calls on a student who has the word made correctly to spell aloud the letters in that word. The letter manipulator moves the letters on the overhead or active board so that everyone has a visual image against which to check their spelling. Students tear the letters apart and arrange them in alphabetical order—vowels first and consonants next.

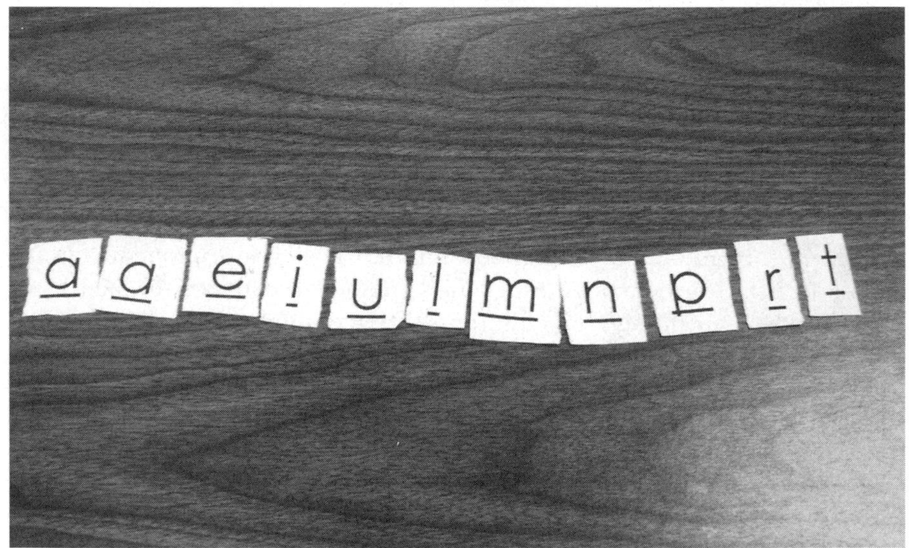

The words the students are going to make are written on index cards. These words will be placed in the pocket chart or along the chalk ledge and will be used for the Sort and Transfer steps of the lesson.

Step 1: Making Words

The teacher begins the lesson by telling students what word to make and how many letters each word requires. She gives a sentence for each word to clarify meaning.

> "Use four letters to spell the word *real*. The creatures in the movie were animated, but they looked very *real*."

Find someone with *real* spelled correctly and have that student spell *real* aloud so that the letter manipulator can spell *real* with the transparency or active board letters.

"Use four letters to spell *ripe*. We pick strawberries when they are *ripe*."
"Spell another four-letter word, *mine*. Would you like to work deep down under the earth in a coal *mine*?"
"Let's spell one more four-letter word, *time*. What *time* do we go to lunch?"
"Add one letter to *time* to spell *timer*. I put the cookies in the oven and set the *timer* for 15 minutes."
"Use five letters again to spell *miner*. I am claustrophobic, so I would not be a good coal *miner*."

Quickly call on someone with the correct spelling to spell the word aloud for the letter manipulator. Keep the pace brisk. Choose your struggling readers to spell words aloud when easy words are being spelled and your advanced readers when harder words are being made.

"Use five letters to spell *ripen*. The strawberries are just beginning to *ripen*."
"Use five letters to spell *paint*. We all love to *paint* in art class."
"Use five letters to spell *plant*. In the spring we will *plant* flowers in our garden."
"Add one letter to *plant* to spell *planet*. Mars is called the red *planet*."
"Use six letters in to spell *unreal*. Everyone said that watching the tornado touch down felt very *unreal*."
"Use six letters to spell *unripe*. Strawberries do not taste good when they are *unripe*."
"Use seven letters to spell *planter*. I plant spring flowers in a hanging *planter*."
"Use the same letters in *planter* to spell *replant*. Every year I *replant* the shrubs that die during the winter."
"Change the first two letters in *replant* to spell *implant*. If your heart does not have a steady beat, doctors can *implant* a pacemaker into your body to regulate your heartbeat."
"Use seven letters to spell *painter*. The *painter* is coming next week to paint the house."
"Use the same seven letters in *painter* to spell *repaint*. After the storm, the roof leaked and we had to *repaint* the kitchen."
"I have just one word left. It is the secret word you can make with all your letters. Move your letter and see if you can figure out the word that can be spelled with all the letters. You have 1 minute to try to figure out the secret word, and then I will give you clues."

Give the students 1 minute to figure out the secret word and then gives clues if needed. "Our secret word today is related to the word *planet*. Start with the word *planet* and add your other letters to it." Let someone who figures it out go to the overhead and spell the secret word—*planetarium*.

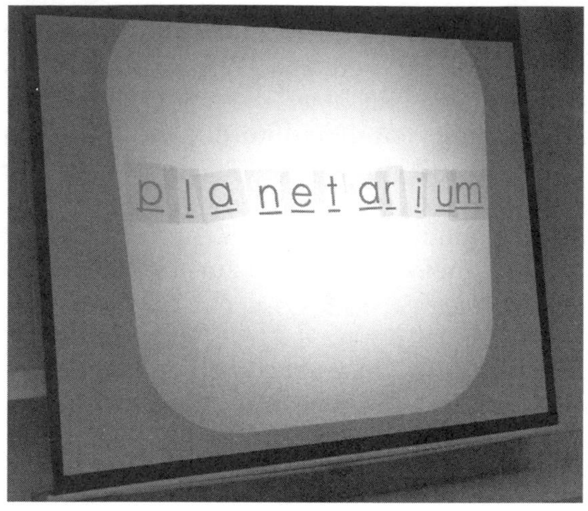

Step 2: Sorting the Related Words

Put the words on index cards in the pocket chart and have the words pronounced. Remind students that related words are words that share a root word and meaning. Choose a set of related words and model for students to use related words in sentences to show how they are related. (Choose the most complex set of words to model.)

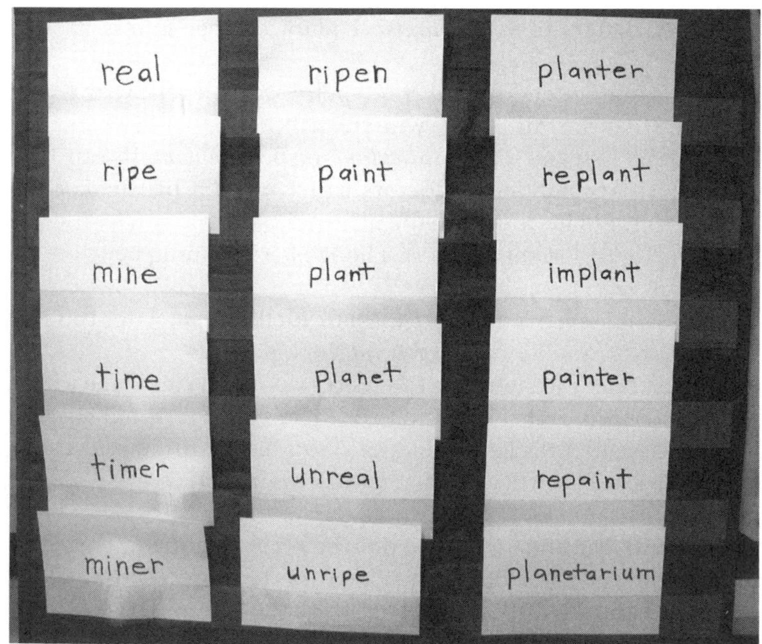

plant planter replant implant

"A *planter* is a container you plant things in. When you *replant* something, you *plant* it again. When you *implant* something, you plant it in something or somebody. The *er* suffix can be a person or a thing. *Re* is a prefix that sometimes means again. *Im* is a prefix that sometimes means in."

Let volunteers choose other sets of related words and help them construct sentences and explain how the prefixes and suffixes change the root words.

paint painter repaint

"A *painter* is a person who *paints.* When you *repaint* something, you *paint* it again. *Er* is a suffix that sometimes means the person who does something. *Re* is a prefix that sometimes means again."

ripe ripen unripe

"The strawberries are starting to *ripen* and will soon be *ripe* enough to eat. *Unripe* strawberries taste terrible! The suffix *en* changes how a word can be used in a sentence. The prefix *un* often turns a word into the opposite meaning."

real unreal

"When you see something that is actually happening it is *real,* but sometimes things are so strange they seem *unreal.* The prefix *un* changes real into the opposite meaning."

time timer

"To *time* the cookies baking, we set the *timer.* The suffix *er* sometimes means a thing."

mine miner

"A *miner* is a person who works in a *mine.* The suffix *er* sometimes means a person."

planet planetarium

"You can see all the different *planets* and how they move at a *planetarium.* Other words that end in *ium* and mean places are *aquarium, terrarium, auditorium, gymnasium,* and *stadium.*"

Sorting the related words, using sentences that show how they are related, and explaining how prefixes and suffixes affect meaning or change how words can be used in a sentence is a crucial part of each Making Words lesson in upper grades. Students often need help in explaining how the prefixes and suffixes work. For less common prefixes and suffixes such as *ium,* it is helpful to point out other words students may know that begin or end with that word part.

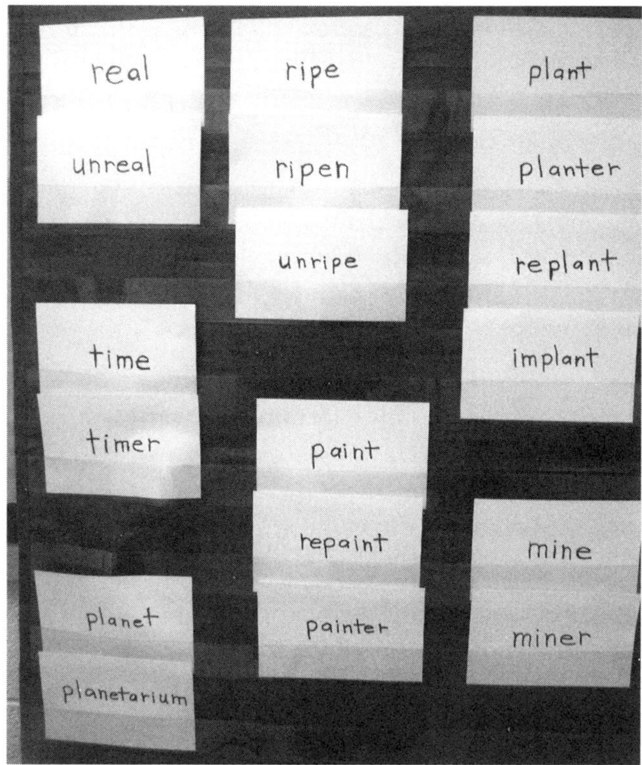

Step 3: Transfer

The Transfer step is the most important of the lesson because it is when we teach students how the prefixes, suffixes, and roots they are learning help them read and spell lots of other words. Once we have sorted all the words into related word sets, we say five or six new words and have students decide which word parts these words share with our related words and how they will help them spell them. It is very important to make this a learning experience, rather than a test. Make sure everyone knows how to spell the new part of the transfer word and which related words will help before letting anyone write the word. Have students number a sheet of paper 1–6. Pronounce a word that follows the pattern of some of the related words.

unripe unreal

Have students use *unripe* and *unreal* to spell other words that begin with *un*. Give them help to spell the root word if needed.

unfair unpainted

Let volunteers tell a sentence that shows the meaning relationship between *fair, unfair; painted, unpainted.* Have students use *repaint* and *replant* to spell other words that begin with *re*. Give them help to spell the root word if needed.

rebuild refill

Let volunteers tell a sentence that shows the meaning relationship between *build, rebuild; fill, refill.*

Have students use *painter, planter, miner,* and *timer* to spell other words that end with *er*, meaning person or thing. Give them help to spell the root word if needed. Point out the spelling change—drop *e*—if necessary.

leader driver

Let volunteers tell a sentence that shows the meaning relationship between *lead, leader; drive, driver.*

1. unfair
2. unpainted
3. rebuild
4. refill
5. leader
6. driver

Word Detectives

Word Detectives is another activity that helps students learn how to use morphemes to decode, spell, and build meaning for big words. When introducing big words to our students, we teach them to ask themselves two questions to "solve the mystery of big words."

> "Do I know any other words that look and sound like this word?"
> "Are any of these look-alike/sound-alike words related to one another?"

The answer to the first question helps students with pronouncing and spelling the word. The answer to the second question helps them discover what, if any, meaning relationships exist between this new word and others words they know. To be most effective, students need to be word detectives throughout the school day in every subject area. Imagine that during math your students encounter the new word *equation*. You demonstrate and give examples of equations and help build meaning for the concept. Finally, you ask your students to pronounce *equation* and to see whether they know any other words that look and sound like *equation*. Students think of words that end like *equation*, such as *addition, multiplication, nation*, and *vacation*. For the beginning chunk, they think of *equal* and *equator*.

You list these words, underlining the parts that are the same and having the students pronounce the words, emphasizing the part that is pronounced the same. Then you point out to students that thinking of a word that looks and sounds the same as a new word will help you quickly remember how to pronounce the new word and will also help you spell the new word.

Next you explain that words, like people, sometimes look and sound alike but are not related. Since this is the first time this analogy is used, you spend some time talking with the students about people with red hair, green eyes, and so on who have some parts that look alike but are not related and others who are:

> "Not all people who look alike are related, but some are. This is how words work too. Words are related if there is something about their meaning that is the same. After we find look-alike, sound-alike words that will help us spell and pronounce new words, we try to think of any ways these words might be in the same meaning family."

With help from you, the students discover that *equal, equator*, and *equation* are related because the meaning of *equal* is in all three. An *equation* has to have *equal* quantities on both sides of the *equal* signs. The *equator* is an imaginary line that divides the earth into two *equal* halves.

Later, during science time, your students are doing some experiments using thermometers and barometers. At the close of the lesson, you point to these words and ask your students to once again be word detectives. They notice that the *meters* chunk is pronounced and spelled the same. You ask the students whether they think these words are just look-alikes or are related to one another. The students conclude that you use them both to measure things and the *meters* chunk must be related to measuring, as in *kilometers*. Students also notice that *thermometer* begins like *thermostat* and decide that *thermometer* and *thermostat* are related because they both involve heat or temperature.

Throughout their school day, children encounter many new big words. Because English is such a morphologically related language, most new words can be connected to other words by their spelling and pronunciation, and many new words have meaning-related words already known to the students. Children who use clues from other big words to figure out the decoding, spelling, and meaning of new big words are being word detectives.

How Making Big Words and Word Detectives Reflects What We Know

Both Making Big Words and Word Detectives help students become sensitive to morphology. They learn how prefixes, suffixes, and roots provide links to the spelling, pronunciation, and meanings of big words. In Word Detectives, because the words chosen always come out of the context of what is being studied, students learn to use morphology and context together as clues to solve the mysteries of big words.

CONCLUSIONS AND LOOKING TO THE FUTURE

This chapter summarized what we know from research about how to teach phonemic awareness and phonics. The key conclusion of this research is that children do need systematic phonics instruction, but there is no one best way to teach phonics. This conclusion is disturbing to those who would like for there to be a specified best way so that everyone could be mandated to do it in that way. In many schools, one approach to phonics has been mandated despite the lack of proof that that approach is any better than others teachers might favor.

In order to improve reading instruction for all children, we need to look to the research on effective literacy instruction (Allington & Johnston, 2002; Pressley, Allington, Wharton-McDonald, Block, & Morrow, 2001). These nationwide studies identified effective first- and fourth-grade classrooms and analyzed the literacy instruction that occurred in those classrooms. They found that there were many differences in these classrooms but also many commonalities. The classrooms of the most effective teachers were characterized by high academic engagement, excellent and positive classroom management, explicit teaching of skills, large amounts of reading and writing, and integration across the curriculum. Within these commonalities, there were huge differences in the way the components were orchestrated. How we teach phonics has not been demonstrated to have a huge effect on achievement, but how we orchestrate classrooms has shown that effect. To improve beginning literacy achievement, we need to continue our efforts to research how to create, maintain, and support excellent classroom teachers.

ENGAGEMENT ACTIVITIES

1. Consider other phonics activities you have done or read about. How well do they reflect what we know about how children learn phonics? Is phonemic awareness developed as an integral part of that activity? Does the activity include a variety of approaches to learning phonics strategies?
2. Almost all the key words encountered in science and social studies are polysyllabic words. These big words are stumbling blocks for many children who don't know how to use prefixes, suffixes, and roots as keys to spelling, decoding, and meaning. Examine the materials and activities you have available for teaching phonics and determine how much attention they pay to helping children discover morphemic links.

REFERENCES

Professional Literature

Allington, R. L., & Johnston, P. H. (2002). *Reading to learn: Lessons from exemplary fourth-grade classrooms.* New York: Guilford Press.

Cunningham, P. M. (2009). *Phonics they use: Words for reading and writing* (5th ed.). Boston: Pearson Education.

Cunningham, P. M., & Hall, D. P. (2009a). *Making words 2nd grade: 100 hands-on lessons for phonemic awareness, phonics, and spelling.* Boston: Pearson Education.

Cunningham, P. M., & Hall, D. P. (2009b). *Making words 5th grade: 50 hands-on lessons for teaching prefixes, suffixes, and roots.* Boston: Pearson Education.

Davis, L. H. (2000). The effects of rime-based analogy training on word reading and spelling of first-grade children with good and poor phonological awareness (doctoral dissertation, Northwestern University). *Dissertation Abstracts International, 61,* 2253A.

Ehri, L. C., & Nunes, S. R. (2002). The role of phonemic awareness in learning to read. *What research has to say about reading instruction* (pp. 110–139). Newark, DE: International Reading Association.

Flesch, R. (1955). *Why Johnny can't read.* New York: Harper & Row.

Juel, C., & Minden-Cupp, C. (2000). Learning to read words: Linguistic units and instructional strategies. *Reading Research Quarterly, 35,* 458–492.

McCandliss, B., Beck, I. L., Sandak, R., & Perfetti, C. (2003). Focusing attention on decoding for children with poor reading skills: Design and preliminary tests of the Word Building intervention. *Scientific Studies of Reading, 7,* 75–104.

McCutchen, D., Green, L., & Abbott R. D. (2008). Children's morphological knowledge: Links to literacy. *Reading Psychology, 29,* 289–314.

Nagy, W., & Anderson, R. C. (1984). How many words are there in printed school English? *Reading Research Quarterly, 19,* 304–330.

National Reading Panel. (2000). *Teaching children to read: An evidence-based assessment of the scientific research literature on reading and its implications for reading instruction* (National Institute of Health Publication No. 00-4769). Washington, DC: National Institute of Child Health and Human Development.

Pressley, M., Allington, R. L., Wharton-McDonald, R., Block, C. C., & Morrow, L. M. (2001). *Learning to read: Lessons from exemplary first-grade classrooms.* New York: Guilford Press.

Stahl, S. A, Duffy-Hester, A. M., & Stahl, K. A. (1998). Everything you wanted to know about phonics (but were afraid to ask). *Reading Research Quarterly, 33,* 338–355.

Yopp, H. K., & Yopp, R. H. (2000). Supporting phonemic awareness development in the classroom. *The Reading Teacher, 54,* 130–143

Young, S. (1994). *The Scholastic rhyming dictionary.* New York: Scholastic.

Children's Literature

Seuss, Dr. (1974). *There's a wocket in my pocket.* New York: Random House.

Slepian, J., & Seidler, A. (1967). *The hungry thing.* New York: Scholastic.

CHAPTER 9

Best Practices in Vocabulary Instruction Revisited

Camille L. Z. Blachowicz
Peter J. Fisher

This chapter will:

- Present research-based guidelines for vocabulary instruction.
- Share the research that underpins each and give examples of instruction reflecting the targeted guideline.
- Describe a classroom that utilizes this type of instruction.
- Share resources for vocabulary instruction.

EVIDENCE-BASED BEST PRACTICES

The term *vocabulary instruction* can encompass a number of activities that occur in a classroom. We often ask teachers to make a list of word-study activities that normally occur during a single day in their classroom. A typical list from a fourth-grade teacher included the following:

- Teach the suggested words prior to the reading selection from the basal.
- Brainstorm synonyms for the word *said* as part of a minilesson in writing.
- List word families as part of spelling instruction.
- Teach the meaning of *quadrant* for word problems in math.

- Have the Mexican American and Arab American students teach the rest of the students the Spanish and Arabic words for *plains, rivers, clouds, mountains,* and *rain* as part of social studies on the Great Plains.
- Develop a semantic web for the Great Plains, including words learned so far in the unit.
- Talk about *honesty* in relation to one student's having "borrowed" a marker from another without permission.
- Clarify the meanings of some difficult words in the teacher read-aloud at the end of the day.
- Assess students' knowledge of key social studies vocabulary.

Clearly, for each of these teaching events, the nature of the learning task was somewhat different. In some cases, students were learning unfamiliar words (the Spanish and Arabic words) for familiar concepts (plains, rivers, etc.), whereas in others they were learning new concepts (quadrant). In addition, we might expect that students would remember some words and use them almost immediately (synonyms for *said*), whereas students might recognize other words in a story but not choose to use them in their own writing (which largely features basal words). Vocabulary instruction occurs in our classrooms every day at a variety of levels and for a variety of purposes. After all, words are the currency of education. However, teachers are increasingly faced with a diverse group of learners in terms of current word knowledge, linguistic background, learning styles, and literacy abilities. It is up to us as teachers to make word learning enjoyable, meaningful, and effective.

How, then, does a teacher meet all these needs in a classroom of diverse learners? Like much in education, there is no simple answer. However, research has suggested several guidelines that apply across most situations (Blachowicz & Fisher, 2000; National Reading Panel, 2000):

- *Guideline 1.* The effective vocabulary teacher builds a word-rich environment in which students are immersed in words for both incidental and intentional learning and the development of "word awareness."
- *Guideline 2.* The effective vocabulary teacher helps students develop as independent word learners.
- *Guideline 3.* The effective vocabulary teacher uses instructional strategies that not only teach vocabulary but also model good word-learning behaviors.
- *Guideline 4.* The effective vocabulary teacher provides explicit instruction for important content and concept vocabulary, drawing on multiple sources of meaning and for relevant high-frequency words.
- *Guideline 5.* The effective vocabulary teacher uses assessment that matches the goal of instruction.
- *Guideline 6.* The effective vocabulary teacher integrates vocabulary instruction across the curriculum.

In the next section, we look at each guideline in turn, presenting an evidence base and then some examples of instruction consistent with this guideline.

VOCABULARY INSTRUCTION: THE EVIDENCE BASE

In today's world, it is important to model good practice in our classrooms and be able to articulate an evidence base for our instruction drawn from research and best practices. The research base on good practice in vocabulary instruction strongly supports the guidelines we have presented, and we examine each in more depth.

> *Guideline 1. The effective vocabulary teacher builds a word-rich environment in which students are immersed in words for both incidental and intentional learning and the development of "word awareness."*

Vocabulary and Emergent Readers

This guideline is supported by research in several areas: the importance of rich oral language in the classroom; the need for wide reading; and the importance of vocabulary learning as a metalinguistic process. Just as teachers use the term *flood of books* to talk about situations in which students have many and varied opportunities to read, so *flood of words* is an important concept for general vocabulary development (Scott, Jamieson-Noel, & Asselin, 2003). Both rich oral and rich book language provide important input for students' vocabulary growth.

The variance in vocabulary knowledge of young children is well established. In 1995 Betty Hart and Todd Risley, two researchers at the University of Kansas who looked at parent–child interactions among different social groups, found some striking differences among preschoolers. On average, professional parents talked to their toddlers more than three times as much as parents of families on welfare did. Not surprisingly, that difference resulted in a big discrepancy in the children's vocabulary size. The average 3-year-old from a welfare-dependent family demonstrated an active vocabulary of around 500 words, whereas a 3-year-old from a professional family demonstrated a vocabulary of more than 1,000 words.

Those differences become more pronounced as children get older—by the time low-income children get to school and start to learn to read, they're already at an enormous disadvantage. It is estimated that children from economically privileged homes enter kindergarten having heard some 30 million more words than students from economically disadvantaged homes. Further, the difference in time spent in "lap reading"—sitting in the lap of an adult and listening to a book being read—may be of the magnitude of 4,000 to 6,000 hours.

Read-alouds, that is, reading aloud to children—sometimes also referred to as shared storybook reading—is a productive means for giving students opportunities to develop new-meaning vocabulary. Because children's books present more advanced and less familiar vocabulary than everyday speech (Cunningham & Stanovich, 1998), listening to books that are read aloud helps students to go beyond their existing oral vocabularies and presents them with new concepts and vocabulary. Discussions after shared storybook reading also give students opportunities to use new vocabulary in the more decontextualized setting of a book discussion.

Numerous studies have documented the fact that young students can learn word meanings incidentally from read-aloud experiences (Blachowicz & Obrochta, 2007; Robbins & Ehri, 1994). This is equally true for young English language learners (Collins, 2010; Silverman, 2007). In school settings, the effect is large for students age 5 and older and smaller for those under age 4. Involving students in discussions during and after listening to a book has also produced significant word learning, especially when the teacher scaffolds this learning by asking questions, adding information, or prompting students to describe what they heard. Whitehurst and his associates (Whitehurst et al., 1994, 1999) have called this process "dialogic reading."

However, teachers are amazed when they hear that storybook reading with young children is not always a positive experience. Some reading situations are less optimal than others, and research also suggests that this scaffolding (providing explanations, asking questions, clarifying) may be more essential to those students who are less likely to learn new vocabulary easily. Children with less rich initial vocabularies are less likely to learn new vocabulary incidentally and need a thoughtful, well-designed scaffolded approach to maximize learning from shared storybook reading (Robbins & Ehri, 1994; Sénéchal, Thomas, & Monker, 1995).

De Temple and Snow (2003) draw the contrast between talk around shared storybook reading that is cognitively challenging and talk that is not. There has been substantial research on the nature and effects of storybook reading in both home and school settings that supports their view and suggests ways in which read-alouds can maximize student vocabulary learning (Neuman & Dickinson, 2001). Some of the findings include:

- Children can learn the meaning of unknown words through incidental exposure during storybook reading.
- With traditional storybook readings, in the absence of scaffolding for those with less rich initial vocabularies, the vocabulary differences between children continue to grow.
- Children learn more words when books are read multiple times.

- Children do not benefit from being talked *at* or read *to*, but from being talked *with* and read *with* in ways requiring their response and activity.
- Natural, scaffolded reading can result in more learning than highly dramatic "performance" reading by the adult.
- Children learn more words when books are read in small groups.

In sum, most researchers agree on several principles related to developing vocabulary with read-aloud storybook reading in schools. First, there should be some direct teaching and explanation of vocabulary during storybook reading in school settings. Second, adult–child discussion should be interactive, and discussion should focus on cognitively challenging ways to interact with the text rather than literal one-word or yes/no questions. The students need to be able to contribute to the discussion in a substantial way, and smaller groups of five or six allow for this type of interaction. Third, the rereading of texts in which vocabulary is repeated can maximize learning; informational texts and text sets can both capitalize on children's interest in "real" things (trucks, dinosaurs, pandas) as well as providing satisfaction on thematically related words. Lastly, the nature of the learning that occurs is different with familiar versus unfamiliar books. In an initial reading the children may focus on the plot or storyline. In subsequent readings the reasons for characters' actions, and especially unfamiliar vocabulary, may become the focus of their interest. Read-alouds can be a potent tool in exposing students to new vocabulary in a meaningful and pleasurable way.

Wide Reading

Wide reading is another hallmark of word learning, with many studies suggesting that word learning occurs normally and incidentally during normal reading (Herman, Anderson, Pearson, & Nagy, 1987; Nagy, Herman, & Anderson, 1985). Anne Cunningham (2005) has done an excellent summary of the research in education and psychology that underpins the aspects of wide reading (such as engagement, repeated exposure to words, etc.) that are beneficial to students. Furthermore, discussion in the classroom (Stahl & Vancil, 1986) and around the dinner table (Snow, 1991) is another correlate of incidental word learning. Although this type of learning through exposure cannot guarantee the learning of specific vocabulary words, it does develop a wide, flexible, and usable general vocabulary.

Models

Teachers should also be models of word learning. We all remember the year we learned many new words in school. We had a teacher who was an avid punster, crossword puzzle aficionado, or otherwise involved in wordplay. Teachers can be sure that they and their classrooms are models of best practices by being good models of enthusiastic and pleasurable word learning. Using word games such as Hinky Pinkies, puns, puzzles, contests, and other playful activities develops this awareness in a playful and motivating way (Blachowicz & Fisher, 2004). In a detailed study of word learning in the middle elementary grades, Beck, Perfetti, and McKeown (1982) found one classroom in which the students outperformed others in word learning. Looking around the classroom, they saw a 79¢ piece of posterboard on the wall, with words entered on it by different students. When the researchers asked about this, they were told by the teacher, "Oh, that's just a little something we do each day. If the kids encounter a new and interesting word, they can tell the rest of the class about it, put it on the chart, and earn points for their team." The students became attuned to listening for new and interesting words, and this interest was validated in the classroom on a regular basis. Techniques such as "word of the day" and "mystery word" are easy, low-maintenance, inexpensive, and time-effective ways of making sure that kids are intentionally exposed to words each day and motivated to do their own word learning.

When the goal is to have students gain control of vocabulary to use for their own expression, students need many experiences that allow them to use words in meaningful ways. Use in writing and conversation, where feedback is available, is essential to durable and deep learning. Creating personal word books and dictionaries is a good first step toward ownership; use in varied situations is a second step. Using new words in discussion, writing, independent projects, and wordplay develops real ownership and moves new words into students' personal vocabularies.

Wordplay

Wordplay is also an important part of the word-rich classroom. The ability to reflect on, manipulate, combine, and recombine the components of words is an important part of vocabulary learning and develops metalinguistic reflection on words as objects to be manipulated intelligently and for humor (Nagy & Scott, 2001; Tunmer, Herriman, & Nesdale, 1988). Phonemic awareness (being able to segment phonemes, such as the *am* in *ambulance*), morphological awareness (of word-part meanings), and syntactic awareness (how a word functions in language) all play important parts in word learning (Carlisle, 1995; Willows & Ryan, 1986). There is also evidence that this type of learning is developmental over the school years (Johnson & Anglin, 1995; Roth, Speece, Cooper, & De la Paz, 1996).

Part of creating a positive environment for word learning involves having activities, games, materials, and other resources that allow students to play with words. Who would not enjoy spending a few minutes each day figuring out a *wuzzle*, or word puzzle? Wuzzles and other word games and puzzles call on students to think flexibly and metacognitively about words. Much of the fun stems from the fact that words can be used in multiple ways with humorous results (see Figure 9.1).

jobsinjobs

Q. Can you tell what phrase this Wuzzle (Word Puzzle) represents?

A. In between jobs

FIGURE 9.1. Wuzzle example.

So, our students need "word-rich" and "word-aware" classrooms, where new vocabulary is presented in rich listening and personal reading experiences, time is taken to stop and discuss new words, language is a part of all activities, and words, dictionaries, puzzles and word games, word calendars, books on riddles, and rhymes round out the environment for enthusiastic word learning.

Guideline 2. The effective vocabulary teacher helps students develop as independent word learners.

Control of Learning

Good learners take control of their own learning. They can select words to study and use context, word structure, and word references to get information about important vocabulary they need to know. Studies that focus on self-selection of vocabulary suggest that when students choose words that they need to learn, they learn the word meanings more successfully and retain the meanings longer than when a teacher chooses the words. Haggard (1982) interviewed adults and secondary school learners about their memories of learning new words and found that these learners most easily retained words that were usable in their peer groups—popular among peers, occurring frequently in their readings, buzzwords in the media. Her subsequent teaching studies involving self-selection of words to be learned (Haggard, 1982, 1985; Ruddell & Shearer, 2002) suggested that the control offered by self-selection is an important factor in building a generalized vocabulary. Moreover, for students for whom English is a second language, some self-selection is critical to getting a true picture of words that confound learning (Jiminez, 1997).

With the popularity of wide reading approaches and cooperative group models of classroom instruction, Fisher, Blachowicz, and Smith (1991) examined the effects of self-selection in cooperative reading groups on word learning. The fourth-grade groups analyzed in this study were highly successful in learning a majority of the words chosen for study. In a later study with fifth- and seventh-grade readers (Blachowicz, Fisher, Costa, & Pozzi, 1993) the results were repeated and new information was added. The teachers who were coresearchers in the study were interested not only in whether the words were learned but also in whether the students chose challenging words for study. In all groups studied, the students consistently chose words at or above grade level for study. These and other studies indicate that self-selection and self-study processes can work effectively in the classroom. Collaborative word choice, with the students selecting some words to be learned and the teacher also contributing words for study, may be called for in content-area learning and with new difficult conceptual topics (Beyersdorfer, 1991). Combined with teacher selection and support, helping students learn to select words for self-study is a powerful tool for independent learning.

Context

Researchers suggest that learning words from context is an important part of vocabulary development but point out that it is unreasonable to expect single new contextual exposures to do the job (Baldwin & Schatz, 1985). Students need to understand context and how to use it.

Although several studies have provided intensive instruction in contextual analysis with mixed results, recent instructional studies suggest that successful context-use instruction involves explicit instruction, good planning, practice and feedback, scaffolding that leads to more student responsibility, and a metacognitive focus (Baumann et al., 2002; Blachowicz & Fisher, 2010; Buikema & Graves, 1993; Kuhn & Stahl, 1998). For example, a teacher might choose particular words from students' reading to teach how to predict meaning and look for clues. Similarly, instruction focusing on structural analysis or morphology (the learning of word parts, such as the Greek roots *tele-* and *graph*) can be helpful in learning new words while reading, as long as a teacher emphasizes problem solving.

Dictionary

Students also need supportive instruction in learning how to use the dictionary, an important word-learning tool. Every teacher who has watched a student struggle to look up a word knows that using a dictionary can be a complex and difficult task. Stories of dictionary use often take on a "kids say the darndest things" aura: The student whose only meaning of *sharp* has to do with good looks feels vindicated by finding "acute" as one meaning for *sharp* in the dictionary ("That sure is acute boy in my class"). Another, noting that *erode* is defined as "eats out," produces the sentence "Since my mom went back to work my family erodes a lot" (Miller & Gildea, 1987). Aside from providing humorous anecdotes for the teacher's room, dictionaries and dictionary use are coming under closer scrutiny by those involved in instruction. Students do not automatically understand how dictionaries work or how they can most effectively take information from them.

The use of morphology—word parts such as prefixes, suffixes, roots, and the other elements needed to break a word's meaning apart—is also an important strategy. Breaking words apart not only helps students learn and remember those specific words but also supplies them with the building blocks to understand new words they encounter (Baumann et al., 2002; Carlisle, 2000; Kieffer & Lesaux, 2007). For morphology instruction, contextual analysis, and work with dictionaries, it is wise to remember to work from the known to the unknown. As students engage in learning any one of these processes, it is important for them to understand the underlying rationale. This is best achieved through exploration of the "how-to" with familiar words and phrases. Once they have mastered easy words, they can practice with more and more difficult words until the process becomes automatic.

A particular instance of morphology instruction with ELL students is the use of cognates. Cognates are words that are similar in their native languages to English forms of words (e.g., *excelente* [Spanish] and *excellent* [English]). Carlo (2009), in her review of the transfer of vocabulary knowledge from one language to another, concluded that, as reading fluency increases, readers may take advantage of their knowledge of cognates to identify the meanings of words in their second language. Research in teaching the use of cognates is not yet advanced enough to determine whether it is effective for all students, although we know it can be effective for some (Carlo, August, & Snow, 2005).

Guideline 3. The effective vocabulary teacher uses instructional strategies that not only teach vocabulary but also model good word-learning behaviors.

The effective vocabulary teacher presents new vocabulary in ways that model good learning. This involves developing learners who are active, who personalize their learning and look for multiple sources of information to build meaning, and who are playful with words.

Good learners are active. As in all learning situations, a hallmark of good instruction is having the learners actively attempt to construct their own meanings. Learning new words as we have new experiences is one of the most durable ways to develop a rich vocabulary. For example, the words *thread, needle, selvage, pattern,* and *dart* may be learned naturally in the context of learning to sew, just as *hit, run, base,* and *fly* take on special meanings for a baseball player. This is particularly important with students whose primary language is not English. They may need the additional contextual help of physical objects and movement to internalize English vocabulary. Another way for students to become actively involved in discovering meaning is by answering questions that ask them to evaluate different features of word meaning (Beck & McKeown, 1983). For example, answering and explaining one's answer to the question "Would a recluse enjoy parties?" helps students focus on the important features of the word *recluse*, a person who prefers to be alone. As noted earlier, discussion is another way to involve learners in examining facets of word meaning.

Graphic Organizers

Making word meanings and relationships visible is another way to involve students actively in constructing word meaning. Semantic webs, maps, organizers, or other relational charts, such as the one in Figure 9.2, not only graphically display attributes of meanings but also provide a memory organizer for later word use. Many studies have shown the efficacy of putting word meaning into a graphic form such as a map or web (Heimlich & Pittelman, 1986) or a semantic feature chart (Pittelman, Heimlich, Berglund, & French, 1991), advanced organizer, or other graphic form. It is critical to note, however, that mere construction of such maps, without discussion, is not effective (Stahl & Vancil, 1986).

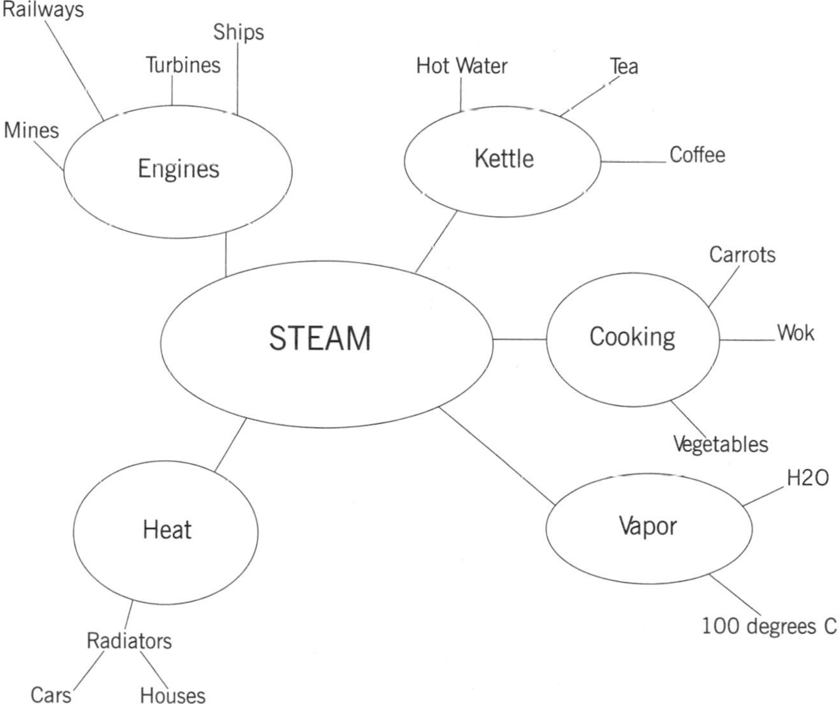

FIGURE 9.2. Wcb/map.

Clustering Techniques

Other approaches that stress actively relating words to one another are clustering strategies that call for students to group words into related sets, brainstorming, grouping and labeling (Marzano & Marzano, 1988), designing concept hierarchies (Wixson, 1986), or constructing definition maps related to conceptual hierarchies (Bannon, Fisher, Pozzi, & Wessel, 1990–1991; Schwartz & Raphael, 1985), mapping words according to their relation to story structure categories (Blachowicz, 1986). All these approaches involve student construction of maps, graphs, charts, webs, or clusters that represent the semantic relatedness of words under study to other words and concepts. Again, discussion, sharing, and use of the words are necessary components of active involvement, as are feedback and scaffolding on the part of the teacher.

Personalizing Learning

Effective learners make learning personal. We have already commented that one of the most durable ways to learn words is in the context of learning some important skill. When we do so, word meanings are personalized by our experiences. Words not learned in firsthand experiences can also be personalized; relating new words to one's own past experiences has been a component of many successful studies. Eeds and Cockrum (1985) had students provide prior knowledge cues for new words, a method related to that used by Carr and Mazur-Stewart (1988), who asked students to construct personal cues to meaning, along with graphic and other methods. Acting out word meaning (Duffelmeyer, 1980) has also led to increased word learning.

Mnemonic Strategies

Creating one's own mnemonic or image is another way to personalize meaning. While active, semantically rich instruction and learning seem best for learning new concepts, tagging a new label onto a well-established concept can be done through the creation of associations. For example, we all know that feeling of being happy, when everything is right with the world, so we have a concept for the word *euphoria.* Mnemonic strategies, those strategies aimed at helping us remember, such as ROY G. BIV for the colors of the spectrum (red, orange, yellow, green, blue, indigo, violet), are time-honored ways to assist memory. Keyword methods are the best known of these word-learning strategies. They involve the creation of a verbal connection, an image, or a picture to help cement the meaning in memory. For example, to remember *phototropism,* the bending of plants toward light, a student created the picture in Figure 9.3 as a visual mnemonic. The verbal labels *photographer* and *tropical plant* aided in memorizing the word; the bending toward the light supplied a visual image to support it. Another student created a keyword sentence, "A photo was taken of the plant bending toward light." When trying to remem-

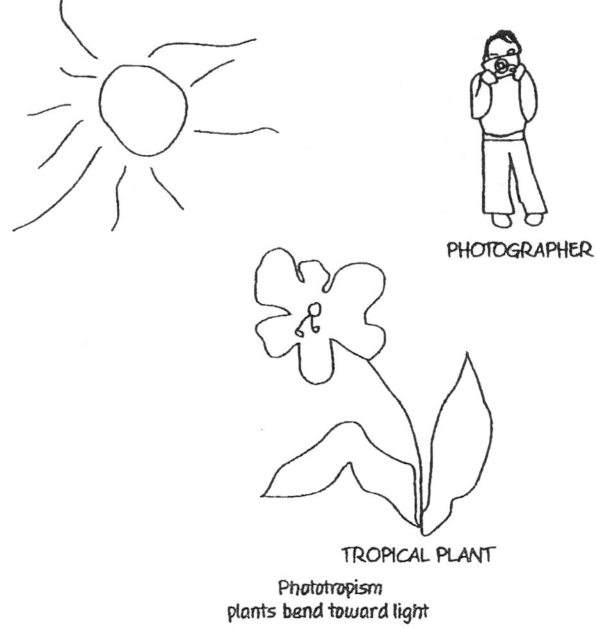

FIGURE 9.3. Keyword for *phototropism.* From Blachowicz and Fisher (2002). Copyright 2002 by Camille Blachowicz. Reprinted by permission.

ber, one student would call up the picture in her mind; the other would think of the sentence, with "photo" providing an acoustic cue and "bending toward light" a meaning clue.

Guideline 4. The effective vocabulary teacher provides explicit instruction for important content and concept vocabulary, drawing on multiple sources of meaning.

Although contextualized word learning in wide reading, discussion, listening, and engaging in firsthand learning provides a great deal of word learning, explicit instruction can also contribute to vocabulary development (Biemiller, 2001). This is most appropriate in the content areas, where students need a shared set of vocabulary to progress in their learning. It is hard to have a discussion about phototropism if the words *plant, sun, bend,* and *light* have not already been established in the learner's vocabulary. Shared content vocabulary is required for group learning.

Numerous studies comparing definitional instruction with incidental learning from context or with no-instruction control conditions support the notion that teaching definitions results in learning. However, students who received instructions that combined definitional information with other active processing, such as adding contextual information, writing contextual discovery, or rich manipulation of words, all exceeded the performance of students who received only definitional instruction (see Blachowicz & Fisher, 2000, for a review of this research). A meta-analysis of studies that compared different types of instruction (Stahl & Fairbanks, 1986) concluded that methods with multiple sources of information for students provide superior word learning. In effective classrooms, students encounter words in context and work to create or understand appropriate definitions, synonyms, and other word relations.

Therefore, teachers can model mature word-learning strategies by helping students gather information across texts and sources. Students should keep looking for different types of information that will flesh out the meaning they need to understand. Students benefit from the following:

- Definitional information
- Contextual information
- Usage examples

They also profit from manipulating words in many contexts.

Definitional information can be provided in many ways. Giving synonyms and antonyms provides information on what a word is or is not. Creating definitions using frames (see Figure 9.4) or other models helps students understand what a dictionary can provide. Example sentences clue students into nuance as well as usage. Semantic maps (as exemplified earlier), webs, feature analysis, and comparing and contrasting words all help students gain definitional information.

Care must be taken that the students see the words in context and have chances to use the words with feedback. Teachers often present usage sentences for choice and discussion. For example, for the word *feedback* the teacher might present the following and ask students to choose the correct usage.

We gave him feedback on his choices.
We were feedbacked by the teacher.

As in all vocabulary activities, discussion is the key. After choice and discussion, the teacher could ask each student to do two things: (1) locate a sentence or paragraph in the text where the word is used and explain the meaning, and/or (2) write and illustrate an original sentence.

One important task in teaching individual words that many teachers have recently faced is teaching academic vocabulary. Although the term "academic vocabulary" can have many meanings, core academic vocabulary can be thought of as words that are used in many content areas. Hiebert and Lubliner (2008) describe academic vocabulary as consisting of four components: content-specific words (such as *equator*), school-task words (such as *learning log*), literary vocabulary (such as *flustered, rambunctious*), and general

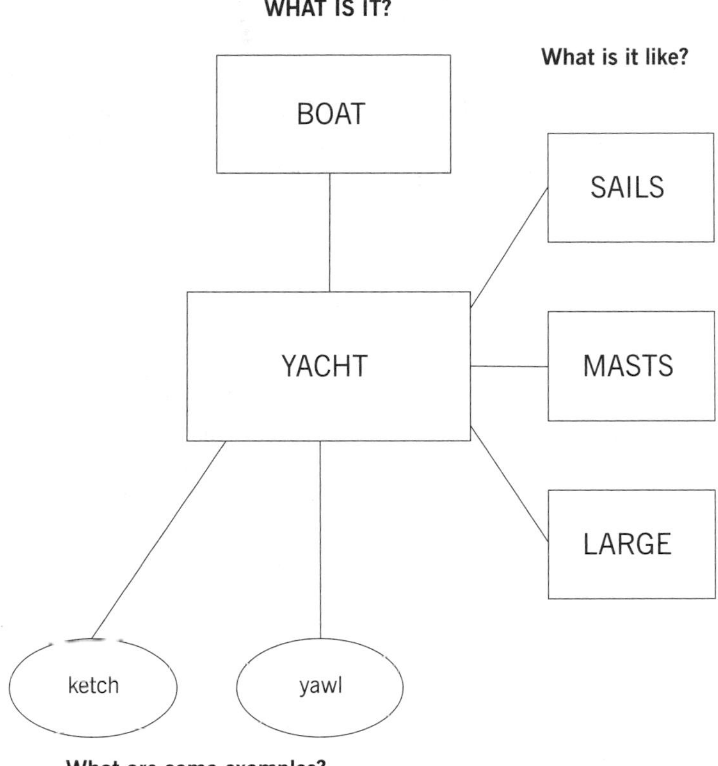

FIGURE 9.4. Concept of definition map.

academic vocabulary (such as *features, reasons*). The rationale for teaching core academic words like *synthesize* and *analyze* is that if students learn their meaning, then when they encounter them in the various content areas they will be better prepared to learn other more important new concepts. Another meaning of academic vocabulary is content words appropriate for a grade level, usually derived from standards for that grade level, such as those provided by Marzano (2004). As far as we know, the principles for teaching individual words apply to teaching both these types of academic vocabulary. In addition, we hope that teachers will pay attention to our next guideline when considering their instruction in this area.

Guideline 5. The effective vocabulary teacher uses assessment that matches the goal of instruction.

Just as we know that the various ways in which we teach students words affects what they learn about them, we are beginning to understand that the ways in which we assess their learning impacts on our understanding of what they have learned. Pearson, Hiebert, and Kamil (2007) have argued that our assessments need to change to match our developing understanding of the relationship between knowledge of vocabulary and comprehension, and how it affects on learning. While their arguments seem to be related mainly to research, theirs is a salutary reminder to teachers that we need to match our assessments to the purposes of instruction. As such, in general, it is helpful to think of two main dimensions for vocabulary knowledge—depth and breadth.

Depth refers to how much is known about a particular word: Can you recognize the meaning in text or conversation, can you use it appropriately, or can you define it? We all have the experience of being asked, "What does *energetic* mean?" and replying, "Well, Lassie is energetic when she runs all over the house and barks at everything." We tend to supply examples to illustrate meaning rather than give a definition. This is probably appropriate in many situations and relies on the questioner's ability to use the context we provide to elaborate on the basic meaning of the word. We often do this even when we could give a definition, but on many occasions we do it because we know how to use a word, perhaps *calligraphy*, but are unsure of the precise meaning. Other times we can understand some of the meaning of a word when we hear or see someone use it—and yet not feel comfortable about using it ourselves. We learn more about words each time we see or hear them; that is, we increase our depth of understanding. In relation to classrooms, it is helpful to consider what level of understanding is needed for successful completion of the task. Perhaps, when reading a particular selection, it is enough to know that a *pallet* is a form of bed, or maybe it is necessary to know what distinguishes it from other beds (it is made of straw) because it is part of a social studies unit that connects living styles to the environment.

Breadth of knowledge of a word is related to depth insofar as it can add layers of understanding, but breadth is concerned primarily with how a word is connected to other words in a domain of learning. For example, do students understand the relations among the words *plains, rivers, mountains, foothills,* and *erosion*? Students in the fourth grade may need to see how each relates to the other when studying a unit on the Great Plains. However, their depth of understanding of *erosion* may be limited as compared to that of a high school geography student or a geomorphologist.

Baker, Simmons, and Kame'enui (1995) have argued that an important principle of vocabulary instruction is that it should be aligned with the depth of word knowledge required in any setting. We understand this to mean that teachers should decide how much students need to know about a word's meaning before teaching it. For example, is it enough that students learn that an *echidna* is a small Australian mammal, or do they need to know more about its appearance and habitat? We would add that the assessment should match the instruction in relation to both depth and breadth of word knowledge. This may sound complicated, but it is not. Many instructional techniques can also be used as assessment techniques, so that a teacher can evaluate a student's understanding in authentic learning situations.

Assessing Vocabulary Breadth

One way to know what students have learned about a broad range of words is to use and analyze pre- and post-instruction graphic organizers that ask students to work with sets of related words. Knowledge ratings, semantic mapping and webbing, Vocab-O-Grams, semantic feature analysis, structured overviews, and other graphic organizers can reveal to a teacher what students have learned about groups of terms. Mapping activities can be done individually or in groups and allow a teacher to keep tabs on word learning without testing. Alternatively, a teacher can test what individuals have learned by presenting graphic organizers that are partially completed.

Assessing Vocabulary Depth

Sometimes, rather than assessing breadth of knowledge, we want to analyze how deeply students understand central terms. If we expect students to have a deep knowledge, such as a definition, an alternative to writing a definition is to have them complete a concept of definition map (Schwartz & Raphael, 1985; see Figure 9.4). Using this alternative allows a teacher to see where students' knowledge is incomplete: Do they know a category, distinguishing characteristics, and examples, or only some of these parts of a definition?

The ability to use a term is often regarded as less difficult than defining it. When you want to know about students' ability to use a new term correctly, rather than resorting to such a simplistic method as "See how many of this week's new words you can use in one story"—a technique sure to produce distorted and contrived usage—you can ask students to use vocabulary in meaningful ways in the context of some larger activities. The most direct way to do this is to ask students to incorporate particular words in their responses to questions, and their summaries and retellings. Observing students' use of words in discussion, in lessons, and in writing is a means of evaluating their vocabulary usage in the most authentic way. Many teachers compose their own "rubrics," or structured ways of looking at vocabulary and rating usage. If you keep a notebook with a page for each student, you can pull out sheets for a few students each day to make observations or enter information on the sheet when you notice something in your daily anecdotal records. In addition to observing students in action in discussion and writing, you might ask students to keep lists of words that interest them and that they encounter in reading. You can designate specific words as journal additions, and review can serve as assessment.

Another alternative for evaluating word usage is to use word monitors for discussion. A student in a discussion group can be designated as a "word monitor" to chart the number of times particular teacher-selected words are used. The monitor for that word can also be charged to survey each student in the group about the word's meaning and ask each to supply a usage for a designated word or words. Records turned into the teacher can be used as assessment.

Some teachers use Word Walls or vocabulary charts as part of assessment. Students can be assigned to construct a collection of new words in a word bank, list, or dictionary, or on a Word Wall or bulletin board. A teacher can have periodic 3-minute meetings in which she selects 10 words from the collections and asks students to use them in a meaningful way.

Along with the use of teacher assessment methods, it may be important to ask students to evaluate themselves in terms of their word learning. Using knowledge ratings and other techniques, you can encourage students to become self-reflective about the words they need to learn and the ways they need to go about learning them.

Finally, for assessing students' ability to recognize a meaning for a word, teacher-constructed tests may be appropriate. These tests can take many forms and usually test recognition (i.e., the ability to select an appropriate answer) rather than the more difficult recall (i.e., the ability to provide a word from memory). Typical teacher-made tests are types of recall assessment that involve defining a word by:

1. Giving/choosing a synonym (a *diadem* is a *crown*).
2. Giving/choosing a classification (a *shrimp* is a *crustacean*).
3. Giving/choosing examples (*flowers* are things, such as daisies, roses, mums).
4. Giving/choosing an explanation of how something is used (a *shovel* is a *tool* used to dig holes).
5. Giving/choosing an opposite.
6. Giving/choosing a definition.
7. Giving/choosing a picture.
8. Giving/choosing a word to complete a context.

Tests that you make for the classroom should be easy and efficient to use. You will also want to ask the following questions:

1. Do the items and the process call on students to do the same things you typically ask them to do in class? If your normal question in class asks that students supply a synonym, then asking for an antonym on a test does not make much sense.
2. Will answering the item provide useful repetition of vocabulary or make students think more deeply about it? If the test item is an exact repetition of something you did earlier, then it may be testing rote memory rather than more creative or extensive thinking.
3. Will the knowledge you draw on be useful and relevant to the course in which the assessment is taking place? If you are testing aspects of

word knowledge not relevant to the topic, your efforts may be counterproductive.

4. Does your test format match your instructional format? If you have stressed usage in instruction, test for usage. If you have emphasized word recognition, test for recognition.

An important part of all assessment is keeping records to show growth and change. Both students and teachers can keep records in the classroom to chart change and growth. Students may use word files and notebooks to record their developing knowledge. These may become part of a portfolio. In addition to test records, you may also want to keep anecdotal records, using the type of techniques already suggested. The records that you keep will help you become a more effective vocabulary teacher by aligning your assessment with instruction and vice versa.

Guideline 6. The effective vocabulary teacher integrates vocabulary instruction across the curriculum.

Knowing about teaching vocabulary is not the same as structuring a sensible classroom approach. It essential that teachers and researchers begin to document what a balanced approach to vocabulary actually looks like in the classroom (Blachowicz, Watts-Taffe, & Fisher, 2006). Some of the most exciting research currently being done is composed of formative studies looking at the implementation of best-practices vocabulary instruction across the curriculum (Baumann, Ware, & Edwards, 2007). The National Reading Panel (2000) emphasized the need for these kinds of studies and currently there are several in process that should provide real data for thinking about classroom instruction for the next edition of this book! Let's look at what some of these classrooms might look like now.

BEST PRACTICES IN ACTION

You can tell that Angela, a fourth-grade teacher, loves words and wordplay from the moment you walk into her classroom. A poster headed "New Words We Like" is displayed prominently on the front wall. It is filled with entries from students, with some words spilling over onto the wall on index cards. For each word, there is an entry, a description of where the student encountered the word, such as the one for *vile*, which the student illustrated with a drawing and verbal description of her sister's shoes (see Figure 9.5). Each student who used the word during the week could add his or her initials to the picture with another example.

In the library area, a shelf of riddle, joke, and pun books holds many well-thumbed volumes, and a "joke of the day" is posted on the wall. The bookcase also has a multitude of dictionaries—sports dictionaries, animal

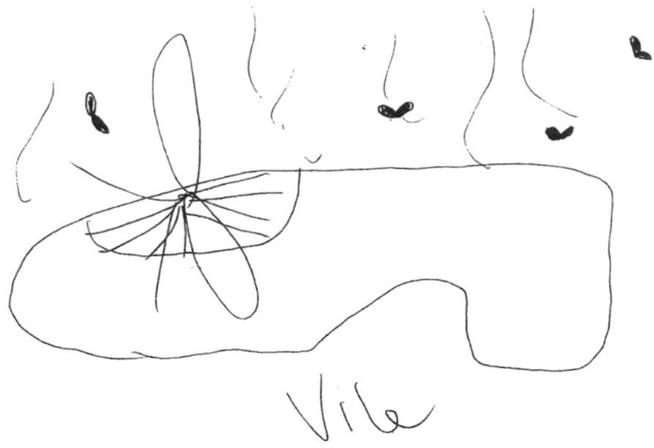

FIGURE 9.5. Personal word record: *vile*. "My brother says my sister's shoes smell vile. *Vile* = really bad, nasty."

dictionaries, dictionaries of tools, and others. On the bottom shelf, a number of word games are stored, including Boggle, Scrabble, Pictionary, and their junior versions. There is also a basket of crossword books nearby and blank forms for making crossword puzzles. The nearby computer has a crossword puzzle program that is well used. There is also a box of disks called "Personal Dictionaries" on which students keep their own word lists. For some, a simple list in table form is used. These can be easily alphabetized and realphabetized with each addition. Other students like to use HyperCard stacks to keep their word files, so that they can re-sort them in different ways.

Rather than having a set of dictionaries stored on her bookshelf, Angela has dictionaries in convenient locations around the room. These range from hardbound collegiate dictionaries to more accessible softbacks at a range of levels. She also has several "learner's dictionaries" (e.g., *American Heritage Dictionary*, 2000), which are intended for students who are learning English. These define words functionally instead of classically, and Angela finds that many students like to use them, not just her English Language Learners (ELL) students.

Angela's day starts with a word of the week, in which she poses a puzzle such as "Would a *ruthless* person be a good social worker?" If some students have a view, they answer and explain their reasoning. If no one has anything to offer, Angela presents the word in a few context sentences and then provides a definition. No more than 5 minutes are spent on this activity, and she varies the format. Sometimes she presents a word as a puzzle, sometimes as a guessing game, and so forth.

Today the class is starting a new unit on whales, so Angela begins with a Vocab-O-Gram (Blachowicz, 1986) brainstorming. She puts up a piece of chart paper (see Figure 9.6) and begins by having students brainstorm the words they already know about whales and enter these words on the chart

Habitat/home	Description/types	Food
Predators/prey	Life/cycle	Other interesting words

FIGURE 9.6. Vocab-O-Gram.

in the categories related to the "grammar" of the selection. As the unit progresses, more and more words will be added, and new categories will be drawn out of the "other interesting words" category. Because she has many ELL students in her class, Angela uses the "Vocabulary Visit" (Blachowicz & Obrochta, 2005) model of scaffolding, recording and revisiting thematic content material over the course of the unit.

In math class, students are busy working on their graphic dictionary of math terms, showing types of angles labeled with their names. In literature time, students are engaged in self-selection words for study from *The Castle in the Attic* (Winthrop, 1986), their core book for the unit. As they read their self-selected books on medieval life, they add to their personal lists.

At the end of each school day, Angela reads from a chapter book that her class has chosen. She asks the students to choose from a list of conceptually rich books that are too difficult for most of the children to read on their own. Each day, at the end of the reading, she asks students to pick a "wonderful word" the author used from that day's reading, and they add it to their wonderful word list. The day ends, as it began, with the wonder of words.

REFLECTIONS AND FUTURE DIRECTIONS

In 2007 minority students made up 40% of K–12 public school enrollment, with about half of those being Latino. While we know all children are language learners, educating an increasingly diverse student population whose first language is not English presents a special challenge, particularly in the area of vocabulary development (Blachowicz & Fisher, 2000). Finding creative and effective means for developing the vocabularies of diverse learners will be a major challenge of this decade. This is a critical issue for equity as well as for instruction.

CONCLUDING COMMENTS

All of us are vocabulary teachers when we work with students in classrooms. We teach them new ways of looking at the world and, in doing so, develop new concepts and understandings. Every day, we teach words in a variety of ways. Our obligation to the students is not just to be vocabulary teachers but to be the best vocabulary teachers that we can be. Following the six evidence-based guidelines will make our classrooms homes for motivated word learners whose interest and skill in learning new words will grow along with their vocabularies.

ENGAGEMENT ACTIVITIES

1. Choose a vocabulary word from a text selection you will use with students. Construct a vocabulary frame for that word (see Figure 9.3 for an example). Then develop three contextual sentences, each of which gives a clue to the meaning. Lastly, develop two usage-choice sentences. Try them out with a classmate or with students in class. Write a reflection on what worked and what did not. How would you modify what you did?
2. Choose a vocabulary website below to use with your students. Describe the directions you would give them to use it. (See the Reading Center website—*www2.nl.edu/reading_center*—for some other sites to start with or search in your browser.)
3. Develop a Vocab-O-Gram for a selection. Use it to select the words you would teach. Try it out with a classmate or with students in class. Write a reflection on what worked and what did not. How would you modify what you did?

RESOURCES FOR FURTHER LEARNING

Books for Further Reading

Allen, J. (1999). *Words, words, words: Teaching vocabulary in grades 4–12.* York, ME: Stenhouse.

Beck, I. L., McKeown, M. G., & Kucan, L. (2002). *Bringing words to life: Robust vocabulary instruction.* New York: Guilford Press.

Blachowicz, C., & Fisher, P. (2010). *Teaching vocabulary in all classrooms* (4th ed.). Columbus, OH: Pearson-Merrill Prentice Hall.

Ganske, K. (2000). *Word journeys: Assessment-guided phonics, spelling, and vocabulary instruction.* New York: Guilford Press.

Graves, M. F. (2006). Vocabulary learning and instruction. New York: Teachers College Press.

Johnson, D. D. (2000). *Vocabulary in the elementary and middle school.* Boston: Allyn & Bacon.

Scott, J. A., Jamieson-Noel, D., & Asselin, M. (2003). Vocabulary instruction throughout the day in twenty-three Canadian upper-elementary classrooms. *Elementary School Journal, 103,* 269–268.

Websites

Research

National Clearing House for English Language Acquisition: A source for research and resources
www.ncela.gwu.ed'u

Teaching Diverse Learners: Publications and resources for ELL instruction
www.alliance.brown.edu/tdl/index.shtml

Games

Vocabulary.com: Vocabulary puzzles and games
www.vocabulary.com

The Word Detective: E-zine with column about words and their meanings
www.word-detective.com

Vocabulary Games: A variety of games at different grade levels
www.vocabulary.co.il

A Word a Day: Receive a word a day via e-mail
www.wordsmith.org/awad

Beat the Dictionary: Online hangman
www.randomhouse.com/features/rhwebsters/game.html

Merriam-Webster Dictionary with online games
www.m-w.com

English Language Learners

Interactive Audio–Picture English Lessons: Interactive instruction for ELLs with pronunciation and pictures
www.web-books.com/Language

EnglishCLUB.com: Grammar and vocabulary activities, word games, pen-pal listings, and question-and-answer service; free classroom handouts for teachers of ELLs.

Interesting Things for ESL Students: Free Web-based textbook and fun study site; daily page for English, proverbs, slang, anagrams, quizzes, and more
www.manythings.org

Lists of Spanish cognates organized around themes
eltmedia.thomsonlearning.com/resource_uploads/downloads/1413014860_30999.pdf

REFERENCES

American Heritage Dictionary for learners of English. (2000). Boston: Houghton Mifflin.

Baker, S. K., Simmons, D. C., & Kame'enui, E. J. (1995). *Vocabulary acquisition: Curricular and instructional implications for diverse learners* (Technical Report No. 14). Eugene, OR: National Center to Improve the Tools of Educators, University of Oregon.

Baldwin, R. S., & Schatz, E. I. (1985). Context clues are ineffective with low frequency words in naturally occurring prose. In J. A. Niles & R. V. Lalik (Eds.), *Issues in literacy: A research perspective* (34th Yearbook of the National Reading Conference) (pp. 132–135). Rochester, NY: National Reading Conference.

Bannon, E., Fisher, P. J. L., Pozzi, L., & Wessel, D. (1990–1991). Effective definitions for word learning. *Journal of Reading, 34,* 301–303.

Baumann, J. F., Edwards, E. C., Font, G., Tereshinski, C. A., Kame'enui, E. J., & Olejnik, S. (2002). Teaching morphemic and contextual analysis to fifth-grade students. *Reading Research Quarterly, 37,* 150–176.

Baumann, J. F., Ware, D., & Edwards, E. C. (2007). "Bumping into spicy, tasty words that catch your tongue.": A formative experiment on vocabulary instruction. *The Reading Teacher, 61*(2), 108–122.

Beck, I. L., & McKeown, M. G. (1983). Learning words well: A program to enhance vocabulary and comprehension. *The Reading Teacher, 36,* 622–625.

Beck, I., Perfetti, C., & McKeown, M. (1982). The effects of long-term vocabulary instruction on lexical access and reading comprehension. *Journal of Educational Psychology, 74,* 506–521.

Beyersdorfer, J. M. (1991). *Middle school students' strategies for selection of vocabulary in science texts.* Unpublished doctoral dissertation, National-Louis University, Evanston, IL.

Biemiller, A. (2001). Teaching vocabulary: Early, direct, and sequential. *American Educator, 25*(1), 24–28,

Blachowicz, C. L. Z. (1986). Making connections: Alternatives to vocabulary notebook. *Journal of Reading, 29,* 643–649.

Blachowicz, C. L. Z., & Fisher, P. J. L. (2000). Vocabulary instruction. In R. Barr, L. Kamil, P. B. Mosenthal, & P. D. Pearson (Eds.), *Handbook of reading research* (Vol. 3, pp. 503–523). New York: Longman.

Blachowicz, C., & Fisher, P. (2004). Putting the "fun" back in fundamental: Wordplay in the classroom. In J. F. Baumann & E. J. Kame'enui (Eds.), *Vocabulary instruction: Research to practice.* New York: Guilford Press.

Blachowicz, C., & Fisher, P. (2010). *Teaching vocabulary in all classrooms* (4th ed.). Boston: Pearson Allyn & Bacon.

Blachowicz, C. L. Z., Fisher, P. J. L., Costa, M., & Pozzi, M. (1993, November). *Researching vocabulary learning in middle school cooperative reading groups: A teacher–researcher collaboration.* Paper presented at the 10th Great Lakes Regional Reading Conference, Chicago.

Blachowicz, C. L. Z., & Obrochta, C. (2005). Vocabulary visits: Developing content vocabulary in the primary grades. *The Reading Teacher, 59,* 262–269.

Blachowicz, C. L. Z., & Obrochta, C. (2007). "Tweaking practice": Modifying read-alouds to enhance content vocabulary learning in grade 1 (National Reading Conference Yearbook). Oak Creek, WI: National Reading Conference.

Blachowicz, C. L. Z., Watts-Taffe, S., & Fisher, P. (2006). *Integrated vocabulary instruc-*

tion: Meeting the needs of diverse learners in grades 1–5. Naperville, IL: Learning Point Associates.

Buikema, J. L., & Graves, M. F. (1993). Teaching students to use context clues to infer word meanings. *Journal of Reading, 36,* 450–457.

Carlisle, J. (1995). Morphological awareness and early reading achievement. In L. Feldman (Ed.), *Morphological aspects of language processing* (pp. 189–209). Hillsdale, NJ: Erlbaum.

Carlisle, J. F. (2000). Awareness of the structure and meaning of morphologically complex words: Impact on reading. *Reading and Writing, 12,* 169–190.

Carlo, M. S., August, D., & Snow, C. E. (2005). Sustained vocabulary-learning strategies for English language learners. In E. H. Hiebert & M. Kamil (Eds.), *Teaching and learning vocabulary: Bringing research to practice* (pp. 137–153). Mahwah, NJ: Erlbaum.

Carlo, M. S. (2009) Cross-language transfer of phonological, orthographic, and semantic knowledge. In L. M. Morrow, R. Rueda, & D. Lapp (Eds.) *Handbook of research on literacy and diversity* (pp. 277–291). New York: Guilford Press.

Carr, E. M., & Mazur-Stewart, M. (1988). The effects of the vocabulary overview guide on vocabulary comprehension and retention. *Journal of Reading Behavior, 20,* 43–62.

Collins, M. F. (2010). ELL preschoolers' English vocabulary acquisition from storybook reading. *Early Childhood Research Quarterly, 25,* 84–97.

Cunningham, A. E. (2005). Vocabulary growth through independent reading and reading aloud to children. In E. H. Hiebert & M. Kamil (Eds.), *Teaching and learning vocabulary: Bringing research to practice* (pp. 45–68). Mahwah, NJ: Erlbaum.

Cunningham, A. E., & Stanovich, K. E. (1998, spring/summer). What reading does for the mind. *American Educator, 22,* 8–17.

De Temple, J., & Snow, C. (2003). Learning words from books. In A. V. Kleeck, S. A. Stahl, & E. B. Bauer (Eds.), *On reading books to children: Parents and teachers* (pp. 16–36). Mahwah, NJ: Erlbaum.

Duffelmeyer, F. A. (1980). The influence of experience-based vocabulary instruction on learning word meanings. *Journal of Reading, 24,* 35–40.

Eeds, M., & Cockrum, W. A. (1985). Teaching word meanings by expanding schemata vs. dictionary work vs. reading in context. *Journal of Reading, 28,* 492–497.

Fisher, P. J. L., Blachowicz, C. L. Z., & Smith, J. C. (1991). Vocabulary learning in literature discussion groups. In J. Zutell & S. McCormick (Eds.), *Learner factors/teacher factors: Issues in literacy research and instruction* (40th Yearbook of the National Reading Conference) (pp. 201–209). Chicago: National Reading Conference.

Haggard, M. R. (1982). The vocabulary self-selection strategy: An active approach to word learning. *Journal of Reading, 26,* 634–642.

Haggard, M. R. (1985). An interactive strategies approach to content reading. *Journal of Reading, 29,* 204–210.

Hart, B., & Risley, T. R. (1995). *Meaningful differences in the everyday experience of young American children.* Baltimore: Brookes.

Heimlich, J. E., & Pittelman, S. D. (1986). *Semantic mapping: Classroom applications.* Newark, DE: International Reading Association.

Herman, P. A., Anderson, R. C., Pearson, P. D., & Nagy, W. E. (1987). Incidental acquisition of word meaning from expositions with varied text features. *Reading Research Quarterly, 22,* 263–284.

Hiebert, E. H., & Lubliner, S. (2008). The nature, learning, and instruction of general academic vocabulary. In A. E. Farstrup & S. J. Samuels (Eds.), *What research has to say about vocabulary instruction* (pp. 106–129). Newark, DE: International Reading Association.

Jiminez, R. J. (1997). The strategic reading abilities and potential of five low-literacy Latina/o readers in middle school. *Reading Research Quarterly, 32,* 224–243.

Johnson, C. J., & Anglin, J. M. (1995). Qualitative developments in the content and form of children's definitions. *Journal of Speech and Hearing Research, 38,* 612–629.

Kieffer, M. J., & Lesaux, N. K. (2007). Breaking down words to build meaning: Morphology, vocabulary, and reading comprehension in the urban classroom. *The Reading Teacher, 61,* 134–144.

Kuhn, M., & Stahl, S. (1998). Teaching children to learn word meanings from context: A synthesis and some questions. *Journal of Literacy Research, 30,* 119–138.

Marzano, R. J. (2004). *Building background knowledge for academic achievement: Research on what works in schools.* Alexandria, VA: Association for Supervision and Curriculum Development.

Marzano, R. J., & Marzano, J. S. (1988). *A cluster approach to elementary vocabulary instruction.* Newark, DE: International Reading Association.

Miller, G. A., & Gildea, P. M. (1987). How children learn words. *Scientific American, 257,* 94–99.

Nagy, W. E., Herman, P. A., & Anderson, R. C. (1985). Learning words from context. *Reading Research Quarterly, 20,* 233–253.

Nagy, W., & Scott, J. (2001). Vocabulary processes. In M. L. Kamil, P. B. Mosenthal, P. D. Pearson, & R. Barr (Eds.), *Handbook of reading research* (Vol. III, pp. 269–283). New York: Longman.

National Reading Panel. (2000). *Report of the National Reading Panel: Teaching children to read.* Washington, DC: National Academy Press.

Neuman, S. B., & Dickinson, D. K. (2001). *Handbook of early literacy research* (Vol. 1). New York: Guilford Press.

Pearson, P. D., Hiebert, E. H., & Kamil, M. L. (2007). Vocabulary assessment: What we know and what we need to learn. *Reading Research Quarterly, 42,* 282–296.

Pittelman, S. D., Heimlich, J. E., Berglund, R. L., & French, M. P. (1991). *Semantic feature analysis: Classroom applications.* Newark, DE: International Reading Association.

Robbins, C., & Ehri, L. C. (1994), Reading storybooks to kindergarteners helps them learn new vocabulary words. *Journal of Educational Psychology, 86,* 54–64.

Roth, F., Speece, D., Cooper, D., & De la Paz, S. (1996). Unresolved mysteries: How do metalinguistic and narrative skills connect with early reading? *Journal of Special Education, 30,* 257–277.

Ruddell, M. R., & Shearer, B. A. (2002). "Extraordinary," "tremendous," "exhilarating," "magnificent": Middle school at-risk students become avid word learners with the vocabulary self-collection strategy (VSS). *Journal of Adolescent and Adult Literacy, 45,* 352–363.

Schwartz, R. M., & Raphael, T. E. (1985). Concept of definition: A key to improving students' vocabulary. *Reading Teacher, 39,* 198–205.

Scott, J., Asselin, M., Henry, S., & Butler, C. (1997, June). *Making rich language visible: Reports from a multidimensional study on word learning.* Paper presented at the annual meeting of the Canadian Society for the Study of Education, St. John's, Newfoundland.

Scott, J. A., Jamieson-Noel, D., & Asselin, M. (2003). Vocabulary instruction throughout the day in 23 Canadian upper-elementary classrooms. *Elementary School Journal, 103,* 269–268.

Sénéchal, M., Thomas, E., & Monker, J. (1995). Individual differences in 5-year-olds' acquisition of vocabulary during storybook reading. *Journal of Educational Psychology, 87,* 218–229.

Silverman, R. D. (2007). Vocabulary development of English-language and English-only learners in kindergarten. *Elementary School Journal, 107,* 365–384.

Snow, C. (1991). The theoretical basis of the home–school study of language and literacy development. *Journal of Research in Childhood Education, 6,* 5–10.

Stahl, S. A., & Fairbanks, M. M. (1986). The effects of vocabulary instruction: A model-based meta-analysis. *Review of Educational Research, 56,* 72–110.

Stahl, S., & Vancil, S. (1986). Discussion is what makes semantic maps work in vocabulary instruction. *Reading Teacher, 40,* 62–69.

Tunmer, W. E., Herriman, M. L., & Nesdale, A. R. (1988). Metalinguistic abilities and beginning reading. *Reading Research Quarterly, 23,* 134–158.

Whitehurst, G. J., Epstein, J. N., Angell, A. L., Payne, A. C., Crone, D. A., & Fischel, J. E. (1994). Outcomes of an emergent literacy intervention in Head Start. *Journal of Educational Psychology, 86,* 542–555.

Whitehurst, G. J., Zevenberg, A. A., Crone, D. A., Schultz, M. D., Velting, O. N., & Fischel, J. E. (1999). Outcomes of an emergent literacy intervention from Head Start through second grade. *Journal of Educational Psychology, 91,* 261–272.

Willows, D. M., & Ryan, E. B. (1986). The development of grammatical sensitivity and its relationship to early reading achievement. *Reading Research Quarterly, 21,* 253–266.

Winthrop, E. (1986). *The castle in the attic.* New York: Yearling Books.

Wixson, K. K. (1986). Vocabulary instruction and children's comprehension of basal stories. *Reading Research Quarterly, 21,* 317–329.

CHAPTER 10

Best Practices in Comprehension Instruction

Janice F. Almasi
Susan J. Hart

This chapter will:

- Describe the role of social context in comprehension instruction.
- Discuss the importance of scaffolding during comprehension instruction.
- Discuss the importance of teaching readers to be strategic versus teaching strategies.
- Assert that metacognition is crucial as readers become transformed into strategic learners.

"I have been a teacher for 26 years and I have seen various reform initiatives come and go. I feel like I have seen it all. But this is the first time that I have felt so heavily mandated in everything I do. Everyone is watching me to see if I follow the prescribed lessons that tell me what strategies to teach on what days and how to introduce and utilize those strategies within my classroom. The sad thing is, though, I am not being watched to see when and how I teach those strategies so the children will benefit. I am being watched so my school can say that every teacher taught a specific comprehension strategy so when testing comes along, if we don't do well, everyone can just say we did what we were told to do."—*Fourth-grade elementary school teacher*

This vignette highlights how many teachers feel within today's educational climate. This teacher's perception of how she is being mandated to teach represents a systemic problem in the approach that schools are taking in how they implement comprehension strategies. The conversation has drastically changed from teaching what is best for the students, in a way that is differentiated to meet every child's needs, to an overarching understanding of teaching that expects all students to learn at the same pace, at the same time, and use the same strategies in the same way. Such a conception of education has removed all notions of context from the discussion surrounding what exemplifies best practices.

This teacher's narrative highlights the importance of changing the conversation surrounding strategy instruction specifically related to comprehension. The first section of this chapter reviews what the current research has to say about comprehension, while the second section describes the fundamental changes that need to take place to recontextualize comprehension as a means of cultivating strategic and reflective learners. The third section highlights small adjustments that can be made within literacy classrooms to foster an environment that is conducive to a "transformational view" of strategy instruction.

EVIDENCE-BASED BEST PRACTICES

Comprehension is critical for successful reading. While the ability to decode words and read with fluency is also necessary for successful reading, and vital *for* comprehension, the ability to decode by itself is not sufficient to ensure successful comprehension. Throughout the 1990s there was pressure to teach all children how to read by grade 3. This led to the No Child Left Behind legislation that ultimately created Reading First. This educational reform shaped the nature of instructional practice in the 2000s and was predicated on the theoretical notion that decoding skills alone, or at least in large part, are sufficient to lead to high levels of comprehension. This theoretical premise derives from automaticity theory (LaBerge & Samuels, 1974; Samuels, 2004) and is known as the bottleneck hypothesis (Fleisher, Jenkins, & Pany, 1979). Hoover and Gough's (1990) "simple view" of reading followed a similar theoretical premise, arguing that skilled reading consisted simply of decoding and linguistic comprehension. While Reading First programs were intended to provide explicit instruction in phonics, phonemic awareness, fluency, vocabulary, *and* comprehension, ensuing instructional practice focused largely on phonics, phonemic awareness, and fluency. Thus instructional practice during that time was guided largely by automaticity theory and the simple view of reading. Ultimately, however, when the final report of Reading First's results were released, findings indicated that these code-based interventions had no significant impact on comprehension for children in grades 1, 2, or 3 (Gamse, Jacob, Horst, Boulay, & Unlu, 2008). Almasi, Palmer, Madden, and Hart's

(2011) recent review of research on interventions that foster narrative comprehension for struggling readers found similar results. Those interventions focused solely on decoding and/or fluency were not as successful at enhancing comprehension as interventions that included both decoding and comprehension instruction. Furthermore, interventions that focused exclusively on comprehension were consistently successful at enhancing comprehension. While decoding is critical for reading, these recent research findings should put to rest the notion that an instructional emphasis on decoding (i.e., phonics and phonemic awareness) by itself, or even in large part, leads to significant effects on comprehension—it does not.

In contrast, successful comprehension instruction *must* consist of instruction that includes explicit instruction focused on comprehension. Most of the comprehension-focused interventions in the Almasi et al. (2011) review sought to improve comprehension via strategy instruction. However, definitions of "strategy" and "strategy instruction" vary widely among practitioners and researchers.

For the purposes of this synthesis, strategies will be defined as cognitive and metacognitive processes that are deliberately and consciously employed as a means of attaining a goal (Almasi, 2003; Hacker, 2004; Paris, Lipson, & Wixson, 1983; Pressley, Borkowski, & Schneider, 1989). Afflerbach, Pearson, and Paris (2008) distinguished strategies from skills by noting that intentionality, awareness, and goal directedness are the hallmarks of strategic action:

> Reading strategies are deliberate, goal-directed attempts to control and modify the reader's efforts to decode text, understand words, and construct meanings of text. Reading skills are automatic actions that result in decoding and comprehension with speed, efficiency, and fluency and usually occur without awareness of the components or control involved. The reader's deliberate control, goal directedness, and awareness define a strategic action. Control and working toward a goal characterize the strategic reader who selects a particular path to a reading goal. (p. 368)

Almasi (2003) focused her definition of strategies as "actions that are selected deliberately by an individual to attain a goal" (p. 1), the key aspect of this definition being that strategic behaviors are actions employed by an agentic individual. Often, educators speak of strategies as if they are nouns rather than actions. This may be because much of the early research on strategy instruction focused on identifying what good and poor readers did while reading to enhance their comprehension. These "good and poor reader studies" helped the field understand what good readers were thinking and doing while reading (e.g., August, Flavell, & Clift, 1984; Davey, 1988; Gambrell, Wilson, & Gantt, 1981; Garner & Kraus, 1981; Garner & Reis, 1981; Paris & Myers, 1981; Recht & Leslie, 1988). Instructional practice based on these findings attempted to teach struggling readers to engage in those strategies that good readers did while reading. This led to a number of research studies in which interventions were aimed at teaching students how to use these strategies. Typically these strategies were taught in isolation and they were taught quickly—sometimes over the course of a few lessons or a few weeks.

Reviews of these studies (e.g., Gersten, Fuchs, Williams, & Baker, 2001; Mastropieri, Scruggs, Bakken, & Whedon, 1996; National Reading Panel, 2000; Paris, Wasik, & Turner, 1991; Pearson & Dole, 1987; Pearson & Fielding, 1991; Pressley, 2000; Pressley, Johnson, Symons, McGoldrick, & Kurita, 1989) identified a number of powerful strategies that had significant effects on comprehension, including comprehension monitoring, constructing mental images, identifying story grammar components, generating questions while reading, and summarizing. Inadvertently, these studies may have led to current instructional practice in which strategies are often taught one at a time and in isolation. The other inadvertent outcome that may have emerged is that, due to the isolated nature of the instruction, teachers often prompted students to employ the strategy rather than encouraging students to make their own decisions about whether to use the strategy. The results of these studies have shown that students are able to learn how to use strategies such as visualizing (Chan, Cole, & Morris, 1990; Flaro, 1987); comprehension monitoring (Baumann, Seifert-Kessell, & Jones, 1992); identifying story grammar (Boulineau, Fore, Hagan-Burke, & Burke, 2004; Newby, Caldwell, & Recht, 1989; Idol, 1987; Idol & Croll, 1987); and summarizing (Borkowski, Weyhing, & Carr, 1988; Mastropieri et al., 2001) to improve short-term comprehension, but over time these comprehension gains were not sustained.

Furthermore, research has also shown that the ability of such short-term, isolated strategy instruction to yield long-term benefits and transfer to all reading contexts is questionable (Almasi et al., 2011; Pressley, 2000). Many of these early studies did not provide students with the type of explicit instruction that enables them to internalize the strategic processing necessary to transfer what they learned to other contexts. Instruction that fosters transfer includes opportunities for readers to talk about not only the strategies they use, but also the conditions under which they may or may not use them. That is, readers must think about and consider where, when, and why they might use a strategy as they make decisions about whether to use it to meet their reading goal.

In short, these early studies focused on teaching students the "strategy" rather than teaching students "to be strategic." Subsequently, teachers have come to focus on strategies as things to be taught, rather than as actions to be fostered. The difference is that strategic actions require intentionality—they require a reader who is actively processing the text and making decisions (Afflerbach et al., 2008; Paris et al., 1991; Pressley, Borkowski, et al., 1989). Such readers continually monitor the reading experience and consciously make decisions as to where, when, how, and why they should apply strategic behaviors and actions (e.g., activating background knowledge to make connections, visualizing, making predictions, setting purposes, identifying text structure, monitoring comprehension, summarizing) as warranted by the conditions surrounding the reading event. Thus teaching readers to be strategic not only involves teaching them about the strategy, but also about the conditions under which one might *use* the strategy. Those conditions include giving consideration to reader factors, textual factors, and contextual factors.

Reader factors include aspects such as reading ability, ethnicity, identity, physiology, socioeconomic status, language, experiences, gender, age, affect, motivation, and fatigue. The characteristics one brings to the reading event influence the meaning one constructs and are unique to each individual (Marshall, 2000).

Textual factors can include both linguistic (e.g., printed or electronic text of any form) and semiotic (e.g., signs, symbols, language, gestures, music, art) forms (Hartman, 1995). Alexander and Jetton (2000) also distinguish between linear and nonlinear texts, the distinguishing feature being that in linear texts processing decisions are left to the reader, whereas in nonlinear texts the discourse processing decisions are in part determined by the computer- or Web-based links associated with a particular text. As well, textual factors include more traditional features such as genre, readability, and concept density.

Contextual factors involve the setting in which the reading event occurs. This means that the reader gives consideration to, and may need to adapt to local, sociocultural, and/or sociohistorical aspects of context (Marshall, 2000). The local setting reflects particular instructional methods, activities, or tasks within a literacy classroom. The literacy classroom is situated within a school, which is situated within a larger community. This local context is situated socioculturally in that it is affiliated with the beliefs, values, rites, and obligations of those living within the larger community and the nation. The local setting is also situated sociohistorically in that the beliefs, values, rites, and obligations that preceded it affect it.

The ability to use a reading strategy to improve comprehension is thus far more difficult when the ultimate goal is to teach students to be strategic. It involves not only teaching students about the strategy, but also about the subtle nuances related to analyzing the reading task and making decisions about which strategies might best be suited for particular purposes, at particular times, and under particular circumstances. Such instruction cannot be done in a couple of lessons. Thus researchers developed interventions that taught readers how to use *sets* of strategies rather than individual strategies. These interventions focused on teaching students how to recognize where and when they should use strategies, how to select from a variety of strategies, and how to determine whether their choices were moving them toward their goal: comprehension (Almasi et al., 2011; National Reading Panel, 2000; Paris et al., 1991; Pressley, 2000). Reciprocal teaching (Palincsar & Brown, 1984), informed strategies for learning (Paris, Cross, & Lipson, 1984; Paris & Jacobs, 1984; Paris & Oka, 1986), and transactional strategies instruction (Anderson, 1992; R. Brown, Pressley, Van Meter, & Schuder, 1996; Pressley,

El-Dinary, et al., 1992) are examples of interventions that teach students not only how to flexibly use a cohesive set of strategies, but also to develop metacognitive awareness of the task and self that fosters self-initiated and self-regulated strategy use. Research has shown that each of these interventions has proven successful with readers at various age levels, and some have shown that they lead to sustained and significant growth in comprehension over time (R. Brown et al., 1996; Van Keer, 2004; Westra & Moore, 1995). Recent research has also indicated that teaching strategies one at a time was not as effective as teaching them as a set as in transactional strategies instruction (Reutzel, Smith, & Fawson, 2005).

As a result of these research findings, core reading programs (i.e., basal reading programs) published in the past decade have incorporated much of the research related to comprehension strategies instruction (Pilonieta, 2010). However, as Dewitz, Jones, and Leahy (2009) found, the five most widely used commercial core reading programs do not provide the type of explicit instruction or the gradual release of responsibility that is foundational to comprehension strategies instruction. Furthermore, Dewitz, Leahy, Jones, and Sullivan (2010) found these publications woefully inadequate in their attempt to provide students with the procedural and conditional knowledge associated with strategy use. What continues to be problematic is that teachers tend to misunderstand what strategic processing involves, focus on isolated strategy use rather than strategic processing, and focus on activities rather than strategies. Teachers may engage students in an activity, but they do not provide the requisite instructional elements to teach *strategic processing*. Very often the teacher actually performs the strategy but does not teach the students how to use the strategy independently. That is, a teacher may set a purpose for reading rather than teach the students how, when, and why they should set their own purposes while reading. Thus students are not actively engaged in the decision-making process regarding what strategies to use and when to use them. As a result they do not learn to become planful, self-regulated readers who possess a repertoire of strategies to assist them as they read. Struggling readers in particular are at a disadvantage in this scenario.

In summary, the previous review of reading comprehension research provided an overview of two generations of comprehension strategies research that has led to two different perspectives on instruction. The first perspective is what we will call the "isolation view," in which strategies are taught in isolation and their use is often prompted by teachers. A common metaphor is that readers acquire a "toolbox" full of different strategies (Almasi, 2003). From this perspective the strategies, or "tools," that are used by the reader are outside of the reader (metaphorically, they are kept in a toolbox or in a tool belt) and accessed when needed. A more knowledgeable other, such as a teacher, might even let you know which tool to select and when to use it: "Today we're going to learn about the parts of a story. Stories include setting, characters, plot, and a solution. Here is a story map for you to fill out after you read the story. It will help you remember what you have read."

The "transformational view," which is what this chapter encourages, is a perspective that emphasizes the importance of teaching strategies in a manner that enables students to *become* strategic. Just as a Transformers action figure can morph from a car to a robot whose body parts can change into a variety of mechanical tools and weapons, readers engage with strategies until they become a part of them. They are no longer reaching for a tool from a toolbox that is outside of them, they actually *are* the tools. The tools are within themselves and the student must consider reader factors, textual factors, and contextual factors to determine what strategy works best in a given situation. The reader actually embodies the tools/strategies. That is, the reader becomes the tools/strategies and the tools/strategies become the reader. The reader is transformed by using the strategies. Teachers from this perspective do not tell readers when to use a strategy; instead, they might say things like, "Today we are going to read a story. What strategies or tools might we use as we are reading to help us understand the story?" This would be followed by a discussion among the students as to different types of strategies that they might use to help them as they read. The section that follows provides further explanation of what these best practices look like in action.

BEST PRACTICES IN ACTION

The lack of coherence between reading programs and research-based strategies instruction has led to a disconnect between content and learning. Core reading programs like the ones evaluated by Dewitz et al. (2009) establish a precedent as to how comprehension instruction will occur within classrooms. Within the environments perpetuated by such reading programs, content is seen as prescriptive. It removes the social context of learning and expects all students to use the same strategies, in the same way, for the same outcome. Learners are viewed as separate from the context of learning. Such separation between content and learning is leading to a different understanding of how people conceptualize the process of learning.

Understanding the various perspectives associated with the learning process are important to consider as best literacy practices are discussed. Underlying these varied perspectives on learning is the manner in which one views the nature of knowledge. In philosophy this is known as epistemology (i.e., the study of the nature and scope of knowledge) (Cunningham & Fitzgerald, 1996). Epistemology has been used within education to explore learning more thoroughly by providing a framework from which belief systems related to knowledge and learning are more readily understood. Specifically, epistemology is focused on three overarching concerns: "what constitutes or counts as knowledge, where knowledge is located, and how knowledge is attained" (p. 40). When discussing the reading programs or strategies instruction, these questions can be used to situate the learner within the process of learning. For example, the first question—*What constitutes or counts as knowledge?*—

relates to how a person situates truth in relation to a learner. Can various learners understand things differently? Can they use a strategy in multiple ways, or is there only one absolute way/place/circumstance in which to use a strategy?

The second question—*Where is knowledge located?*—is important because it asks a person to consider where learners are in relation to what they are learning. Is your goal as a teacher to "fill the vessel," or is your goal as the teacher to "cultivate the mind"? One perspective places knowledge outside of the learner, while the other perspective allows for knowledge to be embodied by the learner.

The final question—*How is knowledge attained?*—is directly related to discovery versus creation as it relates to learning. Within a learning environment, does learning occur through discovery, or is the creation of knowledge emphasized? Can learners find or be given knowledge, or do they have to create understanding for themselves and transform their own thinking before knowledge is created? The first outlook removes the learner from the process of creating knowledge, while the second perspective acknowledges learners as active agents within their own process of creating meaning.

For the purposes of this chapter, the discussion of epistemology is important to highlight the two various perspectives discussed within the first section. One perspective, embraced by the most current reading programs, considers there to be one absolute truth, located outside of the learner, that is waiting to be discovered by the learner. The other viewpoint acknowledges that based on prior experiences there is not going to be an absolute truth, learning does not happen outside of the learner. The learners' experiences and contexts matter as knowledge grows. And finally, knowledge cannot be discovered. True learning does not happen until the learner transforms and begins to embody the strategies they are being shown. They create an understanding about how to affectively utilize each strategy to meet their needs within various contexts. Table 10.1 outlines the conflicting perspectives associated with strategies instruction.

As highlighted in Table 10.1, the recent shift in education has started to change the underlying belief of what is valued within learning. The viewpoint that students are products detached from their own learning processes has overtaken our schools. As the National Reading Panel embraced the five areas of reading development: (1) phonemic awareness, (2) phonics, (3) fluency, (4) vocabulary, and (5) comprehension (National Reading Panel, 2000), reading programs followed in line and perpetuated a decontextualized nature of teaching strategies in isolation (Dewitz et al., 2009). In terms of comprehensive literacy instruction, the push toward prescribed teaching as a means to reach annual yearly progress (AYP) has brought with it a mindset that emphasizes "the simple view" of reading comprehension (Carver, 1993; Hoover & Gough, 1990). Such a developmental perspective stresses individual skills such as decoding, listening, and fluency as steps to achieve comprehension. Hoffman (2009) stated that such a perspective might work for

TABLE 10.1. Dichotomous Perspectives on Strategies Instruction

	Perspective 1: Isolation view (core reading programs)	Perspective 2: Transformational view (strategies instruction model)
What constitutes or counts as knowledge?	One truth.	Multiple ways of knowing are embraced.
Where is knowledge located?	Located outside of learner.	Learning does not happen outside of learner.
How is knowledge attained?	Knowledge is discovered.	Knowledge is created.
Outcome	Heavily prescribed reading environment that views the learner as separate from learning. Learning focused on product not process.	Differentiated instruction is embraced. Use of strategies so learners are empowered to know when and how to use them to best meet their needs within a given context. Learning focused on process, not product.

Note. Based on Cunningham and Fitzgerald (1996).

literacy growth if literacy instruction and literacy learning were not such complex processes. The purpose of this chapter is to extend the conversation of comprehensive literacy instruction to recognize the social context of literacy learning as it relates to reading comprehension. As the research synthesized above has shown, teaching strategies as skills in isolation has not yielded long-term effects on comprehension.

In an effort to get to the root of the instructional problem, rather than focusing on the seven strategies that research has shown are most critical to comprehension, this chapter focuses on how to teach readers to be strategic, while recognizing the social nature of learning by highlighting the following key ingredients as a means of cultivating a classroom culture that values the learning process: (1) context, (2) agency/metacognition, and (3) scaffolding. Figure 10.1 illustrates how these elements work together to create a learning environment that foster independent, self-regulated strategy use.

This chapter attempts to change the conversation related to strategy instruction. Instead of focusing on individual skills and perpetuating the notion that strategies can be taught in isolation, Figure 10.1 highlights the need to shift from a list of seven strategies and associated skills to a more comprehensive and contextual view of how strategies can be implemented within a literacy environment so that students can become strategic and reflective.

The ideas that follow are based on Almasi's (2003) strategy instruction model and will help classroom teachers and interventionists identify critical features necessary for helping readers become strategic.

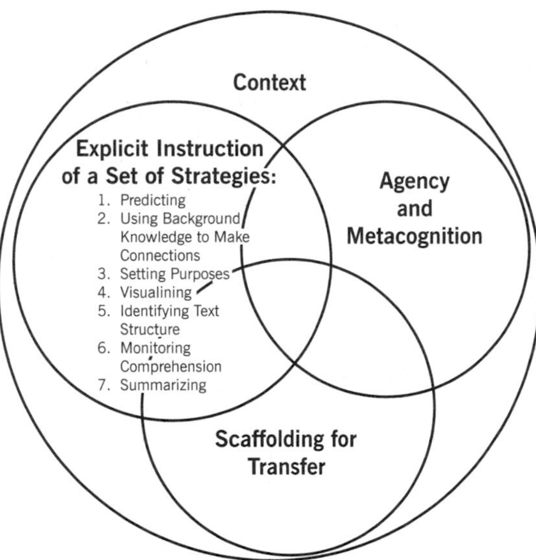

FIGURE 10.1. Key elements in a transformational view of comprehension strategy instruction.

Context

The instructional context in Figure 10.1 represents the overall instructional environment and everything contained within that environment. Context is critical for solid comprehension strategy instruction because it is through context that students become enculturated into the language of strategies, observe strategic behaviors and actions, and participate in strategic processing firsthand. Sociocultural perspectives on learning (e.g., Rogoff, 1990; Vygotsky, 1978) suggest that learning is a "cognitive apprenticeship" that occurs when learners are able to interact socially with others who might guide, support, or stretch their thinking so that they can learn how to use and implement the "tools of culture" (Rogoff, 1990, p. i) that will be needed. In an instructional context focused on comprehension, this means that students learn how to be strategic. The "tools" needed to be strategic in one context or culture might differ from those needed in another. For example, a reader might need different "tools" or act in a different manner when reading in an online environment than when reading traditional text (Coiro & Dobler, 2007; Leu et al., 2008), or when reading in a Western society that places greater value on "school literacy" or "written literacy" than in a society that values "oral literacy," where a higher demand is placed on memory. Johnston (2004) has noted that classrooms are sites where "children are *becoming* literate" (p. 22). It is where they are developing social and personal identities about who they are as readers, writers, and thinkers. It is where they explore, try out, and try on various ways of being, acting, and thinking as they negotiate their own identities. In this sense then, the classroom instructional context is a space in which readers author themselves (Holland, Lachiotte, Skinner, & Cain, 1998), which means there is a great deal of playful experimentation needed, particularly as readers attempt new or different ways of accomplishing tasks and goals. This is not a space where there are "right" or "wrong" ways of "doing" reading or comprehending. It is a space where readers construct and build their own understanding of themselves and of what works for them and under what conditions. Thus the instructional context must be a safe space that is free of the hazards that lead children to become cautious, fearful, anxious, and passive participants in their own learning. Often such hazards arise when children are assessment focused or performance oriented, as Prawat (1989) described them. Their goal might be to "get done," which might lead them to rush through or skim a text so they finish, rather than engage in strategic behaviors that would assist their comprehension but cause them to take longer.

Creating a "safe" environment means creating a space in which it is "OK" to be uncertain or wrong, and in fact it is celebrated when students say, "I don't get it," or "I'm confused." The teacher's response, in a safe space, would be, "Wonderful! Owen, I'm so glad you were able to recognize when your reading doesn't make sense! That shows you are a good reader because you know when the text doesn't make sense! What didn't make sense to you?" In these classrooms, the teacher creates a safe space where students can openly discuss what they don't understand (cf. Almasi, 1995, 1996; Almasi, O'Flahavan, & Arya, 2001; Fall, Webb, & Chudowsky, 2000) and test new or different ways of making sense of text. These safe spaces include lots of opportunities for readers to talk with other readers about what texts they read, what they understood (or did not understand), and how they went about making sense of the text (e.g., what strategic processes they used, when they used them, where they used them, and why they used them). Teachers in these classrooms are not asking comprehension questions or noting who understood and who did not. Instead, teachers who create safe spaces make note of what strategic processing was being done, by whom, and under what circumstances.

In the above scenario, the teacher might ask other students whether they had a similar problem: "Did anyone else have difficulty understanding that part? Let's talk about what strategies we can use to help ourselves when the text doesn't make sense." The teacher might then use the teachable moment to begin a very brief explanation of "fix-up strategies" that we might use when the text doesn't make sense, such as rereading, reading ahead to clarify meaning, or discussing the difficult part with another person.

In addition to creating a safe instructional environment, another critical feature of context focuses on the nature of the instruction itself. Explicit instruction is represented in Figure 10.1 as a key element within the context. It is an aspect that is often heralded as being vital to best practice, but in reality does not occur. Explicit instruction involves teacher modeling, explanation, and think-alouds that help children understand what strategic processes are, how to use them, under what conditions they might be used, and why they might be used. In the research literature this is known as declarative, procedural, and conditional knowledge (Paris et al., 1983). In Figure 10.1 the seven research-based comprehension strategies are represented within explicit instruction as a list, but they should be thought of as a flexible and interconnected set of strategies. Teachers should teach this set of strategies using explanation, modeling, thinking aloud, and long-term guided practice in a variety of settings.

Brown (2008) found that the teachers trained to use transactional strategies instruction (TSI) provided much richer explanations of the processes involved in strategic thinking. The TSI teachers described the reasons for using particular strategies at particular times and the processes underlying their use. They also provided a great deal of modeling and verbalized about the thought processes they used while reading, whereas non-TSI teachers did not. In addition, TSI teachers provided commentary on and elaborated students' thought processes to take advantage of teachable moments.

In the example above, the teacher might provide an explanation of various fix-up strategies and then think aloud about how to use one of them in the context:

> "OK, so Owen said that he didn't understand what the author, Stephen Mooser, meant in the sentence 'Happy HICCUP Halloween.' That is confusing and it doesn't seem to make sense. When we are reading and the text doesn't make sense we can use our fix-up strategies. So I might think, 'Wait a second, that doesn't make sense. I'd better stop and use a fix-up strategy.' One fix-up strategy we can use is to read ahead slowly and see whether the meaning clears up. That just means reading ahead a little further and being very alert and cautious while I read. So as I read ahead slowly, I'm going to keep trying to think of that HICCUP in the middle of the sentence that didn't make sense and see whether the next couple of sentences help clarify the meaning. I'm going to try that."

The teacher would then continue by reading aloud from the text (in this example the text is Stephen Mooser's *The Ghost with the Halloween Hiccups*):

> "[reading aloud] 'Oh my,' said Laura. 'You have the hiccups.' 'All HICCUP day,' said Mr. Penny. [thinking aloud] OK, now I've read ahead a little further to see whether the meaning cleared up. I noticed that Laura told Mr. Penny that he had the hiccups. So I guess that means Mr. Penny has the hiccups. Then there is another odd sentence with HICCUP in the middle of it. I noticed that there are quotation marks around the sentence 'All HICCUP day,' and that usually means someone's talking. So if he has the hiccups and

he's talking . . . well, that reminds me of when I have hiccups. Sometimes if I have hiccups and I try to talk, I hiccup in the middle of the sentence I'm trying to say. Maybe that's it! Could it be that the author, Stephen Mooser, is trying to show us how Mr. Penny was actually talking by inserting an actual HICCUP right in the middle of his sentence? Let me go back and reread that sentence and make a pretend HICCUP in the place where the word *hiccup* is capitalized, 'All [makes a hiccup sound] day.' Does that make sense now?"

In this think-aloud the teacher fluidly integrated several aspects of strategy instruction. She provided a *think-aloud* of what she might think while she was reading if that same sentence didn't make sense to her. Then she included an *explanation* of what one fix-up strategy, reading ahead, is and how to do it. She then *modeled* the fix-up strategy by reading ahead from the spot where Owen had difficulty. After she read aloud she actually used several comprehension strategies—she *summarized* what she read, *made a connection to her background knowledge* about what happens to her when she has the hiccups and then she used the *rereading fix-up strategy* to check (*monitor*) her comprehension.

Ultimately, she is showing the students how to weave together a variety of strategies to make sense of the text—the "read ahead slowly" fix-up strategy gets linked to two of the seven comprehension strategies, "summarization" and "using background knowledge to make connections to bring meaning to the sentence," before she goes back to use the "rereading fix-up strategy" to check her understanding, which is yet another one of the seven comprehension strategies (monitoring comprehension). In this small example we can see how complicated the reading process actually is. When we read successfully we never use just one strategy. Instead, we integrate the entire set of strategies in different combinations.

After the think-aloud, the teacher might turn the conversation back to the students to ask them whether they interpreted the sentence in a different way or used different strategies: "Did anyone understand that sentence in a different way?" "Did anyone use other strategies to help them make sense of that sentence?" By doing this the teacher opens the door to a safe environment where different combinations of strategies can be used and different interpretations of the text are valued. What we see in this example is a teacher who is providing explicit instruction, but she is grounding it in authentic reading experiences and continually turns the context back over to the students.

Another aspect of explicit instruction includes providing lots of guided practice for readers to use and try out ways of recognizing and using strategic behaviors in varied contexts. This guided practice should take place over time and should gradually shift the responsibility for strategic thinking, actions, and behaviors to students so that over time students are able to engage in these processes independently. This is where Dewitz et al. (2009)

found that core reading programs lagged in their attempts at reproducing research-based best practices in comprehension strategy instruction. These programs simply did not provide sufficient opportunities for students to use what they had learned in multiple contexts and under varying conditions. As well, there was too much teacher guidance that did not enable students to assume responsibility for their own learning.

Explicit instruction should also occur in authentic reading contexts. That is, readers need to practice being strategic using authentic texts of all sorts—books, informational texts, comic books, magazines, online texts, newspapers, and so on. Transfer will not occur unless readers have the opportunity to think about how they might be strategic in different contexts (e.g., in school, out of school, in church) and under different circumstances (e.g., when they are fatigued, unmotivated, stressed).

Unlike direct instruction, explicit instruction does not break the reading process down into separate parts or subskills. Each time reading occurs it should reflect the entire reading process with authentic texts. That is, strategic reading requires students to read whole texts—not chunks of texts, or a couple of sentences, or sentences with blanks in them, or words (or parts of words) in isolation. In order for readers to truly understand what it means to be strategic they must encounter the reading process in its complex entirety. It is similar to learning to drive a car. Imagine if we taught teenagers how to drive by having steering practice using fake steering wheels in a classroom. After steering practice, imagine the teacher providing braking practice by having students pumping imaginary brakes, followed by acceleration practice using imaginary accelerator pedals. Inauthentic sites of practice do not provide learners with the realities they will encounter when they have to coordinate all of those separate pieces into a coherent whole while also making decisions about where and when to brake and under what conditions you might need to brake more quickly. So it is with reading and learning to be strategic. We must provide authentic learning contexts in which readers learn to negotiate and manage the entire process all at once. This means being an active participant in the process and learning to make decisions.

Pearson and Dole (1987) have also noted that during explicit instruction there are no "correct" answers. There are multiple sets of strategies, combinations of strategies, and strategic behaviors that can be used to accomplish a given reading task. If we use the driving scenario again, it is similar to using multiple or different routes to arrive at the same place for a meeting. Everyone can arrive at the same place using different paths. So it is with strategic processes in reading. Different readers can use different strategies, combinations of strategies, and strategic behaviors to accomplish the same goal—comprehension of text.

The final feature of explicit instruction is that the feedback that teachers offer should be suggestive rather than corrective. If there are no "correct" answers, then the feedback we offer students should provide alternate suggestions or different ways of approaching the task. We can also provide opportunities for students to share the different strategies they use with each other so they can see how other readers approach the and accomplish tasks.

Agency/Metacognition

Agency refers to the notion that people are active participants in life events, not simply a product of those events (Bandura, 2008). In reading this means that the reader plays an active role in and influences the manner in which the reading event occurs. That is, the reader is an agent who has an influence on how the reading event will proceed and what strategic behaviors and actions will be used. In many classrooms that teach "strategies," however, it is often the teacher who takes on a great deal of authority in terms of making decisions about what strategies will be taught, to whom, with what texts, and when. At times, teachers determine what graphic organizers will be used, with what texts, and when they will be filled out. In a classroom that fosters agency, the teacher enables and empowers students to make such decisions. At the heart of agentic behavior is metacognition. That is, students are able to influence and make decisions about the reading process when they are able to evaluate their progress to determine whether their reading is successful or unsuccessful and make adjustments as needed so that they can reach their goal.

Johnston (2004) suggested ways in which teachers' language can enable agentic behaviors. He noted that teachers foster agency by providing opportunities for students to stop and talk about their thinking. For example, during a read-aloud teachers might stop at points that are particularly thought provoking or that are prime opportunities for predicting and say, "What are you thinking? Share your thoughts with a partner." These stopping points provide an opportunity for children to verbalize their thought processes. This is not simply "sharing." The goal is for students to actually verbalize their thought processes during the reading process. In this way metacognitive awareness is built.

Instructional opportunities that foster verbalization also occur when students are able to figure out something while reading. For example, if a young reader recognizes a word such as *laundry* that they ordinarily would not recognize, the teacher might say, "You figured that out. How did you do that?" As Johnston (2004) has noted, the teacher's question does not have a "correct" answer. Instead, it is an invitation to tell a narrative about how they solved a problem. The story is a process-oriented story in which the student shares the strategy or combination of strategies that he or she used to solve the problem: "Well, I looked at the picture and saw dirty laundry on the floor. Then I noticed a slot in the wall with a word that began with *L* on it. I figured the word must be *laundry*." By verbalizing these thought processes, students see a variety of ways in which they can solve similar problems.

Thus teachers can encourage metacognitive behaviors by asking open-ended questions that encourage students to share their thought processes.

Other examples include, "Why doesn't that make sense to you?" "What did you do to figure that out?" "How did you know that?" Brown's (2008) study showed that TSI teachers tended to ask students to explain their thinking, whereas non-TSI teachers did not. Such questions led the students in the TSI classrooms to clarify and justify their thinking, and they were able to draw on their personal experiences and evidence from the text to do so.

The language that students use to respond to such questions brings awareness to what are typically "covert" or hidden thought processes (Prawat, 1989). The thoughts become objects for others to reflect on and evaluate. Vygotsky (1978) has noted that such "egocentric" speech is the basis for inner speech. When this type of language is in its external and public form it becomes available for everyone to think about. During that thinking, some individuals may think about how that process might be helpful to them: "Oh, I never thought about doing it that way. I'll have to try that." Such reflection then opens the doors for the individual to try it on their own. When learners attempt such behaviors on their own it shows that they are beginning to internalize the process. These attempts, however, also illustrate the need (as mentioned above) for creating a safe space because these initial attempts are just that—initial—and we want students to be willing to take risks to try new ways of thinking and processing text. As students become more metacognitive they are able to recognize when text doesn't make sense, which means they recognize the need for strategic action. Such recognition leads to action, which leads to agency. Students determine whether they need to be strategic, when they need to be strategic, where they need to be strategic, and how to be strategic. Such agentic behavior is necessary to help students transform from passive to active participants in the reading process.

Scaffolding That Leads to Transfer

Decades of research have shown that strategy instruction improves reading comprehension; however, the troublesome aspect is helping readers transfer such instruction to different contexts. Providing sufficient guided practice under varying conditions is critical to transfer. One way to provide such guided practice is by incorporating strategies instruction into every aspect of the classroom, in every content area. This includes creating a safe context and providing opportunities for student verbalization that lead to agency in *every* learning opportunity—during read-alouds, during shared reading, during guided reading, and after independent reading. This form of scaffolding is flexible and might occur during whole-class, small-group, or individualized instruction. TSI is a model of instruction that incorporates these principles into every reading event because the teacher–student and student–student conversations that characterize TSI can occur during the reading of any text, including online reading. The type of teacher scaffolding that occurs during TSI is not preplanned. It requires a trained teacher who is able to identify opportune, teachable moments as students are reading text in authentic contexts. Brown (2008) has noted that teachers gradually release responsibility to students by engaging in think-alouds in which they explain and model their own thought processes to students as described above. TSI teachers grab teachable moments during the course of authentic reading experiences to demonstrate the type of strategic thinking and behaviors in which they naturally engage.

At other times, particularly with struggling readers, scaffolding that leads to transfer needs to be planned more deliberately. During this type of scaffolding the teacher might select a strategy, a combination of strategies, or a strategic behavior on which to focus instruction. These preplanned lessons might be conducted during guided reading groups so that students can practice using the focal strategies with texts at their independent or instructional reading level. This type of instruction should not occur with texts that are at a frustration level for students.

Almasi's (2003) strategy instruction model describes a means of planning instructional lessons so that teacher-scaffolded support is gradually reduced. In this model, two dimensions of scaffolded support are considered: (1) the amount of cognitive effort a reader must expend, and (2) the nature of the instructional tasks and texts used during the lesson (see Figure 10.2). The amount of cognitive effort a reader must expend is greater when the reader must complete the reading tasks independently, because all of the burden for reading and enacting strategic behaviors belongs to the reader; however, the amount of cognitive effort diminishes when the reader can complete the reading task with a partner, a small group, or with the whole class. By using various grouping patterns the teacher can provide guided practice and scaffolding in different ways.

The amount of scaffolded support can also be varied by teaching students how to engage in strategic behaviors using different types of tasks and texts in lessons. If we define "text" broadly so that it includes any sign or symbol that communicates a message, then texts would include movies, cartoons, pictures, wordless picture books, texts that are read aloud, texts read during shared reading, and texts read independently. This broad conceptualization of "text" means that initial strategy lessons can introduce readers to difficult strategies such as comprehension monitoring without requiring them actually to decode the text. In this manner, struggling readers can learn very high-level cognitive strategies at a young age. By introducing readers to strategic processing in this manner it helps them learn the language of being a strategic reader.

Focal lessons aimed at teaching students new strategies or strategic behaviors (e.g., making predictions, monitoring comprehension, summarizing, visualizing, making connections, setting purposes) that they did not previously know about might begin with very concrete lessons using video excerpts from movies or television programs. In this type of lesson teachers can provide explicit instruction for students using "texts" in which the reader can focus solely on the strategic processing rather than having to bear the additional burden of decoding. For example, Mrs. Macklin noticed that her second graders often made "wild" predictions that were based more on their background knowledge and didn't use the text to help form the prediction. She decided to model how to predict by using a video clip from a TV show in which she could stop the video at a highly predictable or "cliff-hanger" point and think aloud about the thoughts going through her mind as she formed a prediction: "Well, I'm really excited to see the next part because I noticed ____________ and that makes me think that ____________ is going to happen next." At this point she might open the discussion up for the students to share their thoughts: "Does anyone else have a prediction about what might happen next in the show?" As students share their ideas, Mrs. Macklin will try to encourage them to verbally share the thought processes they are using as they form their predictions and link those ideas to some evidence in the show that they have already seen: "Oh, you think ____________ is going to happen? What did you notice in the show so far that makes you think that?" Mrs. Macklin would then continue using the think-aloud with whole-class input during this lesson in which the "text" is a TV show. This lesson would be located at point A in Figure 10.2.

After teaching this type of lesson, follow-up guided practice lessons can be planned that vary either the type of text or task (e.g., teaching students how to make predictions with a wordless picture book or during a read-aloud while keeping it as a whole-class or small-group activity so cognitive effort needed will still be low—points B1 and C1 in Figure 10.2) and/or the amount

		Concrete ← → Abstract					
		Event/ Experience	Video/TV	Read-Aloud	Wordless Picture Book	Picture Book	Book
Less Individual Cognitive Effort Needed ↑	Whole Class		A	B1	C1		
	Small Group						
	Trio		B2				
More Individual Cognitive Effort Needed ↓	Pair		C2				
	Individual						D

FIGURE 10.2. Scaffolded instructional support for strategic processing. Adapted from Almasi (2003, p. 63). Copyright 2003 by The Guilford Press. Adapted by permission.

of cognitive effort needed (e.g., making predictions from a video with a partner or independently—points B2 and C2 in Figure 10.2). The goal in this form of scaffolding is to alter the types of texts, tasks, and grouping arrangements during follow-up guided practice sessions so that, over time, we are releasing the responsibility for strategic processing to students. Eventually, students will be using the strategy independently with text written at their instructional level (i.e., making it to point D in Figure 10.2). By planfully mapping out these two dimensions of scaffolding during instruction, responsibility is gradually released to students, which leads to transfer.

In summary, the three key ingredients to support an environment that cultivates strategic and reflective learning are: (1) context, (2) agency/metacognition, and (3) scaffolding. These three components are essential within a setting that values the learning process because they provide a space where students' prior experiences, individual perceptions, and own pace of learning are valued. Such an environment includes:

Context

- The teacher creates a safe environment in which students are able to explore, try out, and try on various ways of being, acting, and thinking.
  - The safe environment is a space where readers construct and build their own understanding of themselves and what works for them under what conditions.
  - In a safe environment there are no "correct" answers.
  - A safe environment celebrates "I don't get it" or "I'm confused" responses—these are teachable moments when learners are becoming strategic.
- The teacher includes explicit instruction, in which he or she explains, models, engages in think-alouds, and provides guided practice in authentic contexts.
- Authentic texts should be used.
- Strategy instruction should involve the whole reading process and use whole texts—not just part of it such as reading a sentence, a sentence with blanks in it, or a paragraph.

Agency/Metacognition

- Reader plays an active role in and influences the manner in which the reading event occurs.
- Students determine when they need to be strategic, where they need to be strategic, and how to be strategic as they transform from passive to active participants in the reading process.
- The goal is for students to verbalize their thought processes during the reading process as they become metacognitive.

Scaffolding

- Scaffolding is flexible and might occur during whole-class, small-group, or individual instruction.
- Scaffolding is incorporated into all content areas and in all teacher–student or student–student conversations.
- The goal is to gradually release the responsibility for strategic processing to students so that eventually they are using the strategy independently at their instructional level. We can do this by gradually:
  - Altering the types of texts used for guided practice.
  - Altering the amount of individual cognitive effort needed during the task.

It is within such an environment that we begin to recognize it is not just about the strategy you teach—environment matters. Research has shown that teaching strategies in isolation is not effective; we must provide a space for students that cultivates their transformation into independent, agentic learners who recognize that context matters as they decide when and how to use strategies that best meet their needs.

REFLECTIONS AND NEW DIRECTIONS

This chapter aimed to change the discourse surrounding comprehension strategy instruction from ideas about how to teach the seven research-based strategies to ideas about how to teach students to be strategic. This focus will hopefully help teachers achieve the most elusive aspect of comprehension instruction: transfer. Transfer happens when students become agentic. They see the value of thinking strategically and use it to make decisions about how to solve problems as they read.

The benefit of this approach to comprehension instruction is that we know it works. The research reviewed in this chapter is quite conclusive that teaching readers to be strategic results in long-term gains in comprehension. There are several limitations to consider, however. One is that learning to teach in this manner is difficult and can take years to learn how to do well (Anderson, 1992; Brown & Coy-Ogan, 1993; Duffy 1993a, 1993b; El-Dinary & Schuder, 1993; Pressley, Schuder, SAIL Teachers, Bergman, & El-Dinary, 1992). Another issue is that most assessments of comprehension focus on the end products of comprehension, which often rely on memory and recall of text and the ability to make inferences. The reliance on literal and inferential questions as the primary means of assessing comprehension means that instruction tends to approximate the text. Assessments that focus more on the processes used to make sense of text would be better aligned with an emphasis on teaching students to be strategic. Currently, we are left to rely on self-reports of strategy use (which are not always reliable) or think-aloud protocols (which are time consuming to administer and labor intensive to code) as the primary means of assessing strategic processing. Developing new forms of assessing strategic processing (and valuing them) would begin to change the instructional emphasis in our schools and classrooms.

CONCLUDING REMARKS

For decades we have emphasized the importance of teaching students comprehension strategies. However, shifting the emphasis from "the strategy" to "the student" is critical. This shift requires teachers to move from focusing on the strategies that are taught to the context in which they are taught. The focus on context ensures that we create learning opportunities that make it safe for readers to try on new ways of thinking and acting. A safe space accompanied by explicit instruction means that the context is ripe for readers to construct meaning and explore their own identities as readers. When we also include lots of opportunities for students to verbalize and share the thought processes they use while reading, this enables them to become more metacognitively aware while reading. Such metacognitive awareness enables readers to evaluate their reading progress and make decisions about what strategic processes may be needed to successfully attain their goals. When readers are active participants who make their own decisions about the reading process they possess agency, which is the key to transformation.

This chapter suggests that by recognizing the underlying belief systems that are perpetuated by various programs, change can begin to occur in educational environments. If learners are valued within their own comprehension instruction, positive change will be reflected in how these students negotiate/identify themselves as learners. By cultivating an environment that values the learner as inextricably linked to their own learning process, their agency will improve and positively affect their ability to transform into lifelong learners who are strategic and reflective.

ENGAGEMENT ACTIVITIES

1. Create a safe environment for strategy use.
2. Teach strategies by using explicit instruction.
3. Include opportunities for student verbalization in all instruction by asking open-ended questions that encourage students to share how they process text.
4. Vary the types of texts and tasks used during instruction.

5. Vary the amount of cognitive effort needed by students in order to release responsibility for strategic processing from teacher to student.

RESOURCES FOR FURTHER LEARNING

Almasi, J. F. (2003). *Teaching strategic processes in reading.* New York: Guilford Press.

Dewitz, P., Leahy, S., Jones, J., & Sullivan, P. M. (2010). *The essential guide to selecting and using core reading programs.* Newark, DE: International Reading Association.

Duffy, G. G. (2003). *Explaining reading: A resource for teaching concepts, skills, and strategies.* New York: Guilford Press.

Johnston, P. H. (2004). *Choice words: How our language affects children's learning.* Portland, ME: Stenhouse.

Pressley, M., & Afflerbach, P. P. (1995). *Verbal protocols of reading: The nature of constructively responsive reading.* Hillsdale, NJ: Erlbaum.

REFERENCES

Afflerbach, P., Pearson, P. D., & Paris, S. G. (2008). Clarifying differences between reading skills and reading strategies. *The Reading Teacher, 61*(5), 364–373.

Alexander, P. A., & Jetton, T. L. (2000). Learning from text: A multidimensional and developmental perspective. In M. L. Kamil, P. B. Mosenthal, P. D. Pearson, & R. Barr (Eds.), *Handbook of reading research* (Vol. 3, pp. 285–310). Mahwah, NJ: Erlbaum.

Almasi, J. F. (1995). The nature of fourth graders' sociocognitive conflicts in peer-led and teacher-led discussions of literature. *Reading Research Quarterly, 30*(3), 314–351.

Almasi, J. F. (1996). A new view of discussion. In L. B. Gambrell & J. F. Almasi (Eds.), *Lively discussions! Fostering engaged readers* (pp. 2–24). Newark, DE: International Reading Association.

Almasi, J. F. (2003). *Teaching strategic processes in reading.* New York: Guilford Press.

Almasi, J. F., O'Flahavan, J. F., & Arya, P. (2001). A comparative analysis of student and teacher development in more proficient and less proficient discussions of literature. *Reading Research Quarterly, 36*(2), 96–120.

Almasi, J. F., Palmer, B. M., Madden, A., & Hart, S. (2011). Interventions to enhance narrative comprehension. In R. Allington & A. McGill-Franzen (Eds.), *Handbook of reading disability research* (pp. 329–344). New York: Routledge.

Anderson, V. (1992). A teacher development project in transactional strategy instruction for teachers of severely reading-disabled adolescents. *Teaching and Teacher Education, 8*(4), 391–403.

August, D. L., Flavell, J. H., & Clift, R. (1984). Comparison of comprehension monitoring of skilled and less-skilled readers. *Reading Research Quarterly, 20*(1), 39–53.

Bandura, A. (2008). Reconstrual of "free will" from the agentic perspective of social cognitive theory. In J. Baer, J. C. Kaufman, & R. F. Baumeister (Eds.), *Are we free? Psychology and free will* (pp. 86–127). New York: Oxford University Press.

Baumann, J. F., Seifert-Kessell, N., & Jones, L. A. (1992). Effect of think-aloud instruction on elementary students' comprehension monitoring abilities. *Journal of Reading Behavior, 24*(2), 143–172.

Borkowski, J. G., Weyhing, R. S., & Carr, M. (1988). Effects of attributional retraining on strategy-based reading comprehension in learning-disabled students. *Journal of Educational Psychology, 80*(1), 46–53.

Boulineau, T., Fore, C., Hagan-Burke, S., & Burke, M. D. (2004). Use of story-mapping to increase the story-grammar text comprehension of elementary students with learning disabilities. *Learning Disability Quarterly, 27*(2), 105–121.

Brown, R. (2008). The road not yet taken: A transactional strategies approach to reading comprehension instruction. *The Reading Teacher, 61*(7), 538–547.

Brown, R., & Coy-Ogan, L. (1993). The evolution of transactional strategies instruction in one teacher's classroom. *The Elementary School Journal, 94*(2), 221–233.

Brown, R., Pressley, M., Van Meter, P., & Schuder, T. (1996). A quasi-experimental validation of transactional strategies instruction with low-achieving second-grade readers. *Journal of Educational Psychology, 88*(1), 18–37.

Carver, R. P. (1993). Merging the simple view of reading with rauding theory. *Journal of Reading Behavior, 25*(4), 439–455.

Chan, L. K. S., Cole, P. G., & Morris, J. N. (1990). Effects of instruction in the use of a visual-imagery strategy on the reading-comprehension competence of disabled and average readers. *Learning Disabilities Quarterly, 13*(1), 2–11.

Coiro, J., & Dobler, E. (2007). Exploring the online comprehension strategies used by sixth-grade skilled readers to search for and locate information on the Internet. *Reading Research Quarterly, 42*, 214–257.

Cunningham, J. W., & Fitzgerald, J. (1996). Epistemology and reading. *Reading Research Quarterly, 31*(1), 36–60.

Davey, B. (1988). The nature of response error for good and poor readers when permitted to reinspect text during question answering. *American Educational Research Journal, 25*(3), 399–414.

Dewitz, P., Jones, J., & Leahy, S. (2009). Comprehension strategy instruction in core reading programs. *Reading Research Quarterly, 44*(2), 102–126.

Dewitz, P., Leahy, S., Jones, J., & Sullivan, P. M. (2010). *The essential guide to selecting and using core reading programs.* Newark, DE: International Reading Association.

Duffy, G. G. (1993a). Rethinking strategy instruction: Four teachers' development and their low achievers' understandings. *The Elementary School Journal, 93*(3), 231–247.

Duffy, G. G. (1993b). Teachers' progress toward becoming expert strategy teachers. *The Elementary School Journal, 94*(2), 109–120.

El-Dinary, P. B., & Schuder, T. (1993). Seven teachers' acceptance of transactional strategies instruction during their first year using it. *The Elementary School Journal, 94*(2), 207–219.

Fall, R., Webb, N. M., & Chudowsky, N. (2000). Group discussion and large-scale language arts assessment: Effects on students' comprehension. *American Educational Research Journal, 37*(4), 911–941.

Flaro, L. (1987). The development and evaluation of a reading comprehension strategy with learning disabled students. *Reading Improvement, 24*, 222–229.

Fleisher, L. S., Jenkins, J. R., & Pany, D. (1979). Effects on poor readers' comprehension of training in rapid decoding. *Reading Research Quarterly, 15*(1), 30–48.

Gambrell, L. B., Wilson, R. M., & Gantt, W. N. (1981). Classroom observations of task-attending behaviors of good and poor readers. *Journal of Educational Research, 74*(6), 400–404.

Gamse, B. C., Jacob, R. T., Horst, M., Boulay, B., & Unlu, F. (2008). *Reading First impact study final report executive summary* (NCEE 2009-4039). Washington, DC: National Center for Education Evaluation and Regional Assistance, Institute of Education Sciences, U.S. Department of Education.

Garner, R., & Kraus, C. (1981). Good and poor comprehender differences in knowing and regulating reading behaviors. *Educational Research Quarterly, 6*(4), 5–12.

Garner, R., & Reis, R. (1981). Monitoring and resolving comprehension obstacles: An investigation of spontaneous text lookbacks among upper-grade good and poor readers. *Reading Research Quarterly, 16*(4), 569–582.

Gersten, R., Fuchs, L. S., Williams, J. P., & Baker, S. (2001). Teaching reading comprehension strategies to students with learning disabilities: A review of research. *Review of Educational Research, 71*(2), 279–320.

Hacker, D. J. (2004). Self-regulated comprehension during normal reading. In R. B. Ruddell & N. J. Unrau (Eds.), *Theoretical models and processes of reading* (5th ed., pp. 755–779). Newark, DE: International Reading Association.

Hartman, D. K. (1995). Eight readers reading: The intertextual links of proficient readers reading multiple passages. *Reading Research Quarterly, 30*(3), 520–561.

Hoffman, J. V. (2009). In search of the simple view of reading comprehension. In S. E. Israel & G. G. Duffy (Eds.), *Handbook of research on reading comprehension* (pp. 54–66). New York: Routledge.

Holland, D., Lachiotte, W., Skinner, D., & Cain, C. (1998). *Identity and agency in cultural worlds.* Cambridge, MA: Harvard University Press.

Hoover, W. A., & Gough, P. (1990). The simple view of reading. *Reading and Writing: An Interdisciplinary Journal, 2,* 127–160.

Idol, L. (1987). Group story mapping: A comprehension strategy for both skilled and unskilled readers. *Journal of Learning Disabilities, 20,* 196–205.

Idol, L., & Croll, V. J. (1987). Story-mapping training as a means of improving reading comprehension. *Learning Disabilities Quarterly, 10*(3), 214–229.

Johnston, P. H. (2004). *Choice words: How our language effects children's learning.* Portland, ME: Stenhouse.

LaBerge, D., & Samuels, S. J. (1974). Toward a theory of automatic processing in reading. *Cognitive Psychology, 6*(2), 293–323.

Leu, D. J., Jr., Coiro, J., Castek, J., Hartman, D. K., Henry, L. A., & Reinking, D. (2008). Research on instruction and assessment in the new literacies of online reading comprehension. In C. C. Block & S. R. Parris (Eds.), Comprehension instruction: Research-based best practices (2nd ed., pp. 321–346). New York: Guilford Press.

Marshall, J. (2000). Research on response to literature. In M. L. Kamil, P. B. Mosenthal, P. D. Pearson, & R. Barr (Eds.), *Handbook of reading research* (Vol. 3, pp. 381–402). Mahwah, NJ: Erlbaum.

Mastropieri, M. A., Scruggs, T. E., Bakken, J. P., & Whedon, C. (1996). Reading comprehension: A synthesis of research in learning disabilities. *Advances in Learning and Behavioral Disabilities, 10B,* 201–227.

Mastropieri, M. A., Scruggs, T., Mohler, L., Beranek, M., Spencer, V., Boon, R. T., et al. (2001). Can middle school students with serious reading difficulties help each other and learn anything? *Learning Disabilities Research and Practice, 16*(2), 18–27.

National Reading Panel. (2000). *Teaching children to read: An evidence-based assessment of the scientific research literature on reading and its implications for reading instruction* (Report of the Subgroups). Washington DC: U. S. Department of Health and Human Services, Public Health Service, National Institutes of Health, and the National Institute of Child Health and Human Development.

Palincsar, A. S., & Brown, A. L. (1984). Reciprocal teaching of comprehension-fostering and comprehension-monitoring activities. *Cognition and Instruction, 1,* 117–175.

Paris, S. G., Cross, D. R., & Lipson, M. E. (1984). Informed strategies for learning: A program to improve children's reading awareness and comprehension. *Journal of Educational Psychology, 76,* 1239–1252.

Paris, S. G., & Jacobs, J. E. (1984). The benefits of informed instruction for children's reading awareness and comprehension skills. *Child Development, 55,* 2083–2093.

Paris, S. G., Lipson, M. Y., & Wixson, K. K. (1983). Becoming a strategic reader. *Contemporary Educational Psychology, 8,* 293–316.

Paris, S. G., & Myers, M. (1981). Comprehension monitoring, memory, and study strategies of good and poor readers. *Journal of Reading Behavior, 13*(1), 5–22.

Paris, S. G., & Oka, E. R. (1986). Children's reading strategies, metacognition, and motivation. *Developmental Review, 6,* 25–56.

Paris, S. G., Wasik, B. A., & Turner, J. C. (1991). The development of strategic readers. In R. Barr, M. L. Kamil, P. Mosenthal, & P. D. Pearson (Eds.), *Handbook of reading research* (Vol. 2, pp. 609–640). White Plains, NY: Longman.

Pearson, P. D., & Dole, J. A. (1987). Explicit comprehension instruction: A review of research and a new conceptualization of instruction. *The Elementary School Journal, 88*(2), 151–165.

Pearson, P. D., & Fielding, L. (1991). Comprehension instruction. In R. Barr, M. L. Kamil, P. Mosenthal, & P. D. Pearson (Eds.), *Handbook of reading research* (Vol. 2, pp. 815–860). White Plains, NY: Longman.

Pilonieta, P. (2010). Instruction of research-based comprehension strategies in basal reading programs. *Reading Psychology, 31,* 150–175.

Prawat, R. S. (1989). Promoting access to knowledge, strategy, and disposition in students: A research synthesis. *Review of Educational Research, 59*(1), 1–41.

Pressley, M. (2000). What should comprehension instruction be the instruction of? In M. L. Kamil, P. B. Mosenthal, P. D. Pearson, & R. Barr (Eds.), *Handbook of reading research* (Vol. 3, pp. 545–561). Mahwah, NJ: Erlbaum.

Pressley, M., Borkowski, J. G., & Schneider, W. (1989). Good information processing: What it is and how education can promote it. *International Journal of Educational Research, 13,* 857–867.

Pressley, M., El-Dinary, P. B., Gaskins, I., Schuder, T., Bergman, J. L., Almasi, J., et al. (1992). Beyond direct explanation: Transactional instruction of reading comprehension strategies. *The Elementary School Journal, 92*(5), 513–555.

Pressley, M., Johnson, C. J., Symons, S., McGoldrick, J. A., & Kurita, J. A. (1989). Strategies that improve children's memory and comprehension of text. *The Elementary School Journal, 90*(1), 3–32.

Pressley, M., Schuder, T., SAIL Teachers, Bergman, J., & El-Dinary, P. B. (1992). A researcher–educator collaborative interview study of transactional comprehension strategies instruction. *Journal of Educational Psychology, 84,* 231–246.

Recht, D. R., & Leslie, L. (1988). Effect of prior knowledge on good and poor readers' memory of text. *Journal of Educational Psychology, 80*(1), 16–20.

Reutzel, D. R., Smith, J. A., & Fawson, P. C. (2005). An evaluation of two approaches for teaching reading comprehension strategies in the primary years using science information texts. *Early Childhood Research Quarterly, 20*(3), 276–305.

Rogoff, B. (1990). *Apprenticeship in thinking: Cognitive development in social context.* New York: Oxford University Press.

Samuels, S. J. (2004). Toward a theory of automatic information processing in reading, revisited. In R. B. Ruddell & N. J. Unrau (Eds.), *Theoretical models and processes of reading* (5th ed., pp. 1127–1148). Newark, DE: International Reading Association.

Van Keer, H. (2004). Fostering reading comprehension in fifth grade by explicit instruction in reading strategies and peer tutoring. *British Journal of Educational Psychology, 74,* 37–70.

Vygotsky, L. S. (1978). *Mind in society.* Cambridge, MA: Harvard University Press.

Westra, J., & Moore, D. (1995). Reciprocal teaching of reading comprehension in a New Zealand high school. *Psychology in the Schools, 32*(3), 225–232.

CHAPTER 11

Best Practices in Fluency Instruction

Melanie R. Kuhn
Timothy Rasinski

This chapter will:

- Discuss the relationship between fluency and the broader reading process.
- Present evidence-based practices for fluency instruction.
- Describe options for assessing reading fluency.
- Suggest future directions for fluency research.

In the years since the National Reading Panel report (2000), fluency has come to be seen as an integral component in reading development and text comprehension. As a result, we have seen it move from a rarely considered aspect of reading development (e.g., Rasinski, Reutzel, Chard, & Linan-Thompson, 2011) to one that has come to dominate literacy learning in many primary and elementary schools (e.g., Kuhn, Schwanenflugel, & Meisinger, 2010). During this same period, a second trend has emerged in many classrooms, that of equating fluent reading with accurate, automatic word recognition (Applegate, Applegate, & Modla, 2009). Although improvement in reading rate is a consequence or indicator of automaticity, instructionally, many educators have come to treat it as the cause of automaticity. This (mis)understanding has been driven, in large part, by a system of assessment that bases student competency on the number of correct words read in a minute.

Indeed, improvements in reading rate seem to be the primary goal of numerous fluency programs. Unfortunately, an exclusive, or even a primary, focus on accurate and automatic word recognition can lead students to a skewed view of what skilled readers do. Furthermore, the dominance of this perspective has led to a demotion in the perceived importance of fluency in the reading process, a reflection that can be seen in the failure to list reading fluency as a hot topic in the most recent survey of "What's hot, what's not" in reading (Cassidy & Cassidy, 2011). From our perspective, neither of the above positions accurately portrays fluency's role in the reading process; that is, fluent reading should neither be the dominating force in the literacy curriculum, nor should it be eliminated from consideration. Instead, we argue that fluency is one of many important components in skilled reading, and its instruction is a valuable element of the literacy curriculum when it is placed in proper perspective. In order to begin determining the appropriate role of fluency instruction, it is important to remember that *two* aspects of fluent reading are integral to literacy development: automaticity (LaBerge & Samuels, 1974) and prosody (Schreiber, 1991). Critically, this understanding is built upon the recognition that fluency is not only characterized by both elements, but that both aspects contribute to a learner's ability to construct meaning from text (Benjamin, Schwanenflugel, & Kuhn, 2009).

Our goals for this chapter, however, are not only to include a discussion of what we consider to be a more appropriate role for fluency instruction in the classroom, but also to provide a range of effective instructional approaches, some of which expand the ways in which fluency can be developed, as well as to review and expand on what constitutes appropriate assessment and to highlight future directions for research that may inform both theory and practice.

EVIDENCE-BASED BEST PRACTICES: A SHORT RESEARCH SYNTHESIS

In order to understand why instruction in reading fluency should involve more than simple speeded word recognition, it is important to consider how both automaticity and prosody contribute to its development. Here we discuss the role of both.

Contribution of Automatic Word Recognition to Comprehension

When it comes to word recognition, proficient readers not only identify words accurately, they also recognize the vast majority of words effortlessly or automatically. In other words, they do not need to spend a great deal of time on word recognition. This is important because, as with any cognitive task, individuals have a limited amount of attention available while reading (e.g., Adams, 1990; Samuels, 2006). As a result, whatever attention they expend on word recognition is, by necessity, attention that is unavailable for comprehension.

On the other hand, because beginning readers are developing their decoding skills, they need to focus a great deal of their attention on word recognition; this means that there is little attention left for the comprehension of texts. What we as educators need to do is devise ways to help students move from purposeful decoding to effortless word identification. There is a general consensus that this can best occur through practice—practice that consists, not only of work on word recognition, but also of the supported reading of a wide variety of connected text (e.g., Kuhn et al., 2010; Rasinski et al., 2011). As learners repeatedly encounter words in print, progressively less attention is required to decode them accurately, so that they eventually become part of a reader's sight word vocabulary, generally over the course of three to eight repetitions (e.g., Torgesen, 2005).

Contribution of Prosody to Reading Fluency

While automaticity has a central role in the development of fluent reading, fluency consists of more than simply reading words quickly and accurately; it also involves prosodic reading, or those melodic elements of language that, when taken together, constitute expressive reading (e.g., Schreiber, 1991). These include the use of intonation, stress, tempo, and appropriate phrasing, and, when they are applied correctly, they ensure that the oral reading of written text takes on the qualities of fluent speech. Furthermore, when readers incorporate prosody into their oral reading, they are providing clues to an otherwise invisible process, that of comprehension. This is because prosodic elements contribute to shades of meaning and a richer understanding of what is written. Furthermore, recent research indicates that prosody contributes to comprehension above and beyond the contribution made by automatic word recognition (Benjamin et al., 2009). While we know that prosody is closely tied to comprehension, the exact nature of the relationship is a matter of additional research (e.g., is the relationship reciprocal, does understanding the text allow for prosody, or does prosody lead to better comprehension?) (Kuhn et al., 2010). No matter what the relationship, however, the use of expression contributes to learners' engagement with text, helping to bring text to life and adding nuance to their reading.

BEST PRACTICES IN ACTION

Fluency Instruction and the Literacy Curriculum

Given that fluency is an important contributor to comprehension, it is critical that we identify effective instructional approaches for the classroom; that is, approaches that go beyond simply asking students to read text rapidly and instead present learners with a richer and more nuanced understanding of skilled reading (Kuhn et al., 2010; Rasinski et al., 2011). Importantly, there are a number of traits that underlie effective fluency instruction in all its forms (Rasinski, 2003). We outline these principles because it is possible to integrate some aspect(s) of these qualities across a range of literacy curricula, depending on the needs of your learners.

In addition, we focus on several approaches that can become an integral part of regular classroom instruction and are designed either for flexible groups (Fluency-Oriented Oral Reading; Kuhn, 2004/2005), for synthesized fluency routines (Fluency Development Lesson; e.g., Rasinski, Padak, Linek, & Sturtevant, 1994), or for shared reading approaches (Fluency-Oriented Reading Instruction; Kuhn & Schwanenflugel, 2007), or, alternatively, are simply activities that prove enjoyable for your students (Reader's Theater; e.g., Griffith & Rasinski, 2004). These approaches can serve as regular components of your lesson plans for younger readers who are making the transition to fluency, or they can be integrated into your literacy curriculum as needed for older struggling readers who have not yet achieved fluency. Importantly, they all have a focus on comprehension and prosody, as well as accuracy; as such, we feel they better represent the type of instruction that leads to the development of skilled reading than does instruction that focuses only on certain surface aspects of reading, such as accuracy and rate.

Principles of Fluency Instruction

Timothy Rasinski (2003) has outlined four basic principles that can help literacy educators develop effective fluency instruction. To begin with, students should have the opportunity to hear their teacher, or some other skilled reader, model fluent reading for them. Such modeling, even if consists of only a few minutes of oral reading a day, provides students with a better sense of what their own reading should sound like, something that is especially important for students whose reading is choppy or monotone. Next, it is critical that students are provided with support while they themselves are reading aloud (this support can come in the form of choral reading with a group, paired reading with a partner, or reading while listening to a prerecorded rendering of the text).

Third, teachers need to help focus students' attention on reading in syntactically appropriate and meaningful phrases. As with modeling, a focus on phrasing helps students develop a more complete understanding of the importance of prosody while simultaneously helping them move beyond reading that is word-by-word or that uses phrasing in ways that fail to replicate language. Finally, it is essential that students have ample opportunities to read text. As with most skills, students become better at reading through practice (Allington, 2009; Samuels, 2006), although the type of practice—and how much support is required—varies depending on the needs of the individual learner and the difficulty of the text.

The four basic principles outlined above can be used independently, or they can be combined to create synergistic instructional routines. However, one aspect of most fluency instruction, repetition, must be reconsidered in light of some recent findings (Kuhn et al., 2010; Mostow & Beck, 2005). First, it is important to stress that repetition does indeed help students develop their automaticity as well as their prosody; this, in turn, helps to ensure that learners become fluent readers. What needs to be reconsidered is not the repetition, per se, but instead how that repetition occurs. That is, repetition can occur through a traditional repeated reading format in which a given text is read several times. Alternatively, it can occur through the single reading of multiple texts. Because of the number of shared words and syntactic constructions in many texts, but especially in selections designed for young readers (Adams, 1990), it is possible for repetition to occur across a range of reading materials. In this scenario, students are likely to see the same words in multiple contexts, for example, words like *the, ran,* and *cat.* Furthermore, evidence indicates that readers may learn words faster when the words are encountered in a variety of contexts rather than when they are seen repeatedly in the same context (Mostow & Beck, 2005). As a result of this expanded understanding, we present several approaches to fluency instruction based on the above principles as well as both the wide and repeated reading of text.

Fluency-Oriented Oral Reading/Wide Fluency-Oriented Oral Reading

As discussed above, for many years repetition was considered a key element in aiding the fluency development of many learners. However, in their review of research on fluency interventions, Melanie Kuhn and Steven Stahl (2003) noted that when students who were using a repeated-readings approach were compared with students who read equivalent amounts of text with support, both groups made equivalent gains. In order to explore this possibility further, Melanie Kuhn (2004/2005) compared two forms of small group fluency instruction with second-grade struggling readers, one using repetition and the other using the wide reading of a number of texts. In addition, she included a group that listened to, but did not read, the texts used by the fluency groups and a control group.

The program involved working with small groups of students (five to six per group) for 15–20 minutes per session three times per week. Because the students were struggling second-grade readers, and because the goal was to scaffold, or support, the students' reading of texts slightly beyond their instructional level, the texts they read ranged from a late first- to an early third-grade reading level (FEP/Booksource, 1998; Fountas & Pinnell, 1999). Titles included books such as *Big Max* (Platt, 1992), *The Golly Sisters Go West* (Byars, 1985), and *Whistle for Willie* (Keats, 1965). The first group of learners used a modified repeated readings technique, or Fluency-Oriented Oral Reading (FOOR). This consisted of echo or choral reading a single trade book three times over the course of a week (i.e., the same book was read for each of the week's three 15–20 minute sessions). The second condition, or Wide FOOR approach, involved a single echo or choral reading of three different texts, or one text for each session. The third group listened to all the stories that were presented to the Wide FOOR group, but did not read the texts themselves, and the control group did not get any extra reading instruction beyond what was already occurring in their classroom.

The approaches were very simple, but the results were quite interesting. Both intervention groups did better than either the control group or the students who simply listened to the texts. That is, the FOOR and the Wide FOOR groups outperformed their peers in terms of word recognition in isolation, prosody, and correct words per minute. However, only the students in the Wide FOOR group made greater growth on comprehension than did their peers. It is possible that this finding resulted from perceived differences in the nature of the tasks; that is, students in the FOOR group may have felt that the implicit purpose of repeatedly reading a text was improvement in word recognition and prosody, while the students in the Wide FOOR group may have felt that the implicit purpose of reading multiple texts also included construction of meaning. It is important to note that, while there was some naturally occurring discussion surrounding the stories, neither comprehension nor vocabulary development were the focus of the lessons. Bearing this in mind, it may be that, by incorporating vocabulary and comprehension instruction into the FOOR and Wide FOOR, teachers could further assist learners in their understanding of the material being read (e.g., see Stahl, 2008).

Fluency Development Lesson

The Fluency Development Lesson (FDL; Rasinski et al., 1994) also integrates several of the principles of effective fluency instruction mentioned earlier into a coherent classroom routine. In the FDL, students work daily with a relatively short text. First, the teacher would read the passage to the students two to three times as they follow along silently. Next, students read the selection chorally as a group, with each student providing oral support for their classmates. Students then divide into pairs and engage in paired repeated reading, with each student reading the text two to three times while a partner follows along silently and provides support and encouragement. After completing this practice, students are offered the chance to perform the daily text for their classmates, alone or in small groups. Finally, the teacher and the students choose words from the text for word study. As an option, students may also take the assigned passage home for further practice with family members.

Implementation of the FDL with second-grade students demonstrated gains in overall fluency and a trend for improved overall achievement in reading (Rasinski et al., 1994). Fast Start (Padak & Rasinski, 2005) is a variation of the FDL for home involvement. In Fast Start, students work with a skilled reader (e.g., parent, caregiver, or even an older sibling) on a daily rhyme or other short text. The skilled reader reads the passage to their child two to three times while pointing to the words; next, the skilled reader and child read the passage together two to three times; then the skilled reader listens to the child read the passage to him or her a couple of times. Finally, the skilled reader and child engage in a brief word-study activity using one or more words from the passage (e.g., if the word *wall* was found in the passage, the skilled reader and child may write and read other words within the same word family—*ball, call, stall, mall,* and so on). In an implementation of Fast Start with first-grade students, Timothy Rasinski and Bruce Stevenson (2005) found that Fast Start had a profound and positive impact on the reading development of the most at-risk students; Fast Start students made nearly twice the gain in word recognition fluency than their peers who received the same instruction in school but did not participate in the program at home.

Fluency-Oriented Reading Instruction/Wide Fluency-Oriented Reading Instruction

Fluency-Oriented Reading Instruction (FORI)/Wide Fluency-Oriented Reading Instruction (Wide FORI) is designed for the shared reading component of your literacy curriculum, but could be modified for small-group instruction and can even be used for tutoring one or two struggling readers. FORI (Stahl & Heubach, 2005) is based on a weekly lesson plan that incorporates echo, choral, and partner reading in a systematic manner. The original intervention took place with second graders who were reading below grade level, and was developed in response to a mandate that teachers use only grade-level texts for their literacy instruction. FORI was created in the hopes that it could provide readers with an approach that would allow these texts to become more accessible. Although the procedure is quite straightforward, it has been shown to be successful with students who are having trouble working with grade-level material and works best with texts that would be classified as somewhat challenging for your learners.

Although the FORI procedure was originally used as a way to cover a selection from a basal reader or literature anthology, it can be used with any text that is part your literacy curriculum, including trade books. However, it is essential that the selection be somewhat challenging for the learners and that each student has a copy of whatever material is being read. In many classrooms, there is a particular story or expository piece that is a required part of the weekly literacy curriculum. As a result, you may feel a corresponding sense of accountability attached to these selections. In practice, this can mean that you dedicate a greater proportion of your class time to their instruction. The FORI procedure allows you to develop meaningful lessons around such selections. At the same time, the approach provides room for integrating additional reading materials—and instructional approaches—into your literacy curriculum as well. In fact, FORI should not be viewed as the only component of your literacy instruction; instead, it is important that you include multiple types of literacy learning, such as small-group and individual reading instruction, opportunities to write, and a focus on word study, as part of a balanced curriculum.

In terms of specifics, FORI involves the teaching of a single challenging text over a 5-day period (see Figure 11.1). The first day begins with the introduction of the week's selection. This can start with the type of activities that you would typically use for your prereading instruction; for example, you may choose to highlight important vocabulary, build background knowledge, or preview the text. However, rather than having the students attempt to read the text themselves on the first day, you should read the selection to them while they follow along in their own copies. This allows your students to concentrate on comprehending the text while you provide them with the pronunciation of any unknown words. Upon completing the first reading of the text, you and your students should discuss the material; this further reinforces the notion that text comprehension is your primary goal. The second day involves an echo reading of the text; this approach can be made even more effective by integrating comprehension questions at natural stopping points throughout the selection (Stahl, 2008).

The third day's lesson is the shortest of the week, consisting of a simple choral reading of the material with your students. Depending on the amount of time you can allocate to your shared reading on this day, you may want to integrate a second choral reading of the material into your instruction. The fourth day involves asking your students to partner read alternating pages of the text. By that time, the students should be fairly comfortable with the text, having encountered it at least three times previously. Furthermore, the support the partners provide each other should allow them to read the text successfully. Depending on how quickly the partners complete their first reading, you may have time for them to reread the selection; for this second reading, the partners would read the pages opposite those they read initially. The last day of the FORI lesson plan consists of simply implementing your usual postreading extension activities; for example, you might ask students to summarize the selection, to complete graphic organizers of the material, or to write in response to the reading (see Figure 11.1 for the weekly lesson plan).

The FORI program provides students with modeling, support or assistance, a focus on appropriate phrasing, and, perhaps most important, ample opportunities to read substantial amounts of connected text. Although some teachers find the format to be a bit tedious, the vast majority of the students actually enjoyed the predictable and consistent routine. What is critical, however, is that the material being used is long enough for your students to read for an extended period (20–40 minutes per day) and that the texts being used are sufficiently challenging for your learners (e.g., grade-level texts if the majority of your students are reading below grade level, and texts that are above grade level if the majority of your students are reading at grade level). When these conditions are in place, FORI has been shown to help students make significant gains in terms of their reading ability.

However, despite the benefits we found for FORI, when comparing it to a wide-reading alternative that used less repetition (Wide FORI), the wide-

Fluency-Oriented Reading Instruction	Monday	Tuesday	Wednesday	Thursday	Friday
Shared reading lesson	• Teacher introduces story (often from basal or literature analogy). • Teacher reads story to class; class discusses story. • Option: Teacher develops graphic organizers. • Option: Class does activities from basal.	• Students practice story. • Teacher and students echo read story.	• Students practice story. • Teacher and students choral read story.	• Students practice story. • Students partner read story.	• Students do extension activities. These may include writing in response to story, etc. • Option: Teacher does running records of children's reading.
Home reading	• Children read 15–30 minutes in a book of their choosing.	• Students take story home and practice reading basal story aloud to someone.	• Students who need more practice take home the basal story—others take book of their choosing.	• Students who need more practice take home the basal story—others take book of their choosing.	• Children read 15–30 minutes in a book of their choosing.

FIGURE 11.1. FORI weekly lesson plan.

reading approach proved to be equally if not more effective at improving students' reading ability. While the Wide FORI method is similar to the original FORI in many ways, three texts, rather than one, are read over the course of a week (see Figure 11.2). This allows learners to encounter many words in multiple contexts and has the potential to expose students to a broader range of concepts as well. This method relates to Gordon Logan's (1997) notion that breadth as well as depth is central to developing automaticity. As was the case in the FORI approach, the primary text for the Wide FORI lessons is usually the basal or literature anthology selection that is required as part of many literacy curricula; however, any shared reading text can be used.

Critically, because the approach involves three texts over the course of a week, the amount of time spent on the first selection is, by necessity, reduced. As a result, you would only spend 3 days on this text, as opposed to the 5 days allotted in the original FORI method. The first day involves prereading activities to introduce the text, reading the selection to your class as your students follow along, and discussing the reading with your learners; the second day consists of echo reading the text, followed by a choral or partner reading if time allows; and the third day centers around implementing whatever extension activities you feel are appropriate for the material (see Days 1, 2, and 5 of the FORI approach, respectively, for a more detailed plan of these days' lessons). The remaining lessons incorporate the reading of a second and third text on Days 4 and 5. These texts should be echo read, and you should follow the reading with a discussion of the selections with your children. Furthermore, if time allows, you should have your students undertake a second reading of the material; whether you decide to have your learners echo, choral, or partner read at this point should depend on your students' comfort with the material, the text difficulty, and the amount of time available. Again, it is essential that the texts be substantive enough to ensure students are spending between 20 and 40 minutes actually engaged in reading.

Reader's Theater: Practice and Performance

Although Reader's Theater is often thought of as the performance of a script (e.g., Rasinski et al., 2011), we enlarge our definition of Reader's Theater to include the reading performance of any text for the purpose of eliciting both efferent and aesthetic responses from the audience. While recitation is another term that has been used in place of Reader's Theater, we prefer Reader's Theater, as recitation implies memorizing a text and performing it from memory. In Reader's Theater, the final performance is read by the performer. Furthermore, the texts used for Reader's Theater are varied and can include scripts, dialogues, monologues, transcripts of interviews, poetry, songs, oratory, journal entries, letters, jokes, chants, cheers, and more.

When employing a Reader's Theater approach to fluency instruction, you should assign (or have your students choose) texts that will eventually be performed by your learners. Students can work individually, in pairs, or in small

Wide Fluency-Oriented Reading Instruction	**Monday**	**Tuesday**	**Wednesday**	**Thursday**	**Friday**
Shared reading lesson	• Teacher introduces story (often from basal or literature anthology). • Teacher reads story to class; class discusses story. • Option: Teacher develops graphic organizers • Option: Class does activities from basal (story 1).	• Students practice story. • Teacher and students echo read story 1. • Option: students do partner reading.	• Students do extension activities. These may include writing in response to story, etc. • Option: Teacher does running records of children's reading.	• Teacher and students echo or choral read trade book (story 2). • Option: Students partner read story 2. • Option: Students do extension activities (writing, etc.).	• Teacher and students echo or choral read trade book (story 3). • Option: Students partner read story 3. • Option: Students do extension activities (writing, etc.).
Home reading	• Children read 15–30 minutes per day in a book of their choosing.	• Students take story home and practice reading basal story aloud to someone.	• Children read 15–30 minutes per day in a book of their choosing.	• Children read 15–30 minutes per day in a book of their choosing.	• Children read 15–30 minutes per day in a book of their choosing.

FIGURE 11.2. Wide FORI weekly lesson plan.

groups to practice and perform their assigned text. Once a text is assigned, your students should rehearse (i.e., engage in repeated readings of) their text over a period of time (usually several days). The goal of the rehearsal is not fast reading, but a prosodic and meaningful oral interpretation of the text. During this rehearsal time the teacher is engaged in modeling the readings, coaching and providing feedback to the students, and setting the stage for the performance. After an appropriate rehearsal period (depending on the length and complexity of the text), the students perform their selections for an audience usually made up of classmates, teacher, parents, and other guests. The cycle of practice and performance should become a classroom routine that is repeated over the following days, weeks, and months.

Reader's Theater, as we describe it here, incorporates the elements or principles of effective fluency instruction that we described earlier—modeling fluent reading, assisted reading, and repeated reading—within an authentic and purposeful framework. Classroom-based research has found that a Reader's Theater approach to fluency instruction leads to significant improvements in reading fluency and overall reading achievement (Griffith & Rasinski, 2004; Martinez, Roser, & Strecker, 1999; Young & Rasinski, 2009). Moreover, the same research has also shown that students, teachers, and parents view Reader's Theater as a highly motivating and engaging reading activity.

Assessing Fluency

Before leaving our discussion on fluency instruction, we consider it important to discuss briefly the two primary ways in which fluent oral reading can be assessed. The first involves the oral reading fluency (ORF) target rate norms (Rasinski, 2004), an assessment designed to determine students' rate (correct words per minute) and word-recognition accuracy. This provides a sense of how students are developing in terms of accurate and automatic word recognition according to both their grade level and the time of year (see Table 11.1). However, we present a caveat when suggesting the use of this approach for evaluating fluency. As we mentioned at the beginning of this chapter, there has been a tendency to equate correct words per minute with fluent reading. We would like to say emphatically that it is not. Automatic word recognition is simply one aspect of fluent reading, albeit an easily measured and recognized one. Unfortunately, the notion that fluency is speeded word recognition has led some students (and some educators; see Applegate et al., 2009) to develop the incorrect belief that fast reading, rather than meaningful reading, is the goal of reading instruction. When using this as a measure of correct words per minute, it is critical that we use it in conjunction with a measure of prosody to help students focus on the meaning of what they are reading, not simply on how quickly they read it.

The second evaluation tool is the National Assessment of Educational Progress's (NAEP) Oral Reading Fluency Scale (NAEP, 1995), a measure that looks at fluency more broadly—incorporating phrasing, smoothness, pace,

TABLE 11.1. Correct Words per Minute by Grade Level

Grade	Fall (wcpm)	Winter (wcpm)	Spring (wcpm)
1	—	10–30	30–60
2	30–60	50–80	70–100
3	50–90	70–100	80–110
4	70–110	80–120	100–140
5	80–120	100–140	110–150
6	100–140	110–150	120–160
7	110–150	120–160	130–170
8	120–160	130–170	140–180

Note. Wcpm, words correct per minute. Adapted from "AIMSweb: Charting the Path to Literacy" (2003; available at *www.aimsweb.com/norms/reading_fluency.htm*). Data are also adapted from Hasbrouck and Tindal (1992).

and expression—and evaluates children's oral reading against a range of behaviors, from reading that is primarily word-by-word and monotonous to reading that incorporates the above attributes in a fluent rendering of a text (see Table 11.2). By using this simple scale (or a variation of the scale) along with the correct words per minute norms, it is possible to decide whether students will benefit from a fluency-oriented instructional approach—either as part of the general literacy curriculum or as part of an intervention designed

TABLE 11.2. National Assessment of Educational Progress's Oral Reading Fluency Scale

Level 4

Reads primarily in larger, meaningful phrase groups. Although some regressions, repetitions, and deviations from text may be present, those do not appear to detract from the overall structure of the story. Preservation of the author's syntax is consistent. Some or most of the story is read with expressive interpretation.

Level 3

Reads primarily in three- or four-word phrase groups. Some smaller groupings may be present. However, the majority of phrasing seems appropriate and preserves the syntax of the author. Little or no expressive interpretation is present.

Level 2

Reads primarily in two-word phrases with some three- or four-word groupings. Some word-by-word reading may be present. Word groupings may seem awkward and unrelated to larger context of sentence or passage.

Level 1

Reads primarily word-by-word. Occasionally two-word or three-word phrases may occur, but these are infrequent and/or they do not preserve meaningful syntax.

Note. Data from National Assessment of Educational Progress (NAEP, 1995).

for individuals or a small group of learners—or whether they have already achieved oral reading fluency and are ready to focus on another aspect of their reading development.

REFLECTIONS AND NEW DIRECTIONS

While we know much about fluency's role in the reading process as well as ways to develop fluency in our learners (including the approaches outlined above; e.g., Kuhn et al., 2010; Rasinski et al., 2011), there are still a number of questions that need to be answered. Perhaps the most important concerns the nature of the relationship between prosody and comprehension. While it is clear that prosody contributes to comprehension beyond that of word recognition (Benjamin et al., 2009), it is less clear whether improvements in comprehension result from improvements in prosody, whether improvements in prosody result from improvements in comprehension, or whether there is an interaction between the two that supports improvements in both aspects of reading development. Given that the primary goal of reading is comprehension, this is a key area for further study.

Second, as was discussed in the *Best Practices in Action* section, recent research (Kuhn et al., 2010; Mostow & Beck, 2005) indicates that improvements in fluency do not result specifically from the repetition of text, but instead from a more generalized increase in the amount of challenging connected text students are responsible for reading with appropriate support. If fluency development can occur simply by increasing the amount of text students read with support, then a range of approaches may be as effective as those discussed here. Research in this area may allow us to create additional instructional approaches while simultaneously developing a better understanding of how fluency contributes to learners' overall reading development.

Along these same lines, the appropriate level of text difficulty used in fluency instruction is an issue worth further consideration. Conventional wisdom suggests that fluency is best developed through practice with easier, independent-level material. However, research by Steven Stahl and Kathleen Heubach (2005), as well as by ourselves and others (e.g., Kuhn, 2004/2005; Hollingsworth, 1970, 1978) have found that greater progress was made when students were given more challenging materials for repeated or scaffolded wide readings.

The nature of the texts provided for fluency instruction is also an issue that requires further study. Some scholars (and many commercial fluency programs) argue that the texts for fluency instruction should contain academic content and be designed to include words that students need to learn to recognize automatically. Other scholars suggest the use of texts that have a strong voice in order to provide opportunities to work on prosody and that are meant to be performed (e.g., poetry, Reader's Theater scripts, songs) in order to provide students with a natural context for repeated readings (i.e., rehearsal).

Fluency is most often thought of as an oral reading phenomenon. Yet most reading done by adults and students beyond the initial stages of reading is silent. Studies have found strong correlations between oral reading fluency and silent reading comprehension (Daane, Campbell, Grigg, Goodman, & Oranje, 2005). And more recently, promising attempts have been made to develop instructional methods for developing silent reading fluency (Rasinski, Samuels, Hiebert, Petscher, & Feller, in press; Reutzel, Jones, Fawson, & Smith, 2008). Still, future research needs to explore further the nature of silent reading fluency and how it may best be taught in classroom and clinical settings.

Finally, while the role of the teacher in fluency instruction is clearly important, it has not been thoroughly investigated. While wide or repeated readings may seem to be primarily, if not entirely, an independent activity, we feel that the teacher plays a significant role in fluency instruction by choosing appropriate texts, modeling fluent reading, encouraging and providing feedback and support for students, and setting the stage for performance (e.g., Rasinski, 2003). Clearly, the appropriate role of the teacher during fluency instruction needs further examination.

CONCLUDING REMARKS

Prior to publication of the National Reading Panel report, fluency was considered to be the "neglected reading goal" (Allington, 1983, p. 556). In recent years, there has been a renewed focus on approaches that assist learners with their fluency development. However, we strongly believe that certain forms of assessment, along with their corresponding practices, have skewed conceptualizations of reading fluency, which in turn have negatively affected the way in which fluency is taught. We believe the approaches and principles presented here provide an alternative that will help you begin to integrate effective fluency instruction into your classroom. By doing so, your students will not only develop automatic word recognition and integrate expression into their oral reading, they also will be better able to read challenging text with understanding, thereby achieving the ultimate goal of reading instruction.

Although several issues related to reading fluency still need to be resolved, we feel strongly that appropriate fluency instruction offers a key to success in reading for many developing and struggling readers. We hope you agree and are willing to give fluency instruction a try!

ENGAGEMENT ACTIVITIES

1. Select a range of texts and follow the format outlined for two of the above approaches (authentic repeated reading, Fluency-Oriented Oral Reading, Fluency Development Lesson, and the

Wide FOOR) for several weeks. See which one your students enjoy more as well as how easy it is to implement these in your classroom!

2. a. Read a story to your students in an expressive voice, then talk with your students about how you used your voice to enhance the meaning of the text. Ask your students if they noticed portions of the text where you changed the tone, pitch, or volume of your voice, or where you sped up or slowed down, or where you had an extended dramatic pause. How did those changes in your voice while reading affect the meaning that students took from your reading?

   b. Read to your students in a slow, robotic manner, or in a very quick but unexpressive way. Ask students whether they found great satisfaction in your reading. Have them discuss why such a reading impairs their understanding of the passage. Help your students see that good, meaningful reading means reading with expression or fluency.

3. Purchase or make an audiotape of a book for an individual student who is a disfluent reader. Allow him or her to listen to the entire book for enjoyment, then ask the learner to listen to and read along with the first few pages several times. When she or he feels ready, have the student read the text aloud to you. You should hear some improvement in oral reading. Encourage the student to continue the process until she or he has mastered the text (or a chapter in the text, depending on the selection).

4. Select two short poems or passages from a story. Try to select passages that have a good sense of voice—that lend themselves well to oral expressive and meaningful reading. Pair up your students and have them practice repeatedly reading the texts using the paired repeated reading approach. Tell them to emphasize expression and their own interpretation of the piece. After the students have had the opportunity to practice their passage, ask for volunteers to perform their interpretation of the piece in front of their classmates.

5. Select a text that your class will be reading. Have each student read a passage from the text out loud to you without practicing it ahead of time. Using the Oral Reading Fluency (ORF) Target Rate Norms and the NAEP Oral Reading Fluency Scale (1995), evaluate their oral reading level. This will give you a sense of which students in your class need to work on their fluency

development in order to succeed with the material you are expected to cover.

RESOURCES FOR FURTHER LEARNING

Professional Books

Johns, J., & Berglund, R. (2010). *Fluency: Differentiated interventions and progress monitoring assessments* (4th ed.). Newark, DE: International Reading Association.

Kuhn, M. (2008). *The how and why of fluency instruction.* New York: Allyn & Bacon.

Kuhn, M., & Schwanenflugel, P. (2007). *Fluency in the classroom.* New York: Guilford Press.

Rasinski, T. V. (Ed.). (2009). *Essential readings in fluency.* Newark, DE: International Reading Association.

Rasinski, T. V. (2010). *The fluent reader* (2nd ed.). New York: Scholastic.

Rasinski, T., Blachowicz, C., & Lems, K. (Eds.). (2005). *Fluency instruction: Research-based best practices.* New York: Guilford Press.

Samuels, S. J., & Farstrup, A. (Ed.) (2006). *What research has to say about fluency instruction.* Newark, DE: International Reading Association.

Children's Books for Building Fluency

Rasinski, T. V. (2008). *Tim Rasinski presents fabulously famous books for building fluency, Library A (grades K–2).* New York: Scholastic.

Rasinski, T. V. (2008). *Tim Rasinski presents fabulously famous books for building fluency, Library B (grades 3–5).* New York: Scholastic.

Rasinski, T. V. (2008). *Tim Rasinski presents fabulously famous books for building fluency, Library C (grades 6–8).* New York: Scholastic.

REFERENCES

Adams, M. J. (1990). *Beginning to read: Thinking and learning about print.* Cambridge, MA: MIT Press.

Allington, R. L. (1983). Fluency: The neglected reading goal. *The Reading Teacher, 36,* 556–561.

Allington, R. L. (2009). If they don't read much . . . 30 years later. In E. H. Hiebert (Ed.), *Reading more, reading better* (pp. 30–54). New York: Guilford Press.

Applegate, M. D., Applegate, A. J., & Modla, V. B. (2009). "She's my best reader; she just can't comprehend": Studying the relationship between fluency and comprehension. *The Reading Teacher, 62* 512–521.

Benjamin, R., Schwanenflugel, P. J., & Kuhn, M. R. (2009, May). *The predictive value of prosody: Differences between simple and difficult texts in the reading of second graders.* Presentation to the College of Education Research Conference, University of Georgia, Athens GA.

Byars, B. (1985). *The Golly sisters go west.* New York: HarperCollins.

Cassidy, J., & Cassidy, D. (2011). What's hot for 2011. *Reading Today, 28*(2), 1, 6–7.

Daane, M. C., Campbell, J. R., Grigg, W. S., Goodman, M. J., & Oranje, A. (2005). *Fourth-grade students reading aloud: NAEP 2002 special study of oral reading.* Washington, DC: U.S. Department of Education, Institute of Education Sciences.

FEP/Booksource. (1998). *1998 books for early childhood to adult.* St. Louis, MO: The Booksource.

Fountas, L. C., & Pinnell, G. S. (1999). *Guided reading: Good first teaching for all children.* Portsmouth, NH: Heinemann.

Griffith, L. W., & Rasinski, T. V. (2004). A focus on fluency: How one teacher incorporated fluency with her reading curriculum. *The Reading Teacher, 58,* 126–137.

Hasbrouck, J. E., & Tindal, G. (1992). Curriculum-based oral reading fluency norms for students in grades 2 through 5. *Teaching Exceptional Children, 24,* 41–44.

Hollingsworth, P. M. (1970). An experiment with the impress method of teaching reading. *The Reading Teacher, 24,* 112–114.

Hollingsworth, P. M. (1978). An experimental approach to the impress method of teaching reading. *The Reading Teacher, 31,* 624–626.

Keats, J. E. (1964). *Whistle for Willie.* New York: Puffin.

Kuhn, M. R. (2004/2005). Helping students become accurate, expressive readers: Fluency instruction for small groups. *The Reading Teacher, 58,* 338–344.

Kuhn, M. R., & Schwanenflugel, P. (2007). *Fluency in the classroom.* New York: Guilford Press.

Kuhn, M. R., Schwanenflugel, P. J., & Meisinger, E. B. (2010). Review of research: Aligning theory and assessment of reading fluency: Automaticity, prosody, and definitions of fluency. *Reading Research Quarterly, 45,* 230–251.

Kuhn, M. R., & Stahl, S. A. (2003). Fluency: A review of developmental and remedial practices. *Journal of Educational Psychology, 95*(1), 3–21.

LaBerge, D., & Samuels, S. J. (1974). Toward a theory of automatic information processing in reading. *Cognitive Psychology, 6,* 293–323.

Logan, G. D. (1997). Automaticity and reading: Perspectives from the instance theory of automatization. *Reading and Writing Quarterly, 13,* 123–146.

Martinez, M., Roser, N., & Strecker, S. (1999). "I never thought I could be a star": A Readers Theatre ticket to reading fluency. *The Reading Teacher, 52,* 326–334.

Mostow, J., & Beck, J. (2005, June). *Micro-analysis of fluency gains in a reading tutor that listens.* Paper presented at the Society for the Scientific Study of Reading, Toronto.

National Assessment of Educational Progress (NAEP). (1995). *Oral Reading Fluency Scale. Listening to children read aloud, 15.* Washington, DC: U.S. Department of Education, National Center for Education Statistics.

National Reading Panel. (2000). *Teaching children to read: An evidence-based assessment of the scientific research literature on reading and its implications for reading instruction. Reports of the subgroups.* (NIH Publication No. 00-4769). Washington, DC: U.S. Government Printing Office.

Padak, N., & Rasinski, T. (2005). *Fast Start for early readers: A research-based, send-home literacy program.* New York: Scholastic.

Pinnell, G. S., Pikulski, J. J., Wixson, K. K., Campbell, J. R., Gough, P. B., & Beatty, A. S. (1995). *Listening to children read aloud: Data from NAEP's integrated reading performance record (IRPR) at Grade 4. The Nation's Report Card* (Report No. 23-FR-04). Washington, DC: Office of Educational Research and Improvement, U.S. Department of Education.

Platt, K. (1992). *Big Max.* New York: HarperCollins.

Rasinski, T. V. (2003). Parental involvement: Key to leaving no child behind in reading. *The New England Reading Association Journal, 39,* 1–5.

Rasinski, T. V. (2004). *Assessing reading fluency.* Honolulu: Pacific Resources for Education and Learning. Available at *www.prel.org/products/re-assessing-fluency.htm.*

Rasinski, T. V., Padak, N. D., Linek, W. L., & Sturtevant, E. (1994). Effects of fluency development on urban second-grade readers. *Journal of Educational Research, 87,* 158–165.

Rasinski, T. V., Reutzel, D. R., Chard, D., & Linan-Thompson, S. (2011). Reading fluency. In M. L. Kamil, P. D. Pearson, E. B. Moje, & P. P. Afflerbach (Eds.), *Handbook of reading research* (Vol. 4, pp. 286–319). New York: Routledge.

Rasinski, T., Samuels, S. J., Hiebert, E., Petscher, Y., & Feller, K. (in press). The relationship between silent reading fluency instructional protocol on students' reading comprehension and achievement in an urban school setting. *Reading Psychology.*

Rasinski, T., & Stevenson, B. (2005). The effects of Fast Start Reading: A fluency-based home involvement reading program on the reading achievement of beginning readers. *Reading Psychology, 26*(2), 109–125.

Reutzel, D. R., Jones, C. D., Fawson, P. C., & Smith, J. A. (2008). Scaffolded silent reading (ScSR): An alternative to guided oral repeated reading that works! *The Reading Teacher, 62,* 194–207.

Samuels, S. J. (2006). Toward a model of reading fluency. In S. J. Samuels & A. E. Farstrup (Eds.), *What research has to say about fluency instruction* (pp. 24–46). Newark, DE: International Reading Association.

Schreiber, P. A. (1991). Understanding prosody's role in reading acquisition. *Theory into Practice, 30,* 158–164.

Stahl, K. A. D. (2008). Creating opportunities for comprehension within fluency-oriented reading. In M. R. Kuhn & P. J. Schwanenflugel (Eds.), *Fluency in the classroom* (pp. 55–74). New York: Guilford Press.

Stahl, S. A., & Heubach, K. (2005). Fluency-oriented reading instruction. *Journal of Literacy Research, 37,* 25–60.

Torgesen, J. (2005, September). *Teaching every child to read: What every teacher needs to know.* Georgia Reading First Preservice Conference, Atlanta.

Young, C., & Rasinski, T. (2009). Implementing readers theatre as an approach to classroom fluency instruction. *The Reading Teacher, 63*(1), 4–13.

CHAPTER 12

Best Practices in Teaching Writing

Karen Bromley

> This chapter will:
>
> - Discuss theory and research on writing.
> - Present evidence-based practices for K–8 writing instruction.
> - Suggest future directions for writing instruction.

Text message: *Hey Glo . . . ty 4 the pb sandwich . . . Wd def < 3 his2. Cant w8 2 come back 2mro. Cu then . . . ps . . . I want 2 c the w8 n c tree 2!*

Translation: *"Hey, Gloria! Thank you for the peanut butter sandwich. Winn Dixie definitely loved his too. Can't wait to come back tomorrow. See you then! P.S. I want to see the wait-and-see tree too!"*

This text message and translation from Opal to Gloria Dump, characters in *Because of Winn-Dixie*, by Kate DiCamillo (2000), are examples of how April, a fourth-grade teacher, connects her students' digital literacies with traditional literacy. April shared this text message and translation with her students after they read a chapter in *Because of Winn-Dixie* and had students create their own messages and translations. Activities like this honor the "out-of-school" literacies many students use today, while providing practice in using standard English. These activities give students choices in what they write, and sharing their writing with each other provides audiences who provide immediate feedback. As well as linking "new" and traditional literacies, activities like this include the important components of effective writing instruction—a purpose for writing, choices in how and what to write, a real audience, and a suggested format.

EVIDENCE-BASED BEST PRACTICES

Writing is a complex interaction of cognitive and physical factors. It involves the hand, eye, and both sides of the brain as one makes connections and constructs meaning. It is a way to explore thinking and create new knowledge. It requires knowing the conventions of grammar, spelling, punctuation, and form. It involves small-muscle development and eye–hand coordination to form letters, words, and paragraphs with a pen, pencil, or on a keyboard. It requires having a vocabulary that permits effective self-expression and communication. Writing can be a personal process done solely for oneself or a social process done for and with others.

Writing Theory

When we apply Cambourne's (1988) model of learning literacy, we have a framework for understanding writing. He suggests that authentic *engagement* accompanied by *immersion* and *demonstration* result in learning. Students learn to write when they are surrounded with examples and models, given expectations, allowed to make decisions and mistakes, given feedback, and allowed time to practice in realistic ways.

Engagement and relevance are basic to Graves's (1983, 1994) model of the writing process that is based on in the recursive steps of *planning, drafting, revising, editing,* and *publishing* for a real audience. This process approach to writing is part of a writing workshop format (Fletcher & Portaluppi, 2001), in which the teacher sets up the structure and allows students plenty of choice in what they write. Atwell's (1998, 2002) well-recognized work with middle school students also supports the use of writing process in a writing workshop format.

Oral language is also an important contributor to writing, because both depend on the same cognitive abilities. Vygotsky (1978) theorized that children's early speech is a precursor to inner speech, which in turn results in the ability to think in words. This self-talk is like an inner commentator that develops into a mature writer's voice. Shanahan (2006) reminds us that no consistent body of research supports the specifics of the relationship, but it is likely that oral language ability is a valuable foundation for writing. Vygotsky (1978) believed thought and knowledge emerge from oral language that is embedded in social interaction. This co-construction of meaning leads to learning. Thus when writing is a social act, it is often stronger because of interactions as students talk and create new meanings together.

Social interaction around a shared experience is the foundation of the language experience approach. When students talk about an experience and that talk is transcribed, they can then read the written story or report. Young children learn how to write and how to read as a result of the social interaction that is part of the language experience approach. With middle school students, similar substantive discussions or "curricular conversations" focused on content can strengthen their writing as well as their reading, speaking, and thinking abilities (Angelis, 2003). This kind of *demonstration* and *immersion* in talking, writing, and reading as students create meaning together is the *engagement* Cambourne (1988) puts at the heart of all learning.

Grammar, Spelling, and Other Conventions

Research shows grammar instruction to have little positive effect on writing. Studies over time indicate that teaching formal grammar to students has "a negligible or even harmful effect on improving students' writing" (Routman, 1996, p. 119). In fact, "a heavy emphasis on mechanics and usage results in significant losses in overall quality" (Hillocks, 1987, p. 74). Thus the National Council of Teachers of English (NCTE) published a resolution urging teachers to discard traditional school grammar instruction (Brozo, 2003).

But, in a climate of standards-based mandated tests that often require students to correct errors, teachers may need to focus student attention on identifying and correcting errors (Smith, Cheville, & Hillocks, 2006). Alerting students to the pattern of errors they commit within and across their own writing assignments is one way to do this. Using strategies for examining and correcting errors gives teachers and students another window into learning about standard grammar and conventions in writing.

Research suggests a strong relationship between spelling and writing (Cunningham & Cunningham, 2010). Good writing depends on the automatic use of spelling skills. When students struggle with spelling, they use up valuable cognitive resources that they might otherwise use for other aspects of writing (Singer & Bashir, 2004). Students who try to use standard spelling but do not possess this skill may labor over every word and use words that they can readily spell rather than words that are more difficult. Thus accurate and automatic spelling can improve fluency (McCutcheon, 2006), and the quality and length of a written piece is affected as well as a writer's confidence.

In fact, Moats (2005–2006) calls for automatic knowledge of spelling and other conventions. She says, "Even more than reading, writing is a mental juggling act that depends on automatic deployment of basic skills such as handwriting, spelling, grammar, and punctuation so that the writer can keep track of such concerns as topic, organization, word choice, and audience needs" (p. 12). Knowledge of conventions is important whether students write with pencil and paper or use a computer and word processor. While grammar checkers may find grammatical problems and spell checkers may correct misspellings of commonly used words, these devices do not catch all errors, and students still need to know standard grammar and spelling.

Berninger and Winn (2006) report that students can become metacognitively aware of their own thinking and may produce better writing when they use a word processor, since it does change some spelling and correct some grammar. Baker (2000) found that word processors eased the difficulties many young children have with fine motor control and helped them better understand revision. Baker also found that, through student interaction with the Internet and the digital world, their writing abilities improved. Students found support for their writing efforts, increased their awareness of audience, and gained useful feedback.

Although vocabulary is not considered a writing convention, it is an important contributor to good writing. Zarry (1999) found that students who received vocabulary instruction that engaged them in playful activities used the words they learned more often in their writing and wrote narratives of a higher quality than students who did not receive such instruction. These students each received a thesaurus and were encouraged to select their own words to use in their writing and create their own definitions and sentences for each word.

Special Populations

Research on gender differences in the writing of elementary and middle school students is striking. On standardized writing tests, girls in the fourth, eighth, and twelfth grades consistently outperformed boys in narrative, persuasive, and informative writing (National Center for Education Statistics, 2002; *nces.ed.gov/nationsreportcard/pubs/*). Peterson (2006) found that boys' writing was more action filled, competitive, and assertive than girls' writing, which was more nurturing and focused on domestic topics. Boys more often wrote in the first person and wrote shorter pieces, while girls wrote in the third person and wrote longer pieces using more adjectives. Girls were more confident and viewed as better writers by both boys and girls.

More recently, NAEP (2008) writing test results (no tests were given to fourth graders) showed the writing skills of eighth and twelfth graders improved in 2007 compared to earlier assessment years, with gains across many student groups. Increases were seen since 2002 in percentages of students scoring at or above the Basic achievement level but not at or above Proficient. Average writing scores increased since 2002 for white, black, and Asian/Pacific Islander students at both grades. The average score for Hispanic eighth graders was higher in 2007 than in both previous assessments. For 12th-grade boys, there was also an increase in average scores since 2002.

But many students from diverse cultural and language backgrounds do not do well on NAEP and other standardized tests. They often come from urban schools in poor communities that lack the resources of more affluent schools. In an analysis of 50 studies of K–12 writing with racial or ethnic minorities, Ball (2006) observed that balancing process and product writing that reflects cultural understandings and influences on students' writing is necessary to help these students meet the demands of school and work.

Studies of students with learning disabilities indicate these students possess limited metacognitive awareness of the knowledge, skills, and strategies necessary to be good writers (Troia, 2006). So writing instruction that incorporates self-monitoring, goal setting, and self-evaluation is important for these students. Troia reported that these students often skip the planning stage, have problems generating and transcribing ideas, and often do not revise. He notes that students with learning disabilities need more time for writing, and they need intensive, individualized, and explicit instruction in self-regulation skills and writing strategies.

This brief discussion examines some of the theory and research evidence that supports writing instruction. In the next section, the classroom practices of several K–8 teachers provide examples of some best practices for sound writing instruction.

BEST PRACTICES IN ACTION

Besides the text messaging and translation activity described earlier, what other effective writing practices does April follow? April uses writing workshop as often as she can even though time pressures to cover required curriculum and prepare students for three state tests make it difficult. She tries to use writing workshop at least three times a week. She says it is hard because she has varied ability levels in her class of 28 students and she rarely has classroom support from the reading team or other professionals.

Here is how April explains writing workshop:

> "At the beginning of the school year I provide each student with a Writer's Workshop Notebook. Then we brainstorm a list of ideas that students can write about. They put this list in their notebook and they can add to it during the year. Each student chooses a topic to write about and they use the writing process to draft, revise, proofread, and edit their piece. Students keep all their work in writing folders."

April teaches minilessons about the writing process when she sees a pattern in students' work.

> "In lessons at the beginning of the year, we focus on capitalization, punctuation, and paragraphing. As the year continues, I teach minilessons on dialogue, the use of quotation marks, how to revise writing, poetry, and past, present, and future tenses. When I teach a minilesson, I expect students to reflect the skill we worked on together in that lesson in their writing."

April often uses the overhead projector or the SMARTboard for these lessons. She says students are glued to lessons on the SMARTboard because they are physically engaged in the lesson.

April uses peer partners so students can give each other feedback that promotes revising. She says:

> "Sometimes I pair my 'high-fliers' with less capable students and have them conference with each other. I find that students often work better with each other than I would have expected. They listen when another child tells them how to make their work better, and when they question each other about clarity, I see good revising. I also require students to reread their work before they conference with me. Many times they find their own spelling and punctuation mistakes. Just taking the time to reread, proofread, and edit makes their work better. I try to conference with each student as they finish a writing piece so they can 'publish' their work."

Thus April relies on oral language, writing process, and social interaction to help develop good writers.

April has three computers in her classroom and she has "fancy writing paper" for students to use for their finished work. She says some students use the computer for the final copy and others hand-write the final copy. Students draw their own illustrations or use clip art.

> "They read their final pieces orally to the class, which is hugely popular. Final pieces are also posted on our hall bulletin board or on a classroom bulletin board for others to read. Overall, most students enjoy having the ability to write about a topic of their choice and follow through to the publishing stage. Most students' writing abilities improve during the year, which also contributes to doing better on the writing portion of our mandated state tests. There are always a few students who continue to struggle with generating ideas and drafting. But for the most part, writer's workshop helps motivate most of my students to produce great writing."

Although testing drives teaching in many classrooms and some teachers have dropped writing workshop, there are teachers like April who want to help students develop as writers first so that achievement on tests is a natural outcome. These teachers use a writing process approach and direct instruction in skills to develop good writers. They believe that when students can articulate ideas confidently and write in organized, fluent, and clear ways, they will do well on mandated writing tests.

Tracy, a curriculum coordinator, says:

> "I have a somewhat negative view of mandated state tests since I see the stress they place on teachers and the imbalance between 'on-demand' writing and planned, thoughtful writing. The tests require the use of text-based details with little opportunity for independent thinking or use of prior knowledge. They send students mixed messages about what reading and writing are *really* all about."

Tracy works with teachers like April and others who want to make writing interesting and authentic as they teach the skills students need to do well on tests. Many of these teachers want to remain loyal to a writing process approach because they believe it develops thoughtful and effective writers. Yet they must also prepare students for "on-demand" writing tasks that include little opportunity for planning and revising. These teachers regularly have students complete "parallel tasks" that mirror the kinds of writing on the tests. But theory and research show that both a writing process approach and direct skill instruction help students become good writers.

Mandated assessments, higher standards, and accountability issues cause some teachers to reduce time for writing, teach writing artificially, and fragment the curriculum (Strickland et al., 2001). In some classrooms, the focus may be away from the writing process and toward writing skills and the written product. While proponents of a process approach to writing instruction are sometimes criticized for overlooking direct instruction, conventions, and legibility, a skills-product approach is sometimes criticized for its teacher centeredness and tendency to overlook student motivation, purpose, and voice. However, good writers need *simultaneous* opportunities to engage in the process and to learn the skills of writing. Casey and Hemenway (2001) conducted a 10-year study of students from third grade to high school graduation, and they found that a balance between structure and freedom results in "more dynamic writers excited about their abilities" (p. 68). Their study suggests that providing instruction that is intentional, socially interactive, and authentic can build a bridge between structure and freedom that supports good writing.

The following discussion explores three areas to include in a best-practices writing program, namely, context for writing, intentional writing instruction, and writing assessment.

Context for Writing

A context or environment for writing that includes individual, physical, and social aspects that affect instruction is critical to best-practices instruction. The individual teacher's attitude and commitment are critical. For example, when teachers identify and commit to improving student writing as a schoolwide goal, the focus of their professional development can be on writing. Teachers can study writing, have conversations about their students' writing, analyze writing tests and test results to see what their students do and don't do, develop writing curricula, and create a vision of exemplary student performance and specify criteria for it. A place to begin to teach writing well is to examine present practices with questions like these:

- What choices do my students have in their writing?
- How much and what kind of writing do they do daily?

- Who do my students write for besides me? What other audiences do they have?
- Who gives students feedback on their writing?
- Are they writing in a variety of formats in all content areas?
- How do I use the writing process? What kind of direct instruction do I provide?
- What opportunities do I provide students to use word processors and e-mail?

Self-evaluation is also important for students because it encourages them to take responsibility for their own writing progress. Periodic self-evaluation with questions like these also helps students reflect and set goals for themselves:

- What do I do well as a writer?
- What is one thing I have learned most recently as a writer?
- What do I need to learn to be a better writer?

Creating a context for writing includes creating a physical environment that is rich with words for students to use when they write. In the following classrooms, two teachers recognize the value of environmental print for teaching reading and writing. In Kelly's first grade, she adds several words to the Word Wall every week so students can use them in their writing. The class composes a daily morning message as they convert spoken language to writing and learn to spell, form letters, and use punctuation. There are printed 5″ × 8″ labels that identify *wastebasket, pencil sharpener,* and other classroom objects. Kelly has a writing corner with baskets of pencils, felt-tip markers, calligraphy pens, colored pencils, ballpoint pens, and paper. In both classrooms, each student has a dictionary and thesaurus. In Sean's sixth-grade classroom, he also has Word Walls for science and social studies terms that are especially helpful for the five English language learners in the class. Sean says Lev, who is newly arrived from Russia, and a buddy use the Word Walls each day as Lev learns English (and his buddy learns some Russian).

Today many classrooms are wired for Internet access like April's, and students use a computer on a regular basis to locate information and plan, draft, revise, and publish their stories, poems, and reports using software such as Inspiration and Publisher. In Sean's classroom, his sixth graders also use Blackboard, an online classroom program where he has his students discuss books they are reading and respond to one another's postings. His struggling writers often use Dragon Naturally Speaking, a speech-to-print software program that eliminates the need for handwriting or keyboarding.

Kelly and Sean set aside blocks of time when students write on topics of their choice during writing workshop. Calkins (1994) suggests that writing workshop should include minilessons, work time for writing, peer conferring and/or response groups, share sessions, and publication celebrations. Teachers who use Atwell's (1998, 2002) and Fletcher and Portaluppi's (2001) model spend an hour a day in writing workshop that includes a brief lesson on a demonstrated need of a group of students. These teachers also spend time sharing and discussing a well-written piece of literature to help students improve their writing and learn to respond to a piece of work. They also integrate writing with content-area learning so students are writing to learn as they are learning to write.

Many teachers encourage buddy reading, discussion, and collaborative writing, which is particularly helpful for students who may have ideas to contribute but who may not yet have the language skills, motivation, or confidence to write without this stimulation. Both students who are learning English and those who struggle are supported and encouraged to develop their abilities when they work in pairs with students who possess strong skills. Kelly and Sean share with their students models of the kinds of writing they expect them to do. They compose reports, poems, and other written forms with the class as a whole so that students have opportunities to learn from one another as they see a piece develop.

Establishing a writing community in the classroom and school is also critical to building a social context and improving student writing. Calling students "authors" and "writers" can have a positive effect on how students view themselves, and whether and how they write. Posting the writing of every student in the class validates them as writers as well. Inviting authors and illustrators of children's books to share their work with students can nudge even the most reluctant writer to write. The entire school can study the work of an author before a visit so students know the author's style and content and can interact in substantive ways with him or her. A visit from an author like Jerry Pallotta (*www.alphabetman.com*), who talks about his writing and shares the many alphabet books he has written, can spark students of all ages to read his work and write like him.

Intentional Writing Instruction

Writers need direct intentional instruction in writing as well as time to write (Tompkins, 2007). Students need to learn how to use the traits of writing effectively: ideas, organization, voice, word choice, sentence fluency, conventions, and presentation (Culham, 2003). They need opportunities for enough instruction, guidance, and practice to allow them to become accomplished. Good writing teachers balance writing process and product as they celebrate and encourage clarity of meaning, creativity, and standard English.

NCTE promotes teaching standard conventions and correctness by having students edit their own writing (Brozo, 2003). Other alternatives to isolated grammar instruction include teaching grammar during writing instruction, having grammar debates, teaching students to use style manuals, creating assignments that require writing for real audiences, and studying grammar controversies (Dunn & Lindblom, 2003). When teachers engage students in the writing process, teach and discuss word usage, and teach students to construct sentences using their own work, students can learn to use grammar and improve their writing.

Many teachers incorporate direct instruction in composing and the conventions of grammar, spelling, form, and handwriting into writing workshop (Peterson, 2000). For example, teaching terms like *purpose, audience, form, voice, noun, verb,* and *adjective* gives students a common vocabulary for discussing and improving their writing. Talking about sentence construction, grammar, and usage makes sense to students when they are writing for a real audience. Many teachers use "fix-the-error exercises" to teach specific grammar skills with examples from real literature that students are familiar with (Kane, 1997). Like April, Kelly, and Sean, they teach minilessons using their own writing and volunteers' writing to show how quotation marks, commas, and periods should be used.

Carol, a seventh-grade teacher who has used writing workshop for several years, begins with a lesson on one aspect of writing that she knows several students need help with, such as organization, run-on sentences, adjectives, verbs, or punctuation. Recently, Carol taught a minilesson on common and proper nouns after noticing the overuse of pronouns in several of her students' narrative stories. Part of the lesson included revising the work of a draft volunteered by a student. On another day she reviewed with the class the function and placement of topic sentences in expository writing and a five-paragraph report (a one-paragraph introduction, three-paragraph body, and one-paragraph conclusion).

Often in a minilesson, teachers share a piece of writing as a model so students know what good writing looks and sounds like (Calkins, 1994; McElveen & Dierking, 2001). Reading and listening to literature also helps students think like writers and write with an audience in mind. Good narrative and expository writing lets students see how an author holds the reader's attention and uses conventions. Then students can begin to use this knowledge in their own writing. For example, one third grader had read several of R. L. Stine's books in which "*THE END*" is used in the final sentence, as in "It doesn't really matter in . . . THE END." The student borrowed this technique and concluded his nonfiction report with "Volcanoes are very cool but when they erupt it's . . . THE END."

To extend her students' writing beyond topics they choose themselves, Carol uses a "genre study" (Calkins, 1994), where students immerse themselves in a particular kind of literature and then write in this form. For example, during recent writing workshops with a group of struggling writers and in conjunction with a science unit on climate change, Carol's students read nonfiction books about the environment, gathered information from a CD-ROM encyclopedia, took an electronic field trip to a weather station, and then created their own informative reports. She compiled these reports into a book that her students shared with a third-grade class. Carol encourages students to coauthor at least one story or report because she believes collaboration is a catalyst for learning.

Moss (2005) shows how even first and second graders can immerse themselves in a genre, such as informational text, and learn to write in that format. Read (2005) found that instructional practices in primary grades underestimate the ability of these students. She says, "Given appropriate instruction in the skills of writing and a topic that they've chosen and find interesting, young students are fully capable of dealing with the complex problems that occur when reading and writing informational texts" (p. 44).

Teachers of writing need to be writers themselves. Tracy, the curriculum coordinator quoted earlier, keeps a personal journal, uses e-mail, and writes curricula, lesson plans, and grant proposals. She believes that writing regularly is a powerful strategy for learning. She says:

> "Writing is a process of constructing meaning, and I never realize what I know until I start writing. I come up with ideas I didn't have before I begin writing. For this reason, I believe every teacher should write, and writing should be part of every content area."

When students write in a variety of forms in the content areas to explain or share information, they also construct new meaning and demonstrate their science and social studies knowledge. Expository writing across the curriculum can take many forms. In first grade, Kelly linked math, social studies, and language arts in a unit called "Quilt Connections." After students had read and heard stories about quilts, researched other cultures' quilts in the library and on the Internet, visited a museum exhibit, and learned about shapes, equal parts, and fractions, a final activity involved creating a quilt. The finished quilt, made of special fabrics and designs contributed by students, went home each day with a different student along with a journal. Students and parents wrote about the quilt in the journal, giving parents an opportunity for involvement in their child's classroom learning.

In third grade, during a study of the Cheyenne, Iroquois, Navaho, Sioux, and Seminole tribes, Mark had his students write daily "on-demand" responses to questions he posed. In this on-demand writing, students have only a short time to think, perhaps list a few ideas, and then write. Mark does not grade this work, but he reads it and responds and/or has students read and respond to one another's entries. Mark's students, like Sean's sixth graders, also engage in writing an occasional "parallel task" that mirrors the kind of writing task found on the state tests. For example, at the conclusion of the study of Indians, Mark's students read a poem and a short nonfiction article about Indian reservations, compared the information offered in each, and wrote an essay from the perspective of a member of one of the tribes they studied. Students compared and contrasted information from both sources and presented their finished pieces to the class.

Writing to explain is part of many mandated math tests. Colleen's eighth-grade students use journals as a way to explain math concepts. This is a way to explore students' thinking, and it is an example of on-demand writing. Colleen's students also write to her in their journals to explain what they believe they do well, what they don't understand, and, for extra credit, how to correct test items they missed. This kind of expository writing exposes students' reasoning so that Colleen can reteach a concept if needed. For Colleen, writing is an assessment tool that helps measure math learning and misconceptions.

Because graphic organizers are visual representations of information that show relationships and contain key vocabulary, they make excellent planning tools for writing (Bromley, 2006; Irwin-DeVitis, Bromley, & Modlo, 1999). They also appear on many mandated tests, thus making it important that even young students learn to use them. For students learning English or those with learning disabilities in literacy, graphic organizers are particularly useful, because they simplify information, use key words, and help organize ideas before writing. For another parallel task, Mark had his students use Venn diagrams and t-charts to compare and contrast a nonfiction selection and poem before writing.

Graphic organizers also support inquiry. For example, in a study of Mexico, Rebecca's second-grade students gathered information from several sources on data charts before they wrote about what they learned. As part of a sixth-grade unit on immigration, Michele's students took the perspective of a person in the story or focused on relationships among characters in *Esperanza Rising* by Pam Muñoz Ryan (2000). Before writing, students used a character map and character relationship map to record evidence and the page numbers where it appeared.

Central to good writing instruction is giving students choices in topics, their own and teacher-provided, because choice in both topic and format builds interest and commitment to writing. For example, to conclude a study of pollution and the environment, Sean and his class identified several writing options. Then students signed up in groups of four for the project they wanted to complete. One group wrote and performed a play, a second group wrote an article for the local newspaper accompanied by digital pictures, two groups created PowerPoint presentations, and another group updated entries on Wikipedia about the effects of river pollution on local bird life.

Research in K–6 classrooms indicates that teachers report an increase in motivation to write when their work is published on the Internet (Karchmer, 2001). In addition to skills in viewing and analyzing, when students do research on the Internet and write for the Web, they build skills in keyboarding, word processing, and navigating with browsers and search engines (Leu, 2000; Owens, Hester, & Teale, 2002; Wepner & Tao, 2002). Both students and teachers use the Internet, CD-ROM encyclopedias, and primary sources on the Web such as historical documents or secondary sources like museum or observatory websites. Some examples follow for using the computer to motivate struggling students and develop better writers:

- Establish electronic key-pal exchanges with students in other states or countries that can be social and/or related to science or social studies. The resulting cross-cultural literacy can benefit everyone involved.
- Have students (in pairs or triads) use Publisher or another software program to create items for a monthly classroom newsletter. Have them insert clip art, pictures, format the text, and send the newsletter electronically to parents or take hard copies home.
- Use digital storytelling (Sylvester & Greenidge, 2009–2010), which is the creation and sharing of a multimedia text consisting of still images and a narrated soundtrack that tells a story or presents a documentary. Visit the Center for Digital Storytelling at *www.storycenter.org* for examples, articles, and resources.
- Alert parents to Internet sites like *www.kidpub.com/kidpub* that publish students' book reviews, poems, short stories.
- Encourage student use of PowerPoint or other presentation software to share their inquiry-driven projects. Visit "Top 9 tips for students—Create classroom presentations worthy of an A" at *presentationsoft.about.com/od/classrooms/tp/student_tips.htmto.*
- Explore other technology like the wiki (meaning "quick" in Hawaiian) (Luce-Kapler, 2007) that requires writing. Wikis are an easily learned, open-source software program that allow all users to access and edit written pages on an ongoing basis.
- Reconnect with your library-media specialist, who can help you and your students learn about podcasting (from the acronym for **p**ersonal-**o**n-**d**emand and broad**casting**) (Smythe & Neufeld, 2010). Podcasting lets students create content quickly and easily.

Writing Assessment

Writing instruction has improved dramatically over the past several decades. Much of this improvement can be attributed to better writing assessments that inform more effective writing instruction. Of course, not all writing needs formal assessment but, whether formal or informal, assessment should be ongoing. Teachers need to assess their writing instruction, and students need to regularly assess their own written products (Bromley, 2007). Portfolios, rubrics, and checklists offer opportunities for writing assessment by both students and teachers.

Students often keep their writing in all its stages in writing folders or portfolios. This collection of work creates a record of student progress and can show a student's growth as a writer. But students need to examine their work, reflect on the patterns they see, and set new goals for themselves as well. Teachers, students, and parents can examine written work in a folder or portfolio to determine what skills a student possesses and needs to develop. As well, conversations with parents and assigning grades are more easily accomplished when there is a body of written work from which to make observations.

Rubrics and checklists can also help identify students' strengths and needs (Bromley, 2007; Tompkins, 2007). Teams of teachers often develop rubrics and checklists based on the priorities for grading a particular project. Even very young writers need feedback in order to understand their writing strengths and the areas where they need to improve. Just saying "Great job!" or "Need to improve" does not help young students know how to be better writers. Young students need feedback on the important aspects of communicating effectively, and a basic checklist or rubric can provide this feedback (see Figures 12.1 and 12.2).

More sophisticated rubrics are appropriate for older students. One project sixth-grade teacher Sean uses to develop students' careful reading and to build expository and persuasive writing skills is the "Classic" Inspiration Project (see Figure 12.3). The project introduces the class to books they may not have read yet and integrates reading, writing, and technology. In this essay students consider whether they believe a book is a "classic" (one that reflects quality, a universal theme, and the potential for longevity). Sean wants students to develop arguments based on evidence and share their arguments with the class. Students read a book and either defend or critique it. In their

My Editing Checklist

Title of my work ________ Name ________ Date ________	Yes	No
1. Did I reread my writing and revise first?		
2. Is my introduction interesting? Does it invite a reader?		
3. Is my writing focused on one idea or topic?		
4. Did I add some words that describe?		
5. Did I delete some unnecessary words		
6. Did I use complete sentences?		
7. Do my sentences begin with capital letters?		
8. Did I check my spelling and make corrections?		
9. Did I check for periods and commas?		
10. Did I indent each paragraph?		
11. Does my conclusion connect to my introduction?		
12. Does my title fit what I wrote about?		

FIGURE 12.1. An editing checklist for young students helps them self-evaluate.

Name ______________________ Date ____________

Rubric for Writing

	Beginning 1	Developing 2	Satisfactory 3	Excellent 4	Points
Content	Random ideas and/or information	A few ideas, some information	Enough ideas/ information to communicate meaning	Communicates meaning clearly and thoroughly	
Order	Ideas not in order	A few ideas in order	Most ideas flow in order from main topic	Ideas flow from main topic to details	
Sentences	Run-ons and fragments	A few complete and some fragments	Mostly complete sentences	Uses complete sentences	
Spelling	Many spelling errors	Some spelling errors	Few spelling errors	No spelling errors	
Punctuation	No punctuation (? , . !)	Some punctuation used correctly	Punctuation is mostly correct	Punctuation used correctly	
Capitals	Uses upper-case letters randomly	Uses some upper-case letters randomly	Begins sentences with upper case	Uses upper case to start names and sentences	
Handwriting	Hard to read, letters formed inconsistently, no spacing	Somewhat legible with some well-formed letters	Mostly legible with spacing and letter forms	Legible, neat, well-formed and spaced letters	
					Total points

FIGURE 12.2. A basic rubric provides feedback to young students on the aspects of good writing.

essays, students use Inspiration software and are graded with the rubric in Figure 12.3. They must produce a pleasing and readable visual layout with appropriate computer graphics and present the finished essays to the class. Sean allocates points for specific components, spelling, layout, and graphics, for a total of 100 points. He often has students give themselves a grade using this rubric. He also identifies a grade and conferences with students to determine whether and how they agree with his assessment, which he believes helps improve their writing and accuracy in self-assessment.

Name____Date________Period_____
Book Title____
Author____

	4	3	2	1
All three components included	• 2 reasons book is a *classic* with examples • 2 exciting or engaging parts • Theme and why it is universal (30 pts.)	3–4 Components explained accurately (25 pts.)	1–2 Components explained accurately (20 pts.)	1 Component explained accurately (10 pts.)
Spelling	All spelling accurate (20 pts.)	All but 1–3 words spelled accurately (17 pts.)	All but 4–5 words spelled accurately (12 pts.)	All but 5 or more words spelled accurately (15 pts.)
Layout	• Flows in a way that is organized and easy to understand • Shows creativity • Graphics do not interfere with info (30 pts.)	• Layout is mostly under-standable • Organiza-tion is present, but little creativity • Some graphics get in way of info (25 pts.)	• Layout is partly under-standable • Weak orga-nization • Little creativity • Graphics interfere with info (20 pts.)	• Layout is confusing • Lacks orga-nization • Graphics interfere with info (15 pts.)
Graphics	• Pictures and graphics used are appropriate • They aid creativity (20 pts.)	• Most pic-tures and graphics used are appropriate (17 pts.)	• Some pictures and graphics are appropriate (12 pts.)	• Pictures and graphics are not appropriate • Pictures and graphics hinder pre-sentation of info (8 pts.)

Comments:

FIGURE 12.3. This rubric combines criteria for writing using digital and standard English.

Sean also has his sixth graders create checklists and rubrics with him because "They seem to understand the assignment better and have confidence that they can achieve a higher grade when they have a say in rubric development." First, he explains the project or writing piece and shares an exemplar. He has students brainstorm characteristics or criteria for an excellent paper. Then, they group the characteristics into categories and rate them for importance. Last, Sean creates a draft, shares it on the overhead, and the class edits it as needed and votes to accept it. When students create criteria for a written piece, such as the Descriptive Writing Checklist in Figure 12.4, Sean feels it has a dramatic effect on the final product. When students have finished writing and revising, they check off the presence of each component and then have a peer read the piece and do the same. Based on this feedback, students revise before they hand the paper to Sean. He says, "You can't possibly do this for every checklist or rubric. But once the process is completed, you can use some of the criteria for other projects or pieces, as I did to create the rubric for this essay" (see Figure 12.5).

Knowing the key components of a good piece of writing provides students with goals for writing and the characteristics of a good report, essay,

Name____________________________Date ________Period_______

Title of Essay____

My Editing Peer______________________________________

Directions: Use this checklist as you work on your essay. Your essay will be scored according to the rubric on the attached sheet.

Literary Style	Self	Peer
Includes title	____	____
Varies sentence structure and length	____	____
Includes at least 2 similes	____	____
Includes at least 1 metaphor	____	____
Uses adjectives, adverbs, and vivid verbs	____	____
Refers to a minimum of 3 senses	____	____
Organization		
Introductory paragraph has a clear topic	____	____
Introductory paragraph grabs the reader's attention	____	____
All paragraphs include a main idea and supporting details	____	____
A clear and logical order of information is evident	____	____
Details let the reader develop a clear mental picture	____	____
Concluding paragraph is a summary and restates the central idea	____	____
Mechanics		
Uses capital letters correctly	____	____
Uses all punctuation correctly	____	____
Essay is free of spelling errors	____	____
Essay is free of run-on sentences and fragments	____	____

FIGURE 12.4. When students help define the criteria, it alerts them to the components of good writing.

Name____________________________________Date__________Period_____

Title of Essay____

	4	3	2	1	0
Descriptive components	Unique language that engages the senses—2 similes, 1 metaphor, adverbs, adjectives, and vivid verbs (35 pts.)	Language is often precise and appropriate. Vivid vocabulary present with 1 missing component (29 pts.)	Some language is precise and appropriate. Vivid vocabulary minimal with 2–3 missing components (25 pts.)	Limited use of vivid vocabulary and figurative language, with 4 or more components missing (21 pts.)	Lacks descriptive components. Not developed as a descriptive writing piece (0 pts.)
Mechanics	Varied sentence structure. All correct grammar, capitals, punctuation (15 pts.)	Most sentences show variety. Correct grammar, capitals, punctuation except 1–2 errors (13 pts.)	Some sentence variety. Correct grammar, capitals, punctuation except 3–4 errors (11 pts.)	Little sentence variety. Correct grammar, capitals, punctuation except 5 or more errors (9 pts.)	No sentence variety. Incomplete sentences. Grammar and other errors hinder message (0 pts.)
Spelling	All spelling correct (15 pts.)	All but 1 word spelled correctly (13 pts.)	All but 2–3 words spelled correctly (11 pts.)	All but 4 or more words spelled correctly (9 pts.)	Many spelling errors that affect message (0 pts.)
Organization	All paragraphs include topic and conclusion sentences with details. Clear connections and smooth transitions (35 pts.)	Most paragraphs include topic and conclusion sentences and details. Some unclear connections and transitions (29 pts.)	Some paragraphs include topic and conclusion sentences and details. Weak organization and sequence of ideas (25 pts.)	Some organization. Transitions and connections not present or weak (21 pts.)	Organization, connections, and transitions not evident (0 pts.)

Comments:

FIGURE 12.5. A rubric that reflects student-created criteria provides feedback on the written product.

letter, PowerPoint presentation, play, or poem, for example, before they write. It also gives the teacher and students an objective way to assess the finished product after writing. Rubrics show teachers what to reteach, and rubrics can help parents understand a student's grade. Of course, teachers don't use them for every piece of writing, but they can improve the quality of writing on key assignments and final projects. Templates found at these websites contain existing criteria that can be used as is or edited:

- Rubistar (*www.rubistar.4teachers.org*)
- Schrock Guide for Educators (*www.school.discovery.com/schrockguide/assess.html*)

Peers can also assess one another's written work and provide feedback (see Figure 12.3). Besides conferencing with students one-on-one, many teachers use peer conferences to give students real and immediate audience feedback on their work. Often, when a student reads his or her work to a peer or hears it read to him or her, the student discovers what to revise. Kelly uses writing groups of two to three students and has students read each other's work and give feedback on drafts. She uses TAG (Tell, Ask, Give), in which peers *tell* the writer one thing they like about a piece, *ask* a question about something they don't understand, and *give* a piece of advice. One student's handwriting improved dramatically when a peer wrote, "You should write neater so I can read it!" When Carol's third graders work in pairs or small groups to give each other feedback, she uses a different version of TAG. She uses the language of PQS (Praise, Question, Suggest). To help frame constructive feedback, both teachers model responses first by thinking aloud about a volunteer's draft and then have students respond to the draft with three statements.

Using a checklist when conferencing with students during writing workshop is a good way to assess and improve writing (see Figure 12.6). April, the fourth-grade teacher who was introduced at the beginning of this chapter, makes conferences a priority. She has a sign-up sheet for conferences, and she tries to see five students for a few minutes every day. To make the most of a conference, April has students arrive with a question they have about their writing, for example, "This sentence doesn't sound right to me. What do you think?" or "Is my introduction strong enough?" Requiring students to reflect on their own work and wonder about some aspect of it shifts responsibility for improved writing to the student. But April also asks pointed questions to prompt each student to rethink and revise his or her writing as well.

Teachers can also assess student writing with tools like the "The Word-Writing CAFÉ" (Leal, 2006), which is a "*C*omplexity, *A*ccuracy, and *F*luency *E*valuation." This group-administered assessment is an inventory of words students know how to write. It is not meant to measure sentence or paragraph creation but rather the ability to write and spell words correctly. It can be used at the beginning, middle, and end of the year to assess what words

Conference Checklist

NAME	M	T	W	Th	F	M	T	W	Th	F	Comments

Minilessons:

✓ Good conference

— Weak conference

〰 Not sure

☺ Shared today

★ Publishing conference

P Published today

☹ Not working

T Helped find topic

FIGURE 12.6. A conference checklist can help keep track of individual and class progress in writing.

students can write in September and how this changes over time. The CAFÉ can also show interests, strengths, and weaknesses (Bromley, Vandenberg, & White, 2007). While the CAFÉ does not measure writing in context, it does show the handwriting, spelling, and number and complexity of vocabulary words students can write.

Along with writing portfolios, rubrics, checklists, peer feedback, and conferencing, students need to become accurate in self-assessment. Students need to regularly ask questions about their writing such as the ones suggested earlier in this chapter. This self-assessment should be ongoing because students improve as writers when they regularly examine their work with an eye toward making it more organized, fluent, and clear.

REFLECTIONS AND FUTURE DIRECTIONS

Today, perhaps more than ever before, technology and the digital world are transforming writing. Writing practices in classrooms of the future will need to reflect the roles computers and the Internet increasingly play in writing that occurs out of school and at work. Although the "new" literacies of e-mail, text messaging, and Twitter do not always conform to standard grammar, spelling, or punctuation, students still need to possess basic skills in the conventions of standard English in order to succeed in many aspects of the adult world. Accountability, mandates, and tests will undoubtedly continue to affect what and how writing is taught. Thus teachers need to be flexible, open to collaboration with others, and creative in blending out-of-school literacies with in-school writing. Research is needed that examines technology, writing, and best-practices instruction for increasingly diverse classrooms. We need to understand better what sound instruction should look like for students who differ in cultural, ethnic, language, learning backgrounds, and gender.

CONCLUDING COMMENTS

The goal of a best-practices writing program ought to be to develop writers who enjoy and learn from writing as they write well in a range of forms for a variety of purposes and audiences. Vygotsky's (1978) ideas about *thought, knowledge,* and *social interaction,* and Cambourne's (1988) model of *engagement* through *immersion* and *demonstration* provide a foundation for this kind of program, as does the research briefly presented in this chapter. Establishing a classroom context for writing, providing intentional instruction, and regularly assessing writing can build student writers who are fluent, competent, and independent. Classroom practices that give students plenty of opportunities for writing and self-assessment at every grade level, both individually and together, are critical in developing strong writers.

ENGAGEMENT ACTIVITIES

1. Read Chapter 6, "Writing and Editing across the Curriculum," from *What Really Matters in Writing: Research-Based Practices across the Elementary Curriculum* (Cunningham & Cunningham, 2010). How would you involve fourth graders in editing their writing for a social studies report?
2. With a group of students, create a rubric or a checklist for something they will write. Using their ideas (and your own), categorize the ideas to create a rubric or checklist. Have you included the 6 + 1 traits (Culham, 2003)? What are the benefits and drawbacks of this activity?
3. Visit *www.readingonline.org* and bookmark this electronic journal of the International Reading Association for future reading. Read an article on the teaching of writing. How does it connect (or not connect) to what you just read in this chapter?

REFERENCES

Angelis, J. (2003). Conversation in the middle school classroom: Developing reading, writing, and other language abilities. *Middle School Journal, 34*(3), 57–61.

Atwell, N. (1998). *In the middle: New understandings about writing, reading and learning* (2nd ed.). Portsmouth, NH: Boynton Cook.

Atwell, N. (2002). *Lessons that change writers.* Portsmouth, NH: Boynton Cook.

Baker, E. A. (2000). Instructional approaches used to integrate literacy and technology. *Reading Online, 4*(1). Retrieved November 21, 2009, from *www.readingonline.org/articles/art_index.asp?HREF=baker/index.html.*

Ball, A. F. (2006). Teaching writing in culturally diverse classrooms. In C. A. MacArthur, S. Graham, & J. Fitzgerald (Eds.), *Handbook of writing research* (pp. 293–310). New York: Guilford Press.

Berninger, V. W., & Winn, W. D. (2006). Implications of advancements in brain research and technology for writing development, writing instruction, and educational evolution. In C. MacArthur, S. Graham, & J. Fitzgerald (Eds.), *Handbook of writing research* (pp. 96–114). New York: Guilford Press.

Bromley, K. (2006). From drawing to digital creations: Graphic organizers in the classroom. In D. S. Strickland & N. Roser (Eds.), *Handbook on teaching literacy through the communicative and visual arts* (Vol. 2, pp. 349–354). Mahwah, NJ: Erlbaum.

Bromley, K. (2007). Assessing student writing. In J. Paratore & R. McCormack (Eds.), *Classroom literacy assessment* (pp. 210–226). New York: Guilford Press.

Bromley, K., Vandenberg, A., & White, J. (2007). What can we learn from the word-writing CAFÉ? *The Reading Teacher, 61*(4), 284–295.

Brozo, W. (2003). Literary license. *Voices from the Middle, 10*(3), 43–45.

Calkins, L. (1994). *The art of teaching writing.* Portsmouth, NH: Heinemann.
Cambourne, B. (1988). *The whole story: Natural learning and the acquisition of literacy in the classroom.* Auckland, New Zealand: Scholastic.
Casey, M., & Hemenway, S. (2001). Structure and freedom: Achieving a balanced writing curriculum. *English Journal, 90*(6), 68–75.
Culham, R. (2003). *6 + 1 traits of writing: The complete guide: Grades 3 and up.* New York: Scholastic.
Cunningham, P. M., & Cunningham, J. W. (2010). *What really matters in writing: Research-based practices across the elementary curriculum.* Boston: Allyn & Bacon.
DiCamillo, K. (2000). *Because of Winn-Dixie.* Cambridge, MA: Candlewick Press.
Dunn, P. A., & Lindblom, K. (2003). Why revitalize grammar? *English Journal, 92*(3), 43–50.
Fletcher, R., & Portaluppi, J. (2001). *Writing workshop: The essential guide.* Portsmouth, NH: Heinemann.
Graves, D. (1983). *Writing: Teachers and children at work.* Portsmouth, NH: Heinemann.
Graves, D. (1994). *A fresh look at writing.* Portsmouth, NH: Heinemann.
Hillocks, G. (1987). Synthesis of research in teaching writing. *Educational Leadership, 11,* 71–82.
Irwin-DeVitis, L., Bromley, K., & Modlo, M. (1999). *50 graphic organizers for reading, writing and more.* New York: Scholastic.
Kane, S. (1997). Favorite sentences: Grammar in action. *The Reading Teacher, 51*(1), 70–72.
Karchmer, R. A. (2001). The journey ahead: Thirteen teachers report how the Internet influences literacy and literacy instruction in their K–12 classrooms. *Reading Research Quarterly, 36*(4), 442–480.
Leal, D. J. (2005). The word-writing CAFÉ: Assessing student writing for complexity, accuracy and fluency. *The Reading Teacher, 59*(4), 340–350.
Leu, D. J. (2000). Our children's future: Changing the focus of literacy and literacy instruction. *The Reading Teacher, 53*(5), 424–429.
Luce-Kapler, R. (2007). Radical change and wikis: Teaching new literacies. *Journal of Adolescent and Adult Literacy, 51*(3), 214–223.
McCutcheon, C. (2006). Cognitive factors in the development of children's writing. In C. A. MacArthur, S. Graham, & J. Fitzgerald (Eds.), *Handbook of writing research* (pp. 115–130). New York: Guilford Press.
McElveen, S. A., & Dierking, C. C. (2001). Children's books as models to teach writing. *The Reading Teacher, 54*(4), 362–364.
Moats, L. C. (2005–2006). How spelling supports reading: And why it is more regular and predictable than you may think. *American Educator,* 12–22, 42–43.
Moss, B. (2005). Making a case and a place for effective content area literacy instruction in the elementary grades. *The Reading Teacher, 59*(1), 46–55.
National Assessment of Educational Progress. (2008). *The Nation's Report Card: Writing 2007.* Retrieved from *nces.ed.gov/nationsreportcard/pubs/main2007/2008468.asp.*
National Center for Education Statistics. (2002). *The nation's report card: Writing 2002.* Retrieved October 26, 2010, from *nces.ed.gov/nationsreportcard/pubs/main2002/2003529.asp#section3.*
Owens, R. F., Hester, J. L., & Teale, W. H. (2002). Where do you want to go today? Inquiry-based learning and technology integration. *The Reading Teacher, 55*(7), 616–641.

Peterson, S. (2000). Yes, we do teach writing conventions! (Though the methods may be unconventional). *Ohio Reading Teacher, 34*(1), 38–44.

Peterson, S. (2006). Influence of gender on writing development. In C. A. MacArthur, S. Graham, & J. Fitzgerald (Eds.), *Handbook of writing research* (pp. 311–323). New York: Guilford Press.

Read, S. (2005). First and second graders writing informational text. *The Reading Teacher, 59*(1), 36–44.

Routman, R. (1996). *Literacy at the crossroads: Crucial talk about reading, writing and other teaching dilemmas.* Portsmouth, NH: Heinemann.

Ryan, P. M. (2000). *Esperanza rising.* New York: Scholastic.

Schrock Guide for Educators. Retrieved from *www.school.discovery.com/schrockguide/assess.html.*

Shanahan, T. (2006). Relations among oral language, reading and writing development. In C. A. MacArthur, S. Graham, & J. Fitzgerald (Eds.), *Handbook of writing research* (pp. 171–186). New York: Guilford Press.

Singer, B., & Bashir, A. (2004). Developmental variations in writing. In C. A. Stone, R. R. Silliman, B. J. Ehren, & K. Apel (Eds.), *Handbook of language and literacy: Development and disorders* (pp. 559–582). New York: Guilford Press.

Smith, M. W., Cheville, J., & Hillocks, G. (2006). I guess I'd better watch my English: Grammars and the teaching of the English language arts. In C. A. MacArthur, S. Graham, & J. Fitzgerald (Eds.), *Handbook of writing research* (pp. 263–274). New York: Guilford Press.

Smythe, S., & Neufeld, P. (2010). Podcast time: Negotiating digital literacies and communities of learning in a middle years ELL classroom. *Journal of Adolescent and Adult Literacy, 53*(6), 488–496.

Strickland, D. S., Bodino, A., Buchan, K., Jones, K. M., Nelson, A., & Rosen, M. (2001). Teaching writing in a time of reform. *The Elementary School Journal, 101*(4), 385–397.

Sylvester, R., & Greenidge, W. (2009–2010). Digital storytelling: Extending the potential for struggling writers. *The Reading Teacher, 63*(4), 284–295.

Tompkins, G. E. (2007). *Teaching writing: Balancing process and product* (5th ed.). Upper Saddle River, NJ: Prentice Hall.

Troia, G. A. (2006). Writing instruction for students with learning disabilities. In C. A. MacArthur, S. Graham, & J. Fitzgerald (Eds.), *Handbook of writing research* (pp. 324–336). New York: Guilford Press.

Vygotsky, L. (1978). *Mind in society.* Cambridge, MA: Harvard University Press.

Wepner, S. B., & Tao, L. (2002). From master teacher to master novice: Shifting responsibilities in technology-infused classrooms. *The Reading Teacher, 55*(7), 642–661.

Zarry, L. (1999). Vocabulary enrichment in composition. *Education, 120,* 267–271.

CHAPTER 13

Best Practices in Literacy Assessment

Peter Afflerbach
Jong-Yun Kim
Maria Elliker Crassas
Byeong-Young Cho

This chapter will:

- Describe the current state of literacy assessment.
- Examine a series of imbalances in current literacy assessment that have an impact on the positive contributions of literacy assessment.
- Suggest means for achieving balance and best practice in literacy assessment.
- Provide examples of balanced approaches and best practices with literacy assessment.

This chapter focuses on classroom-based reading assessments, assessments with considerable promise to enhance the teaching and learning of reading. The chapter begins with an overview of the context in which reading assessment is conceptualized and conducted—the places where curriculum and instruction, teachers and students, and tradition and politics interact. A result of this interaction is that certain reading assessments are privileged and others are underutilized. This creates a series of imbalances in reading assessment. In the chapter we identify areas within reading assessment that are in need of balance, and the means for working toward balance. We describe particular classroom-based assessments that are capable of measuring the depth and breadth of students' reading development, while attaining standards of validity and reliability that are hallmarks of useful reading assessment.

EVIDENCE-BASED BEST PRACTICES

Any consideration of best practices in reading assessment must take into account the contexts (sometimes contentious contexts) in which teaching and learning happen, where reading assessments are proposed, mandated, developed, bought, administered, and used. The current context of reading assessment is marked by imbalance. A significant portion of this imbalance is attributable to the supreme attention given to high-stakes testing and a resultant lack of focus on classroom-based reading assessment that might help change the teaching and learning of reading. Correcting these imbalances can provide one basis for superior teaching and learning, while ignoring them may diminish the achievements of teachers and their students. The most pressing challenges to best practices in classroom assessment of reading relate to a lack of balance in:

- The assessment of reading processes and reading products.
- The assessment of reading skills and strategies and the assessment of how students use what they understand from reading.
- The assessment of single-text reading with reading from multiple sources including Internet/hypertext.
- The assessment of cognitive and affective reading factors.
- Formative reading assessment and summative reading assessment.
- The reading assessment that is done to or for students and reading assessment that is done with and by students.
- The assessment of in-school literacies with out-of-school literacies.
- The demands for teacher and school accountability and professional development opportunities that help teachers develop expertise in reading assessment.

The promise to meet these challenges emanates from the depth and breadth of knowledge we possess about reading (National Assessment Governing Board, 2008; Snow, 2002; Stanovich, 1986) and the means to develop effective assessments related to reading (Darling-Hammond, 2010; Morsy, Kieffer, & Snow, 2010). Never before have we had such detailed understanding of reading and its development, and never before have we possessed as many potentially valid and reliable reading assessment options.

We have rich conceptualizations of reading, its development, and influences on its development. For example, the necessary skills and strategies for accomplished reading are well researched (Pressley & Afflerbach, 1995), providing detail that should inform both our instruction and assessment. Informing our understanding is research from fields as diverse as critical discourse (Rogers, 2003), human development (Alexander, 2005), information processing (LaBerge & Samuels, 1974), sociology and economics (Hart & Risley, 1995), and anthropology (Heath, 1983). Thus our ability to describe the nature of reading and what student readers need to succeed is greatly enhanced, as is our means to provide instruction that fosters student readers' growth.

As our knowledge about reading evolves, so too does our understanding of effective reading assessment. Many forms of reading assessment, informed by research in educational measurement, have the potential to positively influence instruction and learning. Pellegrino, Chudowsky, and Glaser (2001) propose that when we carefully chart the territory of what we will assess, we are then in a good position to produce the assessment materials and procedures that will best demonstrate the nature of students' development. As we have confidence in our full account of the construct of reading and we utilize our knowledge from assessment and psychometrics, we should have confidence in the assessments we design and use. In turn, this should give us confidence in the inferences we make from assessment results. Thoughtful assessment seeks to use knowledge (the collected wisdom) about the construct to be measured and combine this with our best understanding of effective assessment so that the inferences we make from reading assessment information are accurate and useful (Afflerbach, 2007).

Consider an example of how this should work. We know from research that successful developing readers must decode printed text, often relying on phonics early in their reading careers. Part of decoding involves learning to identify pairs of consonants, in isolation and as they appear in words, and knowing the unique sounds that these consonant blends, or digraphs, make. Allowing for dialect variations, we know that the *ch-* consonant digraph makes predictable sounds, and we can design assessments that allow us to measure students' ability to accurately recognize *ch-* in print, to determine its sound counterparts, and to correctly pronounce, or "say" the *ch-* digraph. As we are careful with our understanding of the *ch-* digraph and how we assess students' ability to produce the sounds, we can make accurate inferences about their developing ability to do so. We can examine students' ability to decode the *ch-* digraph using assessments that include words that contain the *ch-* digraph in meaningful text, as the *ch-* digraph occurs in whole words, and with the *ch-* digraph in isolation.

From student performance on these assessments we infer phonics skills and decoding strategies. With confidence in our conceptualization of phonics and confidence in our attempt to assess phonics as students use them, we have confidence in our inferences drawn from assessment results. We can use the results of our assessment in a formative manner, to immediately shape our understanding of the developing reader and related instruction. We can also use the results in a summative manner, as they provide evidence that the student has (or has not) met a key learning goal. Likewise, we understand that students' reading comprehension can be conceptualized as literal, inferential, critical, and evaluative (National Assessment Governing Board, 2008). We can formulate questions that require of students literal, inferential, critical, and evaluative comprehension of the texts they read, and from students' responses make inferences about the development of their reading comprehension (Afflerbach, Cho, & Kim, in press).

As broad as our understanding of reading is, we must strive to develop assessments that describe the complexity of student reading growth. Davis (1998) reminds us that we must be vigilant in our development and use of assessments, and that assessment is always a sample and approximation of the thing we want to describe. As well, Davis notes that many of our assessments are "thin": they yield results that describe only a portion of reading, and this should temper the inferences we make about students' complex growth and learning.

While theoretical and practical knowledge of reading and reading assessment is rich, the implementation of useful and effective reading assessment is impoverished. We have reading assessment habits that may be informed by habit, rather than by current conceptualizations of accomplished reading and effective teaching. Given the considerable advances in our understanding of reading and reading assessment, shouldn't we find it puzzling that our students' adequate yearly progress is measured by tests much like those we took in elementary and middle school? In addition, the use of single test scores to judge students' reading achievement and teachers' accountability skews schools' reading assessment agendas and funding (Afflerbach, 2005). Despite the fact that using single test scores to make highly consequential decisions is indefensible (American Educational Research Association/American Psychological Association/National Council on Measurement in Education, 1999), much school capital is invested in these single-score events. The purchasing, training, practicing, administering, scoring, and teaching related to high-stakes tests each take from limited school resources and create a poverty of alternatives and the means to pursue them.

BEST PRACTICES IN ACTION

Assessment must reflect the evolution of our understanding of the construct of reading, and it must be informed by state-of-the art knowledge in the science of educational measurement. Reading assessment must exhibit a series of balances that produces information useful to different audiences for their different purposes, and it is within classrooms that the promise of reading assessment must be realized. In spite of the considerable growth in our understanding of how to develop and use classroom-based reading assessments (Calfee & Hiebert, 1996), implementation is generally slow.

Effective reading assessment is that which informs important educational decisions. A first concern for classroom teachers is collecting and using reading assessment information that can be used to shape instruction and learning. Consider the students who populate our classrooms. In a classroom of 25 or 30 students, we expect that each will vary in terms of their reading skills and strategies, their prior knowledge for texts, their motivation, and their self-esteem as readers. They will vary in the attributions they make for their reading success or failure, and they will vary in terms of their agency, or the degree to which they feel they are in control of the reading they do. These differences contribute to varied performances and achievement in reading. We need assessments that describe the characteristics of student readers in diverse classrooms, characteristics that can influence their reading achievement. Talented teachers use their understandings of each of these student characteristics to shape reading instruction, and careful classroom-based assessment informs teachers and serves as a basis for this instruction. Throughout reading lessons and on a daily basis, over marking periods, and across the school year, *this is* high-stakes assessment, for without it there is not progress to daily, weekly, and annual reading goals.

Best practices in reading assessment are balanced so that they provide teachers with rich and current information about their students' reading development. Vygotsky (1978) proposes the zone of proximal development as the place in which students learn new things in relation to their knowledge and competencies, and in relation to teachers' instruction and support. If you believe, as we do, that teacher accountability is related to identifying students' zones of proximal development and teaching in these zones, then the centrality of classroom-based assessment is evident. We need regular classroom-based assessments that help us identify teachable moments for each student, that give us the detail we need to effectively teach to students' needs, and that describe the important outcomes of effective reading instruction.

Over the course of a school year, carefully teaching to students' individual needs can obviate the need to teach to the test. We must know where students are in terms of their skill and strategy development, motivation and engagement, prior knowledge for the texts they read, and self-esteem as readers. When reading assessment provides us with this balance of information, we can identify the next steps for student learning and for our teaching. A robust classroom assessment program continually provides detailed information about students' current competencies and next steps: it informs our ongoing work in the zone of proximal development.

Addressing Imbalance in Reading Assessment

In the next section, we describe necessary balances that promote best practices in classroom-based reading assessment. We provide an overview of the specific balance, explain why it is necessary, and describe the means for achieving balance. In doing so, we refer to specific reading assessments that can provide valid and reliable assessment information. These assessments include reading inventories and miscue analysis, performance assessments, teacher questioning, observations and surveys of student growth, and checklists for student self-assessment.

Balancing Assessments That Focus on Reading Processes and Reading Products

All of our reading assessment involves making inferences about students' growth and achievement. We reason about the extent of students' reading development using our assessment of the processes and products of their reading. In general, process assessments focus on students' skills, strategies, and tasks as they unfold. In contrast, product assessments focus on what students produce as a result of reading. Much attention is now given to product assessments, especially tests, and this creates an imbalance that favors product assessment at the expense of process assessment.

Reading processes are those skills and strategies that readers use when they decode words, determine vocabulary meaning, read fluently, and comprehend. Process-oriented reading assessment focuses on the skills and strategies that students use to construct meaning from text. Such assessment allows teachers to assess in the midst of students' reading. For example, as we listen to the student applying phonics knowledge to sound out the *ch-* consonant digraph, we see the student in the midst of using decoding processes. When we observe a student rereading a sentence to clarify the meaning, we are seeing a metacognitive process. Our process assessment helps us determine the skills and strategies that work or do not work as the student attempts to construct meaning. Moreover, assessment of reading processes can be situated in the context of a student actually reading, providing insights into how reading skills and strategies work together.

In contrast, product-oriented reading assessment provides an after-the-fact account of student reading achievement. The information provided by product assessments can help us determine students' achievement in relation to important reading goals, ranging from benchmark reading achievement to content-area learning. Typical reading product assessments are quizzes, tests, and questions related to students' comprehension of text. When we examine test scores, we can make inferences about students' achievement in relation to lesson and unit goals and curriculum standards, but we must make backwards inferences about what worked (or didn't work) as the student read. If we are interested in making inferences about how our instruction contributed (or didn't contribute) to the students' achievement, a similar series of backwards inferences is necessary. This is an important fact about product assessments: they provide relatively limited detail on what students can and can't do as they read. An apt analogy is one in which we try to determine why a basketball team won or lost a game by examining the final score. Certainly the final score is important, but it tells us nothing of the means by which it was achieved. There may be very little for us to go on if we are interested in gaining useful information from the assessment about how to do better.

In contrast, a balance of classroom-based assessment of reading processes can provide us with detailed information on how students process text and construct meaning. Here, our inferences are based on our assessment of the processes themselves. A prime example of assessment that focuses on readers' processes is miscue analyses (Clay, 1993; Goodman & Goodman, 1977), in which the teacher focuses on a student's oral reading behaviors. Assessment here is "online," and we get information about students' reading processes as they read. Accordingly, miscue analysis can illustrate how students decode print, engage prior knowledge, read fluently, construct meaning, and monitor the comprehension process. It can inform the teacher of strengths or weaknesses in sound–symbol correspondences, or in literal and inferential comprehension. The inferences we make about students' strengths and needs comes from the actual account of reading processes. With oral reading data, we may observe that a student is not consistently monitoring comprehension, as the student continues when meaning-changing miscues are made. We are able to pinpoint the problem, and we may be able to provide instruction to address a detailed, precise need based on our process-oriented reading assessment information.

Balancing the Assessment of Reading Skills and Strategies with the Assessment of How Students Use What They Understand from Reading

Students must comprehend the texts they read, and they must also be able to use the information they gain from reading to perform reading-related tasks. Reading assessment focuses on the reader's comprehension of text. We can assess students' ability to determine or construct main ideas, and we can ask students to locate or identify details in texts. When we ask students to summarize the texts they read, we are continuing a focus on constructing meaning. Each of these assessments focuses on comprehension as the final goal of reading. We must remember that reading to answer comprehension questions, while common school practice, is not nearly as common in the reading done outside of school. Thus reading assessment should also focus on how students use their constructed meaning from text in reading-related tasks. When students read guidelines for conducting hands-on experiments to help guide their science inquiry or they read colonists' diaries so that they can create a dramatic presentation on the struggles in Jamestown, reading involves these two goals: to comprehend text and to use what is comprehended in a related task or performance. Of course, such reading is the norm outside of the classroom. So it should be in classrooms.

Performance assessment, a form of authentic assessment, focuses on student reading and the things we expect students to do with knowledge gained from reading (Baxter & Glaser, 1998). For example, fifth-grade students read instructions and guidelines for conducting a hands-on science experiment. Of course, we focus on their comprehension, but we are also very interested in their application of what is learned (or comprehended) when conducting the science experiment. This includes the correct sequencing of steps in scientific inquiry, identification of laboratory tools, and accurately following procedures. The performance assessment accommodates our need to measure and describe the link between comprehension of text and how students use what they comprehend. Performance assessment has the added attraction of using rubrics that help students conceptualize suitable levels of performance at a specific task—they provide students with a blueprint of what they must do to achieve a superior score, and the performance assessment illustrates for students what is needed. The rubric also provides the means for students to check their progress toward a particular performance level and to practice self-assessment. The assessment uncovers the black box of assessment (Black & Wiliam, 1998) and helps students continue to learn how to do assessment for themselves.

Balancing the Assessment of Basic Skills and Strategies with the Assessment of Higher-Order Thinking

Many reading comprehension assessments focus on student understanding of a single text, often with multiple-choice items. After students read a given text, they choose the best answer from among alternatives, with questions focusing on identifying the main idea and inferring vocabulary and sentence meaning. These tests often fail to tap students' higher-order thinking skills and strategies in reading, including their ability to analytically and critically read text materials.

In order to achieve a balance between basic and higher-order skills and strategies in reading, it is important to examine the relationship of reading skills and strategies with higher-order cognitive processes. Bloom's taxonomy (Anderson & Krathwohl, 2001; Bloom, 1956) reminds us that while understanding and remembering text involves basic comprehension, related cognitive processes of applying, analyzing and synthesizing, evaluating represent higher-order thinking in reading, and self-reflecting on these processes at the metacognitive level. We offer two examples of reading assessment that can provide information about students' higher-level thinking: students' generation of critical questions about their reading and composing integrative essays when learning from multiple-source texts.

In order to create critical questions, a student must identify or construct main ideas, determine the author's intention, and use the meaning constructed to formulate questions. For example, based on the students' critical questions, teachers can assess the extent to which a student has understood text and how the student manipulated this understanding to create a meaningful question. Second, writing an integrative essay based on the reading of multiple texts helps us understand higher-order thinking. A student must demonstrate comprehension of each individual text and the ability to combine information from across texts into a coherent whole (Wolfe & Goldman, 2005) in the writing. In this task, a well-developed rubric serves two roles: a scaffolded guide for students' higher-order thinking and a scoring rule for a classroom teacher to assess the students' work. We note that our second example assigns writing a major role and that writing ability may be confounded with reading ability. Such is literacy use outside of the classroom, and efforts to determine the relative contribution of each to student writing are needed.

Without basic skills and strategies in reading, higher-order reading skills and strategies cannot occur: the latter depend, in part, on the former. It may be difficult to draw a strict boundary between basic and higher-order levels in reading, and the assessment of higher-order thinking will also include some basic skills and strategies. Even so, it is our responsibility to conduct reading assessments that tap students' higher-order thinking skills and strategies. Creating balanced reading assessment between basic and higher-order levels of thinking is especially imperative under the current assessment situation that frequently requires students to answer by filling in the short blank or to choose one answer among given choices.

Balancing the Assessment of Single-Text Reading with Reading from Multiple Sources Including Electronic Texts

A predominant goal of reading instruction and assessment is to help readers construct meaning from the text. Most reading assessments of comprehension focus on the understanding of single texts. After reading a single passage, students are asked to determine vocabulary meanings, supporting details and main ideas, and answer literal and inferential questions. This assessment approach focuses on comprehension of single short passages, yet our evolving understanding suggests that accomplished reading in the 21st century may involve more than comprehending a single text.

The environment of reading changes based on developments in informational technology and the Internet and hypertext (Leu, Kinzer, Coiro, & Cammack, 2004). In this changing environment, students must be able to comprehend single texts as well as multiple sources of information from different texts, search and decide which sources are more reliable, and coherently integrate information taken from various sources. Current reading assessments have limited ability to assess this new aspect of reading. The current foci on reading assessment of a single text represents imbalance for two reasons. First, in an authentic reading situation, the texts students encounter may be composed of multiple modalities of information. While reading a textbook or an informational book, readers encounter both verbal and nonverbal information such as graphs, charts, drawings, and maps. The textual information may be composed of nontextual, visual, and auditory information. Second, reading multiple sources of texts may require additional cognitive skills and strategies that cannot be assessed with tests that dwell on the comprehension of single texts. Stahl, Hynd, Britton, McNish, and Bosquet (1996) showed that high school students had difficulty understanding multiple sources of information about a historical event because they lacked sourcing skills to help distinguish multiple source texts, not because they lacked comprehension skills. This difficulty is increased when the texts students read conflict with one another. For example, suppose a student reads two texts. One text argues that human activity is a cause of global warming, while the other refutes the argument. In this situation, reading assessment must describe the student's ability to construct meaning from each text and to identify the relative strengths and weaknesses of claims and evidence presented (Rouet, 2006).

Teachers can assess students' comprehension of multiple texts and print and nonprint information within texts. Using two approaches sketched below, teachers can determine whether students have the knowledge, skills, and strategies to evaluate the usefulness of sources in terms of informativeness and credibility criteria, and to integrate multiple sources of information for coherent understanding. In the first case, teachers can determine whether students are able to evaluate source text information (Wineburg, 1991) by using think-aloud protocols on the assessment tasks. In such tasks, teachers can observe whether students evaluate source information in terms of credibility (e.g., Are you familiar with the author? When was this article published? Does the text come from a source that you trust?) and usefulness of the sources (e.g., Is this text comprehensible? Does this text fit my purpose of reading?). In the second case, teachers can examine how students integrate multiple sources of text information through performance assessments. For instance, given a specific topic such as the Civil War, teachers can prompt students to write integrative essays from two or more different texts and sources of information, including primary and secondary source texts that include both fact and opinion.

Balancing the Assessment of Cognitive and Affective Reading Outcomes and Reader Characteristics

Currently used high-stakes assessments, early-reading screening instruments, and most classroom reading assessments focus on the skills and strategies that make reading comprehension possible. Assessment measures the cognitive development of student readers, but there is little or no attention paid to the factors that can support and enhance reading development. Experienced classroom teachers and parents know that reading skills and strategies are essential to students' reading success, but do not guarantee this success. Successful readers are engaged readers (Guthrie & Wigfield, 1997). These students are motivated to read, they identify themselves as readers, they persevere in the face of reading challenges and they consider reading to be an important part of their daily lives. When we think of our teaching successes, do we think only of students who scored high on tests under our guidance? Or do we also think of students who went from reluctant readers to enthusiastic readers? Do we think of students who evolved from easily discouraged readers to readers whose motivation helped them persevere through reading challenges? Do we remember students who avoided reading at all costs changing to students who learned to love reading? Certainly, we can count such students and our positive influence on them among our most worthy teaching accomplishments.

If we are serious about accountability, we need to have balance in the assessment that demonstrates that high-quality teaching and effective reading programs change student readers' lives. To achieve balance we need assessments that measure and describe student growth that is complementary to reading skill and reading strategy development. This growth can include positive motivation, perseverance in the face of difficulty, appropriate attributions made for reading success and failure, and self-esteem as a reader. We are fortunate to have such measures. For example, we can conduct surveys and inventories of students' reading motivation (Gambrell, Palmer, Codling, & Mazzoni, 1996), attitudes toward reading (McKenna & Kear, 1990), and reading self-concept (Chapman & Tunmer, 1995). Together, these and related assessments can help us understand and describe growth related to the already assessed cognitive development. They move us toward a fuller measure of the accomplishments of students and their teachers.

Balancing Formative Reading Assessment and Summative Reading Assessment

We are a society enamored with numbers. Schools, school districts, classrooms, states, teachers, and students are evaluated and ranked in relation to annual series of tests, or summative reading assessments. These assessments report important summary information about students' reading skills and strategies. They summarize reading achievement as a level, a raw score, and a percentile rank. Summative assessment is important, as it helps us understand whether students reach grade-level benchmarks, unit and lesson goals, and standards in classrooms, districts, and states. However, summative assessment is, by nature, an after-the-fact event. We do not have as rich an opportunity with summative assessment, compared with formative assessment, to inform instruction and to address students' individual needs as they are developing.

In spite of this limitation, summative assessment is used to make highly consequential decisions. Accountability, sanction, reward, school success, and school failure are often determined by single summative assessment scores. This pressure to focus on summative assessment creates an imbalance with formative assessment efforts, the very type of assessment that could help teachers and schools demonstrate accountability on a daily basis. Formative assessment, in contrast, is conducted with the goal of informing our instruction and improving student learning. At the heart of effective reading instruction is the classroom teacher's detailed knowledge of each student. This knowledge is constructed through ongoing formative assessments, conducted across the school day and the school year, like the process-oriented reading assessment discussed earlier in this chapter.

For example, teacher questioning may be tailored so that it provides formative assessment information. The teacher adept at asking questions during instruction can develop a detailed sense of how well students are "getting" the lesson. Teachers' questions can focus on both skills and strategies, cognitive and affective influences on reading achievement, and content-area learning that result from reading. The teacher uses the information provided by students' responses to questions to build a detailed sense of how students are progressing toward lesson goals and where to place an ongoing instructional focus. Consider a third-grade teacher's questions to her students as they read a chapter in a science textbook: What is it? Can you explain your reasoning? How do you know? Where do you get the information contained in your explanation? Questions like these evoke responses that demonstrate the degree of students' understanding. From their responses, the teacher constructs her own understanding of their achievement. And from this understanding comes action: a decision to move ahead or to reteach, a decision to slow the pace of instruction or speed it up, a decision to have more class discussion around the key concept of *ecosystem*.

Formative assessment is conducted in situ, or as the process of teaching and learning unfolds. The degree of detail provided by formative assessment may help a classroom teacher determine a teachable moment, identify the need for reteaching an important concept or skill, or move forward to new instruction with confidence that students possess the requisite knowledge to succeed. Creating balance will result in formative assessment describing students' ongoing reading growth as it occurs, and summative assessment providing summary statements about students' literacy achievement.

Balancing the Reading Assessment That Is Done to or for Students with Reading Assessment That Is Done with and by Students

Many students move through school with reading assessment done to them, or for them. Students read, take a quiz or test, and hand it in. It is evaluated and graded, then returned to the student. The student earns a score but gains no understanding of how assessment works. A result is that many students think of assessment as a "black box" (Black & Wiliam, 1998), and a consequence of this approach to reading assessment is that students do not learn to do reading assessment for themselves. Even as we ask questions in class, without our explanation of why we ask these questions or how we arrive at our evaluations of student responses, students will not understand how the evaluation of their reading is made. Across school years there may be lost opportunities for students to learn to conduct reading assessment on their own, and they remain outsiders to the culture of reading assessment.

Our classroom-based assessment should provide students with the means eventually to assume responsibility for assessing their reading. Accomplished readers regularly assess their ongoing comprehension of text and their progress toward reading-related goals. This ability is not innate—it is learned from models of doing assessment that the students eventually internalize. In fact, a hallmark of successful readers is the ability to monitor their reading and conduct ongoing assessment of reading progress (Pressley & Afflerbach, 1995).

As we strive to create balance, we should provide opportunities in which students learn the value of self-assessment and the means to do accurate and useful assessment for themselves. A good start is modeling simple and straightforward assessment routines and helping students learn to initiate and successfully complete the routines independently. For example, consider the checklist used by a second-grade teacher. As students read, she regularly asks the students to refer to the checklist and engage in the assessment thinking that it requires. She models using the checklist and expects that her students will learn to use as they read independently. The checklist includes the following:

______ I check to see if what I read makes sense.
______ I remind myself why I am reading.
______ I focus on the goal of my reading while I read.
______ I check to see if I can summarize sentences and paragraphs.
______ If reading gets hard, I ask myself if there are any problems.
______ I try to identify the problem.
______ I try to fix the problem.
______ When the problem is fixed, I get back to my reading, making sure I understand what I've read so far.

The teacher also models the use of the checklist by asking related questions of herself when she reads to the students, and thinks aloud about why she asks the questions and her answers to the questions. This predictable presentation of routines can help set developing readers on a healthy path to self-assessment.

The checklist is also scalable: it can be constructed to reflect specific instructional goals. If we are interested in helping students learn to assess critical reading abilities, we may devise a checklist with the following items:

______ I check the text to see if the author provides evidence to support claims.
______ I compare the information in the text with what I already know about the topic.

We do not give up our responsibility to conduct valuable classroom-based reading assessments when we promote student self-assessment. Rather, we look for opportunities when using our assessments to help students learn assessment themselves (Afflerbach, 2002). Creating balance is imperative, for if in all our reading instruction students do not begin learning how to self-assess, how will they ever become truly independent readers?

Balancing Assessment of In-School and Out-of-School Literacy Practices

Out of school, students are constantly involved with text. Whether students are texting, blogging, creating rhymes, journaling, or networking on Facebook and Twitter, they need and acquire specific literacy skills in order to do these things effectively. Yet some of these students do not see themselves as capable in-school readers (Alvermann et al., 2007). They may not realize how frequently and how effectively they use their literacy skills. These students may struggle in traditional school literacy tasks, and we, as educators, may not view them as proficient readers. Students may excel in particular literate behaviors, but these may not have obvious and regular connections to school literacy.

The lack of knowing and understanding students' out-of-school literacies demonstrates how teacher–student relationships may be "'thin' and 'single-stranded'" (Moll, Amanti, Neff, & González, 1992, p. 134). For example, a math teacher might know his student solely by the performance on his or her math test. In another learning situation, an aunt (the teacher) may show her nephew (the student) how to garden. This aunt does not know her nephew based solely on his gardening skills because she spends time with him during family gatherings and knows all of his interests. Moll et al. (1992) found that students had many sources of knowledge outside of the traditional classroom. However, teachers only "knew" their students through their school performances, which were often in limited classroom contexts. Although there are sporadic attempts to know more about students' reading interests and motivations (Gambrell et al., 1996; McKenna & Kear, 1990), the assessment of out-of-school literacies can help us better understand students' daily literacy practices and how we might tap into those literacies in which students are most proficient. Here, assessment helps us better understand the nature of student literacy and not to judge it or rank-order students.

A straightforward means of becoming familiar with students' notions of literacy is to hold conversations about them. Students describe and demonstrate literacy practices, which allows us to determine the commonalities and idiosyncrasies of in-school and out-of-school literacies. A second approach is to have students keep account of their literacy practices. For example, Alvermann et al. (2007) had struggling adolescent readers keep track of their reading outside of school in a daily reading log. Through this documentation, the researchers found that these "struggling readers" looked much more like readers than one would think. Students read and interacted with text in such forms as song lyrics, Internet sites, text in electronic games, and sets of directions. If we allow students to see that they read and use text successfully and in meaningful ways on a regular basis, they may begin to see that they are indeed successful readers. Furthermore, they may see that reading is not just for what they may believe to be limited school practices, but that it has purpose in their lives.

A further means of using assessment to gather information on students' out-of-school literacy is the use of surveys about reading practices. These surveys might include the following questions:

- What do I think a good reader looks like?
- What types of books do I like to read?
- What other types of text do I like to read in school or outside of school? (magazines, websites, texts, etc.)?
- What types of text do I use outside of school on a regular basis?
- How does text connect me with others?
- Why is it important to be able to read and understand text outside of school?
- How is reading and understanding text outside of school important in my life?

These questions help students think about how text is important outside of our classroom doors. They also allow us to see what ideas and definitions of reading students may have, which may open up opportunities for us to broaden those ideas and definitions. Even further, their answers may allow us to bring their outside-of-school reading interests into the classroom. When Moll et al. (1992) investigated students' lives outside of school, they found that one of their students enjoyed selling candy made from Mexico, his home country. Upon discovering this information the research team, which included his teacher, decided to create a unit on candy in his classroom. The unit included defining, categorizing, making (with the help of a parent candy expert), and selling candy. We are also able to provide authentic activities with outside-of-school reading interests. If we find that students are interested in reading song lyrics, we might find that they benefit from analyzing, writing, and performing their own song lyrics. In both cases, students may be quite motivated by such relevant and authentic activities.

Helping students understand that they use literacy skills and strategies and that they are literate is important. By understanding and acknowledging their current practices, we give value to those practices, which may allow them to connect with the in-school literacy practices. For example, teachers might acknowledge the use of blogging and compare it to an opinion column about a current event. To further bridge the gap, we may even want to bring these out-of-school texts into our classrooms. We can instruct and assess students on many of the same reading skills using out-of-school literacies. Assessing students on their interpretations of lyrics of a popular song is much like assessing their interpretations of a poem. By bringing out-of-school literacies in our classrooms and not focusing solely on traditional school-based texts, we gain the ability to capitalize on our students' current literacy interests and strengths. Through the assessment of students' out-of-school literacy practices, educators and students have a more complete picture of students as literate people.

Balancing the Demands for Teacher and School Accountability with Professional Development Opportunities to Develop Expertise in Reading Assessment

Each of the necessary balances described in this chapter depends on teachers' professional development in assessment. Successful classroom-based reading assessment demands teacher expertise, and professional development is an essential component. Accomplished reading teachers and effective schools take accountability to heart every day. This accountability is demonstrated through the care and professionalism with which teachers work with their students. In addition, teacher and school accountability are determined by the results of high-stakes testing. The costs involved in developing, buying, administering, and scoring these assessments are considerable. Unfortunately, the school funds spent on high-stakes tests are taken from otherwise limited school budgets. This means that money spent on tests cannot be spent on initiatives that would actually help teachers become better at classroom-based assessment.

Lack of professional development opportunities prevents many teachers from becoming practicing experts in classroom-based reading assessments (Black & Wiliam, 1998). Teachers become expert at classroom assessment when they are supported by their administrators and school districts (Johnston, 1987). Specifically, professional development can help teachers learn and use effective reading assessment materials and procedures that best inform the daily teaching and learning in the classroom (Stiggins, 1999). Regular and detailed assessments provide information that helps teachers recognize and utilize the teachable moment. These daily successes sum to the accomplished teaching and learning that is reflected in accountability tests. But accountability is not achieved through testing—it is achieved through the hard work that surrounds successful classroom assessment and instruction. Professional development also helps teachers construct reliable product assessments, such as quizzes, tests, and report cards. Professional development helps teachers become educated consumers and users of the variety of reading assessments that are available.

Summary

Effective reading assessment is necessary for reading program success, and balance is necessary for effective reading assessment. Current reading assessment practice reflects a series of imbalances that influence teaching and learning. As teachers, we are challenged to provide effective instruction for all students. Effective instruction depends on assessment that helps teachers and students move toward and attain daily and annual reading goals. This chapter described the balances that must be attained if reading assessment is to reflect our best, most recent understandings of reading and how to measure reading development. We are not wanting for description and detail of how classroom-based reading assessment helps our teaching and how our teaching helps student readers develop. There must be a concerted effort to bring classroom-based reading assessment into the spotlight and, when the time arrives, to be ready to deliver on its promise.

High-quality classroom assessment of reading is as much a product of teacher expertise and effort as it is of political power, popular will, and continuing education. Many people believe that tests are at worst a nuisance and at best a key to school excellence. But a populace that equates testing with best practice in assessment needs further education. As well, full accounting of the costs of current reading assessment programs, especially high-stakes tests, may help the general public understand how much school resources are given to reading assessment that yields information of relatively little use to teachers. Teachers must earn and maintain the trust that is currently given by some to high-stakes standardized tests. If, in correcting an imbalance in our school and classroom, we are able to demonstrate the superior nature of particular reading assessment information, we may gain converts to classroom assessment.

The imbalances identified in this chapter need our attention. Righting these should lead to an assessment program that is more integral to the daily life of teachers, students, and classrooms. When we focus on process assessment, we can accurately determine what aspect of a summarization strategy students do and don't understand. When we assess and determine how a student's motivation grows as the result of mastering the act of reading, we are describing a compelling success story. And when we share our reading assessment knowledge with our students, we prepare them to bring a balanced approach and balanced understanding of the assessment of their own reading, fostering independence.

REFLECTIONS AND FUTURE DIRECTIONS

A balanced approach to classroom reading assessment will be achieved when classroom teachers can conduct assessment in a reliable and valid manner, thus gaining the public trust. Earlier, we sketched the importance of professional development to teachers' growing ability to conduct classroom reading assessments and effectively use their results. However, there is little research that describes how teachers develop as assessment experts, or that demonstrates what type of classroom assessment training most benefits teachers and their students.

A related area for future research and action is the public perception of assessment. We are a society that purports to value scientific inquiry along with research results and agendas for action that are informed by such inquiry and results. Why, then, do our most consequential reading assessments appear relatively uninformed by our most recent understandings? Similarly, why do states and school districts spend the bulk of their assessment budgets on test purchasing, administering, scoring, and reporting? This problem is exacerbated by the federal mandate of testing all students in grades 3–8 in reading, but it existed prior to the passage of No Child Left Behind.

A final area for future research relates to the effects of reading assessment on student reading achievement. Despite the importance of reading assessment in determining student achievement and related consequences, reading assessment itself is not a common focus of research (Afflerbach, Cho, Kim, & Clark, 2010). Reading assessment is used as the measure of student achievement in many research designs. There are few studies that describe how assessment can contribute to student learning and achievement, although work in this area is promising (Black & Wiliam, 2005; Crooks, 1988). Research should help us determine the relationship of reading assessment with students' reading achievement. Classroom-based reading assessments, especially those that focus on formative assessment, assessment of processes, and the application of knowledge gained from reading, should affect teaching and learning as they operate in zones of proximal development.

CONCLUDING COMMENTS

Early in this chapter we framed best practices in reading assessment in relation to balance and imbalance. As we conclude this chapter we are trying to balance concern and optimism. Our concern is fueled by the fact that in the past few years we have witnessed an actual backtracking in reading assessment. Positive developments in assessment, including the use of performance assessments in statewide and large school district testing to measure complexities in students' reading growth (Maryland State Department of Education, 2006; Valencia, Hiebert, & Afflerbach, 1994), are abandoned and left behind as a result of federal law. The many factors that combine in students' successful reading performances are ignored when assessment's exclusive focus is on cognitive gain. And politicians and the general public continue to privilege high-stakes tests over all other forms of reading assessment.

In contrast, our optimism is fueled by the fact that eminently useful reading assessment materials and procedures exist, indicating that part of the hard work is already done. We have the means to develop reading assessment that is central to the identification and accomplishment of teachable moments and reading assessment that reflects student achievement in relation to our most recent understanding of reading. This must be complemented by teachers' professional development and the public commitment to examine our new conceptualizations of reading and reading assessment and to supporting those assessments that best describe students' achievement.

ENGAGEMENT ACTIVITIES

The following activities are designed to encourage readers of this chapter to investigate balance in imbalance in reading assessment:

1. Conduct an inventory of the reading assessments used in your classroom and school. Evaluate the current assessments in relation to the balances described earlier in this chapter. Is there ample opportunity for collecting and using formative assessment information that might inform ongoing reading instruction? Do the assessments provide opportunity to observe students' reading processes, as well as the products of reading? Do assessments help us understand how students develop in areas related to their cognitive growth, motivation, and self-esteem? Is there opportunity for students to learn to self-assess? Look for gaps, redundancies, and how well the collection of reading assessments honors the rich construct of reading. Prepare to use the results of your inventory to argue for change or maintenance of the current assessment program.
2. Conduct task analyses of the reading and reading-related work you ask of your students. When our reading assessments require that students summarize text or locate important details, we should be familiar with the means with which students accomplish this. Task analyses give us detailed knowledge of what we ask students to do. This puts us in a position to assess our assessments. Are they sensitive to all the growth that students may exhibit? Do they favor one type of achievement while ignoring others? Task analyses not only help us determine the suitability of the assessment, they also prompt our attention to aspects of reading strategies and tasks that may be the focus of instruction. Knowing the assessment in this case helps us think about teaching, assessment, and balance in assessment.
3. Learn advocacy for those reading assessments you find most useful. It is important to know the benefits and shortcomings of different reading assessments. Be prepared to demonstrate the particular benefits of an assessment to fellow teachers and administrators. Develop reasoned and detailed explanations of what assessments could do better as a replacement or complement of current materials and procedures, and frame your claims in relation to the different audiences and purposes that reading assessment should serve. Choose a type of

assessment and become expert at it. Demonstrate your expertise at this assessment and demonstrate how it provides valuable assessment information to different audiences in your school community. This, in essence, is the most effective means to create change.

4. Lobby for professional development opportunities that promote teachers' expertise in developing and using high-quality classroom assessments of reading. Can you demonstrate the value of a particular type of reading assessment, such as performance assessment, so that you can then lobby for the need to support teachers in this effort?

REFERENCES

Afflerbach, P. (2002). Teaching reading self-assessment strategies. In C. Block & M. Pressley (Eds.), *Comprehension instruction: Research-based best practices* (pp. 96–111). New York: Guilford Press.

Afflerbach, P. (2005). High stakes testing and reading assessment. *Journal of Literacy Research, 37,* 1–12.

Afflerbach, P. (2007). *Understanding and using reading assessment, K–12.* Newark, DE: International Reading Association.

Afflerbach, P., Cho, B., & Kim, J. (in press). The assessment of higher-order thinking skills in reading. In G. Schraw (Ed.), *Current perspectives on cognition, learning, and instruction: Assessment of higher-order thinking skills.* Omaha, NE: Information Age.

Afflerbach, P., Cho, B., Kim, J., & Clark, S. (2010). Classroom assessment of literacy. In D. Wyse, R. Andrews, & J. Hoffman (Eds.), *The international handbook of English, language and literacy teaching* (pp. 401–412). London: Routledge.

Alexander, P. (2005). *The path to competence: A lifespan developmental perspective on reading.* Retrieved April 2, 2009, from *www.nrconline.org/.*

Alvermann, D. E., Hagood, M. C., Heron-Hruby, A., Hughes, P., Williams, K. B., & Yoon, J. (2007). Telling themselves who they are: What one out-of-school time study revealed about underachieving readers. *Reading Psychology, 28*(1), 31–50.

American Educational Research Association/American Psychological Association/National Council on Measurement in Education. (1999). *The standards for educational and psychological testing.* Washington, DC: Author.

Anderson, L., & Krathwohl, D. (2001). *A taxonomy for learning, teaching, and assessing: A revision of Bloom's taxonomy of educational objectives.* New York: Addison-Wesley/Longman.

Baxter, G., & Glaser, R. (1998). Investigating the cognitive complexity of science assessments. *Educational Measurement: Issues and Practice, 17*(3), 37–45.

Black, P., & Wiliam, D. (1998). Assessment and classroom learning. *Educational Assessment: Principles, Policy, and Practice, 5,* 7–74.

Black, P., & Wiliam, D. (2005). Assessment for learning in the classroom. In J. Gardner (Ed.), *Assessment and learning* (pp. 9–25). London: Sage.

Bloom, B. S. (1956). *Taxonomy of educational objectives. Handbook 1: Cognitive Domain.* New York: McKay.

Calfee, R., & Hiebert, E. (1996). Classroom assessment of reading. In R. Barr, M. Kamil, P. Mosenthal, & D. Pearson (Eds.), *Handbook of reading research* (2nd ed., pp. 281–309). Mahwah, NJ: Erlbaum.

Chapman, J. W., & Tunmer, W. E. (1995). Development of young children's reading self-concepts: An examination of emerging subcomponents and their relationship with reading achievement. *Journal of Educational Psychology, 87,* 154–167.

Clay, M. (1993). *Reading Recovery: A guidebook for teachers in training.* Portsmouth, NH: Heinemann.

Crooks, T. (1988). The impact of classroom evaluation on students. *Review of Educational Research, 58,* 438–481.

Darling-Hammond, L. (2010). *Performance counts: Assessment systems that support high-quality learning.* Washington, DC: Council of Chief State School Officers.

Davis, A. (1998). *The limits of educational assessment.* Oxford, UK: Blackwell.

Gambrell, L., Palmer, B., Codling, R., & Mazzoni, S. (1996). Assessing motivation to read. *The Reading Teacher, 49,* 518–533.

Goodman, K., & Goodman, Y. (1977). Learning about psycholinguistic processes by analyzing oral reading. *Harvard Educational Review, 47,* 317–333.

Guthrie, J., & Wigfield, A. (1997). *Reading engagement: Motivating readers through integrated instruction.* Newark, DE: International Reading Association.

Hart, B., & Risley, T. (1995). *Meaningful differences in the everyday experience of young American children.* Baltimore: Brookes.

Heath, S. (1983). *Ways with words: Language, life and work in communities and classrooms.* Cambridge, UK: Cambridge University Press.

Johnston, P. (1987). Teachers as evaluation experts. *The Reading Teacher, 40,* 744–748.

LaBerge, D., & Samuels, S. (1974). Toward a theory of automatic information processing in reading. *Cognitive Psychology, 6,* 293–323.

Leu, D. J., Jr., Kinzer, C. K., Coiro, J. L., & Cammack, D. W. (2004). Toward a theory of new literacies emerging from the Internet and other information and communication technologies. In R. B. Ruddell & N. Unrau (Eds.), *Theoretical models and processes of reading* (5th ed., pp. 1570–1613). Newark, DE: International Reading Association.

Maryland State Department of Education. (2006). *How did we test what students learned from 1993–2002?* Baltimore: Author.

McKenna, M. C., & Kear, D. J. (1990). Measuring attitude toward reading: A new tool or teachers. *The Reading Teacher, 43,* 626–639.

Moll, L. C., Amanti, C., Neff, D., & González, N. (1992). Funds of knowledge for teaching: Using a qualitative approach to connect homes and classrooms. *Theory into Practice, 31,* 132–141.

Morsy, L., Kieffer, M., & Snow, C. (2010). *Measure for measure: A critical consumer's guide to reading comprehension assessments for adolescents.* New York: Carnegie Corporation.

National Assessment Governing Board. (2008). *Reading framework for the 2009 National Assessment of Educational Progress.* Washington, DC: American Institutes for Research.

Pellegrino, J., Chudowsky, N., & Glaser, R. (2001). *Knowing what students know: The science and design of educational assessment.* Washington, DC: National Academy Press.

Pressley, M., & Afflerbach, P. (1995). *Verbal reports of reading: The nature of constructively responsive reading.* Hillsdale, NJ: Erlbaum.

Rogers, R. (2003). *An introduction to critical discourse analysis in education.* Mahwah, NJ: Erlbaum.

Rouet, J-F. (2006). *The skills of document use: From text comprehension to Web-based learning.* Mahwah, NJ: Erlbaum.

Snow, C. (2002). *Reading for understanding: Toward an R&D program in reading comprehension.* Washington, DC: Rand.

Stahl, S., Hynd, C., Britton, B., McNish, M., & Bosquet, D. (1996). What happens when students read multiple source documents in history? *Reading Research Quarterly, 31,* 430–456.

Stanovich, K. (1986). Matthew effects in reading: Some consequences of individual differences in the acquisition of literacy. *Reading Research Quarterly, 21,* 360–407.

Stiggins, R. (1999). Evaluating classroom assessment training in teacher education. *Educational Measurement: Issues and Practices, 18,* 23–27.

Valencia, S., Hiebert, E., & Afflerbach, P. (1994). *Authentic reading assessment: Practices and possibilities.* Newark, DE: International Reading Association.

Vygotsky, L. (1978). *Mind in society: The development of higher psychological processes.* Cambridge, MA: Harvard University Press.

Wineburg, S. (1991). Historical problem solving: A study of the cognitive processes used in the evaluation of documentary and pictorial evidences. *Journal of Educational Psychology, 83,* 73–87.

Wolfe, M. B. W., & Goldman, S. R. (2005). Relations between adolescents' text processing and reasoning. *Cognition and Instruction, 23,* 467–502.

PART IV

Perspectives on Special Issues

CHAPTER 14

Best Practices in Content-Area Literacy

Douglas Fisher
Nancy Frey

This chapter will:

- Explore the theory, research, and best practices related to content-area literacy.
- Identify and explain effective approaches for teaching content areas other than English language arts.
- Discuss the role of background knowledge in learning content.
- Explore ways to foster transformation of texts in the mind and on paper.

Mauricio is a 10th grader at the school where we teach. We asked him to keep track of all of the things he read for a day. His log included text messages, community signs, a history textbook, MySpace, an online article for his science class, several Google page results, the novel he was reading for English, flyers on the walls of the school announcing various events, and the school newspaper. The vast majority of what Mauricio reads on a daily basis is informational. He mostly reads to find information, some of it by his choice and some of it for school. Luckily, Mauricio has been taught to read for information and easily comprehends the various texts he reads.

Reading for information is a specific kind of reading and one that is very common for most adults. In fact, reading for information accounts for the majority of reading adults do. While reading for information has some core processes in common with reading for pleasure, there are differences that have instructional implications. Getting lost in a story requires a certain set of skills, whether you are 9 or 49, including an understanding of plot-driven literature in which characters interact in specific settings. These narrative structures are useful in that they provide readers with a window and mirror to the world (Cullinan, 1989). It is through a window that literature allows us to learn about people we might never meet and visit places we may never travel to in our lifetimes. And through literature we see and affirm ourselves and people like us, as if in a mirror. Of course, literature can be used to help students understand content as well. For example, students can read historical fiction to broaden their understanding of various time periods.

An understanding of plot-driven narrative texts will not provide the reader with the skills necessary to read for information. Expository, or informational, texts do not rely on plots, settings, and conflicts to make their point. These content-area texts differ in that they attempt to explain the social, physical, and biological world in which we live. They have different text structures, such as problem–solution or cause–effect, and often contain text features such as figures, charts, diagrams, and headings that contain valuable information.

That's not to say informational texts are better. Reading both narrative and expository texts are important; they do different things for our brains. It's just that teaching one, and not the other, is common. As Duke (2000) noted, few informational texts are used in the primary grades. Without experience with informational texts, students struggle in school, and their middle and high school teachers wonder why they can't gain information from the texts they're reading. The solution isn't as easy as assigning more expository texts in the primary grades. Students have to be taught how to read, write, speak, listen, and think in each of the disciplines in which they are expected to perform. In other words, reading like a scientist really is different from reading (or writing, for that matter) like a historian or art critic. The remainder of this chapter focuses on best practices in content-area literacy, a long and distinguished field that has focused on helping teachers and students use literacy across the disciplines.

EVIDENCE-BASED BEST PRACTICES

Early research efforts to understand reading focused on specific processes, such as decoding or comprehension. Much of the early research focused on young students learning to read. The seminal text by Hal Herber (1970) changed that. Herber suggested that researchers and teachers should focus on reading in content areas. Many of the ideas in Herber's book, widely accepted as the first comprehensive text on content-area literacy, are still used today. As we discuss further in the section that follows, there are a number of effective approaches for fostering students' reading, writing, speaking, and listening in every content area. Having said that, there are two areas of research that inform our work today.

For several decades, content-area teachers were told, "Every teacher is a teacher of reading." Unfortunately, this isn't accurate when you consider the complexity of reading process as identified in this book. Reading instruction requires a deep knowledge of language structure and function (Schleppegrell, 2004; Zwiers, 2008). Instead of thinking that every teacher is a reading teacher, today we note "learning is based in language" (Fisher & Ivey, 2005). This is more than a semantic change. It's a conceptual change focused on the things that have to happen in a classroom for students to learn. An understanding that learning is based in language helps teachers structure their instructional time such that students read, write, speak, and not just listen in the classroom. Providing students time to use language as part of their content-area instruction has the power to significantly improve achievement (Zwiers, 2008), especially for English language learners (Short & Fitzsimmons, 2007).

Another difference since Herber's seminal work centers on disciplinary literacy. Shanahan and Shanahan (2008) examined literacy learning and concluded that there are three stages of development: basic literacy, intermediate literacy, and disciplinary literacy (see Figure 14.1). Basic literacy represents the foundational and generalizable skills that are needed for all reading

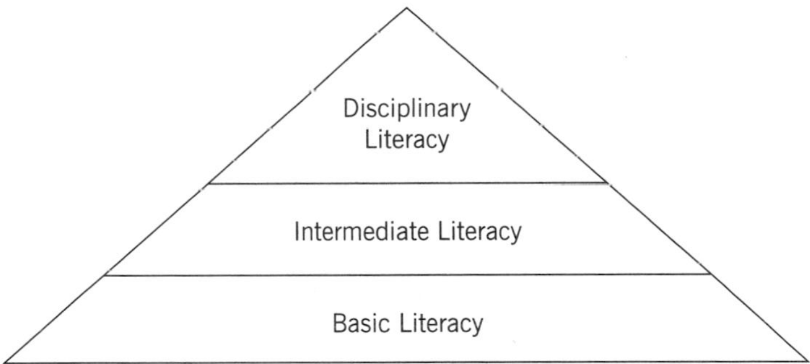

Basic Literacy: Literacy skills such as decoding and knowledge of high-frequency words that underlie virtually all reading tasks.

Intermediate Literacy: Literacy skills common to many tasks, including generic comprehension strategies, common word meanings, and basic fluency.

Disciplinary Literacy: Literacy skills specialized to history, science, mathematics, literature, or other subject matter.

FIGURE 14.1. The increasing specialization of literacy development. From Shanahan and Shanahan (2008, p. 44). Copyright 2008 by President and Fellows of Harvard College. Reprinted by permission.

tasks—decoding skills, comprehension of print and literacy conventions, recognition of high-frequency words, and usual fluency routines.

As students progress beyond this stage—typically in upper primary grades—they move into intermediate literacy. This stage involves the development of skills that allow readers to use some generic skills to understand their literacy tasks. At this stage, students are better able to employ various cognitive comprehension strategies and can utilize fix-up procedures to address misunderstandings. In addition, they are able to take notes, activate background knowledge, summarize their thinking, and so on.

Beyond this stage, disciplinary literacy becomes the focus. The skills involved in this stage are usually not formally taught and are difficult to learn due to the abstract nature of many discipline-specific texts. Moreover, disciplinary literacy is constrained in terms of its applicability to a wide range of reading materials. Specifically, an English teacher who is proficient in teaching literacy skills related to reading classic and contemporary novels may not be so skilled at guiding students to comprehend a technical biology article from a professional journal.

In order for students to gain discipline-specific literacies necessary for content learning, they must be able to transform texts in their minds and on paper. In the next section, we explore instructional practices necessary for this to occur. However, these hinge on two assumptions about text difficulty and reading volume. In the absence of these assumptions, best practices for transforming texts have limited effectiveness.

BEST PRACTICES IN ACTION

In discussing best practices, it is useful to identify assumptions on which these practices are predicated. Our first assumption is related to text difficulty. As Allington (2002) emphatically states, "You can't learn much from books you can't read" (p. 16). In fact, there is no evidence that an 11th-grade learner reading at the fifth-grade level will benefit from reading 11th-grade texts without fairly extensive supports. While discarding the textbook altogether is not advised, a student reading well below grade level is going to need supplemental texts that will allow her to extract information in a meaningful way. Thankfully, readings on a wide range of topics are widely available using digital search engines. In addition, textbook publishers have responded to the demand for a range of texts and modalities. Many adopted programs offer parallel texts written 2 years below grade level, as well as digital versions that are read aloud by a prerecorded voice, allowing the user to follow along in the text. These text-based supports allow struggling readers to benefit more fully from transformational instruction by lowering the barriers presented by texts that are too difficult to read.

Our second assumption is that students read widely. A steady diet of daily reading does wonders for building background knowledge about the range of topics needed across the curriculum (Fisher, Grant, & Ross, 2010). A study of educational success among students in 27 countries found that coming from a home with 500 books was the strongest predictor of a child's level of educational attainment—stronger than parents' occupation, education, or demographics (Evans, Kelley, Sikora, & Treiman, 2010). And while it may not be feasible to stock home libraries, the use of daily opportunities to read from an array of texts has a positive effect on content learning (Pilgreen, 2000). When these two assumptions are in place—texts across a gradient of difficulty and daily opportunities to read—the effects of best practices are magnified.

Transforming Texts in the Mind and on Paper

In order for students for students to learn the concepts of the discipline, they must be able to cognitively transform the information. Educators have long known that learning is an active process that requires the student to manipulate information in order to make it his own (Bransford, Brown, & Cocking, 1999). Inadequate instructional practices rely on transmission rather than transformation of knowledge. We call this "transforming ideas in the mind and on paper" (Fisher, Schell, & Frey, 2004, p. 26) to describe effective instructional practices that foster deep learning. However, it's easy for a good idea to go wrong, and there are numerous bad examples of good ideas. A transmission model of instruction is a retreat from a commitment to foster transformation of information. In each of the following sections, we provide a nonexample and contrast that with a more effective use of an instructional routine.

Developing and Activating Background

Marzano (2004) describes two approaches for developing background knowledge: direct and indirect. Direct approaches immerse the student in the learning moment and include field trips, mentoring and internship relationships, and other methods of experiential learning. Indirect approaches are those that take place in the classroom and do not require relocating students to another environment. These indirect approaches include the aforementioned wide reading, as well as vocabulary instruction.

Vocabulary instruction, which is discussed more thoroughly in another chapter in this book, is essential to content-area learning. Students arrive at the classroom door with incomplete vocabulary knowledge specific to the discipline. This can be misleading for students, who may believe that because they can furnish one definition, they know everything they need to know about the term. This is especially true for multiple-meaning words that are influenced by the context. For instance, the words *root, bark,* and *cone* are as essential to a botany unit as *xylem* and *monocot* (see Figure 14.2). However, neglect of these multiple-meaning words, while favoring the scientific vocabu-

Word	Common term	Scientific term
Tissue	Thin paper; Kleenex	A group of the same type of cells that perform a specific function within an organism
Rod	Any long, cylinder-shaped object; a boy's name	One of the photoreceptors in the eye that distinguish the shapes of objects
Vessel	A container for holding something; a ship	A tube through which a body fluid travels
Culture	The social customs of a group of people	The process of growing living tissue in a laboratory
Petrified	Made rigid with fear	Turned into stone by the replacement of tissue with minerals

FIGURE 14.2. Common and scientific terms in biology.

lary, can create gaps in student knowledge. In turn, this leads to incomplete background knowledge for future learning.

We expand further on this by using a decision-making model for identifying the kind of background knowledge that would be useful for the learner. Depending on the purposes of instruction, some background knowledge might be incidental to the learning, while other background knowledge is essential. Information about the elements of a *pourquoi* folktale is essential background knowledge for understanding a lesson using *Why Mosquitoes Buzz in People's Ears* (Aardema, 1992); knowing about the life cycle of a mosquito is incidental knowledge. Alternatively, a lesson about the spread of malaria makes information about mosquito's life cycle essential, while knowledge about a popular folktale involving the insect is incidental.

While these examples are obvious, it is helpful to utilize a decision-making model to determine what needs to be taught in order to develop the kind of background knowledge students will need to understand the concepts being taught:

- *Representation*: Is it essential?
- *Transmission*: Can it be easily explained, or must it be taught?
- *Transferability*: Will it be used for future understanding?
- *Endurance*: What will be remembered after the details have been forgotten? (Fisher & Frey, 2009, p. 36)

Unfortunately, Mr. Stevenson doesn't use such a model for identifying background knowledge, and therefore spends time developing unnecessary background knowledge while overlooking what his students really do need. His unit about the Revolutionary War included incidental background knowledge about the food and dress of the time, but he missed vital core background knowledge about the varying opinions of the population about whether a spilt from Great Britain was a good idea. Across the hall, Ms. Rochester identified debate and controversy of the time as core knowledge and provided instruction using texts such as *George vs. George: The Revolutionary War as Seen by Both Sides* (Schanzer, 2004). Ms. Rochester divided her class into two groups, and students wrote RAFT responses (Role, Audience, Format, Topic; Santa & Havens, 1995), then debated the prevailing ideas of the time with one another, further developing background knowledge and transforming information (see Figure 14.3). More information about RAFT writing is provided later in this chapter.

Determining what is core and what is incidental also guides what background knowledge should be activated. A hallmark of a novice learner is that they are not good at knowing what information they will need for a task, and therefore they frequently overlook existing knowledge they possess when learning something new (Billingsley & Wildman, 1990; Bransford et al., 1999). In order to spur new learning, activate the background knowledge students will need to use. A simple way of doing so is to begin with a K-W-L chart (Ogle, 1986). A staple of content classrooms, this use of a K-W-L chart invites inquiry through classroom discussion of what is known about a topic and what the class wants to learn. After instruction, the chart is used again to record reflective knowledge about what was learned. In the hands of a skilled teacher, the first column of the chart ("What Do I Know About This Topic?") becomes a tool for activating core background knowledge. However, this isn't a time to rob students of their active role in inquiry. Ms. Wilton applied this process when she told students, "This is what you know about whales, and what you want to know about whales," and then proceeded to write down a series of facts while students sat quietly.

The K-W-L process was used much more effectively by Mr. Lee, who fostered discussion in his U.S. history class when he first asked students about what they knew about the 1960s in America. When some students began offering descriptions of clothing and music from their grandparents' youth, Mr. Lee shaped the conversation to focus their attention on core background

What?	Perspective of Colonists	Perspective of Loyalists
Who?	Last name beginning with A–M	Last name beginning with N–Z
Role	Colonist in support of revolt	Loyalist in support of British citizenship
Audience	Loyalists	Colonists
Format	Letter of protest	Letter of protest
Topic	We should be free!	We're better off remaining British

FIGURE 14.3. RAFT writing for the Revolutionary War.

knowledge. "And what was the reaction of adults to those crazy clothes and loud music?" he asked. Tristan replied, "They didn't like it one bit!" Carmen, whose own family was involved in antiwar activities of the era, offered, "All that was easy to pick on, but what was really scary to the adults was that kids didn't just do what they were told. They had their own opinions." Mr. Lee used this to capture core background knowledge, and wrote on the chart, *Rebelling against beliefs of parents.* To further activate their core background knowledge, he showed them a series of photographs that included student demonstrations at Columbia University, the Watts riots of 1965, and the Kent State shooting in May 1970. "It's about protest," Celeste said, almost to herself. "Tell me more about that," her teacher replied. "Well, yeah, they had flowers in their hair and all that, but really it was about the protests that were happening. The kids didn't like it, and they went out in the street to say so." As Mr. Lee wrote *protest* on the chart, he knew that even though the unit hadn't yet formally begun, he was already refining their ability to draw on what they knew to understand this volatile period in history.

Students first begin to transform information in their minds by making connections to what they already know. This requires them to leverage the *right* background knowledge in order to begin building a schema for new information. This new information can be further transformed on paper through the use of graphic organizers, note-taking and note-making, and writing to learn routines.

Graphic Organizers

Graphic organizers are one way that students can transform the text on paper. Venn diagrams, concept maps, semantic webs, compare-and-contrast charts, cause-and-effect charts, and the like allow students to create visual representations of what they have read. Transforming a piece of text into a graphic and visual form requires that students reread and engage in critical thinking about what they read. Graphic organizers have been used with students of all ages and across the disciplines (Fertig, 2008; Struble, 2007). They have been used with students with disabilities (Gajria, Jitendra, & Sood, 2007), English language learners (Rubinstein-Ávila, 2006), and students identified as gifted and talented (Cassidy, 1989). In summary, graphic organizers are an effective way for students to learn and remember content. Unfortunately, sometimes graphic organizers are simple photocopies and function more like worksheets rather than thinking tools. Let's consider a nonexample and then two effective examples.

The misuse of a graphic organizer occurs when students are asked to copy information onto the tool, often while the teacher does all of the work and thus all of the thinking. For example, the students in Ms. Hardy's class each received a photocopy of a Venn diagram. Following her reading of an informational text that compared cuttlefish and squid, the students copied the information that she wrote and projected with a document camera. By the end of the lesson each student had an exact replica of the teachers' graphic organizer, but they did none of the analysis or thinking. While the product is impressive, the students in Ms. Hardy's class are not benefiting from the use of graphic organizers as a tool for transforming text. They are no more likely to use a Venn diagram when confronted with a text that compares and contrasts information, and they are not very likely to remember the specific information about cuttlefish and squid.

The students in Ms. Epstein's class have a very different experience with graphic organizers. They were taught various tools at the beginning of the year and are encouraged to select a tool that fits with the information presented. During the unit on volcanoes and earthquakes, students are provided with readings from textbooks, the Internet, and a number of additional informational sources. On one particular day, students are reading the textbook in class. Listening in while a group works illustrates the ways in which graphic organizers can be used to ensure understanding. Jessica used a Venn diagram to collection information from the chapter about the similarities and differences between earthquakes and volcanoes. Marco used a flow chart to document the process, which includes similarities between the two actions that occur when tectonic plates move. Daisy created two semantic maps to identify the meanings of the terms, examples of each, as well as the processes that created them. Their discussion highlights the effectiveness of student created graphic organizers.

DAISY: So, the plates kinda rub together for both, right?

MARCO: Yeah, when the plates rub, it's the start of the process. But right here (*pointing to a part of his graphic organizer*), there's a difference. In this direction, you get a volcano but in this direction you get an earthquake. See?

JESSICA: I get it. It's like what I wrote in common. They both have a start with the plates of the Earth. And they both occur around the edges of plates, or breaks in the plates.

DAISY: Yeah, and we got some bad ones. Like the one in San Francisco.

Their conversation continues, and the students regularly refer to the tools they have created. The result of their work was increased understanding of the content as well as reinforced the different ways to transform a text and really understand it.

Graphic organizers do not have to be two-dimensional. Three-dimensional and manipulative graphic organizers are called Foldables™ (Fisher, Zike, & Frey, 2007; *www.dinah.com*). In essence, students fold paper in specific configurations to represent the content or concept. For example, a flipbook made from three pieces of paper provides students with a tool to take notes about the Five Pillars of Islam. A piece of paper held in portrait position and folded in half (called a hot-dog fold) and then cut three times can be used to take notes about the four ways that heat can be transferred. A similar three-tab fold was used by a student in a biology class to take notes about the digestive system (see Figure 14.4). These interactive graphic organizers provide students with a structure that they use to store information, building their schema for later recall and use.

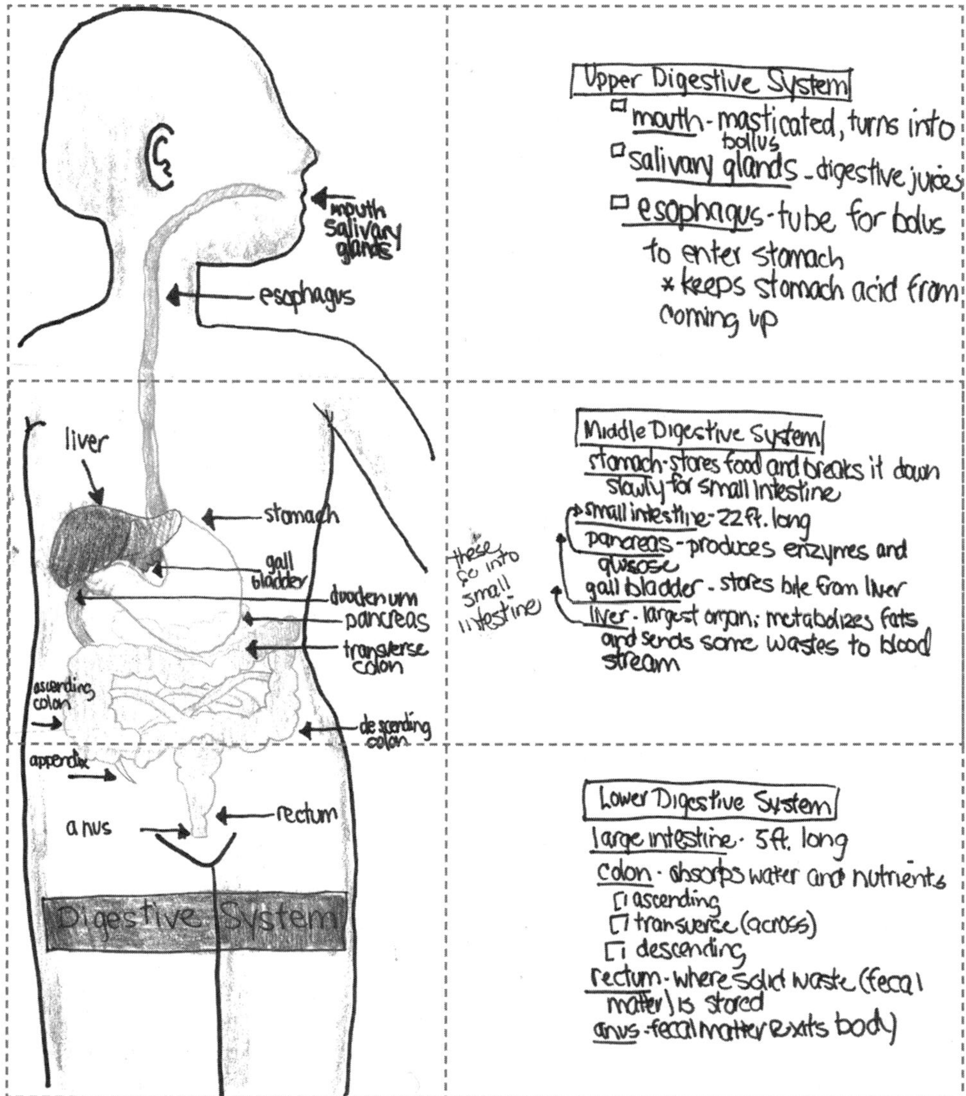

FIGURE 14.4. Foldable from biology.

Note Making

Note making is another way that students can transform the text. Like note taking, which occurs as students listen, note making requires that students identify key ideas and summarize information. In note making, students take a piece of text and distill its essential features, key ideas, or main points to record in their notes (Edge, 1983). Notes should not include all of the information presented, as that would be redundant (the reader could simply reread the text or play the digital recording over). Instead, notes should highlight content and serve an external storage function (Callison, 2003).

While taking notes is a strong predictor test performance (Peverly, Ramaswamy, & Brown, 2007), students often do not know how to take good notes. In a study of the implementation of several content literacy instructional routines, teachers noted that students had difficulty identifying main ideas and summarizing, and that their instruction in taking and making notes improved student performance (Fisher, Frey, & Lapp, 2009).

As with other instructional procedures used to improve students' understanding of the content, note making can go astray. When Mr. Thibodeaux created a "fill-in-the-blank" page for a reading he assigned students, they did not learn to transform the text. Instead, they were on a mission to find the right answer to write on the line. They didn't ever really read the text and certainly didn't think about the information in their quest to finish the task.

When Devon took notes from a primary source document about Mount Vesuvius, he transformed the text and included visuals and words (see Figure 14.5). His teachers taught him how to identify key ideas and summarize through their modeling. For example, several months before Devon's reading about the tragic events in Italy in 79 C.E., his teacher modeled her thinking and note making while reading about the creation of the QWERTY keyboard. Pausing every so often, Devon's teacher makes comments such as, "This seems really important because the author took the time to write about it and include an illustration. I think that will need to be included in my notes." With practice and instruction, students can be taught to store content-area information in their notes, and this process will serve them well, whether they are in a college class or at a business meeting. We all rely on notes as reminders and triggers for our memory.

Writing to Learn

Writing to learn is yet another way for students to transform the text on paper. When students write, they think. Writing requires that students consider what they already know, what they have read, and what they think. Writing to learn is not process writing, meaning that teachers do not evaluate students' writing for mechanics and grammar. Instead, student responses are used to check for understanding that the writer has developed an understanding of the content. As McDermott (2010) noted, "Instead of having students parrot science

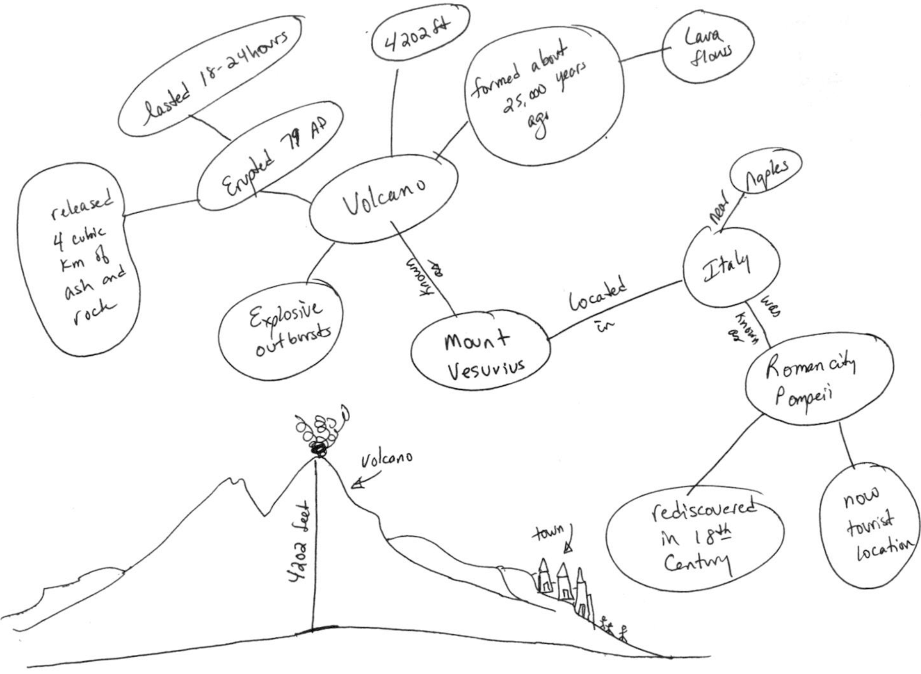

FIGURE 14.5. Devon's notes about Mount Vesuvius.

facts back to the instructor, writing-to-learn activities focus on the production of nontraditional writing assignments—such as poems, brochures, or letters—to develop student understanding (Yore & Treagust, 2006)" (p. 33).

As with all instructional routines designed to improve student performance, writing to learn can be used in ways that are not effective. For example, when Ms. Haddock asked her students to "write about a personal experience with travel," the responses varied widely and were really of no use in activating students' background knowledge about immigration in preparation for their study of *The Circuit* (Jimenez, 1997). In this case, the prompt was not created in such a way as to ensure learning from and while writing. There are a number of prompts that can be used effectively in writing to learn. Fisher and Frey (2008, pp. 174–175) provide the following list of examples:

- *Admit slips.* Upon entering the classroom, students write on an assigned topic such as "What did you notice was important in yesterday's discussion?" or "Explain the difference between jazz and rock."
- *Crystal ball.* Students describe what they think class will be about, what will happen next in the novel they are reading, or the next step in a lab.
- *Found poems.* Students reread an assigned text and find key phrases

that "speak" to them, then arrange these into a poem structure without adding any of their own words (Dunning & Stafford, 1992).
- *Awards.* Students recommend someone or something for an award that the teacher has created, such as "the best artist of the century, living or dead."
- *Cinquains.* A five-line poem in which the first line is the topic (a noun), the second line is description of the topic in two words, the third line is three *–ing* words, the fourth line is a description of the topic in four words, and the final line is a synonym of the topic word from line one.
- *Yesterday's news.* Students summarize the information presented the day before, either from a film, lecture, discussion, or reading.
- *"What-if" scenarios.* Students respond to prompts in which information is changed from what they know and they predict outcomes. For example, students may be asked to respond to "What would be different if the Civil War was fought in 1920?"
- *Take a stand.* Students discuss their opinions about a controversial topic such as "Just because we can, should we clone people?"
- *Letters.* Students write letters to others, including elected officials, family members, friends, or people who made a difference. For example, students may respond to the prompt, "Write a letter to Dr. Martin Luther King, Jr., informing him of the progress we have made on racism since his death."
- *Exit slips.* Used as a closure activity at the end of the period, students write on an assigned prompt such as "The three best things I learned today are . . . "

One of our favorite writing prompts/structures is called RAFT (Santa & Havens, 1995). RAFT is an acronym for:

- *R*ole—What is the role of the writer?
- *A*udience—To whom is the writer writing?
- *F*ormat—What is the format for the writing?
- *T*opic—What is the focus of the writing?

This prompt is very flexible and requires that students think about the content and how to respond to the task at hand. Figure 14.6 contains a number of RAFT prompts from picture books for older readers from different content areas.

REFLECTIONS AND NEW DIRECTIONS

The field of content literacy continues to evolve, and a growing body of research is focused on identifying the nature and characteristics of discipline-

The Midnight Ride of Paul Revere (Longfellow, 1996)
R—Paul Revere
A—William Dawes
F—A secret letter
T—Our plan

Sir Cumference and the First Round Table (Neuschwander, 1997)
R—Sir Cumference
A—Geo of Metry (carpenter)
F—Work order
T—Please make a new table for us

Starry Messenger: Galileo Galilei (Sis, 2000)
R—Galileo
A—Family
F—Letter
T—My life's work

The Flag We Love (Ryan, 1996)
R—Francis Scott Key
A—His family
F—Letter
T—Last night at Ft. McHenry

Sweet Clara and the Freedom Quilt (Hopkinson, 1995)
R—Conductor
A—Traveler
F—Message quilt
T—A safe path through our town

Casey at the Bat (Thayer & Bing, 2001)
R—Sports reporter
A—Mudville fans
F—Newspaper article
T—Mudville loses

You Can't Take a Balloon in the Metropolitan Museum (Weitzman & Glaser, 1998)
R—Balloon
A—Tourists
F—Postcard
T—Why you should visit the Metropolitan

FIGURE 14.6. Sample RAFT prompts.

specific literacies. While much has been written about textbooks in content areas, there is less knowledge in the profession about how content experts read and understand information in their chosen fields. Wineburg (1991) examined the differences between the ways historians and history students read and understood primary source documents, and noted that sourcing was a critical difference between the two groups. Shanahan and Shanahan (2008) have also conducted research on the unique skills content experts use when reading texts. Further pursuit of this line of research would be of benefit to content-area teachers.

A related topic of research is on reading comprehension of digital texts, especially those online. This is an expanding knowledge base in the literacy field, and raises questions about how we use digital texts, with whom, as well as how we teach and assess it (Leu, O'Byrne, Zawilinski, McVerry, & Everett-Cacopardo, 2009). The interactive nature of Internet spaces, commonly referred to as Web 2.0, is challenging how we teach students to find, use, create, and share information (Fisher, Frey, & Gonzalez, 2010).

CONCLUDING REMARKS

Content-area literacy is an important consideration for learners whether they are in preschool or college. Informational texts differ from narrative texts, and students need to be taught to read—and be encouraged to read—both. As we have noted, there are a number of best practices for helping students learn content, all of which have a basis in language. While we no long think of all teachers as teachers of reading, teachers can use reading, writing, speaking, listening, and viewing to ensure student understanding. Content-area literacy draws on each of the literacy components addressed in this book, from decoding to vocabulary to comprehension, to enable readers to make sense of the complex and amazing world around them.

ENGAGEMENT ACTIVITIES

1. Identify the background knowledge necessary to understand this chapter. What is core versus incidental? Do the same thing with an upcoming lesson for your students.
2. Identify the differences in how different content areas approach reading and writing. How do scientists read or write, and how is that different from other disciplines?
3. Use any of the "transforming text" approaches to summarize this chapter. You might create a graphic organizer, take notes,

or summarize your understanding in writing. Share your transformations with others and talk about the differences and similarities you identified.

RESOURCES FOR FURTHER LEARNING

For additional information on instructional approaches for transforming texts, see:

Fisher, D., & Frey, N. (2008). *Improving adolescent literacy: Content area reading strategies at work* (2nd ed.). Upper Saddle River, NJ: Merrill/Prentice Hall.

Frey, N., & Fisher, D. (2007). *Reading for information in elementary school: Content literacy strategies to build comprehension.* Upper Saddle River, NJ: Merrill/Prentice Hall.

For syntheses of information about reading and writing in the content areas, see:

Biancarosa, G., & Snow, C. E. (2004). *Reading Next–A vision for action and research in middle and high school literacy: A Report from Carnegie Corporation of New York.* Washington, DC: Alliance for Excellent Education.

Graham, S., & Perin, D. (2007). *Writing Next: Effective strategies to improve writing of adolescents in middle and high schools* (Carnegie Corporation Report). Washington, DC: Alliance for Excellent Education.

Short, D. J., & Fitzsimmons, S. (2006). *Double the work: Challenges and solutions to acquiring language and academic literacy for adolescent English language learners: A report to the Carnegie Corporation of New York.* Washington, DC: Alliance for Excellent Education.

REFERENCES

Aardema, V. (1992). *Why mosquitoes buzz in people's ears: A West African tale.* New York: Dial.

Allington, R. L. (2002). You can't learn much from books you can't read. *Educational Leadership, 60*(3), 16–19.

Billingsley, B. S., & Wildman, T. M. (1990). Facilitating reading comprehension in learning-disabled students: Metacognitive goals and instructional strategies. *Remedial and Special Education, 11*(2), 18–31.

Bransford, J. D., Brown, A. L., & Cocking, R. C. (Eds.). (1999). *How people learn: Brain, mind, experience, and school.* Washington, DC: National Academy Press.

Callison, D. (2003). Note taking: Different notes for different research stages. *School Library Media Activities Monthly, 19*(7), 33–37, 45.

Cassidy, J. (1989). Using graphic organizers to develop critical thinking. *The Gifted Child Today, 12*, 34–36.

Cullinan, B. E. (1989). *Literature and the child* (2nd ed.). San Diego: Harcourt Brace Jovanovich.

Duke, N. K. (2000). 3.6 minutes per day: The scarcity of informational texts in first grade. *Reading Research Quarterly, 35*, 202–224.

Dunning, S., & Stafford, W. (1992). *Getting the knack: 20 poetry writing exercises.* Urbana, IL: National Council of Teachers of English.

Edge, J. (1983). Reading to take notes and to summarise: A classroom procedure. *Reading in a Foreign Language, 1,* 93–98.

Evans, M. D. R., Kelley, J., Sikora, J., & Treiman, D. J. (2010). Family scholarly culture and educational success: Books and schooling in 27 nations. *Research in Social Stratification and Mobility, 28*(2), 171–197.

Fertig, G. (2008). Using biography to help young learners understand the causes of historical change and continuity. *The Social Studies, 99*(4), 147–154.

Fisher, D., & Frey, N. (2008). *Improving adolescent literacy: Content area reading strategies at work* (2nd ed.). Upper Saddle River, NJ: Merrill/Prentice Hall.

Fisher, D., & Frey, N. (2009). *Background knowledge: The missing piece of the comprehension puzzle.* Portsmouth, NH: Heinemann.

Fisher, D., Frey, N., & Gonzalez, A. (2010). *Literacy 2.0: Reading and writing in 21st-century classrooms.* Bloomington, IN: Solution Tree.

Fisher, D., Frey, N., & Lapp, D. (2009). Meeting AYP in a high need school: A formative experiment. *Journal of Adolescent and Adult Literacy, 52,* 386–396.

Fisher, D., Grant, M., & Ross, D. (2010). Building background knowledge. *The Science Teacher, 77*(1), 23–26.

Fisher, D., & Ivey, G. (2005). Literacy and language as learning in content area classes: A departure from "ever teacher a teacher of reading." *Action in Teacher Education, 27*(2), 3–11.

Fisher, D., Schell, E., & Frey, N. (2004). "In your mind and on the paper": Teaching students to transform (and own) texts. *The Social Studies Review,* 26–31.

Fisher, D., Zike, D., & Frey, N. (2007, August). Foldables: Improving learning with 3-D interactive graphic organizers. *Classroom Notes Plus,* 1–12.

Gajria, M., Jitendra, A., & Sood, S. (2007). Improving comprehension of expository text in students with LD: A research synthesis. *Journal of Learning Disabilities, 40*(3), 210–225.

Herber, H. L. (1970). *Teaching reading in content areas.* Englewood Cliffs, NJ: Prentice Hall.

Hopkinson, D. (1995). *Sweet Clara and the freedom quilt.* New York: Dragonfly.

Jimenez, F. (1997). *The circuit.* Albuquerque: University of New Mexico.

Leu, D. J., O'Byrne, W. I., Zawilinski, L., McVerry, J. G., & Everett-Cacopardo, H. (2009). Expanding the new literacies conversation. *Educational Researcher, 38*(4), 264–269.

Longfellow, H. W. (1996). *The midnight ride of Paul Revere.* New York: Puffin.

Marzano, R. J. (2004). *Building background knowledge for academic achievement: Research on what works in schools.* Alexandria, VA: ASCD.

McDermott, M. (2010). More than writing-to-learn. *The Science Teacher, 77*(1), 32–36.

Neuschwander, C. (1997). *Sir Cumference and the first round table.* Watertown, MA: Charlesbridge.

Ogle, D. M. (1986). K-W-L: A teaching model that develops active reading of expository text. *The Reading Teacher, 39,* 564–570.

Peverly, S., Ramaswamy, V., & Brown, C. (2007). What predicts skill in lecture note taking? *Journal of Educational Psychology, 99*(1), 167–180.

Pilgreen, J. (2000). *The SSR handbook: How to organize and manage a sustained silent reading program.* Portsmouth, NH: Boynton/Cook.

Rubinstein-Ávila, E. (2006). Connecting with Latino learners. *Educational Leadership, 63*(5), 38–43.

Ryan, P. M. (1996). *The flag we love.* Watertown, MA: Charlesbridge.

Santa, C., & Havens, L. (1995). *Creating independence through student-owned strategies: Project CRISS.* Dubuque, IA: Kendall Hunt.

Schanzer, R. (2004). *George vs. George: The Revolutionary War as seen by both sides.* Washington, DC: National Geographic.

Schleppegrell, M. J. (2004). *The language of schooling: A functional linguistics perspective.* Mahwah, NJ: Erlbaum.

Shanahan, T., & Shanahan, C. (2008). Teaching disciplinary literacy to adolescents: Rethinking content-area literacy. *Harvard Educational Review, 78*(1), 40–59.

Short, D. J., & Fitzsimmons, S. (2007). *Double the work: Challenges and solutions to acquiring language and academic literacy for adolescent English language learners: A report to the Carnegie Corporation of New York.* Washington, DC: Alliance for Excellent Education.

Sis, P. (2000). *Starry messenger: Galileo Galilei.* New York: Farrar, Straus & Giroux.

Struble, J. (2007). Using graphic organizers as formative assessment. *Science Scope, 30*(5), 69–71.

Thayer, E. L., & Bing, C. (2001). *Casey at the bat.* San Francisco: Chronicle Books.

Weitzman, J. P., & Glaser, R. (1998). *You can't take a balloon in the metropolitan museum.* New York: Puffin.

Wineburg, S. S. (1991). On the reading of historical texts: Notes on the breach between school and academy. *American Education Research Journal, 28,* 495–519.

Yore, L., & Treagust, D. (2006). Current realities and future possibilities: Language and science literacy—empowering research and informing instruction. *International Journal of Science Education, 28*(2), 291–314.

Zwiers, J. (2008). *Building academic language: Essentials for the content classroom.* San Francisco: Jossey-Bass.

CHAPTER 15

Effective Uses of Technology in Literacy Instruction

Michael C. McKenna
Linda D. Labbo
Kristin Conradi
Jessica Baxter

This chapter will:

- Present a brief history of the use of technology in literacy instruction.
- Describe how the instructional use of technology relates to sociocognitive learning theory.
- Describe research-based classroom practice using technology for beginning readers and skilled readers.
- Investigate how technology can support special populations of readers.
- Suggest how teachers, reading specialists, and reading coaches can successfully embrace technology in the reading curriculum.
- Identify activities for self-reflection and planning.

At the end of the previous school year, when Mr. Moore's principal encouraged each teacher to adopt a new goal for the upcoming year, Mr. Moore decided his would be to incorporate technology in his fifth-grade reading–language arts classes. A teacher for 10 years, he felt his use of technology in the classroom was sorely lacking. The question was where to start. Amid the dizzying array of software applications, Web resources, and hardware, he was at something of a loss. Mr. Moore's situation is hardly unfamiliar to many teachers

> today. Technology is growing at a pace difficult to follow, making many teachers feel sheepishly outdated at best, and inept at worst. Even if we're proficient and comfortable with technology in our own lives, we lack know-how (or confidence!) about how to incorporate it into our classrooms.

In this chapter, we keep teachers like Mr. Moore in mind as we first present a brief history of technology and literacy instruction. We next discuss how incorporating technology aligns with a sociocognitive perspective. We then spend the bulk of the chapter focusing on promising practices for technology use with emerging/beginning readers, proficient readers, and special populations. We end with suggestions for embracing technology in the curriculum and identifying activities for self-reflection and planning.

HISTORY OF TECHNOLOGY IN LITERACY INSTRUCTION

In the 1950s and '60s, computer-assisted instruction (CAI) emerged as field of study, but it had little connection with schools. This was because children had to visit university labs and work at terminals attached to huge mainframe computers. Researchers were confident, however, that as technology improved computers would eventually become practical in schools. Their faith was well founded. Computing technology continued to become "faster, cheaper, smaller, more mobile, and more powerful" (McKenna, 2006, p. ix). The advent of microcomputers in the 1980s made it possible to bring computers into schools for the first time. Two problems soon emerged as educators grappled with the new technology. One was the dilemma of the "digital divide"—the fact that disadvantaged children did not have the same access to computers as their more affluent peers. Although this problem lingers in home environments, there is now an abundance of technology available in most American schools.

The second problem was more basic. What were teachers supposed to do with the computers? What were the wisest applications in an era during which there was no Internet and only rudimentary software? In the 1980s, there were typically too few computers to place even one in every classroom, and so they were placed in labs, where student visits were scheduled on a rotating basis. This made it difficult to integrate computer applications with what was happening in classrooms, and for many teachers that was just as well. Seymour Papert, in *The Children's Machine* (1994), likened computers to invading viruses. Schools reacted much as the body would, he observed, by containing the viruses (in labs) and limiting their contact with the healthy parts of the body (classrooms). The principal software used in school labs involved diagnostic–prescriptive systems that continually assessed students and provided them with activities that corresponded to the results. These elaborate and expensive programs, called integrated learning systems (ILSs), were separate from the classroom materials and curriculum. Although ILSs are still popular, research has not been encouraging. Their repetition of activity formats is a recipe for disengagement, and the tendency of teachers to exercise little involvement has not resulted in the gains that developers had hoped for (Coiro et al., 2003).

Although labs remain popular in many schools, the large number of computers has meant that they are now commonplace in classrooms. Ninety-seven percent of teachers report having at least one computer in their classroom, and 93% of these computers have Internet access (Gray, Thomas, & Lewis, 2010). Just 17 years ago, in 1994, only 3% of classrooms had Internet access (Parsad & Jones, 2005). Over that same interval, software improved markedly in sophistication and scope and is now available on school servers linked in local area networks (LANs). In addition, the broad availability of Internet access has greatly increased the range of activities in which children can be involved.

At the same time, however, Internet access has created an unparalleled dilemma for literacy teachers. The nonlinear environments of the Web require users to apply strategies that have few counterparts in conventional print settings. Teachers have long treated technology as a helpful support for developing traditional print-based literacy. For example, a teacher might place a student in word-recognition software to develop the skills needed to read a book. Increasingly, however, those same skills are likely to be applied in digital settings: reading multiple texts online, interpreting them in conjunction with other media, and navigating among them for a variety of purposes. It is now clear that as technology has evolved it has created new types of literacy demands. Roswell and Lapp (Chapter 16, this volume) deal more with these new literacies, while in this chapter we focus on activities that will develop skills and strategies useful in all settings. In Figure 15.1, we have attempted to illustrate the continuum of literacy skills and strategies related to technology use. Our focus here is toward the left side of this spectrum.

FIGURE 15.1 The range of technology applications for literacy development.

We end this brief history on a note of caution. Although the rise of technology in schools is undeniable, the prevalence of computers in the classroom ensures neither widespread nor effective use of technology. The average student's use of computers in school is still only 12 minutes a week (Wells & Lewis, 2006), and access to computers hardly guarantees meaningful integration (O'Brien & Scharber, 2010). To better understand the barriers to effective applications of technology, we begin by examining the social dynamics of computer use. In the next section, we discuss the integration of computers into the literacy curriculum, framed within a sociocognitive perspective.

SUCCESSFULLY INTEGRATING COMPUTERS INTO THE LITERACY CURRICULUM

We begin by drawing on relevant research and underlying sociocognitive theory (Vygotsky, 1978) to offer suggestions for establishing a classroom environment that promotes demonstration, collaboration, and other forms of social interaction. The evidence is clear that the social environment of the classroom will always play a central role in determining how a computer is used by children in schools (see Kamil, Intrator, & Kim, 2000; Leu, 2000). We believe that, if computers are to adequately support both the conventional and electronic literacy development of children, the computer-related activities must be woven into the fabric of daily classroom routines through planned activities in such areas as (1) teacher-interactive demonstration and (2) diverse collaboration among students and teachers.

Interactive Demonstration and Discussion

Our research (Labbo, Phillips, & Murray, 1995–1996) suggests that teachers can effectively integrate technology by employing interactive demonstrations of classroom computer applications during whole- and small-group lessons. For example, an LCD projector or electronic whiteboard allows a teacher to demonstrate specific features, such as how to navigate through software. However, the makeup of the demonstration should include more than just a teacher explaining or modeling. Rather, demonstrations should combine teacher modeling with opportunities for child involvement. Teachers might solicit children's input during demonstrations of computer use for maintaining a class calendar of events, setting alarm reminders for special class appointments, composing and printing notes to parents, writing the morning message, making class to-do lists, and creating signs for classroom events. In the middle grades, teachers might demonstrate using PowerPoint to craft multimedia reports and presentations. Likewise, a high school math teacher might use a digital tablet to project notes and examples, storing them after class for students to retrieve if they wish.

By socially negotiating the form, content, and context of the demonstration, teachers can help children create a rich schema for employing technology in ways that quite naturally involve many literacy-related activities. Moreover, this schema will, over time, become more sophisticated as teachers present new applications that students assimilate. Thus the perspective we advocate implies much more than perfunctory uses of technology. Computers should be placed as seamlessly as possible into the mainstream of the literacy activities in the classroom. The first step in doing so is an interactive, shared viewing of the computer application using an LCD projector or large monitor. The following steps prepare students to use the software or website effectively:

- First, introduce the title and general purpose of the computer application and demonstrate procedures to open the application. Then state a specific purpose for interacting with the program. Comparing the objectives of different software reveals distinct software functions, such as reading for pleasure, practicing decoding, or playing a game to learn a stated objective.
- Next, model how to navigate through the program. For example, when modeling how to use an electronic text, guide students in how and when to click on words to hear the pronunciation.
- During this modeling, children may be invited to take turns operating the software as a check for understanding. This provides an opportunity for students to offer opinions about the software and develop strategies for making decisions when using the software independently.
- Add procedural reminders during the demonstration, such as how to take turns with computer partners. This helps avoid "mouse wars" that can detract from cooperative learning at the computer (see Labbo, 2000).
- After a shared viewing, encourage the children to critically discuss the information, presentation of the content, and the operation of the program itself. This activity helps students develop the ability to critically analyze software and digital material, just as we hope they will critically examine conventional print materials.

Adult modeling of literacy activities is a major factor in children's acquisition of conventional literacy. Such modeling is no less powerful in the acquisition of digital literacy. As Papert (1980) suggested during the infancy of technology applications, children will use computers in ways they see the adults in their lives using computers. When children dictate personal news to the morning message and watch their words appear on the screen, they have an opportunity to become aware of letter–sound relationships, to be sure, but they also gain a new perspective on what it means to write. Likewise, when children receive an individual printout of the morning message and are invited to circle words, letters, or letter sounds they recognize, it represents an opportunity not only to enrich or refine their conventional literacy knowledge but also to appreciate the interconnectedness of print and digital literacies. Similar benefits of social, interactive digital processes are evident for older children as well. For example, when adults model how to compose e-mails with proper Internet etiquette ("netiquette") or how to evaluate in practical terms the veracity of a website, students' digital literacy knowledge may increase. But through such modeling, teachers also afford their students platforms for productive social interaction within the literate community they are joining.

Diverse Opportunities for Collaboration

Weaving computer-related activities into the classroom culture requires collaboration among students and teachers. From a sociocognitive perspective, we believe that children who observe and interact with teachers and peers during technology demonstrations will internalize relevant vocabulary, develop approaches to problem solving, and encounter action schemes, all of which enable them to use the computer as a tool for thinking, learning, and communicating. Collaborative computer activities are also beneficial because children who collaborate at the computer can simultaneously construct both conventional and digital literacy knowledge. In this section we examine various worthwhile collaborative computer-based applications.

Collaborative writing processes employing paper-and-pencil tools are enhanced by the malleability possible on a computer screen (e.g., cutting and pasting). Other effective collaborations involve digital pen pals, now called keypals. Garner and Gillingham (1998) explained how students use e-mail to communicate effectively with students in various geographic regions. Beach and Lundell (1998) reported that shy students become more interactive and even develop online personalities when they exchange messages through digital communication systems.

Another computer-based collaboration is paired keyboarding. This occurs when a child with knowledge about computer operations and the Internet is paired with another who is less knowledgeable about accessing information from the Internet. Peters (1996) suggested that such interaction can extend the less-knowledgeable partner's zone of proximal development, enabling the child to internalize strategies for successful explorations. Lewis and Fabos (2005) suggest using instant messaging and other socially mediated technologies, such as blogging, to heighten students' analytical thinking skills, which are crucial for critically navigating the vast assortment of online materials. Leu and Leu (2000) argued for a project approach to Internet use because it is naturally collaborative and because students can share their expertise. In the middle grades teachers can use projects with highly motivating possibilities (Miller, 2003), and linking projects to technology appears especially promising.

Teachers should be aware that empowering students to use technology cooperatively can be a demanding task that requires persistence. Yang and Liu (2005) found that it took considerable time and effort for collaborative learning to move beyond the simple skills of technological proficiency to higher-level skills such as synthesizing information. We suggest that teachers remain diligent in training their students to work cooperatively with technology by modeling strategies and cooperative learning procedures, mentoring children's use of strategies, and managing strategy use and computer procedures (see Labbo, 2000, for a detailed description). Purposeful and goal-directed computer tasks encourage better collaboration. This approach helps minimize interpersonal struggles such as "mouse wars" (see Labbo, Sprague, Montero, & Font, 2000, for computer center management tips). Carroll (2004) described how concluding computer projects by asking students to rate their collaborative efforts with a "collaboration rubric" helped students work more effectively (p. 119).

EVIDENCE-BASED BEST PRACTICES

The pace at which technology evolves and changes renders an empirical evidence base almost impossible. By the time research studies are published, the technology used in the study is often antiquated. Nevertheless, researchers have validated a number of instructional practices that we can recommend with confidence. Some of what we recommend in this section hinges on descriptive research alone, but all of our recommendations are consonant with practices in keeping with effective literacy research. We first turn our attention to best practices with emerging and beginning readers. We next focus on technology applications with skilled readers.

Recommended Practices with Emerging and Beginning Readers

In the early days of classroom computer applications, educators often assumed that because computers are sophisticated machines, their principal uses must involve older students. No more! Applications for the youngest children now abound, and their effectiveness behooves teachers in the primary grades to consider them carefully.

Digital Language Experience Approach

Like the traditional Language Experience Approach (LEA), the Digital Language Experience Approach (D-LEA; Labbo, Eakle, & Montero, 2002) provides students with unique contextualized occasions to develop literacy through the dictation of a story that is related to a specific stimulating classroom experience (Stauffer, 1970). However, the literacy learning is enhanced by digital photography and creativity software. The teacher or teaching assistant and a small group of children collaborate to create a digital photo essay enhanced with multimedia features such as those in KidPix (Hickman, 1994), PowerPoint, or Key Note.

D-LEA allows students to compose stories with drawing tools, imported video animations, sounds, speech synthesis, and writing (see also Turbill, 2003; Turbill & Murray, 2006). For example, on the first day the teacher takes a series of photographs of students making a fruit salad. On the second day, students view the pictures, they put them in the correct order of events, and each child dictates at least one sentence describing the activity. Students suggest revisions, the teacher edits the sentences, students decide on a title for the story, and then chorally read the revised text. One the third day, each student reads aloud her screen/page of the D-LEA. Students may record their voices narrating each page and add the sound files to the slide show. On the fourth day, students point to specific letters, words, and punctuation marks that they recognize and then reread the story. On the final day, students present a digital slide show of their D-LEA story to their classmates.

Digital Books

Interactive digital books that provide children with a multimedia experience of stories and literature have come to be known as "talking books." These books may include oral translation of text, interactive pictures, animations, narration, music, sound effects, word games and activities, and speech feedback designed to help children read and understand story components (Lewin, 2000; Littleton, Wood, & Chera, 2006; Ricci & Beal, 2002). Talking books have become widespread, with many parents using them at home. Research has shown potential benefits for incorporating their use in the classroom (Chera & Wood, 2003; Ricci & Beal, 2002; Verhallen, Bus, & de Jong, 2006). Computer centers are an ideal location for engaging young students with electronic texts. Electronic texts include commercially available electronic books, such as the Living Books software series that was developed by Broderbund two decades ago, and Internet texts, such as the electronic books that are available at websites such as *starfall.com, PBSkids.org*, or *Disney.com* free of charge or for a nominal fee.

Students in the preschool or kindergarten classrooms who interact with multimedia books have unique opportunities to have access to books that may be beyond their reading abilities (McKenna & Zucker, 2008). Students may also acquire concepts about print as individual words in a text are highlighted in left-to-right directionality. They may learn new vocabulary words or understand cause-and-effect relationships when text is brought to life by animation and narration. Students who need support with automatic word recognition and decoding can click on words to hear them read aloud, or they can interact with hidden seek-and-find features called hot spots that are embedded within the illustrations. Caution is suggested, because these hidden animations or sound effects can be not only engaging but distracting (see Labbo & Kuhn, 2000). Young students may first explore the book in a spirit of play and later return to the book in a "read-only" manner.

Educational Television

Over the past two decades, children's televised educational programs have become an established technology system that blends entertainment with education. Research indicates that children who consistently view programs such as *Reading Rainbow* and *Sesame Street* perform better on assessments of prereading skills than children who watch less frequently (MacBeth, 1996; Wright et al., 2001). The *WordWorld* (WW) Public Broadcasting System (PBS) television series (see *pbskids.org/wordworld/index_flash.html*) offers an innovative approach for the optimal utilization of media to support emergent and early literacy development, with a particular focus on children from disadvantaged home and community environments. *WordWorld*, an Emmy Award-winning series funded by a U.S. Department of Education Ready to Learn Partnership, was launched in the fall of 2007. The series specifically addresses preschool and beginning readers' literacy development via a scientifically based reading research curriculum delivered through a variety of media, including animated episodes on DVD or television and various hands-on manipulatives such as toys, puzzles, games, and internet activities.

Of note are the WordThings™ and WordFriends™, which are objects or characters that look like and spell out what they are, such as *rug* or *pig*. These animated features (the visual component) of the WW screen architecture are integral to the stories as told through text (the linguistic component), music, and narration (the audio component). The dynamic and multimodal way the letters physically come together to morph into an image of the word (e.g., *d-o-g* takes the shape of a dog, complete with a face, body, legs, and tail) makes it possible for young children to quickly and intuitively connect letters, word spellings, and word names with the objects and meanings represented. Research indicates that prekindergarten children who viewed six episodes within 6 weeks outscored children in control groups on oral vocabulary, recognition of written words, and phonological awareness (Cohen & Hadley, 2010; Labbo, 2009).

Our recent research suggests that teachers play an important role in leveraging the power of the episodes and manipulatives to foster literacy in prekindergarten children before, during, and after viewing, as well as serving as a valuable home–school connection (Labbo, Baxter, & Huddleston, 2010). Recommendations for each phase include the following:

- *Before viewing*: Provide a purpose for the viewing and exploring particular literacy concepts (e.g., letters, rhyming words, or comprehension skills such as predicting) that are presented or are required for understanding the episode.

- *During viewing*: Encourage students to actively participate in the word-building songs and chants or ask guiding questions to encourage higher-order thinking such as inferring.
- *After viewing*: Differentiate extension activities to meet the needs of students of differing ability levels (e.g., some students might focus on letter identification, others might focus on rhyming words or episode reenactments, and still others might draw pictures of their own ideas for WordThings or WordFriends). Read a chant or sing a song from a chart that utilizes the same word families or rhyming words as those that appeared in an episode.

Author's Computer Chair

A useful technique for supporting and celebrating children's development of conventional and digital literacy is to provide a physical space and a time to share and discuss computer activities as in the Author's Computer Chair activity (Labbo, 2004). Our research suggests that that although many of the goals and procedures of the Author's Computer Chair are similar to the traditional Author's Chair that was conceived during the 1980s (see Calkins, 1983; Graves, 1983; Graves & Hansen, 1983), the key difference is that children discuss computer-mediated meaning making.

The Author's Computer Chair is a time of social peer collaboration in which children request feedback and support from peers and teachers during any phase of a computer task. This routinely scheduled time period benefits students as they seek out advice, share knowledge and pointers, and celebrate the completion of a computer activity. (See Labbo, 2004, for guidelines to successfully implement Author's Computer Chair.) For example, a student who is learning how to play an online video game may demonstrate what he has accomplished in the game and also ask for help from other students in the classroom in overcoming difficulties with game play. In these and other instances, the integration of various communicative symbol systems (e.g., print, sound, clip art, animations and video) and digital tools (e.g., word processing, art, e-mail, social networking) support children's development of the language arts of listening, speaking, reading, and writing. However, the convergence of these digital functionalities also fosters cognitive activities, strategic decision making, and affective engagement that challenge and motivate children.

Virtual Field Trips

A virtual field trip (VFT) is an Internet activity that is intended to offer a simulation of a traditional field trip, during which a teacher and parent volunteers guide a classroom of students on an exploratory learning excursion away from a school campus. Traditional field trips offer active hands-on experience with cultural, historic, or scientific resources of a local community.

Field trips are intended to increase student knowledge of a subject and add authenticity to a topic of study. By way of contrast, during a VFT students never leave the classroom, but through interactive multimedia they may experience a local or distant location that is represented in an online site. VFTs are a timely development in light of the lack of funding available for extracurricular activities to many schools.

In a VFT the teacher may serve as a guide who controls the experience and demonstrates interactions with a variety of media, such as video, audio, transcripts of interviews, archival information, and so on (Ritter, 1998; Stevenson, 2001). Students may also submit questions and receive answers from online experts such as historians, scientists, politicians, community workers, museum curators, or astronauts (Owens, Hester, & Teale, 2002). A set of questions that provide guidelines (see *cnx.org/content/m32323/latest*) for determining the potential value of an online VFT site include:

1. Authenticity: Does the site provide enough context to simulate an in-person site visit?
2. Relevance: Is the content available on the site connected to the topic of study?
3. Age-appropriateness: Is the content and the way the content is delivered accessible to the targeted age group?
4. Quality of the resource: Is the information included on the site up-to-date, easy to navigate, and reliable?
5. Feasibility: Is the available technology sufficient to interact with and complete a VFT?

Mobile Devices

Cell phones offer a promising direction for using technology to positively affect children's access to literacy content outside the classroom. It is worth noting that a recent National Health Interview Survey, conducted by the Centers for Disease Control and Prevention in 2009, indicates that "One in four households has a cell phone but no traditional landlines, a trend led by the young and the poor that is showing no sign of abating" (Fram, 2010). Sesame Street Workshop conducted a study in 2006 to determine whether cell phones provide a valuable avenue for providing literacy tips to parents and appealing literacy content to children in families. Three to four times a week for 8 weeks, parents in 80 families received literacy tips from *Sesame Street*'s Maria. Elmo followed with a clip introducing a Letter of the Day and a short video from the *Sesame Street* archives. Parents indicated that they consistently listened to the parenting tips and made their cell phones available to their children, who were excited to view the clips and learn the Letter of the Day (Horowitz et al., 2006).

For a list of additional ideas for integrating technology into beginning readers' literacy curricula, see Figure 15.2.

Instructional area	Suggested application
Phonological awareness	• Use well-designed phonological awareness software such as *DaisyQuest* or *Daisy's Castle* by Blue Wave Software (Pressley, 2006) at the computer center. • Students can use talking electronic books for phonological awareness tasks such as identifying rhyming words and checking by clicking the computer pronunciation (see Labbo, 2000).
Phonics and spelling	• Teachers can type daily Morning Message or student stories using an LCD projector (see Labbo, 2005a) or electronic whiteboard to highlight word features and spelling patterns. • Well-designed decoding software can supplement students' developing phonics skills (see McKenna, 2002, for guidelines to select phonics software aligned with research-based practices; see also Kuhn & Stahl, 2006). • Tutors, paraprofessionals, volunteers, or teachers can create individual student word banks for beginning readers (Bear, Invernizzi, Templeton, & Johnston, 2007), and can store the words electronically using PowerPoint. This is a growing bank of words the child can read automatically in isolation. • Students dictate digital language-experience stories (D-LEA). Print individual copies for isolating words and phonics lessons (see Labbo et al., 2002; Turbill, 2003).
Vocabulary	• Extend themes and concepts with Internet sites, electronic encyclopedias, video streaming, and other multimedia (see Labbo, 2005c, for ideas to support young learners). • Virtual field trips can build vocabulary (Blachowicz & Obrochta, 2005) related to units of study. Use the Internet, electronic encyclopedias, and other media to build prior knowledge and vocabulary that can be saved digitally (see Doe, 2003, for more on virtual field trips). • Use digital photography combined with text to document class field trips and build rich vocabulary in class-authored books (Turbill & Murray, 2006). • Build a collection of useful and important vocabulary in a class database. This resource can include a reference to the text or place where the vocabulary word was first encountered (see Doe, 2003). • Students can build their vocabulary and prior knowledge by going on a virtual scavenger hunt. See Valmont (2003) for a step-by-step guide to creating an HTML document to guide your students to specific websites during a virtual scavenger hunt.
Fluency	• Students can build fluency using electronic texts with computer pronunciations of speech as a model for fluent reading. Speech-recognition software can record and track students' fluency progress (see Adams, 2006). • Repeated readings and echo readings of electronics texts are beneficial for students who need practice reading aloud in a risk-free environment (see Labbo, 2000). • Students can use talking books for Reader's Theater practice (see Labbo, 2000) and then share their performance with an online webcast or podcast of their dramatic reading.

(cont.)

FIGURE 15.2. Suggested applications that integrate technology into literacy instruction. (This list presents examples organized by instructional area.)

Instructional area	Suggested application
Fluency *(cont.)*	• Students can practice repeated readings of literature, digitally record themselves reading the book, and then donate the books and student-authored tapes or CDs to kids in hospitals. Using a class website to spread the word about this community service brings in an authentic audience (see Sangiuliano, 2005).
Comprehension	• Electronic texts at the computer learning center can be coupled with response activities or retellings at the sociodramatic play center to foster comprehension (see Labbo, 2000). • Children can benefit from the meaning making that occurs when they respond to read-alouds or literature using desktop publishing software such as KidPix or Inspiration (see Labbo, 1996). • Internet links to author websites (see Valmont, 2000) can enhance author studies by learning more about the author and his or her writing process or to communicate via e-mail with the author. • Students evaluate and take a critical stance toward digital material, including considerations of credibility of source and potential bias (see Leu, 2000; Morrell, 2002). • Internet, instant messaging, e-mail, and other social media provide opportunities for socially constructed learning (see Lewis & Fabos, 2005).
Writing	• Written responses to stories or process writing techniques such as writing workshop can include computer-based work that constructs knowledge through a variety of symbol systems (see Labbo, 1996, 2003). • Students' poetry creations using the computer can be enriched with symbols, including unique fonts, colors, stamps/clip art, layout templates, animated graphics, and embedded music (see Carroll, 2004). • A variety of open-ended tools for digital publishing facilitate process writing. See Wood (2004, p. 23) for a description of publishing tools. • Electronic keypals via e-mail or other social media can link students and classrooms around the globe. Topics can include literature discussions or common units of study (see Leu, 2002; Wood, 2004). • Teacher- and student-authored classroom websites or blogs can display student work and communicate classroom events (see Chamberlain, 2005; Leu, 2002). • Students conduct research projects using the Internet and present their findings in a multimedia PowerPoint presentation (see Kinzer, 2005). See Morrell (2002) for ideas on critically evaluating pop culture using the Internet and other sources. • Collaborative Internet projects based on traveling stuffed animals (see Leu, 2002) or the Flat Stanley Project can be used to generate online reading and writing experiences (see Hubert, 2005).

FIGURE 15.2. *(cont.)*

Recommended Practices with Skilled Readers

As students become proficient readers, technology not only serves as a tool for continued literacy development, but it can also serve as a platform for using and showcasing literacy skills. The research base for applications with older students lags behind that of technology with younger students. However, Moran, Ferdig, Pearson, Waldrop, and Blomyer (2008) have observed that "While our empirical knowledge may be weak, individuals have used theoretically-based arguments, grounded in case studies, to draw conclusions about the degree to which technology tools can and do support literacy teaching and learning for adolescents" (pp. 12–13). In this section, we draw on research and theory to present ideas for practice with readers in upper elementary, middle, and high school.

Online Discussions

While the important role discussion plays in text comprehension is of little dispute, in-class discussions are often difficult for the teacher to lead (Kucan, 2009). Moving class discussions and literature circles online to a wiki, Google doc, discussion board, or blog can alleviate some of the challenges presented in face-to-face interactions, while also developing students' writing fluency. West (2008) used blogs with her high school students to discuss English literature and found them interacting with the texts in ways they would not have in the classroom. Others have found the online discussions build a sense of community, with students helping each other clarify answers, make connections, and identify literary elements (e.g., Alfassi, 2000; Chamberlain, 2005; English, 2007; Grisham & Wolsey, 2006; Jewell, 2005; Tharp, 2010; Witte, 2007; Zawilinski, 2009). Online discussions can take many different forms. In addition to discussions among classmates, online communication has proven effective between the teacher and student and between students paired up beyond the classroom. Doherty and Mayer (2003) found that establishing purposeful contact between the teacher and students in the middle grades led to stronger relationships between them. In addition, students who received online feedback about their writing did better than students receiving traditional feedback (Carmichael & Alden, 2006). Furthermore, electronic keypals, connecting via e-mail or social media, can link students and classrooms around the globe. Topics can include literature discussions or common units of study (see Barone & Wright, 2008; Leu, 2002; Wood, 2004).

Internet Reciprocal Teaching

Reciprocal teaching (Palincsar & Brown, 1984) is one of the best-researched reading strategies (Rosenshine & Meister, 1994). Based on the fact that reading in internet contexts presents different and unique challenges, Internet reciprocal teaching (IRT; Castek, 2006; Leu et al., 2005) was developed. As in the traditional approach, in IRT students apply four specific reading strategies (predicting, questioning, clarifying, and summarizing) as they work collaboratively to discuss a shared text. Castek (2006) recommends that IRT groups be heterogeneous, recognizing that students with lower reading abilities might actually have higher Internet experience. This mix would invite collaboration and engagement from all. Castek's IRT strategies have been adapted in Figure 15.3. Video clips and examples are available at *ctell1.uconn.edu/IRA/InternetRT.htm.*

Making Videos

Flip cameras, iPods, and cell phones have made video-making ubiquitous (and inexpensive). While making videos is undeniably motivating, Ranker (2007) suggests that the novelty of video-making presents opportunities for students to search for, evaluate, clarify, and revise information. Furthermore, Bruce (2008) found that students traditionally unsuccessful with print nevertheless demonstrated sophisticated and complex composition skills via the medium of video. We discuss two types of videos here.

Predict
- Explain what kinds of information will be contained on this webpage.
- Use cues from the website (illustrations, icons, graphics, or subtitles) to support your prediction.
- Identify which hyperlinks will help you navigate through the text to gather information.
- Describe the types of information you predict will be hyperlinked.

Clarify
- Look for words, phrases, hyperlinks, or electronic features that are not clear.
- Discuss the words, images, animations, or concepts you find confusing or misleading.
- Suggested strategies are examine the context; substitute a synonym; locate the root word, prefix, or suffix and use these pieces as supports; ask others; mark the word to look it up later; if it is a hyperlinked word, examine the link to identify supports that may help you (glossary or other online information source).

Question
- Ask questions that begin with who, what, when, where, why, or how.
- Ask main-idea questions that aid in identifying key concepts.
- Ask questions that have under-the-surface answers.
- Ask questions about the navigational path as it relates to constructing a clear summary.

Summarize
- Include the main ideas, not all the details.
- Keep the summary concise and focused.
- Stick to the point.

FIGURE 15.3. Suggestions for presenting IRT strategies. Based on Castek (2006).

Digital Booktalks. Digital book trailers (Kajder & Young, 2010; Tarasiuk, 2010) are modern versions of book talks. For digital booktalks, students plan, design, and shoot a video aimed at getting their audience to want to read the book. Making one of these requires an array of literacy skills. After students have read a book, they spend time in groups discussing the book and deciding on critical elements to include in the trailer. Then students create scripts (what to say) and storyboards (what to show) that lay out the plan for their video (Kajder, Bull, & Albaugh, 2005). In developing both the script and the storyboard, students must repeatedly return to the text to search for salient details and evaluate critical elements. The process invites extensive planning and revision, and students are motivated by the idea of having a final audience. Teachers might choose simply to show the videos to the class, but Kajder and Young (2010) suggest publishing the trailers in an online forum. This not only asserts authorship of the final product but also provides students with opportunities to return to their work for review and further evaluation. Gunter and Kenny (2008) conducted an exploratory study of the benefits of a Web-based portal housing digital booktalk videos. They found that a commercial portal, Digital Booktalk™, showed promise in matching readers with potential texts.

Digital Storytelling. For teachers feeling skittish about plunging into a video-making process, digital storytelling might be a good way to get their feet wet. A digital story is a series of digital images narrated by means of an audio track (Kajder et al., 2005). These stories can be narrative, historical, or informative (Robin, 2010). As with digital booktalks, students need to create both scripts and storyboards before developing their digital story, tying in both reading and writing skills. Students can compose digital stories using several software programs. In addition, some websites serve as great (and free!) resources. Two include *digitalstorytelling.coe.uh.edu* and *www.primaryaccess.org.*

Watching Videos

Video watching might be perceived as a passive process, but it does not have to be. Teachers can use short videos in the classroom in a number of ways. Bull, Tillman, and Bell (2010) suggest selecting videos that are brief, interesting, and relevant to the topic at hand. Videos can be found on several different venues and Robin and Tillman (2010) provide a number of different suggestions for how to obtain and save the digital videos.

As we discussed in relation to beginning readers, videos can be used for classes to take virtual field trips (VFTs), as a means of activating and building prior knowledge. But videos also present many other opportunities for rich literacy development. Videos can be used for students to practice their critical literacy skills. For example, Parker (2006) notes that his students were better able to demonstrate narrative structure through film than through print composition. Teachers could use video first to point out salient elements of a genre, then have students apply those skills to a print composition. Also, teachers can ask students to compare how a film director's adaptation of a book differs from the author's treatment.

One way for students to compare text with film adaptations is by writing their own narration. Cabat (2009) suggests having students make "yak traks" (p. 57) to accompany video scenes. Yak traks are the audio commentary (or director's cut) often included with DVDs. Cabat suggests having students write their own yak traks to accompany video sequences. After downloading video, the audio can easily be removed using iMovie. Next, students prepare their scripts for audio commentary. This process has a number of benefits. Because students are expected to provide an insider's view to the scene, writing the narration requires them to engage in thoughtful and critical literary analysis, comparing the film version to the text version. Furthermore, because the narration will be added to a video and later viewed by an audience, students are motivated to revise and refine their piece. After writing their script, they can record their narration using either the voice over feature of iMovie or Garage Band.

Hoffner, Baker, and Quinn (2008) suggest incorporating descriptive video to develop students' writing skills. They define it as follows: "Descriptive video (also known as described programming) was developed to give individuals with visual impairments access to visual media such as television programs and films" (p. 576). They suggest that teachers incorporate the detailed nuances provided in the descriptive video to scaffold and build upon students' writing. They also suggest that the teacher should first have students watch one scene of a movie (without the descriptive video) and write a description of what they see. Next, teachers should turn on the descriptive narration of that scene. Students watch the video again before returning to their drafts and revising or expanding their compositions. Students should then compare their two compositions. Descriptive video can be found on select DVDs and from PBS.

Graphic Organizers

As one of the National Reading Panel's seven recommendations on effective reading comprehension instruction (National Reading Panel, 2000), the use of graphic organizers has had a somewhat seamless transition to technology, implemented both through software (e.g., Kidspiration and Inspiration) and hardware (electronic whiteboards). Anderson-Inman and Zeitz (1993) compared the use of electronic concept mapping with a paper-and-pencil approach and found that the ease of revising in the electronic version encouraged more changes.

Jonassen (2006) suggests that the best way to use computers is to use technology-based modeling tools, which he calls "mindtools" (p. 12). Modeling tools help learners build alternative representations of ideas or experiences. For instance, Jonassen describes how using semantic organizers, concept mapping, or databases helps students construct representations of processes and relationships. After reading an expository text, a student could use the computer to develop a concept map to reconstruct the most important concepts from the text. Alternatively, students could collect an index of texts read in a database. Then students can use this archive as a reference for solving problems and answering questions based on ideas they have documented. As these examples illustrate, technology provides enriching methods for students to acquire and manage ideas gained in content-area reading.

Word Processing

We believe that it is important for teachers to provide enough time for children to be able to compose on the computer and not just retype a handwritten draft to be printed. To reap the benefits of technology and, indeed, to prepare children to use the tools of contemporary writing, word processing must be integrated into all phases of the writing process. The computer can function as a digital writing folder or portfolio by storing text files such as reflective journals, topic ideas, responses to books, works in the early draft stage, works to be edited or spell-checked, or works to be read by and responded to by peers. However, unlike a conventional portfolio, the digital version reinforces the idea that electronic writing is never a final product. Each electronic file awaits future modification. Valmont (2003) described teachers who have successfully used technology to encourage older students to write. He illustrates how e-cards (electronic greeting cards) and e-zines (electronic magazines) are motivating opportunities for students to compose. Guzzetti and Gamboa (2004) also studied how adolescent girls use e-zine writing to develop and express their individual identities.

As with the research on beginning readers, how to use technology appropriately with skilled readers is an area where more research is needed. For additional suggestions and strategies for integrating technology and literacy with skilled readers, see Figure 15.3.

DIGITAL APPLICATIONS FOR SPECIAL POPULATIONS

Technology can support the needs of diverse learners. Students at all grade levels who struggle with reading and writing may benefit from particular computer applications. We define special populations broadly to include readers who are not fluent in decoding, reluctant readers, children learning English as a second language, and students who struggle with a particular area of reading and writing. Software applications can make age-appropriate text comprehensible to these learners through a system of built-in supports. Dalton and Strangman (2006) describe this notion in terms of “universal access," the architectural concept that has led to barrier-free construction in buildings to permit easy access by the handicapped. From the outset, it is important to note that the provision of technological support hardly ensures either its use or its effectiveness. Marino (2009) found that though lower-ability students benefitted the most from using technological tools, they were less likely to utilize them. Their effectiveness might depend on the individual (MacArthur, Ferretti, Okolo, & Cavalier, 2001), but it is clear that we need more research into the topic. In their meta-analysis of effective technology and literacy at the middle school level, Moran et al. (2008) found that effect sizes were greater for the interventions focusing on general populations than for those focusing on students with specific needs. They suggested potential issues with engagement and/or appropriate levels of support.

Children who struggle with learning to read may benefit from various types of support available in electronic texts that make the texts accessible. Rather than a traditional instructional or tutorial approach for struggling readers, one that may slow down the pace of instruction (Walmsley & Allington, 1995), supported texts can allow these readers to maintain a pace similar to that of the regular classroom. How readers use supported text will vary with their developmental level. Struggling emergent readers can access the full listening version of a text, whereas readers at later developmental levels who are learning to decode may gain more from resources such as digitized pronunciations of difficult words. More advanced readers who are approaching fluency will have greater recourse to glossary entries, prose simplifications, digitized video clips, and the like as they endeavor to acquire content from expository text (Anderson-Inman & Horney, 1998). At this stage, their comprehension will also benefit from accessing linked resources, such as graphic organizers, databases, or electronic encyclopedias. Because the efficacy of these resources is based on aligning software with a child's stage of reading development, it is essential that assessment be aimed at precisely determining that stage.

This alignment allows teachers to guide the child to the most appropriate use of electronic resources (McKenna, Reinking, Labbo, & Kieffer, 1999; Reinking, Labbo, & McKenna, 2000). Technology for struggling readers must offer resources that meet the needs of the individual learner. Dalton and Strangman (2006) argue that technology should not be approached from the standpoint of one size fits all. They review promising research on hypertext enhanced with learning supports to create a "scaffolded learning environment." Dalton and Strangman's work with a program called Thinking Reader supports a range of learners by offering a text-to-speech function, a multimedia glossary, background knowledge links, and embedded strategy instruction. The software aims to develop metacognitive strategies and increase comprehension by prompting children to "stop and think" or to use comprehension strategies such as predicting, clarifying, questioning, summarizing, making connections, or visualizing. Their research with middle school students reading at or below the 25th percentile rank showed significantly better gains in reading achievement when using Thinking Reader and reciprocal teaching compared with the control group. Dalton and Strangman's (2006) work suggests that digitized, flexible, leveled supports in a hypertext environment can improve students' comprehension skill.

Similarly, Wanzek et al. (2006) synthesized studies exploring the effects of spelling and reading interventions on the spelling of students with learning disabilities. They found that assistive technology (AT), such as word-processing programs that included speech synthesis, word prediction, and spell-checking yielded positive effects on measures of students' spelling accuracy and correction. Simply using a word processor may help. Students were, for example, more likely to correct spelling errors (e.g., Hetzroni & Shrieber, 2004; MacArthur, Graham, Haynes, & De La Paz, 1996).

Many young readers and a small percentage of middle-grade readers require extensive decoding support to read successfully. When using electronic texts, children find they can "read" material that far exceeds their decoding ability because of the support the computer offers. When beginning readers click on unfamiliar words and hear them pronounced, they make substantial gains in sight-word acquisition, provided they can already name letters and recognize word boundaries (Reinking et al., 2000). We have obtained the same results with older struggling readers (McKenna, Cowart, & Watkins, 1997; McKenna & Shaffield, 2002). Hasselbring (1999) provided Start-to-Finish (Don Johnston, Inc.) electronic books to struggling middle-grade readers and reported significantly improved comprehension and motivation. Similarly, McKenna and Shaffield (2002) used WriteOutLoud to create tailored texts (including scanned textbook passages) for a similar sample of students, and observed increased confidence and success as a result of the support received. Electronic supports might trump the benefits of using texts at lower readability levels. Marino, Coyne, and Dunn (2010) assigned struggling eighth-grade readers to two conditions. All students participated in a Web-based inquiry-model science unit, but half were in text adjusted to a fourth-grade reading level. They found that the adjusted reading levels did not bring about significant differences and concluded instead "that other scaffolds included in the technology-based curriculum may have helped students with severe reading difficulties compensate for their limited reading skills" (p. 44).

A future abundance of supported text will mean both advantages and drawbacks for struggling readers. Surely, one of the challenges of electronic literacy is the need for students to develop the ability to navigate strategically through hypermedia environments. Even when these environments are limited to a few helpful sources, the appearance of so many choices can seem like a labyrinth to a struggling reader. On the positive side, students will be able to read text independently that would have frustrated them without the built-in support that McKenna (1998) has called "electronic scaffolding" (p. 47).

Indeed, the notion of the instructional reading level will have to be reexamined in electronic environments, because many struggling readers will be able to read at or near their listening levels (McKenna, Reinking, & Labbo, 1997).

Burns (1996) and Kamil et al. (2000) note that multimedia technology can be used to facilitate the English language acquisition of nonnative speakers. Multimedia resources accommodate the needs of English language learners as they progress in second-language proficiency and gain content-area knowledge. Some electronic books offer the option of listening to the story in Spanish or another language. After using digital storybooks with children who were inexperienced with the mainstream school language, Bus, de Jong, and Verhallen (2006) reported promising results for scaffolding these children's understanding of the story through supportive animations. They concluded that hearing the text in combination with animations bolsters children's ability to derive the meaning of unknown words and sentences. They describe this as an "interactive cycle." Specifically, "when children understand more of the story, they will understand more of the text. When language is better understood this will stimulate their understanding of the story" (Bus et al., 2006, p. 137). More research about the effectiveness of such programs on children's acquisition of a second language and their understanding of specific reading passage content is needed. Notably, speech synthesizer software offers some promising directions for supporting spelling development of English language learners and native-speaking nonfluent writers. Shilling (1997) introduced the use of a basic word-processing program and an external speech synthesis unit that gave children a choice of listening to a word they had attempted to spell on the screen, listening to the entire text they had typed on the screen, or not using speech synthesis at all. Findings suggest that before children consistently benefit from synthesizer software they need to have acquired some basic concepts about print, phonemic awareness, and a notion of the alphabetic principle.

For teachers who are interested in improving their students' fluency, and thereby enhancing comprehension, Adams's (2006) work sheds light on a new technology that has the potential to boost reading while tracking fluency progress: a speech recognition program called Reading Assistant. This promising technology best supports novice and intermediate readers. Such readers already know how to decode but lack automaticity, vocabulary, or comprehension skills. When the child mispronounces a word, Reading Assistant pronounces it correctly and marks the difficult word. When using the read-and-record feature, the speech-recognition layer of the software listens to the student as she or he reads aloud. If the computer detects that the student has stumbled or gotten stuck on a word, it provides assistance. Simultaneously, the computer records the reading and builds an ongoing record of what the student has read and reread, the difficulties the student had, and the progress made. A teacher can access fluency reports and various data that parallel the types of notes taken during a traditional running record. Adams's (2006) initial findings suggested that students who used the speech-recognition program made fluency gains that were significantly greater than children who did not. Furthermore, many students were motivated to use the program because it kept them engaged during rereadings and they could chart their improvements.

For struggling and proficient readers alike, technology often increases student motivation and can boost confidence when children successfully use technology. Our work with Digital Language Experience Approach activities (D-LEA; Labbo et al., 2002) provided a unique opportunity for a struggling reader to envision herself as a literate being, capable of writing and reading. When adding text to a digital photograph of her writing, she exclaimed, "Say, I'm writing! I'm [*verbal emphasis and a pause*] writing! I'm a writer!" (Labbo et al., 2002). It is worth noting that this new self-awareness appeared to foster an elevated level of confidence that resulted in her willingness to participate more actively in literacy activities in the classroom. Kamil et al. (2000) also described consistent findings that computer use in classrooms leads to increased intrinsic motivation, especially when technology gives opportunities to "customize one's work and increase the control, curiosity, and challenge of a task" (p. 778). In their survey of 4,000 students in grades 6–8, Spires, Lee, Turner, and Johnson (2008) found that students ranked working on computers in general and doing research on the Internet as their favorite activities. Gambrell (2006) noted that the Internet in particular holds great capabilities for motivating and engaging students because students can self-select their reading materials and explore others' opinions about texts.

EDUCATOR COLLABORATION TO ENVISION NEW DIGITAL REALITIES

How do you envision the model classroom that successfully integrates technology into literacy instruction? McKenna (2006) described a model primary-level classroom as including "computer-guided word study, electronic storybooks with decoding scaffolds, social interaction guided by software applications, graphics packages to assist children as they illustrate their work, and software designed to reinforce concepts about print" (p. xi). How many of these model classrooms have you visited recently? Despite what is known about effective uses of technology in literacy instruction, it appears that schools are slow to change and that model classrooms are hard to come by. For instance, Turbill and Murray (2006) observed the disinclination of many Australian teachers to integrate technology and commented, "It is our belief that currently most teachers of early literacy view technology as something that their students can 'play' with during 'free time' or as a 'reward' after the real 'work' has been completed" (p. 93). Furthermore, many websites claim to be technological resources for educators but only contribute to the problem by offering little more than drill-and-skill activities or printable blackline images (Turbill & Murray, 2006).

How do you achieve your vision of new digital realities? When integrating technology into the reading curriculum, there is no prescription for how it should occur. Each classroom and school must negotiate the multiple realities that shape their own practice (Labbo & Reinking, 1999). An initial step in the change process may be locating or creating assessments like Turbill and Murray's (2006) "Concepts of Screen," which measures children's basic skill level in using the computer (e.g., use of the mouse, matching cursor and mouse, understanding the function of icons). Assessment data can guide starting points for instruction.

Safe first steps might include adding digital innovations that emulate established effective literacy practices that lend themselves to computer innovation (see Labbo, 2005a, for ideas on digital Morning Message or digital K-W-L charts). Generally, teachers who succeed at making the cutting edge a comfortable place to be are constantly becoming technologically literate and keeping up with technological innovations through activities such as taking educational technology courses, participating in professional development either online or in real time, attending professional conferences, and reading professional articles (Labbo, 2005b). These professional development activities can be a starting point for conceiving new digital realities in one's classroom.

Yet new digital technologies will not transform classrooms if teachers are not interested in and comfortable using them. Coiro (2005) describes teachers' lack of enthusiasm for large-group, workshop-style presentations about technology, in part because this format does not allow teachers to voice their own needs and agendas for professional development. In contrast, she reports teachers' active engagement when they direct literacy-learning Internet projects that are supported by various constituents, including the library media specialist, the principal, and a university researcher. Small-group or online professional development is adaptable to teachers' specific needs and to technological realities. Knobel and Lankshear (2009) recommend professional development wikis. Collaboration can enhance technology-based professional development (see Kinzer, Cammack, Labbo, Teale, & Sanny, 2006), just as collaboration can enrich the process of reflecting on one's practice.

Finally, teachers can collaborate on locating and using Internet resources. They can share useful websites that offer free or inexpensive materials, afford students the chance to engage in interactive activities, and make electronic texts available. We suggest that every teacher maintain a list of such sites, adding to them regularly as they explore and confer with colleagues. The abundance of quality sites has mushroomed in recent years, and for teachers like Mr. Moore who hardly know where to begin, we offer a "starter set" in Figure 15.4.

Readwritethink. IRA's key resource for classroom resources, professional development, and parents (*readwritethink.org*).

Starfall. An excellent source for materials, lesson plans, decodable books designed to teach phonics (*starfall.com*).

The Intersect Digital Library. Extensive library of books with supported text, plus lesson plans and help for creating your own supported texts (*intersect.uoregon.edu*).

IPL2. Formerly the Internet Public Library, this site offers full texts of many public domain books, plus many teacher resources (*ipl.org*).

Reading A–Z. Offers downloadable books for guided reading and phonics. Each book has lesson plans and worksheets and the benchmark books have running record forms (*readinga-z.com*).

Between the Lions. This site is tied to the PBS series of the same name. It features over interactive games and stories based on the series (*pbskids.org/lions*).

Reading Rockets. Gives lots of information for both parents and teachers, including professional-development videos. Operated by WETA, a PBS station in Maryland (*readingrockets.org*).

Make a Comic. User-friendly website that allows students to create comics by dragging and dropping images and text and thought balloons (*makebeliefscomix.com*).

Thinkfinity. This comprehensive website offers lesson plans and ideas for teachers as well as interactive activities for use with students (*thinkfinity.org*).

Read-alouds. This site serves as host to scores of picture books read aloud by various celebrities from the Screen Actors Guild. Extension lessons and activities are also included (*storylineonline.net*).

Florida Center for Reading Research. One of the many useful features of the FCRR site is the wealth of free K-5 downloadable activities in all dimensions of reading (*www.fcrr.org/SCASearch/*).

FIGURE 15.4. Useful websites for classroom resources, student activities, and online texts.

ENGAGEMENT ACTIVITIES

Before reflecting on your next steps to implement technology in your classroom, school, or district, consider these overarching goals for integrating technology into literacy curricula:

1. New digital technologies should be available for literacy instruction.
2. New digital technologies should be used to enhance the goals of conventional literacy instruction.
3. New technologies should be used to positively transform literacy instruction.
4. New technologies should be used to prepare students for the literacy of the future.
5. New technologies should be used to empower students (Labbo & Reinking, 1999, p. 481).

Your school or district may have similar technology goals and standards in place. With these general goals in mind, narrow your focus to your particular role and educational context as you address the following reflection questions.

Teachers

1. What resources can I take advantage of to integrate literacy and technology? Consider the computers and digital tools that are available, the professional development opportunities, and which people have a previous background in technology (e.g., reading specialists, technology coordinators, older students, parent volunteers, university partners).
2. What tools (hardware or software) do I need in order to achieve my literacy and technology goals, how can I get these things, and how much time will be needed?
   a. Hardware/software: digital cameras, LCD projectors, flash drives, literacy software, etc.
   b. Time: time to explore software and available resources, time to plan, and time to collaborate with others.

3. Do I need to seek additional funding through writing grants or seeking donations from local businesses?
4. How will I celebrate and showcase my students' digital work (e.g., organizing technology open houses, writing articles for professional journals, creating classroom websites, blogs, or podcasts)?
5. What is my action plan for implementing technology this year? What steps will I take first? What is my major goal, and how do I need to collaborate to achieve this goal? How will I expand these goals next year?

Reading Coaches and Administrators

1. How can I support teachers as they explore new technologies, trade ideas, and gain mastery of digital innovations?
2. How can I create environments where teachers can experiment with technology together, collaborate, and develop action plans for implementing technology?

AUTHORS' NOTE

Although this chapter contains references to commercial materials, none of the authors has a financial interest in them.

REFERENCES

Adams, M. J. (2006). The promise of automatic speech recognition for fostering literacy growth in children and adults. In M. C. McKenna, L. D. Labbo, R. D. Kieffer, & D. Reinking (Eds.), *International handbook of literacy and technology* (Vol. 2, pp. 109–128). Mahwah, NJ: Erlbaum.

Alfassi, M. (2000). The use of technology (ICT) as a medium for fostering literacy and facilitating discourse within the classroom. *Educational Media International, 37,* 137–148.

Anderson-Inman, L., & Horney, M. A. (1998). Transforming text for at-risk readers. In D. Reinking, M. C. McKenna, L. D. Labbo, & R. D. Kieffer (Eds.), *Handbook of literacy and technology: Transformations in a post-typographic world* (pp. 15–43). Mahwah, NJ: Erlbaum.

Anderson-Inman, L., & Zeitz, L. (1993, August/September). Computer-based concept mapping: Active studying for active learners. *The Computing Teacher, 21*(1), 6–11.

Barone, D., & Wright, T.E. (2009). Literacy instruction with digital and media technologies. *The Reading Teacher, 62,* 292–302.

Beach, R., & Lundell, D. (1998). Early adolescents' use of computer-mediated communication in writing and reading. In D. Reinking, M. C. McKenna, L. D. Labbo, & R. D. Kieffer (Eds.), *Handbook of literacy and technology: Transformations in a post-typographic world* (pp. 93–112). Mahwah, NJ: Erlbaum.

Bear, D. R., Invernizzi, M., Templeton, S., & Johnston, F. (2007). *Words their way: Word study for phonics, vocabulary, and spelling instruction* (4th ed.). Upper Saddle River, NJ: Pearson Education.

Blachowicz, C. L., & Obrochta, C. (2005). Vocabulary visits: Virtual field trips for content vocabulary development. *The Reading Teacher, 59*, 262–268.

Bruce, D. L. (2008). Visualizing literacy: Building bridges with media. *Reading and Writing Quarterly, 24*, 264–282.

Bull, G. L., Tillman, D., & Bell, L. (2010). Communicating with digital video. In L. Bell & G. L. Bull (Eds.), *Teaching with digital video* (pp. 183–193). Washington, DC: International Society for Technology in Education (ISTE).

Burns, D. (1996). Technology in the ESL classroom. *Technology and Learning, 16*(8), 50–52.

Bus, A. G., de Jong, M. T., & Verhallen, M. (2006). CD-ROM talking books: A way to enhance early literacy? In M. C. McKenna, L. D. Labbo, R. D. Kieffer, & D. Reinking (Eds.), *International Handbook of Literacy and Technology* (Vol. 2, pp. 129–142). Mahwah, NJ: Erlbaum.

Cabat, J. H. (2009). "The lash of film": New paradigms of visuality in teaching Shakespeare. *English Journal, 99*(1), 56–57.

Calkins, L. M. (1983). *Lessons from a child.* Portsmouth, NH: Heinemann.

Carmichael, S., & Alden, P. (2006). The advantages of using electronic processes for commenting on and exchanging the written work of students with learning disabilities and/or AD/HD. *Composition Studies, 34*(2), 43–57.

Carroll, M. (2004). *Cartwheels on the keyboard.* Newark, DE: International Reading Association.

Castek, J. (2006, May). *What is Internet Reciprocal Teaching and how do we implement it?* Paper presented at the meeting of the International Reading Association, Chicago.

Chamberlain, C. J. (2005). Literacy and technology: A world of ideas. In R. A. Karchmar, M. H. Mallette, J. Kara-Soteriou, & D. J. Leu (Eds.), *Innovative approaches to literacy education: Using the Internet to support new literacies* (pp. 44–64). Newark, DE: International Reading Association.

Chera, P., & Wood, C. (2003). Animated multimedia "talking books" can promote phonological awareness in children beginning to read. *Learning and Instruction, 13*, 33–52.

Cohen, M., & Hadley, M. (2009). *Evaluation of the educational effectiveness of the WordWorld television series on the early literacy learning of children in pre-K classrooms.* Report for the Reading to Learn Partnership, Ready to Learn Cooperative Agreement, 2005, U. S. Department of Education.

Coiro, J. (2005). Every teacher a Mrs. Rumphis: Empowering teachers with effective professional development. In R. A. Karchmar, M. H. Mallette, J. Kara-Soteriou, & D. J. Leu (Eds.), *Innovative approaches to literacy education: Using the Internet to support new literacies* (pp. 199–219). Newark, DE: International Reading Association.

Coiro, J., Leu, D. J., Jr., Kinzer, C. K., Labbo, L., Teale, W., Bergman, L., et al. (2003, December). *A review of research on literacy and technology: Replicating and extending the NRP subcommittee report on computer technology and reading instruction.* Paper presented at the meeting of the National Reading Conference, Scottsdale, AZ.

Dalton, B., & Strangman, N. (2006). Improving struggling readers' comprehension through scaffolded hypertexts and other computer-based literacy programs. In M. C. McKenna, L. D. Labbo, R. D. Kieffer, & D. Reinking (Eds.), *International handbook of literacy and technology* (Vol. 2, pp. 75–92). Mahwah, NJ: Erlbaum.

Doe, H. M. (2003). *Technology through children's literature: Grades K–5.* Portsmouth, NH: Teacher Ideas Press.

Doherty, C., & Mayer, D. (2003). E-mail as a "contact zone" for teacher–student relationships. *Journal of Adolescent and Adult Literacy, 46,* 592–600.

English, C. (2007). Finding a voice in a threaded discussion group: Talking about literature online. *English Journal, 97*(1), 56–61.

Fram, A. (2010, May 12). *1 in 4 households with cell phone, no landline: Younger people are leading the way to a cell phone-only world.* MSNBC: Technology & Science. Retrieved from *www.msnbc.msn.com/id/37109826.*

Gambrell, L. B. (2006). Technology and the engaged literacy learner. In M. C. McKenna, L. D. Labbo, R. D. Kieffer, & D. Reinking (Eds.), *International handbook of literacy and technology* (Vol. 2, pp. 289–294). Mahwah, NJ: Erlbaum.

Garner, R., & Gillingham, M. G. (1998). The Internet in the classroom: Is it the end of transmission-oriented pedagogy? In D. Reinking, M. C. McKenna, L. D. Labbo, & R. D. Kieffer (Eds.), *Handbook of literacy and technology: Transformations in a post-typographic world* (pp. 221–231). Mahwah, NJ: Erlbaum.

Graves, D. (1983). *Writing: Teachers and children at work.* Portsmouth, NH: Heinemann.

Graves, D., & Hansen, J. (1983). The Author's Chair. *Language Arts, 60,* 176–183.

Gray, L., Thomas, N., & Lewis, L. (2010). *Teachers' use of educational technology in U.S. public schools: 2009* (NCES 2010-040). Washington, DC: National Center for Education Statistics, Institute of Education Sciences, U.S. Department of Education.

Grisham, D. L., & Wolsey, T. D. (2006). Recentering the middle school classroom as a vibrant learning community: Students, literacy, and technology intersect. *Journal of Adolescent and Adult Literacy, 49,* 648–660.

Gunter, G., & Kenny, R. (2008). Digital booktalk: Digital media for reluctant readers. *Contemporary Issues in Technology and Teacher Education, 8*(1), 84–99.

Guzzetti, B. J., & Gamboa, M. (2004). Zines for social justice: Adolescent girls writing on their own. *Reading Research Quarterly, 39,* 406–436.

Hasselbring, T. (1999, May). *The computer doesn't embarrass me.* Paper presented at the meeting of the International Reading Association, San Diego.

Hetzroni, O. E., & Shrieber, B. (2004). Word processing as an assistive technology tool for enhancing outcomes of students with writing disabilities in the general classroom. *Journal of Learning Disabilities, 37*(2), 143–154.

Hickman, C. (1994). *KidPix, Version 2.* Novato, CA: Broderbund Software.

Hoffner, H., Baker, E., & Quinn, K. B. (2008). Lights, cameras, pencils! Using descriptive video to enhance writing. *The Reading Teacher, 61,* 576–579.

Horowitz, J. E., Sosenko, L. D., Hoffman, J. L. S., Ziobrowski, J., Tafoya, A., Haagenson, A., et al. (2006). *Evaluation of the PBS Ready to Learn cell phone study: Learning letters with Elmo.* Los Alimitos, CA: WestEd.

Hubert, D. (2005). The Flat Stanley Project and other authentic applications of technology in the classroom. In R. A. Karchmar, M. H. Mallette, J. Kara-Soteriou,

& D. J. Leu (Eds.), *Innovative approaches to literacy education: Using the Internet to support new literacies* (pp. 121–137). Newark, DE: International Reading Association.

Jewell, V. (2005). Continuing the classroom community: Suggestions for using online discussion boards. *English Journal, 94*(4), 83–87.

Jonassen, D. H. (2006). *Modeling with technology: Mindtools for conceptual change.* Upper Saddle River, NJ: Pearson Education.

Kajder, S., Bull, G., & Albaugh, S. (2005). Constructing digital stories. *Learning and Leading with Technology, 32*(5), 40–42.

Kajder, S., & Young, C. A. (2010). Digital video in English language arts education. In L. Bell & G. L. Bull (Eds.), *Teaching with digital video* (pp. 107–130). Washington, DC: International Society for Technology in Education.

Kamil, M. L., Intrator, S., & Kim, H. S. (2000). Effects of other technologies on literacy and learning. In M. L. Kamil, P. B. Mosenthal, P. D. Pearson, & R. Barr (Eds.), *Handbook of reading research* (Vol. 3, pp. 771–788). Mahwah, NJ: Erlbaum.

Kinzer, C. K. (2005). The intersection of schools, communities, and technology: Recognizing children's use of new literacies. In R. A. Karchmar, M. H. Mallette, J. Kara-Soteriou, & D. J. Leu (Eds.), *Innovative approaches to literacy education: Using the Internet to support new literacies* (pp. 65–82). Newark, DE: International Reading Association.

Kinzer, C. K., Cammack, D. W., Labbo, L. D., Teale, W. H., & Sanny, R. (2006). Using technology to (re)conceptualize preservice literacy teacher education: Considerations of design, pedagogy, and research. In M. C. McKenna, L. D. Labbo, R. D. Kieffer, & D. Reinking (Eds.), *International handbook of literacy and technology* (Vol. 2, pp. 211–233). Mahwah, NJ: Erlbaum.

Knobel, M., & Lankshear, C. (2009). Wikis, digital literacies, and professional growth. *Journal of Adolescent and Adult Literacy, 52,* 631–634.

Kucan, L. (2009). Engaging teachers in investigating their teaching as a linguistic enterprise: The case of comprehension instruction in the context of discussion. *Reading Psychology, 30,* 51–87.

Kuhn, M. R., & Stahl, S. A. (2006). More than skill and drill: Exploring the potential of computers in decoding and fluency instruction. In M. C. McKenna, L. D. Labbo, R. Kieffer, & D. Reinking (Eds.), *International handbook of literacy and technology* (Vol. 2, pp. 295–301). Mahwah, NJ: Erlbaum.

Labbo, L. D. (1996). A semiotic analysis of young children's symbol making in a classroom computer center. *Reading Research Quarterly, 31,* 356–385.

Labbo, L. D. (2000). Twelve things young children can do with a talking book in a classroom computer center. *The Reading Teacher, 53*(7), 542–546.

Labbo, L. D. (2003). The symbol-making machine: Examining the role of electronic symbol making in children's literacy development. In J. C. Richards & M. C. McKenna (Eds.), *Integrating multiple literacies in K–8 classrooms: Cases, commentaries, and practical applications* (pp. 10–17). Mahwah, NJ: Erlbaum.

Labbo, L. D. (2004, April). Author's computer chair [Technology in Literacy department]. *The Reading Teacher, 57*(7), 688–691. Available at *www.readingonline.org/electronic/elec_index.asp?HREF=/electronic/RT/4-04_column/index.html.*

Labbo, L. D. (2005a). Moving from the tried and true to the new: Digital Morning Message. *The Reading Teacher, 58*(8), 782–785.

Labbo, L. D. (2005b). Fundamental qualities of effective Internet literacy instruction: An exploration of worthwhile classroom practices. In R. A. Karchmar, M.

H. Mallette, J. Kara-Soteriou, & D. J. Leu (Eds.), *Innovative approaches to literacy education: Using the Internet to support new literacies* (pp. 165–179). Newark, DE: International Reading Association.

Labbo, L. D. (2005c). Books and computer-response activities that support literacy development. *The Reading Teacher, 59*, 288–292.

Labbo, L. D. (2009). *Opportunities for literacy development with WordWorld PBS, Ready to Read in 3, 4, and 5 year old classrooms.* Report for Athens Clarke County School District, Athens, Georgia.

Labbo, L. D., Baxter, J., & Huddleston, A. (2010, April). *WordWorld goes to school: Lessons learned about media and literacy connections in pre-K3, pre-K4, and kindergarten classrooms.* Poster presented at the meeting of the International Reading Association, Chicago, IL.

Labbo, L. D., Eakle, A. J., & Montero, K. M. (2002, May). Digital language experience approach: Using digital photographs and creativity software as a language experience approach innovation. *Reading Online, 5*(8). Available at *www.readingonline.org/electronic/elec_index.asp?HREF=labbo2/index.html.*

Labbo, L. D., & Kuhn, M. R. (2000). Weaving chains of affect and cognition: A young child's understanding of CD-ROM talking books. *Journal of Literacy Research, 32*, 187–210.

Labbo, L. D., Phillips, M., & Murray, B. (1995–1996). "Writing to read": From inheritance to innovation and invitation. *The Reading Teacher, 49*, 314–321.

Labbo, L. D., & Reinking, D. (1999). Negotiating the multiple realities of technology in literacy research and instruction. *Reading Research Quarterly, 34*, 478–492.

Labbo, L. D., Sprague, L., with Montero, M. K., & Font, G. (2000, July). Connecting a computer center to themes, literature and kindergarteners' literacy needs. *Reading Online, 4*(1). Available at *www.readingonline.org/electronic/elec_index.asp?HREF=labbo/index.html.*

Leu, D. J. (2000). Literacy and technology: Deictic consequences for literacy education in an information age. In M. L. Kamil, P. B. Mosenthal, P. D. Pearson, & R. Barr (Eds.), *Handbook of reading research* (Vol. 3, pp. 745–772). Mahwah, NJ: Erlbaum.

Leu, D. J. (2002). The new literacies: Research on reading instruction with the Internet. In A. E. Farstrup & S. J. Samuels (Eds.), *What research has to say about reading instruction* (pp. 310–336). Newark, DE: International Reading Association.

Leu, D. J., Castek, J., Hartman, D., Coiro, J., Henry, L., & Lyver, S. (2005, October). Examining New Forms of Reading Comprehension During Online Learning. In R. Blomeyer (Chair), *A synthesis of new research on K–12 online learning.* Denver: North American Council for Online Learning Conference. Research synthesis available at *www.ncrel.org/tech/synthesis.*

Leu, D. J., & Leu, D. D. (2000). *Teaching with the Internet: Lessons from the classroom* (3rd ed.). Norwood, MA: Christopher-Gordon.

Lewin, H. (2000). Exploring the effects of talking book software in U.K. primary classrooms. *Journal of Research in Reading, 23*(12), 149–157.

Lewis, C., & Fabos, B. (2005). Instant messaging, literacies, and social identities. *Reading Research Quarterly, 40*, 470–501.

Littleton, K., Wood, C., & Chera, P. (2006). Interactions with talking books: Phonological awareness affects boys' use of talking books. *Journal of Computer Assisted Learning, 22*, 382–390.

MacArthur, C. A., Ferretti, R. P., Okolo, C. M., & Cavalier, A. R. (2001). Technology applications for students with literacy problems: A critical review. *Elementary School Journal, 101*, 273–301.

MacArthur, C. A., Graham, S., Haynes, J. A., & De La Paz, S. (1996). Spelling checkers and students with learning disabilities: Performance comparisons and impact on spelling. *Journal of Special Education, 30*, 35–57.

MacBeth, T. M. (1996). Indirect effects of television: Creativity, persistence, school achievement, and participation in other activities. In T. M. MacBeth (Ed.), *Tuning in to young viewers: Social science perspectives on television* (pp. 149–219). Thousand Oaks, CA: Sage.

Marino, M. T. (2009). Understanding how adolescents with reading difficulties utilize technology-based tools. *Exceptionality, 17*, 88–102.

Marino, M. T., Coyne, M., & Dunn, M. (2010). The effect of technology-based altered readability levels on struggling readers' science comprehension. *Journal of Computers in Mathematics and Science Teaching, 29*(1), 31–49.

McKenna, M. C. (1998). Electronic texts and the transformation of beginning reading. In D. Reinking, M. C. McKenna, L. D. Labbo, & R. D. Kieffer (Eds.), *Handbook of literacy and technology: Transformations in a post-typographic world* (pp. 45–59). Mahwah, NJ: Erlbaum.

McKenna, M. C. (2002). Phonics software for a new millennium. *Reading and Writing Quarterly, 18*, 93–96.

McKenna, M. C. (2006). Introduction: Trends and trajectories of literacy and technology in the new millennium. In M. C. McKenna, L. D. Labbo, R. D. Kieffer, & D. Reinking (Eds.), *International handbook of literacy and technology* (Vol. 2, pp. 1–18). Mahwah, NJ: Erlbaum.

McKenna, M. C., Cowart, E., & Watkins, J. W. (1997, December). *Effects of talking books on the reading growth of problem readers in second grade.* Paper presented at the meeting of the National Reading Conference, Scottsdale, AZ.

McKenna, M. C., Reinking, D., & Labbo, L. D. (1997). Using talking books with reading-disabled students. *Reading and Writing Quarterly, 13*, 185–190.

McKenna, M. C., Reinking, D., Labbo, L. D., & Kieffer, R. D. (1999). The electronic transformation of literacy and its implications for the struggling reader. *Reading and Writing Quarterly, 15*, 111–126.

McKenna, M. C., & Shaffield, M. L. (2002, May). *Creating electronic books and documents for poor decoders.* Paper presented at the meeting of the International Reading Association, San Francisco.

McKenna, M. C., & Zucker, T. A. (2008). Use of electronic storybooks in reading instruction: From theory to practice. In A. G. Bus & S. B. Neuman (Eds.), *Multimedia and literacy development: Improving achievement for young learners.* New York: Taylor and Francis Group.

Miller, S. D. (2003). How high- and low-challenge tasks affect motivation and learning: Implications for struggling learners. *Reading and Writing Quarterly, 19*, 39–57.

Moran, J., Ferdig, R. E., Pearson, P. D., Wardrop, J., & Blomeyer, R. L., Jr. (2008). Technology and reading performance in the middle school grades: A meta-analysis with recommendations for policy and practice. *Journal of Literacy Research, 40*, 6–58.

Morrell, E. (2002). Toward a critical pedagogy of popular culture: Literacy development among urban youth. *Journal of Adolescent and Adult Literacy, 46*, 72–77.

National Reading Panel. (2000). *Teaching children to read: An evidence-based assessment of the scientific research literature on reading and its implications for reading instruction* (NIH Publication No. 00-4769). Washington, DC: U.S. Government Printing Office.

O'Brien, D., & Scharber, C. (2010). Teaching old dogs new tricks: The luxury of digital abundance. *Journal of Adolescent and Adult Literacy, 53,* 600–603.

Owens, R. F., Hester, J. L., & Teale, W. H. (2002). Where do you want to go today? Inquiry-based learning and technology integration: Providing a choice of subjects to study and a range of new technologies with which to study them produced positive results in two programs. *The Reading Teacher, 55*(7), 616–630.

Palincsar, A. S., & Brown, A. L. (1984). Reciprocal teaching of comprehension-fostering and comprehension-monitoring activities. *Cognition and Instruction, 1*(2), 117–175.

Papert, S. (1994). *The children's machine.* New York: Basic Books.

Papert, S. (1980). *Mindstorms.* New York: Basic Books.

Parker, D. (2006). Making it move, making it mean: Animation print literacy and the metafunctions of language. In J. Marsh & E. Millard (Eds.), *Popular literacies, childhood and schooling* (pp. 150–159). New York: Routledge.

Parsad, B., & Jones, J. (2005). *Internet access in U.S. public schools and classrooms: 1994–2003* (NCES 2005-015). Washington, DC: National Center for Education Statistics, U.S. Department of Education.

Peters, J. M. (1996). Paired keyboards as a tool of Internet exploration of 3rd-grade students. *Journal of Educational Computing Research, 14,* 229–242.

Pressley, M. (2006). *Reading instruction that works: The case for balanced teaching* (3rd ed.). New York: Guilford Press.

Ranker, J. (2007). A new perspective on inquiry: A case study of digital video production. *English Journal, 91*(1), 77–82.

Reinking, D., Labbo, L. D., & McKenna, M. C. (2000). From assimilation to accommodation: A developmental framework for integrating digital technologies into literacy research and instruction. *Journal of Reading Research, 23,* 110–122.

Ricci, C. M., & Beal, C. R. (2002). The effect of interactive media on children's story memory. *Journal of Educational Psychology, 94,* 138–144.

Ritter, M. E. (1998, March 12). Virtual field trips: Just like being there. *Teaching with Technology Today, 2,* 2–3. Retrieved October 4, 2003, from *uwsa.edu/ttt/tttv2n4.htm.*

Robin, B. (2010). The educational uses of digital storytelling website: *digitalstorytelling.coe.uh.edu.*

Robin, B., & Tillman, D. (2010). Acquiring digital video. In L. Bell & G. L. Bull (Eds.), *Teaching with digital video.* Washington, DC: International Society for Technology in Education.

Rosenshine, B., & Meister, C. (1994). Reciprocal teaching: A review of the research. *Review of Educational Research, 64,* 479–530.

Sangiuliano, G., (2005). Books on tapes for kids: A language arts–based service-learning project. In R. A. Karchmar, M. H. Mallette, J. Kara-Soteriou, & D. J. Leu (Eds.), *Innovative approaches to literacy education: Using the Internet to support new literacies* (pp. 13–27). Newark, DE: International Reading Association.

Shilling, W. (1997). Young children using computers to make discoveries about written language. *Early Childhood Education Journal, 24,* 253–259.

Spires, H. A., Lee, J. K., Turner, K. A., & Johnson, J. (2008). Having our say: Middle grade students perspectives on school, technologies, and academic engagement. *Journal of Research in Technology and Education, 40*(4), 497–515.

Stauffer, R. G. (1970). *The language-experience approach to the teaching of reading.* New York: Harper & Row.

Stevenson, S. (2001). Discover and create your own field trips. *Multimedia Schools, 8*(4), 40–46.

Tarasiuk, T.J. (2010). Combining traditional and contemporary texts: Moving my English class to the computer lab. *Journal of Adolescent and Adult Literacy, 53,* 543–552.

Tharp, T. L. (2010). "Wiki, wiki, wiki—WHAT?" Assessing online collaborative writing. *English Journal, 99*(5), 40–46.

Turbill, J. (2003, March). Exploring the potential of the digital language experience approach in Australian classrooms. *Reading Online, 6*(7). Available at *www.readingonline.org/international/inter_index.asp?HREF=turbill7.*

Turbill, J., & Murray, J. (2006). Early literacy and new technologies in Australian schools: Policy, research, and practice. In M. C. McKenna, L. D. Labbo, R. D. Kieffer, & D. Reinking, (Eds.), *International handbook of literacy and technology* (Vol. 2, pp. 93–108). Mahwah, NJ: Erlbaum.

Valmont, W. J. (2000). What do teachers do in technology-rich classrooms? In S. B. Wepner, W. J. Valmont, & R. Thurlow (Eds.), *Linking literacy and technology: A guide for K–8 classrooms* (pp. 160–202). Newark, DE: International Reading Association.

Valmont, W. J. (2003). *Technology for literacy teaching and learning.* Boston: Houghton Mifflin.

Verhallen, M. J. A. J., Bus, A. G., & de Jong, M. T. (2006). The promise of multimedia stories for kindergarten children at risk. *Journal of Educational Psychology, 98,* 410–419.

Vygotsky, L. (1978). *Mind in society: The development of higher psychological processes.* Cambridge, MA: Harvard University Press.

Walmsley, S. A., & Allington, R. L. (1995). Redefining and reforming instructional support programs for at-risk students. In R. L. Allington & S. A. Walmsley (Eds.), *No quick fix: Rethinking literacy programs in America's elementary schools* (pp. 19–44). Newark, DE and New York: International Reading Association and Teachers College Press.

Wanzek, J., Vaughn, S., Wexler, J., Swanson, E. A., Edmonds, M., & Kim, A. H. (2006). A synthesis of spelling and reading interventions and their effects on the spelling outcomes of students with LD. *Journal of Learning Disabilities, 39*(6), 528–543.

Wells, J., & Lewis, L. (2006). *Internet access in U.S. public schools and classrooms: 1994–2005* (NCES 2007-020). Washington, DC: National Center for Education Statistics and U.S. Department of Education.

West, K. C. (2008). Weblogs and literary response: Socially situated identities and hybrid social languages in English class blogs. *Journal of Adolescent and Adult Literacy, 51,* 588–598.

Witte, S. (2007). "That's online writing, not boring school writing": Writing with blogs and the Talkback Project. *Journal of Adolescent and Adult Literacy, 51,* 92–96.

Wood, J. M. (2004). *Literacy online: New tools for struggling readers and writers.* Portsmouth, NH: Heinemann.

Wright, J. C., Huston, A. C., Murphy, K. C., St. Peters, M., Pinon, M., Scantlin, R., et al. (2001). The relations of early television viewing to school readiness and vocabulary of children from low-income families: The early window project. *Child Development, 72*, 1347–1366.

Yang, S. C., & Liu, S. F. (2005). The study of interactions and attitudes of third-grade students learning information technology via a cooperative approach. *Computers in Human Behavior, 21*, 45–72.

Zawilinski, L. (2009). HOT blogging: A framework for blogging to promote *h*igher *o*rder *t*hinking. *The Reading Teacher, 62*, 650–661.

CHAPTER 16

New Literacies in Literacy Instruction

Jennifer Rowsell
Diane Lapp

This chapter will:

- Provide background about new literacies.
- Describe and synthesize research and literature on new literacies.
- Discuss some promising approaches and activities to new literacies and what they mean for teachers.
- Offer some resources for future learning.

Consider for a moment the contrast between a basal reader from the 1950s and modern digital environments such as YouTube or Google Earth. There are so many aspects of these two genres that are different from earlier analogues, not the least of which is how they look and what it takes to make them comprehensible. In books and printed texts, alphabetic print dominates with visuals serving a purpose but certainly not a dominant one in conveying meanings. In new and digital media visuals show, tell, and carry meanings. The old wine in new bottles debate (Lankshear & Knobel, 2003) is an important argument when discussing how, in what ways, and when learners think differently in digital environments. However, before presenting the new, it is helpful to revisit the old.

BACKGROUND: THE SOCIAL TURN AS THE BEGINNING OF NEW LITERACIES

During the 1980s and '90s, "new" approaches to understanding and researching literacy became increasingly visible. These "new" approaches have come to be known as "New Literacy Studies," and scholars associated with this area are harbingers of new literacies. The roots of such studies grew out of pioneering research (Barton, 1994; Heath, 1983; Scribner & Cole, 1981; Street, 1984) in communities around the world that looked outside of school walls to explain language and literacy processes. Sometimes referred to as the social turn in literacy, researchers during the 1970s and '80s broadened definitions of literacy at a time when gazes were still fixed on classrooms to explain underachievement in reading and writing. What these early researchers saw then, which is plain to see now, is that literacy varies across contexts and people involved in literacy activities. In this way, literacy is inseparable from practices and the effects of these practices. Or, viewed another way, literacy comes with practical purposes and is always embedded within larger practices.

Contemporary Versions of These Roots

There have been many offshoots to New Literacy Studies. Luke (2000) for years has conducted valuable research that sits on the intersection of critical literacy and New Literacy Studies. Comber, Nixon, and Reid (2007) have worked in primary schools to deconstruct everyday texts to forge critical awareness, and Hicks (2002) published her ethnography of the literate worlds of white working-class families in *Reading Lives*. Similarly, in an ethnographic study Rogers (2003) shared how one African American family had strong and diverse literacy practices, which were not duplicated in the school domain, and were unrecognized by school educators. In Rogers's account, a mismatch was identified between home and school literacy practices, with home literacy practices not being valued by the school. Compton-Lilly's (2007) long ethnography of African American families represents children and adults who confront racism, poverty, and issues of power on a daily basis and how these factors play out in their literacy learning in school. Following a group of learners over a decade, Compton-Lilly's (2007) work demonstrates how learners bring unacknowledged literate strengths into the classroom. Pahl and Rowsell (2005, 2006) have used New Literacy Studies as a framework for research that works at the intersection of New Literacy Studies and multimodality. Their most recent work looks at the concept of *artifactual literacies* (Pahl & Rowsell, 2010) that provides the connecting piece as individuals travel across home and school, and these movements provide their power. Literacies are multilingual and multimodal. "Artifactual literacies" as a concept can take in as its range the movement of artifacts across sites. When students come to encounter multiple literacies, they often do so through artifacts.

THE SEMIOTIC TURN: MULTIMODALITY AS THE KNOWLEDGE SYSTEM

At a time similar to the social turn came a semiotic turn in literacy research that unquestionably affected and still affects new literacies and literacy instruction. Scholars such as Halliday (1984) and Kress (1997) have been connected to the semiotic turn and how semiotics (i.e., the study of signs in society) can help us move from a print-based logic to the introduction of other modalities in digital and print environments. When discourse shifts from print to digital media it becomes easier to use a multiplicity of modes, such as images and sounds, to signify meaning. In contrast with monomodality, or a reliance on pages of dense print limited exclusively to words (Kress & van Leeuwen, 2001), there are two primary affordances enabled by the multimodality of the screen; one is interactivity, or the ability for a producer and user of a text to communicate across texts. The other is the affordance of hypertextuality, or the ability to alter, layer, or reinterpret others' texts.

What brings the social and the semiotic together to make "new" literacies is work that locates literacy in the social (i.e., context, identities, and text) and the multimodal/semiotic. A fitting example of research that merges the social and the semiotic is the work of Dyson and her studies with young children. Developed as the notion of recontextualization, Dyson (2003) uses the concept to describe how children take texts or practices from one domain and move them across sites, combining them up as they do so. When children's texts cross boundaries they can be recontextualized into the new setting. The idea of recontextualization moves a piece of writing that was done in one context to another context, thereby embedding it in a different discursive space.

"Multi" Modes and "Multi" Literacies

Multimodal literacy (Jewitt & Kress, 2003) examines how diverse learners use different modalities fluidly and tacitly to make meaning. For example, when a young child plays video games on the computer, the text uses visuals for understanding and requires the child to click a mouse, listen to the sounds of voices and letters, and enter a variety of texts. Each mode elicits different responses that invite different skills. Theorists in multimodality obfuscate terms such as reading and writing and opt for phrases like "meaning making" to stress that there are so many modalities that we use and face in different genres of texts that demand different kinds of practices—sometimes it is reading written words, while on other occasions it might be listening to a song. Modalities emerge from the interests of a sign maker/producer, and when we make meaning we render these modalities meaningful and remediate them in other contexts for the same or perhaps different purposes. Kress (1997) says:

> Signs arise out of our interest at a given moment, when we represent those features of the object that we regard as defining of that object at that moment (that is, wheels as defining of car). This interest is always complex and has physiological, psychological, emotional, cultural, and social origins. It gets its focus from factors in the environment in which the sign is being made. (p. 11)

With Kress in mind, what is embedded in objects, artifacts, drawings, writing made at home is the context, the sign maker, and the practices used to make the text (Pahl & Rowsell, 2010). Multiliteracies, in slight contrast, argue that design drives communication systems and informs how we make meaning: "As curriculum is a design for social futures, we need to introduce the notion of pedagogy as Design. As educators we need to discuss and to debate the overall shape of that design as we supplement literacy pedagogy in the ways suggested by the notion of Multiliteracies" (Cope & Kalantzis, 2000, p. 19). For instance, a teacher might opt to teach a novel by means of a blog. Using the affordances of technologies of which many students are aware and building on this understanding in the teaching of classical literature is a way of building in a new literacies framework. A key difference between multimodality and multiliteracies is that multiliteracies offers pedagogy premised on design. Multimodality is more provisional and theoretical in its intent, suggesting that the technologies of reading and writing are not solely driven by the written word, but also driven by other modalities that play a role in how we make meaning.

"Digital" Literacies

There has been a spate of research studies that examine the screen and what takes place on screen. Although the New London Group certainly emphasize that the screen governs modern communication and should be our canvas (Kress, 2003), scholars working within the field of digital literacies take on digital spaces as their research terrain (Davies, 2006; Davies & Merchant, 2008; Guzzetti & Gamboa, 2004; Knobel & Lankshear, 2006; Lankshear & Knobel, 2003). Digital spaces range from video game interface to 'zines to blogs and what they look like and what they do. Digital literacies have become a popular field of scholarship and inquiry, especially in piecing together the ramifications of digital literacies for literacy learning and meaning making more generally. Studies looking at blogs or 'zines or video games compel us to see how different ways of understanding discourses, modalities, and ways of thinking feed into our sense making and our construction of knowledge out in the world. Studies that look at the intricacies of digital spaces investigate how they affect users and the kinds of skills that they use when users are in Web space. Over the past 5 years there has been a proliferation of digital literacies studies to confront what we can do about pedagogy, literacy, and assessment in the face of interactive, modally complex Web 2.0 texts.

NEW LITERACIES TODAY

Literacy practices are best understood by examining the environment in which they occur. Digital tools are pervasive, and online spaces offer significant possibilities. Digitally mediated practices like making machima, creating podcasts, contributing to wikis, watching YouTube videos, and playing video games all represent valuable knowledge-making resources that, as suggested by Moss and Lapp (2010a, 2010b) and Frey, Fisher, and Gonzalez (2010), educators can draw on in teaching and learning. Knobel and Lankshear (2006) suggest these be examined through two lenses: "new technical stuff" and "the new ethos stuff" (p. 73). At times, the old-bottle research in new literacies focuses overly on the hardware and software issues rather than learning contexts and interactions. New literacies researchers at times overlook core ethos and knowledge work when they focus overly on technical skills and technology-infusion strategies. New literacies carry different literacy practices and ways of understanding those practices. Literacy in the digital age functions in a different way; new literacies rely on participation structures, remix, collaboration, and design (Cope & Kalantzis, 2000; Kress, 2003; Sheridan & Rowsell, 2010). The term *new literacies* has been associated with certain scholars (Coiro, Knobel, Lankshear, & Leu, 2008; Knobel & Lankshear, 2006), who note that there needs to be theoretical work in digital environments that occurs across diverse fields of study—including computer-mediated communication, second-language research, literacy research, educational technology, and media literacy—and across such traditions as sociolinguistics, psycholinguistics, cognitive theory, and sociocultural theory. They argue that these multiple perspectives are essential to understanding new literacy practices.

Scholars working in new literacies which include codes of meaning making shared through 21st-century literacies such as computer literacy, visual literacy, performative literacy, Internet literacies, digital literacies, information literacy, new media literacies, multiliteracies, and ICT literacies, have offered compelling examples of how multimodal choices that adolescents make when writing online, with words and images, punctuation and links, spelling and color, can teach us something about what they value and what engages them in the writing process. Our intent in this chapter is to illustrate how these new literacies can be remixed with intentional instruction to offer a next generation of best practices.

REMIXING BEST PRACTICES IN ACTION

Remixing Cultural and Social Resources with Literacy

Tenth-grade Andy asked his teacher if, instead of writing an essay to fulfill an assignment that had asked students to describe how significant interactions in their lives had affected them positively or negatively, he might instead share his response through graffiti. His teacher's initial response of "no" changed to "yes" as Andy explained that, through what he termed "responsible graffiti" created on boards, cloth, and paper, he was able to show who he was and what he thought and believed. His teacher realized that the genre of graffiti might provide Andy a personal space, a vehicle through which to communicate by using an alternative code and written convention (Robinson & Robinson, 2003). She was sure a right decision had been made when he further explained that when his "first draft" was a graffiti draft he could turn it more easily into the many essays she assigned.

Listening to Andy, she realized that her definition of the acceptable texts her students were reading and authoring needed to broaden if she were truly intent on accommodating their individual strengths and differences. She decided that her view of acceptable genre and learning experiences should not place social restraints on her students because her intent was indeed to enable them, not stifle them, as learners. She knew that one's ability to read, compare, contrast, and evaluate multiple sources of information was essential for success in reading across many genres (National Reading Panel, 2000). With this new insight about learning and instruction she invited each of the students to share their responses to the prompt through any medium they chose. She was surprised that many still chose to write an essay, while others shared their interpretations of their significant interactions through poetry, rap, photo diaries, scrapbooks, iMovies, and graffiti art. By inviting these students to take the lead in sharing their voices, a constructive yet social practice occurred that both connected and blended the boundaries of their lives and learning both for them and their teacher.

Andy's teacher realized that reading and writing are not isolated literacy tasks that can only be taught and learned through the traditional classroom experiences that were frequently assigned prior to a growing understanding of new literacy learning. Realizing that literacy is a social and cultural practice of meaning making (Cope & Kalantzis, 2000), teachers like her are attempting to design instructional practice that, while maintaining its intent, supports students in gaining and creating meaning through a wide array of texts based on their understandings of the world and their background knowledge and interests (Zimmerman & Hutchins, 2003). As outside-of-school 21st-century literacy practices and demands continue to broaden, the major implication for education is that a primary focus on print-based reading and writing, while vital, is insufficient learning for students.

To accommodate these demands teachers are "remixing what is currently known about very good intentional instruction with the engagement and learning potentials availed through new literacies . . . [in an attempt to] hopefully advance learning for all students and especially those who are not currently experiencing academic success" (Gainer & Lapp, 2010, p. 12). *Remix* is defined by Wikipedia as

> an alternative version of a song, different from the original version. . . . A remixer uses audio mixing to compose an alternate master recording of a

> song, adding or subtracting elements, or simply changing the equalization, dynamics, pitch, tempo, playing time, or almost any other aspect of the various musical components.

While often associated with mixing hip-hop music (Mahiri, 2004), remix continues to expand into many forms of meaning making. In fact, Lessig (2008) suggests that all culture is a remix because meaning is derived through interactions (talking, listening, writing, viewing) as one responds to another while incorporating new knowledge while using prior knowledge. Remixing can be viewed as parallel to Vygotsky's (1978) theory of learning as being socially constructed through a scaffolded base of knowledge, or, as hip-hop artist Daddy-O suggests, it's like sampling portions of various songs and blending or mixing them to create a new one. "We learn a lot from sampling, it's like school for us. When we sample a portion of a song and repeat it over and over we can better understand the matrix of the song" (Rose, 1994, p. 79). To gain an even more thorough understand of what's involved in remixing, you might enjoy *www.youtube.com/watch?v=nS6IC5AWh5c&feature=related*. Before we share an additional example of how to remix what we know about effective intentional instruction with what we are learning as new literacies we offer an explanation of what we view as intentional instruction and why researchers are so essential for successful remixing.

An Example of Remixed, Intentional Instruction

Well-focused, intentional instruction involves the teacher creating a learning experience that is specifically designed to share the information a student needs to continue a positive, well-scaffolded trajectory of knowledge acquisition. Insights about what constitutes these next steps are derived by observing the student's daily performance. It is not a guess; instead, it is a purposeful plan of instruction based on exhibited student behaviors. An effective teacher uses this information to design very purposeful or intentional experiences that support students moving to independence as skilled learners.

For example, prior to Andy's teacher assigning the descriptive writing assignment, which she had originally said could be shared as an essay, poem, or play, she had modeled each of these genres. To do so, she shared mentor texts that she and the students read and analyzed together. Through thinking aloud as she wrote a sample of a targeted genre she also modeled the thinking of an author engaged in writing. She and the students co-constructed a sample of each genre. Then, as students worked individually, as partners, and in small groups first creating oral then written drafts of their meaningful interactions, this teacher was able to continue to actively offer instruction through scaffolded conversational questioning that helped them gain new insights that helped them make connections between their prior and new information. Throughout this experience students conversed and collaborated with their teacher and peers as they developed poetry journals, created dialogue, wrote and performed skits, and studied techniques of descriptive essay writing as their teacher intentionally supported their growing skill development and deepening independence.

This very skilled teacher grew as a professional when she reflected on her instruction and realized that if she were really to support her students' growth as independent learners she must allow them to share their voices through a medium that they selected. To accomplish this she knew that she had to broaden her definition of text and encourage her students to share their voices, their "meanings and messages in all their forms and all their contexts" (Innis, 1985, p. vii) because a person's text represents his view and voice in the world (Bakhtin, 1981), and students in the 21st century have voices that are exponentially shaped by new literacies. As many researchers (Alvermann, Moon, & Hagood, 1999; Heath, 1983; Moje & Thompson, 1996; Street, 1984) have found, student literacies are multiple and they are very able to draw on these to create and share meaning. When educators believe their students are capable of doing so they provide an open gateway for individuals to remix their funds of knowledge (Moll, 2000) as new resources that continually influence their thinking, expression, and critical engagement with learning. As Andy and his teacher evolved and changed, separately and together, their shared classroom time and space were transformed.

Our intent in the following example is to more explicitly illustrate a remix of intentional instruction and new literacy learning during the early years of school. While we have categorized this example according to a grade range, it can easily be adapted for other grades. The content rather than the practice will need to be altered to accommodate the ages and differences of the students.

The Early Years

Instructional Intent: *Understand how authors and illustrators use words and graphics to show how a character changes/develops over time.*

In order to be a writer who can effectively develop a character one first needs a sense of how this is done by other authors. By remixing intentional instruction and new literacies, we offer one example of how this might be taught and learned.

Modeling: Sharing Knowledge

Utilizing a gradual release of instructional frame (Fisher & Frey, 2008; Pearson & Gallagher, 1983; Vygotsky, 1962), Ms. Morris began by modeling for students how an author uses words and illustrations to help readers interpret the characters in a story. To do so she selected *Oh, How I Wished I Could Read,* by John Gile (1995), illustrated by Frank Fiorello. Other books that could have worked just as well are ones like *Curious George,* by Margret and H. A. Rey (1993) that contains many descriptive words and graphics. A picture book like *Doña Flor,* by Pat Mora (2005), that contains wonderful visuals, or others like *Mice and Beans*, by Pam Muñoz Ryan (2005) or *The Relatives Came*, by Cynthia Rylant (2004), that have both wonderful visuals and words. Whichever book you select, it's important to read and think aloud about the pictures and the language while also discussing with the children what they are learning and about how the graphics helped you see how a character changed throughout the book. To keep track of these changes as you talk and think aloud you may want to jot some notes on an interactive graphic organizer called a Foldable™ (*www.dinah.com*) with three sections/flaps. Title the Foldable "How a Character Changes." On one flap of the Foldable write "Beginning," on another "Middle," and on the third "End." Model for the students how, after reading the book cover and the first few pages, you understand a lot about the character. Here's an example of how Ms. Morris modeled this thinking while reading *Oh, How I Wished I Could Read.* First, she showed the cover of the book to the children:

What the pictures show	*What Ms. Morris said*
A boy with a frown on his face sitting on a bench next to a sign that says "WET PAINT"	"I wonder why this boy is so sad. He is sitting on a bench and there's a sign on the bench. The flowers next to the boy look as if they are trying to warn the boy of something. The author is giving me the words, and the illustrator is giving me some visual clues (how he looks) that help me know the boy is sad."

After modeling her initial thinking, Ms. Morris asked the students, "How did the boy look?" When Sylvia responded "sad," Ms. Morris invited the children to fill in their Foldable. Under the first flap (Beginning), students could write the following:

How the Character Changes

Beginning	Middle	End
• Sad		

After reading the first few pages, she stopped on page 5 and further modeled her thinking:

What the pictures show	*What Ms. Morris said*
The boy has a scared and horrible look on his face. His backside is covered in red paint.	"Now I know what the boy was so mad about! The sign on the cover must have said something about the bench having wet paint because the boy has wet red paint all over his backside. No wonder he's so upset. I bet he is upset because he couldn't read the sign and now he is covered in paint. The illustrator gave me clues through his illustrations/pictures."

Again, she paused to converse with students about the word(s) that should be added to their Foldable. Students may draw pictures to describe the words in their Foldable if they are not yet writing.

How the Character Changes

Beginning	Middle	End
• Sad		
• Mad		
• Frustrated		

This kind of thinking aloud and pausing for discussion about the changing character continued throughout the book. After reading aloud, discussing, and adding to their interactive graphic organizer, students had the following:

How the Character Changes

Beginning	Middle	End
• Sad	• Angry	• Feels proud
• Mad	• Determined	• Makes dream come true
• Frustrated	• Wants to learn how to read	• Learns to read

Guided Practice: Assessing, Supporting, Guiding, and Students' Growing Understandings

Now it was time for Ms. Morris to offer more individualized support by giving her students opportunities to acquire and practice the information, language, and insights about the topic and text format that you modeled. As they do so she had an opportunity to provide more individualized support. Once she thought her students had gained a basic understanding of how an author and illustrator use words and graphics to share a character's personality, intentions, and actions over time she had them participate by more interactively reading the book with her. Displaying a page on the document camera she read, stopped, and invited them to partner-talk about the next page while filling in their graphic organizers similar to how she had modeled this for them (see *Oh, How I Wished I Could Read*). As they filled in their graphic organizers she circulated among them, listening in and probing them in ways that allowed her to understand their thinking. This performance information helped her to know what instructional supports to offer that would address students' individual needs. As noted by the following teacher–student(s) exchange, it is during this period of guided practice that teachers are able to offer students the information they need in order to fully comprehend the text and task.

MS. MORRIS: (*Notices that Anthony and Patrick, who are looking at p. 7, which shows a boy with dream bubbles around his head, are not talking about the picture or writing any additional words on their Foldable.*) What do you notice about this boy's face?

ANTHONY: He looks scared.

MS. MORRIS: That's right. Have you ever looked like that? Why do you think he is scared? [Questioning that connects to personal experiences] (*After some wait time when they don't respond, Ms. Morris redirects them as a way to connect author clues to their personal experiences.*) Let's look at the clues the illustrator has given us that will help us know why he is scared. Take a close look at the expression on his face. Think about a time when you may have looked like this. What could he be thinking or feeling? [Questioning and redirecting his attention to textual clues]

PATRICK: Maybe he had a bad dream 'cuz he is still in the bed. I do sometimes.

MS. MORRIS: Good prediction. Let's keep reading to see if that would make sense. (*Continues reading.*)

ANTHONY: (*interrupting Ms. Morris*) You right! You right! He be dreamin'.

MS. MORRIS: I think so too. What helped you to know this? [Probing to model validating one's inferences]

ANTHONY: See those bubbles above the boy's head? That means he was dreaming about something.

PATRICK: Yeah, he's scared of doing what he be dreaming.

MS. MORRIS: Good for you! That's what I also thought. You used all of the clues the illustrator was giving you. So in this first section of your Foldable what do you think you might write?

ANTHONY: You mean in this "beginning" section?

MS. MORRIS: Yes, because it's still the beginning of the book, right?

ANTHONY: Yep, I think we should write *scared.* Maybe I could draw a picture too!

MS. MORRIS: Fantastic idea. And as I continue to read, see if this little boy changes. [Restating purpose or initial instructional intent]

ANTHONY: Yeah, I hope he doesn't stay scared for the whole book!

MS. MORRIS: We'll have to read and look at the illustrations to find out!

This teacher offered this conversational guidance as a way to help Anthony and Patrick use their personal background knowledge bases to connect with the meaning being shared through the visuals. During this guided practice, as she shared additional pages of the book she was also able to move among the students, listening to or observing their thinking as they partner-talked. As suggested by Lapp, Flood, and Goss (2000) and Lapp, Flood, and Moore

(2008), it is during such guided practice that teachers provide individuals or small groups of students the additional cognitive supports they need to maintain their comprehension. This can happen as the teacher asks questions that cause the reader to draw on the needed background knowledge, offers clues that direct or redirect their attention to needed information, or probe them in ways that push their understanding of the new information while supporting their metacognitive growth about how they can independently derive text meaning when the teacher isn't with them.

Collaborative Work: Using New Language and Ideas to Complete a Related Task

Now it was time for the students to use the language and domain knowledge that Ms. Morris shared as they collaborated on related tasks. After modeling how a character changed over time, students, in pairs or small groups, were asked to select a text from the classroom collection of audiobooks or podcasts. They could also visit websites such as *pbskids.org/clifford/index-brd-flash.html* or *pbskids.org/arthur/games/groovygarden/groovygarden.html*. Ms. Morris asked them to put Post-it notes beside words and graphics that helped them get to "know" the selected character over time. She also showed them how, when finished, they could make a Foldable by folding a paper into three sections. In each section she modeled how to use their Post-it notes to draw a picture and/or add descriptive words that illustrated how the character in the book they had chosen had changed over time. She explained that each section should help a future reader know something more about how the character changes. She explained if they were reading *Curious George Rides His Bike* they could show, in one third of the paper, George doing tricks on his bike and then add the word *clever* as a caption. In the next third they could show George delivering papers and add the word *helpful*. The last third could show an additional example of George's curiosity. She explained that, when finished, they would be able to add a final sentence summarizing the illustrations and words. From this *Curious George* text Ms. Morris supported students in concluding that the author had given the reader many examples about George's curiosity: "The author showed me, through the expressions he drew on the characters' faces, that everyone likes George because he is so interested and helpful. What else might we conclude?"

Malik quickly responded, "Everybody likes George cuz he's so curious."

"Yes," said Ashley, "I love curious George."

Ms. Morris said, "Let's write that as a caption that summarizes the book."

As partners collaborated further on their character graphics, captions, and Foldables, Ms. Morris again circulated among them, helping if she saw that they were not able to draw conclusions from the visuals they were creating. As they worked she had another opportunity to work with individuals or groups she felt still needed additional scaffolding of the target information. Once finished, partners or groups were invited to share with another team.

Believing that they had now understood how authors and illustrators use words and graphics to show how a character develops over time, it was time to engage them in tasks that would highlight their independence.

Throughout the guided practice and collaborative work Ms. Morris recursively modeled, assessed, and scaffolded instruction as needed. Prior to assigning these collaborative tasks, she had modeled the concepts and procedures the students needed to succeed. For example in this task, Ms. Morris had previously modeled how to select and use new literacies resources, how to make decisions about changing character personality, how to apply Post-it notes, and create a Foldable. She did so because she believes, as do we, that students should not be held accountable for information that has not been taught.

Independent Work: Owning and Transferring the Newly Acquired Information to Novel Tasks

Now that students had watched and learned as Ms. Morris modeled her thinking, gained more knowledge about character analysis through guided practice, and talked collaboratively about how characters change from the beginning of a text to the end, they were ready to use this knowledge to create a character and show how he had changed over time. Students were invited to create a fictional character, use a personal experience about themselves or someone they knew, or self-select a text written at their independent reading level to create their own Foldable about the main character and how he/she changed from the beginning to the end of the story. Ms. Morris reminded them of a previously shared Foldable that would work well as a three-section flip book where they could draw pictures and/or add words, sentences, and a summary statement. Their performance would, of course, depend on their proficiency level.

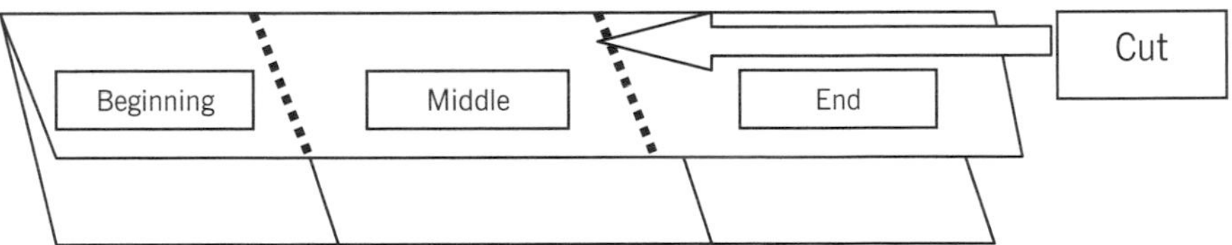

The remixing that occurred in this lesson was illustrated through the interplay of intentional instruction designed to create purposeful learning by utilizing varied text formats and performative tasks. As a result, students created a response that utilized their graphic and written languages. Their new texts, which were an "assemblage of signs" (Chandler, 2002, p. 2), "constructed (and interpreted) with reference to the conventions associated with a genre, and in a particular medium of communication" (p. 3), and shared through their newly designed medium, allowed their teacher to assess if the instructional intent/purpose had been achieved by each.

THINKING ABOUT NEW LITERACIES IN TODAY'S CLASSROOM

Circling back to the basal reader discussed at the beginning of the chapter, we hope these examples have provided firmer ground to stand on when thinking about new literacies in the classroom. New literacies account for the role of written words with visuals. New literacies think about how young, middle, and teenage students compose and read texts onscreen. New literacies incorporate social participation in digital environments as a part of the literacy process. New literacies assess beyond a decoding and encoding of written words by interpreting how students use other modalities of expression and representation in their compositions. New literacies are easily remixed with intentional instruction.

Built on an acknowledgement that literacy takes place everywhere and that the screen increasingly presides over what, how, and when we make meaning with print and other modalities, new literacies scholars and teachers broaden literacy in their classroom to speak to the sophisticated and tech-savvy funds of knowledge (Moll, Amanti, Neff, & Gonzalez, 1992) that our students bring to the classroom. By looking at the theoretical roots of new literacies, we have illustrated how we arrived at new literacies as a promising approach to 21st-century literacy. A central argument in the chapter has been that new literacies scholars, teachers, even learners are redefining what literacy is today and these perspectives hold promise for new literacy pedagogy and policy for the 21st century.

ENGAGEMENT ACTIVITIES

1. Using the lesson examples shared in this chapter, please design a lesson with a specific instructional intent. Next, create a few lines of dialogue to illustrate how you will model target information through a think-aloud. Be sure to check yourself to see that you include statements such as *I think . . . because . . .* This will allow your students to see how an expert thinks and also what causes the student to think in this way.
2. Continuing with the same lesson, design guided, collaborative, and independent tasks that involve students gaining, creating, and sharing information through the use of new literacies. Include a description of why each was selected. Be sure to check yourself to ensure that you provided instruction that supported your students understanding of how to use these. Remember to assess and recursively model as needed.
3. Review the lesson example of Andy. Now use the information shared throughout the chapter regarding new literacies to

explain to a friend why Andy's teacher believed in remixing. Share your thinking through a conversation between Andy's teacher and your friend. Use graffiti to create characters.

REFERENCES

Alvermann, D. E., Moon, J. S., & Hagood, M. C. (1999). *Popular culture in the classroom: Teaching and researching critical media literacy.* Newark, DE: International Reading Association and the National Reading Conference.

Bakhtin, M. M. (1981). *The dialogic imagination: Four essays* (M. Holquist, Ed.; C. Emerson & M. Holquist, Trans.). Austin: University of Texas Press.

Barton, D. (1994). *Literacy: An introduction to the ecology of written language.* Oxford, UK: Wiley-Blackwell.

Chandler, D. (2002). *Semiotics: The basics.* London: Routledge.

Coiro, J., Knobel, M., Lankshear, C., & Leu, D. (2008). *Handbook of research in new literacies.* Mahwah, NJ: Erlbaum.

Comber, B., Nixon, H., & Reid, J. (Eds.). (2007). *Literacies in place: Teaching environmental communication.* Newtown, South Australia: Primary English Teaching Association.

Compton-Lilly, C. (2007). *Rereading families: The literate lives of urban children, the intermediate years.* New York: Teachers College Press.

Cope, B., & Kalantzis, M. (2000). *Multiliteracies: Literacy learning and the design of social futures.* London: Routledge.

Davies, J. (2006). Escaping to the borderlands: An exploration of the internet as a cultural space for teenage wiccan girls. In K. Pahl & J. Roswell (Eds.), *Travel Notes from the New Literacy Studies: Instances of Practice* (pp. 57–72). Clevedon, UK: Multilingual Matters.

Davies, J., & Merchant, G. (2008). *Web 2.0 for schools: Learning and social participation.* New York: Lang.

Dyson, A. H. (2003). *The brothers and sisters learn to write.* New York: Teachers College Press.

Fisher, D., & Frey, N. (2008). *Better learning through structured teaching: A framework for the gradual release of responsibility.* Alexandria VA: Association for Supervision and Curriculum Development

Frey, N., Fisher, D., & Gonzalez, A. (2010). *Literacy 2.0: Reading and writing in 21st-century classrooms.* Bloomington, IN: Solution Tree.

Gainer, J., & Lapp, D. (2010). *Literacy remix: Bridging adolescents' in and out of school literacies.* Newark, DE: International Reading Association.

Gile, J. (Author), & Fiorello, F. (Illustrator). (1995). *Oh, how I wished I could read?* New York: John Gile Communications.

Guzzetti, B., & Gamboa, M. J. (2004). Zines for social justice: Adolescent girls writing on their own. *Reading Research Quarterly, 32*(4), 406–436.

Halliday, M. K. (1984). *The semiotics of culture and language.* London: Pinter.

Heath, S. B. (1983). *Ways with words: Language, life and work in communities and classrooms.* Cambridge, UK: Cambridge University Press.

Hicks, D. (2002). *Reading lives: Working-class children and literacy learning.* New York: Teachers College Press.

Innis, R. (Ed.). (1985). *Semiotics: An introductory anthology.* Bloomington: Indiana University Press.

Jewitt, C., & Kress, K. (2004). *Multimodal literacy.* London: Lang.

Knobel, M., & Lankshear, C. (2006). Weblog worlds and constructions of effective and powerful writing: Cross with care, and only where signs permit. In K. Pahl & J. Rowsell (Eds.), *Travel notes from the new literacy studies* (pp. 72–95). Clevedon, UK: Multilingual Matters.

Kress, G. (1997). *Before writing: Rethinking the paths to literacy.* London: Routledge.

Kress, G. (2003). *Literacy in the new media age.* London: Routledge.

Kress, G., & Van Leeuwen, T. (1996). *Reading images: The grammar of visual design.* London: Routledge.

Kress, G., & Van Leeuwen, T. (2001). *Multimodel discourse: The modes and media of contemporary communication.* New York: Arnold.

Lankshear, C., & Knobel, M. (2003). *New literacies: Changing knowledge and classroom learning.* Berkshire, UK: Open University Press.

Lapp, D., Flood, J., & Goss, K. (2000). Desks don't move—students do: In effective classroom environments. *The Reading Teacher, 54*(1), 31–36.

Lapp, D., Flood, J., & Moore, K. (2008). Differentiating visual, communicative, and performance arts instruction in well-managed classrooms. In J. Flood, S. B. Heath, & D. Lapp (Eds.), *Handbook of research on teaching literacy through the communicative and visual arts* (Vol. 2, pp. 537–544). Mahwah, NJ: Erlbaum.

Lessig, L. (2008). *Remix: Making art and commerce thrive in the hybrid economy.* New York: Penguin.

Luke, A. (2000). Critical literacy in Australia: A matter of context and standpoint. *Journal of Adolescent and Adult Literacy, 43,* 448–457.

Mahiri, J. (2004). *What they don't learn in school: Literacy in the lives of urban youth.* New York: Lang.

Moje, E. B., & Thompson, A. (1996, March). *Sociocultural practices and learning to write in school: Exploring the communicative and transformative potential of gang literacies.* Paper presented at the Conference for Sociocultural Research, Geneva, Switzerland.

Moll, L. (2000). Inspired by Vygotsky: Ethnographic experiments in education. In C. Lee & P. Smagorinsky (Eds.), *Vygotskian perspectives on literacy research: Constructing meaning through collaborative inquiry* (pp. 256–268). Cambridge, UK: Cambridge University Press.

Moll, L., Amanti, C., Neff, D., & Gonzalez, N. (1992). Funds of knowledge for teaching: Using a qualitative approach to connect homes and classrooms. *Theory into Practice, 31,* 132–141.

Mora, P. (Author), & Colon, R. (Illustrator). (2005). *Doña Flor.* New York: Knopf Books for Young Readers.

Moss, B., & Lapp, D. (Eds.). (2010a). *Teaching new literacies in grades K–3.* New York: Guilford Press.

Moss, B., & Lapp, D. (Eds.). (2010b). *Teaching new literacies in grades 4–6.* New York: Guilford Press.

National Reading Panel. (2000). *Teaching children to read: An evidence-based assessment of the scientific research literature on reading and its implications for reading instruction.* Washington, DC: National Institute of Child Health and Human Development.

Pahl, K., & Rowsell, J. (2005). *Literacy and education: The new literacy studies in the classroom.* London: Chapman.

Pahl, K., & Rowsell, J. (Eds.). (2006). *Travel notes from the new literacy studies: Instances of practice.* Clevedon, UK: Multilingual Matters.

Pahl, K., & Rowsell, J. (2010). *Artifactual literacies: Every object tells a story.* New York: Teachers College Press.

Pearson, P. D., & Gallagher, M. (1983). The instruction of reading comprehension. *Contemporary Educational Psychology, 8,* 317–344.

Rey, M., & Rey, H. A. (1993). *Curious George.* New York: Houghton Mifflin.

Robinson, E., & Robinson, S. (2003). *What does it mean? Discourse, text, culture: An introduction.* Sydney, Australia: McGraw-Hill.

Rogers, R. (2004). Storied selves: A critical analysis of adult learners' literate lives. *Reading Research Quarterly, 39*(3), 272–305.

Rose, T. (1994). *Black noise: Rap music and black culture in contemporary America.* Middleton, CT: Wesleyan University Press.

Ryan, P. M. (Author), & Cepeda, J. (Illustrator). (2005). *Mice and beans.* New York: Scholastic.

Rylant, C. (Author), & Kelly-Young, B. (Illustrator). (2004). *The relatives came.* New York: Scholastic.

Scribner, S., & Cole, M. (1981). *The psychology of literacy.* Cambridge, MA: Harvard University Press.

Sheridan, M. P., & Rowsell, J. (2010). *Design literacies: Learning and innovation in the digital age.* London: Routledge.

Street, B. V. (1984). *Literacy in theory and practice.* Cambridge, UK: Cambridge University Press.

Vygotsky, L. S. (1962). *Thought and language.* Cambridge, UK: MIT Press.

Vygotsky, L. S. (1978). *Mind in society: The development of higher psychological processes.* Cambridge, MA: Harvard University Press.

Zimmerman, S., & Hutchins, C. (2003). *Seven keys to comprehension: How to help your kids read it and get it!* New York: Three Rivers Press.

CHAPTER 17

Organizing Effective Literacy Instruction

Differentiating Instruction to Meet Student Needs

D. Ray Reutzel

This chapter will:

- Provide a theoretical and research overview of differentiated literacy instruction.
- Present the essential elements of differentiated literacy instruction.
- Discuss the use of assessment data to inform differentiated literacy instruction.
- Describe the use of different effective literacy instructional practices.
- Offer alternative grouping approaches as a part of differentiated literacy instruction.
- Illustrate the scheduling of the literacy instructional block to support differentiated literacy instruction.

EVIDENCE-BASED BEST PRACTICES: DIFFERENTIATING LITERACY INSTRUCTION

Because teachers' experiences and expertise in managing the complexity of classrooms vary greatly, and because students' needs are equally complex and challenging in today's increasingly diverse classroom environments, the question of how to differentiate instruction is of critical importance for all teachers, novice and experienced alike (Gregory & Chapman, 2006). When teachers determine to differentiate literacy instruction, they consciously or unconsciously add to the complexity of managing the classroom environment while at the same time providing necessary accommodations to meet diverse student needs. The tension between a teacher deciding to increase management complexity and meeting the needs of a diverse student population is a tenuous balancing act (Tomlinson, Brimijoin, & Narvaez, 2008).

For example, let us assume that a teacher has chosen to use whole-class literacy instruction to reduce the complexity of classroom management. The potential moral consequences of such a choice may be that individual student needs are not met or, worse yet, that some children, perhaps the most at risk, may be denied access to literacy knowledge, instruction, and an opportunity to learn (Goodlad & Oakes, 1988; Oakes, 1986, 1988; Walpole & McKenna, 2007). Thus a teacher's decision to use a particular literacy grouping strategy in order to reduce classroom management problems must be made with full appreciation of the potential social, instructional, psychological, and moral outcomes of such a choice on children, not based solely on reducing management complexity. On the other hand, an overtaxed, stressed-out teacher with too many small-group or individual literacy learning activities may not be as emotionally available to sensitively respond to the diverse instructional needs of all children. A workable model for many teachers begins with a simple, limited, and manageable small-group instructional plan. A simple small-group instructional model may then be gradually expanded toward increasing complexity and making use of a wider range of instructional differentiation strategies (including intensive, extensive student progress monitoring assessments and teacher-guided instruction to meet individual differences such as those found currently in response-to-intervention [RTI] models). Doing so provides motivating and engaging classroom instructional environments that are characterized by a clear, bounded, and explicit organizational framework that allocates space efficiently with understood and well-trained rules, directions, schedules, and familiar routines; that fosters social collaboration and interaction; that provides access to coherent knowledge domains and structures; that supports individual literacy learners' development; and that encourages children to become self-regulated and independent literacy learners (Gregory & Chapman, 2006; Morrow, Reutzel, & Casey, 2006; Raphael et al., 2003; Reutzel & Jones, 2010; Tomlinson et al., 2008; Tyner, 2009).

Differentiating literacy instruction implies at least two moral imperatives. First, teachers need to recognize that the process of becoming literate follows a developmental path from the simple to the complex, from the concrete to the symbolic, from the unconventional to the conventional, from the cradle to the grave. Second, the tendency of some schools is to create a "one size fits all" curriculum, which when fully implemented will not meet the needs of all children (Raphael et al., 2003; Tyner, 2009). In order to reach all of the children, teachers must be willing to provide instruction that responds to the needs of each child based on assessment results. To meet the diverse needs of all children, teachers need to know how to effectively assess student learning and implement a variety of effective instructional interventions and management techniques (Tomlinson & McTighe, 2006). In this chapter, primarily because of space constraints, I discuss only a few important ways in which teachers can meet the needs of all children in becoming readers and writers, including (1) providing the essentials of literacy instruction, (2) using assessment data to inform literacy instruction and the use of RTI models, (3) using an array of effective literacy instructional practices, (4) properly grouping participants for differentiated literacy instruction, and (5) scheduling time effectively to support differentiated literacy instruction.

Providing the Essentials of Literacy Instruction

Although attention to the activities, techniques, methods, or the *how* of teaching literacy has shown moderate effects on young children's early literacy learning, teaching the essential elements of reading and writing are of even greater significance (Mathes et al., 2005; Rathvon, 2004; National Early Literacy Panel, 2008). Children, depending on their level of literacy development, need daily, sustained, and high-quality literacy instruction in the following essential elements of literacy instruction: (1) oral language, (2) concepts about print, (3) phonological and phonemic awareness, (4) alphabetic principle to include letter names and sounds and phonics, (5) fluency, (6) vocabulary, (7) comprehension strategies, and (8) writing and spelling to make satisfactory progress in early literacy development. Current research also strongly suggests that these essential elements of reading and writing need to be taught *explicitly*, meaning that teachers need to directly explain, model, and scaffold students' acquisition of these critical components of early literacy (National Early Literacy Panel, 2008; Piasta & Wagner, 2010).

Using Assessment Data to Inform Instruction

"Assessment drives instruction!" is a common, often cynical, saying in educational circles. Although this saying may be true at some level, its implicit message is also highly exaggerated in the best sense of the phrase. For the most part, the role current high-stakes assessment has played in instruction is to lead to reductionist instruction—teachers engaging in instruction that mimics the content and format of the assessment used in a school or state—or, worse yet, engaging in simplistic gimmicks such as giving children food during testing, providing test-prep courses, or offering rewards for high test performance. Thus, as portrayed in this case, assessment is driving instruction in the worst rather than the best sense of the phrase. Conversely, in the recent past it has been rare to observe teachers consistently gathering assessment data for the purpose of monitoring students' progress and then actually using these data to inform the selection of instructional approaches, strategies, interventions, or content. So in the best sense of the phrase where assessment informs instruction, *assessment hasn't been driving instruction!*

It seems that the relationship between assessment and instruction has always been tenuous. In the past, assessment was viewed by many educators as an intrusion into the curriculum and instruction of the classroom rather than as an integral part of selecting and designing instructional interventions. Assessment was viewed much like the common cold; it was something to get over and then go on with normal classroom life. In today's educational context, such a practice is no longer acceptable. Using assessment data is at the very heart of differentiating instruction to meet the diverse literacy learning needs of all students in the classroom and for monitoring students' responses to the instruction provided—often called *response to intervention* (RTI) (Brown-Chidsey & Steege, 2005; Fuchs, Fuchs, & Vaughn, 2008; Haager, Klingner, & Vaughn, 2007; Lipson & Wixson, 2010; Reutzel & Cooter, 2011).

In an RTI teaching and learning environment, assessment in today's classrooms is used for four assessment purposes: (1) screening, (2) diagnostic, (3) progress-monitoring, and (4) outcomes. *Screening assessments* are given to all students to determine whether there are preexisting concerns about each student's literacy development prior to offering instruction. If children perform well on literacy screening assessments, these students are likely to be well served by providing a high-quality classroom core literacy program referred to as *Tier 1* intervention.

On the other hand, if students perform poorly on literacy screening assessments, then this signals the need for additional *diagnostic assessment* to pinpoint the source of the problem so that targeted interventions to address the problem can be designed. *Tier 2* instructional interventions are determined by using the results of screening and diagnostic assessments and are often provided to students in small-group settings within the regular education classroom. In some cases, after or in conjunction with Tier 2 literacy interventions, students are found to be in need of additional special services through the use of progress monitoring assessments. When such is the case, students are referred to *Title I, special education,* or *Tier 3* interventions, to address literacy learning problems. As Tier 1, 2, or 3 interventions are used with students, teachers continuously track their literacy development using *progress monitoring assessments.* Progress monitoring literacy assessments are typically quick, reliable, valid assessments that are administered at frequent intervals. One example of a widely used progress monitoring assessment is DIBELS (Dynamic Indicators of Basic Early Literacy Skills), a set of subtests used to determine the effectiveness of the literacy instruction (Good & Kaminski, 2002; Goodman, 2006). If progress monitoring assessment shows acceptable student literacy growth from a specifically selected and implemented literacy instructional intervention, then one can reasonably conclude that this intervention can continue to be used to effectively boost student progress. If progress monitoring assessment demonstrates little or no student progress, then the literacy instructional intervention employed isn't having the desired effect, and another or additional intervention may be needed to promote students' literacy progress. This cycle of student progress monitoring assessment and refinement of instruction is at the heart of today's RTI approaches. After a prolonged period of instruction has taken place, such as an academic or school year, state and federal laws require that *outcomes assessments* be used to determine the overall effectiveness of school literacy instruction and programs used in schools as compared with other students' literacy achievement nationally or against an established standard at the state or local level.

As a result, assessment in today's classrooms has taken on four different purposes to inform teachers' decisions about which instructional interventions to use with whom, when, and where for teaching specific components of the literacy process. In schools where I routinely work, classroom teachers and literacy coaches use a student assessment data board like the one shown in the photo (see below) during team meetings. Students who fall behind or who achieve below the local, state, or national standards for growth and achievement are individually discussed, and educators make specific plans to help these students make improved literacy progress.

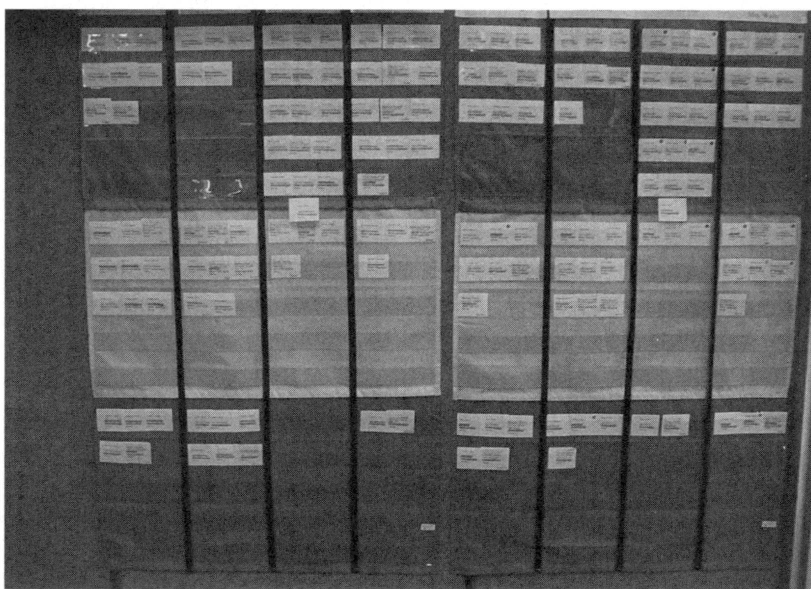

When used to inform instructional decision making, assessment influences classroom teachers' instructional choices and, in the very best sense of the phrase, *assessment drives instruction!*

BEST PRACTICES IN ACTION

Research findings have helped most teachers understand that although some children will learn to read and write from almost any kind or quality of instruction, other students will not learn to read or write well without instruction that is sequenced, systematic, intentional, teacher directed, and explicit (Chall, 2000; Delpit, 1988; Duffy, 2004; National Reading Panel, 2000). Explicit instruction is difficult for most teachers to accomplish, because, as Duffy (2004) points out, "It is often difficult for us to provide explicit explanations for how to read. To do so, we must become aware ourselves of the processes we use as we read. However, because we are expert readers we no longer think about the processes we use to read" (p. 10). As previously noted in this chapter, explicit instruction is composed of three interlocking iterative phases: (1) explanations, (2) modeling, and (3) scaffolding.

What do we do when we *explain* reading or writing concepts, skills, or strategies to children? First, we immerse students in reading or writing! Literacy concepts, skills, or strategies that are learned and practiced in isolation seldom transfer to the act of reading or writing (Taylor, 2008; Taylor, Pearson, Clark, & Walpole, 1999). Second, within a text-based or text-production environment, we explain to students which reading or writing concept, skill, or strategy they are to learn, when or where it will be used in reading or writing, and why learning it is important for becoming a successful reader or writer.

Next, we model for children the application of the literacy concept, skill, or strategy to be taught. To model a literacy concept, skill, or strategy, we must show children how it is to be done, using lots of talking out loud about our thinking as teachers (Oczkus, 2009). Just for a moment, think of a magic show by the renowned magician David Copperfield. You observe his trick of making the Statue of Liberty disappear from New York Harbor and wonder to yourself, "How does he do that?" Well, this is not dissimilar to what the struggling reader or writer is thinking when he or she observes other children reading and writing with ease. Struggling readers and writers just don't know the processes or steps behind the trick of reading and writing. Now imagine you were allowed a backstage pass to have David Copperfield show you step by step how he performed the trick of making the Statue of Liberty disappear. You would then exclaim, "Oh, so *that's* how you do it!" Modeling "thinking by talking out loud about our thinking as teachers" helps students get a grip, as it were, on how to do the thinking in reading or writing that is necessary to acquire and apply a literacy concept, strategy, or skill (Duffy, 2004). In other words, talking aloud about our mental processes when reading or writing helps to make the steps or processes of the reading and writing "magic trick" obvious to students who do not easily or intuitively grasp these processes through normal exposure to reading and writing.

Finally, how does one scaffold or support a student to apply a literacy concept, skill, or strategy independently, effectively, and strategically? At first we provide a great deal of support to help students begin to take ownership of the mental processes used to apply a literacy concept, skill, or strategy. Over time, we reduce the amount of assistance we provide to students as they gradually take ownership for applying reading and writing processes and become increasingly independent, self-regulated readers and writers. Pearson and Gallagher (1983) visually depict in Figure 17.1 this gradual fading of teacher support during the release of a reading or writing concept, strategy, or skill from the teacher to the students' independent and self-regulated application.

Other effective literacy instructional practices in the successful literacy teacher's repertoire include interactive read-aloud, shared reading, small-group differentiated or guided reading, paired or buddy reading, and wide and repeated reading opportunities, modeled writing, interactive writing, and establishing an effective daily opportunity for students to write. Because the constraints of this single chapter do allow sufficient space to discuss each of these instructional practices in detail, we provide the following partial list of resources for learning more about each:

- Interactive read-aloud—Opitz, M. F, & Rasinski, T. V. (2008). *Good-bye round robin: 25 effective oral reading strategies.* Portsmouth, NH: Heinemann.
- Interactive read-aloud—Hickman, P., & Pollard-Durodola, S. D.

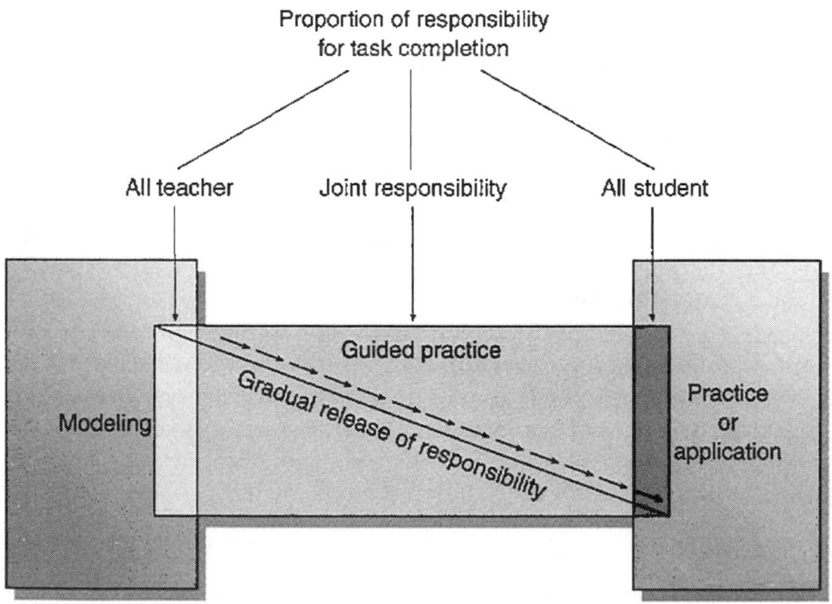

FIGURE 17.1. The gradual release of responsibility model of instruction. From Reutzel and Cooter (2000). Copyright 2000 by Prentice Hall. Reprinted by permission.

(2009). *Dynamic read-aloud strategies for English learners.* Newark, DE: International Reading Association.

- Shared reading—Payne, C. D. (2005). *Shared reading for today's classroom: Lessons and strategies for explicit instruction in comprehension, fluency, word study, and genre.* New York: Scholastic.
- Small-group differentiated reading—Tyner, B. (2009). *Small-group reading instruction: A differentiated teaching model for beginning and struggling readers* (2nd ed.). Newark, DE: International Reading Association.
- Paired reading—Prescott-Griffin, M. L. (2005). *Reader to reader: Building independence through peer partnerships.* Portsmouth, NH: Heinemann.
- Independent reading—Hiebert, E. H., & Reutzel, D. R. (2010). *Revisiting silent reading: New directions for teachers and researchers.* Newark, DE: International Reading Association.
- Modeled and interactive writing—McCarrier, A., Pinnell, G. S., & Fountas, I. C. (2000). *Interactive writing: How language and literacy come together, K–2.* Portsmouth, NH: Heinemann.
- Writers workshop—Widmer, K., & Buxton, S. (2004). *Workshops that work!* New York: Scholastic.

Differentiated Literacy Instruction

Organizing classrooms into smaller groups of children fills the moral imperative often felt by teachers to meet diverse individual student needs (Gregory & Chapman, 2006; Morrow et al., 2005; Tomlinson, 1999, 2003; Tomlinson, Brimijoin, & Naravez, 2008; Tomlinson & Eidson, 2003; Tyner, 2004). However, somewhere between meeting diverse individual needs and managing a full classroom lies an expansive chasm to be bridged, at least in part, by the use of various small-grouping strategies. Individualized instruction, although the ideal, is also for the most part impractical (Pearson, 1985). At the other extreme, the exclusive use of whole-class instruction fails to address individual needs, skills, or performance. It is through using a blend of whole-class, small-group, and individual grouping strategies that teachers can begin to effectively address students' needs, skills, and motivations in becoming readers and writers (Morrow, 2010). In the next section, I discuss a variety of small-group instructional arrangements that provide classroom teachers workable and effective options in addition to whole-class and homogeneous groups.

Response to Intervention: Dynamic Grouping for Differentiated Literacy Instruction

Response-to-intervention (RTI) groups are determined by using progress monitoring data teachers collect at regular intervals (Lipson & Wixson, 2010; Reutzel & Cooter, 2011). Through the use of progress monitoring assessment strategies like running records, anecdotal records, group participation records, and 1-minute fluency samples, teachers determine individual student learning needs. Assessment data groups are formed when progress monitoring data indicate several children share similar learning needs, whether these needs be skill, content, or strategy based. Typically, an assessment data group will include as few as two students or as many as half the class. The purpose of an assessment data group is to teach a temporary group of students a particular literacy skill, concept, or strategy they have yet to learn and apply. The vehicle for instruction within assessment data groups is an explicit concept, skill, or strategy lesson, as previously described in this chapter.

Small-group differentiated literacy instruction, based on an RTI model, is an essential part of an effective literacy program (Fuchs et al., 2008; Lipson & Wixson, 2010; Tyner, 2009). Children are typically placed in differentiated literacy instruction only after they have had ample opportunities as a class group to listen to stories, poems, songs, and so on, and to participate in shared or community-based whole-class literacy experiences. Thus, after teachers have accomplished initial screening assessment of students, built a sense of community, and observed children carefully during the first 4–6 weeks of each new school year, then small- group differentiated literacy instruction can begin in earnest.

Children in differentiated *reading* instructional groups are placed together based on their assessed word-study and text-reading levels. This means that teachers have assessed each child's instructional reading levels in connected texts as well as each child's ability to recognize, decode, and write words. In practice, small-group differentiated reading instruction plays out in a five-part lesson structure: (1) *rereading*—repeated reading of a familiar book or selection; (2) *word bank*—sight word and vocabulary word work; (3) *word study*—spelling and decoding work; (4) *writing*—including interactive and dictation writing; and (5) *new read*—applying previously instructed concepts, skills, and strategies in an unfamiliar book.

At first, dynamic grouping for differentiated reading instruction looks somewhat similar to ability or achievement grouping practices used in decades past. Dynamic grouping for differentiated reading instruction is begun by placing children into small, homogeneous groups. The most important consideration in creating dynamic differentiated reading instructional groups centers on each child's ability to successfully handle and process word decoding and recognition tasks as well as reading within leveled books (Tyner, 2009). Dynamic differentiated reading instruction groups are composed of five to eight children who work together for a finite period of time under the guidance and with the feedback of the teacher. Unlike the static ability groups of yesteryear, dynamic differentiated reading instructional groups change as children make progress during the year, usually changing by months rather than by weeks or days.

Prior to beginning small-group differentiated reading instruction, great care is taken to match children to a book at their instructional level, meaning that children can enjoy and control the reading of the book on their first reading. Instructional-level texts should present children with a reasonable challenge but also with a high degree of success. Typically, children should be able to read 90–95% of the words correctly in an instructional-level book chosen for use in a differentiated reading instruction group. During small-group differentiated reading instruction, teachers teach short lessons and ask students to engage in various word recognition, decoding, spelling, and writing tasks using the five-step cycle previously described.

As teachers work with children in differentiated reading instruction groups, they lead them to understand and strategically use effective reading and writing strategies. Differentiated reading instructional groups also provide a context for systematic skill instruction related specifically to the essential components of reading and writing as well as practicing the application of strategies and skills within the context of reading a leveled book. Small-group differentiated reading instruction is a time to focus instruction directly on student reading skill and strategy development rather than focusing on appreciating and discussing high-quality literature. In fact, the use of leveled books in differentiated reading instruction does not always allow for the use of recognized literature of enduring quality, but rather necessitates using books that are written specifically to support individual readers in their development and use of self-extending and self-regulated reading and writing strategies. When reading leveled texts, whether new to or previously read by the children, teachers use questions, prompts, and comments to help children effectively apply decoding and comprehension strategies they have previously learned in whole-class settings or in their differentiated reading instruction group.

Literature Circles

In literature circles, teachers and children use trade books or literature books, both narrative and expository, as the core for reading instruction. To form literature circles, the teacher has children look through several selected titles of trade books available for small-group instruction. This will mean that multiple copies of each book or title will be needed! It is recommended that teachers purchase about eight copies of each book rather than purchasing classroom sets. Opitz (1998) recommends that books on a common topic or theme called "text sets" be used in literature study groups. At the conclusion of this exploration period, the teacher reads available book titles aloud and asks how many students would like to read each book. In this way teachers can get a quick idea of which available books seem to interest the students most and which engender no interest. The teacher selects from the high-interest trade books three to four titles, depending on how many literature circles he or she can reasonably manage and how many copies of each book are available. Next, the teacher works up a "book talk" on each of the selected books to present to the students the following day. A book talk is a short, interesting introduction to the topic, setting, and problem of a book. After presenting a book talk on each of the books selected, the teacher asks older children to write down the titles of their first two choices. The teacher asks the younger children to come to the chalkboard and sign their names under the photocopied covers of the two books they like best of those presented. Only one literature circle meets each day with the teacher to discuss and respond to a chapter or predetermined number of pages to have been read in a trade book. It is best if the teacher meets with each literature circle after children have indicated their choices to determine how many weeks will be spent reading the book and how many pages per day need to be read to reach that goal. The remaining steps for organizing literature circles are summarized in the following list:

1. Select three or four books children may be interested in reading from the brief interest inventory of literature available in the school or classroom, as described.
2. Introduce each of the books by giving a book talk on each.
3. Invite children to write down the titles of their two top choices.
4. Depending on the number of multiple copies of trade books available, fill each group with those children who have indicated the book as their first choice. Once a group is filled, move the remaining children to their second choice until all children have been invited to attend the group of their first or second choice.
5. Decide how many days or weeks will be spent reading this series of book choices.
6. Meet with each of the literature circles and determine the following:
   a. How many pages per day will need to be read to complete the book in the time allowed.
   b. When the first group meeting will be held. (The teacher meets with only one group per day.)
   c. How children will respond to their reading. This may involve a reading response log, character report cards, or wanted posters.
7. Help children understand when the first or next meeting of their literature circle will be, how many pages in the book will need to be read, and which type of response to the reading—such as group retellings, wanted posters, or a story map—will need to be completed before the meeting of the literature circle.
8. Near the completion of the book, the group may discuss possible extensions of the book to drama, music, art, and other projects.

Peterson and Eeds (1990), in their book *Grand Conversations*, suggest a checklist that teachers may use to track student preparation for and participation in literature circles. I have modified this form to be used with literature circles, as shown in Figure 17.2.

When the literature circle book has been completed, literature circles are disbanded and new groups are formed for selecting and reading a new

Name ______________________ Date ______________

Author ______________________ Title ______________

Preparation for Literature Study

• Brought book to the literature circle.	Yes ___	No ___
• Contributed to developing group reading goals.	Yes ___	No ___
• Completed work according to group goals.	Yes ___	No ___
• Read the assigned pages, chapters, etc., for the goals.	Yes ___	No ___
• Noted places to share (ones of interest, ones that were puzzling, etc.)	Yes ___	No ___
• Completed group response assignments before coming to the day's discussion.	Yes ___	No ___

Participation in the Literature Circle Discussion

• Participated in the discussion.	Weak ___	Good ___	Excellent ___
• Gave quality of verbal responses and contributions.	Weak ___	Good ___	Excellent ___
• Used text to support ideas and assertions.	Weak ___	Good ___	Excellent ___
• Listened to others.	Weak ___	Good ___	Excellent ___

FIGURE 17.2. Record of goal completion and participation in literature circles. Adapted from Peterson and Eeds (1990). Copyright 1990 by Scholastic Canada. Adapted by permission.

series of books. Thus students' interests are engaged by encouraging choice (Raphael et al., 2003), and the problem of static ability grouping plans can be avoided.

Concept-Oriented Reading Instruction: Learning from Information Books

Guthrie et al. (1996) researched a teaching framework called concept-oriented reading instruction (CORI), designed to improve students' learning in science. CORI is easily applied to reading informational books in other content areas. CORI helps students become deeply engaged in learning academic content from informational books (Swan, 2003; Swan, Coddington, & Guthrie, 2010). CORI helps students crystallize and connect new knowledge to what is already known and shows them how to demonstrate their learning to others in some very engaging and interesting ways. The explicit-instruction components of CORI have been shown to be effective with low-achieving students in elementary grades 3 and 5 (Guthrie et al., 1996; Swafford & Bryan, 2000). CORI provides a sound basic platform for teaching and learning in the concept areas that can be modified to suit the teacher's instructional goals.

The CORI instructional framework includes the following: real-world observations, conceptual themes, self-directed learning, explicit instruction on strategies, peer collaboration, and self-expression of learning. The four parts of this instructional model are described next.

- *Part I: Observe and Personalize.* Students are led through hands-on experiences designed to activate their prior knowledge relevant to a new topic and to motivate them to want to know more. After the hands-on experiences, the teacher leads students through a discussion about what they observed and helps them to generate questions for further study.
- *Part II: Search and Retrieve.* In this stage, the teacher demonstrates several search strategies for finding answers to the questions students generated earlier. For each search strategy, the teacher provides a clear description of what it is, models using the strategy with teacher think-alouds, and guides several practice sessions including collaborative group work. Other strategies to be learned include goal setting (what they want to learn), categorizing (learning how information is organized and presented in books and learning how to find information in the library or on the Internet), extracting (taking notes, summarizing, and paraphrasing information), and abstracting (forming generalizations).
- *Part III: Comprehend and Integrate.* Teacher modeling and student discussions focus on the following reading comprehension strategies: comprehension monitoring (metacognition), developing images or graphics, rereading to clarify, and modifying reading rate to match purpose and varying text types. Identification of central ideas and supporting details is also a priority in this phase of CORI. Guthrie et al. (1996) recommend the use of *idea circles* (student-led small-group discussions) and group self-monitoring as ways to transfer learning responsibility to students, leading to more productive discussions. This is especially useful when they discover information that is conflicting or when it contradicts their earlier hypotheses.
- *Part IV: Communication.* The communication phase of CORI focuses on students disseminating to others what they have learned from their study of information texts about a particular topic. They can communicate their new understandings through debates, discussions, or written reports. Some students prefer more creative expressions such as PowerPoint presentations, poetry, dramas, raps, songs, or graphic illustrations.

As with the other phases of CORI, teacher support and modeling are critical in helping students develop effective communication skills to present their new knowledge and strengthen their social development (Swafford & Bryan, 2000). The elements of CORI are summarized in Figure 17.3.

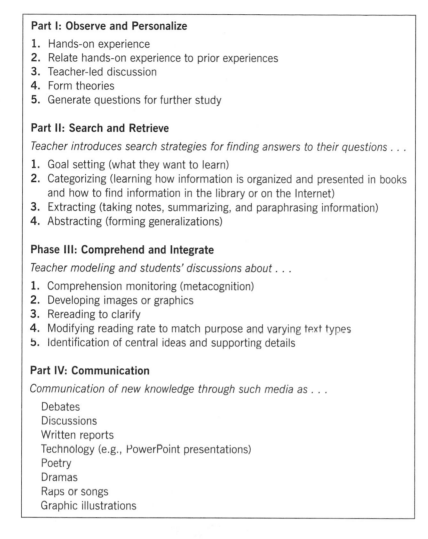

Part I: Observe and Personalize

1. Hands-on experience
2. Relate hands-on experience to prior experiences
3. Teacher-led discussion
4. Form theories
5. Generate questions for further study

Part II: Search and Retrieve

Teacher introduces search strategies for finding answers to their questions . . .

1. Goal setting (what they want to learn)
2. Categorizing (learning how information is organized and presented in books and how to find information in the library or on the Internet)
3. Extracting (taking notes, summarizing, and paraphrasing information)
4. Abstracting (forming generalizations)

Phase III: Comprehend and Integrate

Teacher modeling and students' discussions about . . .

1. Comprehension monitoring (metacognition)
2. Developing images or graphics
3. Rereading to clarify
4. Modifying reading rate to match purpose and varying text types
5. Identification of central ideas and supporting details

Part IV: Communication

Communication of new knowledge through such media as . . .

Debates
Discussions
Written reports
Technology (e.g., PowerPoint presentations)
Poetry
Dramas
Raps or songs
Graphic illustrations

FIGURE 17.3. Phases of CORI of information books. From Reutzel and Cooter (2011, p. 264). Copyright 2011 by Pearson. Reprinted by permission.

The Daily Literacy Block: Organizing an Effective Instructional Routine

Students develop a sense of security when the events of the school day revolve around a sequence of familiar activities. Although variety is the spice of life, we find comfort in familiar instructional routines and schedules in a well-organized classroom (Holdaway, 1984). There are any number of ways to organize the activities and instruction of the school day. However, it is important that children experience a variety of interactive settings in the whole class, in small groups, and individually each day. Groups should be flexible, meet the needs of the students, and involve the "best practices" of literacy instruction. Also, it is important that children receive daily planned, intentional, and explicit instruction in the essential components, strategies, and skills of learning to read and write successfully.

One such approach used to organize the school day is the *five-block schedule* based in part on the recommendations of Shanahan (2004) and also based on the work of Mathes et al. (2005) relating to the value of small-group reading instruction. This organizational framework, the five-block schedule, is a functional and flexible instructional scaffolding used by teachers in classrooms to provide interactive, shared, and small-group differentiated reading and writing experiences for children similar to such other organizational plans as the four-block plan by P. M. Cunningham (Cunningham, Hall, & Defee, 1998).

The five-block schedule is divided into five clearly defined instructional time and activity blocks (1) word work, (2) fluency, (3) writing, (4) comprehension strategy instruction, and (5) small-group differentiated reading instruction. The five-block schedule incorporates into its structure the essential components of reading and writing instruction recommended in this chapter and in several recent national reading research reports, including decoding and word recognition instruction, fluency development, writing, vocabulary and comprehension strategy instruction, and guided reading (August & Shanahan, 2006; National Early Literacy Panel, 2008; National Reading Panel, 2000; Snow, Burns, & Griffin, 1998). The five-block schedule is designed for 180 minutes of allocated daily instructional time. The structure of the time allocations found in the five-block schedule is outlined in Figure 17.4.

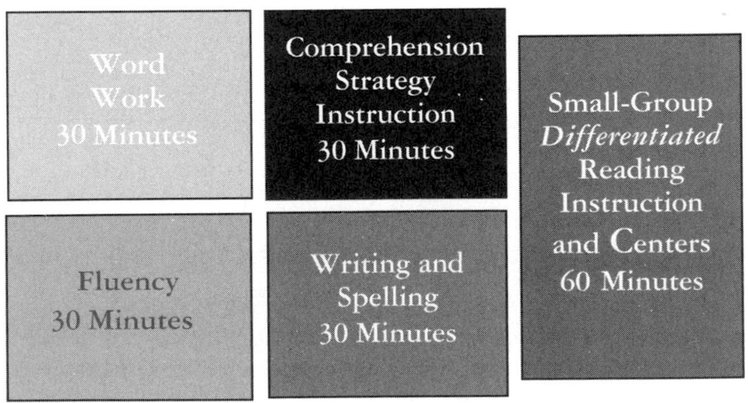

FIGURE 17.4. Five-block schedule for literacy instruction.

Word Work Instruction Block (30 Minutes)

The purpose of the *word work* instructional block is to develop children's (1) phonological and phonemic awareness, (2) concepts about print, (3) letter recognition and production, (4) decoding and word recognition, and (5) spelling concepts, skills, and strategies. Effective instructional practices used within this time allocation include shared reading of enlarged texts, including charts, posters, overhead transparencies, and big books; the co-construction of interactive written sentences and brief stories; making and breaking words using manipulative letters; and choral response techniques use such tools as gel, dry-erase, or magna-doodle boards. I cannot overemphasize the importance of providing the whole class with direct, explicit instruction on each of these word-related skills, strategies, and concepts. Children need clear explanations, "think-alouds" coupled with expert modeling of reading and writing behaviors, and guided application of these concepts, skills, and strategies during this time allocation as well. I also strongly recommend that daily lessons focus on both decoding and spelling, reading and writing processes that help children better understand the reciprocal nature of all reading and writing processes.

Fluency Instruction Block (30 Minutes)

The daily fluency lesson framework begins with an explicit explanation, description, or definition of the importance of reading fluency and the elements, terms, and meta-language of fluent oral reading as defined in the research and professional literature: (1) accuracy, (2) rate, and (3) expression. Children also need to see and hear models of what one means. So the next part of the fluency development lesson framework involves teacher modeling, think-alouds, and demonstration of the elements of fluent oral reading, including examples and intentional miscues (Reutzel, 2006). Teachers select one of the essential elements of oral reading fluency for each lesson (e.g., accuracy). After reading a text aloud to the group of children with accuracy, the teacher reminds them that accurate oral reading is *reading what is on the page.* Next, the teacher performs an inaccurate oral reading of the same text. Once the inaccurate oral reading of this text is complete, the teacher again reminds the children that accurate oral reading is *reading what is on the page.* Next, the teacher invites the children, usually amid snickering and giggles, to comment on the accuracy of the "inaccurate" modeling of oral reading. I have noticed that greater discussion and attention flow from the inaccurate reading than from accurate renditions of text.

After explaining, defining, describing, modeling, demonstrating, and discussing fluent reading, the teacher involves the children in repeated group-guided oral rereadings of the text that has been previously modeled. During this part of the daily fluency lesson, teachers use various formats for choral reading, such as echoic (echo chamber), unison (all together), antiphonal (one side against another), mumble, line-a-child, and so on. For those who are unfamiliar with these choral reading variations, we recommend reading Opitz and Rasinski's (2008) *Good-Bye Round Robin*, or Rasinski's (2003) *The Fluent Reader*. Next in the daily lesson framework, children are involved in paired guided practice and repeated readings of the text previously modeled. Pairs of readers are either same-age peers or older peers from another age- or grade-level classroom. Each pair alternates the roles of reader and listener. After each oral reading by the reader, the listener provides feedback. Guided, oral, repeated reading practice with feedback is one of the practices that produced the largest effect sizes and student gains for fluency practice in the studies analyzed by the National Reading Panel (2000).

Once children sense their emerging fluency, they want to demonstrate it to others. Children love to perform their practiced oral reading for an audience of either parents or other students in the school building. When preparing an oral reading performance, teachers might use one of three well-known oral reading performance approaches: (1) Readers Theater, (2) radio reading, and (3) recitation (Opitz & Rasinski, 2008).

Remember that fluency achieved in one type of task or text type is insufficient and that children require instruction and practice with a variety of reading fluency tasks and a variety of text types and levels of challenge. In grades 2–6 we found that we needed to provide new, fresh, or novel short but high-interest texts for fluency practice nearly every day. In grades K–1, we found that multiple days of fluency practice with the same texts were often needed to move the oral reading of a text to fluency.

Writing Instruction Block (30 Minutes)

The purpose of the *writing* instructional block is to develop children's (1) composition skills, (2) spelling, (3) mechanics, (4) grammatical understandings, and (5) literary and writing genre concepts, skills, and strategies. Effective instructional practices used within this time allocation include modeled writing by the teacher; a writers workshop, including drafting, conferencing, revising, editing, publishing, and disseminating; and direct, explicit whole-class instruction on each of these writing skills, strategies, and concepts. Children need clear explanations, think-alouds coupled with expert modeling of writing behaviors, and guided application of these writing concepts, skills, and strategies during this time allocation as well. I also strongly recommend that daily lessons provide a time allocation for sharing children's writing in an "author's chair" or using some other method of disseminating and sharing children's writing products.

Comprehension Strategy Instruction Block (30 Minutes)

The purpose of the *comprehension strategies* instructional block is to develop children's (1) vocabulary and (2) comprehension concepts, skills, and strategies. Effective instructional practices used within this time segment include explicit instruction of vocabulary concepts, using a variety of methods and requiring a variety of responses (Beck, McKeown, & Kucan, 2002; McKenna, 2002; Stahl & Nagy, 2006); wordplay (Johnson, 2001); and a focus on explicit instruction of comprehension strategies, including questioning, text structure, graphic organizers, inferences, predicting, visual imaging, monitoring, summarizing, and background knowledge activation. Here, too, I cannot overemphasize the importance of providing the whole class with direct explicit instruction on each of these vocabulary and comprehension skills, strategies, and concepts. Children need clear explanations, think-alouds coupled with expert modeling of comprehension thought processes and behaviors, as well as teacher-guided application of these concepts, skills, and strategies in the reading of many texts at different levels and in many genres. It is also strongly recommend that, at some point in time, teachers strongly consider working toward teaching a set or family of multiple comprehension strategies such as *reciprocal teaching* (Palincsar, 2003), CORI (Guthrie, 2003; Swan et al., 2010), and *transactional strategies* (Brown, Pressley, Van Meter, & Schuder, 1996; Reutzel, Smith & Fawson, 2005) to be used collectively and strategically while interacting with a variety of texts over long periods of time (National Reading Panel, 2000; Reutzel et al., 2005).

Small-Group Differentiated Reading Instruction Block (60 Minutes)

Small-group differentiated reading instruction time is divided into three blocks of 20 minutes each. The structure of this time is fairly rigid in the beginning as students learn to rotate from center to center, use their time wisely in completing center tasks, and manage themselves so as to minimize off-task behaviors when they are not in the meeting with the teacher for small- group differentiated reading instruction (Morrow, 2010). Within each 20-minute block of time two major types of activities dominate: *small-group differentiated reading group* and *small groups at learning centers*. The teacher is stationed in the small-group differentiated reading area of the classroom prepared to offer differentiated reading instruction. The children, on the other hand, are called to their small reading group (homogeneous group) from an assigned "center rotation" group (mixed-abilities group). *Learning centers* are teacher-selected, -designed, and -provisioned. Learning centers focus on follow-up activities and tasks drawn from the *word work, fluency, comprehension strategy instruction*, and *writing*. Management of learning centers is a central concern for teachers; they must be designed so that the activities and tasks are clearly understood, independent of teacher supervision, and able to be completed within the time allowed. It is also important that tasks completed in learning centers have a component of accountability and performance. We show in Figure 17.5 two possible approaches for managing learning center group rotations.

Managing the small-group differentiated reading instruction time block is a complex effort for most teachers. We caution teachers against the cre-

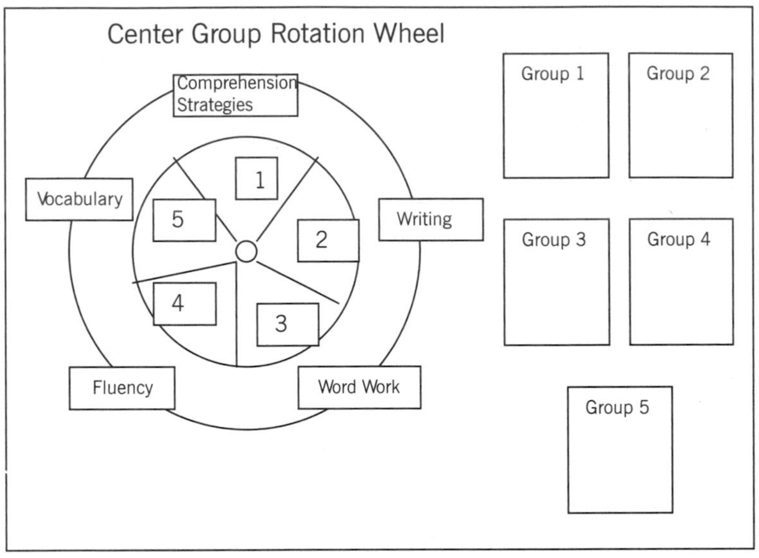

Center Group Management Chart

Working with Comprehension Strategies	Writing	Word Work	Fluency	Vocabulary
1	2	3	4	5
5	1	2	3	4
4	5	1	2	3
3	4	5	1	2
2	3	4	5	1

FIGURE 17.5. Learning center group management/rotation plans.

ation of too many learning centers. In the early part of the year, fewer centers are easier for both teachers and students to handle. As the year progresses, adding a few new centers, especially optional centers, can add variety to this time block. We have also found that very little flexibility is desirable in the group rotation schedule early in the year. As time progresses and children acquire more experience with the rotation among learning centers, we have found it better to assign children specific tasks to be completed during this time period rather than a time-controlled rotation through various learning centers.

REFLECTIONS AND FUTURE DIRECTIONS

Teachers accommodate individual student needs in literacy instruction increasingly by using progress monitoring, screening, diagnostic, and outcomes assessment within an RTI framework. Throughout the history of classroom literacy instruction, several variations on ability grouping and whole-class instruction have persisted despite a large body of relevant research pointing to many negative outcomes for students and teachers related to these grouping strategies. In recent years, however, a number of alternative grouping strategies have emerged— including flexible groups, literature circles, cooperative learning groups, assessment data groups, and dynamic small differentiated or guided reading instruction groups—that offer teachers a wide range of possibilities.

More research is needed to determine the effects of alternative grouping strategies on students' reading growth, engagement, motivation, and achievement. For example, we do not know how homogeneous grouping for small-group differentiated reading instruction affects students' achievement, motivation, engagement, or reading growth as compared with whole-class or homogeneous or heterogeneous grouping strategies singly or in combination. Also, we need to know more about how flexible grouping strategies interact to ameliorate the effects of homogeneous grouping for students with varying needs and abilities.

ENGAGEMENT ACTIVITIES

1. Discuss why learning-disabled students seem to dislike mixed-ability grouping strategies when the research also seems to point to many negative effects for same-ability grouping on struggling students.
2. Observe several levels of dynamic differentiated or guided small-group reading instruction in classrooms and take field notes.

Then interview four or five children in various levels of these groups about their perceptions. Do the typical issues associated with ability grouping seem to be present in the observations and interview responses of the children in these groups?

3. Given a reading or writing task to perform individually or in a cooperative learning group, what is the result on student's performance? Is quality higher or lower? Do individuals or groups use learning time more efficiently? Is the performance or product given to individuals or cooperative learning groups higher or lower? How do children of varying abilities and skill levels feel about the group processes and products?
4. Discuss whether it is important for teachers to know what children are learning from time spent in learning centers. If it is important, how can teachers hold children accountable for learning activities found in typical independent learning centers—like a listening center, for example?
5. Although children often have rich discussions of trade book literature in literature circles, do these arrangements produce better comprehension abilities, larger vocabularies, and greater motivation to read than do whole-class discussions?
6. Discuss and collect data at the local level to determine whether the use of CORI for reading and information texts not only promotes student engagement and motivation but also results in students' extending their background knowledge.

REFERENCES

August, D., & Shanahan, T. (2006). *Developing literacy in second-language learners: A report of the national literacy panel on language-minority children and youth.* Mahwah, NJ: Erlbaum.

Beck, I. L., McKeown, M. G., & Kucan, L. (2002). *Bringing words to life: Robust vocabulary instruction.* New York: Guilford Press.

Brown, R., Pressley, M., Van Meter, P., & Schuder, T. (1996). A quasi-experimental validation of transactional strategies instruction with previously low-achieving second-grade readers. *Journal of Educational Psychology, 88*, 18–37.

Brown-Chidsey, R., & Steege, M. W. (2005). *Response to intervention: Principles and strategies for effective practice.* New York: Guilford Press.

Chall, J. S. (2000). *The academic achievement challenge: What really works in the classroom?* New York: Guilford Press.

Cunningham, P. M., Hall, D. P., & Defee, M. (1998). Nonability-grouped, multilevel instruction: Eight years later. *The Reading Teacher, 51*(8), 652–664.

Delpit, L. D. (1988). Silenced dialogue: Power and pedagogy in educating other people's children. *Harvard Educational Review, 58*, 280–298.

Duffy, G. (2004). *Explaining reading: A resource for teaching concepts, skills, and strategies.* New York: Guilford Press.

Fuchs, D., Fuchs, L. S., & Vaughn, S. (2008). *Response to intervention: A framework for reading educators.* Newark, DE: International Reading Association.

Good, R. H., & Kaminski, R. A. (2002). *Dynamic Indicators of Basic Early Literacy Skills (DIBELS)* (6th ed.). [online]. Retrieved from *dibels.uoregon.edu.*

Goodlad, J. I., & Oakes, J. (1988). We must offer equal access to knowledge. *Educational Leadership, 45*(5), 16–22.

Goodman, K. S. (2006). *The truth about DIBELS: What it is, What it does.* Portsmouth, NH: Heinemann.

Gregory, G. H., & Chapman, C. (2006). *Differentiated instructional strategies: One size doesn't fit all* (2nd ed.). Thousand Oaks, CA: Corwin Press.

Guthrie, J. T. (2003). Concept-oriented reading instruction. In C. E. Snow & A. P. Sweet (Eds.), *Rethinking reading comprehension* (pp. 115–140). New York: Guilford Press.

Guthrie, J. T., Van Meter, P., McCann, A. D., Wigfield, A., Bennett, L., Poundstone, C., et al. (1996). Growth of literacy engagement: Changes in motivations and strategies during concept-oriented reading instruction. *Reading Research Quarterly, 31*(3), 306–332.

Haager, D., Klingner, J., & Vaughn, S. (2007). *Evidence-based reading practices for response to intervention.* Baltimore: Brookes.

Hiebert, E. H., & Reutzel, D. R. (2010). *Revisiting silent reading: New directions for teachers and researchers.* Newark, DE: International Reading Association.

Holdaway, D. (1984). *Stability and change in literacy learning.* Portsmouth, NH: Heinemann.

Johnson, D. D. (2001). *Vocabulary in the elementary and middle school.* Boston: Allyn & Bacon.

Lipson, M. Y., & Wixson, K. K. (2010). *Successful approaches to RTI: Collaborative practices for improving K–12 literacy.* Newark, DE: International Reading Association.

Mathes, P. G., Denton, C. A., Fletcher, J. M., Anthongy, J. L., Francis, D. J., & Schatschneider, C. (2005). The effects of theoretically different instruction and student characteristics on the skills of struggling readers. *Reading Research Quarterly, 40*(2), 148–183.

McKenna, M. C. (2002). *Help for struggling readers: Strategies for grades 3–8.* New York: Guilford Press.

Morrow, L. M. (2010). Preparing centers and a literacy-rich environment for small-group instruction in early reading. In M. C. McKenna, S. Walpole, & Conradi, K. (Eds.), *Promoting early reading: Research, resources and best practices* (pp. 124–141). New York: Guilford Press.

Morrow, L. M., Reutzel, D. R., & Casey, H. (2006). Organization and management of language arts teaching: Classroom environments, grouping practices, and exemplary instruction. In C. Evertson (Ed.), *Handbook of classroom management* (pp. 559–582). Mahwah, NJ: Erlbaum.

National Early Literacy Panel (NELP). (2008). *Developing early literacy: Report of the National Early Literacy Panel.* Washington, DC: National Institute for Literacy.

National Reading Panel. (2000). *Report of the National Reading Panel: Teaching children to read.* Washington, DC: Author.

Oakes, J. (1986). Keeping track: Part 1. The policy and practice of curriculum inequality. *Phi Delta Kappan, 68*(1), 12–17.

Oakes, J. (1988). Beyond tracking. *Educational Horizons, 65*(1), 32–35.

Oczkus, L. (2009). *Interactive think-aloud lessons: 25 surefire ways to engage students and improve comprehension.* New York: Scholastic.

Opitz, M. F. (1998). Text sets: One way to flex your grouping—in first grade, too! *The Reading Teacher, 51*(7), 622–624.

Opitz, M. F., & Rasinski, T. V. (2008). *Good-bye round robin: 25 effective oral reading strategies* (updated ed.). Portsmouth, NH: Heinemann.

Palincsar, A. S. (2003). Collaborative approaches to comprehension instruction. In C. E. Snow & A. P. Sweet (Eds.), *Rethinking reading comprehension* (pp. 99–114). New York: Guilford Press.

Pearson, P. D. (1985). Changing the face of reading comprehension instruction. *The Reading Teacher, 38*(8), 724–738.

Pearson, P. D., & Gallagher, M. C. (1983). The instruction of reading comprehension. *Contemporary Educational Psychology, 8*(3), 317–344.

Peterson, R., & Eeds, M. (1990). *Grand conversations: Literature groups in action.* New York: Scholastic.

Piasta, S. B., & Wagner, R. K. (2010). Developing early literacy skills: A meta-analysis of alphabet learning and instruction. *Reading Research Quarterly, 45*(1), 8–38.

Raphael, T. E., Florio-Ruane, S., Kehus, M. J., George, M., Hasty, N. L., & Highfield, K. (2003). Constructing curriculum for differentiated instruction: Inquiry in the teachers' learning collaborative. In R. L. McCormick & J. R. Paratore (Eds.), *After early intervention, then what? Teaching struggling readers in grades 3 and beyond* (pp. 94–116). Newark, DE: International Reading Association.

Rasinski, T. V. (2003). *The fluent reader: Oral reading strategies for building word recognition, fluency, and comprehension.* New York: Scholastic.

Rathvon, N. (2004). *Early reading assessment: A practitioner's handbook.* New York: Guilford Press.

Reutzel, D. R. (2006). Hey teacher, when you say flu-ency, what do you mean?: Developing fluency and meta-fluency in elementary classrooms. In T. V. Rasinski, C. Blachowicz, & K. Lems (Eds.), *Fluency instruction: Research-based best practices* (pp. 62–85). New York: Guilford Press.

Reutzel, D. R., & Cooter, R. B. (2011). *Strategies for reading assessment and instruction: Helping every child succeed.* Boston, MA: Pearson.

Reutzel, D. R., & Jones, C. D. (2010). Assessing and creating an effective preschool literacy classroom environment. In M. C. McKenna, S. Walpole, & Conradi, K. (Eds.), *Promoting early reading: Research, resources, and best practices* (pp. 175–198). New York: Guilford Press.

Reutzel, D. R., Smith, J. A., & Fawson, P. C. (2005). An evaluation of two approaches for teaching reading comprehension strategies in the primary years using science information texts. *Early Childhood Research Quarterly, 20*(3), 276–305.

Shanahan, T. (2004, November). *How do you raise reading achievement?* Paper presented at the Utah Council of the International Reading Association Meeting, Salt Lake City.

Snow, C. E., Burns, M. S., & Griffin, P. (1998). *Preventing reading failure in young children.* Washington, DC: National Academy Press.

Stahl, S. A., & Nagy, W. E. (2006). *Teaching word meanings.* Mahwah, NJ: Erlbaum.

Swafford, J., & Bryan, J. K. (2000). Instructional strategies for promoting conceptual change: Supporting middle school students. *Reading and Writing Quarterly, 16*(2), 139–161.

Swan, E. A. (2003). *Concept-oriented reading instruction: Engaging classrooms, lifelong learners.* New York: Guilford Press.

Swan, E. A., Coddington, C. S., & Guthrie, J. T. (2010). Motivating silent reading in classrooms. In E. H. Hiebert & D. R. Reutzel (Eds.), *Revisiting silent reading: New directions for teachers and researchers* (pp. 95–111). Newark, DE: International Reading Association.

Taylor, B. M. (2008). Tier 1: Effective classroom reading instruction in the elementary grades. In D. Fuchs, L. S. Fuchs, & S. Vaughn (Eds.), *Response to intervention: A framework for reading educators* (pp. 5–25). Newark, DE: International Reading Association.

Taylor, B. M., Pearson, P. D., Clark, & Walpole, S. (1999). *Beating the odds in teaching all children to read* (CIERA Report No. 2006). Ann Arbor, MI: Center for the Improvement of Early Reading Achievement.

Tomlinson, C. A. (1999). *The differentiated classroom: Responding to the needs of all learners.* Alexandria, VA: Association for Supervision and Curriculum Development.

Tomlinson, C. A. (2003). *Fulfilling the promise of the differentiated classroom: Strategies and tools for responsive teaching.* Alexandria, VA: Association for Supervision and Curriculum Development.

Tomlinson, C. A., Brimijoin, K., & Narvaez, L. (2008). *The differentiated school: Making revolutionary changes in teaching and learning.* Alexandria, VA: Association for Supervision and Curriculum Development.

Tomlinson, C. A., & Eidson, C. C. (2003). *Differentiation in practice: A resource guide for differentiating curriculum, Grades K–5.* Alexandria, VA: Association for Supervision and Curriculum Development.

Tomlinson, C. A., & McTighe, J. (2006). *Integrating differentiated instruction and understanding by design.* Alexandria, VA: Association for Supervision and Curriculum Development.

Tyner, B. (2004). *Small-group reading instruction: A differentiated model for beginning and struggling readers.* Newark, DE: International Reading Association.

Tyner, B. (2009). *Small-group reading instruction: A differentiated model for beginning and struggling readers* (2nd ed.). Newark, DE: International Reading Association.

Walpole, S., & McKenna, M. C. (2007). *Differentiated reading instruction: Strategies for the primary grades.* New York: Guilford Press.

CHAPTER 18

Parent–Teacher Partnerships That Make a Difference in Children's Literacy Achievement

Jeanne R. Paratore
Patricia A. Edwards

This chapter will:

- Provide an overview of the importance of parent involvement in children's literacy development.
- Provide a description of the families that populate our schools.
- Describe new understandings of productive parent–teacher partnerships.
- Share examples of evidence-based programs that meet the varied needs of the families we serve.
- Provide a list of principles to guide teachers as they plan their work with families.

WHY IS PARENT INVOLVEMENT IMPORTANT?

The importance of parent involvement in children's academic success has been well documented and widely accepted. Based on a comprehensive research synthesis, Henderson and Mapp (2002) reported that academic effects are demonstrated across broad and varied measures: students of involved parents have higher rates of school attendance, better social skills and behavior, higher grades and test scores, lower rates of retention, and higher rates of high school graduation and postsecondary study. These findings are further strengthened by additional large-scale studies that postdate Henderson's and Mapp's review. In the largest of these, Houtenville and Conway (2008) sought to determine both educational and economic effects of parent involvement. They analyzed a large dataset (10,382 eighth-grade students) from the National Education Longitudinal Study (NELS). They found parental effort to have significantly positive effects on student achievement, "along the order of four to six years of parental education or more than $1000 in per-pupil spending" (p. 450).

Other recent studies have contributed to deeper understanding of differential effects of parent involvement. Jeynes (2003) conducted a meta-analysis of 20 studies (total sample of 12,000 students) of effects of parent involvement on academic achievement of students of different ethnic backgrounds (African American, Latino, Asian) in grades K–12. Parent involvement had significant positive effects for all racial groups, although these effects were not equal. African American and Latino groups benefited more than Asian Americans. In addition, parent involvement had positive effects on all academic measures (e.g., GPA, achievement tests), but effects were greater on achievement tests than on GPA.

In an experimental longitudinal study of low-income children ($N = 281$) whose parents were involved in an intervention program with services for children (high-quality preschool) and parents (education and job training) during the children's kindergarten year, Dearing, Kreider, Simpkins, and Weiss (2006) found that effects varied by maternal education. That is, although there was no relationship between parent involvement and average literacy performance when parents were relatively more educated, there was a relationship between higher levels of parent involvement and higher levels of literacy performance for children whose parents were less educated. Furthermore, when parent involvement in children's schooling increased between kindergarten and fifth grade, children of both high- and low-education families achieved higher literacy performances, suggesting that benefits accrue when involvement is not only sustained but also heightened. Moreover, despite an achievement gap across children of high- and low-education mothers when parent involvement was low, this gap disappeared when parent involvement levels were high.

The combined evidence supports a clear claim that parent involvement in their children's learning has noteworthy academic benefits for nearly all children. Moreover, when children have mothers with less education, parent involvement exerts an even more powerful influence on children's literacy performance, even eliminating the achievement gap that typically separates the performance of children of low- and high-education mothers.

WHAT IS THE TEACHER'S ROLE IN PARENT INVOLVEMENT?

Few teachers reading the evidence about the importance of parent involvement will be surprised—their own observations and experiences confirm the outcomes of formal investigations. However, many teachers—especially those in low-income communities—believe that the parents of the children with whom they work are disengaged and uninterested in their children's learning (e.g., Compton-Lilly, 2003; Edwards, 2009; Valdés, 1996). Studies indicate that teachers believe so strongly in some parents' lack of interest and motivation related to their children's schooling that they even fail to reach out to them, assuming their efforts will meet with resistance (e.g., Edwards, 2009; Epstein, 1986; Lareau, 1989). Some may be surprised, then, by findings that the actions teachers take are instrumental in levels of parent involvement. Based on evidence collected from a sample of more than 1,200 parents of elementary school children, Epstein (1986) concluded:

> Parents' education did not explain experiences with parent involvement unless teacher practices were taken into account. In the classrooms of teachers who were leaders in the use of parent involvement, parents at all educational levels said they were frequently involved in learning activities at home. (p. 291)

In another study, Sheldon (2003) collected data from 113 public schools in one urban system. He found that high-quality parent involvement programs correlated strongly with the outreach practices, particularly "the depth and breadth of schools' efforts to involve hard-to-reach families and the community in the school and in students' learning" (p. 160). Sheldon further noted:

> The results of multiple regression analyses indicate that, in any given year, the degree to which schools are working to overcome several challenges to equitable parent involvement is associated with students' performance on state tests after accounting for poverty, mobility, and size of the school population. (p. 161)

Moreover, studies indicate that high-quality programs not only increase levels of parent involvement, but also can help parents acquire and use strategies that correlate with higher rates of students' literacy performance (e.g., Arnold, Lonigan, Whitehurst, & Epstein, 1994; Chrispeels & Rivero, 2001; Krol-Sinclair, 1996).

Given the evidence of the importance of parent involvement in children's learning and of the power of the teacher in establishing high levels of involvement and implementation of effective practices, we next turn our attention to developing an understanding of the families we must be prepared to serve.

WHO ARE THE FAMILIES IN OUR SCHOOLS?

As classroom teachers, we observe on a daily basis the changing demographics of our classrooms—our students represent increasingly varied ethnicities and races, countries of origin, first languages, and religions. Also changing, but unseen in the faces and voices of our children, are the structural demographics of the American family, a change so dramatic that Footlick (1990) observed:

> The American family does not exist. Rather, we are creating many American families, of diverse styles and shapes. In unprecedented numbers, our families are unalike: we have mothers working while fathers keep house; fathers and mothers both working away from home; single parents; second marriages bringing children together from unrelated backgrounds; childless couples; unmarried couples, with and without children; gay and lesbian parents. We are living through a period of historic change in American life. (p. 15)

The face of the American family has changed in yet another way: our nation's large cities, and the schools that serve them, are populated by a substantial and growing concentration of persons living in poverty. Many inner-city neighborhoods today include almost exclusively the most disadvantaged segments of the urban minority population, families plagued by persistent poverty and welfare dependency, workers who experience long spells of joblessness, and individuals who, in the face of limited opportunities, turn to street crime and other forms of aberrant behavior (Hays, 2004; Iceland, 2006; Shipler, 2005). Furthermore, although poverty is most often associated with urban areas, DeNavas-Walt, Proctor, and Smith (2009) reported that, overall, 19% of children under age 18 live in poverty, and they noted a higher percentage of such families in rural areas (15.1%) as compared with urban areas (12.9%). Moreover, families living in poverty cross ethnicities and races. In 2008 the overall poverty rate was 13.2%: 24.7% of blacks, 22% of Hispanics, 11% of Asians, and 8.2% of Whites were categorized as poor.

The continued rise in child poverty is attributed to two primary factors: the failure of hourly wages to keep pace with inflation, particularly for young workers and those with less than a college education; and the increase in the number of families headed by a single parent, usually the mother. Mother-only families are at high risk for poverty due to the absence of a second adult earner and the historically lower earning power of women.

Poverty affects children and their school lives in devastating ways. Kozol (1994) poignantly described the lives of homeless children:

> Many of these kids grow up surrounded by infectious illnesses no longer seen in most developed nations. Whooping cough and tuberculosis, once

> regarded as archaic illness, are now familiar in the shelters. Shocking numbers of these children have not been inoculated and for this reason cannot go to school. Those who do are likely to be two years behind grade level . . . many get to class so tired and hungry that they cannot concentrate. Others are ashamed to go to school because of shunning by their peers. Classmates label them "the hotel children" and don't want to sit beside them. Even their teachers sometimes keep their distance. The children look diseased and dirty. Many times they are. Often unable to bathe, they bring the smell of destitution with them into school. There *is* a smell of destitution, I may add. It is the smell of sweat and filth and urine. (p. 77)

Added to this bleak outlook is the problem of underresourced, underperforming schools in high-poverty communities. In one account, Kozol (1994) described a chilling reality for many urban black children and their families:

> On an average morning in Chicago, about 5,700 children in 190 classrooms come to school only to find they have no teacher. Victimized by endemic funding shortages, the system can't afford sufficient substitutes to take the place of missing teachers. "We've been in this typing class a whole semester," says a 15-year-old at Du Sable High, "and they still can't find us a teacher." . . . In a class of 39 children at Chicago's Goudy Elementary School, an adult is screaming at a child: "Keisha, look at me . . . Look me in the eye!" Keisha is fighting with a classmate. Over what? It turns out: over a crayon, said *The Chicago Tribune* in 1988. Last January the underfunded school began rationing supplies. . . . The odds these black kids in Chicago face are only slightly worse than those faced by low-income children all over America. Children like these will be the parents of the year 2000. Many of them will be unable to earn a living and fulfill the obligations of adults; they will see their families disintegrate, their children lost to drugs and destitution. When we later condemn them for "parental failings," as we inevitably will do, we may be forced to stop and remember how we also failed them in the first years of their lives. (p. 75)

There is little reason to believe that this account is outdated. In a report based on school visits conducted between 2000 and 2005 in schools in 11 states, Kozol (2005) found conditions such as these relentlessly persistent in many low-income schools, despite (and, in some cases, Kozol argued, because of) various reform initiatives. Although reports such as these can lead to discouragement and even despair, they should not. There is evidence that excellent schools can make a difference (e.g., Reeves, 2005; Taylor & Pearson, 2002; Teddlie & Stringfield, 1993), especially when teachers add productive parent involvement efforts to the instructional strategies they undertake as part of teaching reform (e.g., Allen, 2007; Chrispeels & Rivero, 2001; McIntyre, 2010; Sheldon, 2003). In the next section, we describe some of the successful efforts.

BEST PRACTICES IN ACTION

Acknowledging, understanding, and acting on the changing characteristics of families and family structures are critical if family involvement is to become a reality in schools. Nieto (1992) noted that the differences in family structures and work patterns make traditional forms of parent involvement (e.g., PTA meetings, help during the day, parent–teacher conferences during school hours, bake sales) a poor fit for many modern parents, and she warned that reliance on only these familiar forms of involvement is a recipe for failure of efforts to increase parent involvement.

But if these forms are outdated, what should we be doing? Hoover-Dempsey and Whitaker (2010) suggested that the answer lies in the creation of invitations for involvement that are thoughtfully matched to parents' time and knowledge; they explained that teachers need to consider the forms of involvement (e.g., conveying high expectations, teaching children at home, attending school meetings, volunteering at school) that fit into parents' family time constraints, and they need to consider what parents may need to know (e.g., specific skill knowledge) to become effectively involved.

Building on Edwards's (2009) identification of fundamental needs of parents who find parent involvement challenging, we have created three major "action" categories that teachers and administrators should attend to as they plan collaborative work with parents. The first category, *developing parent–teacher relationships*, was identified more than three decades ago by Lawrence-Lightfoot (1978) as a partial solution to improving home–school partnerships; nonetheless, attention to relationship building remains insufficient (e.g., Greene & Compton-Lilly, 2011; Lawrence-Lightfoot, 2004; Tutwiler, 1998). Unlike traditional models of parent involvement in which the goal is often to convey to parents information we want them to know, building relationships is grounded in *exchanging*, rather then giving, information. Actions focus on learning from parents (e.g., parents' working schedules and other family responsibilities, parents' understandings of their role in their children's learning) as well as on sharing information with parents (e.g., teachers' preferences for how and when parents should contact them, teachers' expectations for parent involvement). As we seek information, we should pay particular attention to the type of information that will help us to understand the child's cultural and social worlds outside of school, as this will help identify areas of congruence and also areas of potential conflict. This information may be critical to understanding how to connect home and school learning experiences.

In the second category, *understanding school and classroom programs*, we place actions or events that help parents to understand more fully teachers' (and school or district) academic and behavioral expectations. The central purpose of this category is to build parental background knowledge about schools and classrooms so that they understand their children's daily experiences, the tasks and requirements their children describe in their conversations about their school lives, and the tasks and responsibilities teachers ask parents to engage in at home. The third category is *family learning interventions,* that is, specific actions teachers expect parents to take to support their children's school success (e.g., monitoring homework, teaching specific skills, reading to or listening to children read). In the next section, we describe examples of successful home–school partnership initiatives related to each of these categories.

Developing Parent–Teacher Relationships

Perhaps the most well-known and thoroughly studied example of an approach to parent–teacher relationship building is the work of Moll and his colleagues (e.g., González, Moll, & Amanti, 2005; Moll & Cammarota, 2010; Moll & Greenberg, 1991) on identifying *funds of knowledge* present in households of the children we teach. As described by González et al. (2005),

> The concept of *funds of knowledge* . . . is based on a simple premise: People are competent, they have knowledge, and their life experiences have given them that knowledge. Our claim is that firsthand research experiences with families allow one to document this competence and knowledge. It is this engagement that opened up many possibilities for positive pedagogical actions. (p. x)

The Fund of Knowledge project is grounded in "respectful talk between people who are mutually engaged in a constructive conversation" (González et al., 2005, p. 8). Participating teachers learn to visit homes not for the purpose of teaching parents what to do, but instead to deepen their understanding of what parents know and do as part of their daily family, community, and work experiences. To do so they observe, question, and discuss, with a focus on gaining a deeper understanding of their children's lives outside of school. In addition, teachers meet as an after-school study group to discuss their observations and the knowledge they have gained and to articulate how they can act on the information. That is, how can they make connections between children's family and communities lives and what they must learn in school? Participating teachers described their experiences as transformative. One teacher explained:

> Participating in the project helped me to reformulate my concept of culture from being very static to more practice-oriented. This broadened conceptualization turned out to be the key which helped me develop strategies to include the knowledge my students were bringing to school in my classroom practice. (González et al., 2005, pp. 99–100)

A second example of an approach designed to support parent–teacher relationship building, the Parent Story approach, is drawn from the work of Edwards, Pleasants, and Franklin (1999):

> Parent stories can provide teachers with the opportunity to gain a deeper understanding of the "human side" of families and children (i.e., why children behave as they do, children's ways of learning and communicating, some of the problems parents have encountered, and how these problems may have impacted their children's views about school and the schooling process). (p. xviii)

Edwards et al. explained that, through parent stories, teachers have the opportunity to see and understand how home and school cultures may differ and the challenges that the differences create for students; they can learn about individual and social pressures facing families, and they can also learn about parents' aspirations and expectations for their children. Armed with this knowledge, teachers can come to recognize their own strengths and responsibilities in helping parents meet certain challenges, and they can also learn to seek help for issues outside of their expertise.

To collect family stories, Edwards et al. suggest seven major steps. First, teachers seek at least one colleague who is also interested in collecting family stories, so that they can share their experiences—positive and negative—along the way and have a partner with whom to problem solve. Second, teachers systematically review records of each of the children in their classrooms, and, to start, choose one student about whom they have concerns or questions. Third, teachers prepare questions related to 11 categories: (1) parent–child family routines; (2) child's literacy history; (3) teachable moments (e.g., explicit or implicit home learning opportunities); (4) home life (e.g., discipline, parent–child relationship, problems); (5) educational experiences outside of home (e.g., library visits, summer activities); (6) parents' beliefs about their child; (7) child's time with others; (8) parent–child–sibling relationships; (9) parents' hobbies, activities, and interests in books; (10) parent–teacher relationship; and (11) parents' school history and ideas about school. (See Edwards et al., 1999, pp. 36–40 for suggested list of interview questions.) Fourth, teachers identify a time and place to have the conversation with the parent(s), and as they talk, they either tape-record or take written notes to assist them later as they reflect and consider ways to act on the information they gathered. Fifth, teachers review and reflect on the information shared by parents. Edwards et al. provide specific steps to follow, including composing a list of the positive and negative aspects of the "story," recording facts that "stick out" in your mind, and generating new questions. Sixth, the teacher uses his or her notes to develop some instructional ideas to help the child in the classroom and also support learning at home. Seventh, the teacher implements the ideas in the classroom and meets with parents to explain how they might help the child at home.

The Funds of Knowledge and Parent Story approaches are especially comprehensive and potentially very instructive. However, building parent–teacher relationships need not be quite as formal a process as each of these requires. Allen (2007), for example, emphasized ways teachers might take advantage of existing daily and weekly routines to create spaces for conversations with parents. In communities where parents walk their children to school, a teacher positioned at the appropriate location can initiate "hand-off chats" (Allen, 2007, p. 71), sharing information about the child's progress, providing parents an opportunity to ask a question about a homework assignment, and so forth. Other examples include getting-to-know-you conferences with each parent early in the school year, characterized as a "listening conference" (p. 72) during which parents share their knowledge and insights about their children; and a weekly communication about classroom work that includes an envelope containing a sample of children's work, a comment from the teacher about the child's learning progress, and a space for parents to write their own response to the child's work and progress.

As we reflect on these ideas and consider how we, as teachers, can effectively build a classroom culture that leads to productive partnerships with our children's families, we find the comments of Lapp (2010) a clear and helpful reminder of the stance we should take: "As suggested by the African proverb 'he who does not know one thing knows another,' all participants have something to share and therefore all voices should be heard in establishing and maintaining a partnership" (p. 154).

Understanding School and Classroom Programs

We chose two examples of initiatives that were intended, at least partially, to support parents' understanding of school and classroom programs. The first, the Family Fluency Program (Morrow, Kuhn, & Schwanenflugel, 2007) was designed to develop parents' understanding of the classroom reading program and to engage parents as partners to support children's classroom literacy learning. The program comprised two parent workshops. At the first meeting, teachers described the school's reading program and provided a brief demonstration of a typical reading lesson. Using a short reading selection, parents observed how the teacher prompted children to connect the selection to background experiences and to make predictions or ask questions. They also learned about echo reading, choral reading, and partner reading, and about ways to engage children in a discussion of the story. They discussed the purpose of each of the strategies and the ways each is expected to support children's reading achievement. In addition, parents received a handout (in English and in Spanish) that described how to practice the fluency strategies. Next, parents practiced the strategies with each other; following this activity, their children joined them and they practiced the strategies with their children. As the meeting ended, parents were asked to read (at least twice) the stories that would be sent home each week by the classroom teacher and to practice the fluency strategies at least three times each week. At the second workshop, teachers focused on developing parents' understanding of "good" fluency. They played audiotapes of children reading the same selection, one with excellent fluency, one with adequate fluency, and one with poor fluency.

They provided parents with a recorder and audiotapes and suggested that parents record their children's reading so they could compare earlier and later oral readings and evaluate progress. Children again joined the meeting and parents and children together practiced recording the child's reading. Results indicated that participating parents read with their children more than they had before, learned and used strategies to support reading fluency, and recognized and mentioned improvement they saw as they engaged their children in repeated readings.

A second example, the Parent Institute for Quality Education (PIQE; Chrispeels & Rivero, 2001) was designed to increase parent involvement by helping parents to gain a fuller understanding of expectations for their roles and responsibilities in their children's schooling. Consistent with evidence on effective home–school partnerships, PIQE is based on the principle that the parents served (mostly low-income recent immigrants) need information about the educational system, about how to interact with the school, and about how to help their children at home. Parents were invited to attend eight 90-minute sessions, each of which addressed an issue related to one of the principles. Print materials were translated into parents' first language, and during each session, parents talked and interacted with each other and with the instructor about the focal topic. Classes were scheduled in both the morning and evening to accommodate the needs of different families, and classes were taught by instructors fluent in the dominant language of the group of parents. Outcomes, based on presurvey and postsurvey data (collected from 95 families) and interview data (collected from a subsample of 11 families), were noteworthy: parents' understanding of their roles in their children's education grew as they gained new information and, both at home and at school, they acted on their new understanding. Moreover, absent any change in teachers' invitations or active effort, parents increased school involvement in four particular ways: they initiated more communication with the teacher, they provided more positive support to their children, they increased their engagement in teaching activities at home, and they increased requests for information about their children's academic progress.

In each of these examples, outcome data were focused on changes in parent behaviors, rather than changes in children's achievement. However, evidence from other studies (e.g., Houtenville & Conway, 2008; Jeynes, 2003; Sheldon, 2003) of a direct relationship between parent involvement and children's achievement, indicates that interventions that build parents' understanding of school and classroom programs, as these did, are an important part of administrators' and teachers' home–school partnership repertoire.

Supporting Family Learning

Three general findings can be derived from studies of effects of family literacy interventions: first, effective programs not only focus on important literacy content but also support parents' self-efficacy by allocating time to explain, model, and guide parents in implementation of the focal literacy activity (Hoover-Dempsey & Sandler, 1995; Hoover-Dempsey & Whitaker, 2010; Hoover-Dempsey et al., 2005). Second, effective programs consider both short- and long-term effects of focal activities and, in turn, focal activities are thoroughly aligned with this understanding (Sénéchal & Young, 2008). In the early grades, a focus on specific code-related skills will support early literacy achievement, but by themselves, these skills may have little influence on achievement after first grade. Across grade levels, a focus on listening to children read will support children's development of word reading accuracy and fluency (Toomey, 1993), but may have little influence on children's development of vocabulary and concept knowledge. A focus on reading aloud to children beginning in early childhood will support acquisition of vocabulary, language, and concept knowledge that will, in turn, support children's comprehension in grade 2 and beyond, but these abilities may show few effects prior to grade 2 (Whitehurst & Lonigan, 2002). Third, effective parent involvement programs embed literacy events in engaging, high-quality texts and in motivating, interesting, and playful games and activities, and within contexts that are of social importance for family members (Paratore & Yaden, 2010; Roser, 2010).

There are numerous projects and approaches that meet these three criteria (e.g., Edwards, 1994, 1995; Hindin & Paratore, 2007; Jordan, Snow, & Porche, 2000; Paratore, 1993, 2001; Rodriguez-Brown, 2010; Steiner, 2008). We have chosen to share two, each of which demonstrates a different type of intervention approach. The first, Project EASE (Jordan et al., 2000) was designed to focus entirely on supporting the child's literacy learning through parent–child literacy interactions. The second, the Intergenerational Literacy Program (Paratore, 2001), focuses on advancing parents' English language and literacy knowledge, parent–child literacy interactions, and, in turn, children's literacy achievement.

Project EASE (Jordan et al., 2000) was developed as a yearlong literacy intervention program serving families of children entering kindergarten. Project EASE comprised five parent-training sessions (held during the day when children were in school), each organized around a 1-month unit. Each training session provided parents background information related to a focal topic (e.g., vocabulary learning) and guided them in implementing activities designed to promote development of the particular literacy skill or ability (thereby supporting the development of parental self-efficacy). During each of the remaining 3 weeks, parents received a packet containing scripted activities related to the focal topic. Each packet included a book rich in interesting vocabulary and in opportunities for discussion and conversation and suggestions for the types of parent–child interactions that are associated with children's language and literacy learning. At the end of the program, the children were given a battery of language and literacy tasks, and the children of families who participated in the program showed significant gains in vocabulary, narrative understanding, phonemic awareness, and story sequencing.

Moreover, language skills showed the largest effect, a finding that is especially important, given the evidence of the strong relationship between early language knowledge and later reading achievement (Sénéchal, Ouelette, & Rodney, 2006; Whitehurst & Lonigan, 2002). Furthermore, the intervention had the greatest effects on children who scored low at pretest, suggesting the potential for programs of this type to close the achievement gap.

The Intergenerational Literacy Project (ILP) (Paratore, 2001) was designed to serve three purposes: to help parents develop their own literacy, to support the practice of family literacy in the home, and, in turn, to support children's school-based success. The ILP has served more than 2,100 families, almost all new immigrants who journeyed to the United States from 56 different countries. On average, learners have attended school for just over 8 years, although parents' education levels vary widely: more than 15% of learners have gone to school for fewer than 4 years, and more than 14% have attended at least some college. Classes are held four mornings or three evenings per week for 2 hours each day and for 40 weeks each year. Children's classes are offered in both the morning (for preschool children) and the evening (for preschool and school-age children) as well.

Each of the adult literacy classes follows the same basic guidelines—each focuses about half of class time on reading and writing of adult interest and the other half on texts of importance or of interest to child development and child learning. All teachers and tutors are focused on supporting parents' and children's understanding of strategies to improve their reading and writing and application of those strategies in their daily lives and to support children's school success. This understanding is reinforced through several instructional routines. On a daily basis, adult learners report their previous day's literacy activities on a two-sided literacy log. On one side, parents record literacy activities of personal interest, such as reading recipes, holding conversations in English with coworkers, and writing letters. On the other side, learners detail literacy activities that they engaged in with their children, including storybook reading, homework monitoring, and shared TV watching. A few minutes of class time each day is devoted to literacy log sharing, which allows parents to learn from ways in which their peers use literacy at home and helps teachers and tutors build learners' understanding of what constitutes literacy. (If, for example, a parent reports having gone to the supermarket, teachers will tease out how that learner may have interacted with print while shopping.)

A second instructional routine that promotes parents' metacognitive awareness of their own and their children's learning is the use of graphic organizers. Teachers draw learners' attention to how completing the organizer helps them make sense of the text and its structure, and they explain that their children are learning to use the same strategies and tools in school.

Over the years of the project, a diverse collection of assessment practices has been used to monitor and document project outcomes. Short-term outcomes include higher rates of attendance and retention in family literacy classes than those of traditional adult basic education and, in many cases, of other family literacy programs (Paratore, 1993; Paratore, Krol-Sinclair, David, & Schick, 2010; Paratore, Melzi, & Krol-Sinclair, 1999), indicating that daily instructional practices are effective in maintaining parents' motivation to advance their own and their children's literacy knowledge; increased use of reading and writing outside of class to achieve personal goals, thereby making print literacy a more frequent routine in their daily lives; and increased parent–child storybook reading (at least weekly), a practice that has been found to correlate highly with early reading achievement (e.g., Bus, van IJzendoorn, & Pellegrini, 1995). Long-term effects (Paratore et al., 2010) indicate that when children whose parents participated in the ILP are compared with their general-education peers, they have significantly higher rates of school attendance, consistently higher scores on state assessments (in both English language arts and mathematics), higher rates of high school graduation, and higher rates of enrollment in postsecondary education.

SUMMATIVE GUIDING PRINCIPLES

As we look back on the body of evidence related to effects of parent involvement on children's literacy learning, we are struck by two main points. The first is that evidence to support the claim that parental involvement is fundamentally important to children's school success is compelling: across different populations and outcome measures, results consistently favor children whose parents are involved in their learning. The second point is that, especially in communities where parents are poor and linguistically and culturally diverse, the level of parent involvement is not determined by the families' or communities' demographic characteristics, but rather by the actions teachers take to involve parents. As described in the aforementioned examples, at times, administrators and teachers respond to these findings with comprehensive (and often time-consuming) efforts. But one need not start out by attempting a full-scale initiative. To start, we can set the stage for productive parent involvement by adhering to a few basic guiding principles:

1. Productive home–school partnerships are grounded in strong parent–teacher relationships that grow out of interactions that are focused on the *exchange* of information between parents and teachers, such that teachers gain a deeper understanding of the family's routines and interests, their children's particular interests and predispositions, and so forth; and parents gain a deeper understanding about the school, the classroom, and actions they might take to support their children's learning.

2. High levels of parent involvement are associated with effective outreach efforts. These include attention to the particular needs of the families in the community and are typically characterized by flexible scheduling

of events and distribution of notices and materials in the parents' first languages. In addition, teachers and administrators identify and enlist the support of friends, relatives, and community leaders who are influential with a particular family or with the various subcultures within a community.

3. Parental involvement initiatives that have an impact on children's literacy achievement are deliberately focused on the development of particular types of literacy knowledge (e.g., phonological and alphabet knowledge, vocabulary and concept knowledge, comprehension strategies) necessary for school-based literacy success. In addition, teachers and administrators identify the specific knowledge and skills parents need to effectively support children's learning, and they plan and offer workshops and training sessions that support parents' efficacious implementation of the focal activity.

REFLECTIONS AND FUTURE DIRECTIONS

As we think about where we are and where we need to be, we return yet again to the evidence that high levels of parent involvement correlate with greater achievement gains (e.g., Dearing, McCartney, Weiss, Krieder, & Simpkins, 2004; Sheldon, 2003), and that high levels of parent involvement can be realized "when schools take the required steps to develop and implement well-designed partnership activities and programs" (Sanders, Allen-Jones, & Abel, 2002, p. 177). And yet despite this well-documented evidence, inservice teachers are often playing catch-up. Few colleges and universities dedicate a full course on parent involvement as part of their teacher education program (Epstein, 2001), and accordingly, first-year teachers identify their lack of knowledge about how to work with families as one of their greatest needs (Rochkind, Ott, Immerwahr, Doble, & Johnson, 2007). As we look to the future, we see two essential needs. One is to help inservice teachers become familiar with and act on what we know about effective home–school partnerships. The second is to improve the preservice teacher education curriculum such that novice teachers enter the classroom prepared to develop the types of parent–teacher relationships that will enhance children's learning opportunities.

ENGAGEMENT ACTIVITIES

1. In several of the studies, parent involvement efforts were grounded in development of strong parent–teacher relationships. Consider the children in your classroom or your school. What do you know about their lives outside of school? What types of activities might you initiate to establish a trusting relationship and to learn more? Implement one or more of the

activities and then reflect: How might you use the information to make connections between children's home and school lives?

2. One important research finding is that in schools characterized by high levels of parent involvement, teachers and administrators have focused particularly on outreach efforts. Consider the families of the children in your school or classroom. How might you redesign or restructure parent involvement events or activities to accommodate families' needs for flexible time frames, child care, and transportation?
3. Although schools and teachers rely heavily on traditional forms of parental involvement (e.g., monthly newsletter, phone call home, note to parents), there are many other ways to inform parents about the school, the classroom, events, and expectations. Consider the parents in your community and the resources that might be used to improve parent–teacher communication. How might you vary the forms of communication to involve more parents?
4. Research indicates that parents are more involved in parent–child learning activities when they have a clear understanding of what to do and how to do it. Consider a home learning activity that you would like parents to do with their children. Outline the knowledge or skills parents need to effectively implement the activity and develop a plan for coaching parents toward successful implementation.

REFERENCES

Allen, J. (2007). *Creating welcoming schools: A practical guide to home-school partnerships with diverse families.* New York: Teachers College Press.

Arnold, D. H., Lonigan, C. J., Whitehurst, G. J., & Epstein, J. N. (1994). Accelerating language development through picture book reading: Replication and extension to a videotape training format. *Journal of Educational Psychology, 86,* 235–243.

Bus, A. G., van IJzendoorn, M. H., & Pellegrini, A. D. (1995). Joint book reading makes for success in learning to read: A meta-analysis in intergenerational transmission of literacy. *Review of Educational Research, 65,* 1–21.

Chrispeels, J. H., & Rivero, E. (2001). Engaging latino families for student success: How parent education can reshape parents' sense of place in the education of their children. *Peabody Journal of Education, 76*(2), 119–169.

Compton-Lilly, C. (2003). *Reading families: The literate lives of urban children.* New York: Teachers College Press.

Dearing, E., Kreider H., Simpkins, S., & Weiss, H. B. (2006). Family involvement in school and low-income children's literacy: Longitudinal associations between and within families. *Journal of Educational Psychology, 98*(4), 653–664.

Dearing, E., McCartney, K., Weiss, H. B., Krieder, H., & Simpkins, S. (2004). The promotive effects of family educational involvement for low-income children's literacy. *Journal of School Psychology, 42*(6), 445–460.

DeNavas-Walt, C., Proctor, B. D., & Smith, J. C. (2009). *Income, poverty, and health insurance coverage in the United States: 2008* (No. P60-236). Washington, DC: U.S. Census Bureau. Retrieved October 7, 2009, from *www.census.gov/hhes/www/poverty/poverty08html.*

Edwards, P. A. (1994). Responses of teachers and African-American mothers to a book-reading intervention program. In D. K. Dickinson (Ed.), *Bridges to literacy: Children, families, and schools* (pp. 175–210). Cambridge, MA: Blackwell.

Edwards, P. A. (1995). Empowering low-income mothers and fathers to share books with young children. *Reading Teacher, 48*, 558–565.

Edwards, P. A. (2009). *Tapping the potential of parents: A strategic guide to boosting student achievement through family involvement.* New York: Scholastic.

Edwards, P. A., Pleasants, H. M., & Franklin, S. H. (1999). *A path to follow: Learning to listen to parents.* Portsmouth, NH: Heinemann.

Epstein, J. (1986). Parents' reactions to teacher practices of parent involvement. *Elementary School Journal, 86*, 277–294.

Epstein, J. L. (2001). *School, family, and community partnerships: Preparing educators and improving schools.* Boulder, CO: Westview Press.

Footlick, J. K. (1990, Winter/Spring). What happened to the family? [Special issue]. *Newsweek*, pp. 15–20.

González, N., Moll, L. C., & Amanti, C. (2005). *Funds of knowledge: Theorizing practices in households, communities, and classrooms.* Mahwah, NJ: Erlbaum.

Greene, S., & Compton-Lilly, C. (2011). *Connecting home and school: Complexities and considerations in fostering parent involvement and family literacy.* New York: Teachers College Press.

Hays, S. (2004). *Flat broke with children: Women in the age of welfare reform.* Cambridge, UK: Oxford University Press.

Henderson, A. T., & Mapp, K. (2002). *A new wave of evidence: The impact of school, family, and community connections on student achievement.* Austin, Texas: National Center for Family and Community Connections with Schools.

Hindin, A., & Paratore, J. R. (2007). Supporting young children's literacy learning through home–school partnerships: The effectiveness of a home repeated-reading intervention. *Journal of Literacy Research, 39*(3), 307–333.

Houtenville, A. J., & Conway, K. S. (2008). Parental effort, school resources, and student achievement. *The Journal of Human Resources, 43*(2), 437–453.

Hoover-Dempsey, K. V., & Sandler, H. M. (1995). Parental involvement in children's education: Why does it make a difference? *Teacher's College Record, 97*, 310–331.

Hoover-Dempsey, K. V., Walker, J. M. T., Sandler, H. M., Whetsel, D., Green, C. L., Wilkins, A. S., et al. (2005). Why do parents become involved? research findings and implications. *The Elementary School Journal, 106*(2), 105–130.

Hoover-Dempsey, K. V., & Whitaker, M. C. (2010). The parental involvement process: Implications for literacy development. In K. Dunsmore & D. Fisher (Eds.), *Bringing literacy home* (pp. 53–82). Newark, DE: International Reading Association.

Iceland, J. (2006). *Poverty in America: A handbook* (2nd ed.). Berkeley: University of California Press.

Jeynes, W. (2003). A meta-analysis: The effects of parental involvement on minority children's academic involvement. *Education and Urban Society, 35*(1), 202–218.

Jordan, G. E., Snow, C. E., & Porche, M. V. (2000). Project EASE: The effect of a family literacy project on kindergarten students' early literacy skills. *Reading Research Quarterly, 35*(4), 524–546.

Kozol, J. (1994). The new untouchables. In J. Krevotics & E. J. Nussel (Eds.), *Transforming urban education* (pp. 75–78). Boston: Allyn & Bacon.

Kozol, J. (2005). *The shame of the nation.* New York: Crown.

Krol-Sinclair, B. (1996). Connecting home and school literacies: Immigrant parents with limited formal education as classroom storybook readers. In D. J. Leu, C. K. Kinzer, & K. A. Hinchman (Eds.), *Literacies for the 21st century: Research and practice* (pp. 270–283). Chicago: National Reading Conference.

Lapp, D. (2010). Stories, facts, and possibilities: Bridging the home and school worlds for students acquiring a school discourse. In K. Dunsmore & D. Fisher (Eds.), *Bringing literacy home* (pp. 136–160). Newark, DE: International Reading Association.

Lareau, A. (1989). *Home advantage: Social class and parental intervention.* New York: Falmer Press.

Lawrence-Lightfoot, S. (1978). *Worlds apart: Relationships between families and schools.* New York: Basic Books.

Lawrence-Lightfoot, S. L. (2004). *The essential conversation: What parents and teachers can learn from each other.* New York: Random House.

McIntyre, E. (2010). Issues in funds of knowledge teaching and research: Key concepts from a study of appalachian families and schooling. In M. L. Dantas & P. C. Manyak (Eds.), *Home–school connections in a multicultural society: Learning from and with culturally and linguistically diverse families* (pp. 201–217). New York: Routledge.

Moll, L. C., & Cammarota, J. (2010). Cultivating new funds of knowledge through research and practice. In K. Dunsmore & D. Fisher (Eds.), *Bringing literacy home* (pp. 289–305). Newark, DE: International Reading Association.

Moll, L., & Greenberg, J. B. (1991). Creating zones of possibilities: Combining social contexts for instruction. In L. C. Moll (Ed.), *Vygotsky in education* (pp. 319–348). New York: Cambridge University Press.

Morrow, L. M., Kuhn, M. R., & Schwanenflugel, P. J. (2007). The family fluency program. *The Reading Teacher, 60*(4), 322–333.

Nieto, S. (1992). *Affirming diversity: The sociopolitical context of multicultural education.* New York: Longman.

Paratore, J. R. (1993). Influence of an intergenerational approach to literacy on the practice of literacy of parents and their children. In C. Kinzer & D. Leu (Eds.), *Examining central issues in literacy, research, theory, and practice* (pp. 83–91). Chicago: National Reading Conference.

Paratore, J. R. (2001). *Opening doors, opening opportunities: Family literacy in an urban community.* Needham Heights, MA: Allyn & Bacon.

Paratore, J. R., Krol-Sinclair, B., David, B., & Schick, A. (2010). Writing the next chapter in family literacy: Clues to long-term effects. In K. Dunsmore & D. Fisher (Eds.), *Bringing literacy home* (pp. 265–288). Newark, DE: International Reading Association.

Paratore, J. R., Melzi, G., & Krol-Sinclair, B. (1999). *What should we expect of family literacy? experiences of latino children whose parents participate in an intergenerational literacy program.* Newark, DE: International Reading Association.

Paratore, J. R., & Yaden, D. B. (2010). Family literacy on the defensive: The defunding of Even Start—Omen or opportunity? In D. Lapp, D. Fisher, & D. Alvermann (Eds.), *Handbook of research on teaching the English language arts* (3rd ed., pp. 90–96). Newark, DE: International Reading Association.

Reeves, D. B. (2005). High performance in high-poverty schools: 90/90/90 and beyond. In J. Flood & P. L. Anders (Eds.), *Literacy development of students in urban schools: Research and policy* (pp. 362–388). Newark, DE: International Reading Association.

Rochkind, J., Ott, A., Immerwahr, J., Doble, J., & Johnson, J. (2007). *Lessons learned: New teachers talk about their jobs, challenges, and long-range plans. A report from the National Comprehensive Center for Teacher Quality and Public Agenda.* Retrieved July 28, 2010, from *www.publicagenda.org/reports/lessons-learned-new-teachers-talk-about-their-jobs-challenges-and-long-range-plans-issue-no-2.*

Rodriguez-Brown, F. (2010). Latino culture and schooling: Reflections on family literacy with a culturally and linguistically different community. In K. Dusmore & D. Fisher (Eds.), *Bringing literacy home* (pp. 203–225). Newark, DE: International Reading Association.

Roser, N. (2010). Talking over books at home and in school. In K. Dunsmore & D. Fisher (Eds.), *Bringing literacy home* (pp. 104–135). Newark, DE: International Reading Association.

Sanders, M. G., Allen-Jones, G. L., & Abel, Y. (2002). Involving families and communities in the education of children and youth placed at risk. In S. Stringfield & D. Land (Eds.), *Educating at risk students: One hundred-first yearbook of the National Society for the Study of Education, Part II* (pp. 171–188). Chicago: University of Chicago Press.

Sénéchal, M., Ouellette, G., & Rodney, D. (2006). The misunderstood giant: On the predictive role of early vocabulary to future reading. In D. K. Dickinson & S. B. Neuman (Eds.), *Handbook of early literacy research* (pp. 173–182). New York: Guilford Press.

Sénéchal, M., & Young, L. (2008). The effect of family literacy interventions on children's acquisition of reading from kindergarten to grade 3: A meta-analytic review. *Review of Educational Research, 78*(4), 880–907.

Sheldon, S. B. (2003). Linking school–family–community partnerships in urban elementary schools to student achievement on state tests. *The Urban Review, 35*(2), 145–164.

Shipler, D. K. (2005). *The working poor: Invisible in America.* New York: Vintage.

Steiner, L. (2008). *Effects of a school-based parent and teacher intervention to promote first-grade students' literacy achievement.* Unpublished doctoral dissertation, Boston University. Retrieved November 4, 2010, from *proquest.umi.com/pqdweb?did=1514961841&Fmt=7&clientId=3740&RQT=309&VName=PQD.*

Taylor, B. M., & Pearson, P. D. (2002). *Teaching reading: Effective schools, accomplished teachers.* Mahwah, NJ: Erlbaum.

Teddlie, C., & Stringfield, S. (1993). *Schools make a difference: Lessons learned from a 10-year study of school effects.* New York: Teachers College Press.

Toomey, D. (1993). Parents hearing their children read: A review. Rethinking the lessons of the Haringey Project. *Educational Research, 35,* 223–236.

Tutwiler, S. W. (1998). Diversity among families. In M. L. Fuller & G. Olsen (Eds.), *Home–school relations: Working successfully with parents and families* (pp. 40–66). Boston: Allyn & Bacon.

Valdés, G. (1996). *Con respeto: Bridging the differences between culturally diverse families and schools.* New York: Teachers College Press.

Whitehurst, G. J., & Lonigan, C. J. (2002). Emergent literacy: Development from prereaders to readers. In S. B. Neuman & D. K. Dickinson (Eds.), *Handbook of early literacy research* (pp. 11–29). New York: Guilford Press.

CHAPTER 19

Best Practices in Professional Development for Improving Literacy Instruction in Schools

Rita M. Bean
Aimee L. Morewood

> Professional development is not about workshops and courses; rather, it is at its heart the development of habits of learning that are far more likely to be powerful if they present themselves day after day.
>
> —Fullan (2001, p. 253)

This chapter will:

- Provide background about professional development efforts.
- Describe and synthesize the available research and literature about professional development.
- Discuss several promising approaches to professional development and what they mean for teachers and schools.

Over the years, there have been varying views about what matters in terms of improving student achievement in reading. Researchers have studied the effects of various factors, including programs, materials, group size, and teacher quality. Overwhelmingly, there is evidence that teachers are the most important in-school factor contributing to school success (Darling-Hammond, Wei, Andree, Richardson, & Orphanos, 2009; Hanushek, 1992; Rivkin, Hanushek, & Kain, 2005). This finding has led to an emphasis by school districts, states, and the federal government, on providing professional development that enhances teachers' ability to provide effective and evidence-based literacy instruction for students. There tends to be agreement that, even with the most rigorous and comprehensive teacher preparation program, there is a need for ongoing professional development that enables teachers to build on what they know. Just as a physician needs to be current about new treatments or approaches for improving medical care, so too does the teacher, responsible for students' literacy learning, need to be knowledgeable about effective reading practices. In schools today, teachers must continue to learn in order to meet the needs of *all* students, with an emphasis on reducing the achievement gap between the "haves and have nots," in terms of race, culture, socioeconomic status, and language. Likewise, the societal demands that require students to graduate with higher level skills as well as the greater accountability required of teachers has contributed to the need for an investment in ongoing professional development for teachers.

In this chapter, we discuss professional development for improving literacy instruction in schools. We address the following issues and topics:

- *Issues and concerns about professional development.* We begin the chapter with a section that provides necessary background for understanding professional development and the issues related to successful implementation.
- *Evidence-based best practices for professional development.* In this section, we discuss what is known about effective professional development, describing and synthesizing the available research and literature.
- *Best practices in action.* We describe more fully several promising approaches, including literacy coaching, teacher research, and the use of professional learning communities or technology for enhancing teacher learning.
- *Reflections and future directions.*

PROFESSIONAL DEVELOPMENT: ISSUES AND CONCERNS

Guskey (2000) defines professional development as "those processes and activities designed to enhance the professional knowledge, skills, and attitudes of educators so that they might, in turn, improve the learning of students" (p. 16). This definition provides for much variation in how one might envision professional development (e.g., professional reading by individual teachers or groups of teachers, enrollment in university coursework, standalone workshop sessions organized by schools or professional organizations, or a mentoring or coaching approach in which teachers receive support and guidance from another educator in implementing literacy instruction). The focus on student learning is an important aspect of Guskey's definition because it emphasizes student outcomes as a key component for evaluating professional development. Too often, however, the evaluation focus has been on the "happiness" or "satisfaction" of participants. At best, those implementing professional development have looked for changes in teacher knowledge, teacher beliefs, or teacher practices.

Criticisms of professional development are many, and include concerns about its content, delivery, and intensity. Teachers may not feel that the ideas being promoted are worthwhile or that they are able to implement them successfully (Bean, Swan, & Morris, 2002; Morewood & Bean, 2009). Teachers may not receive the learning and support they need to integrate what they are learning into classroom practices. There may be a lack of necessary resources, insufficient feedback and follow-up, or teachers may not see the value in the professional development received. Multiple initiatives being implemented simultaneously may make professional development seem fragmented and contradictory. According to Choy and Ross (1998), districts have a great deal of control in planning professional development for teachers and are responsible for providing much of the professional development that teachers receive. Yet, as reported by Killeen, Monk, and Plecki (2002), from 1992 to 1998 districts devoted only 3% of their total yearly expenditures to professional development. Moreover, teachers reported that the time spent in professional development during the year ranged between 1 and 8 hours (National Center for Educational Statistics [NCES], 2001); yet the Learning First Alliance (2000) suggested 80 hours or more per year for professional development in literacy. The NCES (2001) report also indicated that teachers perceived that time spent in professional development positively influenced their instruction. Furthermore, when teachers perceived the professional development to be relevant, they were willing to spend time engaged in the learning opportunity (Elliott, 2007).

Anders, Hoffman, and Duffy (2000), in their extensive review of what they called "inservice" education, found that studies on this topic represented less than 1% of the total number of studies reported for reading education and indicated that such research was not a top priority for literacy researchers. Recently, however, given the evidence that the quality of teaching affects student learning, there has been an increase in professional development research in many different educational areas, including literacy instruction. Below we describe and summarize that research.

EVIDENCE-BASED PRACTICES FOR PROFESSIONAL DEVELOPMENT RELATED TO LITERACY

Anders et al. (2000), in reviewing the research about professional development in literacy identified six salient features of quality: "intensive/extensive commitments; monitoring/coaching support; reflection and deliberation, dialogue and negotiation; voluntary participation or choice; and collaboration" (p. 730). The National Reading Panel (2000) also analyzed research about professional development related to reading; however, because of the limited number of research studies that met the criteria for inclusion in the report, only a few conclusions were drawn. The writers found that teachers' attitudes and practices did change as a result of professional development, and there was also improvement in student outcomes in several studies. They also concluded that professional development required extensive support and extended periods of training. Their major conclusion was that there is a need for more research in this area, especially research in which the nature of the intervention is described fully.

Research conducted in other subject fields (e.g., math and science) and by those interested in school change have also contributed to the knowledge base about professional development (Desimone, Porter, Garet, Yoon, & Birman, 2002; Garet, Porter, Desimone, Birman, & Yoon, 2001; Richardson & Placier, 2001; Sparks & Loucks-Horsley, 1990; Yoon, Duncan, Lee, Scarloss, & Shapley, 2007). Results of these and other research studies have enabled researchers to identify best practices in PD. These results can be summarized using the three categories of content, context, and process (National Staff Development Council [NSDC], 2001).

Content

Teachers need to know the subject that they are teaching, how to teach it, and how students learn it (American Educational Research Association, 2005; Gabriel, 2010; Morewood, Ankrum, & Bean, 2010; Shulman, 1986). Professional development must be built on a well-conceptualized, in-depth framework that focuses on what teachers need to know about what they are required to teach, *and* how students learn this content. In the literacy area, there are many resources that school district personnel can consult in developing their notions of what content to consider in any professional development program. In Figure 19.1, we identify key reports that may be useful to those seeking up-to-date research findings about specific aspects of literacy.

Schools must also attend to the literacy standards of their district and state; moreover, the Common Core State Standards Initiative for Language Arts (2010), being adopted by many states, will have an impact on what knowledge teachers need to know relative to literacy instruction. Because these standards address literacy across the major academic areas, teachers in these disciplines will also need professional development that helps them understand how to use reading and writing as tools to help students learn the content.

Context

Fullan (2001) has written extensively about the importance of context. What works for one school may not work for another. Professional development needs should be related to school goals and student learning, with a focus on what is or is not happening in teachers' classrooms. Factors such as teacher experiences and abilities, their receptivity and attitude toward change, needs

Biancarosa, G., & Snow, C. (2004). *Reading next: A vision for action and research in middle and high school literacy.* Washington, DC: Alliance for Excellent Education.

Graham, S., & Hebert, M. (2010). *Writing to read: Evidence for how writing can improve reading.* Washington, DC: Alliance for Excellent Education.

Kamil, M. L., Mosenthal, P. B., Pearson, P. D., & Barr, R. (Eds.). (2000). *Handbook of reading research* (Vol. 3). Mahwah, NJ: Erlbaum.

National Early Literacy Panel. (2008). *Developing early literacy: A scientific synthesis of early literacy development and implications for intervention.* Washington, DC: National Institute for Family Literacy and the National Center for Family Literacy.

National Literacy Panel. (2006). *Developing literacy in second-language learners. Report of the National Literacy Panel on Language-Minority Children and Youth* (D. August & T. Shanahan, Eds.). Washington, DC: Center for Applied Linguistics and Erlbaum.

National Reading Panel. (2000). *Teaching children to read: An evidence-based assessment of the scientific research literature on reading and its implication for reading instruction.* Rockville, MD: National Institute of Child Health and Human Development.

FIGURE 19.1. Key research reports.

of the students, and the resources available in the school must be taken into consideration when planning professional development programs. Moreover, successful staff development programs must emphasize the importance of teacher buy-in; that is, teachers understand and value the need for a specific focus. Furthermore, the leadership that exists in the school is important and provides the foundation for change (Marzano, 2003; Smylie, Allensworth, Greenberg, Harris, & Luppescu, 2001).

Lieberman and Miller (1984) indicate that there is a need for both top-down and bottom-up approaches. In other words, there is a need for the district or school to set the general direction or vision for the literacy program and to communicate expectations to the teachers (e.g., top-down). At the same time, effective programs must involve teachers in establishing specific goals and in designing the staff development activities that lead toward achieving the goals (e.g., bottom-up). Another way of thinking about this is to consider Fullan's notion of the need for both pressure and support in any change project or initiative. As Fullan (2001) states, "Pressure without support leads to resistance and alienation; support without pressure leads to drift or waste of resources" (p. 92). Professional development provides the support that teachers need in order to address the goals or vision established for the school and its students.

Processes

Researchers are consistent in their recommendations that the best professional development is job embedded, that is, it is closely related to the classroom work of the teacher. Teachers must be actively involved, and there are benefits when there is collective participation of teachers from the same schools, grades, or departments (Desimone et al., 2002). Moreover, teachers' learning opportunities should be aligned with real work experiences, using actual curriculum materials and assessments.

There is a need for collegial work that requires programs of some duration. Yoon et al. (2007), in analyzing nine studies that met rigorous criteria, including those related to design and outcome measures, found that when teachers received substantial professional development—an average of 49 hours in the nine studies—there was a positive and significant effect on student achievement.

Although there are many approaches or processes that can be used, seldom is one used in isolation. Teachers may attend workshops to gain some initial knowledge about a specific curriculum or instructional approach. However, as illustrated in the classic work of Joyce and Showers (2002), in addition to becoming knowledgeable about a specific educational endeavor and understanding the rationale or theory for it, the following types of support strengthen learning and the potential for transfer of what is learned into classroom practice: demonstration, practice, and coaching that provides teachers with feedback to help them make modifications or adjustments in their instruction. Joyce and Showers (2002) found that when a combination of components was employed, especially peer coaching, there was a real and strong transfer to classroom practice by more than 90% of participants.

A study by Taylor, Pearson, Peterson, and Rodriguez (2005) provides an excellent example of how the important aspects of professional development—content, context, and process—were integrated in a large-scale study. The professional development program was based on the CIERA School Change Framework and was implemented in 13 schools over the course of 2 years. The authors focused on two important bodies of scholarship to build their school reform initiative: knowledge about curriculum and pedagogy in literacy (i.e., what should be taught and how), and research about how to improve schools in general (i.e., effective processes for professional development). These researchers found that the more elements of their CIERA School Framework implemented, the greater the growth in students' reading achievement. Also, there was a larger effect size when data were examined across 2 years rather than 1 year. These findings highlight the necessity of sustained and efforts. As Taylor et al. (2005) state, "Growth in students' reading scores as well as change in classroom teaching practices came in small increments from one year to the next. There were no quick fixes and no magic bullets in these schools—only hard work, persistence, and professional commitment" (p. 64). Taylor et al. (2005) also addressed the importance of sustained collaborative work with colleagues that includes reflection and a commitment to collective problem solving, facilitation and support for teachers (both internal and external), and strong curricular leadership. They also highlighted the importance of refocused classroom instruction based on data about student achievement.

The evidence is clear: Schools need to think about content, context, and process factors when developing professional development programs (NSDC, 2001). They need to recognize that professional development is hard work, it takes time, and it requires a total-school commitment if it is ultimately to improve teacher practices and student achievement.

We used the results of research about professional development to develop a rubric that can be used as a tool for thinking about a school's professional development program for improving literacy and as a means of modifying or adapting that program (see Figure 19.2). The major categories in this rubric are: content, collaboration and sense of community, active learning, duration, and application and feedback opportunities. Although a principal or school leader might complete the rubric independently, it is best if a leadership team at the school discusses each of the items and then completes the rubric. By reviewing the results, the school team has data they can use to make decisions about planning and offering professional development.

In Figure 19.3, we provide a chart that can be used to develop an action plan for the school. By reviewing the scores for the rubric, schools can identify the strengths or weaknesses of their current professional development plan. They can then make decisions about priorities, select dates for accomplishment, and identify individuals responsible for specific tasks and resources needed.

BEST PRACTICES IN ACTION

We discuss four approaches to professional development that seem to show promise in terms of improving classroom instruction in literacy and, ultimately, student learning: literacy coaching, professional learning communities, teacher research, and technology. We chose these four, given their potential and the emerging research that supports efforts using them. All of them could be found in a single comprehensive school professional development program, or a school might choose to emphasize or use one or several approaches (e.g., professional learning communities and literacy coaching). Below we define and describe each approach and provide practical ideas for schools interested in using such an approach.

Literacy Coaching

Coaching is a growing phenomenon in schools today. The concept of coaching, however, is not a new one. As early as the 1980s, Joyce and Showers (2002) were studying the power of coaching, specifically peer coaching, as a means of improving the quality of professional development. At the present time, we find coaches at all levels, K–12, in various subjects (math, science, reading), and there are various models or approaches as to how coaches should function. Some coaching models emphasize the importance of the processes

Rating Scale (To what extent is there evidence that school addresses each of the items in the rubric?)

3	Great extent
2	Some extent
1	Little extent
0	Not present

Content

Score	Description
	School has coherent set of literacy goals and standards across grade levels that can be used as a framework to guide professional development (standards for literacy performance at each grade level have been identified, e.g., what should students know and be able to do?).
	Curriculum and instructional practices are evidence based.
	Curriculum and instructional practices set high expectations for all students.
	Curriculum and instructional practices meet students' needs.
	Multiple sources of data are used to make decisions about curriculum and instructional practices.
	Professional development opportunities enable teachers to gain in-depth understanding of the theory and research underlying practices (why something is important).

_______ or _____ / 18 = _________ %

Collaboration and Sense of Community in the School

Score	Description
	Teachers have decision-making role in what and how they learn.
	There is shared leadership among administrators and teachers when deciding what is necessary to achieve goals set by the school.
	Teachers in the school are given opportunities to work together, interact, network, learn from each other in a collegial manner (in PLCs, grade level meetings, study groups, PDSs, etc.).
	There is a focus on the value of parents and their role as members of the community.
	Teachers are recognized for the work that they do.
	Teachers recognize the importance of ongoing professional learning.

(cont.)

FIGURE 19.2. Rubric to assess professional development program to promote school literacy learning.

	Teachers share leadership in planning and implementation of schoolwide professional development.

________ or _____ / 21 = __________ %

Duration and Amount of Time

Score	Description
	Professional development programs are ongoing and give teachers opportunities to develop in-depth understanding of the content to be learned.
	Teachers have ample contact hours related to the professional development topic.

________ or _____ / 6 = __________ %

Active Learning

Score	Description
	School makes use of new technologies (e.g., blogs, wikis, podcasts, webinars, online course work) in helping teachers achieve their professional goals.
	Teachers use information from their classrooms and students in their professional development work, (e.g., use data, review student work samples, do lesson study).
	Activities are differentiated according to teacher needs and styles of learning.
	Teachers have opportunities to participate in inquiry-based activities that require critical thinking, application, and reflection.
	Teachers have opportunities to practice what they are learning with their peers or in small groups.

________ or _____ / 15 = __________ %

Application and Feedback Opportunities

Score	Description
	Teachers have opportunities to apply what they are learning in their classrooms.
	Teachers interact and reflect with their peers about their experiences in a risk-free environment.
	Feedback is geared toward supporting and guiding teacher practices (it is not evaluative).
	Teachers are recognized for what they know and do.
	Teachers have opportunities to self-evaluate and reflect on their work (video, etc.).
	There are adequate personnel at the school to provide effective professional development (literacy coaches, outside facilitators, university faculty, etc.)

________ or _____ / 18 = __________ %

FIGURE 19.2. *(cont.)*

	Score *N* %	Strength	Need	What should we do? In what order?	Who should do what? What resources are needed?	When should we accomplish our goal?
Content						
Collaboration and sense of community in the school						
Duration and amount of time						
Active learning						
Application and feedback opportunities						

FIGURE 19.3. Action plan for developing a professional development program for improving school literacy learning.

being used. For example, in cognitive coaching (Costa & Garmston, 2002), the emphasis is on teacher choice and reflection, helping teachers move from where they are to where they want to be. In other models, coaches are expected to work with teachers to assure "fidelity to implementation," that is, ensuring that teachers implement the curriculum as expected. Other models, such as content-focused coaching (Staub & West, 2003) define the coach as one who has a deep understanding of the content and knows how to plan lessons in collaboration with teachers to help them become more proficient in their instructional practices and to assure that all students achieve the planned goals. Some writers have a broader view of the coaches' role; that is, coaches, in collaboration with the principal and others, build instructional capacity in the school. These coaches, called "change" or "capacity" coaches (Neufield & Roper, 2003) work with principals and teachers to create a culture or climate that promotes total school reform. Certainly, the model of coaching found in a school has serious implications for what coaches do, how teachers respond to them and their requests, and the degree to which such coaching leads to changes in classroom teaching and student learning.

Also, coaches can be internal to the school or come from an external partner or resource. In LEADERS (Literacy Educators Assessing and Developing Early Reading Success), Bean (2004) discusses a reading initiative that, in addition to regularly scheduled workshops held over a year's time, included coaches or facilitators from the university assigned to schools to assist teachers in their implementation efforts. These facilitators helped with assessment, modeled, co-taught, observed, and provided feedback. They communicated with principals about the program and discussed how they and the university could facilitate program implementation. Because the instructional practices were consistent with those of the school district, the coaches were readily accepted by teachers as an important source of support.

Recent research about coaching has led to positive findings about its effect on classroom practices and student learning (Bean, Draper, Jackson, Vandermolen, & Zigmond, 2010; Biancarosa, Bryk, & Dexter, 2010; L'Allier & Elish-Piper, 2006; Neuman & Cunningham, 2009), while other research has reported mixed or no relationship between coaching and achievement (Garet et al., 2008; Marsh et al., 2008; Shidler, 2009). Given the many factors that influence achievement, the mixed results of studies are not surprising. More effort must be expended in studying exactly how coaching interacts with these other variables, including principal leadership, community relations, the climate of the school, and the instructional guidance or congruence available in the school (Bryk, Sebring, Allensworth, Luppescu, & Easton, 2010). Most educators who write about coaching agree on several key points. One is that the coach does not serve in an evaluative role; rather, the coach is there to support the work of the teacher in a collaborative manner. Second, the role of the literacy coach is to provide the job-embedded professional development that will enhance literacy instruction in the schools and ultimately improve student achievement. The belief is that the presence of a coach will enable teachers to apply more successfully "best" practices in their classrooms. Third, coaches must have the interpersonal and communication skills that enable them to work effectively with other adults. They must have an understanding of adult learning and its relevance to their work. Finally, they must have an in-depth understanding of literacy assessment and instruction if they are going to be able to provide support to teachers. In fact, one of the major roles of coaches is the ability to use data as a means of making instructional decisions (International Reading Association [IRA], 2004).

Coaching certainly exemplifies many important elements of effective professional development: it is job embedded, provides modeling and feedback to teachers, and assists them in implementing effective practices in their classroom. At the same time, coaching presents many challenges, many of which are related to the culture of isolation that exists in schools (e.g., teachers do not understand the role of coaches or their own role as learners). Likewise, coaches may be asked to assume duties that reduce their effectiveness; that is, they may be required to evaluate teachers or serve as quasi-administrators.

We continue to learn more about coaching, given the emphasis on and the extent to which it is being implemented in schools. Such empirical evidence should help schools in thinking about who should coach, what coaching activities are essential, for whom, and under what conditions.

Professional Learning Communities

When teachers work collaboratively with others in the school, evaluating school programs and the allocation of school resources, when they are knowledgeable about resources, school, and community, and work with their peers and with parents, they are considered to be members of a professional learning community (PLC). PLCs allow teachers to have a voice in their learning and in instructional implementation at the school level. Hord (2004) organized the characteristics of professional learning communities into five themes or dimensions: "supportive and shared leadership, shared values and vision, collective learning and application of learning, supportive conditions, and shared practice" (p. 7).

As Fullan and Hargreaves (1996) indicate, efforts to build professional communities must be authentic, not contrived; that is, teacher collaboration must be focused on efforts to achieve school goals and improve teaching practices and student learning. A PLC requires establishing a culture where teachers are involved in decision making and problem solving and where norms of conduct are established by teachers and administrators together (Marzano, 2003). In other words, when teachers, with support from school administration, meet on a regular basis to share and network, there is the opportunity to build a community in which there is an atmosphere of trust, respect, and commitment to providing the best possible educational program for students. Teachers who participate in a PLC have opportunities to engage in conversations about content, curriculum, and pedagogy. They use student work samples, their own lessons or assignments, as well as data about student performance as the catalysts for discussion.

Establishing the school as a PLC can be difficult because of school structures or schedules, especially at the middle and high school levels. Yet schools have generated some creative solutions for finding time for teachers to meet. Some hire substitutes during which time teachers can meet as a group or with a literacy coach or specialist. Others have established days on which there is an early release for students. Teachers in other schools have given up their daily planning period, accumulating the time so that it can be used later for an extended period of professional development. Also, principals have developed schedules in which special subject teachers are assigned to teach all classes at a specific grade level, freeing those teachers to meet for a block of time.

What we know from research is that the interactions and relationships among teachers, administrators, and others that promote trust, a shared vision, and a sense of collective responsibility for the students they teach can make a difference in student learning (Bryk, Sebring, et al., 2010; Leana & Pil, 2006). Leana and Pill (2006) found a significant and positive relationship between strong "social capital" in schools and reading achievement. Nielsen, Barry, and Staab (2008) found that teachers appreciated opportunities to collaborate with their peers and with their coaches.

Other possibilities for building PLCs include curriculum study and development, study groups or book clubs, or involvement in partnerships with universities, for example, professional development schools (PDS). Below, we provide more in-depth information about these approaches to building professional learning communities.

Curriculum Development

When teachers work together to set goals, build curricula, and develop evaluative tools that measure the effects of various curricula, they can develop a strong sense of community and caring for the organization. Such work must be focused on the ultimate outcomes expected—that is, student achievement. Au (2002) describes a process she uses when working in schools to develop effective elementary school reading programs. First, as the leader of the proposed work, she seeks input from teachers about their current thinking on literacy instruction. She then asks teachers to generate descriptions of skilled readers at the various grade levels. Based on the descriptions, teachers, with student input, set goals and determine activities and experiences to achieve those goals. An assessment system with benchmarks is developed, and teachers are asked to establish conditions to support instruction. Finally, teachers summarize and evaluate student learning. Assessment is an important aspect of the process model; teachers analyze student results frequently and use them to reflect on the curriculum and necessary changes. In other words, curriculum building requires that teachers address the following three questions: What are our goals? What will we do to achieve our goals? How do we determine that we have achieved our goals?

Teacher Study Groups

Cramer, Hurst, and Wilson (1996) provide the following definition of a study group: "a collaborative group organized and sustained by teachers to help them strengthen their professional development in areas of common interest. In these groups, teachers remain in charge of their own independent learning but seek to reach personal goals through interaction with others." (p. 7) At times, these study groups occur during school hours, but often they take place after school in more informal settings. Walpole and Beauchat (2008) recommend considering these characteristics for implementing effective study groups: respect, choice, voice, personal connections, and accepting reluctance (pp. 1–5). Although school personnel make the decision about the questions and topics to be addressed in study groups, various materials are available to assist schools in their efforts. For example, the International Reading Association (IRA) has a web link, titled School-Based professional development (IRA, 2010f) (*www.reading.org/General/Publications/PDEditions.aspx*) that has information about IRA books that come with professional development editions including discussion guides, video-book packages, the *Essential Reading Series* (2010b) of articles from the field, and information about IRA journals. Furthermore, IRA (2010a, 2010c, 2010e) offers free podcasts on a variety of topics (*www.reading.org/General/Publications/Podcasts.aspx*), and every month produces a segment for *Reading Radio* (2010d) on timely topics within literacy education.

The advantages of study groups or book clubs are several—they allow teachers to focus on individual goals while interacting on a larger scale with professional colleagues; they reduce the sense of isolation so common in schools; they increase the opportunity for problem solving, inquiry, and reflection; and they acknowledge the teacher as learner (Flood & Lapp, 1994; Lefever-Davis, Wilson, Moore, Kent, & Hopkins, 2003).

Professional Development Schools

The professional development school (PDS) provides a learning community that includes school and university faculty working and learning together. In a PDS, preservice teachers, experienced teachers, administrators, and university faculty work collaboratively to develop a professional philosophy that addresses the complexities between teaching and learning, thus enhancing teacher learning (National Association of Professional Development Schools, 2008; Yendol-Hoppey, Hoppey, & Price, 2010). Teachers have a voice and are actively involved in selecting the focus of discussion and working to improve student learning. Finally, a PDS offers opportunities for coteaching, coplanning, observing, data analysis, and reflection.

Colleges and universities recognize the importance of incorporating more clinical elements into teacher preparation programs by working closely with schools (American Association of Colleges for Teacher Education, 2010; "NCATE Names Expert Panel," 2010). Such partnerships provide a win–win situation for schools and universities. Teachers gain access to resources, information, and professional learning opportunities. University faculty members are provided with opportunities to model in classrooms and to gain a deeper understanding of how theory transfers to practice. Although not all schools can participate in such partnerships because they are not close to a university or college, those that are involved can benefit from this sort of partnership.

Teacher Research

The term *teacher research* has several different meanings and serves as an umbrella term to describe a wide range of activities, which can be traced to the "action" research notion of the 1950s and '60s (Cochran-Smith & Lytle, 1990, p. 3). According to Cochran-Smith and Lytle (1990), teacher research is "systematic, intentional inquiry by teachers" (p. 2). Often, teachers become involved in such research because of their work in a graduate program at a college or university. But teacher research can be school initiated and sustained, especially if teachers and university-based faculty are working together. Richardson and Anders (2005) indicate that "many teachers appear to enjoy and value action research and inquiry as a means of examining their practice" (p. 207). The potential of teacher research has led several organizations to support and sanction teacher research through direct funding. For example, both the National Council of Teachers of English (2010a) (*www.ncte.org/cee/awards/moffett*) and the International Reading Association (2010g; *www.reading.org/Resources/AwardsandGrants/research_teacher_as_researcher.aspx*) provide grants for teachers wishing to undertake action research.

A strength of this approach to professional development is that it allows for teachers to feel a sense of empowerment. Teachers formulate questions for which they want answers. Teacher research also increases the opportunity for teachers to become decision makers, problem solvers, and school leaders. It gives teachers opportunities to interact with an idea or data that promotes reflection and thinking. Most important, it can have an immediate impact on teaching practices and perspectives (Lytle, 2000; Morewood & Bean, 2009; Van Tassell, 2002). Furthermore, if done collaboratively, such research can have great impact on the school as a whole.

Teacher research, however, can be problematic. Often, the results are limited to local context, and therefore quality is difficult to ascertain (Lytle, 2000). Also, if conducted by individuals, results may have limited usefulness; that is, they will not provide the coherent, systematic efforts needed to achieve long-range organizational goals. Finally, teacher research is time consuming, and therefore its implementation by larger groups may be difficult. Nevertheless, for those individuals who undertake such efforts, teacher research has the potential to increase their sense of self-efficacy and professionalism.

Technology

The use of technology—digital as well as online resources—for enhancing teacher learning, has been increasing dramatically during the past 10 years. As explained by the Web-Based Education Commission (2000),

> the Internet is making it possible to connect teachers to each other, giving opportunities for mentoring, collaboration, and formal and informal online learning. Traditional one-size-fits-all professional development workshops are giving way to a new, more teacher-centered, self-directed model of teacher learning. Through the Internet, teachers have access to high-quality online professional development opportunities beyond what the local school or district is able to offer. (p. 60)

Technology provides a means of making professional development more available to teachers. This delivery system allows for differentiation of teacher interests, needs, and pacing. Technology can be used in a variety of ways for professional development. For example, blogs, wikis, podcasts, virtual conferences, webinars, and online courses are all media for professional development. We provide some specific examples of how various technology tools can be incorporated as effective professional development below.

Blogs can be used to facilitate teacher study groups. Teachers can create a blog to facilitate a conversation about a book, eliminating the need for meeting; instead, teachers can participate when they have the time to do so. A free blog creation website is *www.blogger.com/start.*

Wikis can be used to provide teachers with professional development that addresses needs specific to a school. A school could create a wiki where information about a specific topic can be stored for teachers to review. These two websites offer user-friendly ideas about wiki creation: *www.pbwiki.com* and *www.wikispaces.com* .

Podcasts are a way to help school personnel gain access to leading professionals in the literacy field. The podcasts provide up-to-date information about various topics. The International Reading Association has a variety of podcasts such as Reading Radio, Class Acts: Ideas for Teaching Reading and Writing, IRA Insights, and podcasts related to children's literature. These can be found at *www.reading.org/General/Publications/Podcasts.aspx.* The National Council of Teachers of English (2010b) also has podcasts that are recorded from their online book studies. These can be found at *ncte.org/community/book.* Besides online book studies, the National Council of Teachers of English (2010c) also has virtual conferences (i.e., *ncte.org/virtualconf*). And the International Reading Association holds live webinars on various important topics, (e.g., RTI, professional standards; *www.reading.org/General/Conferences/RTIWebinars.aspx*).

Finally, technology offers teachers the ability to locate online courses that fit their needs. According to Allen and Seaman (2007), about 65% of all higher education institutions in the United States are providing online learning opportunities. This extension of professional development beyond traditional opportunities allows teachers and schools to find "what works best" to increase their knowledge of literacy teaching and learning. In addition to the use of online or distance education courses at universities, such experiences are being incorporated into the professional development plans of various states as a means of improving literacy instruction in schools (Bean et al., 2007; Zygouris-Coe, Yao, Tao, Hahs-Vaughn, & Baumbach, 2004). Findings from the Bean et al. (2007) study suggest that teachers' content knowledge increased by participating in the online coursework. Professional development through technology allows teachers to engage in activities at convenient times, and at their own pace; moreover, it can provide for consistency in content and emphasis. Access to information and flexibility are considered to be two main advantages of online learning (Bean et al., 2007; Morewood, 2010). As Owston (1997) indicates, "What the Web can offer that traditional media cannot is information that is instantly available, often very up-to-date, worldwide in scope" (p. 31).

At the same time, these online courses have limitations. Edwards, Cordray, and Dorbolo (2000) point out that "the development of distance-education teaching tools . . . requires even greater attention to detail because students are asked to learn on their own" (p. 388). Brown and Green (2003) also indicate that the lack of modeling may be a problem. If the online experiences do not include opportunities for teachers to "see" something and then discuss their understandings, misinterpretations and incomplete learning may result. Online efforts are not created equal. Just as some materials or approaches may be better in some contexts than in others, so too, are online experiences. Requiring all teachers to participate in the same experiences, regardless of their knowledge base or experience, flies in the face of what is known about effective learning (Bean et al., 2007). Furthermore, unless these online experiences include elements of good instruction and adult learning—such as opportunities for questioning, reflection, feedback, and application to classroom practice—they may not live up to the expectations of those who see them as a primary means of improving teacher practices. The use of technology, although a promising practice, must be studied carefully because the evidence for such professional development is still somewhat thin, and ongoing research efforts must be undertaken, especially given the current emphasis on this approach to teacher learning.

REFLECTIONS AND FUTURE DIRECTIONS FOR RESEARCH

Although we have learned a great deal about professional development during the past 10 years, there is still much more to learn, especially about professional development as it relates to literacy instruction. Much of what we know has been gleaned from the work of researchers who study school change and reform. These theorists and researchers have provided solid evidence about the importance of school culture and collaboration in effecting teacher growth. Indeed, Garmston (2005) states, "Teachers' thoughts, feelings, decisions, and behaviors are influenced more by the culture of the workplace than by their skills, knowledge, and prior or current training. As the work culture of schools changes, so do the schools themselves" (p. x). This powerful statement recognizes the importance of school leadership in professional development. Individual teachers may seek to increase their knowledge and skills through readings, coursework, book clubs, involvement in special initiatives, or projects, but if the achievement of all students in a school is to improve, there must be a concerted effort to provide a strong, comprehensive professional development program that is based on a vision of what literacy instruction means for the students in a specific school, and opportunities for teacher choice in how to achieve that vision. This means that many factors need to be in place: strong leadership, a culture in which teachers see themselves as learners working together to improve literacy of all students in a specific school, and establishing a professional development program that addresses content, process, and context variables. That is, a program must be tailored to meet the needs of students and teachers in a specific school, and be focused on a long-term effort to improve reading achievement.

We also need to continue research efforts to study professional development. Given the many factors that affect successful professional development, such research is complex and requires collaborative efforts of researchers interested in various aspects of teacher learning, literacy instruction and assessment, and school reform or change.

CONCLUSIONS

Professional development is an essential element in any school improvement plan. Effective professional development requires schools to attend to content, context, and process variables. It requires a commitment from all involved in the schools. Effective professional development can and should be structured so that it addresses the identified needs of students in a school; that is, it should be based on the available data about student learning. At the same time, it must be responsive to the teachers in the school and their knowledge about literacy instruction and curriculum. The best professional development is that in which schools function in a collaborative, collegial fashion, in which all personnel strive to achieve the goals for promoting literacy learning.

ENGAGEMENT ACTIVITIES

1. Using a T-chart, list the most effective professional development you have experienced (on one side) and the least effective professional development you have experienced. With a group of colleagues, compare your charts. Are there similarities and/or differences? Example: Best | Worst
2. Using the rubric in Figure 19.2, think about the professional development in your school and how it compares with the criteria identified as important for professional development. Once gaps in the professional development of the school have been identified, create a schoolwide plan to implement change in these areas (Figure 19.3).
3. Interview a principal and/or literacy coach of a school, using the rubric (Figure 19.2), and discuss the professional development in the school. Write a short summary of how the professional development in that school compares with the criteria identified in the rubric.

REFERENCES

Allen, I. E., & Seaman, J. (2007). *Online nation: Five years of growth in online learning.* Needham, MA: Sloan Consortium.

American Association of Colleges for Teacher Education. (2010). *The clinical preparation of teachers: A policy brief.* Washington, DC: Author.

American Educational Research Association. (2005). *Research Points. Teaching teachers: Professional development to improve student achievement* (Vol. 3, Issue 1) [Brochure]. Washington, DC: Author. Retrieved from *www.aera.net.*

Anders, P., Hoffman, J., & Duffy, G. (2000). Teaching teachers to teach reading: Paradigm shifts, persistent problems, and challenges. In M. L. Kamil, P. B. Mosenthal, P. D. Pearson, & R. Barr (Eds.), *Handbook of reading research* (Vol. III, pp. 719–742). Mahwah, NJ: Erlbaum.

Au, K. H. (2002). Elementary programs: Guiding change in a time of standards. In S. B. Wepner, D. S. Strickland, & J. T. Feeley (Eds.), *The administration and supervision of reading programs* (Vol. 3, pp. 42–58). New York: Teachers College Press.

Bean, R. M. (2004). *Reading specialist: Leadership for the classroom, school, and Community.* New York: Guilford Press.

Bean, R. M., Draper, J., Jackson, V., Vandermolen, J., & Zigmond, N. (2010). Coaches and coaching in Reading First schools: A reality check. *The Elementary School Journal, 111*(1), 87–114.

Bean, R., Ezell, H., Heisey, N., Ankrum, J. W., Zigmond, N., & Morewood, A. (2007). Outcomes of online professional development in Pennsylvania. In D. Rowe et al. (Eds.), *56th Yearbook of the National Reading Conference* (pp. 111–112). Oak Creek, WI: National Reading Conference.

Bean, R., Swan, A., & Morris, G. A. (2002). *Tinkering and transforming: A new paradigm for professional development for teachers of beginning teachers.* New Orleans, LA: Annual Meeting of the American Educational Research Association. (ERIC Document Reproduction Service No. ED 465983). Retrieved from *www.eric.ed.gov/ERICWebPortal/search/detailmini.jsp?_nfpb=true&_&ERICExtSearch_SearchValue_0=ED465983&ERICExtSearch_SearchType_0=no&accno=ED465983.*

Biancarosa, G., Bryk, A. S., & Dexter, E. R. (2010). Assessing the value-added effects of literacy collaborative professional development on student learning. *The Elementary School Journal, 111*(1), 7–34.

Biancarosa, G., & Snow, C. E. (2004). *Reading next: A vision for action and research in middle and high school literacy: A report to Carnegie Corporation of New York.* Washington, DC: Alliance for Excellent Education. Retrieved from *www.all4ed.org/files/ReadingNext.pdf.*

Brown, A., & Green, T. (2003). Showing up to class in pajamas (or less!): The fantasies and realities of online professional development courses for teachers. *The Clearing House, 76*(3), 148–151. Retrieved from *heldref-publications.metapress.com.*

Bryk, A. S., Sebring, P. B., Allensworth, E., Luppescu, S., & Easton, J. Q. (2010). *Organizing schools for improvement.* Chicago: The University of Chicago Press.

Choy, S. P., & Ross, M. (1998). *Toward better teaching: Professional development in 1993–94* (NCES No. 98-230). Washington, DC: National Center for Educational Statistics.

Cochran-Smith, M., & Lytle, S. L. (1990). Research on teaching and teacher research: The issues that divide. *Educational Researcher, 19*(2), 2–11.

Common Core State Standards Initiative. (2010). *The standards: English language arts standards.* Washington, DC: Author. Retrieved from *www.corestandards.org/the-standards/english-language-arts-standards.*

Costa, A. L., & Garmston, R. J. (2002). *Cognitive coaching: A foundation for renaissance schools* (2nd ed.). Norwood, MA: Christopher-Gordon.

Cramer, G., Hurst, B., & Wilson, C. (1996). *Teacher study groups for professional development.* Bloomington, IN: Phi Delta Kappa Educational Foundation. (ERIC Document Reproduction Service No. ED 406371). Retrieved from *www.pdkmembers.org.*

Darling-Hammond, L., Wei, R. C., Andree, A., Richardson, N., & Orphanos, S. (2009). *Professional learning in the learning profession: A status report on teacher development in the United States and abroad.* Palo Alto, CA: Stanford University, National Staff Development Council.

Desimone, L. M., Porter, A. C., Garet, M., Yoon, S. K., & Birman, B. F. (2002). Effects of professional development on teachers' instruction: Results from a three-year longitudinal study. *Educational Evaluation and Policy Analysis, 24*(2), 81–112.

Edwards, M. E., Cordray, S., & Dorbolo J. (2000). Unintended benefits of distance-learning technology for traditional classroom teaching. *Teaching Sociology, 28*(4), 386–391. Retrieved from *www.jstor.org.*

Elliott, C. (2007). Action research: Authentic learning transforms student and teacher success. *Journal of Authentic Learning, 4*(1), 34–42. Retrieved from *www.oswego.edu/academics/colleges_and_departments/education/jal/vol4no*1.html.

Flood, J., & Lapp, D. (1994). Teacher book clubs: establishing literature discussion groups for teachers. *The Reading Teacher, 47*(7), 574–576.

Fullan, M. (2001). *The new meaning of educational change* (3rd ed.). New York: Teachers College Press.

Fullan, M., & Hargreaves, A. (1996). *What's worth fighting for in your school.* New York: Teachers College Press.

Gabriel, R. (2010). The case for differentiated professional support: Toward a phase theory of professional development. *Journal of Curriculum and Instruction* [Online], *4*(1). Retrieved from *www.joci.ecu.edu.*

Garet, M. S., Cronen, S., Eaton, M., Kurki, A., Ludwig, M., Jones, W., et al. (2008). *The impact of two professional development interventions on early reading instruction and achievement.* (NCEE 2008-4030). Washington, DC: National Center for Education Evaluation and Regional Assistance, Institute of Education Sciences, U.S. Department of Education.

Garet, M. S., Porter, A. C., Desimone, L., Birman, B. F., & Yoon, S. K. (2001). What makes professional development effective? Results from a national sample of teachers. *American Educational Research Journal, 38*(4), 915–945.

Garmston, R. (2005). *The presenter's fieldbook: A practical guide* (2nd ed.). Norwood, MA: Chistopher-Gordon.

Graham, S., & Hebert, M. (2010). *Writing to read: Evidence for how writing can improve reading. A Carnegie Corporation Time to Act report.* Washington, DC: Alliance for Excellent Education.

Guskey, T. (2000). *Evaluating professional development.* Thousand Oaks, CA: Corwin Press.

Hanushek, E. A. (1992). The trade-off between child quantity and quality. *Journal of Political Economy, 100*(1), 84–117. Retrieved from *www.jstor.org.*

Hord, S. (Ed.). (2004). *Learning together leading together changing schools through professional communities.* New York: Teachers College Press.

International Reading Association. (2004). *The role and qualifications of the reading coach in the United States.* [Brochure]. Newark, DE: Author. Retrieved from *www.reading.org.*

International Reading Association. (2010a). *Class acts: Ideas for teaching reading and writing.* Newark, DE: Author. Retrieved from *www.reading.org/General/Publications/Podcasts.aspx.*

International Reading Association. (2010b). *The Essential Readings series.* Newark, DE: Author. Retrieved from *www.reading.org/General/Publications/Books/EssentialReadings.aspx.*

International Reading Association. (2010c). *IRA Insights.* Newark, DE: Author. Retrieved from *www.reading.org/General/Publications/Podcasts.aspx.*

International Reading Association. (2010d). *Reading Radio.* Newark, DE: Author. Retrieved from *www.reading.org/General/Publications/Podcasts.aspx.*

International Reading Association. (2010e). *Response to intervention (RTI) webinar series.* Newark, DE: Author. Retrieved from *www.reading.org/General/Conferences/RTIWebinars.aspx.*

International Reading Association (2010f). *School Based Professional Development.* Newark, DE: Author. Retrieved from *www.reading.org/General/Publications/PDEditions.aspx.*

International Reading Association. (2010g). *Teacher as Researcher Grant.* Newark, DE: Author. Retrieved from *www.reading.org/Resources/AwardsandGrants/research_teacher_as_researcher.aspx.*

Joyce, B., & Showers, B. (2002). *Student achievement through staff development: Fundamentals of school renewal.* White Plains, NY: Longman.

Kamil, M. L., Mosenthal, P. B., Pearson, P. D., & Barr, R. (Eds.). (2000). *Handbook of reading research* (Vol. 3). Mahwah, NJ: Erlbaum.

Killeen, K. M., Monk, D. H., & Plecki, M. L. (2002). School district spending on professional development: Insights available from national data (1992–1998). *Journal of Education Finance, 28*(1), 25–50. Retrieved from *depts.washington.edu/ctpmail/PDFs/JEFArticle-KKDMMP.pdf.*

L'Allier, S. K., & Elish-Piper, L. (2006, December). *An initial examination of the effects of literacy coaching on student achievement in reading in grades K–3.* Paper presented at the annual conference of the National Reading Conference, Los Angeles.

Leana, C. R., & Pil, F. K. (2006). Social capital and organizational performance: Evidence from urban public schools. *Organization Science, 17*(3), 353–366.

Learning First Alliance. (2000). *Every child reading: A professional development guide.* Baltimore: Author. Retrieved from *www.learningfirst.org/publications/reading/guide/content.html.*

Lefever-Davis, S., Wilson C., Moore E., Kent, A., & Hopkins, S. (2003). Teacher study groups: A strategic approach to promoting students' literacy development. *The Reading Teacher, 56*(8), 782–784. Retrieved from *www.reading.org.*

Lieberman, A., & Miller, L. (1984). School improvement: Themes and variations. *Teachers College Record, 86*(1), 4–19.

Lytle, S. L. (2000). Teacher research in the contact zone. In M. L. Kamil, P. B. Mosenthal, P. D. Pearson, & R. Barr (Eds.), *Handbook of reading research* (Vol. III, pp. 691–718). Mahwah, NJ: Erlbaum.

Marsh, J. A., McCombs, J. L., Lockwood, J. R., Martorell, F., Gershwin, D., Naftel, S., et al. (2008). *Supporting literacy across the sunshine state: A study of Florida middle school reading coaches.* Santa Monica, CA: Rand Corporation.

Marzano, R. J. (2003). *What works in schools: Translating research into action.* Alexandria, VA: Association for Supervision and Curriculum Development.

Morewood, A. L. (2010, April). *Online learning: Is it effective professional development?* Paper presented at the International Reading Association's 55th Annual Conference, Chicago.

Morewood, A. L., Ankrum, J. W., & Bean, R. (2010). Teachers' perceptions of the influence of professional development on their knowledge of content, pedagogy, and curriculum. In S. Szabo, M. B. Sampson, M. M. Foote, & F. Falk-Ross (Eds.), *Mentoring literacy professionals: Continuing the spirit of CRA/ALER after 50 years* (pp. 201–219). Commerce: Texas A&M University–Commerce.

Morewood, A. L., & Bean, R. (2009). Teachers' perceptions of professional development activities in a case study school. In F. Falk-Ross, S. Szabo, M. B. Sampson, & M. M. Foote (Eds.), *Literacy issues during changing times: A call to action* (pp. 248–263). Commerce: Texas A&M University–Commerce.

National Association of Professional Development Schools, Executive Council and Board of Directors. (2008). *What it means to be a professional development school.* Columbia, SC: Author. Retrieved from *www.napds.org.*

National Center for Education Statistics, U.S. Department of Education, Office of Educational Research and Improvement. (2001). *Teacher preparation and professional development: 2000* (NCES 2001-088). Retrieved from *nces.ed.gov/search/?output=xml_no_dtd&site=nces&client=nces&q=Teacher+preparation+and+professional+development%3A++2000+*.

National Council of Teachers of English. (2010a). *CEE James Moffett Award.* Urbana, IL: Author. Retrieved from *www.ncte.org/cee/awards/moffett.*

National Council of Teachers of English. (2010b). *Online study groups.* Urbana, IL: Author. Retrieved from *ncte.org/community/book.*

National Council of Teachers of English. (2010c). *Virtual conference.* Urbana, IL: Author. Retrieved from *ncte.org/virtualconf.*

National Early Literacy Panel. (2008). *Developing early literacy: A scientific synthesis of early literacy development and implications for intervention.* Washington, DC: National Institute for Family Literacy and the National Center for Family Literacy.

National Literacy Panel. (2006). *Developing literacy in second-language learners. Report of the National Literacy Panel on Language-Minority Children and Youth* (D. August & T. Shanahan, Eds.). Washington, DC: Center for Applied Linguistics and Erlbaum.

National Reading Panel. (2000). *Teaching children to read: An evidence-based assessment of the scientific research literature on reading and its implications for reading instruction.* Rockville, MD: National Institute of Child Health and Human Development. Retrieved from *www.nationalreadingpanel.org/Publications/publications.htm.*

National Staff Development Council. (2001). *Standards for staff development, revised.* Retrieved from *www.nsdc.org.*

NCATE names expert panel to explore clinical preparation of U.S. teachers. (2010, February/March). *Reading Today,* p. 8. Retrieved from *www.reading.org.*

Neufield, B., & Roper, D. (2003, June). *Coaching: A strategy for developing instructional capacity.* Providence, RI: Annenberg Institute for School Reform.

Neuman, S., & Cunningham, L. (2009). The impact of professional development and coaching on early language and literacy instructional practices. *American Educational Research Journal.* Retrieved May 27, 2009, from *aerj.aera.net.*

Nielsen, D. C., Barry, A. L., & Staab, P. T. (2008). Teachers' reflections of professional change during a literacy-reform initiative. *Teacher and Teacher Education, 24,* 1288–1303.

Owston, R. D. (1997). The World Wide Web: A technology to enhance teaching and learning? *Educational Researcher, 26*(2), 27–33. Retrieved from *www.jstor.org.*

Richardson, V., & Anders, P. L. (2005). Professional preparation and development of teachers in literacy instruction for urban settings. In J. Flood & P. L. Anders (Eds.), *Literacy development of students in urban schools* (pp. 205–230). Newark, DE: International Reading Association.

Richardson, V., & Placier, P. (2001). Teachers change. In V. Richardson (Ed.), *Handbook of research on teaching* (4th ed., pp. 905–947). Washington, DC: American Educational Research Association.

Rivkin, S. G., Hanushek, E. A., & Kain, J. F. (2005). Teachers, schools and academic achievement. *Econometrica, 73*(2), 417–458. Retrieved from *www.economics.harvard.edu/faculty/staiger/files/HanushekRivkinKain%2BEcta%2B2005.pdf.*

Shidler, L. (2009). The impact of time spent coaching for teacher efficacy on student achievement. *Early Childhood Education Journal, 36,* 453–460.

Shulman, L. S. (1986). Those who understand: Knowledge growth in teaching. *Educational Researcher, 15,* 4–14.

Smylie, M., Allensworth, E., Greenberg, R. C., Harris, R., & Luppescu, S. (2001). *Teacher Professional Development in Chicago: Supporting Effective Practice.* Chicago: Consortium on Chicago School Reform.

Sparks, D., & Loucks-Horsley, S. (1990). Models of staff development. In R. Houston (Ed.), *Handbook of research on teacher education* (pp. 234–250). New York: Macmillan.

Staub, F., & West, L. (2003). *Content-focused coaching: Transforming mathematics lessons*: Portsmouth, NH: Heinemann.

Taylor, B. M., Pearson, P. D., Peterson, D. S., & Rodriguez, M. C. (2005). The CIERA school change framework: An evidence-based approach to professional development and school reading improvement. *Reading Research Quarterly, 40*(1), 40–69.

Van Tassell, M. A. (2002). Getting started on teacher research. In J. M. Irwin (Ed.), *Facilitator's guide* (pp. 20–21). Newark, DE: International Reading Association.

Walpole, S., & Beauchat, K. A. (2008). *Facilitating teacher study groups.* Denver, CO: Literacy Coaching Clearinghouse. Retrieved January 20, 2009, from *www.literacycoachingonline.org.*

Web-Based Education Commission. (2000, December 19). *The power of the Internet for learning: Moving from promise to practice.* Retrieved from *www.ed.gov/offices/AC/WBEC/FinalReport/WBECReport.pdf.*

Yendol-Hoppey, D., Hoppey, D., & Price, T. (2010). Sustaining partnerships. In S. B. Wepner & D. Hopkins (Eds.), *Collaborative leadership in action: Partnering for success in schools* (pp. 74–96). New York: Teachers College Press.

Yoon, K. S., Duncan, T., Lee, S. W.-Y., Scarloss, B., & Shapley, K. (2007). *Reviewing the evidence on how teacher professional development affects students achievement* (Issues & Answers Report, REL 2007-NO. 033). Washington, DC: U.S. Department of Education, Institute of Education Sciences, National Center for Education Evaluation and Regional Assistance, Regional Educational Laboratory Southwest. Retrieved from *ies.ed.gov/ncess/edlabs.*

Zygouris-Coe, V., Yao, Y., Tao, Y., Hahs-Vaughn, D., & Baumbach, D. (2004). *Qualitative evaluation on facilitator's contributions to online professional development.* Chicago: Association for Educational Communications and Technology. (ERIC Document Reproduction Service No. ED 485072) Retrieved from *eric.ed.gov/ERICWebPortal/search/detailmini.jsp?_nfpb=true&_&ERICExtSearch_SearchValue_0=ED485072&ERICExtSearch_SearchType_0=no&accno=ED485072.*

Index

f following a page number indicates a figure; *t following a page number indicates a table.*

F

N

R

T